Thirteenth Edition

Medical Sociology

William C. Cockerham

University of Alabama at Birmingham

Routledge
Taylor & Francis Group

LONDON AND NEW YORK

First published 2016, 2012, 2009 by Pearson Education, Inc.

Published 2016 by Routledge
2 Park Square, Milton Park, Abingdon, Oxon OX14 4RN
711 Third Avenue, New York, NY 10017, USA

Routledge is an imprint of the Taylor & Francis Group, an informa business

ISBN: 9780205896417 (pbk)

Library of Congress Cataloging-in-Publication Data
Cockerham, William C.
  Medical sociology / William C. Cockerham, University of Alabama at Birmingham. —
    Thirteenth edition.
    pages cm
  Includes bibliographical references and index.
  ISBN 0-205-89641-3
  1. Social medicine. I. Title.
  RA418.C657 2015
  362.1--dc23   2014028546

Cover Image: © Allies Interactive

Printed and bound by CPI Group (UK) Ltd, Croydon, CR0 4YY

DEDICATION

To Cynthia, and to Geoffrey, Sean, Scott, and Laura

CONTENTS

PREFACE

This is the thirteenth edition of a book that has been a standard text in medical sociology since it was first published in 1978—obviously a long time ago. The first edition was written on a typewriter (now permanently stored in the basement) in Champaign, Illinois, when I was a new faculty member in sociology and medicine at the University of Illinois. The work is now done on a computer and transmitted electronically to the publisher. The book has obviously stood the test of time as it has held its position for over 35 years in a competitive marketplace and changed significantly over the years as medical sociology itself has changed. This new edition is intended to address the current changes stemming from health care reform in the United States and other issues that constitute the focus of the field today, much as the previous editions discussed what was important at that time.

New to This Edition

- Coverage of Ebola, MERS, and updates on other pandemics (Chapter 1).
- Discussion of obesity as a disease (Chapter 2).
- New information on the decline of life expectancy among rural American white women (Chapter 4).
- New material on biomarkers, gene-environment interaction, and stress (Chapter 5).
- Analysis of the role of the hidden curriculum in medical schools (Chapter 10).
- Extensive review of the Affordable Care Act (Chapter 15).

Past Editions

As noted in other editions, it was an honor to have this book included on the International Sociological Association's list of "Books of the Century" in 2000. And it was 1 of only 10 Western sociology books (the others were all on theory or research methods) selected by Huaxia Publishing House in Beijing in 2000 to be translated into Chinese to meet the growing demand for sociology books in China. The translators were Yang Hui and Zhang Tuohong of Beijing Medical University. The book was also published in English in Beijing in 2005 by the Peking University Press, which further highlights the spread of medical sociology in China. Another Chinese-language version was published in Taiwan by the Wu-Nan Book Company. The book has also been translated into Spanish by Lourdes Lostao of the University of Navarra in Spain and published by Pearson in Madrid. Hojin Park, M.D., translated a Korean edition published in Seoul by ACANET. The growth in translations and readership signals the increasing interest in medical sociology on a global scale.

The Growth of Medical Sociology

The field of medical sociology has undergone considerable modification since the first edition. At that time, much of the research in medical sociology was dependent upon the sponsorship of physicians. A clear division of labor existed between sociologists working in academic departments in universities and those working in health institutions. Today, that situation has changed dramatically. Medical sociology is no longer dependent on the medical profession for funding or focus—although a strong alliance continues to exist in many cases. Having experienced sponsorships and partnerships with medicine in joint faculty positions at the University of Illinois at Urbana-Champaign, and later at the University of Alabama at Birmingham, I can personally attest to and appreciate medicine's significant role in the development of medical sociology. In many ways, this relationship has been more supportive than that of the general discipline of sociology, which did not fully embrace the field until it became too important to ignore.

Medical sociologists now exercise their craft in a variety of settings, as full-fledged professionals, often working as colleagues on research projects with professionals in medicine, public health, nursing, and other health-related fields. Furthermore, research and teaching in medical sociology, in both universities and health institutions, are increasingly similar in the application of sociological theory and usefulness in addressing problems relevant to clinical practice. In sum, medical sociology has evolved into a mature, objective, and independent field of study and work, supported by a vast literature. It constitutes one of the largest and most important subdisciplines in modern sociology.

Medical sociology has also experienced significant growth worldwide. In many countries, including the United States, Canada, Australia, Great Britain, Finland, Germany, and Singapore, medical sociologists are either the largest or one of the largest specialty groups in sociology. The European Society for Health and Medical Sociology is a large and active professional society, as are the medical sociology sections of the American, British, French, German, European, and International sociological associations. American and British medical sociologists have held joint meetings the past few years in London, Edinburgh, Boston, and Belfast, Northern Ireland.

Elsewhere, a growing and active group of medical sociologists from the French Sociological Association is gaining in strength, Canada formed a new Canadian Society for Sociology of Health (CSSH) in 2008, the Japanese Society of Health and Medical Sociology is working to further develop the field in that country and helped plan the 2014 ISA World Congress of Sociology held in Yokohama, while medical sociologists in Latin America hold regional conferences on a regular basis and have their own Spanish-language journals. The field is expanding in Russia, Eastern Europe, India, Africa, and, as noted, in China, as the importance of the subject matter for the people in those countries becomes increasingly apparent. In the meantime, the Research Committee on Health Sociology (RC 15) of the International Sociological Association, which I formerly served as president, met in Montreal in 2008; Jaipur, India in 2009; the ISA World Congress in Gothenburg, Sweden in 2010; the ISA Forum in Buenos Aires, Argentina in 2012; and the 2014 ISA World Congress in Yokohama, Japan to present research findings and network with others in the field. Numerous books, journals, college and university courses, and lecture series in medical sociology now exist in different parts of the world; so it is obvious that medical sociology has a promising future. The publication of a new textbook, *Medical Sociology in Africa* (Amzat and Razum 2014) is evidence of medical sociology's expansion.

Since its inception, the principal goal of this book has been to introduce students to medical sociology and serve as a reference for faculty by presenting the *most* current ideas, issues, concepts, themes, theories, and research findings in the field. This edition—the thirteenth—continues this approach.

Acknowledgments

The material contained in the pages of this book is my own responsibility in terms of perspective, scope, topics, and style of presentation. Nevertheless, I am sincerely grateful to several people for their assistance in preparing the thirteen editions of this book. I would like to acknowledge the insightful comments of those colleagues who served as reviewers. For sharing their views and helping to improve the quality of this book, my appreciation goes to Lori Anderson, Tarleton State University; Melvin Barber, Florida A&M University; Paul Berzina, County College of Morris; Deirdre Bowen, University of Washington; Ann Butzin, Owens State Community College; Herbert Bynder, University of Colorado at Boulder; Christine Caffrey, Miami University (Ohio); Robert Clark, Midwestern State University; John Collette, University of Utah; Spencer Condie, Brigham Young University; Wendy Cook-Mucci, Tennessee Tech University; Morton Creditor, University of Kansas Medical Center; Norman Denzin, University of Illinois at Urbana-Champaign; Nancy DiMonte, Farmingdale State College; Karen A. Donahue, Hanover College; Barry Edmonston, Cornell University; Anne Eisenberg, SUNY-Geneseo; M. David Ermann, University of Delware; and Eliot Freidson, New York University.

Also Reed Geertsen, Utah State University; Sharon Guten, Case Western Reserve University; Deborah Helsel, Fresno State University; Wendell Hester, East Tennessee State University; Brian Hinote, Middle Tennessee State University; Joseph Jones, Portland State University; Daniel J. Klenow, North Dakota State University; Sol Levine, Harvard University and the New England Medical Center; Richard C. Ludtke, University of North Dakota; William Lugo, Eastern Connecticut State University; John Malek-Ahmadi, College of Western Idaho; Duane Matcha, Siena College; Leon Ragonesi, California State University-Dominguez Hills; Robert Terry Russell, College of St. Francis; Alexander Rysman, Northeastern University; Jeffrey Salloway, University of New Hampshire; Anne Saunders, College of St. Francis; Diane Shinberg, Indiana University of Pennsylvania; Neil Smelser, University of California, Berkeley, and Center for the Advanced Study of the Behavioral Sciences, Stanford, CA; Henry Vandenberg, Bridgewater State College; Yvonne Vissing, Salem State College; George J. Warheit, University of Miami (Florida); J. B. Watson, Stephen F. Austin State University; and Raymond Weinstein, University of South Carolina at Aiken.

I would also like to thank Ronald Berkowsky and Bryant Hamby , doctoral students in medical sociology at UAB, who provided valuable assistance in the preparation of this edition.

William C. Cockerham
Birmingham, Alabama

PART 1

Introduction

CHAPTER 1

Medical Sociology

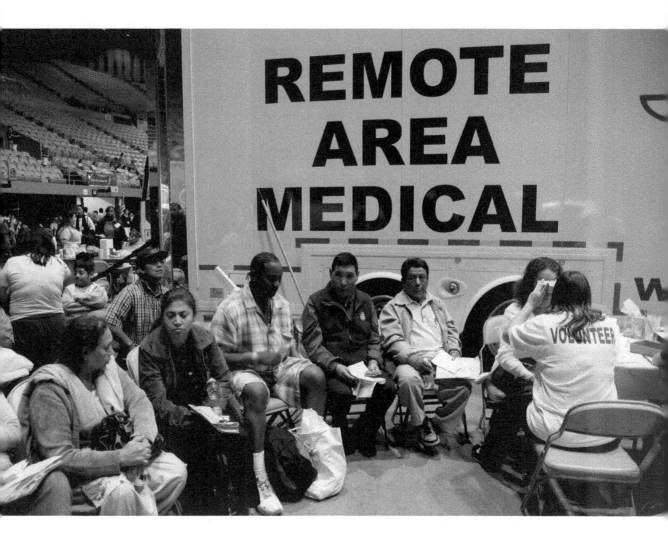

The purpose of this book is to introduce readers to the field of medical sociology. Recognition of the significance of the complex relationship between social factors and the level of health characteristic of various groups and societies has led to the development of medical sociology as a major substantive area within the general field of sociology. As an academic discipline, sociology is concerned with the social causes and consequences of human behavior. Thus, it follows that medical sociology focuses on the social causes and consequences of health and illness. Medical sociology brings sociological perspectives, theories, and methods to the study of health, illness, medical practice, and policy. Areas of investigation include the social causes of health and disease, health disparities, the social behavior of health care personnel and their patients, the social functions of health organizations and institutions, the social patterns of the utilization of health services, social policies toward health, and similar topics. What makes medical sociology important is the critical role social factors play in determining or influencing health outcomes.

The Social Determinants of Health

A major development in the study of health and disease is the growing recognition of the relevance of social determinants. The term *social determinants of health* refers to social practices and conditions (such as lifestyles, living and work situations), class position (income, education, and occupation), stressful circumstances, poverty, and economic (e.g., unemployment, business recessions), political (e.g., policies, government benefits), and religious factors that affect the health of individuals, groups, and communities, either positively or negatively. Social determinants not only foster illness and disability, they also enhance prospects for coping with or preventing disease and maintaining health. Once thought of as secondary or distant influences on health and disease, it now appears that social connections can be a fundamental cause of health problems (Link and Phelan 1995; Phelan and Link 2013). The social context of a person's life determines the risk of exposure, the susceptibility to a disease, and the course and outcome of the affliction—regardless of whether it is infectious, genetic, metabolic, malignant, or degenerative (Holtz et al. 2006). Thus, it can be claimed that "society may indeed make you sick or conversely promote your health" (Cockerham 2013a:1).

For example, in addressing the question of whether or not social factors matter to health, the National Research Council and the Institute of Medicine documented various links between social determinants and health (Woolf and Aron 2013). The most important social factors determining health were found to be income, accumulated wealth, education, occupational characteristics, and social inequality based on race and ethnic group. These variables have direct effects on both unhealthy and healthy lifestyles, high or low risk health behavior, and on living conditions, food security, levels of stresses and strains, social disadvantages over the life course, environmental factors that influence biological outcomes through gene expression, and other connections (Cockerham 2005, 2013a, 2013b; Daw et al. 2013; Frohlich and Abel 2014; Goodman, Joyce, and Smith 2011; Phelan and Link 2013; Phelan, Link, and Tehranifar 2010; Miech et al. 2011; Montez and Zajacova 2013; Sandoval and Esteller 2012; Woolf and Aron 2013; Yang et al. 2013).

Social factors are also important in influencing the manner in which societies organize their resources to cope with health hazards and deliver health care to the population at large. Individuals, groups, and societies typically respond to health problems in a manner consistent with their culture, norms, and values. As Donald Light (Light and Schuller 1986:9) explains, "medical care and health services are acts of political philosophy." Thus, social and political values influence the choices made, institutions formed, and levels of funding provided for health. It is no accident that the United States has its particular form of health care delivery and other nations have their own approaches. Health is not simply a matter of biology but involves a number of factors that are cultural, political, economic, and—especially—social in nature. It is the social aspects of health that are examined in this book.

The Development of Medical Sociology

The earliest works in medical sociology were undertaken by physicians and not by sociologists who tended to ignore the field. John Shaw Billings, organizer of the National Library of Medicine and complier of the *Index Medicus*, had written about hygiene and sociology as early as 1879. The term *medical sociology* first appeared in 1894, in a medical article by Charles McIntire on the importance of social factors in health. Other early work by physicians included essays on the relationship between medicine and society in 1902 by Elizabeth Blackwell, the first woman to graduate from an American medical school (Geneva Medical College in New York), and James Warbasse who wrote a book in 1909 called *Medical Sociology* about physicians as a unique social class. Warbasse also organized a Section on Sociology for the American Public Health Association in 1909 that lacked sociologists and was comprised almost entirely of physicians and social workers (Bloom 2002).

It remained for Michael Davis and Bernard Stern to publish books on health with a sociological perspective. Davis published *Immigrant Health and the Community* in 1921 and Stern's book appeared in 1927, titled *Social Factors in Medical Progress*. A few publications followed in the 1930s, such as Lawrence Henderson's 1935 paper on the physician and patient as a social system that subsequently influenced Talcott Parsons's important conceptualization of the sick role years later. Henderson was a physician and biochemist at Harvard, who became interested in sociological theory and changed careers to teach in the new sociology department when it was formed in the early 1930s (Bloom 2002). Parsons was one of his students.

Medical sociology did not begin in earnest until after World War II, in the late 1940s, when significant amounts of federal funding for sociomedical research first became available. Under the auspices of the National Institute of Mental Health, _____ ce with medicine was in psychiatry. A basis for _____ ts and psychiatrists existed because of earlier _____ ban mental health, conducted by Robert Faris and _____ y significant cooperative effort that followed was _____ *Class and Mental Illness: A Community Study* by _____ k Redlich. This landmark research, conducted in _____ N _____ ed important evidence that social factors could be cor _____ mental disorders and the manner in which people recei _____ in the most socially and economically disadvan- taged _____ und to have the highest rates of mental disorder in gen _____ tes of schizophrenia—the most disabling mental illness— _____ ttracted international attention and is considered one of t _____ of the relationship between mental disorder and social cla _____ y role in the debate during the 1960s, leading to the estab _____ mental health centers in the United States, as did other sign _____ volving sociologists and psychiatrists, such as the Midtown _____ Srole and his colleagues (1962).

Funding from federal and private organizations also helped stimulate coopera- tion between sociologists and physicians, with regard to sociomedical research on problems of physical health. In 1949, the Russell Sage Foundation funded a program to improve the utilization of social science research in medical practice. One result of this effort was the publication of *Social Science in Medicine* (Simmons and Wolff 1954). Other work sponsored by the Sage Foundation came later, including Edward Suchman's book *Sociology and the Field of Public Health* (1963). Thus, when large- scale funding first became available, the direction of work in medical sociology in the United States was toward applied or practical problem solving rather than the development of a theoretical basis for the sociological study of health.

This situation had important consequences for the development of medi- cal sociology. Unlike law, religion, politics, economics, and other social institu- tions, medicine was ignored by sociology's founders in the late nineteenth century because it did not shape the structure and nature of society. Karl Marx's collabora- tor Friedrich Engels (1973) linked the poor health of the English working class to capitalism in a treatise published in 1845, and Emile Durkheim (1951) analyzed European suicide rates in 1897. However, Durkheim, Marx, Max Weber, and other major classical sociological theorists did not concern themselves with the role of medicine in society. Medical sociology did not emerge as an area of study in sociol- ogy until the late 1940s and did not reach a significant level of development until the 1960s. Therefore, the field developed relatively late in the evolution of sociology as a major academic subject and lacked statements on health and illness from the classical theorists. Consequently, medical sociology came of age in an intellectual climate far different from sociology's more traditional specialties, which had direct links to nineteenth- and early twentieth-century social thought. As a result, it faced a set of circumstances in its development different from that of most other major sociological subdisciplines.

A circumstance that particularly affected medical sociology in its early development was the pressure to produce work that can be applied to medical practice and the formulation of health policy. This pressure originated from government agencies and medical sources, both of which either influenced or controlled funding for sociomedical research but had little or no interest in purely theoretical sociological work. Yet the tremendous growth of medical sociology, in both the United States and Europe, would have been difficult without the substantial financial support for applied studies provided by the respective governments. For example, in the United States, where medical sociology has developed most extensively, the emergence of the field was greatly stimulated by the expansion of the National Institutes of Health in the late 1940s. Particularly significant, according to Hollingshead (1973), who participated in some of the early research programs, was the establishment of the National Institute of Mental Health, which was instrumental in encouraging and funding joint social and medical projects. "It was through the impetus provided by this injection of money," notes Malcolm Johnson (1975:229), "that sociologists and medical men changed their affiliations and embraced the field of medical sociology." When Alvin Gouldner (1970) described the social sciences as a well-financed government effort to help cope with the problems of industrial society and the welfare state in the West during the post–World War II era, medical sociology was a prime example.[1]

Parsons

However, a critical event occurred in 1951 that oriented American medical sociology toward theory. This was the appearance, in 1951, of Talcott Parsons's book *The Social System*. This book, written to explain a relatively complex structural-functionalist model of society, in which social systems are linked to corresponding systems of personality and culture, contained Parsons's concept of the sick role. Unlike other major social theorists preceding him, Parsons formulated an analysis of the function of medicine in society. Parsons presented an ideal representation of how people in Western society act when sick. The merit of the concept is that it describes a patterned set of expectations defining the norms and values appropriate to being sick, for both the sick person and others who interact with that person. Parsons also pointed out that physicians are invested by society with the function of social control, similar to the role provided by priests and the police, to serve as a means to control deviance. In the case of the sick role, illness is the deviance, and its undesirable nature reinforces the motivation to be healthy.

In developing his concept of the sick role, Parsons linked his ideas to those of the two most important classical theorists in sociology—Emile Durkheim (1858–1917) of France and Max Weber (1864–1920) of Germany. Parsons was the first to demonstrate the controlling function of medicine in a large social system, and he did so in the context of classical sociological theory. Having a theorist of Parsons's stature rendering the first major theory in medical sociology called attention to

---

[1]For historical discussions of the development of medical sociology, see Samuel Bloom (2002), William Cockerham (2001, 2013a, 2013b), and Fran Collyer (2012).

the young subdiscipline—especially among academic sociologists. Not only was Parsons's concept of the sick role "a penetrating and apt analysis of sickness from a distinctly sociological point of view" (Freidson 1970b:62), but also it was widely believed in the 1950s that Parsons and his students were charting a future course for all of sociology through the insight provided by his model of society.

However, this was not the case, as Parsons's model was severely criticized and his views are no longer widely accepted. Nevertheless, he provided a theoretical approach for medical sociology that brought the subdiscipline the intellectual recognition it needed in its early development in the United States. This is because the institutional support for sociology in America was in universities, where the discipline was established more firmly than elsewhere in the world. Without academic legitimacy and the subsequent participation of such well-known, mainstream academic sociologists in the 1960s, such as Robert Merton, Howard Becker, and Erving Goffman, all of whom published research in the field, medical sociology would lack the early professional credentials and stature it currently has in both academic and applied settings. Parsons's views on society may not be the optimal paradigm for explaining illness, but Parsons was important in the emergence of medical sociology as an academic field.

Practical Application versus Theory

The direction initially taken by medical sociology is summarized by Robert Straus (1957). Straus suggested that medical sociology was divided into two separate but closely interrelated areas—sociology *in* medicine and sociology *of* medicine.

The sociologist in medicine is one who collaborates directly with physicians and other health personnel in studying the social factors that are relevant to a particular health problem. The work of the sociologist in medicine is intended to be directly applicable to patient care or to the solving of a public health problem. Some of the tasks are to analyze the social etiology or causes of health disorders, the differences in social attitudes as they relate to health, and the way in which the incidence and prevalence of a specific health disorder is related to such social variables as age, sex, socioeconomic status, racial/ethnic group identity, education, and occupation. Such an analysis is then intended to be made available to health practitioners to assist them in treating health problems. Thus, sociology in medicine can be characterized as *applied research and analysis primarily motivated by a medical problem,* rather than a sociological problem. Sociologists in medicine usually work in medical schools, nursing schools, public health schools, teaching hospitals, public health agencies, and other health organizations. They may also work for a government agency, such as the U.S. Department of Health and Human Services or the Centers for Disease Control and Prevention, in the capacity of biostatisticians, researchers, health intervention planners, and administrators.

The sociology *of* medicine, however, has a different emphasis. It deals with such factors as the organization, role relationships, norms, values, and beliefs about health as a form of human behavior. The emphasis is on the social processes that occur in health-related situations and how these contribute to our fund of knowledge on medical sociology in particular and to our understanding of social life in general. The sociology of medicine shares the same goals as all other areas of sociology and may consequently be characterized as *research and analysis of the medical or health environment from a sociological perspective.* Most sociologists of medicine are employed as professors in the sociology departments of universities and colleges.

However, problems were created by the division of work in medical sociology into a sociology of medicine and a sociology in medicine. Medical sociologists who were affiliated with departments of sociology in universities were in a stronger position to produce work that satisfied sociologists as good sociology. But sociologists in medical institutions had the advantage of participation in medicine, as well as research opportunities unavailable to those outside medical settings. Tension began to develop between the two groups over whose work was more important. This situation resolved itself as two major trends emerged to significantly reduce differences among medical sociologists. First, an evolution has taken place in medical sociological work generally toward research relevant to health practitioners and policymakers. This development is largely because of the willingness of government agencies and private foundations to fund only health-related research that can help solve problems or improve health conditions. Regardless of whether a medical sociologist works in a health care or academic setting, today much of the research in the field deals with topics that have practical utility. Moreover, many of the better studies, including those in medical settings with a practical focus, also use sociologically based theoretical models to illustrate the utility of their findings.

Second, a growing convergence among medical sociology and the general discipline of sociology took place. This situation is aided by the fact that all sociologists share the same training and methodological strategies in their approach to research. Theoretical foundations common throughout sociology are increasingly reflected in medical sociological work (Cockerham 2001, 2005, 2013a, 2013b, 2013c; Cockerham and Scambler 2010; Collyer 2012; De Maio 2010; Frohlich, Corin, and Potvin 2001; Karlsen and Nazroo 2002; Scambler 2002, 2012; Thoits 2011), while many health issues investigated by medical sociologists call for knowledge of social processes outside of the sociomedical realm. For example, studies of health reform may require consideration of the larger sociological literature on social change, political power, class, and the welfare state, while research on job-related stress requires familiarity with occupational structures. Therefore, as Bernice Pescosolido and Jennie Kronenfeld (1995:24) point out, medical sociologists "need to understand the general nature of social change and social institutions—to recognize, describe, and draw from these changes and institutions implications for health, illness, and healing." Thus, much of the future success of medical sociology is linked to its ability to utilize the findings and perspectives of the larger discipline in its work and to contribute, in turn, to general sociology.

While the division of medical sociology, as outlined by Straus (1957), has lost its distinctiveness in the United States, it never really developed elsewhere in the world. The difference was that in the United States, medical sociology was entrenched early in the universities and elsewhere it was much slower to be university-based, thereby avoiding the schism. By the 1940s and 1950s, several major American sociology departments, including Harvard, Yale, Columbia, and Chicago, offered courses in medical sociology, whereas in Britain, Germany, and other European countries, as well as in Australia, the field was largely centered in medical institutions at this time (Bloom 2002; Collyer 2012). Today, in comparison to the past, medical sociology has achieved a state of development that allows it to investigate health problems from an independent sociological perspective regardless of where the research takes place.

At present, medical sociologists constitute the largest and one of the most active groups of people doing sociological work. Medical sociologists comprise the third-largest section of the American Sociological Association and the largest sections of the British and German sociological associations. About one out of every ten American sociologists is a medical sociologist. In Germany, the German Society for Medical Sociology, an organization solely for persons working in the field of medical sociology, has had more members than the entire German Sociological Association. In Europe, medical sociologists provided the basis for the European Society for Health and Medical Sociology established in 1983. Earlier, in Asia, the Medical Sociology Section of the Sociological Association of Australia and New Zealand had been founded in 1967 and the Japanese Society for Health and Medical Sociology was established in 1974. And, more recently, the Canadian Society for the Sociology of Health was formed in 2008. Additionally, the Research Committee (RC 15) on the Sociology of Health of the International Sociological Association, established in 1959, has members from all over the world. Not only have the numbers of medical sociologists continually increased, but also the scope of matters pertinent to medical sociology has clearly broadened as issues of health, illness, and medicine have become a medium through which general issues and concerns about society have been expressed. One result is that numerous books and scientific journals dealing with medical sociology have been and continue to be published in the United States, Britain, and elsewhere, including Africa (Amzat and Razum 2014). The future of medical sociology itself is very positive. Contemporary medical sociologists are not seriously concerned with whether work is in the sociology of medicine or sociology in medicine, but rather with how much it increases our understanding of the complex relationship between social factors and health.

Defining Health

There is no single, all-purpose definition of health that fits all circumstances, but there are many concepts such as health as normality, the absence of disease, or the ability to function (Blaxter 2010). The World Health Organization (WHO) defines health as a state of complete physical, mental, and social well-being, and not merely the absence of disease or injury. This definition calls attention to the fact that being healthy involves much more than simply not being ill or injured. Being healthy also means being physically fit, having good social relationships with friends and family, being able to function or do things, and having a sense of well-being (Blaxter 2010).

Thomas McKeown (1979) supports the WHO definition when he points out that we know from personal experience that feelings of well-being are more than the perceived absence of disease and disability. Many influences—social, religious, economic, personal, and medical—contribute to such feelings. The role of medicine in this situation is the prevention of illness and premature death, as well as the care of the sick and disabled. Thus, McKeown concludes that medicine's task is not to create happiness but to remove a major source of unhappiness—disease and disability—from people's lives.

However, most studies suggest that laypersons tend to view health as the capacity to carry out their daily activities. That is, many people consider health to be a state of functional fitness and apply this definition to their everyday lives. Good health is clearly a prerequisite for the adequate functioning of any individual or society. If our health is sound, we can engage in numerous types of activities. But if we are ill, distressed, or injured, we face the curtailment of our usual round of daily life, and we may also become so preoccupied with our state of health that other pursuits are of secondary importance or even meaningless. Therefore, as René Dubos (1981) explains, *health can be defined as the ability to function*. This does not mean that healthy people are free from all health problems, but it means that they can function to the point that they can do what they want to do. Ultimately, suggests Dubos, biological success in all of its manifestations is a measure of fitness.

Contrasting Ideas About Health and Social Behavior

Attempts to understand the relationship between social behavior and health have their origin far back in history. Dubos (1969) suggested that primitive humans were similar to animals in that they, too, relied upon their instincts to stay healthy. Yet some primitive humans recognized a cause-and-effect relationship between doing certain things and alleviating symptoms of a disease or improving the condition of a wound. Since there was so much that primitive humans did not understand about the functioning of the body, *magic* became an integral component of the beliefs about the causes and cures of health disorders. In fact, an uncritical acceptance of magic and the supernatural pervaded practically every aspect of primitive life. So it is not surprising that early humans thought that illness was caused by evil spirits. Primitive medicines made from plants or animals were invariably used in combination with some form of ritual to expel the harmful spirit from a diseased body. During the Neolithic age, some 4,000 to 5,000 years ago, people living in what is today the Eastern Mediterranean and North Africa are known to have even engaged in a surgical procedure called *trepanation* or trephining, which consists of a hole being bored in the skull to liberate the evil spirit supposedly contained in a person's head. The finding by anthropologists of more than one hole in some skulls and the lack of signs of osteomyelitis (erosion of bone tissue) suggests that the operation was not always fatal. Some estimates indicate that the mortality rate from trepanation was low, an amazing accomplishment considering the difficulty of the procedure and the crude conditions under which it must have been performed (Porter 1997).

One of the earliest attempts in the Western world to formulate principles of health care, based upon rational thought and the rejection of supernatural phenomena, is found in the work of the Greek physician Hippocrates. Little is known of Hippocrates, who lived around 400 B.C., not even whether he actually authored the collection of books that bears his name. Nevertheless, the writings attributed to him have provided a number of principles underlying modern medical practice. One of his most famous contributions, the Hippocratic Oath, is the foundation of contemporary medical ethics. Among other things, it requires the physician to swear that he or she will help the sick, refrain from intentional wrongdoing or harm, and keep confidential all matters pertaining to the doctor–patient relationship.

Hippocrates also argued that medical knowledge should be derived from an understanding of the natural sciences and the logic of cause-and-effect relationships.

In his classic treatise, *On Airs, Waters, and Places*, Hippocrates pointed out that human well-being is influenced by the totality of environmental factors: living habits or lifestyle, climate, topography of the land, and the quality of air, water, and food. Concerns about health in relation to living habits, lifestyles, and the quality of air, water, and places are still very much with us today. In their intellectual orientation toward disease, Hippocrates and the ancient Greeks held views that were more in line with contemporary thinking about health than was found in the Middle Ages and the Renaissance. Much of the medical knowledge of the ancient world was lost during the Dark Ages that descended on Europe after the fall of the Roman Empire. The knowledge that survived in the West was largely preserved by the Catholic Church. The church took responsibility for dealing with mental suffering and adverse social conditions such as poverty, while physicians focused more or less exclusively on treating physical ailments. The human body was regarded as a machinelike entity that operated according to principles of physics and chemistry. The result was that both Western religion and medical science sponsored the idea "of the body as a machine, of disease as a breakdown of the machine, and of the doctor's task as repair of the machine" (Engel 1977:131).

A few physicians, such as Paracelsus, a famous Swiss doctor who lived in the early sixteenth century, did show interest in understanding more than the physical functioning of the body. Paracelsus demonstrated that specific diseases common among miners were related to their work conditions. But Paracelsus was an exception, and few systematic measures were employed to either research or cope with the effects of adverse social situations on health until the late eighteenth and early nineteenth centuries.

Modern Medicine and Regulation of the Body

Modern medicine traces its birth to Western Europe in the late eighteenth century. In analyzing the development of French medicine at this time, social theorist Michel Foucault (1973) noted the emergence of two distinct trends in medical practice—what he called "medicine of the species" and "medicine of social spaces." Medicine of the species pertained to the strong emphasis in Western medicine upon classifying diseases, diagnosing and treating patients, and finding cures. The human body became an object of study and observation in order that physiological processes could be demystified and brought under medical control. Physicians perfected their so-called clinical gaze, allowing them to observe and perceive bodily functions and dysfunctions within a standardized frame of reference. Clinics were established to both treat patients and train doctors, with the clinic providing the optimal setting for physicians to exercise authority and control over their patients.

The medicine of social spaces was concerned not with curing diseases, but preventing them. Prevention required greater government involvement in regulating the conduct of daily life—especially public hygiene. Physicians served as advisers in the enactment of laws and regulations specifying standards for food, water, and the disposal of wastes. The health of the human body thus became a subject of regulation by medical doctors and civil authorities, as social norms for healthy behavior became more widely established. In such a context, Foucault found that scientific concepts of disease had replaced notions that sickness had metaphysical (religious, magical, superstitious) origins. Disease was no longer considered an entity outside of the existing boundaries of knowledge, but an object to be studied, confronted scientifically, and controlled.

The Public's Health

Awareness that disease could be caused by unhealthy social conditions and lifestyles spread through common sense and practical experience. A most significant development occurred when it was realized that uncontaminated food, water, and air, as well as sanitary living conditions, could reduce the onset and spread of communicable diseases. Prior to the advent of modern medicine, high mortality rates from communicable diseases such as typhus, tuberculosis, scarlet fever, measles, and cholera were significantly lowered in both Europe and North America through improved hygiene and sanitation. Thus, the late eighteenth and early nineteenth centuries are conspicuous for the systematic implementation of public health measures.

Noting the link between social conditions, lifestyles, and health, some nineteenth-century European physicians argued that improvement was necessary in the living situations of the poor. They advocated governmental recognition of the social as well as medical nature of measures undertaken to promote health. Rudolf Virchow, for instance, a prominent German physician known in clinical medicine for the development of cellular pathology, insisted that medicine was a social science. Virchow argued not only that the poor should have quality medical care but also that they should have free choice of a physician. Improved medical care was to go hand in hand with changed social conditions, leading to a better life. However, these proposals had little effect outside Virchow's small circle of colleagues. Virchow's views were simply seen as too liberal by many European rulers and politicians of the period, who feared that social reforms would erode their authority and lead to revolution. There was also a widespread bias in Europe, among the educated classes, in favor of a medical science that did not acknowledge the possible benefits of health measures that were largely social.

This was ironic because several twentieth-century scholars found that the decline in deaths from infectious diseases in the second half of the nineteenth century was mainly because of improvements in diet, housing, public sanitation, and personal hygiene instead of medical innovations (McKeown 1979; Porter 1997). McKeown, for example, notes that the decline in infant mortality was due more to improved nutrition for mothers and better care and feeding for infants than to improved obstetric services. Deaths from typhus also fell dramatically without a specific medical cause. A similar drop in mortality from typhoid and dysentery led McKeown (1979:53) to conclude that "the rapid decline in mortality from diseases spread by water and food since the late nineteenth century owed little to medical intervention."

The Germ Theory of Disease and the Search for "Magic Bullets"

Most physicians in the 1800s were primarily interested in treating patients and improving the state of medical technology. They were not necessarily concerned with social reform. However, the medical doctors of the time had a history of only mixed success in curing human ailments. But as British social historian Roy Porter (1997:428) reported, "the latter part of the nineteenth century brought one of medicine's true revolutions: bacteriology." Louis Pasteur, Robert Koch, and others in bacteriological research decisively confirmed the germ theory of disease and uncovered the cause of a host of diseases, including typhoid, tetanus, and diphtheria, along with the vaccines providing immunity. Alexander Fleming followed up these advances in 1928 with the discovery of penicillin—the first antibiotic. Drug production became industrialized, which allowed mass production. The tremendous progress in the development of internal medicine, anesthesiology, pathology, immunology, and surgical techniques convinced physicians to focus exclusively upon a clinical medicine grounded in exact scientific laboratory procedures. Thus, the practice of medicine in the twentieth century rested solidly upon the premise that every disease had a specific pathogenic cause, the treatment of which could best be accomplished by removing or controlling that cause within a biomedical framework.

As Dubos (1959) pointed out, medicine's thinking was dominated by the search for drugs as "magic bullets" that could be shot into the body to kill or control all health disorders. Because research in microbiology, biochemistry, and related fields resulted in the discovery and production of a large variety of drugs and drug-based techniques for successfully treating many diseases, this approach became medicine's primary method for dealing with the problems it was called upon to treat.

Return to the "Whole Person"

By the late 1960s, polio and smallpox were largely eradicated and infectious diseases had been severely curtailed in most regions of the world. This situation produced a major change in the pattern of diseases, with chronic illnesses—which by definition are long-term and incurable—replacing infectious diseases as the major threats to health. This epidemiological transition occurred initially in industrialized nations and then spread throughout the world. It is characterized by the emergence of chronic diseases such as cancer, heart disease, and stroke as the leading causes of death. Porter (1997) observes, for example, that cancerous tumors were familiar to physicians as far back as ancient Greece and Rome, but today cancer has become much more prevalent as people live longer. Despite the vast sums spent on cancer research, no magic bullet has been found to cure it, although chemotherapy is sometimes successful in shrinking tumors. As for heart disease, Porter notes the comments of a famous British doctor who observed in 1892 that cardiac deaths were "relatively rare." However, within a few decades, coronary heart disease had become the leading cause of death in Western society with the aging of the population. New diagnostic techniques, drugs, and surgical procedures, including heart transplants, bypass surgery, and angioplasty, were developed. Also, as Porter (1997:585) states: "Public understanding of risk factors—smoking, diet, obesity, lack of exercise—improved, and lifestyle shifts made a fundamental contribution to solving the problem." Between 1970 and 1990, heart disease mortality in the United States decreased by 50 percent and is continuing to decline.

The transition to chronic diseases meant that physicians were increasingly called upon to deal with the health problems of the "whole person," which extend well beyond singular causes of disease such as a germ or virus. Contemporary medical doctors are required to treat health disorders more aptly described as "problems in living," dysfunctions that involve multiple factors of causation, not all of them biological in origin. Social and psychological factors influence not only whether or not a person becomes sick but also the form, duration, and intensity of the symptoms. Consequently, modern medicine is increasingly required to develop insights into the behaviors characteristic of the people it treats.

Also, it is not uncommon for an individual suffering from a chronic disease to feel perfectly normal, even when irreversible damage to organs and tissues is occurring. Because of the irremediable damage done to the body by a chronic disease, patients may be required to permanently change their style of living. As Anselm Strauss (1975), one of the pioneers in medical sociology, pointed out long ago, health practitioners need to know how patients with chronic disorders control their symptoms, adjust to changes in their physical condition, and live their lives. This is in addition to all else that physicians need to know about the behavior and lifestyles of individuals that influence whether they are likely to develop chronic disorders in the first place.

According to Porter, it is not only radical thinkers who appealed for a new "wholism" in medical practice, but many of the most respected figures in medicine were insistent that treating the body as a mechanical model would not produce true health. Porter (1997:634) describes the situation as follows:

> Diseases became conceptualized after 1900 as a social no less than a biological phenomenon, to be understood statistically, sociologically, and psychologically— even politically. Medicine's gaze had to incorporate wider questions of income, lifestyle, diet, habit, employment, education and family structure—in short, the entire psychosocial economy. Only thus could medicine meet the challenges of mass society, supplanting laboratory medicine preoccupied with minute investigation of lesions but indifferent as to how they got there.

At this time in history, it is clear that social behavior and social conditions play a critically important role in causing disease. Negative health lifestyles involving poor diets, lack of exercise, smoking, alcohol and drug abuse, stress, and exposure to sexually transmitted diseases like AIDS can lead to sickness, disability, and death. Positive health lifestyles—the reverse of the practices listed above—help lessen the extent of chronic health problems, better control these problems when they appear, or allow the individual to avoid them until the onset of old age. However, adverse social conditions, such as poverty, also promote health problems and reduce life expectancy. Several studies report, for example, that the poor are more likely to engage in practices that induce ill health and less likely to engage in practices that forestall illness-inducing situations (Cockerham 2013a; Pampel and Rogers 2004; Phelan *et al.* 2004; Pampel, Krueger, and Denney 2010).

The poor are exposed to more unhealthy situations in their daily lives and find themselves in circumstances where there is less opportunity for quality health care. They may confront more stress, have inadequate diets and housing, and live in areas where industries pollute the environment with cancer-causing agents or other chemicals causing skin and respiratory disorders. They may have greater exposure to communicable diseases because of crowded living conditions, parasites, insects, and vermin. To be poor by definition means to have less of the good things in life. It also means the possibility of having more of the bad things, and with respect to health problems, this seems to be the case. The poor have the highest rates of disease and disability, including heart disease, of any socioeconomic group (Braveman et al. 2010; Link and Phelan 1995, 2000; Phelan et al. 2004).

The need to understand the impact of lifestyles and social conditions on health has become increasingly important in preventing or coping with modern health disorders. This situation has promoted a closer association between medicine and the behavioral sciences of sociology, anthropology, and psychology. Medical sociologists are increasingly familiar figures, not only in medical schools but also in schools of nursing, dentistry, pharmacy, and public health, as well as in the wards and clinics of teaching hospitals. Medical sociologists now routinely hold joint teaching and research appointments between sociology departments and departments in various health-related educational institutions or are employed full-time in those institutions. They also work full-time in research organizations like the Centers for Disease Control and Prevention (CDC).

The Reemergence of Infectious Diseases

A new challenge for medical sociology is the surprising reemergence of infectious diseases as a major threat to human health, from both natural causes and bioterrorism. As George Armelagos and Kristin Harper (2010) explain, there have been three such disease transitions in human history. The first epidemiological transition occurred some 10,000 years ago when human societies shifted from foraging (hunting and gathering) to agriculture, which was marked by the emergence of novel infectious and nutritional diseases. The second transition began about 200 years ago as improved nutrition and living standards, public health measures, and medical advances in developed societies led to a decline in infectious diseases and a rise in chronic and degenerative diseases. We are now in a third epidemiological transition in which there is a resurgence of infectious diseases previously thought to be under control. Several factors, including globalization, urbanization, and global warming, are contributing to this change. This new transition is a topic that will require increasing attention from researchers in several disciplines, including medical sociology. The term *newly emerging or reemerging infectious diseases* is currently being used to refer to this phenomenon. In the late 1960s there was a widespread belief that some infectious diseases were on the verge of extinction, and the remainder were controllable through immunization or treatment with antibiotics. In 1967, the surgeon general of the United States had, in fact, declared that infectious diseases were no longer a significant problem for Americans, by saying that it was "time to close the book on infectious disease as a major health threat" (Armelagos, Brown, and Turner 2005:755). We now know this was wrong. Some pathogens have shown a remarkable ability to resist antibiotics, certain disease-transmitting insects have successfully resisted pesticides, and humans have created ecological disturbances uncovering new diseases.

For example, some previously unknown and deadly viruses such as HIV, Ebola, Lassa fever, and the Marburg virus have emerged from areas of tropical rain forests or savanna penetrated by increasing numbers of humans. Other epidemics are the result of old diseases resurfacing, such as cholera, yellow fever, polio, and diphtheria. In early period of this century alone, there have been serious outbreaks affecting humans of cholera, Marburg virus, malaria, Rift Valley fever, polio, the West Nile virus, severe acute respiratory syndrome (SARS), swine influenza, avian (bird) influenza, methicillin-resistant Staphylococcus aureus (MRSA), antibiotic staph infections, and MERS (Middle East respiratory syndrome).

Ebola

The potential for the spread of infectious diseases has been significantly enhanced in today's world by the globalization of trade and travel (Cockerham and Cockerham 2010). Air travel, in particular, makes it easy for infected people or shipments of diseased animals to move from one continent to another, spreading their virus as they go. A cough or a sneeze from an infected but symptomless passenger could pass a respiratory infection to another passenger or someone else days after that person reaches his or her destination. A bite, scratch, or exposure to an airborne virus from a diseased animal might produce an infection in a human. For example, the Marburg virus (an airborne and less potent relative of the deadly Ebola virus) is named for an old university town in central Germany where it was first identified in 1967. The virus spread to humans from a shipment of laboratory monkeys from Uganda and infected 31 people, 7 of whom died. In 1989, two shipments of monkeys from the Philippines to a laboratory in Reston, Virginia, arrived with Ebola. In a dramatic series of events, a team of medical scientists and Army personnel contained the virus in the lab facility before it was able to spread to humans in the greater metropolitan area of Washington, D.C. The first shipment of infected monkeys were all killed by lethal injection by a team dressed in space suits, although one monkey temporarily escaped within the facility before being killed. The second shipment was allowed to simply die of the disease. Four human caretakers tested positive for Ebola but did not become sick, and eventually the virus cleared from their blood. According to Richard Preston (1994:361), "they are among the very, very few human survivors of Ebola virus."

However, in 2014, the Ebola virus reached the United States in a human host. Previously Ebola had been confined to rural areas in Africa after it was first identified in 1976. It killed between 50 to 90 percent of its victims. The disease is transmitted through direct contact with a sick person's bodily fluids. Local burial traditions of cleaning, touching, and kissing the deceased, along with caring for the sick, lack of health care facilities, and being ill in unhygienic circumstances promoted infection and death. The 2014 outbreak was the worst ever. The first known victim was a 2-year-old boy who died in a southeast Guinea village. The virus spread into neighboring Sierra Leone and Liberia, and from rural areas into cities. By October, 2014, over 4,600 persons had died, including some 500 doctors and nurses. An infected diplomat from Liberia flew to Nigeria where he spread the disease resulting in eight deaths, including his own. Two sick priests from Spain sent home from Sierra Leone died after infecting a nurse who was the first person to contract Ebola outside of Africa. Three infected American aid workers and a news cameraman in Liberia were evacuated to the United States where they recovered, making it the first time people in the U. S. had ever been hospitalized from Ebola.

However, a traveler from Liberia sick with Ebola walked into a hospital emergency room in Dallas, was misdiagnosed, and mistakenly sent home. The man

BOX 1.1

Camels and the Spread of MERS

Camels have served as a basic mode of transportation in the Middle East for centuries, carrying people, supplies, and trade goods across vast deserts. Camels can also be used as food and a source of milk; additionally, some are prized for their racing ability and there are even camel "beauty" contests to select the best looking camel. Now, in another example of newly emerging diseases in the contemporary world, a recent study has identified dromedary (one-hump) camels as the source of the Middle East respiratory syndrome (MERS) (Alagalli et al. 2014). The MERS virus was first detected in Saudi Arabia in 1992, but was not a serious health threat until it emerged in force in 2012. Some 600 people became sick from it and slightly less than a third died. Besides Saudi Arabia, the disease appeared in Jordan, Qatar, United Arab Emirates, and reached Tunisia in North Africa.

A few cases appeared in Europe among people who had visited sites in the Middle East where the disease was prevalent. In 2014, MERS reached the United States by way of a health care worker who had been employed in Saudi Arabia and traveled to Indiana; he infected a person in Ohio and a person from Saudi Arabia who was visiting Florida. All three survived.

People in close vicinity of infected camels apparently were the first to be exposed to the virus through the camel's respiratory secretions (i.e., coughing, sneezing, snorting, spitting) that traveled through the air and clung to surfaces on landing. How the camels themselves became infected is not known, but it is suspected the MERS virus was transmitted to them from bats. So once again a previously unknown virus appears and this time it seems to have jumped from bats to camels to humans.

---

returned to the hospital days later and died after infecting two nurses who recovered. One of the nurses had earlier traveled to Cleveland potentially exposing her family and several hundred air travelers. CDC had cleared her to fly. Also a lab employee at the Dallas hospital went on a cruise ship to Mexico with 4,000 other passengers, but later tested negative for the disease. A doctor in New York City who was in Guinea, however, tested positive. These incidents set off a major Ebola scare in the United States. The federal government appointed a national Ebola coordinator and limited arriving travelers from West Africa to five airports where they could be monitored, while CDC set up rapid response teams and training programs.

The West Nile Virus

In the United States, another new infectious disease is the West Nile virus, which unexpectedly appeared in New York City in the summer of 1999 and went on to infect people in five northeastern states. The virus was discovered in Uganda in 1937 and was relatively common in the Nile Delta of Egypt. It made birds sick but did not kill them. Something happened to the virus in the Middle East—most likely a genetic mutation that did kill birds and eventually humans and horses—in the early 1990s. Mosquitos become infected when they bite birds that have the disease and, in turn, transmit it to humans when they bite them. In most people, the disease feels like a mild headache, but in the very young, the elderly, and those with weak immune systems, it can turn into encephalitis, causing muscle weakness, seizures, comas, and a cessation of breathing. The mutated strain of the West Nile virus was found in Israel in 1998, when birds began dying. It found its way to the Queens area of New York City the following year, which was the first time the disease had ever been seen in the Western Hemisphere.

How the new strain of the disease reached New York City is unknown, but it probably migrated in the blood of a traveler who went to Queens and was subsequently bitten by mosquitos there. The mosquitos, in turn, began spreading the disease. Dozens of people became sick, and six elderly persons died. The first sign of it was sick and dying birds at the Bronx Zoo, and then two elderly persons were admitted to a hospital in Queens with fever and muscle weakness. Lab samples were sent to the New York State Health Department and the Centers for Disease Control and Prevention (CDC) in Atlanta. As the number of sick persons increased, CDC indicated that their tests showed that the virus was St. Louis encephalitis (a close relative of the West Nile virus). The West Nile virus was not considered, because it had never been known to occur in the United States. New York City initiated an immediate citywide campaign to kill mosquitos as New Yorkers were growing fearful about a potentially dangerous and unknown virus in their midst. All one had to do was to walk outside and be bitten by a mosquito to become sick.

Yet a pathologist at the Bronx Zoo knew St. Louis encephalitis does not normally kill birds. Furthermore, another form of encephalitis, which is deadly to emus, was obviously not the culprit because the zoo's emus were healthy. CDC was again alerted, and new samples were sent to them and to an Army laboratory in Maryland. In the meantime, Central Intelligence Agency officials were becoming concerned about a possible act of bioterrorism, since an unidentified viral agent was obviously active in New York City (Preston 1999). The Army lab and CDC both concluded it was the West Nile virus. Confirmation came a few days later from a lab at the University of California at Irvine that had received brain tissue from some of the people who had died from the disease, sent by the New York State Department of Health. The virus abruptly disappeared, and it remained unclear how it would maintain itself in the North American ecosystem. "In discovering the New World," comments Preston (1999:108), "West Nile has killed a few humans and managed to roil the C.I.A., but now it has more important business—to find a way, somehow, to keep making copies of itself." If the virus migrated south with the birds and found a place to hide for the winter, Preston (1999:108) observes that "the only way we will know is if it comes back next year."

It did come back. By 2002, the West Nile virus had spread to 43 states, and over 3,600 Americans became sick from it in that year. Some 212 died. About 91,000 birds also died, while 13,000 horses became infected, and about one-third of them died. Earlier strains of the virus had not affected horses. Nothing like this has ever been seen before in biological history. Not only did a virus in one hemisphere mutate and jump to another, but in its new environment it finds a host (birds) that has no immunity and spreads via mosquito bites to other species (horses and humans). The epidemic ends with cold weather, and each year it has returned. West Nile virus reached the West Coast of the United States in 2003, when some 9,862 people became sick nationally and 264 died. However, in 2004, the number of people who contracted the disease (8,219) and deaths (182) declined, the decline continued in

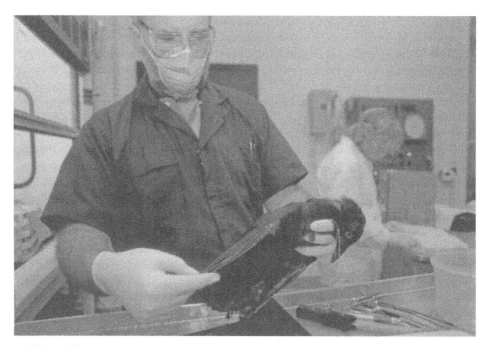

PHOTO 1.2 Wildlife pathologist examines a dead crow for West Nile disease.

2005 (3,000 cases, 119 deaths), rose in 2006 (4,269 cases, 177 deaths), fell again in 2007 (3,623 cases, 124 deaths), and continued to decline in 2008 (1,356 cases, 44 deaths) and 2009 (720 cases, 32 deaths). In 2012, however, the United States saw its largest number of cases and deaths since 2003 (5,674 cases, 286 deaths). The virus now exists in every state, but Alaska and Hawaii.

Sexually Transmitted Diseases

Among infectious diseases, one of the greatest threats worldwide comes from sexually transmitted diseases (STDs). Rates of STDs, such as syphilis and gonorrhea, had significantly decreased in the United States and Western Europe during the twentieth century because of the widespread availability of antibiotics. However, beginning in the 1970s, the prevalence of STDs increased dramatically, as the yet incurable AIDS virus was introduced into human populations in epidemic proportions. In the United States, the STDs of chlamydia, gonorrhea, AIDS, syphilis, and hepatitis B account for nearly 90 percent of cases reported for the country's ten leading infectious diseases.

What happened? What caused the prevalence of STDs to soar around the globe? According to Laurie Garrett (1994), four factors were primarily responsible: (1) the birth control pill that greatly reduced fears of unwanted pregnancy; (2) an ideology of sexual liberation and permissiveness among young urban adults throughout the world; (3) a new pattern of employment in developing nations, in which young males migrate to cities for jobs and return to their villages on weekends to spend time with their spouses and girlfriends, thereby spreading STDs acquired in urban areas to the countryside; and, perhaps most importantly (4) the availability of multiple sexual partners on an unprecedented scale.

Garrett finds that homosexual men in Europe and North America and young heterosexuals in developing countries, especially in Africa, took the greatest advantage of the new sexual climate. Ever-increasing numbers of urban residents, the availability of air travel and mass transit systems allowing people from all over the world to go to cities of their choice, and attitudes of sexual permissiveness all combined to promote the spread of STDs. But the number of sex partners an individual has is the most important risk factor in exposure to infection (Laumann, Gagnon, Michael, and Michaels 1994; Laumann and Michael 2001). As Garrett (1994:610) concludes, the world's leading infectious disease amplifier today is multiple-partner sex:

> At the top of the list has to be sex: specifically, multiple-partner sex. The terrifying pace of emergences and re-emergences of sexually-transmitted diseases all over the world since World War II is testimony to the role that highly sexually active individuals, or places of sexual activity, play in amplifying microbial emergences such as HIV-1, HIV-2, and penicillin-resistant gonorrhea.

Bioterrorism

A relatively new threat of infectious diseases is bioterrorism. Bioterrorism takes place when people knowingly prepare biological agents or gases and use them to deliberately induce illness and death among other people. As Simon Williams (2004) points out, sociology has a vital role to play in assessing bioterrorism with its themes of intentional diseases, fear, security, surveillance, combat, and other issues. There are two categories of bioterrorism: overt and covert (Butler et al. 2002). In cases of overt bioterrorism, the perpetrator announces responsibility for the event or is revealed by the attack, such as the 1995 release of sarin gas in Japan by the Aum Shinrikyo cult in the Tokyo subway. Covert events are characterized by the unannounced or unrecognized release of agents, in which the presence of sick people may be the first sign of an attack. An example is the 1985 outbreak of gastroenteritis in Oregon, caused by a religious cult contaminating several salad bars with salmonella. Another incident of gastroenteritis took place in 1996, when a disgruntled coworker put dysentery bacteria in pastries consumed by staff members in a large medical center laboratory.

A significantly more serious and terrifying covert attack was the use of anthrax sent through the U.S. mail in September through November 2001. This attack came soon after Middle East terrorists hijacked airliners and crashed them into the World Trade Center in New York City and the Pentagon in Washington, D.C., killing some 3,000 people, including the terrorists themselves. Someone then mailed anthrax spores in letters from post offices in New Jersey to certain media outlets and congressional offices. Five people died and eighteen others became sick—some seriously. The first person infected, a female editorial assistant at NBC in New York City, recovered, but her illness was not diagnosed for weeks even though she was treated in two hospital emergency rooms. The possibility of anthrax was not considered by doctors who treated the first victims, because it was so unlikely. It was a disease that doctors had never seen and never thought they would see. But the first person to die, a 63-year-old male photo editor at a Florida tabloid, was confirmed with inhalation anthrax, and the investigation of his death turned into a criminal matter when CDC epidemiologists found spores in the mailroom of the company where he worked. In the following weeks, two male postal workers in Washington, D.C., and an elderly woman in Connecticut who were exposed to contaminated mail died, as did a female hospital worker in New York City whose means of infection remains unknown. Measures were taken to protect postal facilities, and a massive investigation was launched to find the person or persons responsible.

It took seven years and the use of research techniques that did not exist in 2001, but the FBI was able to identify the source of the anthrax in 2008. A sample of the anthrax that killed the first victim was sent to a biologist at Northern Arizona University who had developed a test for identifying various strains. He determined that it was the virulent Ames strain but could not identify from which of the many laboratory cultures of the Ames strain around the world it had originated. Next, the FBI enlisted the aid of the Institute for Genomic Research (TIGR) to decode the DNA sequence of the anthrax genome. The TIGR team decoded the Ames anthrax genome and that of one of the genomes used in the attacks. They were identical, and there were no differences that could link the attack strain to other anthrax cultures. However, an Army microbiologist in Maryland spread some attack spores on a bed of nutrients and found one producing morphotypes or "morphs." The morph was distinct, and the TIGR researchers were able to decode it and found it came from a laboratory flask also at the Army lab in Maryland. The flask was in the custody of a scientist at the lab. He committed suicide as the FBI closed in to arrest him, leaving many questions unanswered.

PHOTO 1.3 A Fire Department hazmat team carries a letter containing a suspicious powder out of a building in Washington, D.C.

However, the resurgence of infectious diseases, from either natural causes or bioterrorism, forecasts a shift in the research perspective of medical sociologists from a relatively exclusive concern with chronic illnesses to considerations of both chronic and communicable diseases. Lifestyles and social behavior play an important role in the transmission of infection, as seen in sexual activities, drug use, travel, dietary habits, living situations, and bioterrorism. Therefore, the study of social factors relevant to the prevention and spread of infectious diseases is likely to take on increased importance for medical sociologists in the twenty-first century.

Bioethics

Another relatively new area of research for medical sociology is bioethics. This is because ethical (or unethical) decisions in medicine can have profound social implications and may reflect discrimination and prejudice against particular social groups. While physicians as a profession receive training in ethics and are expected to always exhibit ethical behavior in relation to their patients, there are rare mishaps. An extreme example is the medical experiments during World War II conducted by Nazi doctors on inmates of their concentration camps. An American example is the infamous Tuskegee Syphilis Study in Alabama in 1932, where a group of infected black men were recruited ostensibly for medical care. They were told their syphilis was being treated, but instead received aspirin, vitamins, and iron tonic so their U.S. Public Health Service doctors could study the course of the disease in their bodies (Bosk 2010; Epstein 2007; Washington 2006). Such gross ethical violations are supposedly in the past and safeguards—such as fully informed voluntary patient consent, acceptable risk–benefit ratios, guaranteed patient anonymity and confidentiality, ethics committees, and compliance oversight by institutional review boards (IRBs)—are now in place for all types of health-related research, including those concerned with medical sociology. The Health Insurance Portability and Accountability Act (HIPAA) of 1996 is important because it regulates the handling of patient data and privacy. However, ethical concerns about clinical care, informed consent, drug testing, and the like still exist (Bosk 2010; Orfali and DeVries 2010; Pence 2007, 2014).

One area of concern is the displacement of a considerable portion of clinical research financed by health care and pharmaceutical corporations away from academic institutions to private, for-profit research firms (Fisher 2006). Formerly, academic research laboratories performed about 70 percent of clinical trials, but today that figure has been reduced to about 30 percent. Private firms have their own review boards or hire commercial boards to expedite approval of funded projects. Consequently, clinical research has been transformed into a business conducted within a market economy, which may weaken the protection of human subjects in the quest for profits (DeVries, Turner, Orfali, and Bosk 2006:669). There can be other ethical problems as well. In 2008, a report published in the *Journal of the American Medical Association* (*JAMA*) disclosed that one drug company (Merck) had its employees prepare (ghostwrite) research manuscripts on a drug they manufactured and then recruited and paid academics to be authors and publish the articles as their work under their name in scientific journals (Ross, Hill, Egilman, and Krumholz 2008). The so-called guest authors did not always disclose drug industry support or their own paid compensation. In this situation, the objectivity of the findings and the integrity of the research process are clearly questionable.

There are many other ethical issues today in medicine that have social implications. These include controversies over stem cell research, which is a rapidly developing area in which human embryonic stem cells are used to regenerate cells and tissue in the body. The potential of stem cells in treating degenerative diseases such as Parkinson's disease and diabetes is held by proponents of such research to be revolutionary, although such claims have yet to be proven (Wainright et al. 2006). An important ethical dispute exists over the question of whether the embryos (fertilized human eggs grown in laboratories) are human beings or simply a collection of scientifically useful cells. The debate over this question temporarily led to the prohibition of embryonic stem cells in clinical research. However, in 2009, the Federal Food and Drug Administration (FDA) approved their use in clinical trials for spinal cord injuries that began in 2010 in a project of great public interest. Controversy is lacking, however, with respect to the use of adult stem cells extracted from a patient's own bone marrow to replace damaged or destroyed bone marrow with healthy bone marrow stem cells.

There are also important ethical questions associated with cloning human material, prenatal genetic screening, and the protection of an individual's genetic information from potential employers and others (Pence 2007). Additional ethical issues include abortion, euthanasia, reproductive technology featuring the fertilization of human eggs in test tubes and their implantation in a woman's uterus, the right to die, and similar questions pertaining to the meaning of life and death. These questions speak to the very nature of what it means to be a social and moral being and member of a just society. Medical sociologists have an important role in this discussion.

Summary

Throughout history, human beings have been interested in and deeply concerned with the effects of the social environment on the health of individuals and the groups to which they belong. Today, it is clear that social factors play a critically important role in health, as the greatest threats to the health and well-being of individuals stem largely from unhealthy lifestyles, high-risk behavior, and disadvantaged living conditions. Sociology's interest in medicine as a unique system of human social behavior and medicine's recognition that sociology can help health practitioners to better understand their patients and provide improved forms of health care have begun to bring about a convergence of the mutual interests of the two disciplines. More and more, medical sociologists are being invited to join the staffs of medical institutions and to participate in medical research projects. Medical sociology courses and degrees are now more frequently offered by universities and colleges. The extensive growth of sociological literature in academic medicine is further evidence of the rising status of the medical sociologist. Although a considerable amount of work remains to be done, the medical sociologist at this time is in the enviable position of participating in and influencing the development of an exciting, significant, and relatively new field.

Critical Thinking Questions

1. Medical sociology largely developed outside of mainstream sociology before becoming fully integrated within the larger discipline. What factors changed its course?
2. Explain why medical sociologists are interested in studying newly emerging infectious diseases. What is sociological about such diseases?

Suggested Readings

Blaxter, Mildred (2010) *Health*, 2nd ed. Cambridge, UK: Polity.
A discussion of the different concepts of health.
Cockerham, William C. (2013) *Social causes of health and disease*, 2nd ed. Cambridge, UK: Polity.
Reviews the evidence of social causality in health and disease.
Cockerham, William C., Robert Dingwall, and Stella R. Quah (eds.). (2014) *Wiley-Blackwell encyclopedia of health, illness, behavior, and society*, 5 vols. Oxford, UK: Wiley-Blackwell.
A comprehensive encyclopedia covering major topics in medical sociology, medical anthropology, medical geography, health psychology, public health, and behavioral medicine.
Pence, Gregory E. (2014) *Medical ethics: Accounts of ground-breaking cases*, 7th ed. New York: McGraw-Hill.
An analysis of famous bioethics cases.

References

Alagalli, Abdulaziz N., Thomas Briese, Nischay Mishra, Vishal Kapoor, Stephen C. Sameroff, Emmie de Witd, Vincent J. Munsterd, Lisa E. Hensleye, Iyad S. Zalmouta, Amit Kapoorc, Jonathan H. Epstein, William B. Karesh, Peter Daszak, Osama B. Mohammed, W. Ian Lipkin (2014) "Middle East respiratory syndrome coronavirus infection in dromedary camels in Saudi Arabia." *mBio* 5. doi: 10.1128/mBio.00884-14.
Amzat, Jimoh, and Oliver Razum (2014) *Medical sociology in Africa*. Dordrecht: Springer.
Armelagos, George J., and Kristin N. Harper (2010) "Emerging infectious diseases, urbanization, and globalization in the time of global warning," pp. 291–311 in *The new Blackwell companion to medical sociology*, W. Cockerham (ed.). Oxford, UK: Wiley-Blackwell.
Armelagos, George J., Peter J. Brown, and Bethany Turner (2005) "Evolutionary, historical and political economic perspectives on health and disease." *Social Science and Medicine* 61: 755–65.
Blaxter, Mildred (2010) *Health*, 2nd ed. Cambridge, UK: Polity.
Bloom, Samuel W. (2002) *The word as scalpel: A history of medical sociology*. New York: Oxford University Press.
Bosk, Charles L. (2010) "Bioethics, raw and cooked: Extraordinary conflict and everyday practice." *Journal of Health and Social Behavior* 51: S133–45.
Braveman, Paula A., Catherine Cubbin, Susan Egerter, David R. Williams, and Elsie Pamuk (2010) "Socioeconomic disparities in health in the United States: What the patterns tell us." *American Journal of Public Health* 100(Supp. 1): S186–S196.
Butler, Jay C., Mitchell L. Cohen, Cindy R. Friedman, Robert M. Scripp, and Craig G. Watz (2002) "Collaboration between public health and law enforcement: New paradigms and partnerships for bioterrorism planning and response." *Emerging Infectious Diseases* 8: 1–9.

Cockerham, Geoffrey B., and William C. Cockerham (2010) *Health and Globalization.* Cambridge, UK: Polity.

Cockerham, William C (2001) "Medical sociology and sociological theory," pp. 3–22 in *The Blackwell companion to medical sociology*, W. Cockerham (ed.). Oxford, UK: Blackwell.

—— (2005) "Health lifestyle theory and the convergence of agency and structure." *Journal of Health and Social Behavior* 46: 51–67.

—— (ed.) (2013a) *Medical sociology on the move: New directions in theory.* Dordrecht: Springer.

—— (2013b) *Social causes of health and disease*, 2nd ed. Cambridge, UK: Polity.

—— (2013c) "Sociological theory in medical sociology in the early twenty-first century." *Social Theory & Health* 3: 241–55.

Cockerham, William C., and Graham Scambler (2010) "Medical sociology and sociological theory," pp. 3–26 in *The new Blackwell companion to medical sociology*, W. Cockerham (ed.). Oxford, UK: Wiley-Blackwell.

Collyer, Fran (2012) *Mapping the sociology of health and medicine: America, Britain and Australia compared.* London: Palgrave Macmillan.

Daw, Jonathan, Michael Shanahan, Kathleen Mullan Harris, Andrew Smolen, Brett Haberstick, and Jason D. Boardman (2013) "Genetic sensitivity to peer behaviors: 5HTTLPR, smoking, and alcohol consumption." *Journal of Health and Social Behavior* 54: 92–108.

DeMaio, Fernando (2010) *Health and social theory.* New York: Palgrave Macmillan.

DeVries, Raymond, Leigh Turner, Kristina Orfali, and Charles Bosk (2006) "Social science and bioethics: The way forward." *Sociology of Health & Illness* 28: 265–77.

Dubos, René (1959) *Mirage of health.* New York: Harper & Row.

—— (1969) *Man, medicine, and environment.* New York: Mentor.

—— (1981) "Health and creative adaptation," pp. 6–13 in *The nation's health*, P. Lee, N. Brown, and I. Red (eds). San Francisco: Boyd & Fraser.

Durkheim, Emile. (1951) *Suicide.* New York: The Free Press.

Engels, Friedrich [1845] (1973) *The condition of the working class in England.* Moscow: Progress Publishers.

Engel, George (1977) "The need for a new medical model: A challenge for biomedicine." *Science* 196: 129–35.

Epstein, Steven (2007) *Inclusion: The politics of difference in medical research.* Chicago: University of Chicago Press.

Fisher, Jill A. (2006) "Co-ordinating 'ethical' trials: The role of research coordinators in the contract research industry." *Sociology of Health & Illness* 28: 678–94.

Foucault, Michel (1973) *The birth of the clinic.* London: Tavistock.

Freidson, Eliot (1970b) *Professional dominance.* Chicago: Aldine.

Frohlich, Katherine L., Ellen Corin, and Louise Potvin (2001) "A theoretical proposal for the relationship between context and disease." *Sociology of Health & Illness* 23: 776–97.

Frohlich, Katherine L., and Thomas Abel (2014) "Environmental justice and health practices: Understanding how health inequities arise at the local level." *Sociology of Health & Illness* 36: 199–212.

Garrett, Laurie (1994) *The coming plague.* New York: Farrar, Straus & Giroux.

Goodman, A., R. Joyce, and J. P. Smith (2011) "The long shadow cast by childhood physical and mental problems on adult life." *Proceedings of the National Academy of Sciences* 108: 6302–37.

Gouldner, Alvin (1970) *The coming crisis of western sociology.* New York: Basic Books.

Hollingshead, August B. (1973) "Medical sociology: A brief review." *Milbank Memorial Fund Quarterly* 51: 531–42.

Holtz, Timothy J., Seth Holmes, Scott Stonington, and Leon Eisenberg (2006) "Health is still so-cial: Contemporary examples in the age of genome." *PLoS Medicine* 3: e419-25.

Johnson, Malcolm (1975) "Medical sociology and sociological theory." *Social Science and Medicine* 9: 227–32.

Karlsen, Saffron, and James Y. Nazroo (2002) "Agency and structure: The impact of ethnic identity and racism on the health of ethnic minority people." *Sociology of Health & Illness* 24: 1–20.

Laumann, Edward O., John H. Gagnon, Robert T. Michael, and Stuart Michaels (1994) *The social organization of sexuality.* Chicago: University of Chicago Press.

Laumann, Edward O., and Robert T. Michael (eds) (2001) Sex, love, and health in America: Private choices and public policies. Chicago: University of Chicago Press.

Light, Donald W., and Alexander Schuller (eds.) (1986) *Political values and health care: The German experience.* Cambridge, MA: MIT Press.

Link, Bruce G., and Jo Phelan (1995) "Social conditions as fundamental causes of diseases." *Journal of Health and Social Behavior* 36(Extra issue): 80–94.

——— (2000) "Evaluating the fundamental cause explanation for social disparities in health," pp. 33–47 in Handbook of medical sociology, 5th ed., C. Bird, P. Conrad, and A. Fremont (eds). Upper Saddle River, NJ: Prentice Hall.

McKeown, Thomas (1979) *The role of medicine.* Oxford, UK: Blackwell.

Miech, Richard, Fred Pampel, Jinyoung Kim, and Richard G. Rogrers (2011) "The enduring association between education and mortality: The role of widening and narrowing disparities. *American Sociological Review* 76: 913–34.

Montez, Jennifer Karas and Anna Zajacova (2013) "Explaining the widening education gap in mortality among U. S. white women." *Journal of Health and Social Behavior* 54: 166–82.

Orfali, Kristina, and Raymond DeVries (2010) "A Sociological gaze on Bioethics," pp. 487–510 in *The new Blackwell companion to medical sociology*, W. Cockerham (ed.). Oxford, UK: Wiley-Blackwell.

Pampel, Fred C., and Richard D. Rogers (2004) "Socioeconomic status, smoking, and health: A test of competing theories of cumulative disadvantage." *Journal of Health and Social Behavior* 45: 306–21.

Pampel, Fred C., Patrick M. Krueger, and Justin T. Denney (2010) "Socioeconomic disparities in health behaviors." *Annual Review of Sociology* 36: 349–370.

Parsons, Talcott (1951) The social system. Glencoe, IL: The Free Press.

Pence, Gregory E. (2007) *Recreating medicine: Ethical issues at the frontiers of medicine.* Lanham, MD: Rowman & Littlefield.

——— (2014) *Medical ethics; Accounts of ground-breaking cases*, 7th ed. New York: McGraw-Hill.

Pescosolido, Bernice A., and Jennie J. Kronenfeld (1995) "Health, illness, and healing in an uncertain era: Challenges from and for medical sociology." *Journal of Health and Social Behavior* 36(Extra issue): 5–35.

Phelan, Jo C., and Bruce G. Link (2013) "Fundamental cause theory," pp. 105–26 in *Medical sociology on the move: New directions in theory*, W. Cockerham (ed.). Dordrecht: Springer.

Phelan, Jo C., Bruce G. Link, Ana Diez-Rouz, Ichiro Kawachi, and Bruce Levin (2004) "'Fundamental causes' of social inequalities in mortality: A test of the theory." *Journal of Health and Social Behavior* 45: 265–85.

Phelan, Jo C., Bruce G. Link, and Parisa Tehranifar (2010) "Social conditions as fundamental causes of health inequalities: Theory, evidence, and policy implications." *Journal of Health and Social Behavior* 51: S28–40.

Porter, Roy (1997) *The greatest benefit to mankind: A medical history of humanity.* New York: W. W. Norton.

Preston, Richard (1994) *The hot zone.* New York: Anchor Books.

———(1999) "West Nile mystery." *New Yorker* (October 18 & 25): 90–108.

Ross, Joseph S., Kevin P. Hill, David S. Egilman, and Harlan M. Krumholz (2008) "Guest authorship and ghostwriting in publications related to rofecoxib." *Journal of the American Medical Association* 299: 1800–12.

Sandoval, J., and M. Esteller (2012) "Cancer epigenomics: Beyond genomics." *Current Opinion in Genetics & Development* 22: 50–55.

Scambler, Graham (2002) *Health and social change: A critical theory.* Buckingham, UK: Open University Press.

——— (2009) "Health-related stigma." Sociology of Health & Illness 31: 441–55.

Simmons, L., and H. Wolff (1954) *Social science in medicine.* New York: Russell Sage.

Srole, Leo, T. S. Langner, S. T. Michael, M. K. Opler, and T. A. C. Rennie (1962) *Mental health in the metropolis: The midtown Manhattan study*, Vol. 1. New York: McGraw-Hill.

Straus, Robert (1957) "The nature and status of medical sociology." *American Sociological Review* 22: 200–204.

Strauss, Anselm (1975) *Chronic illness and the quality of life.* St. Louis: C. V. Mosby.

Suchman, Edward A. (1963) Sociology and the field of public health. New York: Russell Sage.

Thoits, Peggy A. (2011) "Mechanisms linking social ties and support to physical and mental health." *Journal of Health and Social Behavior* 52: 145–61.

Wainright, Steven P., Claire Williams, Mike Michael, Bobbie Farsides, and Alan Cribb (2006) "Ethical boundary-work in the embryonic stem cell laboratory." *Sociology of Health & Illness* 28: 732–48.

Warbasse, James (1909) Medical sociology. New York: Appleton.

Washington, Harriet A. (2006) *Medical apartheid.* New York: Doubleday.

Williams, Simon J. (2004) "Bio-attack or panic attack? Critical reflections on the ill-logic of bioterrorism and biowarfare in late/postmodernity." *Social Theory & Health* 2: 67–93.

Woolf, Steven H., and Laudan Aron (eds.) (2013) *U. S. health in international perspective: Shorter lives, poorer health.* Washington, DC: The National Academies Press.

Yang, Yang Claire, Martha K. McClintock, Michael Kozloski, and Ting Li (2013) "Social isolation and adult mortality: The role of chronic inflammation and sex differences." *Journal of Health and Social Behavior* 54: 183–203.

CHAPTER 2

Epidemiology

Many sociologists working in the health field are epidemiologists. Depending on the particular health hazard being investigated, epidemiology draws upon the knowledge and research techniques of several scientific fields. Besides sociologists, one will find physicians, public health workers, biologists, biochemists, entomologists, ornithologists, mammalogists, veterinarians, demographers, anthropologists, and perhaps even meteorologists (in studies of air pollution) involved in epidemiological work. In its strictest sense, epidemiology is the science of epidemics. However, present-day epidemiologists have broadened their field to include not only epidemic diseases but also all other forms of disease such as chronic ailments like cancer and heart disease, as well as unhealthy behaviors like alcoholism and drug addiction and bodily injury stemming from automobile accidents.

The primary focus of the epidemiologist is not on the individual, but on the health problems of social aggregates or large groups of people. The epidemiologist studies both the origin and distribution of health problems in a population, through the collection of data from many different sources. The next step is the construction of a logical chain of inferences to explain the various factors in a society, or segment of that society, that cause a particular health problem to exist. Epidemiology is one of the most important investigative fields in the study of health and disease and is applied throughout the world to solve health problems.

The role of the epidemiologist can probably be best likened to that of a detective investigating the scene of a crime for clues. The epidemiologist usually begins by examining the sick person or persons and then extends the investigation to the setting where people first became ill and are likely to become ill again. What the epidemiologist is looking for is the common denominator or denominators that link all the victims of a health problem together so that the cause of the problem can be identified and eliminated or controlled.

Epidemiological Measures

Several analytic concepts assist the epidemiologist in describing the health problems of human groups. One of these concepts pertains to the definition of a *case*. A *case*, in epidemiological terms, refers to an episode of a disorder, illness, or injury involving a person. Two other commonly employed concepts are those of *incidence* and *prevalence*. Incidence refers to the number of *new* cases of a specific health disorder occurring within a given population during a stated period of time. The incidence of influenza during a particular month would be the proportion of persons within a population who are reported as having developed the illness during the month in question. Prevalence, in contrast, would be the *total* number of cases of a health disorder that exist at any given time. Prevalence would include new cases, as well as all previously existing cases. Prevalence rates are sometimes expressed as *point prevalence* (the number of cases at a certain point in time, usually a particular day or week), *period prevalence* (the total number of cases during a specified period of time, usually a month or year), or *lifetime prevalence* (the number of people who have had the health problem at least once during their lifetime).

One way to distinguish between incidence and prevalence is to regard incidence as the rate at which cases first appear, while prevalence is the rate at which all cases exist. To illustrate the difference between incidence and prevalence, consider that the incidence of influenza in a community might be low because no new cases had developed. Yet a measure of the disease's prevalence could be a larger figure because it would represent all persons who are currently sick from the illness. For chronic health disorders such as cancer, cases initially reported in terms of incidence for a particular period may be reported later as prevalence because the duration of the disease has caused it to exist for a longer period of time. The cases are simply no longer new. Therefore, the use of data on disease determines whether an analysis should be one of incidence or prevalence. An epidemiologist would use cases denoting incidence if he or she were analyzing the outbreak of a health problem. Cases specifying prevalence would be used to study the overall extent of a disorder.

Regardless of the size of the group under investigation, the epidemiologist is concerned with the computing of ratios. This is done to develop an accurate description of a particular health disorder in relation to a particular population. The epidemiologist accomplishes this task by collecting data from various sources, such as face-to-face interviews or reports rendered by various health practitioners, institutions, and agencies. Once the relevant data are gathered, the epidemiologist computes a ratio, which demonstrates the incidence and/or prevalence of the health problem. The ratio is always expressed as the total number of cases of a disease compared to the total number of people within a population:

$$\frac{\text{Cases}}{\text{Population}}$$

The simplest ratio computed by the epidemiologist is called the *crude rate;* the number of persons (cases) who have the characteristics being measured during a specific unit of time. Typical types of crude rates are birth rates and mortality rates. For example, the crude *mortality* (death) *rate* for a particular year is computed by using the number of deaths in that year as the numerator and the total number of residents in a specific population as the denominator. The results are then multiplied by 1,000, 10,000, or 100,000, depending on whether the mortality rate being calculated is for the number of deaths per 1,000, per 10,000, or per 100,000 people. The formula for computing the crude death rate in the United States for 2014 per 1,000 people would be as follows:

$$\frac{\text{Total deaths, all ages, 2014}}{\text{Estimated U.S. population on June 30, 2014}} \times 1,000 = 2014 \text{ death rate}$$

However, crude death and birth rates are usually too gross a measure to be meaningful for most sociological purposes. Sociologists are typically concerned with the effects of specific variables or social characteristics within a population such as age, sex, race, occupation, or any other measure of significant social differences. *Age-specific rates* are an example of rates used to show differences by age. Age-specific rates are computed in the same way as crude rates, except the numerator and the denominator are confined to a specific age group (a similar method can be used to determine sex-specific rates, race-specific rates, and so forth). To calculate an age-specific rate, the procedure is to subdivide a population by age and then compare the number of cases in this subpopulation with the total number of persons within the subpopulation. For example, if you wanted to compute the age-specific mortality rate for all infants for a particular year in the United States, you would need to know how many infants there were in that year and the number of deaths that occurred in this age-specific group. The *infant mortality rate,* a measure of the deaths of all infants in a geographical area under the age of one year, is a common age-specific rate in epidemiology. You would compute the 2014 U.S. infant mortality rate in the following manner:

$$\frac{\text{Total number of deaths in 2014 among persons aged less than one year}}{\text{Number of live births during 2014}} \times 1000 = 2014 \text{ infant mortality rate}$$

The infant mortality rate has special significance for a society because it is traditionally used as an approximate indicator of a society's standard of living and quality of health care delivery. For instance, the infant mortality rate in the United States in 1900 per 1,000 infants was 162.4. By 1940, this rate had been reduced to 47.0 as living conditions, diet, and health care improved. After World War II, further advances reduced infant mortality rates per 1,000 infants to 29.2 in 1950, 27.0 in 1960, 20.0 in 1970, 12.6 in 1980, 9.2 in 1990, 6.9 in 2000, and 6.1 in 2010. Infant mortality rates have traditionally been lowest in technologically advanced societies such as Japan, Singapore, Western Europe, North America, and Australia. The highest rates are in the developing countries of South Asia and Africa.

The Development of Epidemiology

As a method of measuring diseases in human aggregates, epidemiology has been a relatively recent development. When human beings lived as nomads or in widely scattered and isolated communities, the danger from epidemics was relatively slight. However, once people began to crowd into primitive cities with unsanitary living conditions, the probabilities favoring the development of communicable diseases greatly increased. The crowded conditions of urban living ensured that infectious diseases would spread more quickly and that disease-causing microorganisms would persist within the community for longer periods of time. In addition, the migration of peoples from one region of the world to another spread disease from one geographic area to another. Bubonic plague, for example, apparently reached Europe from China during the fourteenth century, cholera entered Great Britain by way of India in the seventeenth century, and Europeans brought smallpox to the western hemisphere during the exploration and settlement of the New World. Sometimes the New World struck back. The first recorded syphilis epidemic in Europe occurred in 1493—possibly originating with the mutation of a strain of a non-sexually transmitted infection known as yaws that was prevalent in the American tropics. Columbus and his men allegedly brought the infection back with them to Europe from their voyage to America. There is evidence this yaws bacterium mutated into the sexually transmitted syphilis bacterium when it was exposed to a European environment (Harper et al. 2008). History thus reveals numerous examples of explorers and travelers introducing the microorganisms of a dreaded disease to a community of unsuspecting people.

The bubonic plague, which ravaged Europe between 1347 and 1750, marks one of the worst epidemic afflictions in all human history. It is estimated that one-third of the population of Europe, about 20 million people, died during its greatest prevalence (Cantor 2001). During one month (September 1665) in one city (London), approximately 30,000 people were killed by the plague. It was believed that the plague originated in China and reached Europe on a fleet of trading ships from Genoa that stopped in Sicily with dead and dying crewmen who had been infected at a port on the Black Sea. Although the crews were quarantined on their ships, black rats onboard were able to slip ashore unnoticed and their fleas migrated to humans spreading the deadly disease. In an authoritative history describing the plague, it was reported people went to bed feeling well and died in their sleep, doctors died attending their patients, and what made the disease especially terrifying was that no one knew what caused it or how to prevent it (Tuchman 1978). Yet even though the disease affected the rich and poor alike, there was still a *social* difference. The poor were much more likely to die from it than the rich. The wealthy had the advantage of more hygienic living conditions and could escape the pestilence in the cities by going to their country estates.

The cause of the plague was thought by many to be God's wrath upon sinners. However, the realization eventually came that diseases could be transmitted from person to person or between animals and people. Although the flea of the black rat turned out to be the origin of the plague, the pneumonic plague, the most deadly form of the bubonic plague, was transmitted from person to person. What actually ended the plague in about 1750 were significant improvements in public sanitation, along with the appearance in cities of the aggressive brown rat. The brown rat tended to avoid humans, had fleas that were less effective carriers, and drove most of Europe's black rats out of urban areas.

Although the plague is popularly believed to be a disease of the Middle Ages and no longer a major threat to the world's health, its pneumonic version resurfaced in western India in the city of Surat near Mumbai in 1994. Some 6,000 persons were hospitalized and at least 55 died. Many people fled from the area in panic, and some infected persons spread the disease to other locales. Curable if treated early by antibiotics, this modern-day outbreak of a supposedly vanquished ancient disease is a sharp reminder of the relationship between health and social conditions. Surat's population had more than doubled to over two million people in a short period of time, many of them migrants drawn to the area's textile plants and diamond-cutting workshops. About half the population lived in some of the worst and most crowded slums in India. Housing in these shantytowns consisted largely of concrete shells or dwellings made of wood, flattened oil drums, and plastic sheets. There were no sewers, running water, toilets, or garbage removal, and the local river was badly polluted from human waste. Not surprisingly, the densely packed shantytowns were the incubators for the airborne bacteria that was supposedly introduced to Surat by a migrant worker and nurtured into a full-blown epidemic by the social conditions in the city.

Epidemics like the plague have existed for centuries, but the field of epidemiology did not develop as a form of systematic scientific investigation until the nineteenth century. It was not until 1854 that the work of John Snow established the foundation of modern epidemiology. Snow was an English physician who plotted the geographic location of all reported cholera cases in London. He then went out into the neighborhoods of these victims and inquired into their day-to-day behavior. He wanted to know what they ate, what they drank, where they went, and the nature of all their activities. Eventually, Snow began to suspect that cholera was transmitted by water, since the common factor in the daily lives of the victims was getting their water from the Broad Street pump. At that time, London obtained drinking water from several water companies, and a few of these companies apparently were providing water contaminated with cholera bacteria. By closing down the pump on Broad Street, Snow was able to stop the epidemic. He not only established a mode of investigation but also demonstrated that research could lead to positive intervention and that social behavior and the physical environment were both important in the transmission of disease.

At the time of Snow's research, the development of scientific medicine was well under way. The work of Louis Pasteur and his immediate followers, during the latter part of the nineteenth century, revolutionized medical thought with the germ theory of disease stipulating that bacteria were the source of infection in the human body. The findings of Snow, Pasteur, and others provided the epidemiologist with a framework of analysis. Recognition that germs were causal agents of disease served as a precursor to scientific findings that people come into contact with a variety of causal agents. These agents include the following: (1) biological agents, such as bacteria, viruses, or insects; (2) nutritional agents, such as fats and carbohydrates as producers of cholesterol; (3) chemical agents, such as gases and toxic chemicals that pollute the air, water, and land; (4) physical agents, such as climate or vegetation; and (5) social agents, such as occupation, social class and class-based lifestyles, or location of residence.

What a person does, who a person is, and where a person lives can specify what health hazards are most likely to exist in that individual's life. The epidemiologist then identifies a particular host (person or group of persons or animals) most susceptible to these causal agents. Human hosts are examined in terms of characteristics that are both biological (age, sex, degree of immunity, and other physical attributes that promote resistance or susceptibility) and behavioral (habits, customs, and lifestyle). Next, the physical and social environment of the causal agent and the host is explored. The result is intended to be an identification of *what* is causing a group of people to become sick or suffer injury.

The term *social environment* in epidemiological research refers to living conditions, such as poverty or crowding, and also the norms, values, and attitudes that reflect a particular social and cultural context of living. Societies have socially prescribed patterns of behavior and living arrangements, as well as standards pertaining to the use of water, food and food handling, and household and personal hygiene. For example, the plague epidemic in Surat, India, in the mid-1990s, had its origin in unhealthy behavior and overcrowded, unsanitary living conditions. While it might be argued that bacteria caused the plague, not the environment, the environment was necessary for the plague to appear and gain a foothold. The social environment can cause sickness, so information about it can be used to identify the chain of transmission and assist in ascertaining the most effective means of treatment and prevention (Brown 2013).

Since its inception in the 1850s, the science of epidemiology has passed through three eras and is now entering a fourth (Susser and Susser 1996a). First was the *sanitary era* of the early nineteenth century, during which the focus of epidemiological work was largely on sewage and drainage systems, and the major preventive measure was the introduction of sanitation programs. Second was the *infectious disease era* that occurred between the late-nineteenth and mid-twentieth centuries. The principal preventive approach was to break the chain of transmission between the agent and the host. Third is the *chronic disease era* that took place in the second half of the twentieth century. Here the focus was on controlling risk factors by modifying lifestyles (i.e., diet, exercise), agents (i.e., cigarette use), or the environment (i.e., pollution, passive smoking). According to Mervyn Susser and Ezra Susser (1996b:674), the era of the twenty-first century is that of *eco-epidemiology*. Preventive measures are multidisciplinary as scientists from many fields use their techniques to deal with a variety of health problems at the molecular, social behavioral, population, and global levels. Chronic diseases remain the principal threat, but old infectious diseases are reemerging, along with new ones like the West Nile virus, avian flu, Ebola, and SARS.

Disease and Modernization

Although heart disease joins cancer, stroke, and accidents as the leading causes of disability and death in advanced industrial societies, less developed nations in the past showed somewhat different patterns of diseases. In these societies, the traditional diseases of human history, influenced by poor sanitation and malnutrition, often prevailed. Developing nations are traditionally characterized by a high birth rate and a high death rate, with a relatively young population because various diseases do not allow large numbers of people to live a long life.

A major distinction, therefore, in how diseases are distributed among population groups becomes apparent when the health profiles of industrialized societies are compared to those of developing nations. Many epidemiologists insist that there is a regular sequence of health problems corresponding to each stage of a nation's change in social organization from a rural to an urban society and from an agricultural to an industrial producer. For example, Table 2.1 shows the leading causes of death in the United States in 1900 were influenza, pneumonia, and tuberculosis. In 2010, these disorders had been replaced by heart disease, cancer, and respiratory diseases as leading causes of death. Improvements in living conditions and medical technology had all but eliminated disorders such as tuberculosis, gastroenteritis,

TABLE 2.1	The Ten Leading Causes of Death in the United States, 1900 and 2010
1900	**2010**
Influenza and pneumonia	Heart disease
Tuberculosis	Cancer
Gastroenteritis	Respiratory diseases
Heart disease	Cerebrovascular diseases
Cerebral hemorrhage	Accidents
Kidney disease	Alzheimer's disease
Accidents	Diabetes
Cancer	Kidney disease
Diseases of early infancy	Influenza and pneumonia
Diphtheria	Self-harm (suicide)

and diphtheria as major threats to life in 2010, but smoking, excessive consumption of calories and animal fats, stress reactions, and inadequate physical activity had helped promote other health problems, such as heart disease and disorders like cerebrovascular and respiratory diseases.

The same type of pattern has occurred in other countries as they experienced modernization. For instance, in 1920, Jamaica had a level of health similar to that of the poorest country in Africa today. But once development was under way in 1945, Jamaica's traditional pattern of health problems changed. There was a remarkable fall in mortality from infectious diseases and parasitic disorders. There were also declines in other diseases of the digestive and respiratory systems with a communicable component. Life expectancy increased and infant mortality decreased. Death rates from heart disease and cancer rose at the same time. Although modernization was accompanied by greater longevity and a steep decline in infectious diseases, heart disease, cancer, and other physical ailments associated with modern living increased. However, modernization in Jamaica was uneven, as is the case in other developing countries such as Brazil and Mexico. So while overall health dramatically improves in such countries, the poorest segments of the population are left with the greatest exposure to infectious diseases and the more affluent, emerging middle classes have more chronic problems such as heart disease (Armelagos, Brown, and Turner 2005; McKeown 2009).

The Complexity of Modern Ills

Many contemporary epidemiological problems are complex. This is because the major health threat to modern society is from a variety of chronic and degenerative ills related to aging and the effects of human-made environments. Examples of multicausality are seen in heart disease and obesity.

Heart Disease

Heart disease is the leading cause of death in the United States, accounting for more than one-third of all deaths. As shown in the ongoing Framingham, Massachusetts, research project, several factors are responsible for this disease (see http://www .framinghamheartstudy.org). Begun in 1948, this study shows that arteriosclerosis does not strike people at random as they age but that highly susceptible individuals can be identified in advance. Some 5,000 persons initially participated in the study, and 5,000 of their children were added in a second-generation project beginning in 1970. They were all between the ages of 30 and 60 and were free from any form of heart disease at the time of their initial examination. They are given relatively complete physical examinations every two years. The data show that sex (specifically male), advancing age, high blood pressure, cigarette smoking, diabetes, and obesity constitute significant risk factors in whether a person develops heart disease.

The proportion of risk that a person assumes with respect to each of these specific risk factors is unknown. For example, about twice as many males die from heart disease as females. But even though men have the greater overall risk, they are more likely than women to have a favorable prognosis if they survive the first serious heart attack. Furthermore, women with diabetes do not show any special advantage over men when it comes to heart disease. When epidemiologists analyze heart disease they must therefore contend with a variety of relationships between various risk factors.

Although heart disease remains America's leading killer, since the mid-1960s there has been a rapid decline in deaths from the disease for women, and especially men. About 586.8 of every 100,000 persons in the general population died from heart disease in 1950, compared with a rate of 193.6 persons per 100,000 in 2010. Smoking is a leading cause of sudden cardiac death in the United States and quitting smoking nearly eliminates this risk after a year or two. Improved medical services and surgical techniques, modified eating habits, increased exercise, and cholesterol- and blood pressure–reducing drugs are also considered important in the downturn in heart disease rates. Not all cholesterol is bad, however. Low-density lipoprotein (LDL), the so-called "bad" cholesterol, is linked with cardiovascular problems, whereas high-density lipoprotein (HDL) is believed to help the body fight heart disease.

However, as an illustration of change when it comes to modern ills, there is no longer general agreement in the medical literature on the benefits of lowering LDL cholesterol to a specific target level. Over the past several years, the target level for cholesterol has dropped sequentially from 300 mg/dl (milligrams per deciliter of blood) to 190 or below in a one-size-fits-all approach that significantly increased the number of patients diagnosed and treated medically (Welch, Schwartz, and Woloshin 2011). Rather than all patients having the same target goal today, current guidelines based on evidence from randomized controlled trials now recommend primary prevention measures be individually matched to the patient (Martin and Blumenthal 2014). Some patients with near normal cholesterol levels may not be helped by treatment and others may suffer adverse side effects from drug therapy. These side effects, especially from statin drugs, include the possibility of muscle pain and damage, constipation, cognition loss, liver damage, and increases in blood sugar levels heightening risk of Type II diabetes.

When it comes to behavior, certain lifestyles practices are thought to result in a substantially reduced risk of heart disease. Virtually all major health organizations urge people to decrease their consumption of saturated fat, lose excess weight, give up cigarettes, and regularly exercise. Yet even exercise is not a simple variable, as the effects of different types of exercise vary. For example, a major study whose findings remain valid was carried out by Ralph Paffenbarger and his associates in 1986. They investigated the physical activity and lifestyle characteristics of 16,936 Harvard University alumni, age 34 to 74, for a period of 12 to 16 years (1962–1978). It was found that exercise (such as walking, climbing stairs, and playing sports) improved life expectancy for all causes of mortality—but especially for heart disease. Death rates were one-fourth to one-third lower among Harvard alumni who expended 2,000 or more calories in exercise per week than among less active men. Risks of death were highest among those who did not exercise and who also had hypertension and smoked cigarettes. By the age of 80, Paffenbarger et al. estimated that regular exercise provided an additional one to more than two years of longevity. In a subsequent study of Harvard alumni, Paffenbarger and his colleagues (1993) analyzed changes in lifestyle activities and determined that moderately vigorous sports activity was associated with lower rates of deaths from all causes, and particularly from heart disease.

However, Paffenbarger and his associates (Lee, Hsieh, and Paffenbarger 1995; Paffenbarger et al. 1986, 1993) found that light sports such as golf did not influence the incidence of heart disease. Rather, moderately vigorous exercise was required. In general, however, some exercise was found to be better for the health of the men in the study than no exercise, but vigorous exercise made the greatest contribution to reducing heart disease. In sum, the more active the men were, the longer they were likely to live—even if they smoked or were overweight. Active workouts during leisure time are now believed to have a more positive effect on the cardiovascular system than heavy muscular work on the job, since the latter are often associated with the stress of meeting deadlines and time demands.

Obesity

In 2013, the American Medical Association (AMA) officially recognized obesity as a disease—a decision that was partly motivated to encourage physicians to give more attention to it and insurers to pay for treatment (Pollack 2013). Whether or not obesity fully qualifies as a disease remains an open question, however. Some sources, including the AMA's own Council on Science and Public Health disagreed that obesity is a disease, basing their recommendation on criticism of the body mass index (BMI), the most commonly used measure of obesity. People determined to be obese by the BMI may be otherwise healthy and others measured as not obese may have a dangerous level of lower abdomen body fat and metabolic problems linked to excessive weight. Nevertheless, the BMI remains the standard measure for

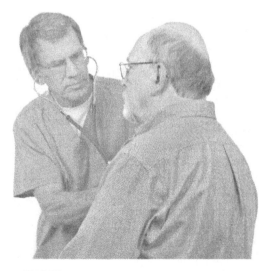

PHOTO 2.2 Men are twice as likely to die from heart disease as women, but they are more likely to have a favorable prognosis if they survive the first serious heart attack.

determining obesity because of its utility in determining the extent of a person's body fat. The AMA's House of Delegates went on to approve the designation of obesity as a disease, a decision that opens the door to increased medical intervention.

The CDC reports that the prevalence of obesity rose nationally from 13.3 percent in 1960–1962 to 34.1 percent in 2003–2006 and to 35.3 percent in 2007–2010, with diet and a lack of physical exercise being primary risk factors (National Center for Health Statistics 2013). The highest percentage of obesity by race and gender in American society in 2010 was estimated to be that of non-Hispanic black females (54.4 percent), followed by women of Mexican origin (45.8 percent), non-Hispanic black males (38.7 percent), Mexican males (36.5 percent), non-Hispanic white males (34.7 percent), and non-Hispanic white females (32.5 percent). People who are extremely obese (with a body mass index [BMI] of 35 and over) are thought to have the highest risk of death, followed (in order) by individuals who are underweight (with a BMI of 18.4 or less), and those who are less obese (BMI 30–34.9). Persons who are overweight but not obese (BMI 25–29.9) seem to have a lower risk of death for reasons yet to be explained than those of normal weight (BMI 18.5–24.9). Having a bit of fat, particularly in old age, may be protective. Nevertheless, obesity is unhealthy and contributes to the deaths of some 400,000 people a year, not only from heart disease, but stroke, diabetes, and other conditions.

Genome studies comparing obese to non-obese individuals have identified specific genes whose mutations are known to trigger obesity in humans, but they cause less than 5 percent of the obesity in the United States (Hu 2008). Environmental factors are important not just in gene-environment interaction, but also because of their independent contributions to excessive weight in the majority of obese people. The importance of the environment has promoted the study of obesity in medical sociology as overeating and weight gain are increasingly linked to social situations. A leading study is that of Nicholas Christakis and Paul Fowler (2007) who investigated the influence of social networks on the spread of obesity with BMI data from 12,067 adults assessed regularly from 1971 to 2003 as part of the Framingham Heart Study. They wanted to determine the extent to which close networks of family and friends influenced weight gain and found that individuals had a 57 percent chance of becoming obese if they had a good friend who also became obese, a 40 percent chance if a sibling became obese, and a 37 percent chance if it was spouse. Whether or not a neighbor gained weight made no difference. Christakis and Fowler conclude that the *nature* of personal ties within a social network is important for a person's weight.

A similar outcome is seen in research showing overweight girls are more likely to try to lose weight if other overweight girls in their school are doing the same thing (Mueller et al. 2010). Other studies show obesity associated with neighborhood racial isolation (Chang, Hillier, and Mehta 2009), adolescent depression (Frisco, Houle, and Martin 2010), immigrant acculturation (Van Hook and Baker 2010), race and income (Ailshire and House 2011), childhood and young adult household income (Schmeer 2010), the health disadvantages of overweight young adults in later life (Zajacova and Burgard 2010), and getting divorced or experiencing widowhood (Umberson, Liu, and Powers 2009). Weight loss associated with divorce tended to be temporary, but it was more enduring with widowhood. In sum, these studies show the relevance of social relationships and settings for a person's weight.

PHOTO 2.3 Smoking is a major risk factor for heart disease.

Turning to global trends, we see that obesity levels are expanding in many countries. For example, a study of body weight in 199 countries, based on BMI scores, found the prevalence of obesity in the world increasing between 1990 and 2008, with the greatest obesity in Oceania (tropical islands in the Pacific ocean) and the lowest in sub-Sahara Africa and Southeast Asia (Finucane et al. 2011). Among high-income countries, the highest increase in BMI scores for men were found in the United States and Australia and the lowest in Brunei, Switzerland, Italy, and France. For women, the highest increases were in the United States, Australia, and New Zealand and the lowest in Italy and Singapore. A study of the rise in obesity in Australia over three generations noted how time pressures, a decline in family dining, convenient solutions to eating (e.g., fast food, take-out, prepackaged foods, eating out), the ease of mobility with automobiles, and the decoupling of exercise from social activity (e.g., dancing, participation in team sports) were factors in weight gain (Banwell, Broom, Davies, and Dixon 2012). Socioeconomic status (SES) is also relevant for body weight in that high SES persons tend to weigh less than those on the bottom of the social scale in advanced societies, but weigh more on average than low SES individuals in developing countries (Pampel, Denney, and Krueger 2010).

Pandemics: HIV/AIDS and Influenza

The struggle against disease never ends. In some ways it becomes more difficult, as disease agents begin operating in more subtle and unanticipated ways, sometimes in relation to certain forms of social behavior and lifestyles. As we know from the first chapter, chronic diseases are not the only major health problems today. Infectious diseases are either returning or are newly emerging through the effects of globalization, urbanization, and global warming (Armelagos and Harper 2010). When epidemics from these diseases break out and literally jump continents, they become pandemics. Pandemics are not regional or local outbreaks of a disease but are epidemics that affect people in many different countries and are the deadliest infectious threat to health in a globalizing world (Cockerham and Cockerham 2010). Consequently, pandemics are a major area of investigation in epidemiology that includes consideration of social behavior. This section will review a lingering pandemic (HIV/AIDS) and a potentially new one (influenza).

HIV/AIDS

AIDS presented a formidable puzzle for epidemiologists to solve. The acquired immunodeficiency syndrome, known as AIDS, is a disease of society in the most profound sense because of its link to specific ways of life. AIDS is a particularly deadly disease that destroys a person's immunity against infection, thereby leaving the

BOX 2.1

Heart Disease, Body Size, Dementia, and the National Football League

The National Institute for Occupational Safety and Health (NIOSH) conducted a study of death rates in 2002 among some 7,000 professional football players in the National Football League (NFL) who played between 1959 and 1988. The study found that former NFL players had a 46 percent lower death rate than men of similar age and race in the current general population and that most players could expect to have a normal life expectancy. Some 189 deaths had been expected and only 103 had occurred. Because the study group contained relatively few men who had reached the age of 50, it will still be several years before researchers can determine their actual average age of death.

However, there was a major exception to the predictions of a normal life expectancy for players at certain team positions. Offensive and defensive linemen were found to have a 52 percent *greater* risk of dying from heart disease than the general population and three times (64 percent) *greater* risk of dying from heart disease than football players at other positions, like quarterbacks, running backs, wide receivers, tight ends, and players in the defensive secondary. Why? The answer is body size. Although obesity has been linked to heart disease in several studies, the NIOSH study provides evidence of one of the strongest associations between body size and heart disease. Offensive linemen in particular were singled out for risk of heart disease, as many routinely weigh as much as 300 pounds. And the number of huge football players is increasing. Today there are about 300 NFL players who weigh at least 300 pounds (a few even weigh 400 pounds) compared to only 50 such players in 1990.

Heart disease is only one health problem facing these large men. Their joints are often not able to withstand the strain of their weight and, after they retire and reach their 40s and 50s, having arthritis becomes likely. The average NFL offensive lineman's career lasts about 3.73 years, but much of what he has to do to maintain such a huge body and subject it to physical punishment on the playing field is cause for significant health problems in later life. These problems exist apart from the potential for injury while playing the sport. Moreover, repeated head trauma from being hit often in the helmet area has been found to cause problems, including depression and dementia, as they age. As an NFL survey released in 2009 showed, retired players ages 32 to 49 were 19 times more likely than the general population in their age group to have memory-related problems, while those 50 and above were five times more likely. The NFL reacted by placing strict penalties on head butts and initiated procedures for the identification and treatment of concussions during games. Improved helmet technology and protective padding to absorb shock were among safety improvements, and in 2013 the NFL awarded $765 million for concussion-related compensation and medical research in response to a lawsuit.

individual defenseless against a variety of afflictions such as cancer, pneumonia, and a host of viruses. AIDS is a virus itself—the human immunodeficiency virus (HIV)—transmitted through sexual intercourse, intravenous drug use, or blood transfusions, or passed to newborn infants by infected mothers.

What makes AIDS a disease of society is that it is lodged in the conduct of social life and sexual activity, and its influence on changing norms, values, sex habits, and lifestyles worldwide has been substantial. Thus, AIDS is no "ordinary" pandemic—it is a lethal illness with far-reaching implications for individuals, families, communities, health care providers and delivery systems, and societies around the globe (Chapman 2000; Ghaziani 2004; De Maio 2014; Kinnell 2001; Scambler 2009). It has become the leading infectious cause of mortality worldwide.

United States

Signs of the disease appeared first in the autumn of 1979. Young homosexual men with a history of promiscuity began showing up at clinics in New York, Los Angeles, and San Francisco with an unusual array of ailments. Some had strange fungal infections and others had rare cancers, such as Kaposi's sarcoma that is found only among elderly men of Mediterranean extraction or young men from equatorial Africa. Some had a deadly pneumonia, *Pneumocystis carinii,* seldom seen except in cancer and organ transplant patients weakened from prolonged treatment with drugs. Information from physicians in Los Angeles and New York City alerted the CDC in Atlanta to the problems in early 1981. Some 50 cases were initially identified around the country, and each of these individuals was interviewed. But what caused the disease and how it could be treated remained unknown as the number of victims began to increase at an alarming rate.

By mid-1984, 4,918 persons in the United States had developed AIDS; many of them died. While homosexual organizations complained that the federal government had little interest in solving the outbreak because most of the victims were gay, a task force was formed at the CDC. At first, it was thought that the cause might be an inhalant, known as "rush" or "poppers," containing either amyl nitrate or butyl nitrate, sometimes used by homosexuals to produce a "high" during sex. But this possibility was ruled out after interviews with gay men who used the inhalants but did not come down with AIDS. This development directed the attention of the investigators toward a virus or some other infectious agent transmitted by sexual contact or dirty needles, since some of the victims used drugs. Support for this theory began to emerge after a few heterosexual drug abusers and a baby in San Francisco, who received blood from a donor with AIDS, contracted the disease. The strongest evidence on the means of transmission came from sexual histories obtained in Los Angeles. AIDS was consistently linked with the sexual encounters of the victims, with the virus possibly entering the bloodstream through the anus. Three different men, for instance, none of whom were acquainted with each other, identified a man in New York City as a sexual partner; he was found to have AIDS.

The next clues were somewhat puzzling because AIDS turned up in immigrants from Haiti, where homosexuality is considered exceptionally taboo. Many of these victims denied they were homosexual or drug users, but additional investigation showed they might have gotten the disease this way. AIDS is believed to have originated in central Africa, and it was theorized that it was carried to Haiti, from where it reached the United States through homosexual contacts. In 2007, evidence from 25-year-old Haitian immigrant blood samples stored in Miami showed that AIDS likely entered the United States through Haiti.

AIDS research has confirmed that the disease is a virus, but attempts to find a cure have not been successful to date, although antiretroviral drug therapy (ART) has been able to successfully postpone the onset of AIDS in many HIV-infected people. Some have argued that HIV/AIDS has undergone a transition from an acute or communicable disease to a chronic disease because it is long-term, incurable, and affects all areas of the infected person's life (Wouters 2011). Yet despite having these characteristics, AIDS is nevertheless infectious.

It is now known that infection occurs when the virus enters the bloodstream, with anal intercourse and intravenous (IV) drug use the most common means of transmission in Western societies. In the United States, CDC data for adult and adolescent males living with HIV/AIDS at the end of 2010 show that approximately 67 percent of all cases reported were homosexual and bisexual men, 13 percent were IV drug users, and 7 percent were homosexuals and IV drug users. Of the remaining male HIV/AIDS cases, 11 percent resulted from heterosexual contacts and less than 2 percent from other causes like blood transfusions. For adult and adolescent females, the majority of HIV/AIDS cases—some 72 percent—are from heterosexual contact with infected males. Another 25 percent of females are infected from IV drug use and about 3 percent from other sources.

Routine, non-intimate contact in the home or workplace with persons with AIDS does not appear to spread the infection. Much of the fear about AIDS arises from the fact that many people who carry the virus are not aware of it. The virus can remain in the body without causing the disease, but among those who do develop AIDS, the average time between infection and diagnosis can be five years or longer. Thus, AIDS carriers can unknowingly infect other people for a number of years, since the only method to determine if a person is HIV-infected in the absence of symptoms is through a blood test. People most at risk for developing AIDS are those who have had multiple sex partners and know little about their partners' past sexual behavior.

Between 1984 and 2007, the total number of AIDS cases in the United States rose from nearly 5,000 to 1,051,875. Some 60 percent died. However, 1995 was the peak year for AIDS mortality as the number of deaths fell from 49,895 that year to 37,221 in 1996, dropped even further to 14,215 in 1999, and stood at 14,561 in 2007. The incidence of AIDS also fell from 60,620 new cases of diagnosed AIDS in 1995 to a revised figure of 56,300 in 2006. Earlier estimates had placed new AIDS cases at around 40,000 annually, but new measurement techniques later showed these figures were too low. Since the late 1990s, the revised data show the number of new infections has remained relatively stable with 55,000 to 58,000 cases annually.

For males, CDC data for 2011 show that non-Hispanic blacks had the highest rate of 112.8 new cases per 100,000 population, followed by Hispanics with 43.4, Native Hawaiians/other Pacific Islanders 34.2, American Indians/Alaska natives 18.0, non-Hispanic whites 14.5, and Asians 13.8. For females, non-Hispanic blacks also have the highest rates at 40.0 cases per 100,000 population in 2011, and Hispanics are next at 7.9, followed by American Indians/Alaska natives (5.5), Native Hawaiian/other Pacific Islanders (3.9), Asians (2.3), and non-Hispanic whites (2.0). In the beginning of the AIDS epidemic, in the mid-1980s, those infected in the United States were principally non-Hispanic white homosexual males. That pattern, however, has altered, and the magnitude of the epidemic shifted especially to African Americans and also to Hispanics.

Table 2.2 shows the mortality rates for AIDS for four selected years: 1987, 1995, 2006, and 2010. Table 2.2 depicts mortality rates for AIDS for non-Hispanic white males, increasing from 8.7 deaths per 100,000 in the general population in 1987 to 20.4 in 1995 before falling to 3.8 in 2006 and to 2.3 by 2010. The highest death rates belong to black males, with a rate of 89.0 per 100,000 in 1995, followed by a decline to 29.8 in 2006 and a further decline to 16.5 in 2010. While there has been an obvious improvement, black male mortality remains the highest

TABLE 2.2	Mortality Rates for AIDS, United States, 1987, 1995, 2006, and 2010			
	(Deaths Per 100,000 Resident Population)			
	1987	1995	2006	2010
Males				
Non-Hispanic White	8.7	20.4	3.8	2.3
Black	26.2	89.0	29.8	16.5
American Indian/Native Alaskan	*	10.5	5.4	2.6
Asian/Pacific Islander	2.5	6.0	1.3	0.7
Hispanic	18.8	40.8	9.3	4.6
Females				
Non-Hispanic White	0.5	2.5	0.7	0.5
Black	4.6	24.4	14.1	7.5
American Indian/Native Alaskan	*	*	1.6	*
Asian/Pacific Islander	*	0.6	0.3	*
Hispanic	2.1	8.8	3.1	1.1

*Less than 20 deaths.

Source: National Center for Health Statistics, 2013.

of any gender and racial group. Hispanic males had a mortality rate of 40.8 in 1995, but 2010 figures show a decline to 4.6. The lowest mortality rates for males are 0.7 per 100,000 for Asians/Pacific Islanders.

For females, Table 2.2 shows that blacks have far higher rates than all other groups, even though there was a decline from 24.4 deaths per 100,000 in 1995 to 7.5 in 2010. Female AIDS mortality for Hispanics in 2010 was 1.1 per 100,000, with even lower death rates for American Indians/Native Alaskans (less than 20 deaths total), non-Hispanic whites (0.5), and Asian/Pacific Islanders (less than 20 deaths total). While the number of new AIDS cases and mortality rates in the United States started to decline in the mid-1990s, the reversal came later and has been much slower for black women, especially those that live in the South. In states like Mississippi and North Carolina, more black women than white men have contracted AIDS. The center of the epidemic among women was initially injection drug–using women in the urban Northeast who got AIDS via contaminated needles, but it is now heterosexual black women in the South. Since 2000, the number of AIDS cases, for both males and females, has increased nearly 30 percent in six Southern states with large black populations: Alabama, Georgia, Louisiana, Mississippi, North Carolina, and South Carolina.

In 2008, the Joint United Nations and World Health Organization Program on HIV/AIDS estimated that 1.4 million North Americans were infected with HIV/AIDS, but no one really knows for sure even today how many persons carry the virus but are not yet ill. Also, no one knows what proportion of those persons who are HIV-positive will ultimately develop AIDS or the extent to which it can be contained without a vaccine that still eludes the best efforts of researchers to develop.

Worldwide

On a worldwide basis, the UN and WHO estimate that 33.3 million people were living with HIV/AIDS in 2009, with 69 percent of those infected living in Africa, south of the Sahara Desert. At least 25 million people have died since 1981. AIDS is believed to have originated in west central Africa in Gabon in one subspecies of chimpanzee (*Pan troglodytes troglodytes*) that somehow transmitted the virus to humans, possibly through blood in hunting, the preparation of chimpanzee meat to eat or sell, or by bites. As long as infections were confined to a few people in remote areas, the virus in humans remained unknown. The earliest infections may have occurred in the 1940s and 1950s, with the earliest confirmed HIV blood sample dating back to 1959 from a Bantu tribesman living in the Congo. It is not known if the man developed AIDS. Migration from rural areas into cities and the increased commercialization of sex in the region caused the disease to spread among Africans, particularly in the eastern and southern parts of the continent, and reach Europe and North America in the 1980s or earlier.

Some 22.5 million people are estimated by the UN and WHO to have HIV/AIDS in Africa south of the Sahara in 2009. African nations such as Botswana, Swaziland, Zimbabwe, and Lesotho have the highest rates per capita of AIDS in the world. Anywhere from 15 to 26 percent of the population in these four countries is HIV-infected. Life expectancy has been reduced to levels not seen since the 1800s and is among the lowest in the world. Elsewhere in the region, the country of South Africa has nearly five million HIV-infected people, which is the highest number of infected persons in any country in the world. Not surprisingly, both population growth and life expectancy are low in Sub-Saharan Africa, although antiretroviral drugs have helped restore longevity to around 50 years in the region. The effects of AIDS on Africa south of the Sahara have been devastating (Hosegood et al. 2007; Timberg and Halperin 2013; van Rensburg 2004).

However, in striking contrast to Western society, AIDS is transmitted in Africa primarily by sexual intercourse among heterosexuals. About 80 percent of all AIDS cases in Africa are believed to result from heterosexual relations. AIDS is especially prevalent among prostitutes, migrant workers, and long-distance truck drivers—but reaches up to include significant numbers of people in upper socioeconomic groups. The migrant labor system in sub-Saharan Africa plays a particularly important role in the transmission of AIDS (Mtika 2007). While African women living in rural areas typically remain in their villages to work and care for their family, African men form a large migrant labor pool seeking greater economic opportunity in mining areas, large commercial farming areas, and large cities. This system of labor promotes long absences from homes, family breakdown, and sexual infidelity. Overall, this situation has helped create a large population that suffers from epidemics of sexually transmitted diseases, thereby making it especially vulnerable to the AIDS virus.

AIDS affects women in Africa more than men, with adult women comprising 60 percent of all persons living with HIV south of the Sahara. A particular problem faced by many African women is a lack of power to negotiate safe sex, either in marriage or outside of it, because of their dependent status in relation to men. Although the passive victim image of African women does not fit all women and some may be active agents of sexuality (Tawfik and Watkins 2007), many African women are at a disadvantage in sexual relationships because of their adverse economic situation (Dodoo, Zulu, and Ezeh 2007). Poverty and the widespread lack of employment opportunities in the business sector make many women highly dependent on their spouses or sexual partners and push others into prostitution, while men can often have multiple wives or partners and divorce easily (Dodoo et al. 2007; Hunter 2007; Jewkes, Levin, and Penn-KeKana 2003).

Why the pattern of AIDS transmission seems to differ so drastically in Africa from that of North America and Europe remains a mystery. Two factors appear to be especially important. One is the low number of circumcised men (circumcision reduces the risk of infection) and the other is multiple sexual partners (Timberg and Halperin 2013). The pattern of gender stratification in which women are severely disadvantaged is likewise a major factor, along with the high prevalence of sexually transmitted diseases generally that enhance the potential for AIDS transmission, and the political violence in many African states that disrupts efforts to maintain stable and healthy relationships (Jewkes et al. 2003; McIntosh and Thomas 2004).

In Europe, the AIDS epidemic has followed the same pattern as in the United States, with the centers of infection found in major cities among homosexual and bisexual men and IV drug users. The UN and WHO estimated in 2009 that 850,000 people were HIV-infected in Western and Central Europe. The highest rates in Western Europe are found in Spain, Italy, France, and the United Kingdom. In Eastern Europe and Central Asia, at least 1.4 million were HIV-infected, with Russia, Estonia, and Ukraine having the highest rates of new infections.

AIDS victims in Asia were few until the late 1980s, when the disease began spreading rapidly. The UN and WHO estimate that 3.8 million people in South and Southeast Asia were HIV-infected in 2009. Similar to Africa, the major source of AIDS in Asia is heterosexual rather than homosexual. Thailand, which has many prostitutes and drug users, is a major center of AIDS. Thailand is the one Asian country that has mounted a major response to the epidemic with a nationwide program of education, condom promotion, and improved treatment for sexually transmitted diseases generally. Other Asian countries like Burma, Indonesia, Cambodia, and Malaysia are now finding that AIDS is entering a new, more visible phase and becoming a major crisis.

Elsewhere in South Asia, AIDS was predicted to spread throughout the population in India to a point that the disease would eventually claim more lives there than in any other country. While the AIDS epidemic is serious, the extent of the problem is currently not as large as expected. India has between 2 and 3 million people infected with HIV, not 4–5 million people as once estimated. Prostitution in large cities like Mumbai and Chennai, and along India's vast system of roadways frequented by some five million truck drivers, appears to be the major chain of transmission (Cornman et al. 2007). Homosexual activity, along with drug use, is also a factor in northeast India. So far, the AIDS epidemic appears to remain largely contained within these high-risk groups of prostitutes, truckers, male homosexuals, and drug users. If not contained, India could become the world center of the AIDS epidemic in the twenty-first century because of its large population.

In East Asia, the number of infected people in 2009 is estimated to be 770,000, mostly in China. The HIV outbreak in China initially occurred in 1989 among IV drug users in Yunnan Province in the southwestern region of the country bordering on the so-called "Golden Triangle" area of Burma, Laos, and Vietnam, where much of the world's heroin is produced (Deng, Li, Sringernyuang, and Zhang 2007; Xiao et al. 2007). By 1995, HIV/AIDS spread to other parts of China as migrant workers spread the disease through drug use and the illicit sex trade. People who become infected with HIV in China are typically subjected to stigma and discrimination that isolates them socially (Deng et al. 2007; Zhou 2007). However, after a slow start, the Chinese government responded to the AIDS menace by launching needle exchange and safe-sex initiatives in provinces where the disease is most prevalent.

Sexual intercourse with female prostitutes in Thailand, the Philippines, and other Asian countries by Japanese men is believed to be a major factor in spreading the disease in Japan, but the prevalence of HIV/AIDS remains small. In the past, the Japanese public has not viewed AIDS as a serious problem, believing it to be associated with other countries and largely confined in Japan to small groups of homosexuals and hemophiliacs (Munakata and Tajima 1996). There is no recent evidence this view has changed. Australia, New Zealand, and nearby islands are considered a separate region in the Pacific area and estimated to have about 60,000 HIV-infected people in 2009, with most cases in Papua New Guinea.

Another part of the world in which AIDS is on the increase is Latin America and the Caribbean. AIDS first appeared among homosexuals and drug users in Haiti, Argentina, and Brazil. It is now spreading throughout the region. Bisexual activity by Latin American men is believed to be important in the infection of a large proportion of females. The UN and WHO estimate that two million Latin Americans are HIV infected, with an additional 230,000 cases in the Caribbean. Brazil has the largest concentration of AIDS cases (an estimated 730,000 people) among Latin American countries, while Haiti, the Dominican Republic, and Jamaica have the highest rates in the Caribbean. HIV is also spreading in rural Mexico, as Mexican male migrants infected in the United States return and spread the disease in their home communities, and Mexican border towns provide conditions for transmission by becoming magnets for prostitutes and drug dealers attracted to the population flow northward and tourists.

AIDS thus stands as an example of how certain types of behavior (especially sexual promiscuity and/or drug use) provide a particular virus with the opportunity to cause a deadly disease. The sociological implications of the AIDS epidemic are enormous and involve not only the widespread modification of sexual behavior but also the deeply discrediting stigma attached to AIDS victims, the social rejection of AIDS patients, the subjective distress associated with becoming an AIDS patient, and the moral and religious debate centering on AIDS as a punishment for a deviant lifestyle (Chapman 2000; Ciambrone 2001; Deng et al. 2007; Zhou 2007; Scambler 2009).

The fact that many people with AIDS are homosexual or bisexual men and IV drug users has promoted widespread stigmatizing, shunning, and discrimination. When a person becomes infected with AIDS, that person in many ways becomes a social outcast—avoided by former friends, acquaintances, and sometimes even family members. People often have a "master status," which is a general status that reflects an individual's most important position in society and typically comes from one's occupation. AIDS, however, can take on the attributes of a master status in that it becomes the single most important social characteristic of an infected person. Regardless of income, education, occupation, or other source of status, persons with AIDS will likely find that having the disease will negatively influence the attitudes and reactions of others (Chapman 2000; Ghaziani 2004; Scambler 2009).

AIDS throws families into crisis as well as it causes family roles and relationships to change (Wouters 2011). Relationships can become strained when families cope with the stigma of AIDS, but families also involve themselves in the care and support of the infected member. For all concerned, this can be an extremely stressful situation. Not only are patients and their families affected, but so are nurses, physicians, and other health care providers who work with AIDS patients (Thomas 2006). Health personnel not only risk exposure to the virus, but they themselves may also be shunned by colleagues and friends, mourn the deaths of patients, and become frustrated at their inability to provide a cure. AIDS is clearly a complex social disease.

Since AIDS results from a private act that has extreme social consequences, serious moral and legal questions also arise about the rights of individuals versus the welfare of society. The central public problem is how to alter behavior that occurs in the most private of settings and whether it can be done in a way that does not violate civil liberties. The current public policy approach to dealing with AIDS is to limit its spread through educational programs stressing safe sex, yet the possibility of quarantines and universal testing remains in the background if the incurable and fatal disease races unchecked through society. However, some state legislatures in the United States have passed laws to protect the public. Several states have laws making it a crime to transmit or knowingly expose other people to HIV/AIDS as well as requiring mandatory testing of prison inmates and pregnant women and notification of partners of infected people. AIDS remains the major public health issue of our time.

Influenza

Influenza presents an especially deadly threat of a pandemic. This disease is common among humans and claims lives every year in every country. Estimating the number of individual flu cases is challenging because many people sick with the flu do not seek medical care and only a small number of those that do seek care are tested. More people who are hospitalized or die of flu-related causes are tested and reported, but sometimes underreporting of hospitalizations and deaths occurs. Nevertheless, the best estimates from CDC suggest that in a typical year, about 36,000 Americans die from the flu and another 200,000 are hospitalized. Should a flu pandemic occur, these figures would be several times higher in the United States and other countries. Influenza pandemics can kill millions of people worldwide when they have little or no immunity against the disease. The great influenza pandemic of 1918 ("Spanish flu"), for example, took 40 million lives globally, while two million people died in 1957 ("Asian flu") and one million in 1968 ("Hong

Kong flu"). Influenza pandemics are unpredictable, occur at irregular intervals, and the potential for one to occur today is high.

The most recent pandemic came in the spring of 2009 when a novel version of the influenza A (H1N1) virus (or swine flu) was first detected in Mexico before spreading to more than 214 countries around the world. Its exact origin has yet to be determined. Many of the initial victims were Mexicans or had visited Mexico as tourists and returned to their countries with the disease. Schools and businesses were closed in Mexico and tourism suffered. The first fatality in the United States was a Mexican child who had accompanied relatives to Texas. Early tests linked the flu to pigs. More extensive tests showed it to be a unique version of influenza consisting of a novel combination of a gene from a Eurasian pig flu with genes from human, bird, and North American pig flu. Although a hybrid, the original name of swine flu stuck in the public mind. Some 257,000 people in the United States were believed to have been hospitalized with H1N1 by early 2010 and 11,200 died. Schools were also closed in parts of the United States, and school activities like sports events postponed or cancelled. People in many countries became more careful about exposure to individuals with flu symptoms. While ultimately the disease was not as dangerous as it could have been, it was still a highly life-threatening occurrence. Estimates vary, but more than 200,000 people worldwide may have died from swine flu or related cardiac problems.

Another version of the influenza A virus is the H5N1 strain known as avian flu. This flu has killed over 200 million birds in Asia and jumped to humans in 1997, causing at least 379 human deaths since 2003. It refuses to disappear and should it mutate or combine with a human influenza virus in a way that would allow it to be readily transmitted from person to person, the world would face a major challenge. Such a pandemic could spread around the globe, passing in waves, and causing millions of people, including health care personnel, to become sick. Some 50 to 80 million people in an unprepared world population could die if the pandemic was similar to the one that occurred in 1918–20. If the 1918 pattern is repeated, people of all ages would be affected, with mortality highest among the young, persons in their 30s, and those over the age of 70. A major problem is the availability of a suitable vaccine. One vaccine considered effective for most types of flu is Oseltamivir ("Tamiflu") that blocks viral replication. But it is effective only if given within 48 hours and depends on adequate global stockpiles.

In early 2014, two new avian flu strains, H7N9 and H10N8, appeared in China. Some 300 persons were reported sick from H7N9 and about a quarter of them had died; only a few people were sick from H10N8. Neither makes poultry sick, making them difficult to monitor and particular concern exists about the possible spread of H7N9. Public health fears about avian flu and its potential to become a pandemic have therefore placed the disease at the forefront of the global health agenda. A major factor in avian flu is the close contact between humans and poultry. A pandemic outbreak in this sector of the economy would not only harm people and birds but also have a dramatic effect on local and global economies and food supplies, as chickens have been particularly susceptible to this disease. While the avian flu virus has not yet been detected in the Western Hemisphere, it may be only a matter of time until it arrives. Despite control measures in the Asian countries where it has infected largely birds, it continues to spread, causing heavy losses to poultry farmers and an occasional human death. Because of the serious health risk it represents, it is monitored closely by national and international health agencies.

Summary

The epidemiologist is like a detective, investigating the scene of a crime in which the criminal is a disease or some other form of health menace. The epidemiologist is primarily concerned not with individuals but with the health profiles of social aggregates or large populations of people. Important tools of the epidemiologist are the ratios used to compute descriptions of mortality, incidence, and prevalence. These rates can be either crude rates or rates reflecting age-specific data, sex-specific data, and so on.

Many diseases in modern society such as coronary heart disease are very complex. The example of AIDS indicates how challenging health problems can be to the practice of epidemiology. Moreover, it has been noted that as underdeveloped societies modernize, the pattern of their diseases changes accordingly. Communicable diseases are replaced by chronic illnesses such as heart disease and cancer. A demanding lifestyle, inadequate diet, smoking, drug and alcohol abuse, obesity, lack of exercise, and exposure to environmental pollution have become the principal risk factors for ill health in modern society. But people can change their behavior and reduce or eliminate their risk of becoming sick.

Critical Thinking Questions

1. Epidemiologists work like detectives solving a crime. What procedures do they use to uncover the causes of a health problem?
2. Recognize how disease patterns are affected by modernization.
3. Explain why heart disease and obesity have complex causes that include social factors. What are these factors and are they important?
4. Define a pandemic and review the social features of AIDS and influenza.

Suggested Readings

De Maio, Fernando (2014) *Global health inequities: A sociological perspective.* New York: Palgrave Macmillan.
Applies epidemiological and sociological concepts to global health disparities
Dingwall, Robert, Lily M. Hoffman, and Karen Staniland (eds.) (2013) *Pandemics and emerging infectious diseases: The sociological agenda.* Oxford, UK: Wiley-Blackwell.
Collection of original articles on pandemics and societal responses to infectious diseases.
Kidder, Tracy (2004) *Mountains beyond mountains: The quest of Dr. Paul Farmer, a man who would cure the world.* New York: Random House.
Story of a medical doctor and his travels to Haiti and other countries to try to improve the health of socially and economically disadvantaged people.
Shim, Janet K. (2014) *Heart-sick: The politics of risk, inequality, and heart disease.* New York: New York University Press.
Discusses the consequences of social differences for heart disease.

References

Ailshire, Jennifer A., and James S. House (2011) "The unequal burden of weight gain: An intersectional approach to understanding social disparities in BMI trajectories from 1986 to 2001/2002." *Social Forces* 90: 397–423.

Armelagos, George J., and Kristin N. Harper (2010) "Emerging infectious diseases, urbanization, and globalization in the time of global warning," pp. 291–311 in *The new Blackwell companion to medical sociology*, W. Cockerham (ed.). Oxford, UK: Wiley-Blackwell.

Armelagos, George J., Peter J. Brown, and Bethany Turner (2005) "Evolutionary, historical and political economic perspectives on health and disease." *Social Science and Medicine* 61: 755–65.

Banwell, Cathy, Dorothy Broom, Anna Davies, and Jane Dixon (2012) *Weight of modernity: An intergenerational study of the rise of obesity.* Dordrecht: Springer.

Brown, Phil (2013) "Integrating medical and environmental sociology with environmental health: Crossing boundaries and building connections through advocacy." *Journal of Health and Social Behavior* 54: 145–64.

Cantor, Norman F. (2001) *In the wake of the plague: The black death and the world it made.* New York: The Free Press.

Chang, Virginia W., Amy F. Hillier, and Neil K. Mehta (2009) "Neighborhood racial isolation, disorder and obesity." *Social Forces* 87: 2063–92.

Chapman, Elizabeth (2000) "Conceptualization of the body for people living with HIV: Issues of touch and contamination." *Sociology of Health & Illness* 22: 840–57.

Christakis, Nicholas A., and James H. Fowler (2007) "The spread of obesity in a large social network over 32 years." *New England Journal of Medicine* 357: 370–79.

Ciambrone, Desirée (2001) "Illness and other assaults on the self: The relative impact of HIV/AIDS on women's lives." *Sociology of Health & Illness* 23: 517–40.

Cockerham, Geoffrey B., and William C. Cockerham (2010) *Health and Globalization.* Cambridge, UK: Polity.

Cornman, Deborah H., Sarah J. Schmiege, Angela Bryan, T. Joseph Benziger, and Jeffrey D. Fisher (2007) "An information-motivation-behavioral skills (IMB) model-based prevention intervention for truck drivers in India." *Social Science and Medicine* 64: 1572–84.

De Maio, Fernando (2014) *Global health inequities: A sociological perspective.* New York: Palgrave Macmillan.

Deng, Rui, Jianghong Li, Luechai Sringernyuang, and Kaining Zhang (2007) "Drug abuse, HIV/AIDS and stigmatization in a Dai community in Yunnan, China." *Social Science and Medicine* 64: 1560–71.

Dodoo, F. Nii-Amoo, Eliya M. Zulu, and Alex C. Ezeh (2007) "Urban-rural differences in the socioeconomic deprivation-sexual behavior link in Kenya." *Social Science and Medicine* 64: 1019–31.

Finucane, M., G. Stevens, M. Cowan, G. Danaei, J. Liu, C. Paciorek, G. Singh, H. Gutierrez, Y. Lu, A. Bahalim, F. Farzadfar, L. Riley, M. Ezzati, and Global Burden of Metabolic Risk Factors of Chronic Diseases Collaborating Group (Body Mass Index) (2011) "National, regional, and global trends in body-mass index since 1981: Systematic analysis of health examination surveys and epidemiological studies with 960 country-years and 9.1 million participants." *Lancet* 377: 557–67.

Frisco, Michelle L., Jason N. Houle, and Molly A. Martin (2010) "The image in the mirror and the number on the scale: Weight, weight perceptions, and adolescent depressive symptoms." *Journal of Health and Social Behavior* 51: 215–28.

Ghaziani, Amin (2004) "Anticipatory and actualized identities: A cultural analysis of the transition from AIDS disability to work." *Sociological Quarterly* 45: 273–301.

Harper, Kristin N., Paolo S. Ocampo, Bret M. Steiner, Robert W. George, Michael S. Silverman, Shelly Bolotin, Allan Pillay, Nigel J. Saunders, and George J. Armelagos (2008) "On the origin of Treponematoses: A phylogenetic approach." *PLoS Neglected Tropical Diseases* 2(1): e148.

Hosegood, Victoria, Eleanor Preston-Whyte, Joanna Busza, Sindile Moitse, and Ian M. Timaeus (2007) "Revealing the full extent of households' experiences of HIV and AIDS in rural South Africa." *Social Science and Medicine* 65: 1249–59.

Hu, F. (ed.). (2008) *Obesity Epidemiology*. New York: Oxford University Press.

Hunter, Mark (2007) "The changing political economy of sex in South Africa: The significance of unemployment and inequalities to the scale of the AIDS pandemic." *Social Science and Medicine* 64: 689–700.

Jewkes, Rachel K., Jonathan B. Levin, and Loveday A. Penn-Kekana (2003) "Gender inequalities, intimate partner violence and HIV preventive practices: Findings of a South African cross-sectional study." *Social Science and Medicine* 56: 125–34.

Kinnell, Ann Marie Kofmehl (2001) " 'So why are you here?' Assessing risk in HIV prevention and test decision counseling." *Sociology of Health & Illness* 23: 447–77.

Lee, I-Min, Chung-Cheng Hsieh, and Ralph S. Paffenbarger (1995) "Exercise intensity and longevity in men." *Journal of the American Medical Association* 273: 1179–84.

Martin, Seth S., and Roger S. Blumenthal (2014) "Concepts and controversies: The 2013 American College of Cardiology/American Heart Association Risk Assessment and Cholesterol Treatment Guidelines." *Annals of Internal Medicine*. Published online 28 January, 2014 doi:10.7326/M13-2805.

McIntosh, William Alex, and John K. Thomas (2004) "Economic and other societal determinants of the prevalence of HIV: A test of competing hypotheses." *Sociological Quarterly* 45: 303–24.

McKeown, Robert E. (2009) "The epidemiologic transition: Changing patterns of mortality and population dynamics." *American Journal of Lifestyle Medicine* 3(1 Supplement): 19S–26S.

Mtika, Mike Mathambo (2007) "Political economy, labor migration, and the AIDS epidemic in rural Malawi." *Social Science and Medicine* 64: 2454–63.

Mueller, Anna S., Jennifer Pearson, Chandra Muller, Kenneth Frank, and Alyn Turner (2010) "Sizing up peers: Adolescent girls' weight control and social comparison in the school context." *Journal of Health and Social Behavior* 51: 64–78.

Munakata, Tsunetsugu, and Kazuo Tajima (1996) "Japanese risk behaviors and their HIV/AIDS-preventive behaviors." *AIDS Education and Prevention* 8: 115–33.

National Center for Health Statistics (2013) *Health United States, 2012*. Washington, DC: U.S. Government Printing Office.

Paffenbarger, Ralph S., Jr., Robert T. Hyde, Alvin L. Wing, and Chung-Cheng Hsieh (1986) "Physical activity, all-cause mortality, and longevity of college alumni." *New England Journal of Medicine* 314: 605–13.

Paffenbarger, Ralph S., Jr., Robert T. Hyde, Alvin Wing, I-Min Lee, Dexter L. Jung, and James Kampert (1993) "The association of changes in physical-activity level and other lifestyle characteristics with mortality among men." *New England Journal of Medicine* 32: 538–45.

Pampel, Fred C., Patrick M. Krueger, and Justin T. Denney (2010) "Socioeconomic disparities in health behaviors." *Annual Review of Sociology* 36: 349–370.

Pollack, Andrew (2013) "A.M.A. recognizes obesity as a disease." *New York Times* (June 19): B1.

Scambler, Graham (2009) "Health-related stigma." *Sociology of Health & Illness* 31: 441–55.

Schmeer, Kammi K. (2010) "Household income during childhood and young adult weight status: Evidence from a nutrition transition setting." *Journal of Health and Social Behavior* 51: 79–91.

Susser, Mervyn, and Ezra Susser (1996a) "Choosing a future for epidemiology: I. Eras and paradigms." *American Journal of Public Health* 86: 668–73.

——— (1996b) "Choosing a future for epidemiology: II. From black box to Chinese boxes and eco-epidemiology." *American Journal of Public Health* 86: 674–77.

Tawfik, Linda, and Susan Cotts Watkins (2007) "Sex in Geneva, sex in Lilongwe, and sex in Balaka." *Social Science and Medicine* 64: 1090–101.

Thomas, Felicity (2006) "Stigma, fatigue and social breakdown: Exploring the impacts of HIV/AIDS on patient and carer well-being in the Caprivi Region, Nambia." *Social Science and Medicine* 63: 3174–87.

Timberg, Craig, and Daniel Halperin (2013) *Tinderbox: How the West sparked the AIDS epidemic and how the world can finally overcome it.* New York: Penguin.

Tuchman, Barbara W. (1978) *A distant mirror: The calamitous 14th century.* New York: Random House.

Umberson, Debra, Hui Liu, and Daniel Powers (2009) "Marital status, marital transitions, and body weight." *Journal of Health and Social Behavior* 50: 327–43.

Van Hook, Jennifer, and Elizabeth Baker (2010) "Big boys and little girls: Gender, acculturation, and weight among children of immigrants." *Journal of Health and Social Behavior* 51: 200–14.

Van Rensburg, Dingie (ed.) (2004) *Health and health care in South Africa.* Hatfield, Pretoria, South Africa: Van Schaik.

Welch, H. Gilbert, Lisa M. Schwartz, and Steven Woloshin (2011) *Overdiagnosed: Making people sick in the pursuit of health.* Boston: Beacon Press.

Wouters, Edwin (2011) "Life with HIV as a chronic illness: A theoretical and methodological framework for antiretroviral treatment studies in resource-limited-settings." *Social Theory & Health* 10: 368–91.

Xiao, Yan, Sibylle Kristensen, Jiangping Sun, Lin Lu, and Sten H. Vermund (2007) "Expansion of HIV/AIDS in China: Lessons from Yunnan province." *Social Science and Medicine* 64: 665–75.

Zajacova, Anna, and Sarah A. Burgard (2010) "Body weight and health from early to mid-adulthood: A longitudinal analysis." *Journal of Health and Social Behavior* 51: 92–107.

Zhou, Yanqui Rachel (2007) "'If you get AIDS . . . You have to endure it alone': Understanding the social construction of AIDS in China." *Social Science and Medicine* 65: 284–95.

CHAPTER 3

The Social Demography of Health: Social Class

To be poor is by definition to have less of the good things in life, including health and longevity. British epidemiologist Michael Marmot (2004:2) illustrates this situation by saying that if you want to get a sense of how socioeconomic status affects health, take a ride on the metro system in Washington, D.C., from the deteriorated neighborhoods southeast of downtown to upscale Montgomery County in Maryland. For every mile traveled, life expectancy for neighborhood residents rises approximately one and one-half years. There is a 20-year gap in life expectancy between the low-income blacks at the beginning of the journey and the wealthy whites at the end. Thus, you see the same 20-year gap in life expectancy within the greater metropolitan area of Washington as you see when you compare the longevity of men in Switzerland in Europe, where males currently have the highest life expectancy in the world at 80.3 years, with men in the country of Sudan in Africa, where male longevity is around 60 years.

In the United States, as well as in virtually all countries without exception, the wealthy are healthier and live longer on average than the poor. It is a sociological fact that the further down one goes in the social structure of a society, the worse the health of the people on that rung of the social ladder. Conversely, the higher one goes in the class structure, the better the overall level of health. This outcome applies to all diseases with few exceptions and throughout the life span (Link and Phelan 1995, 2000; Lutfey and Freese 2005; Phelan et al. 2004; Phelan, Link, and Tehranifer 2010). Consequently, socioeconomic status or social class is the strongest and most consistent predictor of a person's health and life expectancy throughout the world (Bartley 2004; Barr 2008; Braveman et al. 2010; Braveman and Tarimo 2002; Budrys 2003; Carpiano, Link, and Phelan 2008; Cockerham 2013; Goosby 2013; Lahelma 2010; Link, Phelan, Miech, and Westin 2008; Lutfey and Freese 2005; Marmot 2004; Mulatu and Schooler 2002; Pampel, Krueger, and Denney 2010; Olshansky et al. 2012; Phelan et al. 2004; Prus 2007; Saldana-Ruiz et al. 2013; Segall and Fries 2011; Semyonov, Lewin-Epstein, and Maskileyson 2013; Warren 2009; Wermuth 2003).

Even though other social demographic variables such as race, gender, and age also have important effects on health, the explanatory power of class position is evident when it interacts with these other variables to produce differences beyond those already produced. As British sociologist Ivan Reid (1998) pointed out years ago, social class is the most fundamental form of social stratification. "Put as boldly as possible," says Reid (1998:238), "being black, female or elderly and middle class is different from being black, female or elderly and working class."

The Components of Social Class

Before examining the relationship between class and health, it is useful to discuss how sociologists determine a person's class position. A social class is a category or group of people who have approximately the same amount of wealth, status, and power in a society. The various classes are ranked in a hierarchical pattern from top to bottom on the basis of how much wealth, status, and power they have relative to each other and thereby constitute a layered system of socially stratified human beings. The pattern is one of inequality in which classes at the top have the best living conditions and greater access to quality goods and services, while those at the very bottom have none of these things. The relevance of social inequality in the daily lives of most individuals is that it determines their personal opportunities and life experiences in very powerful ways. To be poor by definition means having less of the good things in life and more of the bad things, including more health problems and less longevity.

Different models of class structure exist in medical sociology, including the basic three-class scheme of upper, middle, and lower. However, the model often followed in the United States by medical sociologists who desire greater precision in their analysis evolved out of one suggested by the work of the classical German social theorist Max Weber ([1922] 1978) in the early twentieth century. This is a five-class model consisting of (1) the upper class (extremely wealthy top corporate executives and professionals); (2) the upper-middle class (affluent well-educated professionals and high-level managers); (3) the lower-middle class (office and sales workers, small

PHOTO 3.2 Working-class man smoking on the job.

PHOTO 3.3 Social class is a much stronger predictor of good health than race.

business owners, teachers, managers, etc.); (4) the working class (skilled and higher semiskilled workers, lower-level clerical workers, etc.); and (5) the lower class (less semiskilled and unskilled workers, the chronically unemployed, etc.).

The British have typically focused on occupation to determine class standing. In 2001, social scientists in the United Kingdom adopted the National Statistics Socio-Economic Classification (NS-SEC) scheme as their official measure of class position. This approach was based on differences in employment relationships (such as decision-making autonomy and job security) and work conditions (such as promotion opportunities and influence over the planning of work) that commonly used a seven-class model. This system, however, was merged in 2008 into the European Socio-Economic Classification (ESeC) model using similar criteria of employment relationships to measure class position (Rose and Harrison 2010). The ESeC was designed for use in all countries of the European Union and features a ten-class model: (1) large employers and higher grade professional, managerial, and administrative occupations; (2) lower grade professional, managerial and administrative occupations, and higher grade technical and supervisory occupations; (3) intermediate occupations (such as higher grade white-collar workers); (4) small employers and self-employed occupations, not including agriculture; (5) self-employed occupations, including agriculture; (6) lower technical and supervisory occupations; (7) lower services, sales, and clerical occupations; (8) lower technical occupations; (9) routine occupations with low job security, no career prospects, and closely supervised work; and (10) no occupation and long-term unemployment.

While the Europeans use a person's occupation in determining that individual's location in a class hierarchy, American sociologists use a broader measure of socio-economic status (SES). The concept of SES is derived from ideas about social stratification put forward by Weber ([1922] 1978). Weber agreed with Karl Marx that a basic source of class distinctions was the unequal distribution of material goods and wealth. However, he pointed out that there was more to social stratification than wealth alone and observed that status and power are important as well. Although wealth is an objective dimension of a person's social rank based upon how much money or property he or she possesses, status is a subjective dimension consisting of how much esteem the person is accorded by other people. Status indicates a person's level of social prestige, which may or may not correspond to wealth. In Weber's view, status is derived particularly from social judgments about a person's lifestyle and what he or she consumes and from that person's level of education and occupational prestige. People with similar class standing generally have similar lifestyles.

As for power, Weber defined it as the ability to realize one's will even against the resistance of others. But he was vague about what power meant in relation to status, and most sociologists today agree its contemporary meaning is the amount of political influence a person has. Power is clearly affected by wealth and status, status by wealth and power, and wealth by power and status, so all three variables are interrelated but distinct. Weber advanced the concept of status groups to represent groups of people who are alike with respect to wealth, status, and power.

Yet, the term *status groups* did not replace *social class* in sociology to signify a person's location in a social structure. This is because the term *social class* in its popular usage came to incorporate notions of status and power within it, although Weber himself had not done so. He had viewed classes more strictly as groups with similar income levels distinct from considerations of status. However, as the concept of social class evolved, it took on a more comprehensive meaning that included ratings of status and power. As David Swartz (1997:45) points out, "Status groups and status distinctions are [actually] classes and class distinctions in disguise."

Weber's influence on modern studies of social stratification is nevertheless seen in the widespread use of SES to determine class standing in sociological research. SES consists of three variables: income, occupational prestige, and level of education. The advantage of using this measure in quantitative studies is that income, occupation (through the use of scales ranking occupations in terms of prestige), and years of education can all be assigned numerical values that sort people into social classes based on their scores. Although interrelated, each of these variables reflects different dimensions of a person's position in the class structure of a society. In studies of health and illness, income reflects spending power, housing, diet, and medical care; occupation signifies job status, responsibility at work, physical activity, and health risks associated with one's work; and education is indicative of a person's skills for acquiring positive social, psychological, and economic resources such as good jobs, nice homes, health insurance, access to quality health care, and knowledge about healthy lifestyles (Winkleby, Jatulis, Frank, and Fortmann 1992:816).

While income and occupational status are important, many studies show that education is often an exceptionally strong predictor of good health (Dupre 2007;

Goesling 2007; Jemal et al. 2008; Margolis 2013; Mirowsky and Ross 2003; Olshansky et al. 2012; Pampel et al. 2010; Schnittker 2004). Even in Sweden and the other Scandinavian countries that have high levels of health and a greater distribution of welfare benefits protecting the disadvantaged than found elsewhere, better educated people still have the best health and lowest mortality (Eikemo, Husiman, Bambra, and Kunst 2008). Why is education so significant? It is because well-educated people, especially those with a university education, are generally the best informed about the merits of a healthy lifestyle involving exercise, no smoking, moderate drinking, a healthy diet, and similar practices, along with knowing the advantages of seeking preventive care or medical treatment for health problems when they need it. They are also more likely to have well-paid and more personally satisfying jobs, giving them better control over their lives and the way they live. John Mirowsky and Catherine Ross (2003) note that literally all the pathways from education to health are positive and that higher education and good health generally go together. Mirowsky and Ross (2003:49) state:

> By every measure American adults with college educations enjoy better health than those with lower levels of education. The better-educated feel healthier, have less difficulty with common activities and tasks, more frequently feel vigorous and thriving, less often suffer aches, pains, and malaise, less often feel worried or depressed, carry fewer diagnoses of threatening or debilitating chronic disease, expect to live longer, and probably will live longer.

In a major study in the United States, Ross and Chia-ling Wu (1995) found that well-educated people—in comparison to the less educated—are more likely to have fulfilling, subjectively rewarding jobs, high incomes, less economic hardship, a greater sense of control over their lives and their health, and healthier lifestyles. The Ross and Wu study is important because it shows why the relationship between education and health is particularly strong. This relationship, in fact, gets stronger over the life course, as less-educated persons have increasingly more sickness and disability and die sooner than the well-educated (Dupre 2007; Pudrovska 2014; Robert and House 2000; Ross and Wu 1996).

However, education is not the entire story when it comes to the effects of SES on health. New research is showing that the relationship between income, education, and health changes over the life course, with income becoming more important for health as a person moves toward older age (Herd, Goesling, and House 2007; Kahn and Pearlin 2006; Lynch 2006). For example, Pamela Herd et al. (2007) found in a nationwide study in the United States that education has a significant effect with respect to differences in the onset of chronic disease and physical limitations, but income was more strongly associated with the manner in which the health problems progressed over time. While Herd et al. found that education played a critical role in postponing the onset of poor health, higher educational attainment without higher income did little to help slow the deterioration of health for those persons already in poor health. "Income," say Herd and her colleagues (2007:236), "was dominant in explaining progression from poor health to worse health and especially the progression to death." For low-income persons in poor health, death came quicker than for high-income persons in poor health. Overall, better educated and more affluent people fared the best in health and longevity outcomes. The Herd et al. study did not examine the effects of occupational status, but this research serves as a reminder that while the three SES variables of education, income, and occupational status are interrelated, their effects are not identical or fully overlapping (Adler et al. 1994).

Therefore, as several studies report, lower socioeconomic groups have the poorest health and shortest life spans. These studies have been conducted in the United States (Haas 2006; Herd et al. 2007; Pampel et al. 2010; Phelan et al. 2004; Warren and Hernandez 2007) and other countries, including Canada (Prus 2007; Segall and Fries 2011), Britain (Chandola 2000; Marmot 2004), Britain and Finland (Lahelma, Arber, Rahkonen, and Silventoinen 2000; Rahkonen, Lahelma, Martikainan, and Silventoinen 2002), Germany (Mielck et al. 2000), Spain (Regidor et al. 2002), Spain and France (Lostao, Regidor, Aïach, and Domínguez 2001), Russia and Eastern Europe (Cockerham 2000c, 2007), and even Sweden (Hemström 2005) and Iceland (Olafsdottir 2007), where social equality in living conditions is among the best in the world, and in Europe as a whole (Eikemo et al. 2008). An even more extreme pattern of disadvantages in health and longevity exists among the poor in developing nations in Latin America, South Asia, and especially Africa (Wermuth 2003).

Social-class differences in health affect both men and women, although class distinctions appear to influence male mortality the most (Jemal et al. 2008; McDonough, Williams, House, and Duncan 1999). Class also affects children as income and other features of their parent's SES significantly influence their own level of education, income, and eventual type of work, as seen in evidence linking childhood adversity to poor health later in life (Braveman et al. 2010; Garbarski 2014; Goosby 2013; Haas, Glymour, and Berkman 2011; Turney 2011; Umberson et al. 2014). Regardless of age or gender, people living in poverty and reduced socioeconomic circumstances have the greatest exposure to risk factors that produce ill health. These risk factors are physical (poor sanitation, poor housing, overcrowding, extreme temperatures), chemical (environmental pollution), biological (bacteria, viruses), psychological (stress), economic (low income, lack of health insurance, unhealthy jobs), and lifestyle (poor diets, smoking, alcohol and drug abuse, lack of leisure-time exercise) in origin. Exposure to these factors is generally dependent upon a person's socioeconomic status because individuals at the bottom of the society confront them significantly more often than people residing higher on the social ladder. The closer an individual is to the bottom rung of this ladder, the more likely they will become sick and die younger. Richard Carpiano et al. (2008:232) summarize this situation as follows:

> While volumes of social science research have implicated social class as a critical element in many social and economic outcomes, a substantial body of evidence has also documented its pervasive association with what is arguably one of the most important elements of anyone's life: health. Collectively, this evidence, which spans several centuries, has consistently shown that, across geopolitical place and disease "regime" (infectious, chronic), higher social position (whether conceptualized as social class or socioeconomic status) is associated with lower morbidity and longer life expectancy, and some evidence suggests that this association has even increased in magnitude over time.

Modern Diseases and the Poor

The lower class, even in modern nations, suffers more from the typical diseases of past human existence, such as influenza and tuberculosis, in comparison to the upper and middle classes. Heart disease, in contrast, has traditionally been associated with an affluent way of life. The incidence was usually high in rich countries and low in poor countries. Yet there have been variations with respect to heart disease between different nations and within countries among people of the same ethnic background with different life experiences. Japan, for example, has historically shown a relatively low rate of heart disease. Diet and stress-reducing activities such as periodic group vacations and after-work socializing for Japanese males have been thought to contribute to the low mortality rates from heart disease. In recent years, however, heart disease has been increasing in Japan, especially with the spread of Western eating habits. Westernization of the Japanese diet is considered responsible for the replacement of stroke by heart disease as Japan's second leading cause of death. This pattern underscores the significance of lifestyles in influencing the distribution of disease. As societies change and environments are modified, the style of living and types of activities available to members of the various social classes also change.

Consequently, in the United States there has been a change in the incidence of heart disease, which has declined dramatically in the past 35 years for all Americans, with the decline being greatest among the upper and middle classes. The result is that coronary heart disease is now concentrated more among the poor. The difference is that more obesity, smoking, and stress now occur in the lower class, in addition to higher levels of blood pressure, less leisure-time exercise, and poorer diets. The lower class is disadvantaged not only with respect to heart disease and other chronic health problems, but also in relation to communicable diseases. Lifestyle and social/environmental conditions, along with preventive health measures, primarily determine health status. A healthy lifestyle includes the use of good personal habits such as eating properly, getting enough rest, exercising, and avoiding practices such as smoking, abusing alcohol, and taking drugs. However, the type of lifestyle that promotes a healthy existence is more typical of the upper and middle classes who have the resources to support it. The most important relationship between social class and health is the manner in which social class affects the opportunities that a person has for a generally healthy life. Crowded living conditions, poor diet, inferior housing, low levels of income and education, and increased exposure to violence, alcoholism and problem drinking, smoking, and drug abuse—all combine to decrease the life chances of the poor.

Another problem affecting the health of the poor in the United States is access to quality health care. Before the 1930s, those who were unable to pay for health services were largely dependent on charity. Many of the urban clinics providing treatment for the poor were established and maintained primarily as teaching facilities for medical and nursing students. In such cases, education was the primary goal of the institution, although the provision of charity care was important. Since the 1930s, there has been a considerable increase in the number and types of facilities providing care to the poor in low-income areas. Many communities have hospitals of "last resort" that will take patients lacking the means to pay their bill. Yet despite evidence of more frequent visits to health care providers made possible by health insurance coverage through the government-sponsored programs of Medicaid (for the poor) and Medicare (for the elderly), the poor still have worse health than the affluent and are treated within the framework of welfare medicine.

The Patient Protection and Affordable Care Act passed by Congress in 2010 is intended to reduce the disparities in health insurance by extending coverage to an estimated 32 million previously uninsured Americans. Beginning in 2014, people who could not obtain health insurance because of preexisting medical conditions, have low incomes but are not eligible for Medicaid, or hold jobs with employers who do not offer health care plans and cannot afford to purchase such plans on their own were to be covered. Since the late 1970s, the proportion of people nationally under age 65 with health insurance had declined from around 90 percent to about 86 percent. By 2019, the Affordable Care Act is expected to have reversed this trend by pushing the proportion of the insured up to 95 percent, although it is not certain this goal will be met because of the increased costs of health insurance that resulted for many people who were previously insured, the postponement of mandates requiring small businesses to insure their workers, and other problems that are discussed in Chapter 15.

Obtaining equal access to care by expanding insurance coverage is a major step in improving the health of the general population. However, improved access to health services is only part of the solution for advancing health. Insurance alone is not the primary cause of poor health among the socially and economically disadvantaged. The fact remains that people at the bottom of society have the worst social situations and living conditions that go along with having the worst health. Regardless of what country poor people live in, what type of health insurance they have or do not have, and the level of health care they receive, they still have the worst health of all.

When the question arises about why low SES persons more often behave in ways that harm their health than high SES individuals, part of the explanation is the norms and constraints of the social and physical environments inhabited by the poor. It is much easier to behave in a healthy manner in positive circumstances. Lack of income, health insurance, and knowledge about health, cognitive abilities, the influence of social networks, fewer incentives and motivations for healthy behavior, and much more limited means to reach health goals have also been identified as important for unhealthy behavior (Glied and Lleras-Muney 2008; Pampel et al. 2010).

The lower class is likewise disadvantaged with respect to mental health. The basic finding of most studies is that the highest overall rates of mental disorder are found in the lower class, including schizophrenia—the most severely disabling form of mental illness (Cockerham 2014; Muntaner et al. 2013). Anxiety and depressive disorders, however, tend to be more prevalent among the upper and middle classes, yet the lower class suffers from these problems as well. The reason why mental disorder and social class position are related is not known, but genetics, greater stress in coping with the conditions of poverty (the social causation explanation), and the downward mobility of mentally ill people in society (the social selection explanation) are all used to explain why there is more mental disorder among the poor. Consequently, for mental as well as physical difficulties, socioeconomic factors are major determinants of the types and extent of an individual's health problems.

Given the vast evidence showing that class position determines a person's opportunity for good health and longevity, it appears logical that if differences between social classes decline, overall mortality rates of a population should similarly decline. British health economist Richard Wilkinson (1996) reviewed several international studies and suggested that once countries make the transition to high living standards and achieve a positive level of health, they can continue to increase their wealth but not be any healthier if class differences do not diminish. The key variable, in his opinion, is the degree of social and economic equality within the population; if there is a significant gap in income, education, and living conditions between the rich and the poor, then large-scale health inequalities will exist within the society, even though the overall level of health is generally good. If the gap is small, those health inequalities will likewise be small as seen in countries like Sweden and Norway. Consequently, it is the degree of inequality within a country, not between countries, that determines a population's health. Wilkinson (1996:3) therefore concludes that "in the developed world, it is not the richest countries which have the best health, but the most egalitarian."

Wilkinson's view—known as the "income inequality hypothesis"—initially attracted widespread enthusiasm in medical sociology and public health (De Maio 2010). However, his thesis sparked considerable controversy when several other studies failed to replicate his findings and found his statistical analysis flawed (Eberstadt and Satel 2004; Jen, Jones, and Johnston 2009). Jason Beckfield (2004), for example, replicated previous work in a carefully designed study using a large sample from 115 countries and found no evidence to support the income inequality thesis. Nicholas Eberstadt and Sally Satel (2004) pointed to a persuasive body of scholarship showing that by controlling for household income, living conditions, education, and race, the relationship between income inequality and health either diminishes or disappears completely. Because of the lack of supporting research, Eberstadt and Satel (2004:36) conclude that instead of being a scientific hypothesis, a better way to describe the income inequality hypothesis is to call it "a doctrine in search of data."

Nevertheless, the plight of the poor in relation to health continues to exist as a major social problem throughout the world. Recognition of this situation and efforts to gain greater insight into its causes has made the study of health disparities a major area of research in contemporary medical sociology.

Equality of Care and the Social Gradient in Mortality: The British Experience

Because many health disorders appear to be related to poverty, it is a logical assumption that if poverty were not a factor retarding the availability of quality medical care, the incidence and prevalence of illness in the lower social classes would be reduced. Following World War II, socialized medicine was introduced in Great Britain to provide the lower classes with the same medical care available to the upper classes. It should be noted, however, that poverty and social class differences remained—only health care was supposedly equalized. Results have shown that the equalization of health care alone has not reduced the disparity in health between social classes. Mortality rates remained higher for the lower classes. Despite free health care, financial hardship in Britain today means going without holidays and not having adequate clothing or regular access to fresh fruits and vegetables (Dolan 2007). It also means substandard housing and menial jobs. Britain's experiment failed to reduce health disparities precisely because living conditions and lifestyles could not be equalized; the environment of poverty and poor nutrition continued to adversely affect lower-class health.

Also, as Alan Dolan (2007) observed in a study of working-class men in the British city of Coventry, men with the lowest incomes and poorest living conditions experienced stress and anxiety related to their treatment by other people. Their low social position not only blocked educational and employment opportunities, but they also reported disdainful treatment from welfare agencies and persons in more privileged positions that often left them feeling frustrated and lacking in self-worth. "This study suggests," states Dolan (2007:726), "that people at the bottom of the social hierarchy endure both the direct consequences of their poverty as well as the effects of living in a society that makes them feel intensely aware of their relative position; not only do they feel undervalued and excluded, but they *are* undervalued and excluded." Adverse material circumstances not only hampered their ability to live in a healthy manner but also subjected them to stress because of it.

Health in Britain improved significantly for all social classes during the twentieth century, but mostly for the upper classes, in a trend that has continued in the twenty-first century. The lower classes had shown several health disadvantages, such as higher infant mortality, lower birth weight, more chronic disability, more absence from work owing to illness, lower life expectancy, and higher ratios of risk factors such as obesity and smoking. Reid (1998) attributes the health differences between the classes to a combination of factors, namely, wealth, personal habits, diet, home environment, exercise, mental stress, and differing occupational hazards. He also points out that the lower classes visit physicians more often than the other classes. This trend, which is similar to that today in Britain, as well as in the United States, is consistent with the fact that the lower classes have more health problems.

Wilkinson (1996) explains that prior to the 1980s, it was widely assumed in Britain that society was becoming more egalitarian. Social class differences were believed to be less important because of the growth of welfare services. This assumption was shattered, however, by the publication of the Black Report in 1980, which not only found that there were very large differences between mortality rates among occupational groups but also that these differences were not declining. British workers in lower-status occupations were clearly not living as long as those persons at the top of the occupational scale, and this trend was not improving. The lower class had the highest rates of illness, disability, and infant mortality, as well as the lowest life expectancy. The lower class also used prenatal and preventive health care services less frequently than members of more affluent classes. So while medical care was equalized and subsequently utilized more often by the poor, the use of services was significantly more toward treatment of existing health problems than prevention. The Black Report provided strong evidence that the lower a person is on the social scale, the less healthy that person is likely to be and the sooner he or she can expect to die.

Among the better studies researching this situation is that of Marmot (2004) and his colleagues (1984, 1991), who investigated the mortality of over 17,000 British male civil government employees. Known as the Whitehall studies, this research provided especially strong evidence of social class differences in mortality. The men were classified according to their job, with senior administrators ranked at the top, followed by professionals/executives, clerical, and other (which consisted of jobs lowest in status, such as messengers and other unskilled manual workers). In the first study, these men, whose ages at the time ranged from 40 to 64, were initially interviewed in the late 1960s with respect to their health habits and then reinvestigated ten years later in relation to mortality. Regardless of the cause, those with the highest occupational rank had the lowest percentage of deaths, and the percentages increased across job categories with the lowest-ranked occupations having the highest percentage of deaths. In other words, the lower the job status, the higher the mortality.

Marmot (1996) notes that it seemed unlikely at the time that social class differences in deaths would be as large for the civil servants as they were for the country as a whole. This assumption was made because the civil service jobs were all stable, provided financial security, and presumably were free of chemical and physical hazards. Yet Marmot (1996:43) indicates that he and his associates were surprised to discover that the difference in mortality between the bottom and top grades of the civil service was larger than the difference between the lower and upper classes in British society as a whole. They therefore conducted a second Whitehall study to check their results and found the same pattern. As in the first study, each group had higher mortality than the one above it in the social hierarchy. In a continuation of this research, there is now a Whitehall III study intended to further advance our understanding of class effects on mortality.

An intriguing aspect of this research is the finding of a social gradient in mortality across job positions linked to differences in hierarchy rather than deprivation. As noted, these men all had stable, secure, and hazard-free jobs. They were all white-collar workers, most were Anglo-Saxon, many wore the same dark suits and had similar haircuts, and the majority were upper or lower middle class (Epstein 1998). They all had access to free health care provided by the British National Health Service. There were some differences, however, as those with the highest-ranked job positions had larger houses, all owned cars, and they smoked less and were slimmer overall. And, of course, the men in the highest jobs lived longer than those in the next highest, and so on as the same pattern was repeated down the civil service ranks. The mortality of everyone working at Whitehall was affected by their social position, not just those at the bottom of the hierarchy. The administrators who designed the policies and the strategies for carrying them out were about 50 percent less likely to die of a heart attack than the department heads who worked just under them, three times less likely than the clerks, and four times less likely than the assistant clerks and data processors (Epstein 1998).

If the social gradient thesis is extended to the United States, then we find, as shown in Figure 3.1, that the highest social strata (the upper class) lives longer than the next highest (the upper middle class), although both are affluent and neither is materially deprived. And the upper middle class lives longer than the lower middle class and so on down the social scale until the lower class is reached. So it is not

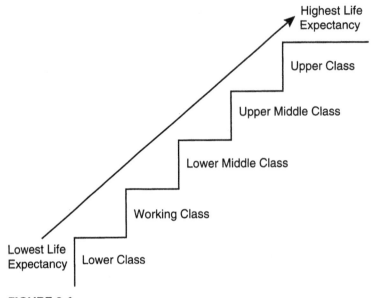

FIGURE 3.1

The Social Gradient in Life Expectancy

only the case that people at the top of society live longer than those at the bottom but also that the different classes live less longer than those higher than them and have greater longevity than those below them.

The reasons for the existence of this gradient are not yet fully known, but relevant research in the United States, Canada, Japan, and elsewhere centers on differences between socioeconomic groups and classes in self-esteem and stress levels (Evans, Barer, and Marmor 1994), the effects of income inequality (Beckfield 2004; McLeod, Nonnemaker, and Call 2004; Wilkinson 1996), deprivation through the life course (Power and Hertzman 1997), and health lifestyles and social support (Cockerham, Hattori, and Yamori 2000). The causality debate surrounding the social gradient thesis "is not a boxing match," states James Smith (1999:165), "in which a knockout blow will eventually be delivered." The answer is likely to be a combination of factors because the relationship between class position and health is complex and is ultimately to be found in the social environment (Marmot et al. 1998).

What is also suggested by studies such as those of Marmot and his colleagues is that medical care alone cannot counter the adverse effects of class position on health. The evidence is clear that a significant gap in health and life expectancy continues to persist in Britain—despite improved access to medical care (Bradby 2012; Marmot 2004). Britain's extension of free health care to the general population at the point of contact between patient and provider had equalized access to health services for everyone. A major assumption, as noted, was that the provision of quality care to all classes would improve levels of health throughout society, as poverty would no longer prevent someone from obtaining professional medical treatment. Health did improve for all classes, but we now know that differences between the social classes remain. In other words, everyone in Britain tended to live longer, but the upper classes continued to live longer than anyone else. This occurred even though over time the lower classes began using medical services more than the middle and upper classes. Medical care alone was unable to overcome the adverse effects of living conditions and negative lifestyles though it obviously had positive effects. This outcome underscores the importance of the social determinants of health.

Neighborhood Disadvantage

A class-related area of emerging research in medical sociology is "neighborhood disadvantage," which focuses on unhealthy urban living conditions. Cities contain the best that human society has to offer in terms of jobs, arts and entertainment, and amenities, but they also include pockets of the worst social and living environments. Neighborhoods contribute to good health or, conversely, harm it (Bernard et al. 2007). Examples of neighborhood characteristics that can be either health promoting or health damaging are found in the work of Sally Macintyre and her colleagues (Macintyre, Ellaway, and Cummins 2002). They determined there are five features of neighborhoods that can affect health: (1) the physical environment; (2) surroundings at home, work, and play; (3) services provided to support people like schools, street cleaning and garbage pickup, police, hospitals, and health and welfare services; (4) the sociocultural aspects of the neighborhood such as its norms and values, economic, political, and religious features, level of civility and public safety, and networks of support; and (5) the reputation of an area that signifies its esteem, quality of material infrastructure, level of morale, and how it is perceived by residents and nonresidents.

Catherine Ross (2000) observes that neighborhoods can be rated on a continuum in terms of order and disorder that are visible to its residents. Orderly neighborhoods are clean and safe, houses and buildings are well maintained, and residents are respectful of each other and each other's property. Disorderly neighborhoods reflect a breakdown in social order, as there is noise, litter, poorly maintained houses and buildings, vandalism, graffiti, fear, and crime. Many families with children in such neighborhoods are one-parent families headed by females. Ross asked whether people who live in disadvantaged neighborhoods suffer psychologically as a result of their environment and found the answer to be yes.

While low education and income, unemployment, and not being married were stressful in themselves in disadvantaged neighborhoods, her study in Illinois found that the daily environment of disorder, crime, and danger were associated with feeling run-down, hopeless, sad, tired, and depressed. However, people living in advantaged neighborhoods that were clean and safe showed low levels of depression. Subsequent research by Ross and John Mirowsky (2001, 2009) found that residents of disadvantaged neighborhoods in Illinois felt less healthy and had more chronic health problems. They observed that the residents in these neighborhoods lived in a stressful environment characterized by crime, incivility, and harassment and argued that the long-term exposure to these conditions impaired their physical and mental health.

Additional research on low-income women receiving welfare support in Chicago, Boston, and San Antonio found that chronic stressors in disadvantaged neighborhoods had negative consequences for the health of its residents (Hill, Ross, and Angel 2005), including the promotion of heavy drinking (Hill and Angel 2005). Other research in Chicago found that low SES on the part of the residents and their neighborhood perceptions could be correlated with negative self-rated health (Wen, Hawkley, and Cacioppo 2006) and that neighborhood effects on health extended into later life (Wen and Christakis 2006). There was also a significantly higher prevalence of hypertension in disadvantaged Chicago neighborhoods (Morenoff et al. 2007) and early risk of exposure to sexually transmitted diseases (Browning, Burrington, Leventhal, and Brooks-Gunn 2008).

In a nationwide study, Liam Downey and Marieke van Willigen (2005) determined that residential proximity to industrial activity is stressful for the inhabitants, adding yet another category to the list of stress-promoting neighborhood variables. In Detroit, neighborhood disadvantage has been linked to psychological distress (Schulz et al. 2000) and adult drug use (Boardman et al. 2001), while in Chicago people in poor neighborhoods were found to have lower levels of cortisol secretion that decreased energy and the strength of the body's ability to respond to inflammation (Karb, Elliott, Dowd, and Morenoff 2012) . Elsewhere, in Baltimore, people in disadvantaged neighborhoods had more depression (Latkin and Curry 2003), but mental health among black women was found to improve after moving from high poverty to low poverty neighborhoods (Turney, Kissane, and Edin 2013); in New York City, Puerto Rican and black households in neighborhoods with deteriorated housing and low social cohesion showed high levels of asthma (Rosenbaum 2008), and, in a national study of adolescents in low-income neighborhoods, there was more alcohol and cigarette consumption (Chuang, Ennett, Bauman, and Foshee 2005). Research in California, by Marissa King and Peter Bearman (2011) found that even though the socioeconomic status of neighborhoods change over time, as does the prevalence of autism, neighborhood effects on autism diagnoses remained strong for children born to parents with fewer socioeconomic resources.

Conversely, in Chicago, residents of affluent neighborhoods rated their health significantly better than people in disadvantaged neighborhoods (Browning and Cagney 2003). Other research using a nationwide data set show that people growing up in affluent neighborhoods surrounded by comparative advantages report better health over the life course than those who grew up in disadvantaged neighborhoods (Vartanian and Houser 2010). This is not surprising because these neighborhoods have healthier living conditions and significantly better access to health care. James Kirby and Toshiko Kaneda (2005, 2006) found that living in disadvantaged neighborhoods reduces the likelihood of having a regular source of health services and obtaining preventive care, while increasing the probability of having unmet medical needs. Overall, the studies reported in this section illustrate the effects of the structural characteristics of neighborhoods on the physical and mental health of the people who live in them.

As Leonard Pearlin and his colleagues (Pearlin, Schieman, Fazio, and Meersman 2005:208) explain:

> . . . the pattern of status attainments can funnel people into the contexts that surround their lives, most conspicuously the neighborhoods in which they come to reside. When neighborhoods are predominantly populated by people possessing little economic or social capital, they have a notable impact on health independent of individual-level socioeconomic status.

SES as a Fundamental Cause of Sickness And Mortality

Studies of neighborhood disadvantage join with other research on the powerful effects of social class on health to illustrate the importance of social structural factors in disease causation. That is, there are social conditions that make people sick (Cockerham 2013). The enduring association of low SES with illness, disability, and death has led Bruce Link and Jo Phelan (Link and Phelan 1995, 2000; Link et al. 2008; Phelan et al. 2004; Phelan et al. 2010; Phelan and Link 2013) to propose that SES is a "fundamental cause" of mortality. This is an important proposition because most researchers in the past viewed SES as a factor contributing to poor health and mortality, not as a direct cause. However, the persistent association of SES with a variety of disease patterns during changing historical periods increasingly pointed toward SES as having a causal role. In order for a social variable to qualify as a cause of sickness and mortality, Link and Phelan (1995:87) hypothesize that it must:

1. influence multiple diseases;
2. affect these diseases through multiple pathways of risks;
3. be reproduced over time; and
4. involve access to resources that can be used to avoid risks or minimize the consequences of disease if it occurs.

SES or social class meets all four of these criteria because a person's class position influences multiple diseases in multiple ways, the association has endured for centuries, and higher SES persons have the resources to better avoid health problems or minimize them when they occur. Historical accounts of the black plague in the fourteenth century, for example, describe how the poor at that time were more heavily afflicted than the rich and suffered the most in an association that continues today (Tuchman 1978). Numerous studies have linked low SES with poor health and high mortality throughout the life course (Carpiano et al. 2008; Cockerham 2013; Herd et al. 2007; Link and Phelan 1995; Lutfey and Freese 2005; Lynch 2006; Olafsdottir 2007; Prus 2007; Robert and House 2000; Warren and Hernandez 2007). Even though the poor live longer now than the wealthy in past periods of history, people in the upper social strata still live the longest on average than people in the strata just below them and so on down the social scale until the bottom of society is reached. The degree of socioeconomic resources a person has or does not have, such as money, knowledge, status, power, and social connections, either protects health or causes premature mortality. Phelan et al. (2004:267) find that these resources directly shape individual health behaviors by influencing whether people know about, have access to, can afford, and are motivated to engage in health-promoting practices, as well as determining access to jobs, neighborhoods, and social networks that vary dramatically in the amount of risk and protection they provide.

In short, Phelan and her associates conclude that there is a long and detailed list of mechanisms linking socioeconomic status with mortality. Included is a sense of personal "control" over one's life because people with such control typically feel good about themselves, handle stress better, and have the capability and living situations to adopt healthy lifestyles (Link and Phelan 2000; Mirowsky and Ross 2003).

This situation may especially apply to people in powerful social positions. "Social power," states Link and Phelan (2000:37), "allows one to feel in control, and feeling in control provides a sense of security and well being that is [health-promoting]." Persons at the bottom of society are less able to control their lives, have fewer resources to cope with stress, live in more unhealthy situations, face powerful constraints in choosing a healthy way of life, and die earlier.

The notion that social factors *cause* rather than merely contribute to health and mortality is a relatively recent finding that is gaining support not only in medical sociology, but medicine and public health through studies on health disparities (Braveman et al. 2010; Carpiano et al. 2008; Cockerham 2013; Herd et al. 2007; Lutfey and Freese 2005; Phelan et al. 2004; Phelan et al. 2010). One study providing supporting evidence is that of Phelan et al. (2004), who investigated causes of death data on 370,930 subjects from the U.S. National Longitudinal Mortality Study. This research found a strong relationship between SES and deaths from preventable causes. Persons with higher SES had significantly higher probabilities of survival from preventable causes because they were able to use their resources (money, knowledge, etc.) to obtain what they needed to live longer. Conversely, the lower the SES, the more likely the person was to die from something that could have been otherwise prevented. The deliberate use of socioeconomic resources was found to be a critical factor in maintaining the differential in mortality. The same pattern is seen in a nationwide study by Virginia Chang and Diane Lauderdale (2009), who found that individuals with high socioeconomic status were significantly more likely to have reversed their formerly high levels of cholesterol through the use of statin drugs to the point that low SES persons are now more likely to have high cholesterol.

Another supportive study is that of Karen Lutfey and Jeremy Freese (2005) of patients at two diabetes clinics in a large Midwestern city. One clinic (Park Clinic) had a primarily white, upper- and middle-class clientele, while the other (County Clinic) served a largely minority, working-class, and uninsured population. This study focused on the control of blood sugar (glucose) levels that is essential for the survival of diabetics, as high glucose levels significantly increase the risk of complications such as kidney damage, heart disease, stroke, blindness, and amputations. High SES patients had much better continuity of care in that they usually saw the same physician. This was not the case at County Clinic, where the physicians were on rotation and dependent on whatever information about the patient was retold by the patient and entered (or not entered) in their chart.

The County Clinic patients also faced financial, occupational, and social network constraints. While the cost of care was subsidized by the state, low-income County Clinic patients had to provide documentation of residency, earnings, and whether they had insurance to qualify, and this took about three months to process. They also did not have the financial resources to assist them in maintaining glucose control, such as paying for insulin pumps that the Park Clinic patients could purchase when needed. Additionally, the low SES patients at County Clinic were more likely to have jobs less hospitable to storing insulin (which requires refrigeration) and maintaining glucose control. Some worked as manual laborers and others had night shifts that interfered with medication schedules. Moreover, patients taking state-subsidized medications could only get their prescriptions refilled in person at the clinic pharmacy, which was time consuming and took time away from jobs. As one County Clinic physician lamented:

> What a travesty. If you gave a businessman a prescription that had to be refilled every month, and he had to stop what he was doing and go to the store and stand there in front of a pharmacist for 30 minutes, 40 minutes he'd say, "Either you give me something that's appropriate, or I'm firing you as my physician." And here [at County] we give patients their prescription and say "Come back every month and stand here. Come back on the bus and get your prescriptions filled." Gimme a break. If that doesn't interfere with compliance, I don't know what does. (Lutfey and Freese 2005:1355)

In addition, the low SES patients had less social support, particularly single mothers with children, less motivation to take responsibility for their treatment regimens, significantly longer waits for their doctor appointments, more transportation problems in getting to the clinic, and knew less about diabetes. They were much less likely to join health clubs for exercise and eat healthily, as well as make other health lifestyle adjustments. Not surprising, Lutfey and Freese found that the higher SES patients in Park Clinic had significantly better glucose management, and one could argue, as they do, that the cause was social.

Other recent findings supporting the "fundamental causes" thesis analyzes the effects of education and income on health (Herd et al. 2007; Link et al. 2008), the enduring association of education with mortality (Miech, Pampel, Kim, and Rogers 2011), disparities in lung and pancreatic cancer mortality (Rubin, Clouston, and Link 2014), colorectal cancer mortality (Saldana-Ruiz et al. 2013), and the use of welfare state benefits to equalize health resources in Iceland (Olafsdottir 2007), as well as the unchanging profile of socioeconomic inequalities in sickness and mortality over the course of the twentieth century (Warren and Hernandez 2007). What these studies and others discussed in this section show is that class is the strongest predictor of health, disease causation, and mortality. This is particularly evident when social gradients in mortality universally display a hierarchical gradient from low to high in death rates along class lines. The *enduring* outcome of good health at the top of society and worse health in descending order toward the bottom marks class as a fundamental social cause of health, disease, and death (Cockerham 2013). Recognition of the causal properties of social variables in health matters has been slow in coming, but there is growing evidence that this is indeed the case.

Summary

Social class is the most powerful social determinant of health and disease. In the United States, medical sociologists often use the concept of socioeconomic status or SES to determine a person's class position. SES consists of three interrelated but distinct variables: income, education, and occupational status. Each can exercise significant influence on health outcomes, but education usually is especially influential in health matters. Virtually all studies show that persons in the lower class have the worst health and highest mortality within any class structure. A social gradient in health and mortality has been clearly identified in which health is best at the top of society, and then deteriorates with each step downward in a class hierarchy.

In Great Britain, socialized medicine failed to reduce health differentials between the social classes because social class differences themselves were not reduced. Equal access to medical care could not, by itself, overcome all of the adverse effects of poverty on health. Recent studies are now showing class position to be a fundamental cause of both good and bad health.

Critical Thinking Questions

1. What are the components of socioeconomic status? Describe the significance of each component for a person's health.
2. Describe the social gradient in mortality. What causes this gradient to exist?
3. How do neighborhoods affect the health of the people who live in them?
4. What are the steps determining whether or not socioeconomic status is a fundamental cause of disease?

Suggested Readings

Cockerham, William C. (2013) *Social causes of health and illness*, 2nd ed. Cambridge, UK: Polity.
Advances the argument that social variables can be direct causes of health and disease.
Marmot, Michael (2004) *The status syndrome*. New York: Times Books.
Discusses how social standing affects health and longevity.

References

Adler, Nancy E., Thomas Boyce, Margaret A. Chesney, Sheldon Cohen, Susan Folkman, Robert L. Kahn, and S. Leonard Syme (1994) "Socioeconomic status and health: The challenge of the gradient." *American Psychologist* 10: 15–24.
Barr, Donald A. (2008) *Health disparities in the United States*. Baltimore: Johns Hopkins University Press.
Bartley, Mel (2004) *Health inequality*. Cambridge, UK: Polity.
Beckfield, Jason (2004) "Does income inequality harm health? New cross-national evidence." *Journal of Health and Social Behavior* 45: 231–48.
Bernard, Paul, Rana Charafeddine, Katherine L. Frohlich, Mark Daniel, Yan Kestens, and Louise Potvin (2007) "Health inequalities and place: A theoretical conception of neighbourhood." *Social Science and Medicine* 65: 1839–52.
Boardman, Jason S., Brian Karl Finch, Christopher G. Ellison, David R. Williams, and James S. Jackson (2001) "Neighborhood disadvantage, stress, and drug use among adults." *Journal of Health and Social Behavior* 42: 151–65.
Bradby, Hannah (2012) *Medicine, health and society*. London: Sage.
Braveman, Paula A., Catherine Cubbin, Susan Egerter, David R. Williams, and Elsie Pamuk (2010) "Socioeconomic disparities in health in the United States: What the patterns tell us." *American Journal of Public Health* 100 (1 Supplement): S186–S196.
Braveman, Paula A., and Eleuther Tarimo (2002) "Social inequalities in health within countries: Not only an issue for affluent nations." *Social Science and Medicine* 54: 1621–35.
Browning, Christopher R., and Kathleen A. Cagney (2003) "Moving beyond poverty: Neighborhood structure, social process, and health." *Journal of Health and Social Behavior* 44: 552–71.

Browning, Christopher R., Lori A. Burrington, Tama Leventhal, and Jeanne Brooks-Gunn (2008) "Neighborhood structural inequality, collective efficacy, and sexual risk behavior among urban youth." *Journal of Health and Social Behavior* 49: 269–85.

Budrys, Grace (2003) *Unequal health.* Lanham, MD: Rowman & Littlefield.

Carpiano, Richard M., Bruce G. Link, and Jo C. Phelan (2008) "Social inequality and health: Future directions for the fundamental cause explanation," pp. 232–63 in *Social class: How does it work?* A. Lareau and D. Conley (eds). New York: Russell Sage.

Chandola, Tarani (2000) "Social class differences in mortality using the new UK National Statistics Socio-Economic Classification." *Social Science and Medicine* 50: 641–49.

Chang, Virginia W., and Diane S. Lauderdale (2009) "Fundamental cause theory, technological innovation, and health disparities: The case of cholesterol in the era of statins." *Journal of Health and Social Behavior* 50: 245–60.

Chuang, Ying-Chih, Susan T. Ennett, Karl E. Bauman, and Vangie A. Foshee (2005) "Neighborhood influences on adolescent cigarette and alcohol use: Mediating effects through parent and peer behaviors." *Journal of Health and Social Behavior* 46: 187–204.

Cockerham, William C. (2000) "Health lifestyles in Russia." *Social Science and Medicine* 51: 1313–24.

———— (2007) "Health lifestyles and the absence of the Russian middle class." *Sociology of Health & Illness* 29: 457–73.

———— (2013) *Social causes of health and disease,* 2nd ed. Cambridge, UK: Polity.

———— (2014) *Sociology of mental disorder,* 9th ed. Upper Saddle River, NJ: Pearson Prentice Hall.

Cockerham, William C., Hiroyuki Hattori, and Yukio Yamori (2000) "The social gradient in life expectancy: The contrary case of Okinawa in Japan." *Social Science and Medicine* 51: 115–22.

De Maio, Fernando (2010) *Health and social theory.* New York: Palgrave Macmillan.

Dolan, Alan (2007) " 'Good luck to them if they get it': Exploring working class men's understandings and experiences of income inequality and material standards." *Sociology of Health & Illness* 29: 711–29.

Downey, Liam, and Marieke van Willigen (2005) "Environmental stressors: The mental health impacts of living near industrial activity." *Journal of Health and Social Behavior* 46: 289–305.

Dupre, Matthew E. (2007) "Educational differences in age-related patterns of disease: Reconsidering the cumulative disadvantage and age-as-leveler hypotheses." *Journal of Health and Social Behavior* 48: 1–15.

Eberstadt, Nicholas, and Sally Satel (2004) *Health and the income inequality hypothesis.* Washington, DC: AEI Press.

Eikemo, Terje A., Martijn Huisman, Clare Bambra, and Anton E. Kunst (2008) "Health inequalities according to educational level in different welfare regimes: A comparison of 23 European countries." *Sociology of Health & Illness* 30: 565–82.

Epstein, Helen (1998) "Life and death on the social ladder." *New York Review of Books* (July 16): 26–30.

Evans, Robert G., Morris L. Barer, and Theodore R. Marmor (eds) (1994) *Why are some people healthy and others not? The determinants of the health of populations.* New York: Aldine de Gruyter.

Garbarski, Dana (2014) "The interplay between child and maternal health: Reciprocal relationships and cumulative disadvantage during childhood and adolescence." *Journal of Health and Social Behavior* 55: 91–106.

Glied, Sherry and Adriana Lleras-Muney (2008) "Technological innovation and inequality in Health." *Demography* 45: 761–71.

Goesling, Brian (2007) "The rising significance of education for health?" *Social Forces* 85: 1621–44.

Goosby, Bridget J. (2013) "Early life course pathways of adult depression and chronic pain." *Journal of Health and Social Behavior* 54: 75–91.

Haas, Steven A. (2006) "Health selection and the process of social stratification: The effect of childhood health on socioeconomic attainment." *Journal of Health and Social Behavior* 47: 339–54.

Haas, Steven A., M. Maria Glymour, and Lisa F. Berkman (2011) "Childhood health and labor market inequality over the life course." *Journal of Health and Social Behavior* 52: 298–313.

Hemström, Örjan (2005) "Society, health, and health care in Sweden," pp. 298–318 in *The Blackwell companion to medical sociology*, W. Cockerham (ed.). Oxford, UK: Blackwell.

Herd, Pamela A., Brian Goesling, and James S. House (2007) "Socioeconomic position and health: The differential effects of education versus income on the onset versus progression of health problems." *Journal of Health and Social Behavior* 48: 223–38.

Hill, Terrence D., Catherine E. Ross, and Ronald J. Angel (2005) "Neighborhood disorder, psychophysiological distress, and health." *Journal of Health and Social Behavior* 46: 170–86.

Hill, Terrence D., and Ronald J. Angel (2005) "Neighborhood disorder, psychological distress, and heavy drinking." *Social Science and Medicine* 61: 965–75.

Jemal, Ahmedin, Michael J. Thun, Elizabeth E. Ward, Jane Henley, Vilma E. Cokkinides, and Taylor E. Murray (2008) "Mortality from leading causes by education and race in the United States, 2001." *American Journal of Preventive Medicine* 34: 1–8.

Jen, Min Hua, Kelvyn Jones, and Ron Johnston (2009) "Global variations in health: Evaluating Wilkinson's income in equality hypothesis using the World Values Survey." *Social Science and Medicine* 68: 643–53.

Kahn, Joan R., and Leonard I. Pearlin (2006) "Financial strain over the life course and health among older adults." *Journal of Health and Social Behavior*47: 17–31.

Karb, Rebecca A., Michael R. Elliott, Jennifer Dowd, and Jeffrey D. Morenoff (2012) "Neighborhood-level stressors, social support, and diurnal patterns of cortisol: The Chicago Community Adult Health Study." *Social Science and Medicine* 75: 1038-47.

King, Marissa D., and Peter S. Bearman (2011) "Socioeconomic status and the increased prevalence of autism in California." *American Sociological Review* 76: 320–46.

Kirby, James B., and Toshiko Kaneda (2005) "Neighborhood socioeconomic disadvantage and access to health care." *Journal of Health and Social Behavior* 46: 15–31.

_____ (2006) "Access to health care: Does neighborhood residential instability matter?" *Journal of Health and Social Behavior* 47: 142–55.

Lahelma, Eero, Sara Arber, Ossi Rahkonen, and Eva Silventoinen (2002) "Multiple roles and health among British and Finnish women: The influence of socioeconomic circumstances." *Social Science and Medicine* 54: 727–40.

Lahelma, Eero (2010) "Health and social stratification," pp. 71–96 in *The new Blackwell companion to medical sociology*, W. Cockerham (ed.). Oxford, UK: Blackwell.

Latkin, Carol A., and Aaron D. Curry (2003) "Stressful neighborhoods and depression: A prospective study of the impact of neighborhood disorder." *Journal of Health and Social Behavior* 44: 34–44.

Link, Bruce G., and Jo Phelan (1995) "Social conditions as fundamental causes of diseases." *Journal of Health and Social Behavior* 36(Extra issue): 80–94.

_____ (2000) "Evaluating the fundamental cause explanation for social disparities in health," pp. 33–47 in *Handbook of medical sociology*, 5th ed., C. Bird, P. Conrad, and A. Fremont (eds). Upper Saddle River, NJ: Prentice Hall.

Link, Bruce G., Jo C. Phelan, Richard Miech, and Emily Leckman Westin (2008) "The resources that matter: Fundamental social causes of health disparities and the challenge of intelligence." *Journal of Health and Social Behavior* 49: 72–91.

Lostao, Lourdes, Enrique Regidor, Pierre Aïach, and Vicente Domínguez (2001) "Social inequalities in ischaemic heart and cerebrovascular disease mortality in men: Spain and France, 1980–1982 and 1988–1990." *Social Science and Medicine* 52: 1879–87.

Lutfey, Karen, and Jeremy Freese (2005) "Toward some fundamentals of fundamental causality: Socioeconomic status and health in the routine clinic visit for diabetes." *American Journal of Sociology* 110: 1326–72.

Lynch, Scott M. (2006) "Explaining life course and cohort variation in the relationship between education and health: The role of income." *Journal of Health and Social Behavior* 47: 324–38.

Macintyre, Sally, Anne Ellaway, and Steven Cummins (2002) "Place effects on health: How can we conceptualise, operationalise, and measure them?" *Social Science and Medicine* 60: 313–17.

Margolis, Rachel (2013) "Educational differences in healthy behavior changes and adherence among middle-aged Americans." *Journal of Health and Social Behavior* 54: 353–68.

Marmot, Michael G. (2004) *The status syndrome*. New York: Times Books.

Marmot, Michael G., George Davey Smith, Stephen Stansfeld, Chandra Patel, Fiona North, Jenny Head, Ian White, Eric Brunner, and Amanda Feeney (1991) "Health inequalities among British civil servants: The Whitehall II study." *Lancet* 337: 1387–92.

Marmot, Michael G., M. J. Shipley, and Geoffrey Rose (1984) "Inequalities in death—Specific explanations of a general pattern." *Lancet* 83: 1003–1006.

McDonough, Peggy, David R. Williams, James S. House, and Greg J. Duncan (1999) "Gender and the socioeconomic gradient in mortality." *Journal of Health and Health Behavior* 40: 17–31.

McLeod, Jane D., James M. Nonnemaker, and Kathleen Theide Call (2004) "Income inequality, race, and child well-being: An aggregate analysis in the 50 United States." *Journal of Health and Social Behavior* 45: 249–64.

Miech, Richard, Fred Pampel, Jinyoung Kim, and Richard G. Rogrers (2011) "The enduring association between education and mortality: The role of widening and narrowing disparities." *American Sociological Review* 76: 913–34.

Mielck, Andreas, Adrienne Cavelaars, Uwe Helmert, Karl Martin, Olaf Winkelhake, and Anton E. Kunst (2000) "Comparison of health inequalities between East and West Germany." *European Journal of Public Health* 10: 262–67.

Mirowsky, John, and Catherine E. Ross (2003) *Education, social status, and health*. New York: Aldine de Gruyter.

Morenoff, Jeffrey D., James S. House, Ben B. Hansen, David R. Williams, George A. Kaplan, and Haslyn E. Hunte (2007) "Understanding social disparities in hypertension prevalence, awareness, treatment, and control: The role of neighborhood context." *Social Science and Medicine* 65: 1853–66.

Mulatu, Mesfin Samuel, and Carmi Schooler (2002) "Causal connections between socioeconomic status and health: Reciprocal effects and mediating mechanisms." *Journal of Health and Social Behavior* 43: 22–41.

Muntaner, Carles, Edwin Ng, Christopher Vanroelen, Sharon Christ, and William W. Eaton (2013) "Social stratification, social closure, and social class as determinants of mental health disparities," pp. 205–28 in *Handbook of the sociology of mental health*, 2nd ed., C. Aneshensel, J. Phelan, and A. Bierman (eds.). Dordrecht: Springer.

Olafsdottir, Sigrun (2007) "Fundamental causes of health disparities: Stratification: The welfare state, and health in the United States and Iceland." *Journal of Health and Social Behavior* 48: 239–53.

Olshansky, S. Jay, Toni Antonucci, Lisa Berkman, Robert Binstock, A. Boersch-Supan, J. Cacioppo, B. Carnes, L. Carstensen, L. Fried, D. Goldman, J. Jackson, M. Kohli, J. Rother, Y. Zheng, and J. Rowe. (2012) "Differences in life expectancy due to race and educational differences are widening, and many may not catch up." *Health Affairs* 31: 1803–13.

Pampel, Fred C., Patrick M. Krueger, and Justin T. Denney (2010) "Socioeconomic disparities in health behaviors." *Annual Review of Sociology* 36: 349–370.

Pearlin, Leonard I., Scott Schieman, Elena M. Fazio, and Stephen C. Meersman (2005) "Stress, health, and the life course: Some conceptual perspectives." *Journal of Health and Social Behavior* 46: 205–19.

Phelan, Jo C. and Bruce G. Link (2013) "Fundamental cause theory," pp. 105-26 in *Medical so-ciology on the move: New directions in theory*, W. Cockerham (ed.). Dordrecht: Springer.

Phelan, Jo C., Bruce G. Link, Ana Diez-Rouz, Ichiro Kawachi, and Bruce Levin (2004) " 'Fundamental causes' of social inequalities in mortality: A test of the theory." *Journal of Health and Social Behavior* 45: 265–85.

Phelan, Jo C., Bruce G. Link, and Parisa Tehranifar (2010) "Social conditions as fundamental causes of health inequalities: Theory, evidence, and policy implications." *Journal of Health and Social Behavior* 51: S28–40.

Power, C., and C. Hertzman (1997) "Social and behavioral pathways linking early life and adult disease." *British Medical Bulletin* 53: 210–21.

Prus, Steven G. (2007) "Age, SES, and health: A population level analysis of health inequalities over the life course." *Sociology of Health & Illness* 29: 275–96.

Pudrovska, Tetyana (2014) "Early-life socioeconomic status and mortality at three life course stages: An increasing within-cohort inequality." *Journal of Health and Social Behavior* 55: 181–95.

Rahkonen, Ossi, Eero Lahelma, P. Martikainan, and K. Silventoinen (2002) "Determinants of health inequalities by income from the 1980s to the 1990s in Finland." *Journal of Epidemiology and Community Health* 56: 442–43.

Regidor, Enrique, Juan L. Gutie'rrez-Fisac, Carmen Rodriguez, Vicente Dominguez, M. Elisa Calle, and Pedro Navarro (2002) "Comparing social inequalities in health in Spain: 1987 and 1995/97." *Social Science and Medicine* 54: 1323–32.

Reid, Ivan (1998) *Social class differences in Britain.* Cambridge, UK: Polity.

Robert, Stephanie A., and James S. House (2000) "Socioeconomic inequalities in health: An enduring sociological problem," pp. 79–97 in *Handbook of medical sociology*, 5th ed., C. Bird, P. Conrad, and A. Fremont (eds). Upper Saddle River, NJ: Prentice Hall.

Rose, David, and Eric Harrison (eds.) (2010) *Social class in Europe: An introduction to the European socio-economic classification.* London: Routledge.

Rosenbaum, Emily (2008) "Racial/ethnic differences in asthma prevalence: The role of housing and neighborhood environments." *Journal of Health and Social Behavior* 49: 131–45.

Ross, Catherine E. (2000) "Neighborhood disadvantage and adult depression." *Journal of Health and Social Behavior* 41: 177–87.

Ross, Catherine E., and Chia-ling Wu (1995) "The links between education and health." *American Sociological Review* 60: 719–45.

Ross, Catherine E., and John Mirowsky (2001) "Neighborhood disadvantage, disorder, and health." *Journal of Health and Social Behavior* 42: 258–76.

——— (2009) "Neighborhood disorder, subjective alienation, and distress." *Journal of Health and Social Behavior* 50: 49–64.

Rubin, Marcie S., Sean Clouston, and Bruce G. Link (2014) "A fundamental cause approach to the study of disparities in lung cancer and pancreatic cancer mortality in the United States." *Social Science and Medicine* 100: 54–61.

Saldana-Ruiz, Nallely, Sean A. P. Clouston, Marcie S. Rubin, Cynthia G. Colen, and Bruce G. Link (2013) "Fundamental causes of colorectal cancer mortality in the United States: Understanding the importance of socioeconomic status in creating inequality in mortality." *American Journal of Public Health* 103: 99–104.

Schnittker, Jason (2004) "Education and the changing shape of the income gradient in health." *Journal of Health and Social Behavior* 45: 286–305.

Schulz, Amy, David Williams, Babara Israel, Adam Becker, Edith Parker, Sherman A. James, and James Jackson (2000) "Unfair treatment, neighborhood effects, and mental health in the Detroit metropolitan area." *Journal of Health and Social Behavior* 42: 314–32.

Segall, Alexander, and Christopher J. Fries (2011) *Pursing health and wellness: Healthy societies, healthy people.* Toronto: Oxford University Press.

Semyonov, Moshe, Noah Lewin-Epstein, and Dina Maskileyson (2013) "Where wealth matters more for health: The wealth-health gradient in 16 countries." *Social Science and Medicine* 81: 10–17.

Smith, James P. (1999) "Healthy bodies and thick wallets: The dual relation between health and economic status." *Journal of Economic Perspectives* 13: 146–66.

Swartz, David (1997) *Culture and power: The sociology of Pierre Bourdieu.* Chicago: University of Chicago Press.

Tuchman, Barbara W. (1978) *A distant mirror: The calamitous 14th century.* New York: Random House.

Turney, Kristin (2011) "Maternal depression and childhood health inequalities." *Journal of Health and Social Behavior* 52: 314–32.

Turney, Kristin, Rebecca Kissane, and Kathryn Edin (2013) "After moving to opportunity: How moving to a low-poverty neighborhood improves mental health among African American women." *Society and Mental Health* 3: 1–21.

Umberson, Debra, Kristi Williams, Patricia A. Thomas, Hui Liu, and Mieke Beth Thomeer (2014) "Race, gender, and chains of disadvantage: Childhood adversity, social relationships, and health." *Journal of Health and Social Behavior* 55: 20–38.

Vartanian, Thomas P., and Linda Houser (2010) "The effects of childhood neighborhood conditions on self-reports of adult health." *Journal of Health and Social Behavior* 51: 291–306.

Warren, John Robert (2009) "Socioeconomic status and health across the life course: A test of the social causation and health selection hypothesis." *Social Forces* 87: 2125–54.

Warren, John Robert, and Elaine M. Hernandez (2007) "Did socioeconomic inequalities in morbidity and mortality change in the United States over the course of the twentieth century?" *Journal of Health and Social Behavior* 48: 335–51.

Weber, Max (1978) *Economy and society,* 2 vols., G. Roth and C. Wittich (eds). Berkeley: University of California Press.

Wen, Ming, Louise C. Hawkley, and John T. Cacioppo (2006) "Objective and perceived neighborhood environment, individual SES and psychosocial factors, and self-rated health: An analysis of older adults in Cook County, Illinois." *Social Science and Medicine* 63: 2575–90.

Wen, Ming, and Nicholas A. Christakis (2006) "Prospective effect of community distress and subcultural orientation on mortality following life-threatening diseases in later life." *Sociology of Health & Illness* 28: 558–82.

Wermuth, Laurie (2003) *Global inequality and human needs.* Boston: Allyn and Bacon.

Wilkinson, Richard G. (1996) *Unhealthy societies.* London: Routledge.

Winkleby, Marilyn A., Darius E. Jatulis, Erica Frank, and Stephen P. Fortmann (1992) "Socioeconomic status and health: How education, income, and occupation contribute to risk factors for cardiovascular disease." *American Journal of Public Health* 82: 816–20.

CHAPTER 4

The Social Demography of Health: Gender, Age, and Race

Three of the most important variables employed in epidemiological research are gender, age, and race. It has been found that each of these variables represents differences between people that can be correlated with health and life expectancy. The purpose of this chapter will be to examine these variables and assess their relationship to health from a sociological perspective.

Gender

Declining Female Life Expectancy and the Narrowing Gender Gap in Longevity

In 2008, a nationwide study of mortality at the county level in the United States revealed the shocking finding that life expectancy for about 19 percent of the nation's women compared to 4 percent of men had declined significantly (1.3 years or more) between 1983 and 1999 (Ezzati, Friedman, Kulkarni, and Murray 2008). Overall, longevity for women had fallen appreciably in 180 counties and less steeply in another 783 counties. For men, life expectancy had declined significantly during the same period in only 11 counties, with smaller decreases in some 48 counties. These counties were primarily located in the Deep South, Appalachia, Texas, and the lower Midwest. The decline was greatest in rural, low-income female populations and included both blacks and whites. The downturn in female mortality was largely because of a rise in chronic diseases related to smoking, being overweight or obese, and having high blood pressure. Between 1961 and 1983, *none* of the nation's 3,141 counties had a significant decline in life expectancy as reductions in heart disease generally increased life for both sexes. However, after 1983, the loss of longevity for females in certain low-income counties emerged and is counter to past trends.

To have this happen in the wealthiest country in the world, with the highest spending on health care, was unexpected. A key factor appeared to be the long-term effects of smoking on women, although other factors such as high-fat diets and lack of exercise may be important as well. Regardless of the reason, the transition from no decline in 1961–1983 to a worsening of life expectancy for some people in a large number of low-income counties between 1983 and 1999 is particularly troubling because of what it signifies for the health of disadvantaged segments of the population—especially low-income women (Ezzati et al. 2008:8).

To more fully assess this trend, more recent mortality data needed to be analyzed. Subsequent research indeed confirms the narrowing of the gender gap in longevity (Montez and Zajacova 2013; Olshansky et al. 2012; Wang et al. 2013). Moreover, the greatest declines in life expectancy were found among non-Hispanic white women with less than a high school education. Jay Olshansky and his colleagues (2012) determined that longevity for low-educated white women fell five years between 1990 and 2008. White men without a high school education lost three years of life expectancy during this period. The result was that in 2008, white males who did not complete high school had a life expectancy equal to all men born in the United States in 1972 and their similarly low-educated white female counterparts had the life expectancy of all women born in 1964. College-educated black and Hispanic men and women lived longer than both their less-educated racial counterparts and less-educated whites, but the differences between whites were more extreme. Olshansky et al. (2012) point out that while the relationship between education and longevity is complicated by race, not having a college or postgraduate degree has a greater negative effect on life expectancy for whites than in the past. Those at the bottom of the class structure are experiencing either a decrease or a slow rate of increase in longevity relative to those at the top. White women in low-income, rural counties seem to be the most affected.

Jennifer Montez and Anna Zajacova (2013) examined mortality risks among non-Hispanic white women and found that the odds of dying were 37 percent greater for those with low levels of education than women with a college education in 1997–2001 and 66 percent greater in 2002–2006. While mortality for college-educated white women declined, it remained stable for those who were high school graduates, and *increased* for those without a high school diploma. Being a lower-educated white woman means living a shorter life than anyone else. In investigating the causes, little support was found for social and psychological factors (e.g., marital status, psychological distress), but adverse economic factors (e.g., unemployment, low paying jobs) and poor health behaviors or lifestyles (e.g., obesity, smoking, alcohol use) were important. Long-term unemployment and how that affects income, living standards, self-esteem, and control over one's life, and especially smoking were the strongest predictors of the early mortality.

What these studies reveal is that since the mid-1980s, life expectancy for some women, especially rural, low-income, poorly educated white women, has surprisingly decreased. The general pattern is depicted in Figure 4.1 showing counties in the United States with either a significant decrease, no significant change, or significant increase in life expectancy by gender for the period 1985–2010. For males, Figure 4.1 shows that life expectancy has significantly increased in most counties, while a lack of change or a decrease characterizes the outcome for women in many counties. Decreases for women are particularly clustered in Oklahoma, Texas, and parts of various Southern states.

This research is part of the renewed interest in investigating the health differences between men and women because of changes in the way that people now live. The lives of men and women used to be more predictable in that men typically behaved in certain distinct ways and women in others. Thus, gender differences in activities, goals, and life expectancy were taken for granted and more or less anticipated. But patterns are emerging that show Americans moving toward greater

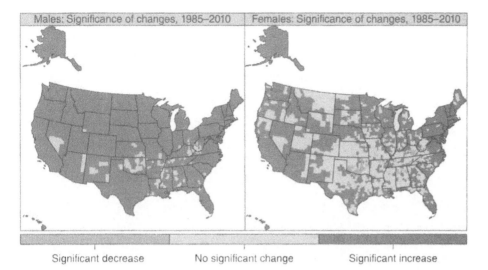

FIGURE 4.1

Map of the United States Showing Significant Changes in Life Expectancy by Gender, 1985–2010.

Source: Institute for Health Metrics and Evaluation, 2013.

equality in mortality between the sexes. This possibility is based upon evidence that gender differences for some life-threatening afflictions such as heart disease and diabetes are smaller than previously assumed (Gorman and Read 2006) and that life expectancy for some women of low socio-economic status has declined (Ezzati et al. 2008; Montez and Zajacova 2013; Olshansky et al. 2012; Wang et al. 2013).

The pattern of change is shown in Table 4.1 depicting life expectancy at birth for both sexes and the gender gap in longevity for selected years from 1930 to 2010. Table 4.1 shows the historic female advantage in life expectancy increased from 3.5 years in 1930 to 7.6 years in 1970, when the gap begins to decrease, falling slightly to 7.4 years in 1980, 7.0 years in 1990, 5.2 years in 2000, and dropping marginally to 4.8 years in 2010. Both men and women had their greatest gains in life expectancy during the 1940s, when males acquired an average of 4.8 additional years and females 5.9 years. But Table 4.1 indicates that the situation changed during the 1970s, and men went on to show their greatest gain (2.3 years) over women (0.5 years) between 1990 and 2000. It is apparent from Table 4.1 that a long-term reversal in the gender gap in longevity surfaced in the late twentieth century and produced a slow but continuing trend toward convergence. The trend appears to be decelerating in the 2000s, possibly because female age cohorts who started smoking in large numbers in the 1940s and 1950s had died.

Going back in history to preindustrial societies, the life expectancies of men and women were approximately the same. This was the situation until about 1850, when women began living longer on average than men and were the primary beneficiaries of modernization with respect to longevity. The only exception worldwide is now in a few countries such as Botswana, the Central African Republic, Qatar, and Tonga where male life expectancy is equal to or greater than that of women by a slight margin. In Western nations, from the 1880s to the 1970s, female longevity

			Life Expectancy at Birth			
Year	All	Male	Male Gain Over Previous Decade	Female	Female Gain Over Previous Decade	Male–Female Gap
1930	59.7	58.1	—	61.6	—	3.5
1940	62.9	60.8	2.7	65.2	3.6	4.4
1950	68.2	65.6	4.8	71.1	5.9	5.5
1960	69.7	66.6	1.0	73.1	2.0	6.5
1970	70.8	67.1	0.5	74.7	1.6	7.6
1980	73.7	70.0	2.9	77.4	2.7	7.4
1990	75.4	71.8	1.8	78.8	1.4	7.0
2000	76.8	74.1	2.3	79.3	0.5	5.2
2010	78.7	76.2	2.1	81.0	1.7	4.8

TABLE 4.1   The Gender Gap in Life Expectancy at Birth, United States, 1930–2010

Note: Life expectancies for 2000–2010 were calculated using a revised methodology.
Source: CDC, National Vital Statistics Reports, 2013.

gradually increased relative to that of men over the ninety-year period. In the United States, Canada, Australia, and Western Europe, the gender gap between females and males in life expectancy reached its historical peak in the 1970s. The female advantage at this time ranged between six and eight years in the various countries, including the United States where the gender gap reached its highest point of 7.8 years in 1979. However, in the 1980s the gender gap began to narrow, and this trend has continued ever since, not just in the United States but in other Western nations as well. As British medical sociologist Ellen Annandale (2010:103) points out: "These international comparisons relate to only some parts of the world, but they are instructive because they draw our attention to the sensitivity of health to social change, often over relatively short periods, and to the variable impacts of such change on men and women."

Dramatic changes have occurred in both family and work situations for American women beginning in the middle of the twentieth century. Prior to this time, public sentiment had favored women staying at home, having children, and taking care of the household. The norms governing gender relations were similar to those in Britain during Victorian times, which focused women on the private sphere of domestic labor and men on the public sphere of paid work (Collins 2009). However, this situation was overturned by new developments. First, World War II initiated the long-term, massive migration of women into the labor force, and their participation never returned to prewar rates. About three-quarters of all working-age women are now employed outside the home in the United States. However, most research shows that while women's work hours and responsibilities increased, men's time adding to the household labor did not substantially rise in response (Percheski 2008). As Catherine Ross, John Mirowsky, and Patricia Ulbrich (1983:681) determined years ago, "if a married woman gets a job to bolster the family income or find self-expression through occupational achievement, or both, she finds that the wife is now more like a husband but the husband is not more like a wife." Therefore, while women were finding meaningful work and entering more jobs and occupations, many had a "second shift," working for pay during the day and working for the family each evening (Hochschild 1989). As work roles changed, divorce rates and single-parent households headed by females also increased.

Male–Female Life Expectancy

Although the gender gap has narrowed in recent decades, it should not be forgotten that male death rates still exceed those of females at all ages and for the leading causes of death such as heart disease, cancer, cerebrovascular diseases (stroke), accidents, and pneumonia. Women tend to suffer from more frequent illnesses and disability, but their usual health disorders are not as serious or as life threatening as those encountered by men. Yet women, especially in later life, also die from the same illnesses as men. For example, heart disease is the leading cause of death for women after age 66, but becomes the number-one killer of men after age 39.

As of 2010, the most recent year data are available as this book goes to press, average life expectancy in the United States of non-Hispanic white females was 81.1 years compared to 76.4 years for non-Hispanic white males. The same gender advantage applies to non-Hispanic black females, who had an average life expectancy in 2010 of 77.7 years compared to 71.4 years for non-Hispanic black males, while among Hispanics—who have the highest life expectancy of all—females lived 83.8 years compared to 78.5 years for males. However, as Olshansky et al. (2012) caution, this result for Hispanics may be somewhat skewed by the influx of immigrants who are typically healthier and better educated than those left behind in the country of origin and whose mortality tends to be 10–20 percent lower than Hispanics born in the United States. Also, on retirement some return to their home country and their deaths are not registered in the United States. Conversely, there has been a surge in the number of U.S.-born Hispanics in the general population whose higher mortality relative to new immigrants may impact on future longevity patterns.

Nevertheless, we know that females live longer than males, even though males are closing the gap somewhat. Male inferiority in terms of life expectancy results from the combined effects of (1) biological and (2) social-psychological factors. The male of the human species is biologically disadvantaged compared to the female. The fact that the male is weaker physiologically than the female is demonstrated by higher mortality rates from the prenatal and neonatal stages of life onward. Although the percentages may vary somewhat from year to year, the chances of dying during the prenatal stage are greater among males than females and significantly greater during the neonatal (newborn) stage. Examples of neonatal disorders more common to male than female babies are such afflictions as hyaline membrane disease (a respiratory disease) and pyloric stenosis (a disorder of the pyloric muscle affecting the emptying of the stomach). Neonatal males are also more prone to certain circulatory disorders of the aorta and pulmonary artery and are subject to more severe bacterial infections. Females are less likely to get childhood leukemia and have a better chance for survival when they do. As an organism, the male appears to be more vulnerable than the female, even before being exposed to the differential social roles and stress situations of later life.

Social and psychological influences also play an important part in the determination of life expectancy. We know that men who are "macho" and express strong masculinity tend to take less care of their health than those with moderate masculinity (Dolan 2007; Springer and Mouzon 2011). Also men tend to be more aggressive than women in both work and play and more likely to engage in risky behavior (Cockerham 2006). Accidents, for example, cause more deaths among males than females, which reflects a difference in sex roles. High accident rates among males may be attributed to the male's increased exposure to dangerous activities, especially those arising from high-risk occupations. For example, the average accidental death rate for all U.S. occupations in 2012 was 3.2 per 100,000 workers. However, the most dangerous job in the United States (according to the Bureau of Labor Statistics) is that of logging workers who have a death rate of 127.8 per 100,000 workers. Next is commercial fishermen with 117 deaths per 100,000 workers, with Alaskan commercial fishermen, especially those who fish for crabs and work in a cold northern climate having the most dangerous jobs in the fishing business. Winter storms, ice building up on boats causing them to capsize, and falling overboard into extremely cold water can all be fatal. The next most dangerous occupation is aircraft pilots and flight engineers, followed by (in order), roofers, structural iron/steel workers, refuse and recyclable materials collectors, electrical power-line workers, truck drivers, farmers and ranchers, and construction workers. Mostly men perform these jobs. Being president of the United States is also hazardous as only about one out of three U.S. presidents has lived to enjoy a normal life expectancy.

A factor contributing to both male and female mortality rates may be occupational competition and the pressure associated with a job. The lifestyle of the business executive or professional with an orientation toward "career" and drive toward "success," marks of the upwardly mobile middle-class individual, is thought to contribute strongly to the development of stress among such men and, more recently, women. Middle-aged professional males, and to a growing extent, females, in the United States today are noted by life insurance companies as a high-risk group, particularly if they smoke, are overweight, and tend to overwork. Thus, it would seem that traditional male roles and the psychodynamics of male competitiveness when adopted by females are capable of affecting longevity for both genders. Alcohol use, particularly heavy use, has also been identified as a risk factor for some diseases (such as cirrhosis of the liver) and deaths from automobile accidents. Men and boys continue to drink more frequently and drink larger quantities at one time than women and girls. Driving at high speeds and participating in violent sports are likewise more common for males. Thus, when occupational hazards are added, men are at greater risk of dying prematurely than women, although this situation affects more women than in the past.

This seems to be the case as women move into high-risk occupations, and ambitious female executives and professionals experience career pressures. For example, in Canada, a study of the mortality rates of medical school class presidents over the course of a century at the University of Toronto found that the presidents had significantly more professional accomplishments than classmates during their careers. They also lived 2.4 years less on average. About one-third of the sample were women and another third were nonwhite, so gender and race were not determining factors nor was medical care since they all had a high level of access to it. The researchers (Redelmeier and Kwong 2004:2541) concluded that "the difference in survival suggests that the type of medical professional who accepts major added responsibilities might also be the type who neglects to look after his or her own health."

In other research in the United States, it was found that women in higher status occupations (professional and managerial) had significantly higher risks (ranging from 57–89 percent) of breast cancer than housewives and women in lower status occupations (Pudrovska, Carr, McFarland, and Collins 2013). It was suggested this outcome was primarily because of the assertion of job authority by the women who found the experience stressful. These stresses were believed to promote the onset of breast cancer later in life through the exposure of breast tissue to the adverse effects of chronically elevated cortisol. The women in the study cohort had entered high status job positions in the 1970s where they experienced prejudice and discrimination stemming from prevailing cultural stereotypes that men were better leaders than women.

While men generally have a higher rate of mortality, women appear to have a higher morbidity or sickness rate. According to the National Center for Health Statistics (2013), females have higher rates of acute illness—namely, infectious and parasitic diseases and digestive and respiratory conditions. The only category of acute health problems in which males had a higher incidence was injuries. Males, however, tended to not stay in bed with injuries as much as females. The rate for acute conditions not related to pregnancy is 11 times greater for females than males.

As for chronic (long-term) conditions, females show higher rates of hypertension, thyroid, anemia, gallbladder conditions, chronic enteritis and colitis, migraine headaches, arthritis, diabetes, diseases of the urinary system, and some skin conditions. Males, on the other hand, have more losses of limbs, gout, emphysema, AIDS, and heart disease. Males have higher rates of cancer at the youngest and oldest ages. Women have the highest incidence rates between the ages of 20 and 55. Overall, men are more likely to die from cancer. The pattern that emerges from these differences is that women are more likely to have a higher prevalence of chronic conditions that are not a leading cause of death (except for diabetes), whereas men have more of the chronic health problems that end one's life.

Women also exhibit much greater use of health services than men (National Center for Health Statistics 2013). Men, on the other hand, may try to be "macho" about their health and avoid seeking preventive care since it is considered be a feminine behavior (Springer and Mouzon 2011). The greater use of medical care by women is a consistent pattern, even when the utilization of maternity services is excluded from analysis. Furthermore, as Judith Auerbach and Anne Figert (1995) explain, women are the primary caretakers for sick people—in both the family and society at large—as well as the major consumers of health care for themselves and others. "Women," state Auerbach and Figert (1995:122), "urge their loved ones to seek medical care; they make the doctors' appointments for their family members; and they purchase and replenish over-the-counter medicines for the family's bathroom medicine cabinet." They are also more likely to leave work to take care of a sick child, monitor the health status of extended family members, and take care of elderly relatives. In sum, women have more physical ailments than men, and spend considerably more time taking care of themselves and others.

It appears there is an inverse relationship between mortality and morbidity when gender differences are considered. Women may be sick more often, but usually live longer. Men may be sick less often, but die sooner. The possibility exists that women do not have more sickness but are just more sensitive to their bodily discomforts and more willing to report their symptoms to others. However, the best evidence indicates that overall differences in morbidity are real (Bird and Rieker 2008; Budrys 2003; National Center for Health Statistics 2013; Rieker and Bird 2000). Regardless of whether the reasons for greater morbidity are mostly social and psychological, or mostly physical, the end result is the same: Females report more illness and disability and, consequently, show a greater loss of productivity—whether their work is in the home or outside it. Employers cannot rely on females as readily as they can on males to be at work or to feel like working while they are there. Females also spend more days at home in a sick role.

Since good health is generally considered to be a highly significant component of a good life, females are at a disadvantage compared to males. "Higher female morbidity, compared to males," as Lois Verbrugge (1976:401) observed many years ago, "means that females experience a less comfortable and satisfying life with regard to a cherished attribute. They simply do not feel as well as often as males." We know that *healthy* life expectancy decreases as life expectancy increases, so that the extra years of life a woman has may not necessarily be spent in good health (Annandale 2010). While the same pattern would be thought to apply equally to men, both male life expectancy and healthy longevity relative to females have increased (Bird and Rieker 2008). Thus, those men who do reach older ages appear to be in better health overall than their female counterparts.

While females are biologically stronger at birth, less often exposed to danger and highly stressful occupations, more sensitive to their bodily states, and possibly enhance their life expectancy through increased use of medical services, the female advantage in longevity may be a mixed blessing. Women not only appear to feel physically ill more often than men, but many studies confirm that depression and anxiety are more prevalent among women, as is discussed in a later subsection. Female longevity also means that more women than men are faced with important decisions about remarriage, employment, family life, and dealing with loneliness after the death of a spouse.

Some data now exist with respect to the possible effects on female life expectancy posed by their increased participation in the labor force and changes in lifestyles. Studies of self-rated health typically show women rating their own health less positively than men do; however, recent research finds college-educated women employed outside the home increasingly more likely to report their health is good (Schnittker 2007). As for types of jobs and lifestyle changes, women today, as compared to the 1970s, are more likely to work in occupations that were once exclusively male and have lifestyles consistent with the norms of these occupations. It will be several years, until the present cohort of adult women dies, before these effects on women's health can be fully determined. Although, it is evident now that a decline in life expectancy for some low-income women is taking place, this trend seems linked more to being unemployed or underemployed than having a job (Ezzati et al. 2008; Montez and Zajacova 2013).

Smoking

More than 440,000 Americans die each year from smoking-related diseases. These diseases include not only lung cancer, but also numerous other cancers, including cancers of the esophagus, throat, bladder and cervix, as well as chronic obstructive pulmonary disease (COPD), chronic heart and cardiovascular diseases, and other fatal afflictions. In the United States, smoking causes a man to lose an average of 13.5 years of life and a woman 14.5 years. American women did not begin smoking in large numbers until World War II, when they entered civilian workplaces as replacements for men in the military. When women were empowered by the greater equality that came with employment outside the home, their smoking rates increased dramatically. Female rates of lung cancer, accordingly, rose from 5.8 deaths per 100,000 in 1950 to 37.9 in 2010. Lung cancer ranked eighth among cancer deaths for women in 1961, but moved up to first by 1986, where it remains today. Deaths from lung cancer now account for 26 percent of all cancer deaths among women, making it apparent that women are now more likely to die of lung cancer than men. This rise is attributed to an aging of female cohorts with a high prevalence of cigarette smoking.

This situation is also seen in relation to COPD that permanently damages the lungs and is typically caused by smoking. It is an example of a disease whose female victims now outnumber the males that are killed by it. This disease was once prevalent among older men, but has emerged today as increasingly fatal for women. It is often diagnosed late because people think they run out of breath because they are aging or are out of shape. The disease kills over 138,000 Americans annually and is the third leading cause of death in the United States. More women than men die or are hospitalized from it every year since 1998. This is seen in Figure 4.2, showing mortality

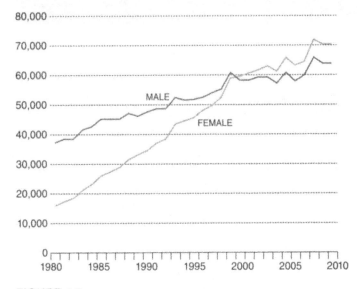

FIGURE 4.2

Mortality from COPD for Males and Females, United States, 1980–2010.

Source: Centers for Disease Control and Prevention, 2013.

from COPD for men increasing until the late 1990s and then beginning to decline, while deaths for women have increased steadily and now exceed those of men.

However, the current trend in the United States is toward a decrease in smoking for both sexes. As shown in Table 4.2, the proportion of men who smoke in the United States declined from 51.2 percent in 1965 to 21.1 percent in 2011. The percentage of white male smokers had declined to 21.4 percent and black males

PHOTO 4.2 Males are more likely to quit smoking than females.

TABLE 4.2	Percentage of Current Cigarette Smokers by Sex and Race, United States (Selected Years, 1965–2011)*							
	1965	1979	1985	1990	1995	2000	2005	2011
Male	51.2	37.0	32.2	28.0	26.5	25.2	23.4	21.1
White	50.4	36.4	31.3	27.6	26.2	25.4	23.3	21.4
Black	58.8	43.9	40.2	32.8	29.4	25.7	25.9	23.2
Female	33.7	30.1	27.9	22.9	22.7	21.1	18.3	16.8
White	33.9	30.3	27.9	23.5	23.4	22.0	19.1	17.7
Black	31.8	30.5	30.9	20.8	23.5	20.7	17.1	15.2

*Eighteen years of age and over, age adjusted. Data for 1995 and earlier are not strictly comparable to later years because of a 1997 questionnaire redesign.
Source: National Center for Health Statistics, 2013.

to 23.2 percent. Table 4.2 shows that the proportion of women smoking dropped from 33.7 percent in 1965 to 16.8 percent in 2011. Whereas smoking by males began declining in the 1970s, the percentage of female smokers did not decrease significantly until the late 1980s and has decreased much more slowly than that of males. Table 4.2 shows the percentage of smokers among white females has decreased steadily over the years but still remains higher than that of black females with some 17.7 percent of white women smoking in 2011 compared to 15.2 percent of black women. Overall, smoking cessation has been more pronounced among men than women. Quitting smoking, even past the age of 50, tends to increase longevity, but the death toll continues to rise each year as the habits of the past have their effects.

Prior to 1999, Hispanics were counted as either white or black and not as a separate racial category by the National Center for Health Statistics. Smoking percentages for Hispanic males were estimated to be 24.4 percent and for Hispanic females 13.7 percent in 1995–1998. Race-specific measures calculated in 2009–2011 for Hispanics show male smoking had declined to 16.4 percent and female smoking had dropped to 9.0 percent. Consequently, it appears that Hispanics have lower rates of smoking than either non-Hispanic whites or blacks.

BOX 4.1

Second-Hand Smoking

In Helena, Montana, in June 2002, the community voted to ban smoking in all public places, including restaurants, bars, and casinos (Ellis 2003). Shortly thereafter, physicians at the local hospital observed that admissions for heart attacks were declining, and they initiated a study with the cooperation of the University of California at San Francisco to find out why. They determined that there was no change in heart attack rates for patients who lived outside the city but that a 58 percent reduction in rates had occurred for city residents in only six months following the smoking ban. The researchers concluded that the reduction was largely because of preventing the exposure of nonsmokers to cigarette smoke in public places. Smokers affect the quality of air inhaled by everyone in enclosed locations like homes, offices, automobiles, bars, and restaurants. The culprit is the irritant and carcinogenic material ("tar") released by burning tobacco in the smoke that is inhaled by both smokers and the nonsmokers around them.

This is why second-hand or passive smoking is so dangerous. Eight hours of working in a smoky bar is the equivalent of smoking a pack of cigarettes a day. Nonsmokers who work in such places are twice as likely to develop lung cancer as nonsmokers working elsewhere. Only 30 minutes exposure to second-hand smoke causes blood platelets to become stickier, which makes it easier to form clots that can block arteries and cause heart attacks. Consequently, many cities and countries in the world today have banned smoking in bars, restaurants, and public places. However, the Montana State Legislature, under pressure from tobacco lobbyists and the Montana Tavern Association, rescinded the smoking ban in Helena six months later (December 2002). Heart attack rates in the city jumped up almost as quickly as they had come down. Finally, in 2005, the legislature passed the Montana Clean Air Act that banned smoking in buildings open to the public, but agreed to a compromise that allowed smoking in bars and casinos to continue until 2009 at which time smoking bans finally went into effect in all public places.

Mental Health

As for mental health, major differences exist between men and women in the pattern of mental disorders they experience. This is particularly the case for depressive and anxiety disorders that are more prevalent among women than men, while men have more personality disorders, which consist largely of impaired personality traits, and more substance-related disorders from alcohol and drug use (Cockerham 2014; Hopcroft and Bradley 2007; Rosenfield and Mouzon 2013; Rosenfield and Smith 2010; Roxburgh 2009). Thus it appears that women have a tendency to *internalize* their feelings of distress by turning them inward on themselves resulting in more anxiety and depression, whereas men tend to *externalize* their distresses through greater substance use and personality disorders that are upsetting to others (Longest and Thoits 2012; Rosenfield, Lennon, and White 2005; Rosenfield and Mouzon 2013).

This pattern is seen both in the United States and in other countries around the globe (Cockerham 2014; Desjarlais, Eisenberg, Good, and Kleinman 1995). For example, Rosemary Hopcroft and Dana Bradley (2007), studied depression in 29 countries in different regions of the world and in none of the countries were men more depressed than women. Tendencies toward depression and anxiety that fall short of mental disorders in the full-blown clinical sense, but nonetheless cause people to feel psychologically distressed, are also more common among women than men (Mirowsky and Ross 2004).

Therefore, as Sarah Rosenfield (1989:77) pointed out years ago, the differences in mental health between men and women exist "across cultures, over time, in different age groups, in rural as well as urban areas, and in treated as well as untreated populations." These differences appear to be related to both biological and sociocultural factors. Much of this research in sociology focuses on the everyday social roles of women. Women employed outside the home tend to show less psychological distress than housewives but more distress than employed men. Often working wives have to maintain the house as well as perform satisfactorily on the job, in addition to caring for children. In essence, these demands are tantamount to having two jobs. It may be that working wives are under greater strain than their husbands, although both employed men and women generally have fewer health problems than the unemployed.

However, there is research showing employment outside the home has tended to enhance the overall psychological well-being of women (Frech and Damaske 2012; Williams 2003). This is especially the case if they are able to exercise some control over what they do at work. However, many jobs that women perform have low levels of complexity, which can reduce the possibilities for satisfaction (Wickrama, Lorenz, Conger, and Elder 1997), while perceived sex discrimination and/or sexual harassment on the job can add stress to the work environment (Houle et al. 2011; Pavalko, Mossakowski, and Hamilton 2003). Consequently, the degree to which employment outside the home has resulted in positive levels of mental health for women generally has not been fully ascertained. What is clear is that increased employment for women has not had a widespread negative impact on the psychological well-being of women, although some women as well as men are adversely affected by job-related stressors.

As for marriage, the quality of the relationship with the spouse appears especially important in maintaining a positive level of mental health (Frech and Williams 2007; Umberson et al. 2006). Certainly psychological difficulties and strain can exist within marriages, with either one or both of the spouses and other family members being affected (Ailshire and Burgard 2012; Uecker 2012; Umberson et al. 2006). When it comes to depression, for example, there is research showing spouses do affect each other, with the link between spouses' depressive symptoms primarily flowing from the wife to the husband (Thomeer, Umberson, and Pudrovska 2013). Most studies, however, find that marriage can bring mental health benefits in the form of social, emotional, and economic support to both spouses and the research literature in medical sociology generally holds that marriage is beneficial for both physical and mental health (Avison and Comeau 2013; Roxburgh 2009; Simon 2002; Spence, Adkins, and Dupre 2011; Umberson, Thomeer, and Williams 2013; Williams 2003).

Some women are no doubt content to be wives and mothers, while other women may find more satisfaction in establishing a career outside the home or combining a job with being a housewife. But others may experience conflict between being a homemaker or a career person—or being both. Yet, whether in the home or on the job, the lives of women are often dependent on what others (usually men) do; hence, they cannot control the possibilities for satisfaction as much as men can. Married women tend to have less control over their lives because of the demands of marriage and family and dependence on the careers of their husbands. This lack of control has been found to make women particularly susceptible to psychological distress (Mirowsky and Ross 2004). Therefore, in comparison to men, women are more prone to psychological distress in general and to anxiety and depression in particular. The social role of the woman appears highly significant in this outcome.

Age

A number of factors including improved medical care, nutrition and health lifestyles, sanitation, and housing have combined over the course of more than a century to help prolong lives for most Americans. In 2010, for example, the average infant in the United States could expect to live for 78.7 years. This figure represents an increase in longevity of approximately 60 percent since 1900, when life expectancy was 47.3 years. Less than one-half of all children born in 1900 could expect to reach age 65, whereas today at least 80 percent can expect to live to age 65, and one-third will live to be at least 85 years of age. The rise in life expectancy has brought a corresponding increase in the growth of the elderly population. Men and women are living to 65 years of age and older in greater numbers and proportions than ever before. In 1940, the elderly (those 65 and over) constituted 9 million people or about 7 percent of the total population. By 2000, their number had increased to 34.9 million or 12.4 percent of the population. Projections for 2015 place the number of elderly at over 47 million.

The twentieth century can be described as a period of rapid growth of the aged population worldwide, and this trend is continuing into the twenty-first century. In the United States, not only are people living longer, but the fertility rate entered a period of decline beginning in 1958 until stabilizing at about 2.1 births per woman of child-bearing age. A declining death rate coupled with a steady birth rate has resulted in a much higher proportion of older Americans in relation to the total population. Table 4.3 illustrates this trend by showing that in 1900 only 4 percent of the total U.S. population was age 65 or above. By 2000, however, older Americans constituted 12.4 percent of the total population, and by 2050 it is projected that 21 percent of all Americans will be in this age bracket. That is, persons above age 65 will make up one-fifth of the population. Beginning in 2010, a dramatic surge in the number of elderly Americans is expected to occur as the leading edge of the baby boom generation reaches 65 years of age. This upsurge will continue until 2030, at which time the number of elderly will stabilize at around 20 percent of the total population. Obviously, Americans are living longer, and the percentage of the elderly in the population is significantly increasing.

Such a trend will undoubtedly bring about a marked change in American society in general and in health care delivery in particular. The aged population will be healthier, better educated, and more affluent than any cohort of elderly persons in the past. They are likely to have not only a higher standard of living but also increased political power because of their larger numbers and experience with the political process. As a result, they will have the political clout to bring about legislation for public services to meet their social and health needs. Even though elderly Americans will be healthier than ever before, more pressure is likely to be put on health care delivery systems and public health insurance, namely, Medicare, to keep them fit. However, the need for health services becomes greater as one ages, because even minor ailments can more easily develop into serious problems or linger longer than usual. Demands for health and other services for the aged are thus likely to increase in accordance with their proportion of the population.

Pressure also will be put upon the Social Security system to maintain or increase payments for old-age benefits. With relatively fewer children resulting from the baby boom generation that was born between 1946 and 1964 and is now passing through middle and late middle age, the financing of old-age benefits will require increasingly more money in the future from a smaller working population. In 1955, for example, there were 8.6 taxpayers per Social Security beneficiary, but by 2005 the ratio was 2.7 taxpayers per retiree. By 2035, the ratio will drop to about 1.9 taxpayers for every retiree. Major adjustments in the financing and provision of services for the elderly in the United States appear certain.

TABLE 4.3	Percentage of Total U.S. Population Age Sixty-Five and Over for Selected Years							
	1900	**1930**	**1950**	**1970**	**1980**	**2000**	**2020 (Projected)**	**2050 (Projected)**
Percent age 65 and over	4.0	5.4	8.1	9.7	11.2	12.4	16.8	21.0

Source: U.S. Bureau of the Census, 2013.

These trends are important because when people become elderly they require a greater share of public services. In developed nations, the care of the elderly has generally shifted from being a family responsibility to being more of a societal responsibility. This change has come about for a number of reasons. One reason is the decline of the extended family, in which multiple generations of a single family continued to live with or near each other. It is replaced by the nuclear family, that is, a family consisting of one couple and their children that can affect the amount of support immediately available to elderly family members—especially if they live far away. Other reasons include the high cost of health and nursing care, the type and degree of care required, and the increase in the number of persons needing such care. Although many old people will be relatively healthy in old age, there will come a time when their health will fail, bringing about the requirement for extended care and greater public expenditures to meet this need.

Adequate health care for the aged is a particularly significant goal for public policy because the single most important determinant of the quality of an elderly person's life is health. Older people who are unhealthy lead relatively shorter and less satisfactory lives than older people who are healthy, feel good, and have the physical capability to pursue their chosen activities. Especially among the elderly, health matters affect all other areas of life. Interestingly, older people often rate their health in a positive fashion. But how can this be, since health deteriorates with age? Several studies have investigated this situation and find that many elderly nevertheless rate their health status as very good despite their age (Baron-Epel and Kaplan 2001).

The question arises as to whether such self-assessments are accurate measures of a person's health. This is an important question because the accuracy of survey respondents' reports of objective conditions affects virtually all fields of sociology. However, extensive analysis of health self-ratings shows that such ratings are indeed valid and reliable and match up as well as or even better than physician evaluations (Ferraro and Farmer 1999; Idler and Benyamini 1997; Mirowsky 1999). Most people appear to make accurate assessments of their physical state based on how they feel and function. As for the elderly, those who rate their health high are usually older than those who rate their health less positively. It may seem incongruent that many older people tend to rate their health positively, in spite of the fact that health declines with age. The reason is that judgments concerning one's health by aged individuals are relative. That is, in assessing their health, aged persons often compare themselves with others of their own age and gender and perhaps also in relation to the expectations others have of their health.

High self-ratings of health by the elderly are likely to be rationalized in two ways. First, simply surviving to old age in a condition reasonably free of serious illness or disability would be evidence of relatively good health. Some of their classmates from school and peers may already have died. Second, subjective responses to a health problem tend to be determined by how much of a person's life is disrupted by the condition, and elderly people typically do not maintain a highly active level of functioning. Thus, the aged are able to perceive their health as good if they can perform their usual daily activities successfully. As people become older, they tend to change their definition of what it is to be healthy to fit their circumstances.

Of course, the health of elderly people on the whole is not actually better than that of young adults in general. This fact is apparent when age differences in overall physical condition, stamina, hand and eye coordination, hearing and vision, capacity for healing from disease and injury, and prevalence of chronic diseases are considered. Although there are exceptions, older people generally cannot pursue a highly active physical lifestyle to the same extent as someone much younger. Rather, it is that the health of many older people is quite good for their age. When this happens, chronological age is not necessarily a reliable predictor when advanced medical procedures such as angioplasty and ICD (internal cardioverter defibrilator) implantations are needed and used if the benefits outweigh the risks (Shim, Russ, and Kaufman 2006).

The health of some older people, however, may easily be poor. The fact remains that health deteriorates with age, and this deterioration occurs later in some people than in others. But eventually everyone's health declines if they live long enough. The key to a positive quality of life in old age appears to be that of maintaining one's health as long as possible and as close as possible to the time of one's death.

The most prevalent health problem of persons above the age of 65 is arthritis. Next is hypertension, followed by hearing impairment, heart disease, cataracts, and orthopedic impairments. With an increasingly older population, these disorders will require greater attention from health care delivery services. So there will be something of a paradox in that the aged are likely to be healthier than previous generations, but they will be placing greater demands on the health care system (since there will be more of them) to help keep them that way.

Race

A major reflection of social inequality in the United States is the differences among the health profiles of racial groups. Asian Americans have typically enjoyed high levels of health, with blacks being especially disadvantaged. Hispanics and Native Americans also have health disadvantages. Comparisons of the health of racial minorities with that of non-Hispanic whites in the United States will be reviewed in this section. When it comes to race, however, the United States is undergoing a significant transition in which the majority non-Hispanic white population is declining in numbers, while the Hispanic population has replaced non-Hispanic blacks as the largest minority group and is reducing the majority status of non-Hispanic whites. This development represents a profound demographic shift in American society.

For example, in 2010, non-Hispanic whites constituted 66.2 percent of the population, followed by Hispanics (14.8 percent), blacks (12.2 percent), Asians and Pacific Islanders (4.3 percent), people of two or more races (1.8 percent), and Native Americans/Alaska Natives (0.7 percent). In 2060, nearly one out of every three Americans (30.6 percent) will be Hispanic because of high birth rates and immigration. The non-Hispanic white population will have declined to 42.6 percent, with the proportion of blacks increasing slightly to 14.7 percent, the Asian population rising to 8.2 percent, persons of two or more races reaching 6.4 percent, and American Indians/Native Alaskans increasing to 1.5 percent. As of 2043, the U.S. Census Bureau projects that racial minorities will be the majority as the proportion of non-Hispanic whites falls below 50 percent of the population.

It needs to also be noted that many minority group persons and their families live in disadvantaged socioeconomic circumstances that are a powerful negative influence on health. In 2012, some 27.6 percent of all non-Hispanic blacks, compared to 25.3 percent of Hispanics, 12.3 percent of Asians/Pacific Islanders, and 9.8 percent of non-Hispanic whites had incomes on or below the poverty line of $23,492 annual income for a family of four.

Black Americans

A comparison of the life expectancy of black and white Americans indicates that black males are the most disadvantaged with respect to longevity. Table 4.4 shows that the black male with a life expectancy of 71.8 years in 2010 lives, on average, about 4.7 years less than the white male (76.5 years) and 9.5 years less than the white female (81.3 years). The white female had a life expectancy in 2010 approximately 3.3 years greater than the black female (78.0 years).

Underlying the lessened life expectancy of blacks is a higher prevalence of several life-threatening illnesses, such as AIDS, cancer, heart disease, and hypertension (Brown, O'Rand, and Adkins 2012; Farmer and Ferraro 2005; Hattery and Smith 2011; Spalter-Roth, Lowenthal, and Rubio 2005; Williams 2012). Hypertension or high blood pressure has been a particular health problem for blacks. Some 24 and 20 percent of all white males and females, respectively, above the age of 20, have hypertension compared to over 30 percent of all black males and females in the same age category. The end result is that proportionately more black people

TABLE 4.4	Average Number of Years of Life Expectancy in the United States by Race and Sex, since 1900			
Year	White Males	White Females	Black Males	Black Females
1900	46.6	48.7	32.5*	33.5*
1950	66.5	72.2	59.1	62.9
1960	67.4	74.1	61.1	66.3
1970	68.0	75.6	60.0	68.3
1980	70.7	78.1	63.8	72.5
1990	72.7	79.4	64.5	73.6
2000	74.7	79.9	68.2	75.1
2010	76.5	81.3	71.8	78.0

*Includes all nonwhites.
Source: National Center for Health Statistics, 2013.

than white have hypertension over the life course. Various hypotheses have been suggested to explain this situation:

1. The genetic hypothesis argues that blacks are genetically different from whites in ways that predispose them to hypertension.
2. The physical exertion hypothesis postulates that blacks are more likely than whites to be engaged in manual labor and that greater physical exertion leads to high mortality from hypertension.
3. The associated disorder hypothesis asserts that blacks are more prone to diseases such as pyelonephritis and syphilis that may result in secondary hypertension.
4. The psychological stress hypothesis theorizes that blacks are severely frustrated by racial discrimination and that this stress and the repressed aggression associated with it lead to a higher prevalence of hypertension.
5. The diet hypothesis emphasizes that blacks may have dietary patterns that increase their susceptibility to hypertension.
6. The medical care hypothesis argues that blacks receive poorer medical care than whites and that this results in greater morbidity and mortality from hypertensive disease and perhaps a higher prevalence of secondary hypertension.

Some research suggests that the genetic hypothesis and the psychological stress hypothesis contribute the most to providing an answer, since blacks in general—not just low-income blacks—have higher rates of hypertension than whites. There is evidence from a study in Atlanta showing measures of hypertension significantly increasing among a sample of African Americans, with higher levels of stress following episodes of racist/discriminatory encounters at work with whites and Hispanics as well as other African Americans (Din-Dzietham, Nembhard, Collins, and Davis 2004). Although the exact cause of higher rates of hypertension among blacks has yet to be determined, research suggests an important role for stress associated with racism (Brown et al. 2012). Socioeconomic factors also seem particularly important, because low-income blacks have more hypertension than affluent blacks. Although rates of hypertension among blacks have declined since 1960, hypertension remains a major contributor to African American mortality from kidney disease, heart disease, and stroke. More research is needed to uncover the exact source.

Blacks also differ from whites and other races in relation to health problems other than hypertension. The extent of the disparity is shown in Table 4.5, which compares the mortality rate for selected causes of death for non-Hispanic whites, non-Hispanic blacks, Hispanics, Asians/Pacific Islanders, and American Indians/ Alaska natives in 2010. For all causes, Table 4.5 shows that non-Hispanic blacks have the highest death rates of 898.2 per 100,000, followed by non-Hispanic whites (755.0), American Indians/Alaska natives (628.3), Hispanics (558.6), and Asian/Pacific Islanders (424.3). Non-Hispanic blacks have the highest mortality rates for each specific cause of death shown in Table 4.5, except for pulmonary (lung) disease and suicide that is higher among non-Hispanic whites, and liver disease and cirrhosis and accidents that are higher among American Indians/ Alaska natives. Particularly striking are the exceptionally high death rates for non-Hispanic blacks for heart disease, cerebrovascular diseases (stroke), cancer, homicide, and AIDS. American Indians/Alaska natives traditionally had the highest mortality rates for diabetes in the past, but non-Hispanic blacks had highest rates

TABLE 4.5	Age-Adjusted Death Rates for Selected Causes of Death, According to Race, United States, 2010*				
	Non-Hispanic Whites	Non-Hispanic Blacks	Hispanics	Asian/Pacific Islanders	American Indian/ Alaska Native
All causes	755.0	898.2	558.6	424.3	628.3
Heart disease	179.9	224.9	132.8	100.9	128.6
Cerebrovascular diseases	37.8	53.0	32.1	37.0	28.1
Cancer	176.5	203.8	119.7	108.9	122.4
Pulmonary disease	46.6	29.0	19.6	13.9	33.8
Pneumonia and influenza	14.9	16.8	15.0	14.4	15.9
Liver disease and cirrhosis	9.4	6.7	13.7	3.2	22.8
Diabetes	18.2	38.7	27.1	15.5	36.4
Accidents	42.4	31.3	25.8	15.0	46.9
Suicide	15.0	5.2	5.9	6.2	10.8
Homicide	3.3	17.7	5.3	1.8	5.7
AIDS	2.5	11.6	2.8	0.4	1.6

*Deaths per 100,000 resident population.
Source: National Center for Health Statistics, 2013.

in 2010. Asians/Pacific Islanders, in contrast, have the lowest mortality rates, or close to it, for all causes of death.

When it comes to infant mortality, blacks are again disadvantaged. Black infants have traditionally had almost twice as high an infant mortality rate as white infants. In 1960, as shown in Table 4.6, there were approximately 43 infant deaths per 1,000 black infants compared to an infant mortality rate of 22.9 among whites. Although rates of infant mortality have declined significantly for both races since 1960, the same gap (almost twice as high) remains, as the most recent data for 2008 show an infant mortality rate of 12.4 for blacks versus 5.6 for non-Hispanic whites. A major factor causing this difference is poverty. Blacks are overrepresented among the poor, and the poor have the highest rates of infant mortality regardless of race (Olshansky et al. 2012).

The adverse health situation of black Americans identifies a pattern that is generally produced by socioeconomic, not biological factors (Barr 2008; Hattery and Smith 2011; Issacs and Schroeder 2004; Rosich and Hankin 2010; Williams and Sternthal 2010). This does not mean that race and biology are unimportant when it comes to disease, as genetic research shows a few notable exceptions. For example, a gene variation, usually absent in non-Hispanic whites and Hispanics, but found in African Americans, increases the risk of developing a rare type of abnormal cardiac rhythm or heartbeat that can be fatal (Splawski et al. 2002). Sickle cell anemia is also more prevalent among people of African origin.

However, the concept of race in relation to health does not simply identify homogenous groups linked by a common biological inheritance. Rather, race represents the convergence of biological factors with geographic origins, and multiple cultural, economic, political, and legal variables, as well as racism, on health (Bradby and Nazroo 2010). Research shows, for example, that perceptions of racism and racial harassment are associated with poor physical and mental health (Bratter and Gorman 2011; Brown et al. 2012; Grollman 2012, 2014; Jackson and Cummings 2011; Karlsen and Nazroo 2002; Miller, Rote, and Keith 2013; Williams 2012; Williams and Mohammed 2009). Even when social situations are not overtly racist, "hyper-vigilant" minority persons may nevertheless be *constantly* on alert for subtle signs of racism. In such circumstances, the body's physiological defenses against disease are worn down by continuous exposure to perceived discrimination (Das 2013; Hayward, Crimmins, Miles, and Yang 2000).

But the most important overall factor in health outcomes for blacks and members of other races is socioeconomic status. Study after study confirms this (Braveman et al. 2010; Jackson and Cummings 2011; Williams and Sternthal 2010). Research by Mark Hayward and his colleagues (Hayward et al. 2000), for example, demonstrates that a racial gap in health between middle-aged blacks and whites exists for chronic health problems, with blacks living shorter lives and having more chronic conditions during their life span. Debra Umberson and her colleagues (2013) found childhood adversity associated with strained adult relationships and worse health among black men in comparison to white men later in life. Socioeconomic factors such as poverty, marginal employment, low incomes, segregated living conditions, and inadequate education are more common among blacks than whites and are features of socioeconomic stratification known to cause poor health (Cockerham 2013; Montez and Zajacova 2013; Olshansky et al. 2012; Phelan et al. 2004). Blacks are more likely than whites, for example, to live in disadvantaged neighborhoods characterized by disrepair, crime, danger, public drinking and drug use, and incivility. The daily stress associated with these neighborhood conditions has been linked to worse health on the part of the residents (Ross and Mirowsky 2001). Living in less safe neighborhoods also explains why adult blacks are less likely than nonblacks to show participation in vigorous exercise as an outdoor activity and such neighborhoods are also less likely to have indoor facilities for exercise (Grzywacz and Marks 2001; Saint Onge and Krueger 2011). Socioeconomic conditions not only reduce opportunities for exercise but they also promote risk behaviors. There is strong evidence that many blacks are at risk because of smoking, alcohol intake, excess weight and obesity that contribute to high blood pressure, high cholesterol levels, and diabetes (LeClere, Rogers, and Peters 1998; Williams 2012; Winkleby, Kraemer, Ahn, and Varady 1998).

Not only do adult blacks get less exercise than whites (Grzywacz and Marks 2001; Saint Onge and Krueger 2011), but consumer research shows they also tend to be heavy purchasers of frozen and canned foods, pork products, and starchy foods high in salt and fats (Barboza 2000; Hattery and Smith 2011). Whites, overall, tend to have healthier diets than blacks. Research in California, for example, shows that cost is not the primary reason for black–white differences in fruit and vegetable consumption; rather, culture (in personal taste and food preparation habits) and knowledge about the nutritional benefits of these foods were the major source of the dissimilarity (Bahr 2007). Blacks were significantly more likely than whites to report they or their families did not like the taste, were not in the habit of eating them, and believed they consumed enough fruits and vegetables. Hispanics buy more vegetables than blacks, but they additionally purchase large amounts of items high in saturated fats such as lard and refried beans. Consequently, the lower an individual's income, the more likely they are to be obese, and this is especially true for blacks and to a lesser extent for Hispanics (Boardman, Saint Onge, Rogers, and Denney 2005; Carr and Friedman 2005; Robert and Reither 2004). Being obese is not only unhealthy, but it is also socially stigmatizing for individuals of any race who are severely overweight (Carr and Friedman 2005; Mustillo, Hendrix, and Schafer 2012), although blacks may feel less stigma than whites about obesity (Mustillo, Budd, and Hendrix 2013). Thus, obesity adversely affects both physical and psychological well-being.

Significant health problems for African Americans include sexually transmitted diseases (STDs), such as syphilis and gonorrhea. There are no known biological reasons why racial or ethnic factors should enhance the risk of STDs and being poor and living in disadvantaged neighborhoods is not the entire answer, as many Hispanics are poor but have lower STDs rates. In addition to poverty, joblessness, minimal access to health care, and a reluctance to seek treatment for STDs because of stigma, segregation is also a factor. Edward Laumann and Yoosik Youm (2001) find that blacks have the highest rates of STDs because of the "intra-racial network effect." They point out that blacks are more segregated than other racial/ethnic groups in American society, and the high number of sexual contacts between an infected black core and its periphery of yet uninfected black sexual partners tends to contain the infection within the black population. Laumann and Youm determined that even though a peripheral (uninfected) African American has only one sex partner, the chance that partner is from a core (infected) group is five times higher than it is for peripheral whites and four times higher for peripheral Hispanics.

Another important health problem for blacks is the availability of medical treatment. There is evidence in recent years that the gap between blacks and whites for basic health care has narrowed, but this is not the case for more complex forms of treatment. Blacks, for example, are much less likely than whites to have heart bypass surgery, appendectomies, and other surgical care, and they receive fewer tests and drugs for heart disease, breast cancer, and diabetes (Jha et al. 2005; Stepanikova 2012; Trivedi, Zaslavsky, Schneider, and Ayanian 2005; Vaccarino et al. 2005; Williams 2012). The availability of physicians and hospitals providing quality care where blacks live is a major reason for the differences in care. For example, the few cardiac surgeons in predominantly black communities—especially in rural areas—help explain why blacks receive fewer coronary artery bypass operations than whites. It also needs to be noted that lack of financial resources and information about health is an important barrier to health care for low-income blacks, as it is for poor people of any race.

Ultimately, what makes race important in a causal sense for health is its close association with class circumstances. Subtract affluence or lack thereof from considerations of race, and the causal strength of race in health and disease is severely minimized. This does not mean that race by itself lacks any significance for health. Race continues to matter to some degree, for example in studies of self-rated health (Farmer and Ferraro 2005), low birth-weight babies (Conley, Strully, and Bennett 2003), and serious health conditions (Brown et al. 2012), as class is unable to completely explain racial differences (Brown et al. 2012; Williams 2012; Williams and Sternthal 2010). Conley et al. (2003:34) go so far as to claim that "almost all studies that factor out socioeconomic status are plagued with some level of unexplained racial variance" and that "race does not seem to be entirely reducible to class with regard to health." While the extent to which this may be the case is not clear, it is the rule rather than the exception that almost every study nevertheless shows that class has a significantly more powerful effect on health than race even though race may independently produce some effects (Erving 2011; Issacs and Schroeder 2004; Williams and Sternthal 2010). Pamela Jackson and Jason Cummings (2011), for example, found evidence that middle-class blacks were generally healthier than whites and blacks in the lower class. Rather, they see that class differences in health apply to all races.

Many African Americans have taken advantage of the increased opportunities stemming from the civil rights movement of the 1960s and significantly improved their life circumstances by acquiring the incomes, education, and quality of life of affluent whites. According to William Julius Wilson (1991, 1996), the social conditions available to poor, urban, isolated blacks who inhabit the core of the nation's central cities have worsened. Rates of unemployment, out-of-wedlock births, households headed by females, dependency on welfare, and violent crimes have increased

PHOTO 4.3 Black males have the lowest life expectancy in American society. Disadvantaged socioeconomic circumstances play a key role in this situation.

to their highest levels ever. While noting the importance of racism and discrimination, Wilson blames this development primarily on the increasing isolation of lower-class African Americans in a changing economy. He points out that both middle- and working-class blacks have moved out of ghetto neighborhoods in the inner city in search of safe places to live and better schools for their children. They have left behind a concentration of the most disadvantaged segments of the African American population—an underclass—whose social and economic isolation is more pronounced than ever before.

At the same time, the American economy shifted from a manufacturing- to a predominantly service and information-oriented base. This situation has produced extraordinary rates of joblessness for those persons (many of them low-income blacks) who lack the education and job skills needed to adapt to these economic changes. Consequently, the inner-city black poor rank among the most disadvantaged groups in American society. This disadvantage extends to health and longevity on a regular basis as discussed above. Several studies, as noted, show that differences in life expectancy between blacks and whites can be explained almost entirely by socioeconomic factors (Hayward et al. 2000; Jackson and Cummings 2011; Warner and Hayward 2006; Williams and Sternthal 2010). According to Stephanie Robert and James House (2000:84): "In sum, race and socioeconomic position are inextricably linked to each other and to health, and hence one cannot be considered without the other."

Hispanic Americans

As noted, Hispanics are the largest racial/ethnic minority group in American society and their numbers continue to grow. About a fourth of all Hispanics in the United States have an income below the poverty line. When it comes to health, comparative health data on Hispanics are limited because, until 1976, federal, state, and local agencies included Hispanics with non-Hispanic whites in the white category. Hispanics were also not included as a separate category on death certificates nationally until 1988. There are data showing that, in comparison to non-Hispanic whites, Hispanics have more diabetes, hypertension, tuberculosis, STDs, alcoholism, cirrhosis of the liver, homicide, and AIDS (Rogers, Hummer, and Nam 2000). This pattern is reflected in Table 4.5 showing Hispanics having higher mortality rates than non-Hispanic whites in 2010 for liver disease, diabetes, homicide, and slightly more for AIDS.

There is, however, the "Hispanic paradox" in that Hispanics have lower mortality rates than non-Hispanic whites at most ages despite their lower socioeconomic status and levels of health insurance in the United States, along with higher life expectancy (Morales et al. 2002; Williams and Sternthal 2010). There is evidence that Hispanics are less likely than non-Hispanic whites to smoke cigarettes, as well as being more likely to have diets high in fiber and protein and occupations high in physical activity (Morales et al. 2002). The overall health profile of Hispanics is also better than that of non-Hispanic blacks (Huie, Hummer, and Rogers 2002; Padilla, Boardman, Hummer, and Espitia 2002). Table 4.5 shows, for example, that Hispanics have lower mortality rates than either non-Hispanic whites or blacks for heart disease, cancer, cerebrovascular diseases, pulmonary diseases, and pneumonia and influenza. Additionally, Hispanic immigrants are generally in good health when they arrive in the United States (Lopez-Gonzalez, Aravena, and Hummer 2005; Read and Reynolds 2012).

However, one important factor that makes the "Hispanic paradox" less of a paradox is that the Hispanic population in the United States is relatively young because of a high birth rate and large-scale immigration from Mexico and Central America that consists mainly of young adults. Consequently, Hispanics have far fewer numbers of people currently in late middle and old age, when heart disease and cancer are most prevalent. In time, the paradox may disappear as disadvantaged social conditions take their toll on health over the life course.

Hispanics are also more likely than non-Hispanics to be without a regular source of health care and to use hospital emergency rooms as their primary source of medical services. They are more likely than any other racial/ethnic group in American society to not have health insurance and many face cultural and language barriers in health care settings. Among Hispanics, Puerto Ricans report the worst health status and Cubans the best, with Mexican Americans and other Hispanics in the middle.

Native Americans

Native Americans, consisting of American Indians and native Alaskans, have shown a dramatic improvement in their overall level of health in the last 40 years. For example, the health of elderly native Alaskans is not significantly different from elderly whites in Alaska. Moreover, in 1950, the infant mortality rate for American Indians and native Alaskans was 82.1 per 1,000 live births. In 2008, the mortality rate had dropped to 8.4 per 1,000 births. Adult mortality rates from heart disease and stroke are not exceptionally high, but heart disease is still the leading cause of death for Native Americans, followed by cancer and accidents. Cancer is the leading cause of death for Alaska natives. In fact, native Alaskans have a 30 percent higher risk of dying from cancer than the non-Hispanic white population in the United States. Over 40 percent of native Alaskan men smoke, and, not surprisingly, lung cancer takes the most lives in this population group.

American Indians have high mortality rates from diabetes, second only to blacks. One tribe, the Pimas, has the highest rates of diabetes in the world. Diabetes among Pima Indians is 10 to 15 times higher than the general American population. The complications of diabetes take a further toll on Indians by increasing the probability of kidney disease, blindness, and heart disease. Indians also suffer more dysentery, strep throat, and hepatitis than other Americans. Other significant health problems of American Indians are alcoholism, tuberculosis, dietary deficiency, cirrhosis of the liver, and gastrointestinal bleeding. In addition, chronic otitis media, a severe ear ailment that arises when simple ear infections are not treated, occurs among 10 percent of all Indian children. Also, more American Indians die from accidents, primarily automobile accidents, than members of any other racial group in the United States. Many accidents are alcohol-related. Other difficulties include severe psychological distress, perhaps beyond those of other racial groups (Walls and Whitbeck 2011). So while American Indians have experienced a significant improvement in their overall level of health, important problems remain.

Another major problem for Indians and Alaska native males is suicide. American Indian and Alaska native male suicide victims are typically younger than those in the general population, with suicide peaking at ages 15 to 45, compared with the non-Indian population in which suicides usually occur after the age of 40. For 15- to 24-year-old males, the mortality rate from suicide during 2010 was 30.6 per 100,000, compared to 10.5 for the U.S. population as a whole in this male age cohort (National Center for Health Statistics 2013). Non-Hispanic white males were second in suicides in this age group, with a death rate of 20.4 per 100,000, followed by blacks (11.1), Asian and Pacific Islanders (10.9), and Hispanics (10.7). American Indian and Alaskan Natives also have the highest rates of suicide for 15- to 24-year-old females at 5.9 per 100,000 as compared to non-Hispanic whites (4.4), Asian and Pacific Islanders (3.5), Hispanics (3.1), and blacks (2.0). In addition to particularly high rates of diabetes, accidents, and suicides, Indians have an exceptionally high prevalence of alcoholism, with many Indian families affected either directly or indirectly by the alcohol abuse of one or more of its members (Cheadle and Whitbeck 2011). Nearly eight percent of all American Indians/Alaska Natives age 18 and over qualify as heavy drinkers compared to 5.6 percent of non-Hispanic whites, 3.6 percent of non-Hispanic blacks, and 3.1 percent of Hispanics (National Center for Health Statistics 2013).

Asian Americans

Another example of the importance of socioeconomic factors in relation to health is found by examining data that include Asian Americans. Asian Americans have the highest levels of income, education, and employment of any racial/ethnic minority group in the United States, often exceeding levels achieved by the white population. Consequently, it is not surprising that the lowest age-adjusted mortality rates in the United States are those of Asian Americans. Asians and Pacific Islanders in the United States showed an age-adjusted mortality rate in 2010 of 424.3 per 100,000, which was the lowest of any racial/ethnic group in the nation. Heart disease is the leading cause of death for Asians, but mortality from this disease is less than that of whites and other minorities. Deaths from cancer, stroke, automobile accidents, AIDS, and homicide are lowest as well. Overall, Asians and Pacific Islanders are the healthiest racial group in American society when mortality rates are considered.

When infant mortality rates for the United States are reviewed, the health advantage of Asian Americans becomes even more apparent. Table 4.6 shows Asian Americans and Pacific Islanders with the lowest rates. According to Table 4.6, infant mortality in the United States has drastically declined since 1950. The most striking decline, as previously noted, has been that of American Indians from 82.1 deaths per 1,000 live births in 1950 to 8.4 in 2008, the most recent year comparative data are available. The decline for Asians/Pacific Islanders has been almost as great in terms of relative proportion, but the rates were much smaller to begin with and therefore not as dramatic. Table 4.6 shows that in 2008, blacks had the highest infant mortality rates (12.4 per 1,000), followed by Native Americans (8.4), non-Hispanic whites (5.6), Hispanics (5.6), and Asians/Pacific Islanders (4.5).

TABLE 4.6	Infant Mortality Rates by Race, United States, Selected Years 1950–2008*				
		Race			
Year	Black	American Indian/ Alaska Native	Asian/Pacific Islander	Hispanic	White
1950	43.9	82.1	—	—	26.8
1960	44.3	49.3	—	—	22.9
1970	32.6	22.0	—	—	17.8
1977	23.6	15.6	—	—	12.3
1985	18.6	13.1	7.8	8.8	8.9[†]
1990	16.9	13.1	6.6	7.5	7.3[†]
1995	14.6	9.0	5.3	6.3	6.3[†]
2000	13.5	8.3	4.9	5.6	5.7[†]
2008	12.4	8.4	4.5	5.6	5.6[†]

*Infant mortality rate is the number of deaths for infants under one year of age per 1,000 live births.
†Non-Hispanic whites.
Source: National Center for Health Statistics, 2013.

Besides illustrating the low infant mortality rates of Asians and Pacific Islanders, Table 4.6 also indicates some other patterns of interest. In 1950, Native Americans had the highest infant mortality rates—almost twice as high as that of blacks. By 1970, Native American infant mortality rates had dropped so sharply that they were lower than the rates for blacks. While infant mortality rates for blacks had declined by more than two-thirds (43.9 versus 12.4) between 1950 and 2008, the black rate was over twice as high as that of non-Hispanic whites (26.8 versus 5.6) in 2008. Hence, the size of gap between black and white infant mortality rates has remained relatively constant, even though infant deaths from both racial groups have fallen.

Although infant mortality rates are only one indicator of health in a society, they are nevertheless an important measure of the quality of life available to a population. Such rates, along with other data discussed in this section, point toward the fact that Asian Americans enjoy the best health in the United States.

Race: Conclusion

Some afflictions such as hypertension, diabetes, and sickle cell anemia have a genetic basis, but living conditions associated with poverty influence the onset and course of most physical health problems (Hayward et al. 2000; McDonough and Berglund 2003; Olshansky et al. 2012; Phelan et al. 2004). Tuberculosis, for example, had nearly disappeared in the United States but resurfaced in the late 1980s and early 1990s with the greatest concentration among the poor. Alcoholism, drug abuse, suicide, homicide, lead poisoning, and influenza and pneumonia, along with heart disease and cancer, are more prevalent among the lower class (Braveman et al. 2010; Braveman and Tarimo 2002; Lahelma 2010; Link and Phelan 2000; Mirowsky, Ross, and Reynolds 2000; Mulatu and Schooler 2002; Robert and House 2000; Wermuth 2003). Race becomes an especially significant variable for physical health in American society, because many racial minority persons occupy a disadvantaged social and economic position. This is particularly the case for blacks (Brown et al. 2012; Hayward et al. 2000; Williams 2012). As previously noted, the differences in life expectancy of blacks and whites can largely be explained by differences in socioeconomic status and what that implies in relation to differences in healthy lifestyles, living conditions, and access to quality medical care.

When it comes to mental health, there is little or no support for the claim that there is a significant difference among races in overall rates of mental disorder, except the relatively low rates for Asian Americans (Cockerham 2014; Williams, Costa, and Leavell 2010). A few studies have found some black populations with more depressed moods than whites (George and Lynch 2003; Gore and Aseltine 2003), but this is not surprising given their increased exposure to race-related and generic stress (Brown 2003:293). Other research finds that poverty causes greater behavioral problems among white than black children (McLeod and Nonnemaker 2000) and greater psychological distress among low-status whites than low-status blacks in disadvantaged urban neighborhoods (Boardman et al. 2001; Schulz et al. 2000). However, findings that there are racial differences in mental health in some situations does not rule out the general finding that there is no overall difference between blacks and whites. Socioeconomic status appears to be a much stronger variable than race in explaining differences in mental disorder.

Furthermore, the time is here when racial/ethnic health differences in the United States will no longer be based primarily on comparisons between whites and blacks but will be multiracial. The Hispanic population has become an increasingly separate and major comparison group in studies of health issues, while Asians/Pacific Islanders will represent a much larger and more important racial category than in the past.

Summary

This chapter has discussed the social demography of health from the standpoint of age, gender, and race. The section on age disclosed that as more persons live to older ages in American society, marked changes are likely to occur in society in general and health care delivery in particular. The new generation of the aged, however, will be the most affluent, educated, and healthy in American history. As for gender differences, females have a very definite advantage over males with regard to life expectancy although men are slowly closing the gap. This advantage involves both biological and social-psychological factors. White Americans also have a definite advantage in health over nonwhite Americans, with the exception of Asians. However, the most significant sociodemographic variable affecting nonwhites is that they are likely to be poor, and poverty, as far as healthy living conditions and medical care is concerned, may be equated with second-rate circumstances. An exception is Hispanics, who have lower mortality for many health problems such as heart disease and cancer than non-Hispanic whites and blacks. This constitutes a "Hispanic paradox" in that many Hispanics live in disadvantaged circumstances, have low rates of health insurance, and lack regular medical care. One explanation of this paradox is that the Hispanic population in the United States is relatively young, and large numbers have not reached the ages in which heart disease and cancer are most prevalent.

Critical Thinking Questions

1. What are the major differences between the health of men and women? What are some of the underlying causes of these differences?
2. What are some of the reasons that Americans are living longer today than ever before? What are some of the effects of a growing elderly population on society?
3. Race is a complex concept that affects health in equally complex ways; what are some of these?

Suggested Readings

Bird, Chloe E., and Patricia P. Rieker (2008) *Gender and health: The effects of constrained choices and social policies.* Cambridge, UK: Cambridge University Press.
An analysis of the effects of social structure on the health choices of women.
Epstein, Steven (2007) *Inclusion: The politics of difference in medical research.* Chicago: University of Chicago Press.
A social history of the politics of achieving gender and racial diversity among persons serving as test subjects in medical research in the United States.
Lemelle, Anthony, Wornie Reed, and Sandra Taylor (eds.) (2011) *Handbook of African American Health.* Dordrecht: Springer.
Discusses African American health issues and interventions.
Washington, Harriet A. (2006) *Medical apartheid.* New York: Doubleday.
A discussion of racism in medicine.

References

Ailshire, Jennifer A., and Sarah A. Burgard (2012) "Family relationships and troubled sleep among U.S. adults." *Journal of Health and Social behavior* 53: 248–62.
Annandale, Ellen C. (2010) "Health status and gender," pp. 97–112 in *The new Blackwell companion to medical sociology*, W. Cockerham (ed.). Oxford, UK: Oxford University Press.
Auerbach, Judith, and Anne Figert (1995) "Women's health research: Public policy and sociology." *Journal of Health and Social Behavior* 36(Extra issue): 115–31.
Avison, William R., and Jinette Comeau (2013) "The impact of mental illness on the family," pp. 543–62 in *Handbook of the sociology of mental health*, 2nd ed., C. Aneshensel, J. Phelan, and A. Bierman (eds.). Dordrecht: Springer.
Bahr, Peter Riley (2007) "Race and nutrition: An investigation of black-white differences in health-related nutritional behaviours." *Sociology of Health & Illness* 29: 831–56.
Barboza, David (2000) "Rampant obesity, a debilitating reality for the urban poor." *New York Times* (December 26): D5.
Baron-Epel, Orna, and Giora Kaplan (2001) "General subjective status or age-related subjective health: Does it make a difference?" *Social Science and Medicine* 53: 1373–81.
Barr, Donald A. (2008) *Health disparities in the United States.* Baltimore: Johns Hopkins University Press.

Bird, Chloe E., and Patricia P. Rieker (2008) *Gender and health: The effects of constrained choices and social policies.* Cambridge, UK: Cambridge University Press.

Boardman, Jason D., Jarron M. Saint Onge, Richard G. Rogers, and Justin T. Denney (2005) "Race differentials in obesity: The impact of place." *Journal of Health and Social Behavior* 46: 229–43.

Boardman, Jason S., Brian Karl Finch, Christopher G. Ellison, David R. Williams, and James S. Jackson (2001) "Neighborhood disadvantage, stress, and drug use among adults." *Journal of Health and Social Behavior* 42: 151–65.

Bradby, Hannah, and James Y. Nazroo (2010) "Health, ethnicity, and race," pp. 113–29 in *The new Blackwell companion to medical sociology*, W. Cockerham (ed.). Oxford, UK: Wiley-Blackwell.

Bratter, Jennifer L., and Bridgert K. Gorman (2011) "Is discrimination an equal opportunity risk? Socioeconomic status and health status among blacks and whites." *Journal of Health and Social Behavior* 52: 365–82.

Braveman, Paula A., Catherine Cubbin, Susan Egerter, David R. Williams, and Elsie Pamuk (2010) "Socioeconomic disparities in health in the United States: What the patterns tell us." *American Journal of Public Health* 100(Suppl. 1): S186–S196.

Braveman, Paula, And Eleuther Tarimo (2002) "Social inequalities in health within countries: Not only an issue for affluent nations." Social Science and Medicine 54: 1621–35.

Brown, Tony N. (2003) "Critical race theory speaks to the sociology of mental health: Mental health problems produced by racial stratification." *Journal of Health and Social Behavior* 44: 292–301.

Brown, Tyson H., Angela M. O'Rand, and Daniel E. Adkins (2012) "Race-ethnicity and health trajectories: Test of three hypotheses across multiple groups and health outcomes." *Journal of Health and Social Behavior* 53: 359–77.

Budrys, Grace (2003) *Unequal health.* Lanham, MD: Rowman & Littlefield.

Carr, Deborah, and Michael A. Friedman (2005) "Is obesity stigmatizing? Body weight, perceived discrimination, and psychological well-being." *Journal of Health and Social Behavior* 46: 244–59.

Cheadle, Jacob E., and Les B. Whitbeck (2011) "Alcohol use trajectories and problem drinking over the course of adolescence: A study of North American indigenous youth and their caretakers." *Journal of Health and Social Behavior* 52: 228–45.

Cockerham, William C. (2006) *Society of risk-takers: Living life on the edge.* New York: Worth.

———. (2013) *Social causes of health and disease,* 2nd ed. Cambridge, UK: Polity.

———. (2014) *Sociology of mental disorder,* 9th ed. Upper Saddle River, NJ: Pearson Prentice Hall.

Collins, Gail (2009) *When everything changed: The amazing journey of American women from 1960 to the present.* New York: Little, Brown.

Conley, Dalton, Kate W. Strully, and Neil G. Bennett (2003) *The starting gate: Birth weight and life chances.* Berkeley: University of California Press.

Das, Aniruddhas (2013) "How does race get 'under the skin'?: Inflammation, weathering, and metabolic problems in late life." *Social Science and Medicine* 77: 75–83.

Desjarlais, Robert, Leon Eisenberg, Byron Good, and Arthur Kleinman (1995) *World mental health: Problems and priorities in low-income countries.* New York: Oxford University Press.

Din-Dzietham, Rebecca, Wendy N. Nembhard, Rakale Collins, and Sharon K. Davis (2004) "Perceived stress following race-based discrimination at work is associated with hypertension in African-Americans. The metro Atlanta heart disease study, 1999–2001." *Social Science and Medicine* 58: 449–61.

Dolan, Alan (2007) " 'Good luck to them if they get it': Exploring working class men's understandings and experiences of income inequality and material standards." *Sociology of Health & Illness* 29: 711–29.

Ellis, Rosemary (2003) "The secondhand smoking gun." *New York Times* (October 15): A23.

Erving, Christy L. (2011) "Gender and physical health: A study of African American and Caribbean black adults." *Journal of Health and Social Behavior* 52: 383–99.

Ezzati, Majid, Ari B. Friedman, Sandeep C. Kulkarni, and Christopher J. L. Murray (2008) "The reversal of fortunes: Trends in county mortality and cross-county mortality disparities in the United States." *PLoS Medicine* 5: e66/001–0011.

Farmer, Melissa, and Kenneth F. Ferraro (2005) "Are racial disparities in health conditional on socioeconomic status?" *Social Science and Medicine* 60: 191–204.

Ferraro, Kenneth F., and Melissa M. Farmer (1999) "Utility of health data from social surveys: Is there a gold standard for measuring morbidity?" *American Sociological Review* 64: 303–15.

Frech, Adrianne, and Sarah Damaske (2012) "The relationship between mothers' work pathways and physical and mental health." *Journal of Health and Social Behavior* 53: 396–412.

Frech, Adrianne, and Kristi Williams (2007) "Depression and the psychological benefits of entering marriage." Journal of Health and Social Behavior 48: 149–63.

George, Linda K., and Scott M. Lynch (2003) "Race differences in depressive symptoms: A dynamic perspective on stress and vulnerability." *Journal of Health and Social Behavior* 44: 353–69.

Gore, Susan, and Robert H. Aseltine, Jr. (2003) "Race and ethnic differences in depressed mood following the transition from high school." *Journal of Health and Social Behavior* 44: 370–89.

Gorman, Bridget K., and Jen'nan Ghazal Read (2006) "Gender disparities in adult health: An examination of three measures of morbidity." *Journal of Health and Social Behavior* 47: 95–110.

Grollman, Eric Anthony (2012) "Multiple forms of perceived discrimination and health among adolescents and young adults." *Journal of Health and Social Behavior* 53: 199–214.

—— (2014) "Multiple disadvantaged statuses and health: The role of multiple forms of discrimination." *Journal of Health and Social Behavior* 55: 3–19.

Grzywacz, Joseph G., and Nadine F. Marks (2001) "Social inequalities and exercise during adulthood: Toward an ecological perspective." *Journal of Health and Social Behavior* 42: 202–20.

Hattery, Angela J., and Earl Smith (2011) "Health, nutrition, access to healthy food and well-being among African Americans," pp. 47–59 in *Handbook of African American health*, A. Lemelle, W. Reed, and S. Taylor (eds.). Dordrecht: Springer.

Hayward, Mark D., Eileen M. Crimmins, Toni P. Miles, and Yu Yang (2000) "The significance of socioeconomic status in explaining the racial gap in chronic health conditions." *American Sociological Review* 65: 910–30.

Hochschild, Arlie (1989) *The second shift: Working parents and the revolution at home.* New York: Viking.

Hopcroft, Rosemary L., and Dana Burr Bradley (2007) "The sex difference in depression across 29 countries." *Social Forces* 85: 1483–1508.

Houle, Jason N., Jeremy Staff, Jeylan T. Mortimer, Christopher Uggen, and Amy Blackstone (2011) "The impact of sexual harassment on depressive symptoms during the early occupational career." *Society and Mental Health* 2: 89–105.

Huie, Stephanie A. Bond, Robert A. Hummer, and Richard G. Rogers (2002) "Individual and contextual risks of death among race and ethnic groups in the United States." *Journal of Health and Social Behavior* 43: 350–81.

Idler, Ellen L., and Yael Benyamini (1997) "Self-rated health and mortality: A review of twenty-seven community studies." *Journal of Health and Social Behavior* 38: 21–37.

Institute for Health Metrics and Evaluation. (2013) *The State of US Health: Innovations, Insights, and Recommendations from the Global Burden of Disease Study*. Seattle, WA: IHME.

Issacs, Stephen L., and Steven A. Schroeder (2004). "Class—the ignored determinant of the nation's health." *New England Journal of Medicine* 351: 1137–42.

Jackson, Pamela Braboy, and Jason Cummings (2011) "Health disparities and the black middle class: Overview, empirical findings, and research agenda," pp. 383–410 in *Handbook of the sociology of health, illness, and healing*, B. Pescosolido, J. Martin, J. McLeod, and A. Rogers (eds.). Dordrecht: Springer.

Jha, Ashish K., Ellitt S. Fisher, Zhonghe Li, F. John Oray, and Arnold M. Epstein (2005) "Racial trends in the use of major procedures among the elderly." *New England Journal of Medicine* 353: 683–91.

Karlsen, Saffron, and James Y. Nazroo (2002) "Agency and structure: The impact of ethnic identity and racism on the health of ethnic minority people." *Sociology of Health & Illness* 24: 1–20.

Lahelma, Eero (2010) "Health and social stratification," pp. 71–96 in *The new Blackwell companion to medical sociology*, W. Cockerham (ed.). Oxford, UK: Blackwell.

Laumann, Edward O., and Yoosik Youm (2001) "Racial/ethnic group differences in the prevalence of sexually-transmitted diseases in the United States: A network explanation," pp. 327–51 in *Sex, love, and health in America: Private choices and public policies*, E. Laumann and R. Michael (eds). Chicago: University of Chicago Press.

LeClere, Felicia B., Richard G. Rogers, and Kimberly Peters (1998) "Neighborhood social context and racial differences in women's heart disease mortality." *Journal of Health and Social Behavior* 39: 91–107.

Link, Bruce G., and Jo Phelan (2000) "Evaluating the fundamental cause explanation for social disparities in health," pp. 33–47 in *Handbook of medical sociology*, 5th ed., C. Bird, P. Conrad, and A. Fremont (eds). Upper Saddle River, NJ: Prentice Hall.

Longest, Kyle C., and Peggy A. Thoits (2012) "Gender, the stress process, and health." *Society and Mental Health* 2:177–206.

Lopez-Gonzalez, Lorena, Veronica C. Aravena, and Robert A. Hummer (2005) "Immigrant acculturation, gender and health behavior: A research note." *Social Forces* 84: 581–93.

McDonough, Peggy, and Pat Berglund (2003) "Histories of poverty and self-rated health trajectories." *Journal of Health and Social Behavior* 44: 198–214.

McLeod, Jane D., and James M. Nonnemaker (2000) "Poverty and child emotional and behavioral problems: Racial/ethnic differences in processes and effects." *Journal of Health and Social Behavior* 41: 137–61.

Miller, Byron, Sunshine M. Rote, and Verna M. Keith (2013) "Coping with racial discrimination: Assessing the vulnerability of African Americans and the mediated moderation of psychosocial resources." *Society and Mental Health* 3:133–50.

Mirowsky, John (1999) "Subjective life expectancy in the U.S.: Correspondence to actuarial estimates by age, sex, and race." *Social Science and Medicine* 49: 967–79.

Mirowsky, John, and Catherine E. Ross (2004) *Social causes of psychological distress*, 2nd ed. New York: Aldine de Gruyter.

Mirowsky, John, Catherine E. Ross, and John Reynolds (2000) "Links between social status and health status," pp. 47–67 in *Handbook of medical sociology*, 5th ed., C. Bird, P. Conrad, and A. Fremont (eds). Upper Saddle River, NJ: Prentice Hall.

Montez, Jennifer Karas, and Anna Zajacova (2013) "Explaining the widening education gap in mortality among U.S. white women." *Journal of Health and Social Behavior* 54: 166–82.

Morales, L. S., M. Lara, R. S. Kingston, R. O. Valdez, and J. J. Escarce (2002) "Socioeconomic, cultural, and behavioral, factors affecting Hispanic health outcomes." *Journal of Health Care for the Poor and Underserved* 13: 477–503.

Mulatu, Mesfin Samuel, and Carmi Schooler (2002) "Causal connections between socioeconomic status and health: Reciprocal effects and mediating mechanisms." *Journal of Health and Social Behavior* 43: 22–41.

Mustillo, Sarah A., Kristen Budd, and Kimber Hendrix (2013) "Obesity, labeling, and psychological distress in late-childhood and adolescent black and white girls: The distal effects of stigma." *Social Psychology* 76: 268–89.

Mustillo, Sarah A., Kimber Hendrix, and Markus H. Schafer (2012) "Trajectories of body mass and self-concept in black and white girls: The lingering effects of stigma." *Journal of Health and Social Behavior* 53: 2–16.

National Center for Health Statistics (2013) *Health United States, 2012*. Washington, DC: U.S. Government Printing Office.

Olshansky, S. Jay, Toni Antonucci, Lisa Berkman, Robert Binstock, Axel Boersch-Supan, John T. Cacioppo, Bruce A. Carnes, Laura L. Carstensen, Linda P. Fried, Dana P. Goldman, James Jackson, Martin Kohli, John Rother, Yuhui Zheng, and John Rowe (2012) "Differences in life expectancy due to race and educational differences are widening, and many may not catch up." *Health Affairs* 31: 1803–13.

Padilla, Yolanda C., Jason D. Boardman, Robert A. Hummer, and Marilyn Espitia (2002) "Is the Mexican American 'Epidemiologic paradox' advantage at birth maintained through early childhood?" *Social Forces* 80: 1101–23.

Pavalko, Eliza, Krysia Mossakowski, and Vanessa J. Hamilton (2003) "Does perceived discrimination affect health? Longitudinal relationships between work discrimination and women's physical and emotional health." *Journal of Health and Social Behavior* 44: 18–33.

Percheski, Christine. (2008) "Opting out? Cohort differences in professional women's employment rates from 1900 to 2005." *American Sociological Review* 73:497–517.

Phelan, Jo C., Bruce G. Link, Ana Diez-Rouz, Ichiro Kawachi, and Bruce Levin (2004) " 'Fundamental causes' of social inequalities in mortality: A test of the theory." *Journal of Health and Social Behavior* 45: 265–85.

Pudrovska, Tetyana, Deborah Carr, Michael McFarland, and Caitlyn Collins (2013) "Higher-Status Occupation and Breast Cancer: A Life-Course Stress Approach." *Social Science and Medicine* 89: 53–61.

Read, Jen'nan Ghazal, and Megan M. Reynolds (2012) "Gender differences in immigrant health: The case of Mexican and Middle Eastern immigrants." *Journal of Health and Social Behavior* 53: 99–123.

Redelmeier, Donald A., and Jeffrey C. Kwong (2004) "Death rates of medical school class presidents." *Social Science and Medicine* 8: 2537–43.

Rieker, Partricia P., and Chloe E. Bird (2000) "Sociological explanations of gender differences in mental and physical health," in *Handbook of medical sociology*, 5th ed., C. Bird, P. Conrad, and A. Fremont (eds). Upper Saddle River, NJ: Prentice Hall.

Robert, Stephanie A., and James S. House (2000) "Socioeconomic inequalities in health: An enduring sociological problem," pp. 79–97 in *Handbook of medical sociology*, 5th ed., C. Bird, P. Conrad, and A. Fremont (eds). Upper Saddle River, NJ: Prentice Hall.

Robert, Stephanie A., and Eric N. Reither (2004) "A multilevel analysis of race, community disadvantage, and body mass index among adults in the US." *Social Science and Medicine* 59: 2421–34.

Rogers, Richard G., Robert A. Hummer, and Charles B. Nam (2000) *Living and dying in the USA: Behavioral, health, and social differentials of adult mortality*. New York: Academic Press.

Rosenfield, Sarah (1989) "The effects of women's employment: Personal control and sex differences in mental health." *Journal of Health and Social Behavior* 30: 77–91.

Rosenfield, Sarah, Mary Claire Lennon, and Helen Raskin White (2005) "The self and mental health: Self-salience and the emergence of internalizing and externalizing problems." *Journal of Health and Social Behavior* 46: 323–40.

Rosenfield, Sarah, and Dawne Mouzon (2013) "Gender and mental health," pp. 277–96 in *Handbook of the sociology of mental health*, 2nd ed., C. Aneshensel, J. Phelan, and A. Bierman (eds.). Dordrecht: Springer.

Rosenfield, Sarah and Dena Smith (2010) "Gender and mental health: Do men and women have different amounts or types of problems?" pp. 256–67 in A handbook for the study of mental health: Social contexts, theories, and systems, 2nd ed., T. Scheid and T. Brown (eds). Cambridge, UK: Cambridge University Press.

Rosich, Katherine J., and Janet R. Hankin (2010) "Executive summary: What do we know? Key findings from 50 years of medical sociology." *Journal of Health and Social Behavior* 51: S1–9.

Ross, Catherine E., and John Mirowsky (2001) "Neighborhood disadvantage, disorder, and health." *Journal of Health and Social Behavior* 42: 258–76.

Ross, Catherine E., John Mirowsky, and Patricia Ulbrich (1983) "Distress and the traditional female role: A comparison of Mexicans and Anglos." *American Journal of Sociology* 89: 560–682.

Roxburgh, Susan (2009) "Untangling inequalities: Gender, race, and socioeconomic differences in depression." *Sociological Forum* 24: 357–81.

Saint Onge, Jarron M., and Patrick M. Krueger. (2011) "Education and racial-ethnic differences in types of exercise in the United States." *Journal of Health and Social Behavior* 52: 197–211.

Schnittker, Jason (2007) "Working more and feeling better: Women's health, employment, and family life, 1974–2004." *American Sociological Review* 72: 221–38.

Schulz, Amy, David Williams, Babara Israel, Adam Becker, Edith Parker, Sherman A. James, and James Jackson (2000) "Unfair treatment, neighborhood effects, and mental health in the Detroit metropolitan area." *Journal of Health and Social Behavior* 42: 314–32.

Shim, Janet K., Ann J. Russ, and Sharon R. Kaufman (2006) "Risk, life extension and the pursuit of medical possibility." *Sociology of Health & Illness* 28: 479–502.

Simon, Robin W. (2002) "Revisiting the relationships among gender, marital status, and mental health." *American Journal of Sociology* 107: 1065–96.

Spalter-Roth, Roberta, Terri Ann Lowenthal, and Mercedes Rubio (2005) *Race, ethnicity, and the health of Americans.* Washington, DC: American Sociological Association.

Spence, Naomi J., Daniel E. Adkins, and Matthew E. Dupre (2011) "Racial differences in depression trajectories among older women: Socioeconomic, family, and health influences." *Journal of Health and Social Behavior* 52:444–59.

Splawski, I., K. Timothy, M. Tateyama, C. Clancy, A. Malhorta, A. Beggs, F. Cappuccio, G. Sagnella, R. Kass, and M. Keating (2002) "Variant of SCN5A Sodium Channel implicated in risk of cardiac arrhythmia." *Science* 297: 1333–36.

Springer, Kristen W., and Dawne M. Mouzon (2011) "'Macho men' and preventive health care." *Journal of Health and Social Behavior* 52:212–27.

Stepanikova, Irena (2012) "Racial-ethnic biases, time pressure, and medical decisions." *Journal of Health and Social* 54: 329–43.

Thomeer, Mieke Beth, Debra Umberson, and Tetyana Pudrovska (2013) "Marital processes around depression: A gendered and relational perspective." *Society and Mental Health* 3: 151–69.

Trivedi, Amal N., Alan M. Zaslavsky, Eric C. Schneider, and John Z. Ayanian (2005) "Trends in the quality of care and racial disparities in Medicare managed care." *New England Journal of Medicine* 353: 692–700.

Uecker, Jeremy E. (2012) "Marriage and mental health among young adults." *Journal of Health and Social Behavior* 53: 67–83.

Umberson, Debra, Kristi Williams, Daniel A. Powers, Hui Liu, and Belinda Needham (2006) "You make me sick: Marital quality and health over the life course." *Journal of Health and Social Behavior* 47: 1–16.

Umberson, Debra, Mieke Beth Thomeer, and Kristi Williams (2013) "Family status and mental health: Recent advances and future directions," pp. 405–31 in *Handbook of the sociology of mental health,* 2nd ed., C. Aneshensel, J. Phelan, and A. Bierman (eds.). Dordrecht: Springer.

U.S. Bureau of the Census (2013) *Statistical abstract of the United States, 2012.* Washington, DC: U.S. Government Printing Office.

Vaccarino, Viola, Saif S. Rathore, Nanette K. Wenger, Paul D. Frederick, Jerome L. Abramson, Hal V. Barron, Ajay Manhapra, Susmita Malik, and Harlan M. Krumholz (2005) "Sex and racial differences in the management of myocardial infection, 1994 through 2002." *New England Journal of Medicine* 353: 671–82.

Verbrugge, Lois M. (1976) "Females and illness: Recent trends in sex differences in the United States." *Journal of Health and Social Behavior* 17: 387–403.

Walls, Melissa L., and Les B. Whitbeck (2011) "Distress among indigenous North Americans: Generalized and culturally relevant stressors." *Society and Mental Health* 1:124–36.

Wang, Haidong, Austin E. Schumacher, Carly E. Levitz, Ali H. Mokdad, and Christopher J. L. Murray (2013) "Left behind: Widening disparities for males and females in U.S. county life expectancy, 1985–2010." *Population Health Metrics* 11: 8 doi:10.1186/1478-7954-11-8.

Warner, David F., and Mark D. Hayward (2006) "Early-life origins of the race gap in men's mortality." *Journal of Health and Social Behavior* 47: 209–26.

Wermuth, Laurie (2003) *Global inequality and human needs.* Boston: Allyn and Bacon.

Wickrama, K. A. S., Frederick O. Lorenz, Rand D. Conger, and Glen H. Elder, Jr. (1997) "Linking occupational conditions to physical health through marital, social, and intrapersonal processes." *Journal of Health and Social Behavior* 38: 363–75.

Williams, David R. (2012) "Miles to go before we sleep: Racial inequities in health." *Journal of Health and Social Behavior* 53: 279–95.

Williams, David R., and Michelle Sternthal (2010) "Understanding racial-ethnic disparities in health: Sociological contributions." *Journal of Health and Social Behavior* 51: S15–27.

Williams, David R., and Selina A. Mohammed (2009) "Discrimination and racial disparities in health: Evidence and needed research." *Journal of Behavioral Medicine* 32: 20–47.

Williams, David R., Manuela Costa, and Jacinta P. Leavell (2010) "Race and mental health: Patterns and approaches," pp. 268–92 in *A handbook for the study of mental health: Social contexts, theories, and systems*, T. Scheid and T. Brown (eds). Cambridge, UK: Cambridge University Press.

Williams, Kristi (2003) "Has the future of marriage arrived? A contemporary examination of gender, marriage, and psychological well-being." *Journal of Health and Social Behavior* 44: 470–87.

Wilson, William Julius (1991) "Studying inner-city social dislocations: The challenge of public agenda research." *American Sociological Review* 56: 1–14.

—— (1996) *When work disappears: The world of the new urban poor.* New York: Knopf.

Winkleby, Marilyn A., Helena C. Kraemer, David K. Ahn, and Ann N. Varady (1998) "Ethnic and socioeconomic differences in cardiovascular disease risk factors: Findings for women from the Third National Health and Nutrition Examination." *JAMA* 280: 356–62.

PART 2

Health and Illness

CHAPTER 5

Social Stress and Health

Social influences upon the onset and subsequent course of a particular disease are not limited to variables such as age, sex, race, social class, and living conditions as they relate to lifestyle, habits, and customs. It is also important to recognize that interaction between the human mind and body represents a critical factor in regard to health. Social situations can cause severe stress that, in turn, affects health and longevity. In a review of stress research, Peggy Thoits (2010) concludes that (1) the impact of stress on health is substantial, (2) exposure to it is unequally distributed in the population (some people and groups experience more stress than others), (3) members of racial minority groups are burdened by additional stress from discrimination, (4) stress can continue over the life course contributing to differences in health between disadvantaged and advantaged groups, and (5) the impact of stress is reduced when people possess high levels of personal mastery (being in control of situations), self-esteem, and social support.

Stress can be defined as a heightened mind–body reaction to stimuli inducing fear or anxiety in the individual. Stress typically starts with a situation that people find threatening or burdensome. Examples of stressful situations that can affect physical and mental health include unpleasant working conditions (Burgard and Ailshire 2009; Marchand, Demers, and Durand 2005; Siegrist 2010a, 2010b), financial strain (Angel, Frisco, Angel, and Chiriboga 2003; Drentea 2000; Drentea and Lavrakas 2000; Drentea and Reynolds 2012; Kahn and Pearlin 2006), job loss (Burgard, Brand, and House 2007), divorce (Lorenz, Wickrama, Conger, and Elder 2006; Wade and Prevalin 2004; Williams and Umberson 2004), migration (Cao, Hwang, and Xi 2012; Shuval 2005), imprisonment (Massoglia 2008; Schnittker and John 2007), death of a spouse (Young and Foy 2013), and racial discrimination (Bratter and Gorman 2011; Brown, O'Rand, and Atkin 2012; Grollman 2012; Miller, Rote, and Keith 2013; Williams 2012; Williams and Mohammed 2009). A review of selected sociological theories by Charles Cooley, William I. Thomas, Erving Goffman, and Emile Durkheim illustrates how social processes, from the standpoint of both the individual and society, promote stress.

Cooley, Thomas, and Goffman: Symbolic Interaction

Cooley, Thomas, and Goffman reflect the symbolic interactionist approach to human behavior. Based upon the work of George Herbert Mead (1865–1931), this approach sees the individual as a creative, thinking organism who is able to choose his or her behavior instead of reacting more or less mechanically to the influence of social processes (Mead 1934). That is, people define the situations they are in and respond on the basis of their definition. This approach assumes that all behavior is self-directed on the basis of common understandings symbolized by language that are shared, communicated, and manipulated by interacting human beings in social situations. Of special relevance to a sociological understanding of stress is Charles H. Cooley's (1864–1929) theory of the "Looking-Glass Self." Cooley (1964) maintained that our self-concepts are the result of social interaction in which we see ourselves reflected in other people. Cooley compares the reflection of our self in others to our reflections in a looking glass:

> Each to each a looking glass
> Reflects the other that doth pass.

Cooley's looking-glass self-concept has three basic components: (1) we see ourselves in our imagination as we think we appear to the other person; (2) we see in our imagination the other person's judgment of ourselves; and (3) as a result of what we see in our imagination about how we are viewed by the other person, we experience some sort of self-feeling, such as satisfaction, pride, or humiliation. The contribution of this theory to an understanding of stress is that an individual's perception of himself or herself as a social object depends on the reaction of other people. Obviously stress could result from the failure of the other person (the observer) to reflect a self-image consistent with that intended by the individual (the subject). Stress can therefore be seen as having a very definite social and personal component based on perceptions that people have in social situations.

The work of William I. Thomas (1863–1947) is also relevant in its understanding of crisis as residing in the individual's "definition of the situation" (Volkart 1951). Thomas stated that as long as definitions of a social situation remain relatively constant, behavior would generally be orderly. However, when rival definitions appear and habitual behavior becomes disrupted, a sense of disorganization and uncertainty may be anticipated. The ability of an individual to cope with a crisis situation will be strongly related to socialization experiences that have taught the person how to cope with new situations.

Consequently, Thomas makes two particularly important contributions concerning stress. First, he notes that the same crisis *will not produce the same effect uniformly in all people*. Second, he explains that adjustment to and control of a crisis situation result from an individual's ability to compare a present situation with similar ones in the past and to revise judgment and action upon the basis of past experience. The outcome of a particular situation depends, therefore, upon an individual's definition of that situation and upon how that individual comes to terms with it. As David Mechanic (1978:293) states, "Thomas's concept of crisis is important because it emphasizes that crises lie not in situations, but in the interaction between a situation and a person's capacities to meet it."

Erving Goffman (1922–1982) is noted for the dramaturgical or "life as theatre" approach. Goffman (1959) believed that in order for social interaction to be possible, people need information about the other participants. Such information is obtained through: (1) a person's appearance; (2) past experience with similar individuals; (3) the social setting; and (4) of most importance, the information a person communicates about himself or herself through words and actions. This fourth category of information is decisive because it is subject to control by the individual and represents the impression the person is trying to project—which others may come to accept. This information is significant because it helps to define a situation by enabling others to know in advance what a person expects of them and what they may expect of him or her. Goffman calls this process "impression management."

Goffman says people live in worlds of social encounters in which they act out a line of behavior. This is a pattern of verbal and nonverbal acts by which individuals express their view of a situation and their evaluation of the participants, particularly themselves. The positive social value that individuals claim for themselves, by the line that others assume they have taken during a particular encounter, is termed a *face*. This face is an image of self that is projected by the individual to other people. One's face is one's most personal possession and is the center of security and pleasure. Goffman is quick to point out that a person's face is only on loan from society and can be withdrawn if the person conducts himself or herself in an inappropriate manner. A person may be in the "wrong face" when information about that person's social worth cannot be integrated into his or her line of behavior. However, a person may be "out of face" when he or she participates in an encounter, without the line of behavior that participants in the particular situation would be expected to take.

Goffman further explains that the maintenance of face is a condition of interaction, not its objective. This is so because one's face is a constant factor that is taken for granted in interaction. When people engage in "face-work," they are taking action to make their activities consistent with the face they are projecting. This is important because every member of a social group is expected to have some knowledge of face-work and some experience in its use, such as the exercise of social skills like tact. Goffman sees almost all acts involving other people as being influenced by considerations of face. For example, a person is given a chance to quit a job rather than be fired. People are therefore aware of the interpretations that others have placed upon their behavior and the interpretations that they themselves should place upon their behavior. Consequently, Goffman's view of the self is that it has two distinct roles in social interaction: (1) the self as an image of an individual formed from the flow of events in an encounter; and (2) the self as a kind of player in a ritual game who copes judgmentally with a situation. This aspect of Goffman's work identifies the calculative element in dealings between people and presents them as information managers and strategists maneuvering for gain in social situations.

Goffman's principal contribution to our understanding of stress arises from his claim that the self is a sacred object. The self is more important than anything else to us, because it represents who we are and is always with us. For someone to challenge the integrity of that self as a social object can be an embarrassing situation. Each self is special, and in social relationships that very special self we have tried to nourish and protect for a lifetime is put on display. Goffman has said that role-specific behavior is based not upon the functional requirements of a particular role but upon the *appearance* of having discharged a role's requirements. Thus, stress could be induced when people fail in their performance. Otherwise, people might not be so willing to take such great care in how they act out lines of behavior considered appropriate to their situation.

The symbolic interaction perspective, as reflected in the work of Cooley, Thomas, and Goffman, contributes to our understanding of stress, by identifying the key variable in the stress experience: the perception of the individual. People vary in their interpretation of situations, but ultimately it is the way in which they perceive the strains and conflicts in their roles, tasks, personal relationships, and other aspects of their life situation that causes them to feel stressed. How people feel about themselves (Cooley), define situations (Thomas), or manage impressions (Goffman) can lead to the creation of stressful conditions. People typically cope with stress by trying to change their situation, manage the meaning of the situation, or keep the symptoms of stress within manageable bounds (Pearlin 1989).

Durkheim: The Larger Society

While symbolic interaction theory emphasizes interpersonal forms of interaction, the French sociologist Emile Durkheim (1858–1917) focuses on the influence of the larger society on individuals. Durkheim was concerned with those social processes and constraints that integrate individuals into the larger social community. He believed that when a society was strongly integrated, it held individuals firmly under its control (Durkheim 1950, 1956). Individuals were integrated into a society as a result of their acceptance of community values, which were reinforced through social interaction with others believing in the same value system. Especially important were participation in events celebrating a society's traditions and also involvement in work activities.

As members of society, individuals were constrained in their behavior by laws and customs. These constraints were "social facts," which Durkheim (1950:13) defined as "every way of acting, fixed or not, capable of exercising on the individual an external constraint." What Durkheim suggests is that society has an existence outside of and above the individual. Values, norms, and other social influences descend on the individual to shape his or her behavior. Social control is, therefore, real and external to the individual.

Among Durkheim's works, the most pertinent to an understanding of the social determinants of stress is his 1897 study *Suicide* (1951). In explaining the differential rates of suicide among various religious and occupational groupings, Durkheim suggested that suicide was not entirely a matter of free choice by individuals. He believed that suicide was a social fact explainable in terms of social causes. He distinguished between three major types of suicide, each dependent upon the relationship of the individual to society. He suggested a fourth type of suicide, fatalistic suicide, where people kill themselves because their situation is hopeless, but he never fully developed the concept. The three major types are (1) egoistic suicide, in which people become detached from society and, suddenly finding themselves on their own, are overwhelmed by the resulting stress; (2) anomic suicide, in which people suffer a sudden dislocation of normative systems where their norms and values are no longer relevant, so that controls of society no longer restrain them from taking their lives; and (3) altruistic suicide, in which people feel themselves so strongly integrated into a demanding society that their only escape seems to be suicide.

Durkheim's typology of suicide suggests how a society might induce enough stress among people to cause them to take their lives. Egoistic suicide is a result of stress brought about by the separation of a strongly integrated individual from his or her group. Durkheim uses the example of the military officer who is retired and suddenly left without the group ties that typically regulated his or her behavior.

Egoistic suicide is based upon the overstimulation of a person's intelligence by the realization that he or she has been deprived of collective activity and meaning. Anomic suicide is characterized by an overstimulation of emotion and a corresponding freedom from society's restraints. It is a result of sudden change that includes the breakdown of values and norms by which a person has lived his or her life. Sudden wealth or sudden poverty, for example, could disrupt the usual normative patterns and induce a state of anomie or normlessness. In this situation, a chronic lack of regulation results in a state of restlessness, unbounded ambition, or perhaps crisis, in which norms no longer bind one to society.

While egoistic and anomic forms of suicide are both due to "society's insufficient presence in individuals" (Durkheim 1951:256), altruistic suicide represents the strong presence of a social system encouraging suicide among certain groups. Suicide in the altruistic form could be characterized as the avoidance of stress by people who prefer to conform to a society's normative system rather than risk the stress of opposing it. Examples of altruistic suicide are the practice of hara-kiri in Japan, where certain failures on the part of an individual are expected to be properly redressed by his or her suicide, or the traditional Hindu custom of the widow committing ritual suicide at her husband's funeral. In these two situations, people sense social pressure for them to take their own lives.

Although altruistic suicide is relatively rare, stories do appear in the mass media of people killing themselves for reasons that could be considered egoistic or anomic. Yet the significance of Durkheim's orientation toward social processes for the understanding of the stress phenomenon extends well beyond the issue of suicide, since this is only one of many possible ways a person might find to cope with social and psychological stress. What is particularly insightful is Durkheim's notion of the capability of the larger society to create stressful situations where people are forced to respond to conditions not of their own choosing.

For example, in a series of studies decades ago, M. Harvey Brenner (1987a, 1987b) linked increased incidence of heart disease, stroke, kidney failure, mental illness, and even infant mortality in the United States and several Western European countries to downturns in the economy. Brenner's thesis is that there are few areas of our lives not intimately affected by the state of the economy. He argues that economic recession increases the amount of stress on an individual by comparing economic cycles with health statistics. Brenner found that heart attacks increase during periods of recession. Usually the first wave of deaths follows the recession by three years, with a second wave occurring five to seven years after the recession. The lag was thought to be due to the length of time it takes for heart disease to cause death. Waves of kidney failure deaths generally lagged two years behind a recession, while death from strokes took about two to four years following an economic downturn. Infant mortality rates were also higher during periods of recession, according to Brenner. Mothers suffering from the stresses of the recession tended to have higher blood pressure and be less healthy themselves, thereby giving birth to children whose chances for survival had likewise been weakened.

What causes stress during an economic recession was the intensified struggle for the basic necessities of life (food, clothing, shelter, health care, and education for children) and a possible loss of self-satisfaction and social status associated with unemployment while trying to survive on savings and welfare. These stresses were often found to be enhanced by a rise in drinking and smoking at the same time. What is happening, suggests Brenner, is that social stress from economic conditions increases exposure to the major risk factors known to accompany many health disorders.

Earlier, Brenner (1973) focused on the relationship between the economy and mental health. He examined rates of employment and mental hospital admissions in New York over a period of 127 years from 1841 to 1968. He believed that regardless of the number and combination of factors that predispose certain individuals toward becoming mentally ill, a question that needed to be answered was why mental disorder appears *when* it does. Brenner found that rates of mental hospitalization increased during economic downturns and decreased during upturns, thereby suggesting that economic factors may precipitate mental disorder.

Brenner provided two explanations for his findings. He preferred a "provocation" hypothesis that stress resulting from being dislocated from one's usual lifestyle or prevented from improving it during a downward shift in the economy caused vulnerable people to reach the point at which they required hospitalization in a mental institution. Another explanation is also possible, described by Brenner as an "uncovering" hypothesis. This alternate view suggests that economic downturns do not promote mental disorder but simply "uncover" those people already mentally ill by stripping them of their existing economic resources. These people who are mentally "borderline" may be able to support themselves during periods of economic affluence, only to become the first to lose their jobs when times are bad. In fact, in a declining economic cycle, mental hospitals may be an attractive source of food and shelter for such individuals.

Although Brenner prefers the hypothesis that economic downturns "provoke" mental disorder, his data also support the finding that such downturns "uncover" mentally disordered people. While it was never determined whether "provocation" or "uncovering" is actually at work, both hypotheses may be relevant. The importance of Brenner's work is that it shows that downward trends in economic activity may stress certain people to the point that they require mental hospitalization, particularly those with the fewest financial resources.

The research of Brenner and others (Burgard et al. 2007; Burgard and Ailshire 2009; Lam, Fan, and Moen 2014; Tausig and Fenwick 1999) demonstrates how large-scale societal processes, specifically those of economic change, can be correlated with adverse physical and mental health. The relationship, however, is complex. It is difficult to substantiate a precise, cause-and-effect relationship between a major social event such as an economic depression and health problems of a particular individual, because of the wide range of variables that may intervene in the individual's situation and modify the effect. Possible intervening variables include social support, personality, genetics, or social class. For example, social support (feelings of being loved, accepted, cared for, and needed by others) can act as a buffer against stress (Thoits 2010, 2011; Turner and Turner 2013). Social support is typically obtained within families. It can also be acquired through the community by individuals who live alone, by way of social interaction with friends, relationships at one's place of religious worship, and involvement in local groups and clubs. Those persons with strong social support tend to cope with stress better than those with little or no support. Nevertheless, the fact remains that social and economic conditions, beyond the direct influence or control of the average person, can create stressful circumstances that force people to respond to them. For vulnerable people, the stressful circumstances can lead to ill health.

Stress

The theories of Durkheim, Cooley, Thomas, and Goffman demonstrate a relationship between social interaction and stress, but they do not explain the effect of stress upon the human body. Embarrassment and psychological discomfort can be socially painful, yet the effects of stress can transcend the social situation and cause physiological damage as well. Hence, a physiological perspective of stress must be considered.

Walter Cannon (1932) believed that the real measure of health is not the absence of disease but the ability of the human organism to function effectively within a given environment. This belief was based upon the observation that the human body undergoes continuous adaptation to its environment in response to weather, microorganisms, chemical irritants and pollutants, and the psychological pressures of daily life. Cannon called this process of physiological adaptation *homeostasis*, which is derived from the Greek and means "staying the same." Homeostasis refers to the maintenance of a relatively constant condition. For example, when the body becomes cold, heat is produced; when the body is threatened by bacteria, antibodies are produced to fight the germs; and when the body is threatened by an attack from another human being, the body prepares itself either to fight or to run.

As an organism, the human body is thus prepared to meet both internal and external threats to survival, whether these threats are real or symbolic. A person may react with fear to an actual object or to a symbol of that object—for example, a bear versus a bear's footprint. In the second case, the fear is not of the footprint but of the bear that the footprint symbolizes. Threats in contemporary urban societies could include types of stimuli such as heavy traffic, loud noises, or competition at work, all of which can produce emotional stress related more to a situation than to a specific person or object.

Whether the stressful situation actually induces physiological change depends upon an individual's perception of the stress stimulus and the personal meaning that the stimulus holds. A person's reaction, for instance, may not correspond to the actual reality of the dangers that the stimulus represents—that is, a person may overreact or underreact. Thus, an individual's subjective interpretation of a social situation is the trigger that produces physiological responses. Situations themselves cannot always be assumed beforehand to produce physiological changes.

Physiological Responses to Stress

Cannon (1932) formulated the concept of the "fight or flight" pattern of physiological change to illustrate how the body copes with stress resulting from a social situation. When a person experiences fear or anxiety, the body undergoes physiological changes that prepare it for vigorous effort and the effect of possible injury. Physiological changes in the body, as a result of stressful situations, primarily involve the autonomic and neuroendocrine systems. The autonomic nervous system controls heart rate, blood pressure, and gastrointestinal functions—processes that occur automatically and are not under the voluntary control of the central nervous system. The autonomic nervous system is delicately balanced between relaxation and stimulation and is activated primarily through the hypothalamus, located in the central ventral portion of the brain. It is composed of two major divisions, the para- sympathetic and the sympathetic systems. The parasympathetic system is dominant when there is no emergency and regulates the vegetative processes of the body such as the storing of sugar in the liver, the constriction of the pupil of the eye in response to intense light, and the decreasing of heart rate. When there is an emergency, the sympa- thetic system governs the body's autonomic functions and increases the heart rate so that blood flows swiftly to the organs and muscles that are needed in defense. It also inhibits bowel movements and dilates the pupil of the eye to improve sight.

Besides the autonomic nervous system, the endocrine glands perform an import- ant role in the body's physiological reaction to stress. The neuroendocrine system consists of the adrenal and pituitary glands, the parathyroids, the islets of Langer- hans, and the gonads. They secrete hormones directly into the bloodstream because they lack ducts to carry their hormones to particular glands. The two glands that are the most responsive to stress situations are the adrenal and pituitary glands. The adrenal gland secretes two hormones, epinephrine and norepinephrine, under stim- ulation from the hypothalamus. Epinephrine accelerates the heart rate and helps to distribute blood to the heart, lungs, central nervous system, and limbs. It also makes the blood coagulate more readily so that as little blood as possible will be lost in case of injury. Norepinephrine raises blood pressure and joins with epinephrine to mobilize fatty acids in the bloodstream for use as energy. The function of the pitu- itary gland is, upon stimulation by the hypothalamus, to secrete hormones that, in turn, stimulate other endocrine glands to secrete their hormones.

Originally, most medical scientists believed that only the adrenal gland was in- volved in stress reaction. However, in 1936, Hans Selye demonstrated the existence of a pituitary–adrenal cortical axis as having a profound effect upon body metabo- lism, though it now seems that the entire endocrine system, not just the pituitary and adrenal glands, is involved in some manner in stress reaction. Under acute stimulus, hormone secretions by the endocrine glands increase; under calming influences, secre- tions decrease. Selye (1956) developed a theory known as the *general adaptation syn- drome* (GAS) to explain this process. He believed that after an initial alarm reaction, a second stage of resistance to prolonged stress was accomplished primarily through increased activity of the anterior pituitary and adrenal cortex. If stress continued and pituitary and adrenal defenses were consumed, Selye indicated that a person would enter a third stage of exhaustion. He described this third stage as a kind of premature aging due to wear and tear on the body. Airline Geronimus and colleagues (2006) use the term "weathering" to depict this stage of premature aging in their research and use it to describe the effects of racial discrimination on disadvantaged blacks over time who showed signs of aging earlier than significantly older whites.

Most threats in modern society are symbolic, not physical, and they do not usu- ally require a physical response. Today, the human organism faces emotional threats with the same physical system used to fight enemies, yet modern society disapproves of such physical responses as fighting. Socially the human organism is often left with no course of action, perhaps not even verbal insults. This inability to respond externally leaves the body physiologically mobilized for action that never comes, a readiness that can result in damage to the body over time.

Biomarkers

The discussion thus far has pointed out that an inability to manage the social, psychological, and emotional aspects of life—to respond suitably to a social situation—can cause a physiological reaction to stressful circumstances (House 2002; McFarland and Hayward 2014; Siegrist 2010a, 2010b; Turner 2013). Such reactions include cardiovascular complications and hypertension, peptic ulcers, muscular pain, compulsive vomiting, asthma, migraine headaches, and other health problems. Some researchers utilize *biomarkers* to ascertain physiological responses to stressful social conditions. Biomarkers are clinical assessments (e.g., blood pressure, urine analysis, blood tests for cholesterol and c-reactive protein, waist-hip ratios) of individuals independent of their self-reports and perhaps even awareness that such conditions exist within their body. While an individual knows he or she lives in disadvantaged social circumstances, that person may not be aware that they have high blood pressure, inflammation, or some other adverse physiological response to their social situation that biomarkers uncover.

Johannes Siegrist (2010a, 2010b) documented the relationship between stress and the onset of cardiovascular disease among German male blue-collar workers and middle managers. These studies demonstrated the effects of stress on the cardiovascular system through blood and urine samples and blood pressure readings, as well as measures of life satisfaction, work load, job security, coping styles, emotional distress, and sleep disturbances. Siegrist found that high personal effort (competitiveness and work-related over-commitment) and low gain (poor promotion prospects, no merit raises, and a blocked career)—what he calls the effort–reward imbalance model—are associated over time with higher risk of heart disease. Workers whose jobs required strong effort that resulted in little reward were most likely to have cardiovascular disease.

Teresa Seeman and her colleagues (2008) focused on allostatic load, which refers to the cumulative wear and tear on the body's organic systems as it repeatedly adapts to chronic stressors. That is, the allostatic load becomes heavier as the body's defenses against persistent stress are worn down over time. Seeman et al. determined that long-term stresses associated with low socioeconomic status (SES) were consistently and negatively associated with increased allostatic loads promoting cardiovascular, metabolic, and inflammatory risks. Other research found that lower SES persons carry a significantly greater allostatic load in late life than higher SES individuals and their adverse life experiences in the lower class have a cumulative negative effect on their health (Gruenewald et al. 2012). Geronimus et al. (2006), as previously noted, observed a similar "weathering" of the body (premature aging) among disadvantaged blacks in the United States, as did R. Jay Turner (2013) in analyzing negative health outcomes among African Americans and the poor. There is also evidence that chronic stress associated with disadvantaged social circumstances initiates differences in cell aging much earlier among low SES children, thereby triggering premature aging long before the onset of diseases associated with old age (Needham et al. 2012).

In other research, Aniruddha Das (2013) found chronic inflammation, described as a "weathering" effect, prevalent among a nationwide sample of older adult black men as a result of stress that was cumulative (repeated over time) and multidimensional (in differing life situations). These long-term and varied stresses leading to chronic inflammation in the body were depicted as a way that race gets "under the skin" through discriminatory experiences. Therefore, as Turner (2013:181) points out, considerable evidence has been forthcoming in the past two decades to show that the task of persistently coping with chronic stressors can have a profound adverse effect on a person's health as seen through physiological differences between chronically stressed persons and those with little or no such stressors in their life.

Social Factors and Stress

A considerable amount of empirical research exists in medical sociology dealing with stress and stress-related topics. Selected findings will be reviewed here, to include relevant research on social stressors, stress adaptations, group influences, social capital, changes in life events, and socioeconomic status. The intent of this section is to show how contemporary sociologists are helping to improve our understanding of stress.

Social Stressors

Leonard Pearlin (1989) identified two major types of social stressors: life events and chronic strains. First, there is the stress of life events such as divorce, marriage, or losing one's job. Typically, the stress associated with life events originates in negative situations (such as heavy debt), but on certain occasions it may come from positive circumstances (such as weddings). Second, are the chronic strains that are relatively enduring conflicts, problems, and threats, which many people face on a daily basis. Chronic strain includes role overload, such as the strain associated with work and being a parent or trying to advance one's career over the life course. It also involves conflicts within role sets, such as those between husbands and wives, inter-role conflict where a person has too many roles, role captivity in which a person is an unwilling incumbent of a role such as being trapped in an unpleasant job or marriage, or role restructuring in which a person changes relationships within roles (Avison, Ali, and Walters 2007; Avison and Thomas 2010; Henretta 2007; Pavalko, Gong, and Long 2007; Schieman, Whitestone, and van Gundy 2006; Thoits 2013; Umberson et al. 2006). As Pearlin (1989:245) observes, role strains can have serious effects on individuals because the roles themselves are important, especially when they involve jobs, marriage, and parenthood.

Although chronic strain tends to have stronger effects on health than a life event since it constitutes a stressful burden that continues over time, such strain can nevertheless be caused by life events and this is especially the case if the life events have negative consequences for the people experiencing them (Turner 2003; Turner and Avison 2003). Consequently, both chronic strain and life events can be inter-related as well as stressful.

Stress Adaptation

Many years ago, Mechanic (1962, 1978) attempted to explain the stress experience from the standpoint of both society and the individual. He draws on the work of

BOX 5.1

Stress, Age, and Debt

Does high debt cause anxiety? Patricia Drentea (2000; Drentea and Reynolds 2012) studied this situation in two different age groups. She found in a statewide survey in Ohio that age makes a difference in that younger people were more likely to be stressed over high credit card debt than older people. A major reason as to why this is the case appeared to be low income. Younger people usually have less money, and Drentea found that anxiety increased when the ratio of debt to income is greatest. This was especially likely if the person was in default. Drentea explains that younger people in the United States have come of age during a period of unprecedented growth in materialism, thereby promoting a culture of consumerism. Buying goods and services now and postponing paying for them is common. Moreover, debt anxiety is more typical among younger adults, in part because they are undergoing significant job and family transitions—a situation that is made more

difficult by economic hardship. Consequently, anxiety during young adulthood may be associated with the amount of debt that is incurred.

However, in subsequent research, Drentea and John Reynolds (2012) investigated the burden of heavy debt among a largely elderly low-income population in Miami-Dade County in Florida. They found that a high level of indebtedness from not only credit cards, but also mortgages, loans, and other sources, resulted in worry, anxiety, anger, and depression. This age group struggled to live on a fixed income and feared never being able to pay off their debts. While credit card debt particularly worries young adults and high debt in general promotes distress among low SES elderly, it is clear that heavy debt and limited financial resources are highly stressful regardless of age. Drentea's research helps us to understand the relationship between stress, age, and indebtedness.

William I. Thomas (Volkart 1951), who pointed out that the meaning of crisis lies not in the situation but rather in the interaction between the situation and the person's ability to rise above it. The outcome or effect of a crisis depends on how well a person comes to terms with the circumstances and adapts to it. Mechanic believes that in social situations people not only have different skills and abilities in coping with problems, but different perceptions. Furthermore, not everyone has an equal degree of control in managing emotional situations or the same motivation and personal involvement. In analyzing any particular situation, an observer must consider individual differences in how threats are assessed and the resources available to deal with it (McLeod 2012).

Extending his concept of stress from the individual to societal components, Mechanic states that a person's ability to cope with problems is influenced by a society's preparatory institutions, such as schools and the family, two entities designed to develop skills and competencies in dealing with society's needs. A person's emotional control and ability to cope are also related to society's incentive systems—that is, society's rewards (or punishments) for those who did (or did not) control their behavior in accordance with societal norms. As for a person's involvement or motivation in a situation, Mechanic explains that society's evaluative institutions provide norms of approval or disapproval for following particular courses of action.

Hence, the extent of physiological damage or change within an individual depends on the following: (1) the stimulus situation, which includes the importance of the situation to the individual; (2) an individual's capacity to deal with the stimulus situation, such as the influence of genetic factors, personal skills, innate abilities, and past experiences; (3) the individual's preparation by society to meet problems; and (4) the influence of society's approved norms of behavior. Mechanic (1962:8) emphasizes the contribution of society toward an individual's adaptation to stress by stating "that whether or not a person experiences stress will depend on the means, largely learned, that [the person] has available to deal with his [or her] life situation."

Mechanic's model represents an important contribution toward our understanding of stress. It shows the importance of adaptation and explaining how that adaptation is based on an individual's perception of life situations, combined with his or her degree of preparation by society to cope with stressful circumstances. Mechanic thus identifies adaptability as the key variable in whether a person will eventually suffer organic damage. This view is consistent with Peggy Thoits's (2006) finding that people are not necessarily passive when faced with stressful situations but often work to resolve the problems causing them stress.

Stress and the Social Group

People's perceptions of an event may be influenced by their intelligence, past experience, socialization, and awareness of stimuli, but the influence of group membership is also important. It has been several decades since Gordon Moss (1973) illustrated the significance of group membership in helping individuals cope with information they find stressful. His work is still relevant as he found that stress and physiological change are likely to occur when people experience information that goes against their beliefs or desires. Moss notes that information processing produces changes in the central nervous system, the autonomic nervous system, and the neuroendocrine system, all of which can alter the susceptibility to disease among certain people. The most vulnerable persons are those whose physiological responses are easily elicited and likely to be more pronounced and prolonged. Moss emphasizes the advantages of group membership in providing social support for the individual. Subjective feelings of belonging, being accepted, and being needed have consistently shown themselves to be crucial in the development of feelings of well-being and the relieving of symptoms of tension. Thus, Moss's work joins that of others (Avison et al. 2007; Thoits 2010, 2011, 2013) to show how the social support rendered by families and groups helps reduce the potentially harmful effects of stress upon the body and mind.

Furthermore, there is often a tendency among members of small groups to develop a consensus about how social events should be perceived. This process minimizes individual differences, reduces uncertainty, and maintains group conformity. Conformity to group-approved attitudes and definitions has long been hypothesized in sociology and social psychology as reducing anxiety, by ensuring acceptance from persons and groups important to the individual. Much of human behavior is seen as the result of an individual's search for relief from anxiety, by conforming to authority and group norms.

Social Capital

The importance of group and organizational membership for the physical and mental health of individuals is seen in the growing interest in the concept of social capital in medical sociology. As Bryan Turner (2004:13) defines it, social capital is "the social investments of individuals in society in terms of their membership in formal and informal groups, networks, and institutions." He points out that the degree to which an individual is socially integrated with parents, neighborhood, community groups, churches, clubs, voluntary service organizations, and so on provides an objective measure of that person's social capital. Nan Lin (2001; Song, Son, and Lin 2010) likewise sees social capital as an investment in social relations that people can use as a buffer against stress and depression, while French sociologist Pierre Bourdieu (1986) viewed it as a resource that accrues to individuals through their memberships in social groups.

Yet, social capital is not just a property of individuals; it is also a characteristic of social networks from which individuals draw psychological and material benefits. According to Bourdieu (1993:2), one can get an intuitive idea of social capital by saying that it is what ordinary language calls "connections." While Bourdieu emphasizes the resources of networks, Robert Putnam (2000) emphasizes the cohesion of networks. Putnam defines social capital as a community-level resource reflected in social relationships involving not only networks but also norms and levels of trust. He maintains that the positive influences of social capital on health are derived from enhanced self-esteem, sense of support, access to group and organizational resources, and its buffering qualities in stressful situations. Social connectedness, in Putnam's view, is one of the most powerful determinants of health. After reviewing several studies, he found that people who are socially disconnected are between two and five times more likely to die from all causes when compared with similar individuals having close ties to family and friends.

The difference between social capital and the concept of social support discussed earlier is that the latter pertains to how much the individual feels loved and supported by other people such as family members, while the former is the quality of a person's social connections and integration into a wider community. The importance of social capital in health outcomes is seen in the well-known public health study in the 1950s and 1960s in the small Italian American community of Roseto, Pennsylvania (Lasker, Egolf, and Wolf 1994). Heart attacks in this community were 50 percent less than in four surrounding towns. The only difference was that Roseto had a tradition of strong family and social ties, church participation, and marriage within the same ethnic group. However, once upwardly mobile young adults in Roseto started departing from local traditions such as ethnic intermarriage and church and club memberships, with many younger adults leaving to seek higher paying and more rewarding jobs elsewhere, mortality from heart disease surpassed that of the other communities. The results of this study and others suggest that people embedded in supportive social relationships providing high levels of social capital have better health and longevity (Browning and Cagney 2002; Mohnen et al. 2011; Song et al. 2010) and less psychological distress (Hughes, Kiecolt, and Keith 2014; Song 2011). However, findings on the relationship between social capital and health outcomes have not always been consistent and are affected by the difficulty in measuring a variable with multiple—individual, group, community, and so on—conceptual levels. But the concept has grown in popularity and is a promising area of research in medical sociology.

Stress and Socioeconomic Status

As we know, socioeconomic status plays an important role in the stress process. The previous section on biomarkers reviewed studies showing that lower SES persons had higher allostatic loads from stress and greater premature aging (Seeman et al. 2008; Turner 2013). The lower class is characterized as being subject to the most stress and having the fewest resources to cope with it (Avison and Thomas 2010; Cockerham 2014; Downey and van Willigen 2005; Grzywacz, Almeida, Neupert, and Ettner 2004; Lantz, House, Mero, and Williams 2005; McLeod 2012; Thoits 2010). After reviewing numerous studies of both humans and primates, Robert Evans (1994) determined that social rank could be correlated with the ability to handle stress. The higher one's position in a social hierarchy, the better one deals with stressful situations and the effects of stress on the body. This advantage decreases proportionally the lower one goes down the social ladder.

Consequently, Evans, Morris Barer, and Theodore Marmor (1994) suggest that stress is the principal cause of the social gradient in mortality. As discussed in Chapter 3, the TheWhitehall studies of Michael Marmot (2004), including those with his colleagues (1984, 1991), provided strong evidence that the association of socioeconomic status with health occurs at every level of the social hierarchy. The upper class was found to live longer than the upper middle class who, in turn, live longer than the lower middle class and so on—until the lower class is reached, who have the lowest life expectancy of all. What is important is not just the difference between the top and bottom of society but the fact that people at the top enjoy better health and longevity than those just below them, even though both groups are affluent.

In Evans's (1994) view, stress is the culprit in that the levels of stress experienced, the amount of resources available to cope with stress, and the degree of control over one's life situation vary by social class position. Therefore, Evans concludes that it is the quality of the "microenvironment" (defined as social relations at home and work) that facilitates the transfer of strain from stressful life events. It is the ability to transfer or buffer the effects of stress, not simply being wealthy, that ultimately determines the extent of the effects of stress on the body. It is not certain, however, whether the social gradient in life expectancy is caused by stress or other factors such as class differences in health lifestyles and social support or some other factor or combination of factors (Cockerham, Hattori, and Yamori 2000). This line of inquiry in stress research requires more investigation.

Life Changes

Another important area of stress research charts significant changes in a person's life experiences. Research in this area has generally focused on the reactions of people both to extreme situations, such as wars and natural disasters, and to ordinary life events. This research is reviewed in the next two subsections.

Extreme Situations

Extreme situations such as natural disasters appear to be a likely source of stress because of the great anxiety people usually attach to being caught in such circumstances. But a common misconception about disasters is that people flee in panic from the site of a potential disaster area. In reality, it is usually difficult to get people to evacuate their homes, even when the possibility of damage or destruction is imminent. This was evident in New Orleans in 2005, when some people resisted evacuation after the flooding of the city by Hurricane Katrina, three years later in 2008 when Hurricane Ike destroyed much of Galveston, Texas, and again in 2012 when Hurricane Sandy hit the eastern seaboard causing its most extensive damage in New Jersey and New York. A few people are even attracted to potential disasters and take risks to see a tidal wave, tornado, or hurricane. Trying to view a disaster and being a victim of one, however, are two entirely different matters. Past research has shown that such extreme situations as earthquakes, tsunamis, tornados, and hurricanes can induce considerable stress (Frankenberg, Nobles, and Sumantri 2012; Haines, Hurlbert, and Beggs 1996)—a fact that was unhappily verified by Hurricane Katrina when it smashed into New Orleans, displacing thousands of people and causing at least 1,833 deaths. Mass media reports commonly show or describe people in large-scale disasters as experiencing intense feelings of grief, loss, anguish, and despair.

Thus, there is sound reason for understanding the social and psychological consequences of disasters, especially from the standpoint of developing and implementing programs to assist disaster victims. Among survivors of the terrorist attack of September 11, 2001, on the World Trade Center in New York City, the impact of the trauma on many of those who were the most intensely exposed was still apparent 5 to 6 years later (Brackbill et al. 2013). In another study of the aftermath of the attack, Hannah Knudsen and her colleagues (2005) investigated the immediate and long-term consequences on the mental health of a national sample of American workers. While there was an increase in symptoms of depression during the four weeks after the attack, the symptoms subsided thereafter and subsequently returned to pre-September 11 levels. Changes in alcohol consumption were modest, and the researchers concluded that there was no lasting and measurable effect. Consequently, the level of exposure to a traumatic event makes a difference with respect to the duration of symptoms, with those experiencing it firsthand having the most lasting emotional distress.

There is almost unanimous agreement among researchers that disasters do promote acute psychological stress, emotional difficulties, and anxiety related to coping with grief, property damage, financial loss, and adverse living conditions. Kathleen Tierney and Barbara Baisden (1979:36) state that "while few researchers would claim that disasters create severe and chronic mental illness on a wide scale, victim populations *do* seem to undergo considerable stress and strain and *do* experience varying degrees of concern, worry, depression, and anxiety, together with numerous problems in living and adjustment in postdisaster." Groups of people with special needs in the aftermath of disasters are usually children and the elderly. Older people, in particular, find it difficult to adjust to change after a disaster. Low-income groups also present special problems in that often they are left without any material resources and become especially dependent on aid. This was the case in New Orleans

PHOTO 5.2 Crowd gathered outside the Louisiana Superdome in New Orleans awaiting evacuation in the aftermath of Hurricane Katrina in 2005. Exposure to extreme situations like natural disasters can be highly stressful, but the psychological impact on individuals is usually short-term.

and the adjoining Gulf coast after the flooding and destruction from Hurricane Katrina's winds.

This is not to say that everyone who experiences disasters firsthand succumbs to psychological trauma—quite the contrary. A pattern that emerges in studies of natural disasters and psychopathology is that the disaster experience, though severe, is usually short in duration except for the most deeply traumatized, and the effects on mental health tend to be short term and self-limiting (Tierney and Baisden 1979; Haines et al. 1996). Exceptions are highly traumatizing events like the World Trade Center attack (Brackbill et al. 2013) and when whole communities are destroyed, as seen when Indonesia (2004) and Japan (2011) were struck by huge tsunamis (Frankenberg et al. 2012). The question arises about the possible effects of stress in extreme situations lasting long periods of time, such as the experiences of people exposed to the brutalities of Nazi concentration camps and the horrors of war. There is evidence that many concentration camp survivors suffered persistent emotional problems and were particularly prone to physical illness and early death (Eitinger 1964, 1973). However, as Aaron Antonovsky (1979) noted, other concentration camp survivors adjusted to the effects of having been subjected to a most terrible experience and went on to live lives that were essentially normal.

When considering what differentiates people who are generally vulnerable to stress-related health problems (not just concentration camp survivors) from those who are not so vulnerable, Antonovsky argues that a strong sense of coherence is the key factor. Coherence, in his view, is a personal orientation that allows an individual to view the world with feelings of confidence, faith in the predictability of events, and a notion that things will most likely work out reasonably well. One achieves this sense of coherence as a result of life experiences in which one meets challenges, participates in shaping outcomes (usually satisfactory), and copes with varying degrees of stimuli. Hence, the person has the resources to cope with unexpected situations if they arise. However, people whose lives are so routine and completely predictable, that their sense of coherence as previously defined is weakened, will find it difficult to handle unpleasant surprises and events. They are likely to be more susceptible to stress-induced health dysfunctions as they are overwhelmed by events. What Antonovsky appears to be saying is that people who have the capability to come to terms with their unpleasant situation rather than to be overcome by it are those who are most likely to emerge in a healthy condition.

A similar conclusion can be made about soldiers fighting in combat. Environmental stresses faced by combat infantrymen are among the hardest faced by anyone. These stresses include the overt threat of death or injury, the sight and sounds of death and dying people, battle noise, fatigue, loss of sleep, deprivation of family relationships, and exposure to rain, mud, insects, heat, or cold—all occasioned by deliberate exposure to the most extreme forms of violence intentionally directed at the soldier by the opposing side. Sociologist Charles Moskos (1970) compared life in combat with the Hobbesian analogy of primitive life—both can be nasty, brutish, and short. Yet, somehow men generally come to terms with the circumstances, since most combat soldiers do not become psychiatric casualties. Two factors may be largely responsible. First is the existence of group demands for discipline and efficiency under fire. Observing helicopter ambulance crews and Green Berets in the Vietnam War, Peter Bourne (1970), a psychiatrist, found these soldiers were subject to strong group pressures to be technically proficient. This finding was particularly true of the Green Berets, who urged their detachment leaders to prove themselves in combat in order to be worthy of their role. Although at times this social pressure added to the stress of the leaders, when the entire group faced an enemy threat, there was unusual group cohesion and considerable conformity in the manner in which the threat was perceived and handled.

Second, Bourne suggests that there is a further psychological mobilization of an internal discipline in which the individual soldier employs a sense of personal invulnerability, the use of action to reduce tension, and a lack of personal introspection to perceive the environment in such a way that personal threat is reduced. Whether Bourne's findings are representative of other types of combat soldiers is subject to question, since helicopter ambulance crews and Green Berets are highly self-selected volunteers for hazardous duty. Nevertheless, Bourne's study supports the conclusion that one of the most efficient techniques that allows soldiers generally to adjust to battle is to interpret combat not as a continued threat of personal injury or death but as a sequence of demands to be responded to by precise military performances. In failing to find significant physiological change (excretion of adrenal cortical steroids) occurring among most soldiers during life-threatening situations, Bourne suggests that the men allowed their behavior under stress to be modified by social and psychological influences, which significantly affected physiological responses to objective threats from the environment.

There is, however, the possibility of relatively long-lasting effects of stress from combat and other extreme situations, such as posttraumatic stress disorders consisting of intense feelings of demoralization, guilt, anger, active expression of hostility, and perceived hostility from others. Yet, for most people, the effects of stress resulting from exposure to extreme situations are usually temporary and disappear after a while. Many people are not emotionally affected at all, even though the circumstances are exceedingly stressful. There is also research showing that people who master a crisis benefit from the experience by feeling good about themselves afterward (Reynolds and Turner 2008). Consequently, as Bruce Dohrenwend (1975:384) once pointed out, if stressful situations play a major role in causing mental disturbance, the relevant events must be the more ordinary and frequent experiences in people's lives, such as marriage, birth of a first child, death of a loved one, loss of a job, and so on. Though such events are not extraordinary in a large population, they are extraordinary in the lives of the individuals who experience them.

Life Events

Life events research does not focus on one particular life event (e.g., exposure to combat) and claim that it is more stressful than another life event (e.g., unemployment). Rather, it is based on the assumption that the *accumulation* of several events in a person's life eventually builds up to a stressful impact. However, what types of events, in what combinations, over what periods of time, and under what circumstances promote stress-induced health problems is not at all clear at the present time.

For example, an important area of contention in life events research is the issue of whether any type of change in one's life, either pleasant or unpleasant, produces significant stress or whether stress is largely a result of unpleasant events only. Considerable evidence supports the idea that any type of environmental change that requires the individual to adapt can produce a specific stress response (Selye 1956). However, most research clearly comes down on the side of unpleasant events as being of prime importance (Thoits 1995, 2010). This is seen in research conducted in Puerto Rico many years ago by Lloyd Rogler and August Hollingshead (1965). They compared a matched set of 20 lower-class "well" families with 20 "sick" families (defined as having either the husband or wife or both diagnosed as schizophrenic). Based upon recall of life events by the subjects and others in the community, the study found no significant differences in the family lives of the normals and schizophrenics during childhood and adolescence. Members of both groups were exposed to the same conditions of poverty, family instability, and lower-class socialization. There was also a lack of difference in their respective adult lives, with the notable exception that for those persons who became schizophrenic, there was a recent and discernible period—*prior to the appearance of overt symptomatology*—during which they were engulfed by a series of insoluble and mutually reinforcing problems. Schizophrenia thus seemed to originate from being placed in an intolerable dilemma brought on by adverse life events, largely stemming from intense family and sexual conflicts related to unemployment and restricted life opportunities.

Robert Lauer (1974) investigated whether the rate or speed of change and the type of change, either positive or negative, were the most important variables in stress produced by change. Though stress was directly related to the perceived rate of change, his findings indicated that the effect of rapid change could be moderated by whether the change was perceived to be desirable. Rapid change and undesirability were the most stressful conditions. The undesirability of life events seems to predict distress better than change alone does (Mirowsky and Ross 2004). The effects of desirable events and change per se do not seem to be as stressful as the occurrence of undesirable events. For example, losing one's job is an undesirable life event that can have potentially harmful effects on a person's physical and mental well-being (Turner 1995). Reemployment, however, produces positive emotional effects, leading to the conclusion that the worst psychological effects of job loss can be minimized if opportunities exist for reemployment (Kessler, Turner, and House 1989).

When it comes to health in general, research by Allan McFarlane and his colleagues (1983) in Canada found that undesirable life events cause the most stress, which, in turn, causes poorer health. What determined the impact of life events on health was the perception of the nature of the change by the individual. Events considered to be undesirable and not controllable by the respondents were consistently followed by an increase in reports of distress, symptoms of illness, and physician visits. People may be particularly prone to seek out the services of a physician after experiencing a stressful life event.

Besides the type of change and the speed with which it occurs, the extent to which change affects a person's life may also be important. Libby Ruch (1977) investigated this nearly 40 years ago and suggested that life change actually has three dimensions: (1) the degree of change evoked; (2) the undesirability of change; and (3) the aspect of one's life that is affected (e.g., personal, occupational). But Ruch found that the degree of change is more significant than either desirability or the area of life affected. That is, the greater the change, the more likely stress will result. Although too much change may indeed be stressful, too little change in a person's life may also induce stress (Wildman and Johnson 1977).

Life events research entails serious challenges in accurately measuring the presumed relationship between stress and particular life experiences. One measure is the Social Readjustment Rating Scale developed by Thomas Holmes and Robert Rahe (1967). This scale is based on the assumption that change, no matter how good or bad, demands a certain degree of adjustment on the part of an individual—the greater the adjustment, the greater the stress. Holmes and Rahe carried their analysis one step further and suggested that changes in life events occur in a cumulative pattern that can eventually build to a stressful impact. Thus, the type of change does not matter so much. The extent to which the change disrupts normal patterns of life is important.

The Social Readjustment Rating Scale lists certain life events that are associated with varying amounts of disruption in the life of an average person. It was constructed by having hundreds of people of different social backgrounds rank the relative amount of adjustment accompanying a particular life experience. Death of a spouse is ranked highest, with a relative stress value of 100; divorce is second with a value of 73; marriage ranks seventh with a value of 50; retirement is tenth with a value of 45; taking a vacation is ranked forty-first with a value of 13; and so forth. Holmes and Rahe call each stress value a "life change" unit. They suggest that as the total value of life change units mounts, the probability of having a serious illness also increases, particularly if a person accumulates too many life change units in too short a time. If an individual accumulates 200 or more life change units within the period of a year, Holmes and Rahe believe such a person will risk a serious disorder.

Although once used extensively and found to measure stress and life events as well as or better than other scales, the Social Readjustment Rating Scale nevertheless contains some serious flaws. For example, the scale may not adequately account for differences in the relative importance of various life events among ethnic and cultural subgroups (Turner and Avison 2003). In other words, the scale measures the amount of change rather than the meaning of the event to the individual. Also some life events, such as divorce, may result from stress rather than cause it. This situation confounds the relationships being measured.

Another problem is that the scale does not account for intervening variables, such as social support from other people, which might modify the effects of stress for many individuals. While interaction with others can be stressful because of

PHOTO 5.3 The Holmes and Rahe Social Readjustment Rating Scale measures the stress associated with various life events, such as divorce.

personal conflicts, conflicting expectations, or excessive demands to achieve or maintain a certain level of performance, there is little doubt that supportive interpersonal influences help reduce stressful feelings. Life events that are successfully resolved may not be stressful. That is, it may be the case that mastery of an event provides a buffer to stress because successful resolution constitutes a personally meaningful positive experience. This situation may substantially counterbalance the stress associated with the event (Reynolds and Turner 2008).

Some research also maintains that chronic strain is a more negative influence on mental health than negative life events (Turner 2003, 2013; Turner and Avison 2003), which may be the case in some situations. However, as noted earlier, chronic strain can be intertwined with negative life events when the stress associated with those events is long-lasting. The stressful effects of marital separation or divorce, which are both negative life events, can indeed be a chronic strain centered around impaired long-term role relationships, particularly if separation from children is involved. Obviously, life events research is in need of more extensive development. The relationship between stress and life events as a precipitating factor in causing or contributing to the onset of physical and mental disorders is a highly complex phenomenon and not easily amenable to a simple cause-and-effect explanation.

Nevertheless, progress has been made in improving measures of stressful life events, and work in this regard continues today. Current findings indicate that those at the lower end of the socioeconomic ladder are particularly vulnerable to the emotional effects of undesirable life events (Lantz et al. 2005). People higher in the class structure may be better able to reduce their stress by taking vacations, obtaining professional help, changing jobs, etc. There may also be important differences between men and women, with men more likely to be distressed by work and finances and women by negative events in the family (Conger et al. 1993). Consequently, there is general recognition in the behavioral sciences that psychological distress is a negative influence on health and life events can indeed be distressful. Debate is no longer centered on whether life events are important in influencing health; rather, the focus is upon determining in which specific ways they are important.

Gene-Environment Interaction

A promising new area of research on stress in medical sociology is gene-environment interaction, investigating the sensitivity of genes to the environment and the environmental control of genetic expression. While it has long been known that stressful situations in a person's life can stimulate genetic predispositions toward mental and physical health problems, it is only been in the past decade or so—following completion of the Human Genome Project in 2003—that studies of gene-environment interaction have increased in medical sociology. Mapping all the genes in the human genome was one of the greatest scientific accomplishments in the modern era and allows researchers to locate specific disease-causing genes and formulate treatments. With respect to stress, an influential paper by Avshalom Caspi and colleagues (2003) determined that when the short allele (a variant or alternate form of a gene) of the 5-HTTLPR gene is affected by stressful environments, a person with one or more copies of it is more prone to depression than those who do not carry the short allele. Among people who had experienced four or more stressful life events, some 43 percent with two short alleles and 33 percent with one short allele developed a major depression. Persons with two long alleles, however, were more or less immune to genetic influences associated with stressful life events. The evidence of the link between a particular type of genetic variation and the social environment provided by this study led to more research in this area.

For example, Jonathan Daw and his colleagues (2013) found a relationship between the short allele in the 5HTTLPR gene, school smoking and drinking norms, and whether or not individuals smoked and drank alcohol. In this study the normative level of smoking and consuming alcohol in a school was the environmental variable. Other studies have examined the interaction between genes and the environment in relation to smoking (Boardman, Blalock, and Pampel 2010) and alcoholism (Pescosolido et al. 2008). While research on gene-environment interaction in medical sociology is still in its infancy and its characterization of the social environment needs to be expanded, this type of research is likely to become increasingly more common in future (Boardman, Daw, and Freese 2013).

A different but related area of research is the study of gene-environment correlations, which usually focus on the genetic control over exposure to the environment. Jason Schnittker (2010) investigated gene-environment correlations in relation to different sources of stress, including unemployment, discrimination, marital problems, poor neighborhood safety, and other unpleasant social situations. He found that such correlations differed according to the source of the stress and genetic influences were stronger for major episodes of depression than relatively mild depressive symptoms. This type of research helps identify areas in which genes do or do not matter in sociological studies of stress.

Summary

The study of the relationship between social factors and stress-related diseases has advanced significantly, but the precise nature of this link is not yet fully understood. It is clear from existing studies, however, that the experience of stress is a subjective response on the part of an individual as a result of exposure to certain social experiences and environments. Before an assessment can be made of the effect of stress upon an individual, it will be necessary to know: (1) the nature of the threat; (2) the social environment within which the threat appears; (3) the psychological style and personality of the individual involved; (4) the subjective definition of the threat by the individual; (5) the social influences acting upon the individual, particularly the social and psychological support offered by group membership; and (6) the duration of the threat. Obviously, stress research represents a complex investigative effort that has extended into studies of life events and gene-environment interaction. The potential contribution of such research to both the social and medical sciences is great. Stress research offers opportunities to learn more about disease processes, as well as the reactions of people to challenging situations.

Critical Thinking Questions

1. Define stress and explain how it affects the body.
2. What are social stressors? Name two of them and explain how they are interrelated.
3. In what ways are social situations stressful? Do ordinary life events cause stress, even those that are positive like weddings and vacations?

Suggested Readings

Aneshensel, Carola S., Jo C. Phelan, and Alex Bierman (eds.) (2013) *Handbook of the sociology of mental health*, 2nd ed. Dordrecht: Springer.
Contains revised chapters on the stress process with a focus on mental illness.
Boardman, Jason D., Jonathan Daw, and Jeremy Freese (2013) "Defining the environment in gene-environment research: Lessons from social epidemiology." *American Journal of Public Health* 103: S61-S72.
A sociological view of the environment in gene-environment interaction studies.

References

Angel, Ronald J., Michelle Frisco, Jacquelin L. Angel, and David Chiriboga (2003) "Financial strain and health among elderly Mexican-origin individuals." *Journal of Health and Social Behavior* 44: 536–51.
Antonovsky, Aaron (1979) *Health, stress, and coping*. San Francisco: Jossey-Bass.
Avison, William R., Jenifer Ali, and David Walters (2007) "Family structure, stress, and psychological distress: A demonstration of the impact of differential exposure." *Journal of Health and Social Behavior* 48: 301–17.
Avison, William R., and Stephanie S. Thomas (2010) "Stress," pp. 242–67 in *The new Blackwell companion to medical sociology*, W. Cockerham (ed.). Oxford, UK: Wiley-Blackwell.
Boardman, Jason D., Casey L. Blalock, and Fred C. Pampel (2010) "Trends in the genetic influences on smoking." *Journal of Health and Social Behavior* 51:108–23.
Boardman, Jason D., Jonathan Daw, and Jeremy Freese (2013) "Defining the environment in gene-environment research: Lessons from social epidemiology." *American Journal of Public Health* 103: S61-S72.
Bourdieu, Pierre (1986) "Forms of capital," pp. 241–58 in *Handbook of theory and research in education*, J. Richardson (ed.). New York: Greenwood.
——— (1993) *Sociology in question*, R. Nice (trans.). London: Sage.
Bourne, Peter (1970) *Men, stress, and Vietnam*. Boston: Little, Brown.
Brackbill, Robert M., Steven D. Stellman, Sharon E. Perlman, Deboraj J. Walker, and Mark R. Farfel (2013) "Mental health of those directly exposed to the World Trade Center disaster: Unmet mental health care need, mental health treatment service use, and quality of life." *Social Science and Medicine* 81: 110–14.
Bratter, Jennifer L., and Bridgert K. Gorman (2011) "Is discrimination an equal opportunity risk? Socioeconomic status and health status among blacks and whites." *Journal of Health and Social Behavior* 52: 365–82.
Brenner, M. Harvey (1973) *Mental illness and the economy*. Cambridge, MA: Harvard University Press.
——— (1987a) "Economic change, alcohol consumption and disease mortality in nine industrialized countries." *Social Science and Medicine* 25: 119–32.
——— (1987b) "Relation of economic change to Swedish health and social well-being, 1950–1980." *Social Science and Medicine* 25: 183–96.

Brown, Tyson H., Angela M. O'Rand, and Daniel E. Atkin (2012) "Race-ethnicity and health trajectories: Test of three hypotheses across multiple groups and health outcomes." *Journal of Health and Social Behavior* 53: 359–77.

Browning, Christopher R., and Kathleen A. Cagney (2002) "Neighborhood structural disadvantage, collective efficacy, and self-rated health in a physical setting." *Journal of Health and Social Behavior* 43: 383–99.

Burgard, Sarah A., Jennie E. Brand, and James S. House (2007) "Toward a better estimation of the effect of job loss on health." *Journal of Health and Social Behavior* 48: 369–84.

Burgard, Sarah A., and Jennifer A. Ailshire (2009) "Putting work to bed: Stressful experiences on the job and sleep quality." *Journal of Health and Social Behavior* 50: 476–92.

Cannon, Walter B. (1932) *The wisdom of the body.* New York: W. W. Norton.

Cao, Yue, Sean-Shong Hwang, and Juan Xi (2012) "Project-induced displacement, secondary stressors, and health." *Social Science and Medicine* 74: 1130–38.

Caspi, Avshalom, Karen Sugden, Terrie E. Moffitt, Alan Taylor, Ian W. Craig, HonaLee Harrington, Joseph McClay, Jonathan Mill, Judy Martin, Antony Braithwaite, Richie Poulton. (2003) "Influence of life stress on depression: Moderation by a polymorphism in the 5-HTT gene." *Science* 301: 386–89.

Cockerham, William C. (2014) *Sociology of mental disorder*, 9th ed. Upper Saddle River, NJ: Pearson Prentice Hall.

Cockerham, William C., Hiroyuki Hattori, and Yukio Yamori (2000) "The social gradient in life expectancy: The contrary case of Okinawa in Japan." *Social Science and Medicine* 51: 115–22.

Conger, Rand D., Frederick O. Lorenz, Glen H. Elder, Jr., Ronald L. Simons, and Xiaojia Ge (1993) "Husband and wife differences in response to undesirable life events." *Journal of Health and Social Behavior* 34: 71–88.

Cooley, Charles H. (1964) *Human nature and the social order.* New York: Schocken.

Das, Aniruddha (2013) "How does race get 'under the skin'?: Inflammation, weathering, and metabolic problems in late life." *Social Science and Medicine* 77: 75–83.

Daw, Jonathan, Michael Shanahan, Kathleen Mullan Harris, Andrew Smolen, Brett Haberstick, and Jason D. Boardman (2013) "Genetic sensitivity to peer behaviors: 5HTTLPR, smoking, and alcohol consumption." *Journal of Health and Social Behavior* 54: 92–108.

Dohrenwend, Bruce P. (1975) "Sociocultural and social-psychological factors in the genesis of mental disorders." *Journal of Health and Social Behavior* 16: 365–92.

Downey, Liam, and Marieke van Willigen (2005) "Environmental stressors: The mental health impacts of living near industrial activity." *Journal of Health and Social Behavior* 46: 289–305.

Drentea, Patricia (2000) "Age, debt, and anxiety." *Journal of Health and Social Behavior* 41: 437–50.

Drentea, Patricia, and John P. Reynolds (2012) "Neither a borrower nor lender be: The relative importance of debt and SES for mental health among older adults." *Journal of Aging and Health* 24: 673–95.

Drentea, Patricia, and Paul J. Lavrakas (2000) "Over the limit: The association among health, race, and debt." *Social Science and Medicine* 50: 517–29.

Durkheim, Emile (1950) *The rules of sociological method.* New York: The Free Press.

——— (1951) Suicide. New York: The Free Press.

——— (1956) *The division of labor in society.* New York: The Free Press.

Eitinger, L. (1964) *Concentration camp survivors in Norway and Israel.* London: Allen & Unwin.

——— (1973) "A follow-up of the Norwegian concentration camp survivors." *Israel Annals of Psychiatry and Related Disciplines* 11: 199–209.

Evans, Robert G. (1994) "Introduction," pp. 3–26 in *Why are some people healthy and others not? The determinants of the health of populations*, R. Evans, M. Barer, and T. Marmor (eds). New York: Aldine de Gruyter.

Evans, Robert G., Morris L. Barer, and Theodore R. Marmor (eds.) (1994) *Why are some people healthy and others not? The determinants of the health of populations*. New York: Aldine de Gruyter.

Frankenberg, Elizabeth, Jenna Nobles, and Cecep Sumantri (2012) "Community destruction and traumatic stress in post-tsunami Indonesia." *Journal of Health and Social Behavior* 53: 498–514.

Geronimus, Airline T., Margaret Hicken, Dayna Keene, and John Bound (2006) "Weathering and age patterns of allostatic load scores among blacks and whites in the United States." *American Journal of Public Health* 96: 826–33.

Goffman, Erving (1959) *The presentation of self in everyday life*. New York: Anchor.

Grollman, Eric Anthony (2012) "Multiple forms of perceived discrimination and health among adolescents and young adults." *Journal of Health and Social Behavior* 53: 199–214.

Gruenewald, Tara L., Arun S. Karlamangla, Perry Hu, Sharon Stein-Merkin, Carolyn Crandall, Brandon Koretz, and Teresa Seeman (2012) "History of socioeconomic disadvantage and allostatic load in later life." *Social Science and medicine* 74: 75–83.

Grzywacz, Joseph G., David M. Almeida, Shevaun D. Neupert, and Susan L. Ettner (2004) "Socioeconomic status and health: A micro-level analysis of exposure and vulnerability to daily stressors." *Journal of Health and Social Behavior* 45: 1–16.

Haines, Valerie A., Jeanne S. Hurlbert, and John J. Beggs (1996) "Exploring the determinants of support provision: Provider characteristics, personal networks, community contexts, and support following life events." *Journal of Health and Social Behavior* 37: 252–64.

Henretta, John C. (2007) "Early childbearing, marital status, and women's health and mortality after age 50." *Journal of Health and Social Behavior* 48: 254–66.

Holmes, T. H., and R. H. Rahe (1967) "The social readjustment rating scale." *Journal of Psychosomatic Research* 11: 213–25.

House, James S. (2002) "Understanding social factors and inequalities in health: 20th century progress and 21st century prospects." *Journal of Health and Social Behavior* 43: 125–42.

Hughes, Michael, K. Jill Kiecolt, and Verna A. Keith (2014) "How racial identity moderates the impact of financial stress on mental health among African Americans." *Society and Mental Health* 4:38–54.

Kahn, Joan R., and Leonard I. Pearlin (2006) "Financial strain over the life course and health among older adults." *Journal of Health and Social Behavior* 47: 17–31.

Kessler, Ronald C., J. Blake Turner, and James S. House (1989) "Unemployment, reemployment, and emotional functioning in a community sample." *American Sociological Review* 54: 648–57.

Knudsen, Hannah K., Paul M. Roman, J. Aaron Johnson, and Lori J. Ducharme (2005) "A changed America? The effects of September 11th on depressive symptoms and alcohol consumption." *Journal of Health and Social Behavior* 46: 260–73.

Lam, Jack, Wen Fan, and Phyllis Moen (2014) "Is insecurity worse for well-being in turbulent times? Mental health in context." *Society and Mental Health* 4: 55–73.

Lantz, Paula M., James S. House, Richard P. Mero, and David R. Williams (2005) "Stress, life events, and socioeconomic disparities in health: Results from the Americans' changing lives study." *Journal of Health and Social Behavior* 46: 274–88.

Lasker, J. N., B. P. Egolf, and S. Wolf (1994) "Community, social change, and mortality." *Social Science and Medicine* 39: 53–62.

Lauer, Robert (1974) "Rate of change and stress." *Social Forces* 52: 510–16.

Lin, Nan (2001) *Social capital: A theory of social structure and action*. Cambridge, UK: Cambridge University Press.

Lorenz, Frederick O., K. A. S. Wickrama, Rand D. Conger, and Glen H. Elder, Jr. (2006) "The short-term and decade long-term effects of divorce on women's mid-life health." *Journal of Health and Social Behavior* 47: 111–25.

Marchand, Alain, Andrée Demers, and Pierre Durand (2005) "Does work really cause distress? The contribution of occupational structure and work organization to the experience of psychological distress." *Social Science and Medicine* 61: 1–14.

Marmot, M. G. (2004) *The status syndrome.* New York: Times Books.

Marmot, M. G., George Davey Smith, Stephen Stansfeld, Chandra Patel, Fiona North, Jenny Head, Ian White, Eric Brunner, and Amanda Feeney (1991) "Health inequalities among British civil servants: The Whitehall II study." *Lancet* 337: 1387–92.

Marmot, M. G., M. J. Shipley, and Geoffrey Rose (1984) "Inequalities in death—Specific explanations of a general pattern." *Lancet* 83: 1003–6.

Massoglia, Michael (2008) "Incarceration as exposure: The prison, infectious disease, and other stress-related illnesses." *Journal of Health and Social Behavior* 49: 56–71.

McFarland, Michael J., and Mark D. Hayward (2014) "Poverty and awakening cortisol in adolescence: The importance of timing in early life." *Society and Mental Health* 4: 21–37.

McFarlane, Allan H., Geoffrey R. Norman, David L. Streiner, and Ranjan G. Roy (1983) "The process of social stress: Stable, reciprocal, and mediating relationships." *Journal of Health and Social Behavior* 24: 160–73.

McLeod, Jane D. (2012) "The meanings of stress: Expanding the stress process model." *Society and Mental Health* 2: 172–86.

Mead, George Herbert (1934) *Mind, self, and society.* Chicago: University of Chicago Press.

Mechanic, David (1962) *Students under stress: A study of the social psychology of adaptation.* New York: The Free Press.

—— (1978) *Medical sociology,* 2nd ed. New York: The Free Press.

Miller, Byron, Sunshine M. Rote, and Verna M. Keith (2013) "Coping with racial discrimination: Assessing the vulnerability of African Americans and the mediated moderation of psychosocial resources." *Society and Mental Health* 3:133–50.

Mirowsky, John, and Catherine E. Ross (2004) *Social causes of psychological distress,* 2nd ed. New York: Aldine de Gruyter.

Mohnen, Sigrid M., Peter P. Groenewegen, Beate Völker, and Henk Flap (2011) "Neighborhood social capital and individual health." *Social Science and Medicine* 72: 660–67.

Moskos, Charles C., Jr. (1970) *The American enlisted man.* New York: Russell Sage.

Moss, Gordon E. (1973) *Illness, immunity, and social interaction.* New York: Wiley.

Needham, Belinda L., Jose R. Fernandez, Jue Lin, Elissa S. Epel, and Elizabeth H. Blackburn (2012) "Socioeconomic status and cell aging in children." *Social Science and Medicine* 74: 1948–51.

Pavalko, Eliza K., Fang Gong, and J. Scott Long (2007) "Women's work, cohort change, and health." *Journal of Health and Social Behavior* 48: 352–68.

Pearlin, Leonard I. (1989) "The sociological study of stress." *Journal of Health and Social Behavior* 30: 241–56.

Pescosolido, Bernice A., Brea L. Perry, J. Scott Long, Jack K. Martin, John I. Nurnberger, Jr., and Victor Hesselbrock (2008) "Under the influence of genetics: How transdisciplinarity leads us to rethink social pathways to illness." *American Journal of Sociology* 114: S171–202.

Putnam, Robert (2000) *Bowling alone: The collapse and revival of American community.* New York: Simon and Schuster.

Reynolds, John R., and R. Jay Turner (2008) "Major life events: Their personal meaning, resolution, and mental health significance." *Journal of Health and Social Behavior* 49: k3rex 223–37.

Rogler, Lloyd H., and August B. Hollingshead (1965) *Trapped: Families and schizophrenia.* New York: Wiley.

Ruch, Libby O. (1977) "Multidimensional analysis of the concept of life change." *Journal of Health and Social Behavior* 18: 71–83.

Schieman, Scott, Yuko Kurashina Whitestone, and Karen van Gundy (2006) "The nature of work and the stress of higher status." *Journal of Health and Social behavior* 47: 242–57.

Schnittker, Jason (2010) "Gene-environment correlations in the stress-depression relationship." *Journal of Health and Social Behavior* 51: 229–43.

Schnittker, Jason, and Andrea John (2007) "Enduring stigma: The long-term effects of incarceration on health." *Journal of Health and Social Behavior* 48: 115–30.

Seeman, T., S. Merkin, E. Crimmins, B. Koretz, S. Charnette, and A. Karlamangia (2008) "Education, income, and ethnic differences in cumulative risk profiles in a national sample of U. S. adults: NHANES III (1988–1994)." *Social Science and Medicine* 66: 72–97.

Selye, Hans (1956) *The stress of life.* New York: McGraw-Hill.

Shuval, Judith T. (2005) "Migration, health, and stress," pp. 126–43 in *The Blackwell companion to medical sociology,* W. Cockerham (ed.). Oxford, UK: Blackwell.

Siegrist, Johannes (2010a) "Stress in the workplace," pp. 268–87 in *The new Blackwell companion to medical sociology,* W. Cockerham (ed.). Oxford, UK: Blackwell.

Siegrist, Johannes (2010b) "Effort-reward imbalance at work and cardiovascular disease." *International Journal of Occupational Medicine and Environmental Health* 23: 279-85.

Song, Lijun (2011) "Social capital and psychological distress." *Journal of Health and Social Behavior* 52: 478–92.

Song, Lijun, Joonmo Son, and Nan Lin (2010) "Social capital and health," pp. 184–210 in *The new Blackwell companion to medical sociology,* W. Cockerham (ed.). Oxford, UK: Wiley-Blackwell.

Tausig, Mark, and Rudy Fenwick (1999) "Recession and well-being." *Journal of Health and Social Behavior* 40: 1–16.

Thoits, Peggy A. (1995) "Stress, coping, and social support processes: Where are we? What next?" *Journal of Health and Social Behavior* 36(Extra issue): 53–79.

——— (2006) "Personal agency in the stress process." *Journal of Health and Social Behavior* 47: 309–23.

——— (2010) "Stress and health: Major findings and policy implications." *Journal of Health and Social Behavior* 51: S41–53.

——— (2011) "Mechanisms linking social ties and support to physical and mental health." *Journal of Health and Social Behavior* 52: 145–61.

——— (2013) "Self-identity, stress, and mental health," pp. 357–78 in *Handbook of the sociology of mental health,* 2nd ed., C. Aneshensel, J. Phelan, and A. Bierman (eds.). Dordrecht: Springer.

Tierney, Kathleen J., and Barbara Baisden (1979) *Crisis intervention programs for disaster victims: A source book and manual for smaller communities.* Rockville, MD: National Institute of Mental Health.

Turner, Bryan S. (2004) *The new medical sociology.* New York: W. W. Norton.

Turner, J. Blake (1995) "Economic context and the health effects of unemployment." *Journal of Health and Social Behavior* 36: 213–29.

Turner, J. Blake and R. Jay Turner (2013) "Social relations, social integration, and social support," pp. 341–56 in *Handbook of the sociology of mental health,* 2nd ed., C. Aneshensel, J. Phelan, and A. Bierman (eds.). Dordrecht: Springer.

Turner, R. Jay (2003) "The pursuit of socially modifiable contingencies in mental health." *Journal of Health and Social Behavior* 44: 1–17.

——— (2013) "Understanding health disparities: The relevance of the stress process model." *Society and Mental Health* 3: 170–86.

Turner, R. Jay, and William R. Avison (2003) "Status variations in stress exposure: Implications for the interpretation of research on race, socioeconomic status, and gender." *Journal of Health and Social Behavior* 44: 488–505.

Umberson, Debra, Kristi Williams, Daniel A. Powers, Hui Liu, and Belinda Needham (2006) "You make me sick: Marital quality and health over the life course." *Journal of Health and Social Behavior* 47: 1–16.

Volkart, E. H. (ed.) (1951) *Social behavior and personality.* New York: Social Science Research Council.

Wade, Terrance J., and David J. Prevalin (2004) "Marital transitions and mental health." *Journal of Health and Social Behavior* 45: 155–70.

Wildman, Richard C., and David Richard Johnson (1977) "Life change and Langner's 22-item mental health index: A study and partial replication." *Journal of Health and Social Behavior* 18: 179–88.

Williams, David R. (2012) "Miles to go before we sleep: Racial inequities in health." *Journal of Health and Social Behavior* 53: 279–95.

Williams, David R., and Selina A. Mohammed (2009) "Discrimination and racial disparities in health: Evidence and needed research." *Journal of Behavioral Medicine* 32: 20–47.

Williams, Kristi, and Debra Umberson (2004) "Marital status, marital transitions, and health: A gendered life course perspective." *Journal of Health and Social Behavior* 45: 81–98.

Young, Wendy B., and Steven L. Foy (2013) "The influence of meaning-making after spousal loss on trajectories of psychological distress." *Society and Mental Health* 3: 187–202.

CHAPTER 6

Health Behavior and Lifestyles

Before discussing the behavior of people who feel sick and are in need of medical treatment, we will examine the behavior of healthy people who try to remain that way. This is a major area of investigation in medical sociology, because health-oriented behavior does not pertain just to those activities concerned with recovering from disease or injury. It also involves the kinds of things that healthy people do to stay healthy and prevent health afflictions. Living a healthy lifestyle and maintaining one's own health in the process is a common component of daily life for many people. Consequently, medical sociologists divide health-oriented behavior into two general categories: health behavior and illness behavior.

Illness behavior is the activity undertaken by a person who feels ill for the purpose of defining that illness and seeking relief from it (Kasl and Cobb 1966). Health behavior, in contrast, is defined as the activity undertaken by individuals for the purpose of maintaining or enhancing their health, preventing health problems, or achieving a positive body image (Cockerham 2000). This definition of health behavior does not limit participation to healthy people trying to stay healthy. Instead, it includes people in good health, as well as the physically handicapped and persons with chronic illnesses such as diabetes and heart disease, who seek to control or contain their affliction through diet, exercise, and other positive forms of health behavior. It also includes persons who are motivated to look and feel good, rather than only be healthy. For example, we know from past studies that the health goals of some people are focused on enhancing their bodily appearance and physical condition to appear attractive and successful or to create an optimal self, not just be free of illness (Brooks 2010; Fishman, Settersten, and Flatt 2009; Kinnunen 2010). For most people, however, their health behavior is primarily intended to maintain their health and prolong their lives (Cockerham 2013b). Yet regardless of the underlying motivation, it is clear that health-promoting behavior and lifestyles are commonplace in advanced societies, as seen in the reduction in heart disease, declines in smoking, and increased life expectancy.

In this chapter, we will review the research pertaining to health behavior and lifestyles. The focus in medical sociology is not on the health behavior of a particular individual, but on the transformation of this behavior into its collective form—health lifestyles that characterize the health practices of particular groups and social classes. The first part of the discussion will focus on the health lifestyles that people pursue on their own, more or less independently of the medical profession. The second part will review the health behavior of people that places them in direct contact with physicians and other health personnel for preventive care intended to maintain their health and reduce the future risk of illness.

Health Lifestyles

Health lifestyles are collective patterns of health-related behavior based on choices from options available to people according to their life chances. A person's life chances are largely determined by his or her class position that either enables or constrains health lifestyle choices. The behaviors that are generated from these choices can have either positive or negative consequences on body and mind but nonetheless form an overall pattern of health practices that constitute a lifestyle. Health lifestyles include contact with medical professionals for checkups and preventive care, but the majority of activities take place outside the health care delivery system. These activities typically consist of choices and practices, influenced by the individual's probabilities for realizing them, that range from brushing one's teeth and using automobile seat belts to relaxing at health spas. For most people, health lifestyles involve daily decisions about food, exercise, relaxation, personal hygiene, risk of accidents, coping with stress, smoking, alcohol and drug use, as well as having physical checkups.

According to the World Health Organization (WHO 1986), significant improvements in health in the nineteenth century were brought about by what might be called "engineering methods"—the building of safe water supplies and sewers and the production of cheap food for urban areas through the use of mechanized agriculture. These methods continue to improve the health of people in underdeveloped areas of the world. The first 60 years of the twentieth century was the "medical era," in which the dominant approach to health was mass vaccination and the extensive use of antibiotics to combat infection. WHO suggests that in the present period of history, advanced societies are entering into a "postmedical era" in which physical well-being is largely undermined by social and environmental factors. These factors include certain types of individual behavior (e.g., smoking, overeating), failures of social organization (e.g., loneliness), economic factors (e.g., poverty), and the physical environment (e.g., pollution) that are not amenable to direct improvement by medicine. WHO (1986:117) concludes: "Whereas in the 'medical era' health policy has been concerned mainly with how medical care is to be provided and paid for, in the new 'post-medical' era it will focus on the attainment of good health and well-being."

And that is essentially what is happening today as the role of health lifestyles in improving the health of people in a postmedical situation is gaining in significance. Robert Crawford (1984) helps us to understand why this is the case. First, as Crawford points out, there has been a growing recognition among the general public that the major disease patterns have changed from acute or infectious illnesses to chronic diseases—such as heart disease, cancer, and diabetes—that medicine cannot cure. Second, numerous health problems, such as AIDS and cigarette-induced lung cancer, are caused by particular styles of living. Third, there has been a virtual campaign by the mass media and health care providers emphasizing lifestyle change and individual responsibility for health. The result has been a growing awareness that medicine is no longer the automatic answer to dealing with all threats to one's health. Therefore, strategies on the part of individuals to adopt a healthier lifestyle have gained in popularity. As Crawford explains, when threats to health persist in the environment and medicine cannot provide a cure, self-control over the range of personal behaviors that affect health is the only remaining option. This means the person will be confronted with the decision to acquire or maintain a healthy lifestyle or disregard the situation and perhaps be at greater risk for poor health.

Weber: Lifestyles

Before discussing health lifestyles, it is useful to review the work of German sociologist Max Weber (1864–1920). Weber is one of the most influential sociological theorists of all time, and his views on lifestyles in general help place the concept of a "health lifestyle" in perspective. Weber's notion of lifestyles appears in his discussion of status groups in his classic work *Economy and Society* (1978), originally published in 1922. Karl Marx had earlier suggested that a person's social class position is determined exclusively by his or her degree of access to a society's means of production. In other words, Marx claimed that one's location in a class structure results strictly from how much of society's goods and services that person is able to command. However, in Weber's view, Marx's concept of class is not the whole story in determining someone's social rank; rather, as discussed in Chapter 3, status (prestige) and power (political influence) are also important. Weber focused primarily on the difference between class and status in his analysis. He pointed out that while class was an objective dimension of social life signified by how much money and property a person has, status was subjective in that it consists of the amount of esteem a person is accorded by other people. Typically, a person's occupation, income, and level of education are the basis of such esteem.

A status group (or more popularly, a social class) refers to people who share similar material circumstances, prestige, education, and political influence. Moreover, members of the same status group share a similar lifestyle. In fact, a particular lifestyle is what distinguishes one status group from another. People with high socioeconomic status clearly lead a different style of life than those at the bottom of society and those somewhere in the middle. Weber also made the pertinent observation that lifestyles are not based upon what one produces but upon what one consumes. That is, one's lifestyle is a reflection of the types and amounts of goods and services one uses or consumes. Thus, for Weber, the difference between status groups does not lie in their relationship to the means of production as suggested by Marx but in their relationship to the means of consumption.

This view applies to health lifestyles because when someone pursues a healthy style of life, that person is attempting to produce good health according to his or her degree of motivation, effort, and capabilities. Yet the aim of this activity, as Weber's insight suggests, is ultimately one of consumption. People attempt to maintain or enhance their health to use it for some purpose, such as a longer life, work, sexual attractiveness, or enhanced enjoyment of their physical being. Alphonse d'Houtaud and Mark Field (1984) found in a study in France many years ago that health was conceptualized as something to be cultivated for increased vitality and enjoyment of life among the upper and middle classes and for the ability to continue to work among lower-class persons. The lower class viewed health largely as a means to an end (work), while persons with higher socioeconomic status regarded health as an end in itself (vitality and enjoyment). In both situations, health was something that was to be consumed, not simply produced. Furthermore, in producing a healthy lifestyle, the individual often *consumes* various goods and services, such as athletic clothing and equipment, healthy food and drink, vitamins, possibly sport club memberships, vacations for rest and relaxation, and the like.

Crawford (1984) suggests that health has indeed become a metaphor for consumption. That is, good health is a form of release in that it provides a person with the freedom to consume to satisfy personal needs. Furthermore, Crawford claims that the abundance of news and commentary in the media on lifestyles and health has reduced complacency about staying healthy. He notes that the media has declared health and fitness activity to be a lifestyle in itself. An important response to this situation is the virtual flood of commercial products (running shoes, workout clothes, exercise machines, health foods, and so on) to help the individual "manufacture" health. As Crawford (1984:76) points out, "the complex ideologies of health are picked up, magnified, and given commodity form by the image-makers." Commercial products associated with fitness not only produce profits, but they also reinforce the general idea that health and fitness constitute a practical goal to be achieved through the use of these products.

Weber did not ignore the socioeconomic conditions necessary for a specific lifestyle. Weber deliberately used three distinct terms to express his view of lifestyles: *Lebensstil* (lifestyle), *Lebensführung* (life conduct), and *Lebenschancen* (life chances). As shown in Figure 6.1, *Lebensführung* and *Lebenschancen* are the two components of *Lebensstil* (Abel and Cockerham 1993; Cockerham, Abel, and Lüschen 1993). *Lebensführung*, or life conduct, refers to the choices that people have in the lifestyles they wish to adopt, but the potential for realizing these choices is influenced by their *Lebenschancen*, or life chances. Ralf Dahrendorf (1979:73) notes that Weber is ambiguous about what he really means by *life chances*, but the best interpretation he found is that life chances are the "probability of finding satisfaction for interests, wants, and needs." For Weber, the notion of life chances therefore refers to the probability of acquiring a particular lifestyle, which means the person must have the financial resources, status, rights, and social relationships that support the chosen lifestyle. One's life chances are shaped by one's socioeconomic circumstances.

Of course, the life chances that enhance participation in a healthy lifestyle are greatest among upper and middle socioeconomic groups who have the best resources to support their lifestyle choices. Yet, it was Weber's contention that lifestyles frequently spread beyond the groups in which they originate (Bendix 1960).

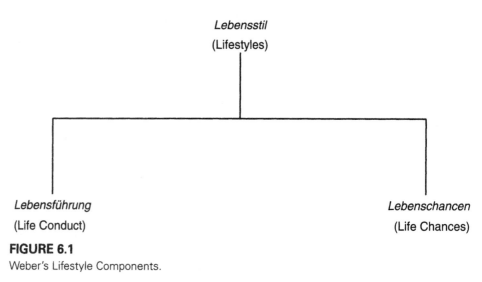

Lebensstil
(Lifestyles)

Lebensführung
(Life Conduct)

Lebenschancen
(Life Chances)

FIGURE 6.1
Weber's Lifestyle Components.

A good example is the spread of the Protestant ethic (a lifestyle emphasizing thrift, effort, and the value of work as a good in itself) into the general culture of Western society. One result is that, in the modern world, the Protestant ethic is no longer distinctive to Protestants, or the West. While lifestyles set people apart, Weber suggests that lifestyles can also spread across society. And there is evidence that health lifestyles—emphasizing exercise, sports, a healthy diet, avoidance of unhealthy practices such as smoking, and so on, which had their origin in the upper middle class—spread across class boundaries in Western society (Cockerham 2013a). Most people try to do at least something (even if it is just eating sensibly, not smoking, getting enough sleep, or relaxing) to protect their health.

Weber's ideas about lifestyles are important for several reasons. First, as discussed in Chapter 3, his work led to the development of the concept of "socioeconomic status," or SES in sociology, as the most accurate reflection of a person's social class position. The location of a person in the social hierarchy of society is determined not by income alone but typically by a combination of three indicators: income, education, and occupational status. Second, lifestyle is a reflection of a person's status in society, and lifestyles are based on what people consume rather than what they produce. Third, lifestyles are based upon choices, but these choices are dependent upon the individual's potential for realizing them. And this potential is usually determined by the person's socioeconomic circumstances. Fourth, although particular lifestyles characterize particular socioeconomic groups, some lifestyles spread across class boundaries and gain influence in the wider society.

Therefore, when it comes to health lifestyles, Weber's work suggests that, while such lifestyles are oriented toward producing health, the aim of the activity is ultimately toward its consumption as people try to be healthy so they can use their health to live longer, enjoy life, be able to keep on working, and so forth. Furthermore, while health lifestyles seem to be most characteristic of the upper and middle classes, the potential exists for them to spread across social boundaries. The quality of participation may differ significantly, but the level of participation in advanced societies may be spreading nonetheless. Regardless of one's particular socioeconomic position, an important feature of modern society appears to be the tendency for many people to adopt a healthy lifestyle within the limits of their circumstances and opportunities.

Of all the socioeconomic groups, however, the poor are especially disadvantaged in relation to positive health lifestyles. As K. A. S. Wickrama and his associates (1999:260) explain, "socially disadvantaged individuals have less access to health information and resources; they have less control over sleeping hours, and food choices; and they are more likely to live in a social environment where unhealthy eating, smoking and heavy drinking are normality, making the formation of risky lifestyles more probable." As one low-income diabetic woman told by a physician to avoid eating sweets put it:

> "Listen, if I want to eat a piece of cake, I'm going to eat it," she said. "No doctor can tell me what to eat. I'm going to eat, because I'm hungry. We got too much to worry about. We got to worry about tomorrow. We got to worry about the rent. We got to worry about our jobs. I'm not going to worry about a piece of cake." (Kleinfield 2006:A20)

Among the behavioral practices affecting health, for example, smoking cigarettes and cigars has the largest number of adverse consequences. Heart disease, stroke, atherosclerosis, and respiratory diseases, along with lung, throat, and other cancers, are all directly associated with smoking. The poor show the highest proportion of smokers followed (in descending order) by the near-poor, middle-income groups, and high-income groups. About twice the proportion of poor persons smoke compared to persons with high incomes. As Fred Pampel (2009:526) explains, "the problem of tobacco use has special relevance to low socioeconomic status groups."

A seminal study of the relationship between social class and lifestyles is that of French sociologist Pierre Bourdieu, reported in his book *Distinction* (1984). Bourdieu investigated class competition and reproduction as expressed in cultural tastes, styles, and practices. He analyzed eating habits and sports preferences that described how a *habitus,* or class-related set of durable dispositions to act in particular ways, shaped health lifestyles. The dispositions generated by the habitus produce lifestyle practices for individuals that are similar to those of other people in their social class and distinctive from people in other classes. Persons from the same class tend to share the same habitus because they typically have similar upbringing (socialization) and experiences in life. They are socialized to prefer their lifestyle preferences over those of other classes. For example, Bourdieu found that the French working class enjoyed soccer, while people in the professions (upper middle class) liked tennis and sailing. As for food, the working class typically favored foods that were cheap, nutritious, and abundant, while professional people were more concerned about body image and opted for foods that were light, tasty, and low in calories.

Bourdieu formulated the notion of "distance from necessity" that is a key explanation of class differences in lifestyles. He found that the more distant a person is from having to obtain economic necessity, the more freedom and time that person has to develop and refine personal tastes in line with a more privileged class status. Lower social strata, in turn, tend to adopt the tastes consistent with their class position, in which acquiring items of necessity such as food and shelter is paramount. Thus, the lower class prefers abundant, cheap beers to expensive wines, bulky meals that are filling instead of lighter foods, and so on.

Although socioeconomic status is the most important factor in lifestyle selection and participation, it is not the sole determinant of lifestyles. Since Weber's time, other research has shown that more is involved in lifestyle selection than social class, and this generalization is particularly true of health lifestyles (Frohlich and Abel 2014; Veenstra and Burnett 2014). What is suggested by these findings is that any concept of health lifestyles needs to go beyond socioeconomic status and consider other variables that also influence health practices such as age and gender.

A Theory of Health Lifestyles

Drawing upon the theoretical perspectives of Weber and Bourdieu, the author (Cockerham 2005, 2010; 2013a, 2013b) formulated an initial theory of health lifestyles, encompassing a broad range of relevant variables. Beginning with Box 1, the top box in Figure 6.2, four categories of social structural variables are listed that shape health lifestyles: (1) class circumstances; (2) age, gender, and race/ethnicity; (3) collectivities; and (4) living conditions. The first category is class circumstances,

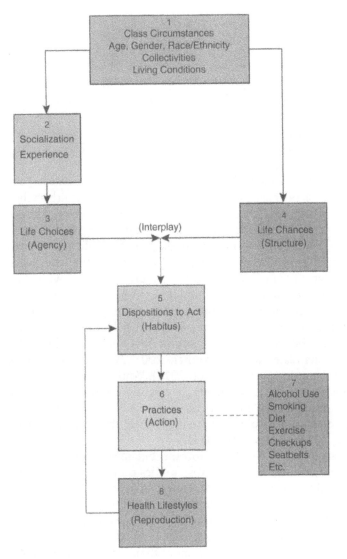

FIGURE 6.2

A Theory of Health Lifestyles.

which has the most decisive influence on lifestyle forms (Cockerham 2013a, 2013b; Jones et al. 2011; Petev 2013). The lifestyles of the upper and upper-middle classes are the healthiest and those of the lower class the least healthy. Virtually every study confirms this in every country where such research has taken place. These classes have healthier diets, little smoking, less problem drinking, more leisure-time exercise, utilize preventive care more frequently, greater opportunities for rest, relaxation, and coping with stress, and make healthy changes in their behavior much more rapidly when diagnosed with a health problem (Antunes 2011; Guptil, Copelton, and Lucal 2013; Jones et al. 2011; Margolis 2013; Pampel 2013; Pechey et al. 2013; Saint Onge and Krueger 2011).

For example, Rachel Pechy et al. (2013) found in their study of 25,000 British households that food purchasing in the lower class was characterized by less energy from healthier food categories and more energy from less healthy products, namely sweet snacks and puddings, processed potatoes, and low-fiber bread products. The extent of the differences was more widespread than reported in previous studies. As for smoking cigarettes, Pampel (2009) found in the United States that it was becoming a lower class characteristic, as did Martin Jarvis and Jane Wardle (1999) earlier in Britain. Other studies of health-promoting leisure-time exercise in American society note the class differences in participation as well, with higher SES groups the most active (Grzywacz and Marks 2001; Saint Onge and Krueger 2011).

As for the second category in Box 1, that of age, gender, and race/ethnicity, age affects health lifestyles because people tend to take better care of their health as they grow older. They do this by showing more careful food selection, more relaxation, and either abstinence or reduced use of tobacco and alcohol. Exercise, however, tends to decline with age. Yet despite a tendency among older people generally to live more healthily, Ian Rees Jones and his colleagues (2011) found that the health lifestyles of men entering later life in Britain remain strongly associated with class position. That is, class-based health lifestyles in middle age become "locked-in" by old age. Gender is highly significant in that women eat more healthy foods, smoke less, visit doctors more often for preventive care, wear seat belts more frequently when they drive, and with the exception of exercise have more healthier lifestyles overall than men (Annandale 2010; Cockerham 2005, 2010, 2013a, 2013b; Grzywacz and Marks 2001; Springer and Mouzon 2011). While both age and gender have important explanatory power, social class exercises a powerful influence on age and gender, since adults on the higher rungs of the social ladder have more healthier lifestyles, regardless of how old they are or whether they are male or female (Cockerham 2013a, 2013b; Jones et al. 2011).

Race and ethnicity are presumed to be important, but there is little research showing the extent to which this is the case. Most studies on race address differences in sickness and mortality rather than health lifestyle practices. There are some exceptions, however. Non-Hispanic whites in the United States tend to have healthier diets than non-Hispanic blacks (Hattery and Smith 2011) and exercise more than blacks and Hispanics (Grzywacz and Marks 2001; Saint Onge and Krueger 2011), but whites, in turn, also smoke and drink more than blacks and Hispanics (Cockerham 2006; Pampel 2009)—so racial data on health lifestyle practices show mixed outcomes. There is strong evidence that racial disparities in health are largely but not exclusively determined by class position in that racial minorities are over-represented in disadvantaged socioeconomic circumstances (Bradby and Nazroo 2010; Karlsen and Nazroo 2002).

The next category in Box 1 is collectivities. Collectivities are groups of people linked through particular relationships, such as kinship, work, religion, and politics. Their shared norms, values, ideals, and social perspectives reflect a particular collective viewpoint capable of influencing the health lifestyles of their members. Religion is a prime example of such a collectivity. Several studies suggest that religious attitudes and behaviors have a positive effect on numerous health-related activities (Idler 2010; Hill et al. 2007; Musick, House, and Williams 2004). These include prohibitions on smoking, drinking, and multiple sexual relationships and

PHOTO 6.2 Exercise is one of the most important components of a positive health lifestyle.

the promotion of nutrition, hygiene, and exercise. Living conditions are a category of structural variables in Box 1 pertaining to differences in the quality of housing and access to basic utilities (i.e., electricity, gas, heating, sewers, indoor plumbing, safe piped water), neighborhood facilities (i.e., grocery stores, parks, recreation), and personal safety. To date there has been little research linking living conditions to health lifestyles, but the connection is important. Mildred Blaxter (1990) found, in her nationwide British survey, that the conditions within which a person lives can have either a positive or a negative impact on implementing a healthy lifestyle.

Class circumstances and the other structural variables shown in Box 1 provide the social context for socialization and experience, as depicted by the arrow leading to Box 2. While primary socialization is the imposition of society's norms and values on the individual usually by family members and secondary socialization results from later (adult) training, experience is the learned outcome of day-to-day activities that occurs through social interaction and the practical exercise of agency. In sociology, *agency* is a term referring to the process by which people critically evaluate and choose their course of action. Experience provides the essential basis for agency's practical and evaluative dimensions to evolve over time as people learn from what they do. Figure 6.2 shows that socialization and experience (Box 2) provides the basis for making life choices (agency) in Box 3. As previously noted, the term *life choices* was introduced by Weber and refers to the self-direction of one's behavior.

The structural categories listed in Box 1 comprise a person's life chances, as shown in Box 4. Life chances represent structure in a Weberian context. Weber's thesis is that a person's life chances are socially determined and an individual's social structure is the arrangement of those chances. The arrows in Figure 6.2 indicate the interplay between life choices (Box 3) and life chances (Box 4). Choices and chances interact to determine a person's health lifestyle, as life chances either enable or constrain the choices made. Figure 6.2 shows that the interaction between life choices and life chances produces dispositions toward particular forms of action (Box 5). These dispositions constitute a "habitus" as suggested by Bourdieu. As noted, *habitus* is a term used to indicate a person's habitual outlook on the world, what some might call a "cognitive map" or set of perceptions that routinely guides and evaluates choices and options. The dispositions toward action provided by the habitus tend to be compatible with the behavioral guidelines set by the wider society. Therefore, usual and practical modes of behaving—not unpredictable novelty—typically occur.

Dispositions to act (Box 5) produce practices (action) that are represented in Box 6. Common practices measured in studies of health lifestyles are shown in Box 7. The practices may be either positive or negative but nonetheless comprise a person's overall pattern of health lifestyles, as represented in Box 8. Action or inaction, with respect to a particular health practice, leads to its reproduction, modification, or nullification by the habitus through a feedback process. This is seen in Figure 6.2 by the arrow showing movement from Box 8 back to Box 5. This is consistent with Bourdieu's assertion that when dispositions are acted upon they tend to reproduce or modify the habitus from which they are derived. Overall, this theory is an initial representation of the health lifestyle phenomenon and is intended to display how social structures influence individual participation in such lifestyles.

Health Lifestyles: A Final Note on the Influence of Social Class

In past historical periods, people seem to have taken their health more or less for granted (Crawford 1984). That is, a person was either healthy or unhealthy and that was simply the way life had turned out. In contemporary society, health has become an achievement—something people are supposed to work toward having by personally making an effort to maintain or improve it. This observation does not mean that everyone is trying to live in a healthy manner, but many people are, and they include persons in all social strata. However, the quality of participation is likely to be severely affected by class position and that position in the case of lower

BOX 6.1

The Healthiest States

Trying to lead a healthy lifestyle? According to the Government Guide (www.americashealthrankings .org), where you live makes a difference. The healthiest state in 2013 was Hawaii, followed by Vermont. The least healthy was Mississippi. The state rankings are based on 24 factors: percentage of current smokers, percentage of binge drinkers, drug-related deaths rate, percentage of obese adults, percentage of adults who report doing no physical activity/exercise, percentage of incoming 9th graders who graduate high school in 4 years, violent crime rate, occupational fatality rate, percentage of children under 18 living in poverty, incidence scores for infectious diseases (like chlamydia), average exposure to particulate matter of 2.5 microns or less (i.e., air pollution), percentage of population without health insurance, amount of public health funding, percentage of children receiving recommended immunizations, percentage of adolescents who receive recommended immunizations, percentage of infants born with low birthweight, number of primary care physicians per 100,000 population, number of dentists per 100,000 population, and discharge rate related to preventable hospitalizations. State rankings for 2013 and 2012 are shown as follows:

2013 Rank	State	2012 Rank	Change	2013 Rank	State	2012 Rank	Change
1	Hawaii	1	—	22	South Dakota	23	1
2	Vermont	2	—	23	Montana	28	5
3	Minnesota	3	—	24	Maryland	20	−4
4	Massachusetts	4	—	25	Alaska	24	−1
5	New Hampshire	5	—	26	Virginia	22	−4
6	Utah	6	—	27	Kansas	27	—
7	Connecticut	7	—	28	Arizona	26	−2
8	Colorado	9	1	29	Pennsylvania	29	—
9	North Dakota	8	−1	30	Illinois	30	—
10	New Jersey	10	—	31	Delaware	32	1
11	Nebraska	11	—	32	New Mexico	36	4
12	Idaho	19	7	33	Florida	31	−2
13	Oregon	14	1	34	Michigan	33	−1
14	Washington	12	−2	35	North Carolina	34	−1
15	New York	18	3	36	Texas	35	−1
16	Maine	15	−1	37	Nevada	37	—
17	Wyoming	25	8	38	Georgia	39	1
18	Iowa	17	−1	39	Missouri	40	1
19	Rhode Island	16	−3	40	Ohio	38	−2
20	Wisconsin	13	−7	41	Indiana	41	—
21	California	21	—	42	Tennessee	42	—

2013 Rank	State	2012 Rank	Change	2013 Rank	State	2012 Rank	Change
43	South Carolina	44	1	47	Alabama	45	−2
44	Oklahoma	46	2	48	Louisiana	49	1
45	Kentucky	43	−2	49	Arkansas	48	−1
46	West Virginia	47	1	50	Mississippi	50	—

social strata can preclude or undermine health lifestyle practices. It is much harder to live healthily in unhealthy living conditions. Affluent people can command the best resources in dieting and exercise and find it easier to give up smoking, since cigarette use, as noted previously, is less common in the upper and upper-middle classes. Moderate drinking, routine physical exams, and preventive care by physicians are also more prevalent. And day-to-day living conditions at home and work are likely to have fewer health risks.

Moreover, people in higher social classes have experienced greater life chances and acquired a stronger sense of control over life situations than individuals in the classes below them (Mirowsky and Ross 2003; Savage, Dumas, and Stuart 2013). A major outcome of these cumulative experiences and the perceptions associated with them is that planning and effort typically produce the desired result. While many lower-class people may try to live a healthy lifestyle, others may be less likely to expect that their efforts to maintain their health will be successful and be either passive or less active than the classes above them in practicing good health habits. When disadvantaged life changes reduce the opportunities for positive health behaviors and lifestyles or reduce their effectiveness, the impact of agency or choice on the part of individuals is minimized. Consequently, class more than just matters when it comes to health lifestyles; it remains the dominant variable.

Preventive Care

As noted earlier in this chapter, health lifestyles generally take place outside of the formal health care delivery system, as people pursue their everyday lives in their usual social environment. However, an important facet of health behavior includes contact by healthy people with physicians and other health personnel for preventive care. Preventive care refers to routine physical examinations, immunizations, prenatal care, dental checkups, screening for heart disease, cancer, and other potential afflictions, and other services intended to ensure good health and prevent disease—or minimize the effects of illness if it occurs.

While there is evidence that participation in health lifestyles that do not involve contact with physicians and other health personnel can spread across social class boundaries, there is other evidence showing that the poor remain least likely to use preventive care (Snead and Cockerham 2002). Low-income women receive less prenatal care, low-income children are significantly more likely to have never had

PHOTO 6.3 Heavy drinking and smoking are highly negative health lifestyle practices because they are addictive and promote heart disease, cancer, and several other serious threats to good health.

a routine physical examination, and other measures such as dental care, breast examinations, and childhood immunizations are considerably less common among the poor. The reason for this situation is that many low-income persons do not have a regular source of medical care, health facilities may not be near at hand, and costs not covered by health insurance may have to be paid out of the individual's own pocket—and this factor can be a significant barrier in visiting the doctor when one feels well. Moreover, for people without any health insurance, going to the doctor for preventive care may be an unaffordable luxury.

The underutilization of preventive care among the poor is common, not just in the United States but also in several European countries, where the lower class has been found to use preventive medical and dental services significantly less frequently

(Lahelma 2010). Consequently, it can be argued that preventive care is a behavior pattern most characteristic of the upper and middle classes in advanced societies. When explanations are sought for the significant disparity in health and life expectancy between the affluent and the poor in the world today, the conditions of living associated with poverty and the lack of preventive care among the lower classes are major factors.

Summary

Health behavior is the activity undertaken by individuals for the purpose of maintaining or enhancing their health, preventing health problems, or achieving a positive body image. Health lifestyles, in turn, are collective ways of living that promote good health and longer life expectancy. Health lifestyles include contact with physicians and other health personnel, but the majority of activities take place outside of formal health care delivery systems. These activities include a proper diet, weight control, exercise, rest and relaxation, and the avoidance of stress and alcohol and drug abuse.

Max Weber, one of the most important theorists in the history of sociological thought, analyzed the general role of lifestyles in society and found that while particular socioeconomic status groups are characterized by their own lifestyles, some lifestyles spread across social boundaries. This is the case with health lifestyles that are now common throughout society—although the quality of participation undoubtedly declines the lower a person's location in a class structure. Weber also observed that lifestyles are based on what people consume rather than what they produce. And, while health lifestyles help produce good health, the aim of such lifestyles is ultimately one of consumption as health is used to avoid disease, live longer, feel better, work, or have a pleasing physical appearance.

The work of Weber and Bourdieu contributes to a model of health lifestyles formulated by the author. This model shows how particular structural variables influence health lifestyle choices, with class circumstances depicted as an especially strong variable. Another important facet of health behavior is preventive care that involves contact by healthy people with health care providers. Preventive care consists of routine physical examinations, dental care, screening for various diseases, immunizations, and so on, intended to prevent or reduce the chance of illness or minimize its effects. Throughout the world, it appears that lower-class persons are significantly less likely to receive preventive care.

Critical Thinking Questions

1. Compare a health behavior to a health lifestyle. What is the difference?
2. Weber and Bourdieu have both contributed theoretical insights to our general understanding of lifestyles. How are these insights incorporated into Cockerham's model of health lifestyles?

Suggested Readings

Brandt, Allan M. (2007) *The cigarette century: The rise, fall, and deadly persistence of the product that defined America*: New York: Basic Books.

A history of the role of the cigarette in American culture.

Cockerham, William C. (2013) *Social causes of health and disease*, 2nd ed. Cambridge, UK: Polity.

Provides an updated account of the relationship between class and health lifestyles.

References

Abel, Thomas, and William C. Cockerham (1993) "Lifestyle or lebensführung? Critical remarks on the mistranslation of Weber's 'class, status, party.' " *Sociological Quarterly* 34: 551–56.

Annandale, Ellen C. (2010) "Health status and gender," pp. 97–112 in *The new Blackwell companion to medical sociology*, W. Cockerham (ed.). Oxford, UK: Oxford University Press.

Antunes, Ricardo Jorge (2011) "The social space of health inequalities in Portugal." *Social Theory & Health* 9: 393–409.

Bendix, Reinhold (1960) *Max Weber: An intellectual portrait*. New York: Doubleday.

Blaxter, Mildred (1990) *Health and lifestyles*. London: Tavistock.

Bourdieu, Pierre (1984) Distinction: A social critique of the judgement of taste, R. Nice (trans.). Cambridge, MA: Harvard University Press.

Bradby, Hannah, and James Y. Nazroo (2010) "Health, Ethnicity, and Race," pp. 113–29 in *The new Blackwell companion to medical sociology*, W. Cockerham (ed.). Oxford, UK: Wiley-Blackwell.

Brooks, Abigail T. (2010) "Aesthetic anti-aging surgery and technology: Women's friend or foe?" *Sociology of Health & Illness* 32: 238–57.

Cockerham, William C. (2000) "The sociology of health behavior and health lifestyles," pp. 159–72 in *Handbook of medical sociology*, 5th ed., C. Bird, P. Conrad, and A. Fremont (eds.). Upper Saddle River, NJ: Prentice Hall.

—— (2005) "Health lifestyle theory and the convergence of agency and structure." *Journal of Health and Social Behavior* 46: 51–67.

—— (2006) *Society of risk-takers: Living life on the edge*. New York: Worth.

—— (2010) "Health lifestyles: Bringing structure back," pp. 159–83 in *The new Blackwell companion to medical sociology*, W. Cockerham (ed.). Oxford, UK: Wiley-Blackwell.

—— (2013a) *Social causes of health and disease*, 2nd ed. Cambridge, UK: Polity.

—— (2013b) "Bourdieu and an update of health lifestyle theory," pp. 127–54 in *Medical sociology on the move: New directions in theory*. Dordrecht: Springer.

Cockerham, William C., Thomas Abel, and Gunther Lüschen (1993) "Max Weber, formal rationality, and health lifestyles." *Sociological Quarterly* 34: 413–25.

Crawford, Robert (1984) "A cultural account of health: Control, release, and the social body," pp. 60–103 in *Issues in the political economy of health care*, J. McKinley (ed.). New York: Tavistock.

Dahrendorf, Ralf (1979) *Life chances*. Chicago: University of Chicago Press.

D'Houtaud Alphonse, and Mark G. Field (1984) "The image of health: Variations in perception by social class in a French population." *Sociology of Health & Illness* 6: 30–59.

Fishman, Jennifer R., Richard A. Settersten, Jr., and Michael A. Flatt (2009) "In the vanguard of biomedicine? The curious and contradictory case of anti-ageing medicine." *Sociology of Health & Illness* 32: 197–210.

Frohlich, Katherine L., and Thomas Abel (2014) "Environmental justice and health practices: Understanding how health inequities arise at the local level." *Sociology of Health & Illness* 36: 199–212.

Grzywacz, Joseph G., and Nadine F. Marks (2001) "Social inequalities and exercise during adulthood: Toward an ecological perspective." *Journal of Health and Social Behavior* 42: 202–20.

Guptil, Amy E., Denise A. Copelton, and Betsy Lucal (2013) *Food & Society*. Cambridge, UK: Polity.

Hattery, Angela J., and Earl Smith (2011) "Health, nutrition, access to healthy food and well-being among African Americans," pp. 47–59 in *Handbook of African American Health*, A. Lemelle, W. Reed, and S. Taylor (eds.). Dordrecht: Springer.

Hill, Terrence, Amy Burdette, Christopher Ellison, and Marc Music. 2007. "Religious Involvement and Healthy Lifestyles: Evidence from the Survey of Texas Adults." *Annals of Behavioral Medicine* 34:217-222.

Idler, Ellen L. (2010) "Health and religion," pp. 133–58 in *The new Blackwell companion to medical sociology*, W. Cockerham (ed.). Oxford, UK: Wiley-Blackwell.

Jarvis, Martin J., and Jane Wardle (1999) "Social patterning of individual health behaviours: The case of cigarette smoking," pp. 240–55 in *The social determinants of health*, M. Marmot and R. Wilkinson (eds.). Oxford, UK: Oxford University Press.

Jones, Ian Rees, Olia Papacosta, Peter H. Whincup, S. Goya Wannamethee, and Richard W. Morries (2011) "Class and lifestyle 'lock-in' among middle-aged and older men: A multiple correspondence analysis of the British Regional Heart Study." *Sociology of Health & Illness* 33: 399–419.

Karlsen, Saffron, and James Y. Nazroo (2002) "Agency and structure: The impact of ethnic identity and racism on the health of ethnic minority people." *Sociology of Health & Illness* 24: 1–20.

Kasl, S., and S. Cobb (1966) "Health behavior, illness behavior, and sick role behavior." *Archives of Environmental Health* 12: 246–66.

Kinnunen, Taina (2010) "'A second youth': Pursuing happiness and respectability through cosmetic surgery in Finland." *Sociology of Health & Illness* 32: 258–71.

Kleinfield, N. R. (2006) "Living at an epicenter of diabetes, defiance, and despair." *New York Times* (January 10): A1, A20.

Lahelma, Eero (2010) "Health and social stratification," pp. 71–96 in *The new Blackwell companion to medical sociology*, W. Cockerham (ed.). Oxford, UK: Blackwell.

Margolis, Rachel (2013) "Educational differences in healthy behavior changes and adherence among middle-aged Americans." *Journal of Health and Social Behavior* 54: 353–68.

Mirowsky, John, and Catherine E. Ross (2003) *Education, social status, and health*. New York: Aldine de Gruyter.

Musick, Marc A., James S. House, and David R. Williams (2004) "Attendance at religious services and mortality in a national sample." *Journal of Health and Social Behavior* 45: 198–213.

Pampel, Fred C. (2009) "The persistence of educational differences in smoking." *Social Problems* 56: 526–42.

——— (2013) "Does reading keep you thin? Leisure activities, cultural tastes, and body weight in comparative perspective." *Sociology of Health & Illness* 34: 396–411.

Pechey, Rachel, Susan A. Jebb, Michael P. Kelly, Eva Almiron-Roig, Susana Conde, Ryota Nakamura, Ian Shemilt, Marc Suhrcke, and Theresa M. Marteau (2013) "Socioeconomic differences in purchases of more vs. less healthy foods and beverages: Analysis of over 25,000 British households in 2010." *Social Science and Medicine* 92: 22–26.

Petev, Ivaylo D. (2013) "The association of social class and lifestyles: Persistence in American sociability, 1974 to 2010." *American Sociological Review* 78: 633–61.

Saint Onge, Jarron M., and Patrick M. Krueger (2011) "Education and racial-ethnic differences in types of exercise in the United States." *Journal of Health and Social Behavior* 52: 197–211.

Savage, Mathieu, Alex Dumas, and Stephen A. Stuart (2013) "Fatlism and short-termism as cultural barriers to cardiac rehabilitation among underprivileged men." *Sociology of Health & Illness* 35: 1211–26.

Snead, M. Christine, and William C. Cockerham (2002) "Health lifestyles and social class in the deep South." *Research in the Sociology of Health Care* 20: 107–22.

Springer, Kristen W., and Dawne M. Mouzon (2011) "'Macho men' and preventive health care." *Journal of Health and Social Behavior* 52: 212–27.

Veenstra, Gerry, and Patrick John Burnett (2014) "A relational approach to health practices: Towards transcending the agency-structure divide." *Sociology of Health & Illness* 36: 187–98.

Weber, Max (1978) *Economy and society*, 2 vols, G. Roth and C. Wittich (eds). Berkeley: University of California Press.

Wickrama, K. A. S., Rand D. Conger, Lora Ebert Wallace, and Glen H. Elder, Jr. (1999) "The intergenerational transmission of health-risk behaviors: Adolescent lifestyles and gender moderating effects." *Journal of Health and Social Behavior* 40: 258–72.

World Health Organization (1986) "Lifestyles and health." *Social Science and Medicine* 22: 117–24.

CHAPTER 7

Illness Behavior

LEARNING OBJECTIVES

■ Define illness behavior.

■ Describe how sociodemographic variables influence the utilization of professional health care.

Illness behavior, in comparison to health behavior, is the activity undertaken by a person who feels ill for the purpose of defining that illness and seeking relief from it (Kasl and Cobb 1966). According to David Mechanic (1995:1208): "Illness behavior refers to the varying ways individuals respond to bodily indications, how they monitor internal states, define and interpret symptoms, make attributions, take remedial actions and utilize various sources of informal and formal care." Some people recognize particular physical symptoms such as pain, a high fever, or nausea and seek out a physician for treatment. Others with similar symptoms may attempt self-medication or dismiss the symptoms as not needing attention.

We know that bodily changes—symptoms of illness that are disruptive, painful, and visible—are the basic determinants of medical help seeking, and this is especially the case if the discomfort is severe. But sometimes physical changes are not obvious, particularly in the early stages of chronic diseases. The initial sign of diseases such as heart disease, diabetes, and cancer may depend on relatively subtle bodily changes experienced in daily life such as heavy fatigue, physical weakness, or extreme thirst before bedtime. Thus, subjective interpretations of feeling states can be medically significant.

For those individuals and groups concerned with the planning, organization, and implementation of health care delivery systems, the identification of social factors that encourage or discourage a person from seeking medical treatment is of great significance. An understanding of the help-seeking process in medicine can have a tremendous impact upon the structuring of health services for people living in a community, in terms of both providing better medical care and making that care more accessible to the people who need it.

The focus of this chapter is on reviewing the social factors influencing the decisions of the ill to use professional medical services. First, self-care will be examined. Next, selected sociodemographic variables are discussed. These, however, explain only that variations in health services utilization exist, rather than why *they exist. Thus, our third topic will be selected social-psychological models of medical help seeking. Only when certain conditions are satisfied in a person's mind can we expect him or her to go to the doctor.*

Self-Care

Self-care is the most common response to symptoms of illness by people throughout the world. Self-care includes taking preventive measures (such as consuming vitamin supplements), self-treatment of symptoms (such as taking home remedies or over-the-counter drugs), and managing diagnosed chronic conditions (for instance, use of insulin by a diabetic or blood thinners for heart patients to prevent clots). As a way of acting in relation to one's health, self-care consists of both health and illness behavior. It essentially consists of a layperson's preventing, detecting, and treating his or her health problems. Self-care may involve consultation with health care providers and use of their assistance. What makes self-care distinctive is that it is self-initiated and self-managed. In modern societies, a number of factors have promoted self-care on the part of laypersons. These factors include: (1) the high cost of medical care; (2) dissatisfaction with medical care that is depersonalized; (3) recognition of the limits of modern medicine; (4) the increasing awareness of alternative healing practices; (5) heightened consciousness of the effects of lifestyles on health; and (6) a desire to be in control of one's own health when feasible (Segall and Goldstein 1989). When an individual's symptoms are familiar, the type of care needed and the likely outcome are known, and a physician is not required, that person is likely to engage in self-care. Self-care, in fact, is universal. People have been doing it for centuries, and it is made easier today by access to the Internet with its abundance of medical information (Stevenson et al. 2003).

Yet, self-care is not an action that is completely independent of the medical profession. People engage in self-care in a manner consistent with medical norms, values, and information. Often medical advice guides the actions taken (Calnan et al. 2007; Stevenson et al. 2003). When laypersons lack knowledge, competence, or experience to proceed, or are simply more comfortable in allowing professionals to handle matters, they turn to doctors. The remainder of this chapter will discuss the social processes involved in seeking help from a physician.

Sociodemographic Variables

A significant portion of past research in medical sociology has concerned itself with the effect of sociodemographic variables on the utilization of health care services. The reader should keep in mind that help-seeking behavior often involves interaction between several variables acting in combination to influence specific outcomes in specific social situations. Nonetheless, studies of the effects of particular sociodemographic variables, such as age, gender, ethnicity, and socioeconomic status, help explain how they relate to the behavior of people seeking medical care.

Age and Gender

The findings for age and gender have been consistent: Use of health services is greater for females than for males and is greatest for the elderly. Perhaps, it is obvious that people more than 65 years of age are in poorer health and are hospitalized more often than the other age groups. It is also clear that elderly people are more likely to visit physicians than younger people. Because older people are more likely both to be physically disabled or ill and to have public insurance (Medicare) coverage, they tend to visit doctors fairly often. One recent change, however, is seen among adults in the 18- to 64-year-old age group whose visits to physicians declined from 4.8 to 3.9 per year in 2001–2010. The reasons for this downturn are not fully known, but contributing factors possibly included good health, lack of health insurance, and higher costs. A study in Michigan of persons between the ages of 19 and 64 following the 2008–2009 economic recession found that people heavily in debt had often foregone medical care (Kalousova and Burgard 2013). Medical debt appeared to be a special type of debt in that it is unplanned, unwanted, and can easily exceed a person's ability to pay if uninsured or underinsured. People carrying heavy debt loads were seen to avoid medical care if possible when it means more debt.

As indicated in Chapter 4 on the social demography of health, it is also clear from existing data that females report a higher morbidity and, even after correcting for maternity, have a higher rate of hospital admissions (National Center for Health Statistics 2013; Weiss and Lonnquist 2012). If the extent of knowledge about the symptoms of an illness is considered, it also appears that women generally know more about health matters than men and take better care of themselves. In addition, the number of females in a household appears to be related to the number of physician visits for that household. That is, the larger the number of females in a particular household, the greater the number of visits to physicians.

Females exhibit a lifelong pattern of visiting doctors more often than do males. There are three peaks in the visitation pattern for females. Initially, there are high rates during childhood, followed by a decline until a second rise during the childbearing years. After age 35, there is once again a decline, but physician visits by females steadily increase after age 45. For males, there are high rates of visits during childhood, followed by comparatively low rates of physician visits until a gradual increase begins at age 45. Pregnancy and associated conditions do result in especially high rates of visits to physicians for women between the ages of 15 and 45, but the woman's reproductive role accounts for less than 20 percent of all doctor visits. The higher visit rates by women are primarily the result of their greater number of ailments (Young 2004). More frequent utilization of physicians may have a substantial benefit for women in that they receive, on the average, earlier diagnosis and treatment for illness than men.

Ethnicity

Several early studies in medical sociology attempted to relate a person's utilization of health care services to his or her cultural background. One of the most systematic studies was Edward Suchman's (1965) investigation of the extent of the belief in and acceptance of modern medicine among several ethnic groups in New York City. Suchman sought to link individual medical orientations and behaviors to specific types of social relationships and their corresponding group structures. He believed the interplay of group relationships with an individual's personal orientation toward medicine affected his or her health-seeking behavior.

Suchman categorized people as belonging to either cosmopolitan (sophisticated) or parochial (unsophisticated) groups. Persons in a parochial group were found to have close and exclusive relationships with family, friends, and members of their ethnic group and to display limited knowledge of disease, skepticism of medical care, and high dependency in illness. They were more likely than the cosmopolitan group to delay in seeking medical care and more likely to rely on a "lay-referral system" in coping with their symptoms of illness. A lay-referral system consists of nonprofessionals—family members, friends, or neighbors—who assist individuals in interpreting their symptoms and in recommending a course of action. The concept of the lay-referral system originated with Eliot Freidson (1960), who described the process of seeking medical help as involving a group of potential consultants, beginning in the nuclear family and extending outward to more select, authoritative laypersons, until the "professional" practitioner is reached. Freidson suggests that when cultural definitions of illness contradict professional definitions, the referral process will often not lead to the professional practitioner. The highest degree of resistance to using medical services in a lay-referral structure was found in lower-class neighborhoods characterized by a strong ethnic identification and extended family relationships. The decision to seek out a physician is based not just on professional standards of appropriate illness behavior but also on lay norms, and the two may be in conflict.

By contrast, the cosmopolitan group in Suchman's study demonstrated low ethnic exclusivity, less limited friendship systems, and fewer authoritarian family relationships. Additionally, they were more likely than the parochial group to know something about disease, to trust health professionals, and to be less dependent on others while sick.

Social Networks What is suggested by Suchman's (1965) study is that, under certain conditions, close and ethnically exclusive social relationships tend to channel help-seeking behavior, at least initially, toward the group rather than professional health care delivery systems. Yet, Reed Geertsen and associates (1975) replicated Suchman's study in Salt Lake City ten years later and found an opposite trend. They observed that the Mormon community, with its strong values concerning good health and education and its emphasis upon family and tradition, demonstrated that group closeness and exclusivity can increase, rather than decrease, the likelihood of an individual responding to professional health resources. They concluded that people who belong to close and exclusive groups, especially tradition- and authority-oriented families, are (1) more likely to respond to a health problem by seeking medical care if it is consistent with their cultural beliefs and practices *or* (2) less likely to seek medical care if their cultural beliefs support skepticism and distrust of professional medicine.

Geertsen and colleagues focused on the family rather than the ethnic group, as the critical social unit in determining help-seeking behavior. The family is the person's first significant social group and usually the primary source of societal values. Thus, knowledge of disease and family authority appear as key intervening variables in a person's medical orientation, as knowledge assists in recognition of symptoms, while family authority impels the sick person into the professional health care system. Alternatively, less knowledge about disease and/or weak family authority could act as inhibiting factors in obtaining professional treatment and cause the individual to jeopardize his or her health condition.

What is suggested here is that the family represents a social experience that influences how a particular person perceives his or her health situation. Individuals are born into a family of significant others—significant because they provide the child with a specific social identity. This identity includes not only an appraisal of the child's physical and intellectual characteristics but also knowledge concerning the social history of a particular family and group with all that means in terms of social status, perspective, and cultural background. As the child becomes older and takes as his or her own the values and opinions of the immediate family or group, or those of the wider society as presented through the mediating perspective of the family, the child is considered to be properly socialized in that he or she behaves in accordance with group-approved views.

Admittedly, children can either accept or reject the social perspective put forth by their family as representative of their own social reality; yet the choices offered to them in the process of their socialization are set by adults who determine what information is provided and in what form it is presented. Thus, although children may not be entirely passive in the socialization experience, what is important, as Peter Berger and Thomas Luckmann (1967) explain, is that they have no choice in the selection of their significant others so that identification with them is quasi-automatic. This further means that children's internalization of their family's interpretation of social reality is quasi-inevitable. While this initial social world presented to children by their significant others may be weakened by later social relationships, it can nevertheless be a lasting influence on them. Parental influence, for example, has been found to be the most important and persistent influence on the preventive health beliefs of their children (Lau, Quadrel, and Hartman 1990) and significant in shaping their health lifestyles as well (Cockerham 2005, 2013a, 2013b; Tilson et al. 2004; Wickrama et al. 1999).

Therefore, it is not surprising that a person's family or social group often guides the perceptual process or signals the perspective from which the total society is viewed. For this reason, some studies in medical sociology have emphasized the social network as a major factor in help-related behavior (Calnan et al. 2007; Christakis and Fowler 2007, 2008; Pescosolido 1992; Umberson and Montez 2010). A social network refers to the social relationships a person has during day-to-day interaction, which serve as the normal avenue for the exchange of opinion, information, and affection. Typically, the social network is composed of family, relatives, and friends that comprise the individual's immediate social world, although the concept of a social network can be expanded to include increasingly larger units of society. The influence of the social network on health can be either good or bad, depending on the network's norms, values, and cultural background (Umberson and Montez 2010).

The role of the social network is to suggest, advise, influence, or coerce an individual into taking or not taking particular courses of action. This is seen in studies of obesity and smoking by Nicholas Christakis and James Fowler (2007, 2008) based on data from the Framingham Heart Study. They found that obese persons were highly likely to have social networks of family and friends who were similarly obese people with shared outlooks and that smoking behavior likewise spreads through ties in groups of interconnected people. Persons who stopped smoking successfully were embedded in social networks that stopped smoking together. Those who still smoked and remained in the network were more likely to be found at the periphery of the group, rather than the center. The findings suggested that decisions to cease smoking were not made solely by isolated persons but reflected collective choices made by groups of people connected to each other. Christakis and Fowler (2008:2256–57) conclude:

> This phenomenon may be especially likely in the case of smoking, since smoking is often deemed an explicitly social—and hence shared—behavior. Consequently, when a smoker runs out of easily available contacts with whom he or she can smoke, he or she may be more likely to quit.

While developing a theory of help-seeking behavior, Bernice Pescosolido (1992) stressed the importance of social networks in obtaining medical care. She developed a list of the various options and choices that people in virtually all societies can potentially turn to for consultation when ill. The most obvious choice is the modern medical practitioner, especially MDs. But the realities of the marketplace, such as insufficient income or health insurance, may push the individual elsewhere. Therefore, alternative medical practitioners, such as faith healers or chiropractors, may be a possibility. Nonmedical professionals such as social workers, clergy, and teachers represent another option, along with lay advisers such as family members, or self-care, or perhaps no choices are available.

Pescosolido points out that people often seek advice and help from a variety of sources, until the situation is resolved. She finds that it is through contact with other people that individuals deal with their illnesses and obtain support for medical and emotional problems. "Individuals in social networks," says Pescosolido (1992:1113), "are more than an influence on help seeking, they *are* caregivers and advisors, part of a 'therapy managing group.'" Consequently, the strategies that people employ for seeking health care are socially organized around the opportunities they have for interacting with people in a position to help.

As for ethnicity, its influence on physician utilization appears largely limited to its role in providing a cultural context for decision making within social networks. A variable that particularly confounds the effects of ethnicity on help seeking is socioeconomic status. The higher an individual's socioeconomic position, the less ethnic the person often becomes (Hollingshead and Redlich 1958). In other words, middle-class Americans of European, African, Hispanic, Asian, and native-origin descent tend to reflect the same middle-class norms and values as part of their mutual participation in middle-class society. Included in this pattern are similar perspectives toward the utilization of health services. This situation suggests that the direct effects of ethnicity on decision making concerning health care are largely confined to the lower class, as Suchman's (1965) work indicated. Studies of low-income racial/ethnic minorities in the United States seem to support this conclusion. The next three sections will discuss some of this research.

Health Insurance Coverage To place this discussion of medical care in perspective, we should first note the extent of health insurance coverage in the United States by race. Persons age 65 and over are eligible for Medicare, and this has not changed under the 2010 health care reform legislation. The major type of health insurance for the remainder of the American population (under the age of 65) is private insurance paid for by the individual, the individual's employer, or some combination thereof. Beginning in 2014, private insurance programs changed significantly in that persons with preexisting medical conditions can no longer be denied coverage because of those conditions, a basic level of benefits set by the federal government must be provided in all plans, and those not covered by their employer are supposed to be able to purchase affordable coverage through their state insurance exchange, which will offer a variety of plans and costs. The lowest-income families may qualify for Medicaid, the public health insurance program for the poor that was expanded by some states making more people eligible in those jurisdictions. As of 2015 (a year's delay), most Americans would be required by law to purchase health insurance or pay a fine. Medium and large businesses also face fines for non-compliance that are discussed in Chapter 15. Government subsidies are available to help small businesses with 50 or fewer employees buy insurance for their workers and to help qualified individuals. Those who presently have health insurance may keep their coverage or purchase a plan from state exchanges, although many found the cost of new health insurance plans was more expensive than anticipated.

Table 7.1 lists the proportion of health insurance coverage for persons under age 65, according to race for 2010. Some 61.7 percent have private health insurance; 16.9 percent have Medicaid; 3.2 percent have some other type of public health insurance, such as military or Veterans Administration (TRICARE) health benefits; and 18.2 percent have no health insurance. Table 7.1 also shows that 64.9 percent of all non-Hispanic whites have private health insurance, compared to 44.8 percent of non-Hispanic blacks. As for other races, Table 7.1 shows that 68.1 percent of Asians have private health insurance in comparison to 31.7 percent of American Indians/Native Alaskans and 36.8 percent of Hispanics.

For Medicaid, Table 7.1 shows some 30.4 percent of all non-Hispanic blacks were covered by this type of insurance in 2010, along with 28.6 percent of Hispanics, and 21.6 percent of all American Indians/Native Alaskans. Some 14.5 percent of all non-Hispanic whites and 12.0 percent of Asians received Medicaid. For those persons without any type of health insurance coverage, Table 7.1 shows that, among non-Hispanics, some 17.6 percent of whites and 20.6 percent of blacks fall into this category. However, the most striking disclosure is that the proportion of American Indians/Alaskan Natives and Hispanic without health insurance was 44.0 percent and 32.0 percent, respectively, the largest percentage by far of any ethnic groups in American society.

The figure of 18.2 percent without health insurance for the nation as a whole in 2010 compares to the figure of 16.8 percent in 2000, 13.9 percent for 1990, and 11.6 percent for 1980; thus, it is clear that the proportion of persons in the total U.S. population lacking insurance coverage for health care had worsened in the twenty-first century. The uninsured include persons working in low-income jobs, whose employers do not provide health insurance benefits for their employees. This would include many Hispanics and Native Americans as well as people from all other racial and ethnic groups. These are the near poor who have a job and make

TABLE 7.1 Health Insurance Coverage for Persons Under 65 Years of Age, Hispanic Origin, and Race, United States, 2010.

Insurance Type	Total United States	White Non-Hispanic	Black Non-Hispanic	Hispanics	Asians	American Indian/ Alaskan Native
Private	61.7%	64.9%	44.8%	36.8%	68.1%	31.7%
Medicaid	16.9	14.5	30.4	28.6	12.0	21.6
Other public	3.2	3.0	4.2	2.6	2.8	2.7
Uninsured	18.2	17.6	20.6	32.0	17.1	44.0

Source: National Center for Health Statistics, 2013.

enough money to be disqualified from welfare programs such as Medicaid but who nevertheless are unable to purchase private health insurance because it remained too expensive for their low level of wages. As Karen Seccombe and Cheryl Amey (1995:179) pointed out years ago, the working poor were "playing by the 'rules' of the health insurance coverage scheme in this country by possessing employment and they are productive members of our economic system, yet they are without coverage for themselves and for their families."

But not all uninsured were among the near-poor. Some were healthy young adults who chose not to pay for health insurance as it was too expensive and they felt there was little likelihood they would need it. Others had moderate or high family incomes, but they had preexisting health conditions and could not get health insurance other than high-priced individual policies. In some cases, higher health care costs drove up premiums, causing employers or workers or both to find health insurance too costly. The economic downturn of 2008–2009 also contributed to a significant decline in health insurance coverage when many people lost their jobs and their health benefits. The goal of the 2010 health care reform legislation was to extend coverage to the large group of uninsured. Consequently, once the provisions of the law are fully implemented, the percentage of the uninsured should theoretically decrease with a significant rise in the percent of persons with private health insurance and a smaller increase for those with Medicaid. Others will have moved to Medicare as the large baby boomer generation enters into the retirement years.

African Americans Many years ago, preventive medicine was largely a white middle-class concept that provided a patient with an elaborate structure of routine prenatal and postnatal care, pediatric services, dental care, immunizations, and screening for the presence of disease. Low-income blacks, like low-income whites, visited doctors only when they were sick or injured, which meant that many blacks did not use preventive services. For those living at a subsistence level, the only options were welfare medicine, which by its very nature is typically bureaucratic and impersonal, or no professional care at all.

However, while some blacks, namely those without any type of health insurance coverage, remain underserved with respect to professional medical care, the overall pattern of physician utilization by blacks has changed dramatically in the last few decades and should continue to change with health care reform. Prior to the mid-1970s, blacks tended to visit doctors significantly less often than whites and showed more negative attitudes toward seeking help from them. This is no longer the case.

Hispanics Studies investigating the utilization of professional health services in the United States show that Mexican Americans have the lowest rates of any racial/ethnic minority group (Angel and Angel 2009). Mexican Americans have somewhat lower rates than non-Hispanic whites and blacks for visits to physicians and substantially lower rates for routine physical and eye examinations. Mexican Americans have higher rates for visits to dentists than African Americans, but these rates are markedly lower than those for non-Hispanic whites. Lower utilization rates for Mexican Americans seem to be largely a function of socioeconomic status (lower income and education) rather than ethnicity or status as illegal immigrants in some cases. Low rates of health insurance coverage are undoubtedly a major factor as well.

Mexican Americans are among those most likely to report that they could not afford health insurance as the main reason they do not have coverage. The low rates of private health insurance among Mexican Americans and other Hispanics also result from low income, low education, and employment in businesses that generally do not provide such coverage. According to Ronald and Jacqueline Angel (2009), Mexican Americans are concentrated in low wage jobs in which insurance benefits are less common and are less likely than any other group to be employed in managerial and professional positions. Another factor in the low rates of physician utilization by Mexican Americans in particular is the paucity of Hispanic health professionals. Only some 5 percent of all American physicians are of Hispanic origin, and the percentage of Hispanic dentists, nurses, pharmacists, and therapists is even lower—about 3 percent of the national total.

Socioeconomic Status

Another major approach to the study of help-seeking behavior has been its correlation with socioeconomic status. Several years ago, it was generally believed that lower-class persons tended to underutilize health services because of the financial cost and/or culture of poverty. The culture of poverty, as summarized many years ago by Thomas Rundall and John Wheeler (1979), is a phenomenon in which poverty, over time, influences the development of certain social and psychological traits among those immersed within it. These traits include dependence, fatalism, inability to delay gratification, and a lower value placed on health (being sick is not especially unusual). This, in turn, tends to reinforce the poor person's disadvantaged social position. The seminal study, showing how the poor had developed a different perspective concerning their interpretations of symptoms, was Earl Koos's *The Health of Regionville* (1954). Koos conducted his study in a small community in New York, where he found it possible to rank the local residents into three distinct socioeconomic classes. Class I consisted of the most successful people in town in terms of financial assets. Class II represented middle-class wage earners who were the majority of citizens, while Class III represented the least-skilled workers and poorest members of the community.

Members of each socioeconomic class were asked to indicate whether certain easily recognized symptoms were considered to be significant enough to be brought to the attention of a doctor. Class I respondents demonstrated a much higher level of recognition of the importance of symptoms than either Class II or Class III. Only two of the symptoms, loss of appetite and backache, were reported by less than three-fourths of Class I as needing medical attention. Otherwise, almost all Class I respondents were prepared to go to a physician if a symptom appeared. For only one symptom, persistent coughing, did Class I respondents not have the highest percentage, and this difference was negligible. Class III respondents, in contrast, showed a marked indifference to most symptoms. Seventy-five percent of the lower-class respondents considered 10 of the 17 symptoms not serious enough to warrant medical attention. Only three symptoms (excessive vaginal bleeding and blood in stool and urine) achieved a response of 50 percent or more, and all of these were associated with unexplained bleeding.

Thus, in Regionville at the time of Koos's study in the early 1950s, symptoms did not necessarily lead to seeking medical treatment among the lower class. In addition, Class III persons were inhibited from seeking treatment because of cost, fear, and relative need as related to age and the role of the sick person. The very young, the elderly, and breadwinners were most likely to receive medical attention among the poor. Another important factor in help-seeking behavior for Class III persons was group expectations about symptoms, further suggesting the importance of the social network. Backache, for example, was a symptom the poor commonly defined as not being a serious ailment. For the poor, having a backache was nothing unusual.

At the time, Koos's study helped establish the premise that lower-class persons are less likely than others to recognize various symptoms as requiring medical treatment and that these beliefs contribute to differences in the actual use of services. This premise was supported by the conclusions of surveys by the National Center for Health Statistics in 1960 and 1965, which found that higher-income persons were visiting physicians to a much greater extent than middle or lower-income persons in that order.

In 1968, however, the National Center found a changing pattern of physician utilization. It was now the middle-income group who had become the underutilizers. Highest rates of physician visits were for persons with either the lowest level of income or the highest level. The increased rate for the low-income group was largely because of Medicaid and Medicare health insurance programs. Medicaid, administered at the state level, provides coverage intended to help pay the cost of health care for the poor. Medicare, a federal program, provides coverage for the elderly, who are overrepresented in the low-income group.

Between 1963 and 1970, as the effects of Medicaid and Medicare became evident, the use of physician services by low-income persons increased to the point where the significance of the relationship between income and utilization was greatly diminished. In fact, by 1970, it could be demonstrated that the poor had higher rates of physician use than any other income group. For example, according to data collected by Ronald Andersen and Odin Anderson (1979) for selected years between 1928 and 1974, the low-income group had the lowest rates of physician utilization from 1928 to 1931. The middle-income group ranked in the middle, and the high-income group had the highest number of visits. This pattern remained until 1970, when the low-income group emerged with the highest rates, followed by the high-income group and the middle-income group. The present pattern indicates the lowest-income group visits physicians most often, followed by middle-income groups. The highest-income group visits doctors the least. The pattern of physician utilization by social class has completely reversed itself since the 1950s.

Even though the poor are visiting doctors in greater numbers, this does not mean that they use the same sources of medical treatment in proportions equal to those of higher-income groups. Differences between income groups in regard to where they seek care are obvious and consistent. People with higher incomes are more likely than those with lower incomes to have received medical services in private doctors' offices and group practices or over the telephone. However, the reverse situation is true for other sources of care. People with lower incomes are more likely to contact hospital outpatient clinics or emergency rooms. Although people of all income groups use each source, a pattern emerges of a dual health care system—a "private" system with a greater proportion of the higher-income groups and a "public" system with a preponderance of lower-income groups on Medicaid. In the public system, the patient is likely to receive care in less quality facilities, spend longer amounts of time in waiting rooms, not have a personal physician, cope more with bureaucratic agencies, and return after treatment to a living situation that is less conducive to good health.

Furthermore, when actual need for health services is taken into account, low-income persons appear to use fewer services relative to their needs. Diana Dutton (1978) pointed out several years ago in a well-known study that statistics showing increased use of health services by the poor could be misleading. She argued that the poor have higher rates of disability because of illness and that the poor also tend to be more likely to seek symptomatic care. The nonpoor, in turn, are more likely to seek preventive care, which is aimed at keeping healthy people well, instead of waiting to seek help when symptoms appear. Thus, the poor appear to have more sickness and, despite the significant increase in use of services, did not obtain as much health care as they actually need. Using data collected in Washington, D.C., Dutton tested three different explanations concerning why the poor would show lower rates for use of health services in relation to actual need than the nonpoor: (1) financial coverage; (2) the culture of poverty; and (3) the systems barrier.

The financial coverage explanation consists of the claim that the poor cannot afford to purchase the services they need—the cost is high, income is low, and insurance programs are inadequate. Dutton found this explanation to be weak. Public health insurance, notably Medicaid, had stimulated use of services by the poor to a much greater extent than private health insurance had done for the nonpoor. Unlike many private insurance plans, Medicaid paid for most physician services and thereby promoted physician utilization. Conversely, private insurance, with the exception of prepaid plans, had less impact on seeking physician services.

The culture of poverty explanation is derived from the premise that attitudes characteristic of poor people tend to retard use of services. For example, the poor may view society and professional medical practices as less than positive as a result of their life experiences. The poor may also be more willing to ignore illness or not define it as such because they must continue to function to meet the demands of survival. Dutton found the culture of poverty explanation to have some validity when combined with measures of income. As income decreased, belief in preventive checkups and professional health orientation also decreased, while degree of social alienation increased. "Of course," says Dutton (1978:359), "these differences may not reflect cultural variation so much as realistic adaptation to economic circumstances; preventive care may well be less important than paying the rent, and purchasing a thermometer may be viewed as an unaffordable luxury." Nevertheless, Dutton argues that attitudes related to the culture of poverty do play an important role in explaining differences in the use of health services between income groups, particularly the use of preventive care.

PHOTO 7.2 The poor have the highest rates of physician utilization. They are most likely to not have a personal physician and to routinely seek care in hospital outpatient clinics and emergency rooms.

In Dutton's view, the strongest explanation for low use of services by the poor in relation to need was the systems barrier explanation. This explanation focused on organizational barriers inherent in the more "public" system of health care typically used by the poor, such as hospital outpatient clinics and emergency rooms. This type of barrier not only pertains to difficulty in locating and traveling to a particular source of care but also includes the general atmosphere of the treatment setting, which in itself may be impersonal and alienating. For example, as Anselm Strauss (1970) observed, hospitals and clinics are organized for staff efficiency in rendering care and can confuse patients unfamiliar with how large organizations get work done with their huge size, similar décor making it easy to get lost, time-consuming bureaucratic procedures, long waits for service, and lack of explanations for inconvenience.

Dutton (1978) found from her research that low-income patients in public health care systems confronted a lack of preventive examinations (physicians had little time for counseling patients or providing preventive care), high charges for services, long waiting times, and relatively poor patient–physician relationships. Dutton's (1978:361–62) position was that this situation posed a highly significant barrier that discouraged low-income patients "from seeking care, *above and beyond* the deterrent effects of inadequate financial coverage and negative attitudes toward professional health care." Low utilization was therefore seen as a normal response to an unpleasant experience.

The majority of people in the Dutton study were black. Subsequent research by Rundall and Wheeler (1979), on the effect of income on use of preventive care, involved a sample of respondents in Michigan, who were mostly white. Dutton's findings were confirmed. There was no support for the financial coverage explanation. There was some support for the culture of poverty explanation in that the poor perceived themselves as relatively less susceptible to illness (they could tolerate unhealthy conditions) and therefore were less likely to seek preventive services. However, there was strong support for the systems barrier explanation. People with relatively high incomes were more likely to have a regular source of care, and those individuals with a regular source of care were more likely to use preventive services.

Having a regular source of care has been identified as an important variable in help-seeking behavior. This situation implies that the patient is relatively comfortable with the relationship and has trust in the physician's skills at diagnosis and treatment. Low-income people receiving medical care in the public sector are less likely to have a personal physician and must be treated by whichever physician happens to be on duty in a hospital or clinic. If they have to maneuver between several clinics and public assistance agencies to obtain either treatment or authorization for treatment, low-income people are subject to even more fragmented pathways to health care.

Future Patterns of Physician Utilization by Social Class

Studies conducted in the 1950s and 1960s suggest that the culture of poverty produces beliefs and values inhibiting the use of physician services (Koos 1954; Suchman 1965; Zola 1966). According to this argument, disadvantaged groups hold beliefs that are not consistent with scientific medicine—the poor are skeptical about medical care and less sensitive to the meaning of symptoms. The potential strength of these attitudes is evident in research reported by Mervyn Susser and William Watson (1971) on physician utilization in Great Britain during the first 10 to 15 years after the introduction of socialized medicine. Even though improved medical care was available at no cost, the poor continued to persist in using self-treatment and to delay seeking professional care. Susser and Watson suggested that despite the change in the availability of services, cultural change lagged behind. Thus, it appears that beliefs can have an impact on the use of physician services that is independent of financial constraints and the structural organization of services.

One would expect, however, that removing the financial barriers to health care might eventually alter the attitudes of people in the lower social classes accordingly. With increasing opportunities for the less privileged to receive health care, such as socialized medicine in Great Britain and the availability of Medicare and Medicaid in the United States, it seems likely that the attitudes of the less privileged would become more positive. Because the utilization rates of the poor have increased significantly over the past 40 years, their attitudes about going to the doctor should also have changed.

The author and his colleagues (Sharp, Ross, and Cockerham 1983) investigated this situation several years ago and found that blacks and people with less education have positive attitudes toward visiting physicians and are more likely than whites and people with more education to think that various symptoms are serious enough to warrant the attention of a doctor. These data suggest that as blacks and less-educated individuals have gained more equitable access to the health care system with the advent of Medicare and Medicaid, their beliefs did change in a direction that encourages physician utilization. At the same time, the well-educated may be more discriminating in deciding which symptoms warrant seeing a physician.

What is suggested by this finding is that there is more of a consumer orientation toward health among socially advantaged persons. In a free-market situation where health care is a commodity to be purchased, health consumers typically have more freedom to choose their source and mode of health care than is usually the case in a system of socialized medicine. Laypersons, as Freidson's (1960) discussion of the lay-referral system made clear, do judge technical performance and the quality of service provided by physicians and hospitals regardless of whether they are trained to do so. And they make decisions about doctors and hospitals based on these evaluations, usually in consultation with their friends and relatives. As Peter Conrad (2007:138) points out:

> As health care becomes more commodified [more of a commodity] and subject to market forces, medical care has become more like other products and services. We are now consumers, choosing health insurance plans, purchasing health care in the marketplace, and selecting institutions of care. Hospitals and health care institutions now compete for patients as consumers.

The trend toward consumerism in medicine is similar to consumerism in other aspects of life, in which people make informed choices about the services available to them. This orientation is more likely a feature characteristic of middle- and upper-class persons than the socially and economically disadvantaged. Dutton (1978) has noted that the United States has a two-track or two-tiered system of health care delivery—one private and the other public. What we may be seeing is that those persons at the bottom of society, who are the major participants in the public track, have a much greater willingness to turn the responsibility for their health over to their doctors and health care delivery system itself. This development is consistent with research investigating Talcott Parsons's (1951) concept of the sick role, where it was found that persons on the lower level of income are most likely to agree that people have a right not to be held responsible for their illnesses.

Arnold Arluke and his associates (1979:34) suggest that acceptance of the notion that illness is not the responsibility of the sick person may be related to broader social class differences in imputation of responsibility. That is, many lower-class persons may tend to have a more passive orientation toward life in general and less willingness to take control of problems. Certainly this is what is shown by research using locus-of-control measures, in which it is reported that members of the lowest socioeconomic group have more fatalistic attitudes and are more accepting of external forces like luck or fate controlling their lives (Wheaton 1980). An external locus of control is the belief that one is more or less at the mercy of the environment, fate, or other more powerful people, while an internal locus of control, in contrast, is the belief that one can master, control, or effectively alter the environment (Seeman and Evans 1962). People with a strong internal locus of control tend to take a very active role in coping with problems, including health problems, than those with an external locus of control. Among studies that have used a locus-of-control measure in relation to physical health, Melvin and Teresa Seeman (1983) found that a low sense of internal control could be significantly associated with less self-initiated preventive care, less optimism about the effectiveness of early treatment, poorer self-rated health, more illness and bed confinement, and greater dependence on physicians.

In other research, the author and his colleagues (Cockerham, Lueschen, Kunz, and Spaeth 1986) found important differences between socioeconomic groups with respect to symptom perception, physician utilization, and sense of control over their health situation. Persons with higher socioeconomic status were more consumer-minded and expressed greater personal responsibility for their own health. The poor were less discriminating in deciding which symptoms warranted a doctor's attention. When ill, the poor reported they visited doctors more or less routinely, even for minor ailments, while the more affluent appeared more likely to engage in self-treatment or to recognize minor ailments as self-limiting and likely to disappear in a day or two without a physician's services. The poor also expressed a decreased sense of personal control over their health. Thus, the poor seemed to be relatively passive recipients of professional health services with a significantly greater likelihood of investing responsibility for their own health in doctors and the health care system than in themselves.

Consequently, when it comes to the self-management of one's health, studies such as the one just mentioned point to an interesting contrast in the health

BOX 7.1

Fatalism in Cardiac Rehabilitation

In Québec, Canada, Mathieu Savage, Alex Dumas, and Stephen Stuart (2013) studied a group of lower class men of French heritage undergoing rehabilitation following hospitalization for a heart attack. In reviewing past research, they found that such socioeconomically deprived men tended to maintain their previous unhealthy lifestyles even after a heart attack and were less likely than more affluent men to survive more than a year after cardiac surgery. These men had all experienced unemployment, worked in low level jobs, and many had a difficult life and lived alone. They shared a highly fatalistic outlook, feeling they had little or no control over their lives. As one of the men in the study said: "I live day-to-day. If I get up tomorrow morning, I'm OK. If I don't get up. I don't get up" (Savage et al. 2013:1222).

Previous attempts to stop smoking and quit eating foods high in saturated fats before their heart attacks had failed and now, after their surgery, they still clung to their past practices—even if unhealthy—because it provided a sense of security and happiness in the face of pessimism about their future. Most continued smoking after their heart surgery, even though they were supposed to quit. Those who tried to follow some of the heart protective guidelines faced difficulties in doing so because the disadvantaged environment in which they lived reminded them of their poor prospects for achieving success in anything, including good health. This study shows the relevance of class culture in health outcomes, as the class-based fatalism of these socially disadvantaged men undermined any motivation they might have to change their unhealthy behavior.

practices of the poor. Persons in lower socioeconomic groups may be attempting to participate in middle-class health lifestyles in accordance with their level of capability, but adopting a distinctly more dependent posture in interacting with physicians and the health care system. If middle-class values have spread to the lower class in regard to health-advancing behavior, why have they not also spread in relation to coping with medical doctors and institutions?

The answer seems to lie within the cultural context of both poverty and medical practice. The culture of poverty tends to promote feelings of dependence and fatalism. Thus, the poor are especially disadvantaged when they interact with physicians as authority figures and are confronted with modern medical technology. The development of a large array of medical equipment and procedures has increasingly taken away the self-management of health from laypersons, but particularly from those at the bottom of society with their more limited levels of education and experience with technology. When direct collaboration with medical practitioners is required, the poor become even more dependent.

However, other better-educated persons have reacted to the professional dominance of physicians, with increased skepticism of physicians' service orientation and an emerging belief that physicians should not always be completely in charge of the physician–patient relationship when it can lead to over diagnosis and unnecessary tests and treatment that run up costs (Welch et al. 2011). They have assumed more of a consumer position with regard to health care. That is, patients as consumers are making decisions on their own about which steps are most appropriate for them in dealing with doctors and maintaining their health. In doing so, they are becoming more questioning of physicians and replacing the traditional old-fashioned physician–patient relationship in which the doctor decides everything for one of provider–consumer in which the patient participates in decision-making about his or her health.

This leads us to consider the influence of the culture of medicine. The culture of medicine has not traditionally promoted equality for laypersons when direct physician–patient interaction is required because the doctor was the expert and used his or her authority over the patient for insuring compliance to medical advice. This situation now appears to be undergoing change in contemporary medical environments. Instead, many physicians involve their patients in deciding about treatment options by explaining the benefits and shortcomings of alternates, along with recommendations. Patients with few years of education, however, remain the most dependent.

The trend for the immediate future in the use of physician services seems to be one in which the more affluent and better educated are likely to be more discriminating in their use of doctors. They likely will take a consumer approach, shopping for the appropriate services, making their own decisions about their symptoms and what they mean, and dealing with physicians on a more equal basis than before. Conversely, the poor appear likely to continue seeing doctors more frequently than members of the other social strata, both because they have more illness and disability and because they have more of a tendency to invest responsibility for their problems in their physicians and the health care delivery system. In doing so, they appear less likely to question the authority or judgments of doctors.

Recognizing and Coping with Illness Symptoms

Several studies suggest that laypersons generally conceive of health as the relative absence of the symptoms of illness, a feeling of physical and mental equilibrium or well-being, being able to carry out one's daily tasks, or some combination of the preceding (Blaxter 2010). Conversely, to be ill means the presence of symptoms, feeling bad and in a state of disequilibrium, and functional incapacitation (not being able to carry out one's usual activities). Thus, what laypersons recognize as illness is in part deviance from a standard of normality established by common sense and everyday experience.

Yet, as Mechanic (1978) has noted, recognition of a symptom, while certainly a necessary condition to motivate help-seeking behavior, is not in itself sufficient for a definition of illness. Some illnesses, such as appendicitis, may have obvious symptoms, while other illnesses, such as the early stages of cancer, may not. Also there are cases of persons who, despite symptoms, delay seeking health care. Cancer patients have been known to avoid cancer-screening procedures because of their anxiety about learning the truth and being forced to confront what it means to have cancer. Therefore, the characteristics of illness recognition and illness danger can be significant influences on the manner in which people perceive a disease.

Mechanic (1978:268–69) suggests that whether a person will seek medical care is based on ten determinants: (1) visibility and recognition of symptoms; (2) the extent to which the symptoms are perceived as dangerous; (3) the extent to which symptoms disrupt family, work, and other social activities; (4) the frequency and persistence of symptoms; (5) amount of tolerance for the symptoms; (6) available information, knowledge, and cultural assumptions; (7) basic needs that lead to denial; (8) other needs competing with illness responses; (9) competing interpretations that can be given to the symptoms once they are recognized; and (10) availability of treatment resources, physical proximity, and psychological and financial costs of taking action.

In addition to describing these ten determinants of help-seeking behavior, Mechanic explains that they operate at two distinct levels: other-defined and self-defined. The other-defined level is, of course, the process by which other people attempt to define an individual's symptoms as illness and call those symptoms to the attention of that person. Self-defined is where the individual defines his or her own symptoms. The ten determinants and two levels of definition interact to influence a person to seek or not seek help for a health problem.

The central theme that forms a backdrop for Mechanic's general theory of help seeking is that illness behavior is a culturally and socially learned response. A person responds to symptoms according to his or her definition of the situation. This definition may be influenced by the definitions of others but is largely shaped by learning, socialization, and past experience, as mediated by a person's social and cultural background. The role of culture in shaping our understanding of illness and responses to it is profound (Quah 2010). Even pain and the attempt to understand it as an objective condition within the body is grounded in cultural meanings about what pain is and how it should be dealt with (Kugelmann 1999; Radley 1994; Zborowski 1952; Zola 1966). As Alan Radley (Radley 1994; Radley and Billig 1996) points out, a person's beliefs about health and illness are based upon that

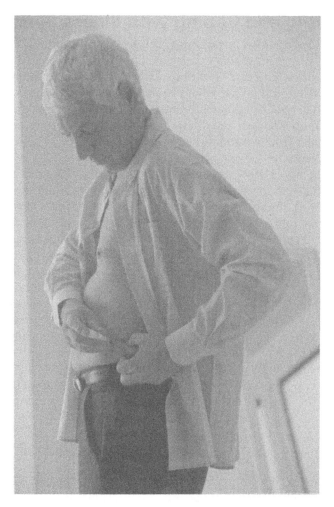

PHOTO 7.3 A diabetic injects himself with insulin. About 21 million Americans have diabetes, which is becoming one of the nation's most important health problems. CDC estimates that about one of every three children born in the United States will become diabetic.

individual's understanding of the world he or she lives in and his or her place in it. "This means," states Radley (1994:62), "that they draw upon a stock of knowledge about sickness, and about its bodily signs, that owes much to their cultural setting."

Summary

This chapter has reviewed the major theories and findings of medical sociology concerning the process of seeking medical care and the utilization of health care services. While there is no single theory or approach that has earned general consensus, the existing literature reveals the two most important variables in health care utilization to be the perceived severity of symptoms and the ability to pay for the rendering of services.

Social-psychological models of help-seeking behavior have emphasized the importance of self-perception as it relates to a person's understanding of a particular symptom. Especially important is whether the person perceives himself or herself as able to perform normal social roles. Studies concentrating on ethnicity as a factor have pointed to the role of the social network in influencing the perceptual process according to the network's own sociocultural orientation. Although some patients, notably cancer patients, may delay seeing a doctor because they are fearful about having their perceptions confirmed, the generalization can be made that the more symptoms are perceived as representing a serious illness, the more likely it is that a person will seek professional services.

The ability to pay for health services has traditionally accounted for significant socioeconomic differences in health care utilization. Today, it appears that public health insurance and social welfare monies have enabled the poor to visit physicians more frequently than higher-income groups. However, whether increased physician visitation has resulted in a corresponding rise in the quality of health care provided to the poor remains to be determined. Then, too, the poor still reside in an environment of poverty that perpetuates their increased risk to health hazards. Among those persons without public health insurance—those covered by private health insurance plans that still leave considerable cost for the individual consumer or those without any health insurance—the ability to pay remains an important obstacle to help-seeking behavior. This chapter also discussed the sociodemographic variables of age and gender, which were found to be consistent predictors of seeking medical care. Elderly persons and females generally report more illness than younger persons and males and tend to consult physicians more readily.

Critical Thinking Questions

1. How does illness behavior differ from health behavior?
2. How do socioeconomic variables affect illness?
3. The pattern of health insurance in the United States varies according to race. Describe this pattern and explain whether the Affordable Care Act will change it in future years.
4. Do different social classes have different patterns of health care utilization? If so, describe them. Did Medicare and Medicaid play a role in changing this pattern? If, so what was it?

Suggested Readings

Wheatley, Elizabeth E. (2006) *Bodies at risk: An ethnography of heart disease.* Aldershot, UK: Ashgate.
A sociological account of how patients in the United States cope with heart disease.

References

Andersen, Ronald, and Odin W. Anderson (1979) "Trends in the use of health services," pp. 371–91 in *Handbook of medical sociology*, 3rd ed., H. Freeman, S. Levine, and L. Reeder (eds.). Englewood Cliffs, NJ: Prentice Hall.

Angel, Ronald, and Jacqueline L. Angel (2009) *Hispanic families at risk*. Dordrecht: Springer.

Arluke, Arnold, Louanne Kennedy, and Ronald C. Kessler (1979) "Reexamining the sick-role concept: An empirical assessment." *Journal of Health and Social Behavior* 20: 30–36.

Berger, Peter L., and Thomas Luckmann (1967) *The social construction of reality*. New York: Anchor.

Blaxter, Mildred (2010) *Health*, 2nd ed. Cambridge, UK: Polity.

Calnan, M., D. Wainright, C. O'Neill, A. Winterbottom, and C. Watkins (2007) "Illness action rediscovered: A case study of upper limb pain." *Sociology of Health & Illness* 29: 321–46.

Christakis, Nicholas A., and James H. Fowler (2007) "The spread of obesity in a large social network over 32 years." *New England Journal of Medicine* 357: 370–79.

—— (2008) "The collective dynamics of smoking in a large social network." *New England Journal of Medicine* 358: 2249–58.

Cockerham, William C. (2005) "Health lifestyle theory and the convergence of agency and structure." *Journal of Health and Social Behavior* 46: 51–67.

—— (2013a) *Social causes of health and disease*, 2nd ed. Cambridge, UK: Polity.

—— (2013b) "Bourdieu and an update of health lifestyle theory," pp. 127–54 in *Medical sociology on the move: New directions in theory*. Dordrecht: Springer.

Cockerham, William C., Guenther Lueschen, Gerhard Kunz, and Joe L. Spaeth (1986) "Social stratification and self-management of health." *Journal of Health and Social Behavior* 27: 1–14.

Conrad, Peter (2007) *The medicalization of society: On the transformation of human conditions into treatable disorders*. Baltimore: Johns Hopkins University Press.

Dutton, Diana B. (1978) "Explaining the low use of health services by the poor: Costs, attitudes, or delivery systems?" *American Sociological Review* 43: 348–68.

Freidson, Eliot (1960) "Client control and medical practice." *American Journal of Sociology* 65: 374–82.

Geertsen, Reed, Melville R. Klauber, Mark Rindflesh, Robert L. Kane, and Robert Gray (1975) "A re-examination of Suchman's views on social factors in health care utilization." *Journal of Health and Social Behavior* 16: 226–37.

Hill, Terrence, Amy Burdette, Christopher Ellison, and Marc Musik (2007) "Religious Involvement and Healthy Lifestyles: Evidence from the Survey of Texas Adults." *Annals of Behavioral Medicine* 34: 217–222.

Hollingshead, August B., and Frederick C. Redlich (1958) *Social class and mental illness: A community study*. New York: John Wiley.

Kalousova, Lucie, and Sarah A. Burgard (2013) "Debt and foregone medical care." *Journal of Health and Social Behavior* 54: 204–20.

Kasl, S., and S. Cobb (1966) "Health behavior, illness behavior, and sick role behavior." *Archives of Environmental Health* 12: 246–66.

Koos, Earl (1954) *The health of Regionville*. New York: Columbia University Press.

Kugelmann, Robert (1999) "Complaining about chronic pain." *Social Science and Medicine* 49: 1663–76.

Lau, Richard R., Marilyn Jacobs Quadrel, and Karen A. Hartman (1990) "Development and change of young adults' preventive health beliefs and behavior: Influence from parents and peers." *Journal of Health and Social Behavior* 31: 240–59.

Mechanic, David (1978) *Medical sociology*, 2nd ed. New York: The Free Press.

—— (1995) "Sociological dimensions of illness behavior." *Social Science and Medicine* 41: 1207–16.

National center for Health Statistics (2013) *Health United States*, 2012. Washington, D.C.: U. S. Government Printing Office.

Parsons, Talcott (1951) *The social system.* Glencoe, IL: The Free Press.

Pescosolido, Bernice A. (1992) "Beyond rational choice: The social dynamics of how people seek help." *American Journal of Sociology* 97: 1096–138.

Quah, Stella R. (2010) "Health and culture," pp. 27–46 in *The new Blackwell companion to medical sociology*, W. Cockerham (ed.). Oxford, UK: Blackwell.

Radley, Alan (1994) *Making sense of illness: The social psychology of health and disease.* London: Sage.

Radley, Alan, and Michael Billig (1996) "Accounts of health and illness: Dilemmas and representations." *Sociology of Health & Illness* 18: 220–40.

Rundall, Thomas G., and John R. C. Wheeler (1979) "The effect of income on use of preventive care: An evaluation of alternative explanations." *Journal of Health and Social Behavior* 20: 397–406.

Savage, Mathieu, Alex Dumas, and Stephen A. Stuart (2013) "Fatlism and short-termism as cultural barriers to cardiac rehabilitation among underprivileged men." *Sociology of Health & Illness* 35: 1211–26.

Seccombe, Karen, and Cheryl Amey (1995) "Playing by the rules and losing: Health insurance and the working poor." *Journal of Health and Social Behavior* 36: 168–81.

Seeman, Melvin, and J. W. Evans (1962) "Alienation and social learning in a hospital setting." *American Sociological Review* 27: 772–782.

Seeman, Melvin, and Teresa E. Seeman (1983) "Health behavior and personal autonomy: A longitudinal study of the sense of control in illness." *Journal of Health and Social Behavior* 24: 144–60.

Segall, Alexander, and Jay Goldstein (1989) "Exploring the correlates of self-provided health care behaviour." *Social Science and Medicine* 29: 153–61.

Sharp, Kimberly, Catherine E. Ross, and William C. Cockerham (1983) "Symptoms, beliefs, and use of physician services among the disadvantaged." *Journal of Health and Social Behavior* 24: 255–63.

Stevenson, Fiona A., Nicky Britten, Christine A. Barry, Colin P. Bradley, and Nick Barber (2003) "Self-treatment and its discussion in medical consultations: How is medical pluralism managed in practice?" *Social Science and Medicine* 57: 513–27.

Strauss, Anselm (1970) "Medical ghettos," pp. 9–26 in *Where medicine fails*, A. Strauss (ed.). Chicago: Aldine.

Suchman, Edward A. (1965) "Social patterns of illness and medical care." *Journal of Health and Social Behavior* 6: 2–16.

Susser, M. W., and W. Watson (1971) *Sociology in medicine*, 2nd ed. New York: Oxford University Press.

Tilson, Elizabeth C., Colleen M. McBride, Issac M. Lipkus, and Richard F. Catalano (2004) "Testing the Interaction between Parent-Child Relationship Factors and Smoking to Predict Youth Smoking." *Journal of Adolescent Health* 35(3): 182–189.

Umberson, Debra, and Jennifer Karas Montez (2010) "Social relationships and health: A flashpoint for health policy." *Journal of Health and Social Behavior* 51: S54–66.

Weiss, Gregory L. and Lynne E. Lonnquist (2012) *The sociology of health, healing, and disease*, 7th ed. Upper Saddle River, NJ: Pearson Prentice-Hall.

Welch, H. Gilbert, Lisa M. Schwartz, and Steven Woloshin (2011) *Overdiagnosed: Making people sick in the pursuit of health.* Boston: Beacon Press.

Wheaton, Blair (1980) "The sociogenesis of psychological disorder: An attributional theory." *Journal of Health and Social Behavior* 21: 100–24.

Wickrama, K. A. S., Rand D. Conger, Lora Ebert Wallace, and Glen H. Elder, Jr. (1999) "The intergenerational transmission of health-risk behaviors: Adolescent lifestyles and gender moderating effects." *Journal of Health and Social Behavior* 40: 258–72.

Young, J. T. (2004) "Illness behaviour: A selective review and synthesis." *Sociology of Health & Illnesss* 26: 1–31.

Zborowski, Mark (1952) "Cultural components in responses to pain." *Journal of Social Issues* 8: 16–30.

Zola, Irving K. (1966) "Culture and symptoms: An analysis of patients' presenting complaints." *American Sociological Review* 31: 615–30.

PART 3

Seeking Health Care

CHAPTER 8

The Sick Role

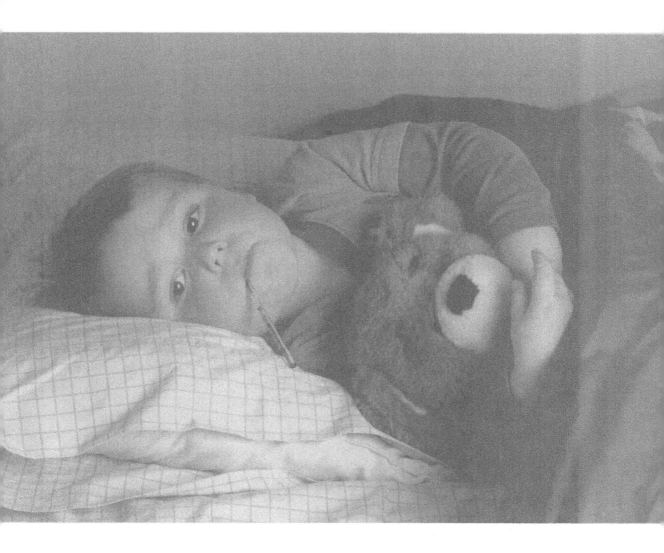

LEARNING OBJECTIVES

- Explain why illness is considered a form of deviance.

- List the four basic categories of Parsons's sick role concept.

- Account for the expansion of medicalization.

- Define stigma and explain its function.

Each society's definition of illness becomes institutionalized within its cultural patterns, so that one measure of social development is a culture's conception of illness. In primitive societies, illness was defined as an autonomous force or "being," such as an evil spirit that attacked people and settled within their bodies to cause them pain or death. During the Middle Ages, some people defined illness as a punishment for sins, and care of the sick was regarded as religious charity. Today, illness is defined as a state or condition of suffering as the result of a disease or sickness. This definition is based on the modern scientific view that an illness is an abnormal biological affliction or mental abnormality with a cause, a characteristic train of symptoms, and a method of treatment.

Illness as Deviance

The medical view of illness is that of deviance from a biological norm of health and feelings of well-being. This view involves the presence of a pathogenic mechanism within the body that can be objectively documented. The diagnosis of a disease, for example, results from a correlation of observable symptoms with knowledge about the physiological functioning of the human being. Ideally, a person is defined as ill when his or her symptoms, complaints, or the results of a physical examination and/or laboratory tests indicate an abnormality. The traditional identifying criteria for disease are (1) the patient's experience of subjective feelings of sickness; (2) the finding by the physician through examination and/or laboratory tests or other indicators that the patient has a disordered function of the body; and (3) the patient's symptoms conforming to a recognizable clinical pattern. The clinical pattern is a representation of a model or theory of disease held by the diagnostician. In diagnosis, logic is the basic tool.

The physician's function in the treatment of illness initially involves arriving at a diagnosis and then applying remedial action to the health disorder in such a way as to return the patient to as normal a state as possible. The evaluation of illness by the physician contains the medical definition of what is good, desirable, and normal as opposed to what is bad, undesirable, and abnormal. This evaluation is interpreted within the context of existing medical knowledge and the physician's experience. On this basis, the medical profession formulates medical rules defining biological deviance and seeks to enforce them by virtue of its authority to treat those persons defined as sick.

In medical sociology, the term *disease* has been characterized as an adverse physical state, consisting of a physiological dysfunction within an individual; an *illness* as a subjective state, pertaining to an individual's psychological awareness of having a disease and usually causing that person to modify his or her behavior; and *sickness* as a social state, signifying an impaired social role for those who are ill. Although a major area of interest in medical sociology is illness behavior, the concept of sickness is of special interest, because it involves analysis of factors that are distinctly sociological—namely, the expectations and normative behavior that the wider society has for people who are defined as sick.

Sociologists have typically viewed sickness as a form of deviant behavior. This view was initially formulated by Talcott Parsons (1951) in his concept of the sick role, which describes the normative behavior a person typically adopts when feeling sick. Parsons saw being sick as a disturbance in the "normal" condition of the human being, both biologically *and* socially. Previously, the sociological study of health and illness had relied on a medical perspective in which efforts in studying sickness were limited to correlating social factors with biological factors—based on references provided by health practitioners. This medically oriented approach emphasized the physiological reality of the human organism but neglected the sociological reality that a person is sick when he or she *acts* sick.

The basis for describing illness as a form of deviant behavior lies in the sociological definition of deviance as any act or behavior that violates the social norms within a given social system. Thus, deviant behavior is not simply a variation from a statistical average. Instead, a pronouncement of deviant behavior involves making a *social judgment* about what is right and proper behavior according to a social norm. Norms reflect expectations of appropriate behavior shared by people in specific social settings, or they may be more general expectations of behavior common to a wide variety of social situations. Conformity to prevailing norms is generally rewarded by group acceptance and approval of behavior. Deviation from a norm, however, can lead to disapproval of behavior, punishment, or other forms of social sanctions being applied against the offender. Norms allow for variations of behavior within a permissible range, but deviant behavior typically violates the range of permissible behavior and elicits a negative response from other people. Most theories of deviant behavior in sociology are concerned with behavior common in crime, delinquency, mental disorders, alcoholism, and drug addiction. These forms of behavior typically *offend* someone.

It should be noted that not all forms of deviant behavior produce undesirable consequences for a society. Deviance from the usual norms in such fields as art, music, theater, literature, and dance often provides very positive rewards both for the creative deviant and society. However, sickness as deviance is regarded as an undesirable circumstance for both the sick person and society. For the sick person, being sick obviously can mean discomfort and either permanent or temporary disruption of normal biological and social functioning, including death. Sickness also entails the risk of economic hardship for the sick person's family. For society, sickness can mean a reduction in the ability of a social group or organization to carry out its usual tasks and perform its normal social functions.

Sociologists have suggested that the explanation for sickness as a *social* event can be found outside of biology and medicine, by including sickness within the general category of deviant behavior. The early causal theories of deviance in sociology were essentially biological models that defined the source of deviance as something inherent in certain individuals. Undesirable behavior was thought to be caused by the genetic inheritance of criminal traits or perhaps a capricious genetic combination. The biological view of deviance has been generally rejected by contemporary sociologists because concentrating exclusively on the physiology of the individual completely overlooks the implications of social norms and social judgments about an individual's behavior.

In turn, these social judgments are influenced by various aspects of social change. For example, in past agrarian societies, illness occurred largely in small-group contexts, such as the family. It was a common occurrence, and the roles of being sick or attending to sick people were part of a role-set that included expectable variations in behavior as well as "normal" behavior. However, far-reaching changes occurred with industrialization: the decline of large families, changing theories in the treatment of disease, the development of an extensive menu of disease-fighting drugs, and the evolution of complex medical techniques that often require hospitalization. These developments have drawn disease out of the area of the expectable into a highly specialized, institutionalized context. Similarly, the methods of dealing with sick people have changed, often transferring them to the care of specialists who operate outside the context of the familiar and over whom ordinary people have few powers of control. This transfer itself, coupled with our submission to hospital routines and medical procedures, creates a specialized set of circumstances that lead to a definition of sickness as deviance. The physically sick, like the insane and criminals, represent a social category of people removed from the mainstream of society, if their illness is judged severe enough. Of course, the insane and criminals are generally much more stigmatized by society than the physically sick, but the point is that the pattern of treatment (removal from society and treatment by specialists) allows the person who is physically sick to be similar—though not identical—to an insane person who goes to an asylum or a criminal who goes to prison. Since the methods for dealing with the ill, the criminal, or the insane are in certain respects similar, we can see a basis for defining sickness as deviance.

The Functionalist Approach to Deviance

While sociologists have generally rejected biological models of deviance, functionalism—also referred to as structural functionalism—stressing societal-level processes, systems, equilibrium, and interrelationships, represents an early sociological homeostatic approach to deviance. This model is not organic or physiological. It does not find the causes of deviant behavior in individual needs, drives, instincts, genetic combinations, or any other purely individual patterns. It does find the source of deviant behavior in the relationships between individuals and social systems. This approach is based on the view that society is held together in a state of equilibrium by harmonious patterns of shared norms and values. What makes social life possible is the expectation that people will behave in accordance with the norms and values common to their particular social system. This process is "functional" because it results in social harmony and counterbalances "dysfunctional" processes, such as crime and mental illness, which disrupt the social order. The tendency of a society toward self-maintenance through equilibrium is similar to the biological concept of homeostasis, in which the human body attempts to regulate physiological (internal) conditions within a relatively constant range to maintain bodily functioning. A person may suffer from warts, indigestion, a broken leg, or perhaps even from a nonmalignant cancer and still be healthy. Likewise, a social system is viewed in the functionalist perspective as maintaining social functioning by regulating its various parts within a relatively constant range. A social system may have problems with crime and delinquency but still be "healthy" because of its overall capacity to function efficiently.

Functionalist theory depicts social systems as composed of closely interconnected parts and that changes, decisions, and definitions made in one part of the system inevitably affect to some degree all other parts of that system. Thus, a person's position within the social system subjects him or her to events and stresses originating in remote areas of the system. Behavior that is adaptive from one's own perspective and peculiar circumstances—like turning to crime—may be regarded as deviant by society at large. The individual then has the choice of continuing the adaptive behavior and being defined as deviant or trying to change that behavior, even though the person sees it as necessary for his or her own survival. Such people run the risk of confrontation with those authorities, such as psychiatrists, the police, and the courts, charged with controlling or eliminating dysfunctional social processes. Thus, deviance in a social system is reduced through the application of social sanctions against the offender. These sanctions include the use of jails, prisons, and mental hospitals to remove the deviant from society to ensure social order and cohesion.

According to functionalist theory, sickness is dysfunctional because it likewise threatens to interfere with the stability of the social system. Sick people are unable to perform their daily tasks and thus become an obstacle to the efficient functioning of society. The medical profession responds to offset the dysfunctional aspects of sickness by curing, controlling, or preventing disease and by establishing technology by which handicapped persons can assist in self-maintenance and in maintenance of the social system. This analytical approach is the basis for Parsons's theory of the sick role—a central concept in medical sociology.

However, at the time, in the 1950s, when Parsons formulated his concept, functionalism was *the* leading theoretical perspective in all of sociology, including medical sociology. This theoretical dominance did not last long, however. Functionalism provided a static image of society consisting of powerful social structures highly resistant to change; moreover, its emphasis on consensus, stability, order, and balance seemed to justify the maintenance of the status quo that perpetuated social inequalities and the power of already existing elite groups. Many sociologists could not agree with this view. Theorists who studied conflict found functionalism additionally lacking because it did not adequately consider conflict as a source of social change, especially rapid and revolutionary change. Symbolic interaction attacked functionalism for its disregard of creativity and innovation at the individual and small-group level.

Consequently, at the beginning of the twenty-first century, functionalism was essentially a dead theory or at least had become what George Ritzer and William Yagatich (2012:105) describe as a "zombie theory" existing with a bare minimum of life. That is, the theory still exists and is found in textbooks, but for all practical purposes is no longer used. Why then, would an entire chapter in this book be devoted to the sick role? The reason is that the sick role concept still provides a basic framework for explaining much of the behavior of the sick in society. While functionalist theory has generally been discarded, the sick role concept survives.

The Sick Role

Talcott Parsons (1902–1978) introduced his concept of the sick role in his book *The Social System* (1951), which was written to explain a complex functionalist model of society. In this model, social systems were linked to systems of personality and culture, to form a basis for social order. Unlike other major social theorists preceding him, Parsons included an analysis of the function of medicine in his theory of society and, in doing so, was led to consider the role of the sick person in relation to the social system within which that person lived. The result is a concept that represents the most consistent approach to explaining the behavior characteristic of sick people in Western society.

Parsons's concept of the sick role is based on the assumption that being sick is not a deliberate and knowing choice of the sick person, though illness may occur as a result of motivated exposure to infection or injury. Thus, while the criminal is thought to violate social norms because he or she "wants to," the sick person is considered deviant only because he or she "cannot help it." Parsons warns, however, that some people may be attracted to the sick role to have their lapse of normal responsibilities approved. Generally, society accounts for the distinction between deviant roles by punishing the criminal and providing therapeutic care for the sick. Both processes function to reduce deviancy and change conditions that interfere with conformity to social norms. Both processes also require the intervention of social agencies, law enforcement, or medicine, to control deviant behavior. Being sick, Parsons argues, is not just experiencing the physical condition of a sick state;

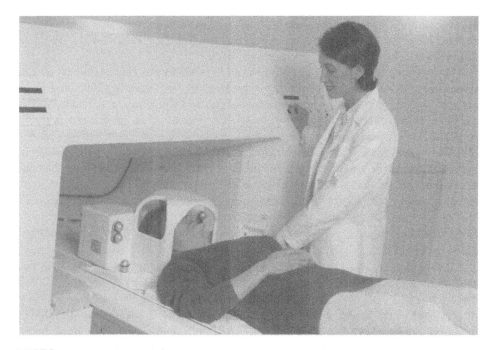

PHOTO 8.2 According to the sick role, a patient should try to get well and seek technically competent help. This photo shows a woman being prepared for magnetic resonance imaging (MRI).

rather, it constitutes a social role because it involves behavior based on institutional expectations and is reinforced by the norms of society corresponding to these expectations.

A major expectation concerning the sick is that they are unable to take care of themselves. It thus becomes necessary for the sick to seek medical advice and cooperate with medical experts. This behavior is predicated on the assumption made by Parsons that being sick is an undesirable state and the sick person wants to get well.

Parsons insists that sickness is dysfunctional because it represents a mode of response to social pressure that permits the evasion of social responsibilities. A person may desire to retain the sick role more or less permanently because of what Parsons calls a "secondary gain," which is the exemption from normal obligations and the gaining of other privileges commonly accorded to the sick. Hence, medical practice becomes a mechanism by which a social system seeks to control the illnesses of its deviant sick by returning them to as normal a state of functioning as possible.

The specific aspects of Parsons's concept of the sick role can be described in four basic categories:

1. *The sick person is exempt from "normal" social roles.* An individual's illness is grounds for his or her exemption from normal role performance and social responsibilities. This exemption, however, is relative to the nature and severity of the illness. The more severe the illness, the greater the exemption. Exemption requires legitimating by the physician as the authority on what constitutes sickness. Legitimation serves the social function of protecting society against malingering.
2. *The sick person is not responsible for his or her condition.* An individual's illness is usually thought to be beyond his or her own control. A morbid condition of the body needs to be changed and some curative process, apart from personal will power or motivation, is needed to get well.
3. *The sick person should try to get well.* The first two aspects of the sick role are conditional on the third aspect, which is recognition by the sick person that being sick is undesirable. Exemption from normal responsibilities is temporary and conditional on the desire to regain normal health. Thus, the sick person has an obligation to get well.
4. *The sick person should seek technically competent help and cooperate with the physician.* The obligation to get well involves a further obligation on the part of the sick person to seek technically competent help, usually from a physician. The sick person is also expected to cooperate with the physician in the process of trying to get well.

Parsons's concept of the sick role is based on the classical social theory of Emile Durkheim and Max Weber and the psychoanalytic theory of Sigmund Freud. Psychoanalytic theories of the structure of the personality (i.e., id, ego, and superego) and the unconscious assisted Parsons in developing his thoughts on individual motivation. The sick person is presumably motivated to recover (as a result of socialization and the influence of the superego) and yet may perhaps also be motivated, either consciously or unconsciously, to desire the "secondary gain" of privileges and exemptions from daily tasks that accompany the sick role.

Durkheim's ideas on the function of moral (ethical) authority and Weber's views on religious values are utilized by Parsons in describing the role of the physician. The physician, according to Parsons, is invested with the function of social control. This function, which is similar to that provided historically by priests and which originated in religion, is intended to control deviance. In this case, illness with its dysfunctional nature is the deviance. The designation of illness as an undesirable and illegitimate state is considered by Parsons to have the greatest implications for the healthy, in that it reinforces their motivation to stay well. All of this is reflected in the position of health as an important social value in American society and the manner in which people are socialized to accept this value. By incorporating a consideration of health and illness into his analysis of social systems, Parsons was the first to demonstrate the function of medicine as a form of social control and did so within the parameters of classical sociological theory.

The Physician–Patient Role Relationship

A major contribution of Parsons's concept of the sick role is its description of a patterned set of expectations that define the norms and values appropriate to being sick in Western culture, both for the individual and for others who interact with the sick person. Thus, the sick role views the patient–physician relationship within a framework of social roles, attitudes, and activities that both parties bring to the situation. This approach allows us, with some exceptions, to both understand and predict the behavior of the ill in Western society. The patient–physician role, like all other roles, involves a basic mutuality—that is, each participant in the social situation is expected to be familiar with both his or her own and others' expectations of behavior and the probable sequence of social acts to be followed. *The sick role evokes a set of patterned expectations that define the norms and values appropriate to being sick, both for the individual and for others who interact with the person.* Neither party can define his or her role independently of the role partner. The full meaning of "acting like a physician" depends on the patient's conception of what a physician is in terms of the social role. The physician's role is, as Parsons tells us, to return the sick person to his or her normal state of functioning.

The role of the patient likewise depends on the conception that the physician holds of the patient's role. According to Parsons, the patient is expected to recognize that being sick is unpleasant and that he or she has an obligation to get well by seeking the physician's help. The patient–physician role relationship is therefore not a spontaneous form of social interaction. It is a well-defined encounter consisting of two or more persons whose object is the health of a single individual. It is also a situation that is too important to be left to undefined forms of behavior. For this reason, patients and physicians tend to act in a stable and predictable manner.

The patient–physician relationship is intended by society to be therapeutic in nature. The patient has a need for technical services from the physician, and the physician is the technical expert who is qualified and defined by society as prepared to help the patient. The goal of the patient–physician encounter is thus to promote some significant change for the better in the patient's health.

Although the patient–physician relationship involves mutuality in the form of behavioral expectations, the status and power of the parties are not equal. The role of the physician is based on an imbalance of power and the technical expertise favorable exclusively to the physician. This imbalance is necessary because the physician needs leverage in his or her relationship with the patient to promote positive changes in the patient's health. Accomplishment of this goal sometimes requires procedures that can be painful or discomforting to the patient, yet the patient may be required to accept and follow the treatment plan if the physician is to be effective. The physician exercises leverage through three basic techniques: (1) professional prestige, (2) situational authority, and (3) situational dependency of the patient.

A physician's professional prestige rests on the technical qualifications and certification by society as a healer. The physician's situational power refers to the physician's having what the patient wants and needs. By contrast, the patient is dependent because he or she lacks the expertise required to treat the health disorder.

The role of the physician is also enhanced by a certain mystique reflecting faith in the power to heal. This aspect of the physician role results from the dependence of the patient on the physician for life-and-death decisions. Since the physician has the responsibility to "do everything possible" and because the survival of the patient may be at issue, the patient may be likely to regard the physician with a strong emotional attachment in the hope or belief that the physician has a "gift" or natural skill in the healing arts. Since medical practice is sometimes characterized by uncertainty, a physician's presumed talent can be a very important dimension in the patient–physician relationship. Exact proof of the existence of many minor ailments and most chronic diseases may not be possible, or attempts to establish such proof may not be justifiable because of the hazards to the patient involved in the investigation. Despite the great advancement of the science of medicine, the physician must still sometimes act on the basis of a hunch.

An interesting analogue to the patient–physician relationship is the child–parent relationship. For some people, an illness can foster a childlike state of dependency. However, while the role of the child is an immature role, the role of the patient represents a "disturbed" maturity (Wilson 1970). Both the child and the sick person lack the capacity to perform the usual functions of the adult in everyday life, and both are dependent on a stronger and more adequate person to take care of them. Also the physician can be like a parent figure, in that he or she provides support and controls rewards significant to the dependent party. The primary reward for the child would be approval, while the primary reward for the sick person would be to get well. Yet, the physician and the parent are unlike in the magnitude of their involvement with the dependent party and the depth of their emotional feelings. Obviously, the states of childhood and patienthood are not totally similar, yet the similarity is a striking one. This is because the extremely sick person who is helpless, technically incompetent in treating his or her disorder, and perhaps emotionally disturbed over his or her condition of illness, can be very dependent and fully capable of acting in childlike ways.

According to Eliot Freidson (1970:206), physicians create the social possibilities for acting sick because they are society's authority on what "illness really is." They decide who is sick and what should be done about it. In essence, physicians are "gatekeepers" to most professional health resources, since these resources (such as prescription drugs and hospitals) cannot be used without their permission. Thus, Freidson argues that the behavior of the physician and others in the health field constitutes the embodiment of certain dominant values in society. These dominant values were described by Parsons (1951, 1979) and include the idea that health is positive and should be sought after. Stipulated in his concept of the sick role is that the sick person is expected to cooperate with the physician and *work* to achieve his or her own recovery and return to normal functioning.

Research Applications of the Sick Role

Parsons's concept of the sick role, as Freidson (1970:228) has explained, represents "a penetrating and apt analysis of sickness from a distinctly sociological point of view." This comment is particularly appropriate when it is recognized that the sick role has stimulated a considerable body of research in medical sociology. To mention only a few studies, Paul Chalfant and Richard Kurtz (1971) utilized Parsons's sick-role concept in explaining social workers' denial of the sick role to alcoholics. Social workers in this study felt that drinking was motivated behavior and that alcoholics could avoid their disorder if they desired to do so. Hence, the alcoholic was not entitled to exemption from normal responsibilities. In Norway, Claire Glenton (2003) found that back sufferers wanted access to the sick role for the benefits it provided, but often their status could not be legitimatized because physicians were unable to provide a clear identification of the source of the pain. The lack of a medical diagnosis kept them going back to their doctors over time for more examinations and perpetuated in a state of dependence on the physician.

Another application of the sick role is found in Stephen Cole and Robert LeJeune's (1972) study of welfare mothers. Cole and LeJeune observed that among welfare mothers in New York City, the general norm was to accept the dominant cultural view that being on welfare is a result of personal failure. Welfare mothers who had given up hope of getting off welfare were prone to adopt the sick role to legitimize their self-defined failure. This study concluded that the sick role may provide a "substitute" status by way of exemption from normal role responsibilities for persons who lack other socially approved statuses. What is implied here is that certain people may use the sick role because it is less stigmatizing than being regarded a failure.

A similar finding was noted in a study by Arnold Arluke, Louanne Kennedy, and Ronald Kessler (1979) of 1,000 patients discharged from two large New York City hospitals. Arluke and his colleagues found that low-income and elderly patients are most likely to agree that a person has the right not to be held responsible for his or her illness. For some elderly people, it was believed that the sick role provided an excuse for being dependent. Consequently, these elderly people were most unwilling to give up the role. Younger people were most likely to agree that a person has the duty to try to get well.

In other research, Brea Perry (2011) found in a nationwide sample that persons with symptoms of severe mental disorder were accorded the sick role by core members of their social network of family and friends. In Illinois, the author and his associates (Cockerham, Creditor, Creditor, and Imrey 1980) studied the manner in which physicians treated their own minor ailments. The doctors tended to adopt aspects of the sick role by engaging in actions requiring a physician (or, in this case, being one), such as taking prescription drugs or ordering diagnostic tests on themselves. Elsewhere, in Israel, David Rier (2000), a seriously ill medical sociologist who had previously been critical of Parsons's concept of the sick role in his lectures,

BOX 8.1

The Sick Role in an Intensive Care Unit

David Rier (2000), a medical sociologist, was admitted to an intensive care unit suffering from a severe case of pneumonia. He woke up one morning so weak, he said he could not think clearly and had a high fever, chills, and difficulty breathing. Two days later, he entered the hospital. "For a medical sociologist, being ill offers a priceless opportunity to engage in the most intimate manner possible, with the subject of my life's work," Rier (2000:71) commented. Only a few days earlier in class, he had criticized Parsons's concept of the sick role, by claiming Parsons's view of physicians was too paternalistic, assumed too readily that patients should place their trust in doctors, and paid insufficient attention to the patient's perspective and ability to challenge, negotiate, collaborate, or circumvent physicians. Parsons's model of the doctor–patient relationship seemed to reflect the 1950s, not the twenty-first century.

Rier almost died. In fact, he said that he could feel himself slipping away, as he became sicker and weaker and had to be put on a respirator to breathe. At this point, he thought about dying ("*There's* something I've never done before," he told himself) and it did not seem to him to be all that difficult. He could just relax and let go. But he thought of his family and told himself he was going to make it. All he had to do was lie there and keep breathing and rely on the medical staff to get him out of this situation. Rier survived. As for the sick role, he had a much better opinion of it. He found that, as Parsons suggests, he had to trust his doctors. His perspective on his treatment was unimportant at the time, and challenging or negotiating was senseless. He was completely in the hands of his physicians and cooperated with their procedures as best he could to get well.

found that the doctor–patient relationship in intensive care was much as Parsons described. "As for myself," states Rier (2000:75), "in what is the most lasting result of my unaccustomed passivity in the ICU [intensive care unit], my illness provoked me to reassess the critique of Parsons I had been teaching only weeks before."

Medicalization

Implicit in Parsons' concept of sickness as a form of deviance is the idea that medicine is (and should be) an institution for the social control of deviant behavior. That is, it is medicine's task to control abnormal behavior by medical means on behalf of society. Bryan Turner (1996) points out that regulation of the human body is in the interest of society because of the need to protect the public's health, the economy, and the social order. Turner notes that disease can be contained by way of social hygiene and education in appropriate lifestyles. Yet, people can also knowingly jeopardize their health through lifestyle habits such as drug addiction, overeating, smoking, lack of exercise, and alcoholism. These behaviors, he continues, either are already regarded as socially deviant or are well on the way to becoming regarded as such. When certain behaviors threaten the health of people and the well-being of society, the state may be required to intervene, such as banning cigarette smoking from public places. Consequently, it is Turner's (1996:214) position that "medicine is essentially social medicine, because it is a practice which regulates social activities under the auspices of the state." Therefore, to the extent that the control of human behavior is the basis of social organization and the control of deviant behavior is becoming the function of the medical profession, Parsons's concept of the sick role helps us understand medicine's role in promoting social stability.

However, some medical sociologists have expressed concern that medicine has taken responsibility for an ever greater proportion of deviant behaviors and bodily conditions by defining them as medical problems (Clarke and Shim 2011; Clarke et al. 2003; Conrad 1975, 2005, 2007, 2013; Conrad and Leiter 2004; Davis 2010; Freidson 1970; Gallagher and Sionean 2004). Acts that might have been defined as sin or crime and controlled by the church or the law are increasingly regarded as illnesses to be controlled through medical treatment, as are certain physical differences like short stature, small female breasts, and male baldness. This trend is known as "medicalization" and occurs when non-medical problems are defined as problems that need to be treated medically, usually as an illnesses or disorder of some type (Conrad 2007:4; Conrad and Leiter 2004:158). "Medicalization," according to Joseph Davis (2010:211), "is the name for the process by which medical definitions and practices are applied to behaviors, psychological phenomena, and somatic experiences not previously within the conceptual or therapeutic scope of medicine." As Thomas Szasz (1974:44–45) put it, "with increasing zeal, physicians and especially psychiatrists began to call 'illness' . . . anything and everything in which they could detect any sign of malfunctioning, based on no matter what the norm."

These comments call attention to the trend toward making sickness and deviance not only synonymous but also toward treating deviance exclusively in a medical mode. Rick Mayes and Allan Horwitz (2005) observed that the American Psychiatric Association's *Diagnostic and Statistical Manual of Mental Disorders* first published in 1952 listed 106 mental disorders and was 130 pages in length. The fourth edition published in 1994 and revised in 2000 had 297 disorders and consisted of 886 pages, while the fifth edition released in 2013 has 341 disorders and 992 pages. Clearly, there has been a proliferation of diagnoses in psychiatry, including problems such as "oppositional defiant disorder" (defiant acts by children, such as losing tempers or being annoying, angry, or spiteful) that would appear to be dubious without evidence of other more abnormal behavior and others such as "binge eating disorder" and "cannabis withdrawal" that arguably have questionable validity as a mental disorder (Cockerham 2014). "Disorder of written expression" (bad writing) was fortunately removed from DSM-5. Some critics, such as Andrew Twaddle (1973:756), have gone so far as to claim that "there are few, if any, problems of human behavior that some group does not think of as medical problems." Freidson (1970) has likewise argued that medicine has established a jurisdiction far wider than justified by its demonstrable capacity to "cure."

Nonetheless, the medical profession has been successful in gaining authority to define aberrant behaviors and even naturally occurring physical conditions such as aging as illness—problems best handled by the physician. For example, hyperactivity at school by children is defined as Attention-Deficit/Hyperactivity Disorder (ADHD) and requires Ritalin; menopause is treated with estrogen replacement therapy, whose side effects were determined a few years later to promote even greater risk from blood clots, stroke, heart disease, and breast cancer; being short in stature necessitates growth hormones for the person afflicted with below average height; and male baldness is slowed or prevented by using Propecia and lost hair is restored by surgical transplants (Conrad 2007). There was a time when hyperactivity, menopause, shortness, and baldness were not medical conditions. A similar trend is seen in studies of mental health showing psychiatry transforming normal sorrow into clinically treated depression and natural anxiety into an anxiety disorder (Horwitz and Wakefield 2007, 2012).

Of course, for some people, new medical treatments for previously untreated conditions can be positive, such as the development of Viagra and similar drugs for erectile dysfunction. However, current accounts of medicalization describe an even greater expansion of this process. This outcome has led Adele Clarke and her colleagues (2003:161; Clarke and Shim 2011) to declare that the growth of medical jurisdiction over social problems is "one of the most potent transformations of the last half of the twentieth century in the West." Whereas medicalization has traditionally been a means by which professional medicine acquired increasingly more problems to treat, Clarke et al. (2003) suggest that major technological and scientific advances in biomedicine are taking this capability even further and producing what she and her colleagues refer to as "biomedicalization." Biomedicalization consists of the capability of computer information and new technologies to extend medical surveillance and treatment interventions well beyond past boundaries, by the use of genetics, bioengineering, chemoprevention, individualized drugs, multiple sources of information, patient data banks, digitized patient records, and other innovations. Also important in this process is the Internet, advertising, consumerism, and the role of pharmaceutical companies in marketing their products.

The increasing commercialization of health products and services in the expansion of the medical marketplace has been noted by other medical sociologists (Conrad 2007; Conrad and Leiter 2004; Davis 2010; Gallagher and Sionean 2004; Light 2010). Peter Conrad and Valerie Leiter (2004) observe that insurance companies can counteract medicalization by restricting access, but there are other forces facilitating the process. Conrad (2005, 2007) finds that the engines pushing medicalization have changed, with biotechnology, consumers, and managed care now being the driving forces. "Doctors," Conrad (2005:10) states, "are still the gatekeepers for medical treatment, but their role is more subordinate in the expansion or contraction of medicalization." He notes that biotechnology has long been associated with medicalization, and the pharmaceutical industry is playing an increasingly central role in promoting its products directly to consumers, while in the future the impact of genetics may be substantial. Already, we are seeing the use of the term *pharmaceuticalization* of society to describe the growth of the drug markets internationally through large-scale advertising campaigns directed to both physicians and the public at large, including drugs for non-medical (enhancement) purposes (Williams, Martin, and Gabe 2011).

In the meantime, consumers have become major players in the health marketplace through their purchase of health insurance plans, health products, and the like, and their demand for these products also fuels medicalization. The Internet, in particular, has led to easier consumer access to health-related goods. Managed care, in turn, has become the dominant form of health care delivery in the United States, which makes insurance companies as third-party payers important in both bolstering medicalization through its coverage of particular services and a constraint in placing limitations on those services. Thus managed care plays an important role in the medicalization process. Although medicalization is prevalent in the United States, observes Conrad (2007), it is increasingly an international phenomenon with multinational drug companies leading the way. While public and professional medical concern about medicalization may be growing, the process it represents is still a powerful influence on behavior and our understanding of it has its origins in Parsons's work.

Criticism of the Sick Role

Although Parsons's concept of the sick role has demonstrated research utility as a framework for explaining illness-related behavior and has become a basic concept in medical sociology, the model has some serious defects that have led some sociologists to suggest that it should be abandoned. Parsons's sick-role theory can be criticized because of (1) behavioral variation, (2) types of diseases, (3) the patient–physician relationship, and (4) the sick role's middle-class orientation.

Behavioral Variation

Much of the criticism of the sick-role theory has been directed toward its lack of uniformity among various persons and social groups. In a random sample of people living in New York City, Gerald Gordon (1966) found at least two distinct and unrelated statuses and complementary role expectations associated with being sick. When a prognosis was believed to be serious and uncertain, expectations of behavior generally conformed to Parsons's description of the sick role. However, when a prognosis was known and not serious, the notion of an "impaired role" emerged from Gordon's data, which required normal role responsibilities and rejected role exemptions despite sickness.

Twaddle (1969) reported at least seven configurations of the sick role, with Parsons's model being only one, in a study of Rhode Island married couples in late middle age. The exact configuration of the alternative sick roles discovered by Twaddle depended in part on cultural values and whether a person defined himself or herself as "sick." Not only were there differing personal definitions of "being sick" but also not all of the respondents stated they expected to get well and not all of them cooperated with the physician. Twaddle found that the sick role, as defined by Parsons, was much more applicable to Jews than to either Protestants or Italian Catholics. Jews were more likely to see themselves as being sick, as expecting to get well, and as cooperating with the physician. Protestants were the most resistant to seeing a physician, and Italian Catholics were generally the least cooperative with the physician. There were also other important ethnocultural differences in the Twaddle study. Protestants, for example, were much more likely to regard functional incapacity (usually an inability to work) as the first sign of illness, while Italian Catholics were more likely to emphasize changes in feeling states such as pain. Jews, however, tended to emphasize fear of eventual outcomes, rather than feeling states or functional incapacities.

A well-known study by Mark Zborowski (1952) demonstrated important group differences pertaining to pain. While pain is clearly a biological phenomenon, Zborowski observed that responses to pain are not always biological but vary among ethnocultural groups. Zborowski's sample consisted of 87 male patients and 16 healthy males in New York City, who were primarily of Jewish, Italian, and "Old

American" ethnic backgrounds. The so-called Old Americans were defined as white, native-born, and usually Protestant patients whose families had lived at least two generations in the United States; they also did not identify with any particular foreign nationality. All of the patients suffered from neurological ailments, such as herniated discs or spinal lesions, which represented disorders where the pain involved would vary only within fairly narrow limits.

Although the level of pain was thought to be generally similar, Zborowski found significant variation in the responses to pain. Jews and Italians tended to be more sensitive to pain and more prone to exaggerate the experience of pain than Old Americans. While Jews and Italians were similar in responding to pain in the hospital, the two ethnic groups differed in the home setting. At home, the Italian acted strong and authoritative, but in the hospital he was highly emotional. The Jewish patient was emotional in both settings. Zborowski observed that Jewish patients also used their suffering as a device for manipulating the behavior of others. But once satisfied that adequate care was being provided, the Jewish patient tended to become more restrained in his response.

In contrast, the Old American patients tried to conform to the medical image of the ideal patient. They cooperated with hospital personnel and avoided being a nuisance as much as possible. The Old American patients also avoided expressing pain in public, and when examined by the physician, they tended to assume the role of a detached observer by becoming unemotional and attempting to provide an efficient description of their internal state to aid in a correct diagnosis. If their pain was too much for them to control, they would withdraw to their rooms and express their pain privately.

The attitudes toward pain also varied. Zborowski reported that Italians were more concerned with the discomfort of the pain itself and were relatively satisfied and happy when immediate relief was provided. The Italian patient also tended to display a confident attitude toward the physician. The Jewish patient, however, was not particularly confident about his physician, and he seemed to be more concerned about the significance of his pain for his general state of health rather than about any specific and immediate discomfort. While Italian patients sought pain killers, Jewish patients were reluctant to take drugs because they were apprehensive about the habit-forming characteristics of the drugs. The Old Americans, like the Jews, were also primarily concerned about what pain signified for their general state of health, but unlike the Jews, they were optimistic about the power of medicine and its ability to provide a cure. Hence, they displayed great confidence in the decisions made by the physicians.

In an effort to explain these ethnocultural differences, Zborowski offered the opinion that Jewish and Italian mothers demonstrated overprotective and overemotional attitudes about their sons' health and that this socialization experience fostered the development of anxieties regarding pain among Jewish and Italian patients. Zborowski believed that Jewish and Italian parents had tended to prevent physical injury to their sons by discouraging them from playing rough games and sports, whereas Old American parents, on the other hand, had socialized their sons to expect to get hurt in sports and to fight back. Old American boys were taught "not to be sissies," "not to cry," and "to take pain like a man." If such a child were actually injured, he was expected not to get emotional but to seek proper treatment immediately.

Research by John Campbell (1978), involving a sample of 264 children and their mothers in Washington, D.C., supports Zborowski's findings in regard to the responses of the Old Americans. Although Campbell did not focus on the role of ethnicity, his data showed that those children who were older and whose parents were of higher socioeconomic background tended to take a "stiff-upper-lip" or "business-as-usual" approach to illness. "This Spartan orientation," says Campbell (1978:46), "bears more than a passing resemblance to the responses to pain that Zborowski described as typifying his 'Old American' subjects—responses that tended to be approved by members of the medical profession—who themselves, perhaps not coincidently, would be assigned to higher SES [socioeconomic status] levels." According to Campbell, parents *do* make a difference when it comes to socializing their children to handle their emotions and reject the sick role.

As for other studies of ethnic variation, Irving Zola's (1966) comparison of American patients of Irish, Italian, and Anglo-Saxon descent at two hospitals in Boston also supported Zborowski's findings. In general, the Italians tended to dramatize their symptoms, while Zola found that the Irish would often deny their symptoms and the Anglo-Saxons would speak of their health problems in a detached and neutral manner lacking in anxiety. Zola concluded that there were indeed distinct differences between cultural groups and the way in which they communicated complaints about their health.

Besides ethnic variation, there may be other ways in which people interpret the sick role. One study has shown that, among heart patients having surgery, women tend to adopt the sick role more frequently than men and to be less ready to resume their work roles after surgery (Brown and Rawlinson 1977). Thus, there may be differences by gender in regard to acceptance of the sick role as well. Emil Berkanovic (1972) studied sick-role conceptions among Los Angeles city employees several years ago. Although his sample cannot claim to be representative of city employees generally, his findings do suggest that some people feel they are able to define appropriate illness behavior under certain circumstances. These people do not reject medical theories of illness but simply feel competent to decide the correct behavior for the sick person, provided the symptoms are recognized and the outcome of the illness is known. Berkanovic points out that often the physician is consulted only as a last resort and only after all other sources of health information fail to provide an adequate explanation.

What is indicated by all of these studies is that Parsons's concept of the sick role does not account for all of the considerable variations in the way people view sickness and define appropriate sick-role behavior for themselves and others.

Type of Disease

The second major category of criticism regarding Parsons's concept of the sick role is that it seems to apply only to acute diseases, which by their nature are temporary, usually recognizable by laypersons, and readily overcome with a physician's help. Yet chronic diseases, such as cancer, heart disease, diabetes, and Alzheimer's disease, are by definition not temporary, and the patient cannot be expected to get well as Parsons's model suggests, no matter how willing the patient may be to cooperate with the physician. Therefore, temporary exemptions from normal role responsibilities for the chronic patient may be impossible.

Research on patients with chronic disorders has shown that some perceive the sick role differently from patients with acute illnesses (Radley 1994). These were chronic patients faced with the impossibility of resuming normal roles and the necessity of adjusting their activities to a permanent health disorder. Yet Carl May (2011) observes that the increase in the prevalence of chronic diseases since the 1950s has brought major changes on the part of both health care providers and patients that include an extended sick role. Patients often need to work (e.g., pursue a healthy lifestyle, regularly take prescribed drugs, and the like) to control the symptoms of chronic disease and the provision of professional health care often requires a team approach on the part of providers to ensure a comprehensive regimen of care—all of which places the patient in a long-term sick role including a prolonged dependent status. Some persons with chronic health problems view the sick role along the same lines as described by Parsons, as found in Glenton's (2003) study of back pain sufferers who wanted to adopt the traditional sick role.

In a reconsideration of the sick role, Parsons (1975) argued that even if the goal of a complete recovery is impractical, many chronic diseases can be "managed" so that the patient is able to maintain a relatively normal pattern of physiological and social functioning. While diabetes, for example, cannot be cured in the sense that pneumonia can, Parsons insists that a chronic disease such as diabetes should not be placed in a totally different category from that of "curable" diseases, if the patient can be returned to a normal range of functioning. True, this explanation may allow the sick-role concept to account for some chronic disorders; still it cannot be applied to a wide range of illness situations such as the bedridden patient, the terminally ill patient, and the HIV-infected patient (Crossley 1998). The conclusion is that Parsons's sick role is applicable to acute diseases and applies to some but not all circumstances pertaining to chronic illnesses.

Problems also arise in applying the sick role to the mentally ill, in that while the sick role stipulates a person should seek professional care, people who go to psychiatrists for help may be stigmatized for doing just that. People who admit to a history of mental illness often have problems finding jobs, and a considerable body of research literature describes the difficulties former mental patients have in coping with rejection from other people. In addition, many mental hospital patients refuse to accept the idea that they are mentally ill, and most patients, rather than voluntarily seeking help, are admitted to mental institutions involuntarily (Cockerham 2014).

Patient–Physician Role Relationship

A third major area of criticism of Parsons's sick-role model is that it is based on a traditional one-to-one interaction between a patient and a physician. This form of interaction is common because the usual setting is the physician's office, where Parsons's version of the sick role is conceptualized. It is the setting where the physician has maximum control. Yet, quite different patterns of interaction may emerge in the hospital, where perhaps a team of physicians and other members of the hospital staff are involved. In the hospital, the physician is one of several physicians and is subject to organizational constraints and policies. If the patient is at home, the patient–physician relationship may also again vary, because the patient and his or her family can much more clearly influence the interaction.

In addition, the pattern of relationships outlined in Parsons's sick role is modified if the client is a target of preventive techniques rather than strictly therapeutic measures. A considerable portion of contemporary medical practice is concerned, not with restoring a single patient to normal social functioning but with maintaining and improving public health. The patient–physician relationship is different when the target is a group of individuals, particularly if the health problem is not a disabling illness but a behavioral problem such as smoking cigarettes or an environmental problem such as water or air pollution. In this situation, the physician or health practitioner must usually be persuasive rather than authoritative, since he or she lacks the leverage to control the client group. The physician must convince the group that certain actions, such as physical examinations or X-ray examinations for tuberculosis, are good for them. In defense of Parsons's sick role, however, it should be noted that the behavior needing to be changed in such cases is often "normal" rather than "sick."

Middle-Class Orientation

Finally, it should be noted that Parsons's sick-role model is a middle-class pattern of behavior. It emphasizes the merits of individual responsibility and the deliberate striving toward good health and a return to normality. It is oriented to the middle-class assumption that rational problem solving is the only viable behavior in the face of difficulty and that effort will result in positive gain. It fails to take into account what it is like to live in an environment of poverty, where success is the exception to the rule.

Also, many people in the lower socioeconomic classes may tend to deny the sick role, not only because they may not have the opportunity to enjoy typically middle-class secondary gains but also because the functional incapacity of the poor person may render him or her less likely to be able to earn a living or survive in conditions of poverty. Therefore, people living in a poverty environment might work, regardless of how sick they might be, as long as they feel able to perform some of their work activities.

Yet, it should be noted that even though the notion of "striving toward good health" reflects a middle-class orientation, the lower class uses the sick role to justify their disadvantaged social position (Arluke et al. 1979; Cole and LeJeune 1972). That is, some poor people claim they are poor because they are sick, and being sick (and poor) is not their fault. While being sick and working to get well may be typical of the middle class, being sick and using the sick role to excuse one's circumstances in life appear more common among the lower class.

Parsons's Sick Role: Conclusion

Despite the considerable criticism of Parsons's sick-role concept found in sociological literature, it should be noted that this model represents a significant contribution to medical sociology. Parsons insists that illness is a form of deviance and that as such it is necessary for a society to return the sick to their normal social functioning. Thus, Parsons views medicine as a mechanism by which a society attempts to control deviance and maintain social stability. In light of the trend toward classifying more and more social problems as medical problems, Parsons's explanation of the function of medicine has broad implications for the future treatment of deviants in our society.

While recognizing that some criticisms of Parsons's theory are valid, we should note that at least some of this criticism is based on a misunderstanding of Parsons. Apparently, some critics incorrectly assume that Parsons viewed the sick role as a fixed, mechanical kind of "cage" that would produce similarities of behavior among sick people, regardless of variant cultural backgrounds and different personal learning experiences. Instead, what Parsons has given us is an "ideal type" of the sick role. By definition, ideal types do not exist in reality. They are abstractions, erected by emphasizing selected aspects of behavior typical in certain contexts, and they serve as bases for comparing and differentiating concrete behaviors occurring in similar situations in different sociocultural circumstances. Perhaps, Eugene Gallagher (1976) said it best when he pointed out that whoever acquires a sociologically informed understanding of health and illness in contemporary society soon realizes how significantly sociological analysis has benefited from Parsons's formulation of the sick role and how, in comparison, many criticisms of it seem petty.

Therefore, it can be concluded that Parsons's model is a useful and viable framework of sociological analysis within certain contexts. Although the theory is an insufficient explanation of all illness behavior, it does describe many general similarities and should not be abandoned. In fact, writing in a later article, Parsons (1975) admitted that he did not believe it was ever his intention to make his concept cover the whole range of phenomena associated with the sick role. Two possibilities exist: (1) using the model as an "ideal type" with which various forms of illness behavior can be contrasted or (2) expanding the concept to account for conditions generally common to most illness situations.

Labeling Theory

By failing to account for the behavioral variations within the sick role, the functionalist approach to illness has not accounted for some aspects of acting sick. Chapter 7, on illness behavior, pointed out that two people having much the same symptoms may behave quite differently. One person may become concerned and seek medical treatment, while another person may ignore the symptoms completely. Individual strategies in coping with illness vary from passive cooperation to positive action to get well and from fear at being diagnosed as ill to actual pleasure in anticipation of secondary gains (Lipowski 1970). Several sociologists, including Freidson (1970), have taken the position that illness as deviant behavior is relative and must be seen as such—this is the perspective of labeling theory.

Labeling theory is based on the concept that what is regarded as deviant behavior by one person or social group may not be so regarded by other persons or social groups. Howard Becker (1973), one of the leading proponents of labeling theory, illustrates the concept in his study of marijuana users. His analysis reveals a discrepancy in American society between those people who insist that smoking marijuana is harmful and that use of the drug should be illegal and those who support a norm favoring marijuana smoking and who believe that use of the drug should be legalized. While the wider society views marijuana smoking as deviant (Colorado nevertheless was the first state to legalize the sale of marijuana in 2013), groups of marijuana smokers view their behavior as socially acceptable.

Becker's position is that deviance is created by social groups who make rules or norms. Infractions of these rules or norms constitute deviant behavior. Accordingly, deviance is not a quality of the act a person commits but instead is a consequence of the definition applied to that act by other people. The critical variable in understanding deviance is the social audience, because the audience determines what is and what is not deviant behavior.

The applicability of labeling theory as a vehicle for explaining illness behavior is that, while disease may be a biological state existing independently of human knowledge, sickness is a social state created and formed by human perception. Thus, as Freidson (1970) has pointed out, when a veterinarian diagnoses a cow's condition as an illness, the diagnosis itself does not change the cow's behavior. But when a physician diagnoses a human's condition as illness, the diagnosis can and often does change the sick person's behavior. Thus, illness is seen by labeling theorists as a condition created by human beings in accordance with their understanding of the situation.

For example, among the Kuba people of Sumatra, skin diseases and injuries to the skin are common because of a difficult jungle environment. A person suffering from a skin disease would not be considered to be sick among the Kuba because the condition, while unhealthy, is not considered abnormal. In parts of Africa, such afflictions as hookworms or mild malaria may not be considered abnormal because they are so common. Examples such as this have led to the realization that an essentially unhealthy state may not always be equated with illness when the people involved are able to function effectively and the presence of the disorder does not affect the normal rhythm of daily life. Therefore, judgments concerning what is sickness and what is deviant behavior are relative and depend on the social situations in which people live.

Labeling Theory and Illness Behavior

Labeling theory has so far failed to develop a theory of illness behavior comparable to Parsons's model. The closest equivalent deriving from the symbolic interactionist view (labeling theory) is that of Freidson (1970). Freidson indicates that the key to distinguishing among sick roles is the notion of legitimacy. He maintains that in illness states, there are three types of legitimacy, which involve either a minor or serious deviation. (1) *Conditional legitimacy,* where the deviants are temporarily exempted from normal obligations and gain some extra privileges on the proviso that they seek help to rid themselves of their deviance. A cold would be a minor deviation and pneumonia serious in this category. (2) *Unconditional legitimacy,* where the deviants are exempted permanently from normal obligations and are granted additional privileges in view of the hopeless nature of their deviance. Terminal cancer falls in this category. (3) *Illegitimacy,* where the deviants are exempted from some normal obligations by virtue of their deviance, for which they are technically not responsible, but gain few if any privileges and take on handicaps such as stigma. A stammer would be minor and epilepsy serious.

Freidson's classification system implies that there are different consequences for the individual and that his or her treatment by other people depends on the label of definition applied to the deviant's health disorder by others. Freidson's model accounts for the problematic aspects of illness relative to social situations. A person with a skin disease in the Kuba tribe or a person with hookworms in Africa could be classified as unconditionally legitimate, for example, because the afflicted person would gain no special privileges or changes in obligations, since the disorder would be common to most people who functioned normally in their society. A person with cancer, in contrast, would gain a permanent exemption from normal obligations because of the seriousness of his or her condition.

Freidson's concept, however, is strictly theoretical and has not been extensively tested. Whether it can account for variations in illness behavior remains a matter of speculation. While Freidson's model is useful in categorizing illness behavior, it fails to explain differences in the way people define themselves as being sick and in need of professional medical care. As discussed earlier, some people ignore their symptoms and others engage in self-care or seek professional help. The merit of Freidson's model, however, is that it does go beyond Parsons's concept of the sick role, by describing different types of illness and pointing out that illness is a socially created label. Of course, some may argue that there is a biological reality constituting a disease, regardless of how people define it; however, social definitions of the disease determine the ways in which societies and people within those societies respond to it.

Criticism of Labeling Theory

The labeling approach stresses that judgments of what is deviance are relative, depending on the perceptions of others. Therefore, the critical variable in understanding deviant behavior is the social audience that has knowledge of the act in question, because the audience determines what is and what is not deviance. But despite its merits in providing a framework to analyze the variety of perceptions people may hold about deviance, labeling theory contains some shortcomings.

First, labeling theory does not explain what causes deviance, other than the reaction of other people to it. Few would deny that groups create deviance when they establish norms. Admittedly, the reaction of an "audience" to variant types of behavior influences the individual's self-concept and also influences society's response. But a label in itself does not cause deviance. Some situations—murder, burglary, drug addiction, and suicide—are generally defined by most people as deviant, yet people do these things regardless of how they are labeled, and their reasons for doing so may have nothing to do with the label that is attached to them. Second, if deviant acts and actors share common characteristics other than societal reaction, these common characteristics are not considered, defined or explained. Yet, people committing deviant acts may share many similarities such as stress, poverty, age, peer group relations, and family background. These characteristics may be as important as, if not more important than, the reaction of the social audience.

Therefore, Jack Gibbs (1971) raised the important question asking *what* is being explained by labeling theory—deviant behavior or *reactions* to deviant behavior? It is likely the latter. Third, labeling theory does not explain why certain people commit deviant acts and others in the same circumstances do not. All this seems to pose the question of whether societal reaction alone is sufficient to explain deviant behavior. The answer seems to be that it is not. In a later reconsideration, Becker (1973:179) agreed that labeling theory "cannot possibly be considered as the sole explanation of what alleged deviants actually do."

Labeling Theory: Conclusion

When compared to Parsons's concept of the sick role, labeling theory does address itself to the specific variations in illness behavior that seem to be present among differing socioeconomic and ethnocultural groups in American society. It also provides a framework of analysis for illness behavior according to the definition and perception of particular social groups and allows the social scientist to account for differences between social settings and types of illnesses as well. Over and against these advantages, labeling theory suffers from vagueness in its conceptualization, namely, what causes deviance other than societal reaction—which has little or nothing to do with disease. While Freidson's model has potential, it has not attracted the attention accorded to Parsons's sick role. But most importantly, there is serious doubt whether societal reactions in and of themselves are sufficient to explain the generalities of behavior occurring among the sick.

Sickness as Social Deviance?

This chapter has discussed the various approaches to sickness as deviance. The question remains whether this perspective of sickness is useful or adequate for sociological studies. The conceptualization of sickness as deviant behavior does make sickness a sociologically relevant variable, but it also restricts the analysis of sickness to the framework of a social event. This is in accordance with the major intention of the sickness-as-deviance perspective in sociology—to focus exclusively on the social properties of being ill and thus to exclude biological properties definable only by the physician. Yet, by dwelling exclusively on the social properties of sickness, the deviance perspective severely limits its capacity to deal with the biological aspects of sickness as a condition of suffering.

It can also be argued that, while deviance is behavior contrary to the normative expectations of society, sickness itself does not counteract social norms. The members of any society are expected to become ill now and then during their lives. People who are sick are different from the norm of wellness, but this situation does not make them a bad person, as the concept of deviance implies. However, when people are sick, they are not themselves. They are different (abnormal) in a negative sort of way that most people would prefer to avoid—just as they would like to avoid going to prison. Not only do sick people feel bad, but they may be physically disabled as well. They may also experience mental dysfunctions. According to Eric Cassell (1985), people with serious physical illnesses often lose their sense of perspective and are unable to think about situations from more than a single viewpoint—namely, how they feel. Their ability to reason and make decisions may change, and they may become heavily dependent on doctors and others to take care of them. They may also become so self-absorbed and childlike in that they focus exclusively on themselves and ignore the outside world.

Kathy Charmaz (1983, 1991) has suggested that the chronically ill also experience a negative sense of self because their illness restricts their activities, isolates them from other people, discredits them by lessening their sense of worth, and causes them to be a burden to others. Some persons may, in fact, feel stigmatized as a result of their illness, as seen in accounts of persons with physical handicaps (Zola 1982), epilepsy (Scambler and Hopkins 1986), AIDS (Chapman 2000; Ciambrone 2001; Ezzy 2000), and other problems such as diabetes, end-stage renal disease, Parkinson's disease, and multiple sclerosis (Roth and Conrad 1987). Effects such as these would seem to place the ill in a position of deviance with respect to their sense of self, relations with other people, and role in society.

Therefore, when the sick role is considered along with society's method of dealing with the sick (i.e., placing them under the control of doctors, putting them in hospitals), the concept of sickness as deviance may well apply. In the absence of other theoretical concepts in medical sociology that would provide a better approach to understanding the sociological aspects of illness, the illness-as-deviance perspective still remains the best sociological thinking on the subject.

Being Sick and Disabled

Everyone becomes ill at some time. Susan Sontag, in her book *Illness as Metaphor* (1978:3), put it this way:

> Illness is the night-side of life, a more onerous citizenship. Everyone who is born holds dual citizenship, in the kingdom of the well and in the kingdom of the sick. Although we prefer to use only the good passport, sooner or later each of us is obligated, at least for a spell, to identify ourselves as citizens of that other place.

As citizens of that other place—the realm of sickness—we typically feel bad or weak or both. We are unable to feel normal because we experience a sense of being less than our usual self. As Peter Freund and Meredith McGuire (1999:132) explain, "illness is upsetting because it is experienced as a threat to the order and meanings by which people make sense of their lives." What Freund and McGuire are saying is that illness disrupts our daily routine, causes various degrees of suffering, and threatens our ability to plan for the future and control our activities. To be sick is to envy those who are well or envy our own past periods of wellness and hopefully be able to look forward to their return. The latter may not be possible if one has an incurable chronic condition. For example, in a study of HIV-positive homosexual men in New York City, Karolyn Siegel and Beatrice Krauss (1991) found that having AIDS meant having to confront the possibility of a curtailed life span, dealing with reactions to having a highly discrediting and stigmatized illness, and developing strategies for maintaining physical and emotional health. Being sick can clearly be an undesirable state, despite the exemption from one's usual activities that are an inherent feature of the sick role.

As previously noted, there are two types of illness conditions. One is acute illness, which typically refers to the sudden onset or sharp increase in pain, discomfort, or inflammation. Usually such problems last only a relatively short time and either disappear after a few days or are moderated or cured by medical treatment. An acute illness is often communicable and can be passed from one person to another, such as colds, flu, measles, and chicken pox. The other form of sickness is chronic illness, which is usually slow in developing, long in duration, and typically incurable. Chronic illnesses are not usually communicable, although there are exceptions, such as AIDS. Chronic disorders develop within the individual rather than being passed directly from someone else and are usually associated with genetic, environmental, and lifestyle influences. If the chronic disease is life-threatening, such as cancer, diabetes, or heart disease, the afflicted person is likely to eventually die from it. Other chronic conditions, like arthritis, are uncomfortable but not life-threatening.

Regardless of whether one's affliction is acute or chronic, when people suffer, their sense of personal competency can be adversely affected. Freund and McGuire (1999) point out that an illness can be particularly damaging to a person's concept of self when it is experienced as overwhelming, unpredictable, and uncontrollable because it paralyzes the ability to act and manage one's life normally. Very sick people often sense a degree of alienation or psychological separation from their body, because it no longer feels normal or functions adequately (Ezzy 2000; Freund and McGuire 1999; Kelly and Field 1996). People who are sick often withdraw from others because they feel bad and are unable to pursue normal social relations. They often lose the ability to find pleasure, appreciate beauty, or be frivolous (Radley 1999).

Persons with chronic disorders, particularly those who are physically handicapped, are faced with additional problems of altered mobility, a negative body image, and stigma (Bell 2000; Bury 1997, 2000; Chapman 2000; Ciambrone 2001; Ferraro, Farmer, and Wybraniec 1997; Radley 1994; Schieman and Turner 1998; Williams 1999, 2000; Yoshida 1993). Consequently, Zola (1982, 1989) points out that the problems facing someone with a physical impairment are not just medical but include social, attitudinal, economic, and other adjustments. Simply moving about can be a major challenge. Scott Shieman and Heather Turner (1998), for example, found in a study in Canada that disabled persons, as they age, lose their sense of mastery and being in control of their lives. Being both old and disabled is characterized as a "double disadvantage." "As age increases," state Schieman and Turner (1998:171), "age and disability jointly combine so that the disabled become even more disadvantaged in mastery relative to the nondisabled."

Elsewhere, Kathy Charmaz (1983, 1991) observed in a study of chronically ill persons in northern California that such individuals frequently experience a deteriorating former self-image and are unable to assume an equally valued new one. As a result of their illness or disability, they live restricted lives, are socially isolated, are devalued as less than normal, and feel they are a burden to others. All the factors combine to reduce their sense of self-worth, unless some alternative means of satisfaction could be found. Most disabled and many chronically ill individuals are forced by their physical condition to reconstruct their sense of self and personal history—owing to what Michael Bury (1997:123) calls a "biographical disruption"—to account for themselves as physically impaired persons (Bell 2000; Bury 2000; Radley 1994; Williams 1999, 2000). As Bury (2000:177) concludes: "Alterations in the body interact with the wider society in cultural and structural contexts that go beyond practical consequences to issues of appearance, social performance, and thus identity."

Anselm Strauss (1975) explains that the chief business of a chronically ill person is not just to stay alive or keep his or her symptoms under control but also to live as normally as possible. A lifelong illness, in Strauss's view, requires lifelong work to control its course, manage its symptoms, and live with the disability. In this context, the sick role that the person assumes is a permanent condition.

Stigma

Some sick or physically handicapped people may be stigmatized if their affliction is unpleasant for other people, because of how they appear, smell, or behave. Stigma, as defined by Erving Goffman (1963:3), is "an attribute that is deeply discrediting." Goffman explains that the term *stigma* originated with the ancient Greeks, who used it to refer to marks on the body that represented something bad or immoral about the person. Usually, the marks were brands cut or burned into the body to identify the bearer as a criminal, slave, or traitor. People encountering such a person were expected to avoid them. In contemporary society, Goffman explains there are three main forms of stigma: (1) abominations of the body, such as various types of physical deformities; (2) blemishes of individual character—that is, mental disorder, sexually transmitted diseases (STDs), alcoholism, and suicidal tendencies; and (3) the tribal stigmas of race, religion, and nationality. People with such attributes are those who are different from the majority of other people, but different in a negative way and are subjected to discrimination because of it. Goffman's primary interest was in analyzing the structure of social interaction, which in the case of stigma and other social phenomena, was inherent in the rules or norms shaping the interaction (Scambler 2009).

People who are physically handicapped typically fall into the first category of "abomination of the body." They may be stigmatized and excluded from the company of the nonhandicapped because their physical deformity makes others around them feel uncomfortable. Persons with STDs can also be characterized as having an abomination of the body, but physical evidence of their disease can usually be concealed by clothing. Persons with STDs, however, are often stigmatized as having "a blemish of character" as people often think such diseases are usually acquired through immoral sexual acts (i.e., outside of wedlock, with disreputable persons, etc.). People who are mentally ill are likewise stigmatized in the "blemish of character" category as they are subjected to cultural stereotypes depicting them as incompetent or dangerous. This stigma can influence the individual's own behavior and act as a barrier to seeking help for mental symptoms, since awareness of being treated for such symptoms can negatively affect judgments of family, friends, co-workers and others, such as potential employers, about the person (Perry 2011; Pescosolido 2013).

As Goffman points out, stigma represents a rupture between an individual's *virtual* and *actual* social identity that is regarded in some way as failing. That is, there is a serious discrepancy between what a person should be and what a person actually is. This failing places the person in a social category of people whose body and perhaps character are tainted. Stigmatized people may try to compensate for their stigma by "passing" as normal as much as they can. Goffman, for example, notes the situation of a badly burned real estate salesman who arranges to meet his clients by approaching them from a distance, so they can have time to adjust to his appearance by the time he arrives in their presence.

However, stigma—even though it is imposed on the individual by other people—can obviously have a negative effect on the self-concepts of those stigmatized. People so stigmatized feel devalued and less than normal in public situations. Betsy Fife and Eric Wright (2000) investigated this situation by examining the impact of stigma on self-esteem and body image by type of illness, namely HIV/AIDS and cancer. They found clear evidence that stigma is a central force in the lives of people with both types of illnesses. Persons with HIV/AIDS reported somewhat stronger feelings of stigma, which is not surprising considering the adverse public characterization often applied to those infected through IV drug use and homosexuality. But persons with cancer also felt stigmatized and sensed social rejection as well as an impaired body image. The more severe the illness, the greater the difficulty in concealing it and, hence, the stronger the feelings of perceived stigma in both groups. Stigma is an example of how feelings about one's illness by the individual and other people negatively affect the self-esteem of those afflicted.

Ultimately, as Daniel Reidpath and his associates (2005:468–69) point out, stigma affects health situations in four ways. First, the psychological stress experienced by stigmatized people may have adverse consequences for their health. Second, fear of being stigmatized and the subsequent discrimination may cause some people to avoid or delay seeking health care if they either have a health problem (like obesity) or suspect they might have a stigmatizing disease (such as HIV/AIDS). Third, a stigmatized individual may experience adverse reactions from others in health care settings, like shunning by some staff members or possibly refusal to treat someone who is, for example, HIV-positive. And fourth, Reidpath et al. suggest that communities may be slow in providing infrastructure (e.g., clinic, hospitals) or allocate lesser quality facilities if they are to primarily provide services to a stigmatized group. While one might argue that stigma should not exist in relation to health matters, it obviously does nonetheless.

Summary

Two major theories have been advanced to date to explain the relationship between illness and society. Parsons's concept of the sick role has had the greatest impact on sociological perspectives thus far, but Freidson's labeling theory approach also represents an important contribution.

Parsons's concept of the sick role includes the following postulates: (1) An individual's illness is grounds for exemption from normal responsibilities and obligations; (2) an individual's illness is not his or her fault and he or she needs help to get well; (3) the sick person has an obligation to get well because being sick is undesirable; and (4) the obligation to get well subsumes the more specific obligation of the sick person to seek technically competent help. Parsons also demonstrates the utility of medicine as an institution of social control by virtue of its mission of treating the deviant sick.

Although Parsons's concept of the sick role has provided a useful framework for understanding illness behavior, it has not been generally sufficient because of its failure (1) to explain the variation within illness behavior, (2) to apply to chronic illness, (3) to account for the variety of settings and situations affecting the patient–physician relationship, and (4) to explain the behavior of lower-class patients. Nonetheless, if we realize the limitations of Parsons's sick-role theory, we can continue to apply it to behavior as an ideal-type model.

The labeling approach to illness, as formulated by Freidson, provides a useful orientation for analyzing the problematic aspects of illness behavior and the social meaning of disease. However, a definitive sick-role theory using labeling theory has yet to be developed. Both Parsons's sick-role concept and Freidson's labeling theory are formulated within the framework of an illness-as-deviance perspective, and currently this view contains the best work on the sociological aspects of being sick. For the chronically ill, the sick role can be a permanent state.

Critical Thinking Questions

1. Should illness be considered a form of deviant behavior or something else? Defend your answer.
2. Parsons's concept of the sick role has four basic categories. What are they and what do they describe?
3. Define medicalization and explain how it works.
4. There are several criticisms of the sick role. Should the concept be abandoned?

Suggested Readings

Conrad, Peter (2007) *The medicalization of society*. Baltimore, MD: Johns Hopkins University Press.

The definitive account of the transformation of what were once considered normal human conditions into medical problems.

Pescosolido, Bernice A. (2013) "The public stigma of mental illness: What do we think; what do we know; what can we prove?" *Journal of Health and Social Behavior* 54: 1–21.

An excellent current review of the research literature on stigma and mental disorder.

Welch, H. Gilbert, Lisa M. Schwartz, and Steven Woloshin (2011) *Over-Diagnosed: Making people sick in the pursuit of health*. Boston: Beacon.

Discusses the trend toward over-diagnosis in American medicine by which advances in medical technology and science result in ever narrower definitions of normal that turn increasingly more people into patients.

References

Arluke, Arnold, Louanne Kennedy, and Ronald C. Kessler (1979) "Reexamining the sick-role concept: An empirical assessment." *Journal of Health and Social Behavior* 20: 30–36.

Becker, Howard S. (1973) *Outsiders: Studies in the sociology of deviance*, 2nd ed. New York: The Free Press.

Bell, Susan E. (2000) "Experiencing illness in/and narrative," pp. 184–99 in *Handbook of medical sociology*, 5th ed., C. Bird, P. Conrad, and A. Fremont (eds). Upper Saddle River, NJ: Prentice Hall.

Berkanovic, Emil (1972) "Lay conceptions of the sick role." *Social Forces* 51: 53–63.

Brown, Julia S., and May E. Rawlinson (1977) "Sex differences in sick role rejection and in work performance following cardiac surgery." *Journal of Health and Social Behavior* 18: 276–92.

Bury, Michael (1997) *Health and illness in a changing society*. London: Routledge.

——— (2000) "On chronic illness and disability," pp. 173–83 in *Handbook of medical sociology*, 5th ed., C. Bird, P. Conrad, and A. Fremont (eds). Upper Saddle River, NJ: Prentice Hall.

Campbell, John D. (1978) "The child in the sick role: Contributions of age, sex, parental status, and parental values." *Journal of Health and Social Behavior* 19: 35–51.

Cassell, Eric J. (1985) *Talking with patients*, Vol. 2. Cambridge, MA: MIT Press.

Chalfant, H. Paul, and Richard Kurtz (1971) "Alcoholics and the sick role: Assessments by social workers." *Journal of Health and Social Behavior* 12: 66–72.

Chapman, Elizabeth (2000) "Conceptualization of the body for people living with HIV: Issues of touch and contamination." *Sociology of Health & Illness* 22: 840–57.

Charmaz, Kathy (1983) "Loss of self: A fundamental form of suffering in the chronically ill." *Sociology of Health & Illness* 5: 168–95.

——— (1991) *Good days, bad days: The self in chronic illness and time*. New Brunswick, NJ: Rutgers University Press.

Ciambrone, Desirée (2001) "Illness and other assaults on the self: The relative impact of HIV/AIDS on women's lives." *Sociology of Health & Illness* 23: 517–40.

Clarke, Adele E., and Janet K. Shim (2011) "Medicalization and biomedicalization revisited: Technoscience and transformations of health, illness, and American medicine," pp. 173–200 in *Handbook of the sociology of health, illness, and healing*, B. Pescosolido, J. Martin, J. McLeod, and A. Rogers (eds.). Dordrecht: Springer.

Clarke, Adele E., Janet K. Shim, Laura Mamo, Jennifer Ruth Fosket, and Jennifer R. Fishman (2003) "Biomedicalization: Technoscientific transformation of health, illness, and U.S. biomedicine." *American Sociological Review* 68: 161–94.

Cockerham, William C. (2014) *Sociology of mental disorder*, 9th ed. Upper Saddle River, NJ: Pearson Prentice Hall.

Cockerham, William C., Morton C. Creditor, Una K. Creditor, and Peter B. Imrey (1980) "Minor ailments and illness behavior among physicians." *Medical Care* 18: 164–73.

Cole, Stephen, and Robert LeJeune (1972) "Illness and the legitimation of failure." *American Sociological Review* 37: 347–56.

Conrad, Peter (1975) "The discovery of hyperkinesis: Note on the medicalization of deviant behavior." *Social Problems* 23: 12–21.

——— (2005) "The shifting engines of medicalization." *Journal of Health and Social Behavior* 46: 3–14.

——— (2007) *The medicalization of society: On the transformation of human conditions into treatable disorders*. Baltimore: Johns Hopkins University Press.

———— (2013) "Medicalization: Changing contours, characteristics, and contexts," pp. 195–214 in *Medical sociology on the move: New directions in theory*, W. Cockerham (ed.). Dordrecht: Springer.

Conrad, Peter, and Valerie Leiter (2004) "Medicalization, markets and consumers." *Journal of Health and Social Behavior* 45(Extra issue): 158–76.

Crossley, Michele (1998) " 'Sick role' or 'empowerment'? The ambiguities of life with an HIV positive diagnosis." *Sociology of Health & Illness* 20: 507–31.

Davis, Joseph E. (2010) "Medicalization, social control, and the relief of suffering," pp. 211–41 in *The New Blackwell Companion to Medical Sociology*, W. Cockerham (ed.). Oxford, UK: Wiley-Blackwell.

Ezzy, Douglas (2000) "Illness narratives: Time, hope and HIV." *Social Science and Medicine* 50: 605–17.

Ferraro, Kenneth F., Melissa M. Farmer, and John A. Wybraniec (1997) "Health trajectories: Long-term dynamics among black and white adults." *Journal of Health and Social Behavior* 38: 38–54.

Fife, Betsy L., and Eric R. Wright (2000) "The dimensionality of stigma: A comparison of its impact on the self of persons with HIV/AIDS and cancer." *Journal of Health and Social Behavior* 41: 50–67.

Freidson, Eliot (1970) *Profession of medicine*. New York: Dodd, Mead.

Freund, Peter E. S., and Meredith B. McGuire (1999) *Health, illness, and the social body*, 3rd ed. Englewood Cliffs, NJ: Prentice Hall.

Gallagher, Eugene B. C. (1976) "Lines of reconstruction and extension in the Parsonian sociology of illness." *Social Science and Medicine* 10: 207–18.

Gallagher, Eugene B. C., and Kristina Sionean (2004) "Where medicalization boulevard meets commercialization alley." *Journal of Policy Studies* 16: 53–62.

Gibbs, Jack (1971) "A critique of the labeling perspective," pp. 193–205 in *The study of social problems*, E. Rubington and M. S. Weinberg (eds.). New York: Oxford University Press.

Glenton, Claire (2003) "Chronic back pain sufferers—striving for the sick role." *Social Science and Medicine* 57: 2243–52.

Goffman, Erving (1963) *Stigma: Notes on the management of a spoiled identity*. Englewood Cliffs, NJ: Prentice-Hall.

Gordon, Gerald (1966) *Role theory and illness*. New Haven, CT: College and University Press.

Horwitz, Allan V., and Jerome C. Wakefied (2007) *The loss of sadness: How psychiatry transformed normal sorrow into depressive disorder*. New York: Oxford University Press.

———— (2012) All we have to fear: Psychiatry's transformation of natural anxieties into mental dis-order. New York: Oxford University Press.

Kelly, Michael P., and David Field (1996) "Medical sociology, chronic illness and the body." *Sociology of Health & Illness* 18: 241–57.

Light, Donald W. (ed.) (2010) *The risks of prescription drugs*. New York: Columbia University Press.

Lipowski, Z. J. (1970) "Physical illness, the individual and the coping process." *Psychiatry in Medicine* 1: 91–101.

May, Carl (2011) "Mundane medicine, therapeutic relationships, and the clinical encounter: Current and future agendas for sociology," pp. 309–22 in *Handbook of the sociology of health, illness, and healing*, B. Pescosolido, J. Martin, J. McLeod, and A. Rogers (eds.). Dordrecht: Springer.

Mayes, Rick, and Allan Horwitz (2005) "DSM-III and the revolution in the classification of mental illness." *Journal of the History of Behavioral Sciences* 41: 249–68.

Parsons, Talcott (1951) *The social system.* Glencoe, IL: The Free Press.

——— (1975) "The sick role and role of the physician reconsidered." *Milbank Memorial Fund Quarterly* 53: 257–78.

——— (1979) "Definitions of health and illness in light of American values and social structure," pp. 120–44 in *Patients, physicians, and illness*, 3rd ed., E. Jaco (ed.). New York: The Free Press.

Perry, Brea L. (2011) "The labeling paradox: Stigma, the sick role, and social networks in mental illness." *Journal of Health and Social Behavior* 52: 460–77.

——— (2013) "The public stigma of mental illness: What do we think; what do we know; what can we prove?" *Journal of Health and Social Behavior* 54: 1–24.

Radley, Alan (1994) *Making sense of illness: The social psychology of health and disease.* London: Sage.

——— (1999) "The aesthetics of illness: Narrative, horror and the sublime." *Sociology of Health & Illness* 21: 778–96.

Reidpath, Daniel D., Kit Y. Chan, Sandra M. Gifford, and Pascale Allotey (2005) " 'He hath the French pox': Stigma, social value and social exclusion." *Sociology of Health & Illness* 27: 468–89.

Rier, David A. (2000) "The missing voice of the critically ill: A medical sociologist's first-person account." *Sociology of Health & Illness* 22: 68–93.

Ritzer, George, and William Yagatich (2012) "Contemporary sociological theory," pp. 98–118 in *The Wiley-Blackwell companion to sociology*, G. Ritzer (ed.). Oxford, UK: Wiley-Blackwell.

Roth, Julius, and Peter Conrad (eds.) (1987) *The experience and management of chronic illness.* Newbury Park, CA: Sage.

Scambler, Graham (2009) "Health-related stigma." *Sociology of Health & Illness* 31: 441–55.

Scambler, Graham, and Anthony Hopkins (1986) "Being epileptic: Coming to terms with stigma." *Sociology of Health & Illness* 8: 26–43.

Schieman, Scott, and Heather A. Turner (1998) "Age, disability, and the sense of mastery." *Journal of Health and Social Behavior* 39: 169–86.

Siegel, Karolyn, and Beatrice J. Krauss (1991) "Living with HIV infection: Adaptive tasks of seropositive gay men." *Journal of Health and Social Behavior* 32: 17–32.

Sontag, Susan (1978) *Illness as metaphor.* New York: Farrar, Straus, & Giroux.

Strauss, Anselm (1975) *Chronic illness and the quality of life.* St. Louis: C. V. Mosby.

Szasz, Thomas S. (1974) *The myth of mental illness*, rev. ed. New York: Harper & Row.

Turner, Bryan S. (1996) *The body and society*, 2nd ed. Oxford, UK: Blackwell.

Twaddle, Andrew (1969) "Health decisions and sick role variations: An exploration." *Journal of Health and Social Behavior* 10: 105–14.

——— (1973) "Illness and deviance." *Social Science and Medicine* 7: 751–62.

Williams, Simon J. (1999) "Is anybody there? Critical realism, chronic illness and the disability debate." *Sociology of Health & Illness* 21: 797–819.

——— (2000) "Chronic illness as biographical disruption or biographical disruption as chronic illness?" *Sociology of Health & Illness* 22: 40–67.

Williams, Simon J., Paul Martin, and Jonathan Gabe (2011) "The pharmaceuticalisation of society? A framework for analysis." *Sociology of Health & Illness* 33: 710–25.

Wilson, Robert N. (1970) *The sociology of health.* New York: Random House.

Yoshida, Karen K. (1993) "Reshaping of self: A pendular reconstruction of self and identity among adults with traumatic spinal cord injury." *Sociology of Health & Illness* 15: 217–45.

Zborowski, Mark (1952) "Cultural components in responses to pain." *Journal of Social Issues* 8: 16–30.

Zola, Irving K. (1966) "Culture and symptoms: An analysis of patients' presenting complaints." *American Sociological Review* 31: 615–30.

———. (1982) *Missing pieces: A chronicle of living with a disability.* Philadelphia: Temple University Press.

——— (1989) "Toward the necessary universalizing of a disability policy." *Milbank Quarterly* 67, Supp. 2: 401–28.

CHAPTER 9

Doctor–Patient Interaction

Talcott Parsons's (1951) concept of the sick role provides some basic guidelines for understanding doctor–patient interaction. Parsons explains that the relationship between a physician and his or her patient is one that is oriented toward the doctor helping the patient deal effectively with a health problem. The physician has the dominant role because he or she is the one invested with professional medical training and expertise. The patient holds a subordinate position oriented toward accepting, rejecting, or negotiating the recommendation for treatment being offered. In the case of a medical emergency, however, the options of rejection or negotiation on the part of the patient may be quickly discarded, as the patient's medical needs require prompt and decisive action from the doctor.

Parsons's concept of the sick role details the obligations of patients and physicians toward each other. Patients cooperate with doctors, and doctors attempt to return patients to as normal a level of functioning as possible. When people visit doctors for treatment and medical advice, doctors usually (but not always) take some type of action to satisfy the patient's expectations. Eliot Freidson (1970) suggests that physicians tend to have a bias in favor of finding illness in their patients. He cites the medical decision rule *as the guiding principle behind everyday medical practice. The medical decision rule, described by Thomas Scheff (1966), is the notion that since the work of the physician is for the good of the patient, physicians tend to impute illness to their patients rather than to deny it and risk overlooking or missing it. Although this approach may promote tendencies to prescribe drugs and order laboratory tests and X-rays, such consequences should not be surprising. Patients desire and demand services, and physicians are trained to meet these demands. As Freidson (1970:258) points out: "While the physician's job is to make decisions, including the decision not to do anything, the fact seems to be that the everyday practitioner feels impelled to do something when [patients] are in distress."*

The distress may not be only physical; purely psychological needs can trigger a visit to a doctor as well. Therefore, to assume that interaction between physicians and patients always follows a preset course, in which all parties work together under the same set of mutual understandings, overlooks the potential for misunderstanding, uncertainty, or disregard of the physician's method of treatment by the patient. The quality of physician–patient interaction is sometimes problematic, but it is nevertheless important because of its potential for affecting the care being provided. This chapter will review models of interaction, misunderstandings in communication, cultural differences in presenting symptoms, and problems in patient compliance. These topics are of interest to sociologists because physician–patient interaction constitutes a structured relationship and mode of discourse that is inherently social. It is the patient's experience with the illness, including the relationship with the physician that allows the person to socially construct his or her understanding of an affliction and how to deal with it (Conrad and Barker 2010).

Models of Interaction

Since Parsons formulated his concept of the sick role, two additional perspectives on physician–patient interaction have added to our understanding of the experience. These are the views of Szasz and Hollender and of Hayes-Bautista. Thomas Szasz and Marc Hollender (1956), both physicians, take the position that the seriousness of the patient's symptoms is the determining factor in doctor–patient interaction. Depending on the severity of symptoms, Szasz and Hollender argue that physician–patient interaction falls into one of three possible models: activity–passivity, guidance–cooperation, and mutual participation.

The *activity–passivity model* applies when the patient is seriously ill or being treated on an emergency basis in a state of relative helplessness, because of a severe injury or lack of consciousness. Typically, the situation is critical as the physician works in a state of high activity to stabilize the patient's condition. Decision making and power in the relationship are all on the side of the doctor, as the patient is passive and contributes little or nothing to the interaction.

The *guidance–cooperation model* arises most often when the patient has an acute, often infectious illness, such as the flu or measles. The patient knows what is going on and can cooperate with the physician by following his or her guidance in the matter, but the physician makes the decisions.

The *mutual participation model* applies to the management of chronic illness in which the patient works with the doctor as a full participant in controlling the affliction. Often the patient modifies his or her lifestyle by making adjustments in diet or giving up smoking and is responsible for taking medication according to a prescribed schedule and seeking periodic checkups. The patient with diabetes or heart disease would be in this category. What Szasz and Hollender accomplish is to show how the physician–patient relationship is affected by the severity of the patient's symptoms.

David Hayes-Bautista (1976a, 1976b) focuses on the manner in which patients try to modify treatment prescribed by a physician. Hayes-Bautista finds that either they try to convince the physician that the treatment is not working or they counter the treatment with actions of their own, such as deliberately reducing the amount of medication they are supposed to take or increasing it. Physicians respond by pointing out their expertise, that the patient's health can be threatened if the treatment is not followed, that the treatment is correct but progress may be slow, or simply appeal to the patient to comply. As Karen Lutfey (2005) found in a study of two diabetes clinics, the physicians had to take on a variety of roles—educator, detective, negotiator, salesperson, cheerleader, and police officer—to induce patient adherence to their treatment regimens. Therefore, the relevance of the Hayes-Bautista model for understanding the doctor–patient relationship is the view of the interaction as a process of negotiation, rather than the physician simply giving orders and the patient following them in an automatic, unquestioning manner. The model is limited, however, to those situations in which the patient is not satisfied with treatment and wants to persuade the doctor to change it.

What is suggested by the Szasz and Hollender and Hayes-Bautista models is that in nonemergency situations, patients often do not act passively when interacting with their doctors in health matters. Patients ask questions, seek explanations, and make judgments about the appropriateness of the information and treatment physicians provide. They may or may not do what they are told by doctors or follow exact orders with respect to the medications that are prescribed. Patients also check the information they get on the Internet, both before and after they consult with their doctors (Barker 2008). But the interaction that takes place appears to be strongly affected by social class differences. Lower-class persons tend to be more passive in dealing with doctors as authority figures and show a decreased sense of personal control over health matters. People with middle and upper socioeconomic status, however, tend to be more consumer-oriented as discerning seekers of health care and active participants in the physician–patient encounter (Cockerham et al. 1986). This circumstance suggests that it is middle- and upper-class patients who are most likely to try to negotiate with doctors and involve themselves as partners in decision making about their medical problem, while lower-class persons stand as more or less accepting recipients of professional health services.

In an early study of consumerism in the doctor–patient encounter, Marie Haug and Bebe Lavin (1981, 1983) found that better educated and younger adults tended to be more skeptical of physician motives in providing treatment. They were more likely to question whether the physician was ordering tests and providing services primarily to help the patient or to make money. These persons strongly believed that decision making in the doctor–patient relationship should not be left entirely to the doctor.

However, it should be noted that despite the general trend toward greater patient equality with the physician in making decisions about one's own health, there are clearly times when patients do not desire to accept responsibility or are unable to do so. There are also times when physicians exert their authority and make decisions regardless of the patient's desires and those of the patient's family to have some say in the treatment. In these situations, the activity–passivity model overrides the mutual participation model. For example, as noted in the previous chapter, David Rier (2000), a medical sociologist critically ill from an acute respiratory and kidney failure, found that Parsons's concept of the sick role was highly applicable to his condition of dependency on doctors in an intensive care unit (ICU). He was so seriously ill, and perhaps near death at one point, that he simply had to trust his doctors. Rier found that notions of negotiation and partnership have only limited relevance to critically ill patients. Such patients often lacked the strength and motivation to either challenge or collaborate with their doctors and their condition could significantly constrain treatment options.

In another study, Rose Weitz (1999) found that ICU doctors, treating her brother-in-law, Brian, who was badly burned in an industrial accident, were unwilling to share decision-making authority. These doctors defined informed consent (a one-word assent given by the barely conscious Brian) as giving them complete authority to make all decisions and initiate aggressive procedures without informing the family. Brian never regained consciousness and died three and one-half weeks later. Although Brian's wife, Lisa, was acknowledged by the physicians as having the authority to give them permission before beginning various treatments, they generally ignored her. When they did speak to the family, they favored talking to Brian's father, who was a confident and wealthy businessman. Yet the father did not receive more information than the others nor was he offered any greater involvement in decision making. The family became cynical about the medical care provided, thinking that the doctors were more interested in their careers or their status than the welfare of their patients.

Besides ICU physicians, surgeons are also known for trying to retain decision-making authority for themselves and to present information to their patients and their families that justifies action (Katz 1999). Patients can feel pressured to just go along with what the surgeon orders. But in some instances, patients and/or their families opt for the decision-making role instead. Pearl Katz reports on an 80-year-old woman who was diagnosed with gallstones. Her surgeon offered to make the decision himself to approve an operation. "If you want to leave the decision to me," stated the surgeon, "I'll make it" (Katz 1999:120). But the woman's son took the decision-making authority away from the doctor. According to Katz (1999:120):

> The son responded, "I don't think that you, me, or my wife has the right to make that decision. It's not proper for anyone to make that decision. Whatever needs to be discussed should be discussed with her and decided by her."

When a patient is extremely ill or there is an emergency, doctors sometimes have to make life-saving decisions about patients quickly, with no time for consultation. In such circumstances, the professional power and authority of physicians is fully exercised, and this may be the case regardless of what the patient or the family might eventually say—since the doctor can assert that he or she has a moral responsibility to treat the affliction. Some physicians may just be generally unwilling to involve patients and their families in decision making, even if the circumstances warrant it (Katz 1999; Weitz 1999). However, despite such exceptions, mutual participation is the norm in most doctor–patient interaction (Boyer and Lutfey 2010; Cockerham et al. 1986a; Frank 1991; Warren, Weitz, and Kulis 1998). This is seen in a review of the research on doctor–patient role relationships by Carol Boyer and Karen Lutfey (2010). They found that patients today have become more active in the relationship, seek multiple forms of care (i.e., acute, chronic, preventive, and palliative), often have needs that are long-term because of chronic illnesses, and have risk-based strategies in that they wish to avoid risks of particular diseases in living their lives. Physicians, conversely, find more actors (e.g., managed care systems, insurance companies, government regulations) intervening in their relationships with patients, are less paternalistic toward them, and more willing to share decision-making with them. Mary Warren et al. (1998), for example, found in a study of physicians in Arizona that the context in which they practiced medicine has changed dramatically in the last 20 years. Among the changes was greater equality in the doctor–patient relationship. Warren and her colleagues (1998:364) state:

> Our data suggest that this context has changed to such an extent that regardless of age or years in practice, many physicians accept a somewhat more collaborative relationship with patients as the norm rather than invidiously comparing their position to those of physicians in some ideal past. . . . Similarly, physicians now accept that patients will seek medical knowledge and desire to participate in medical decisions and thus do not find such patients an impediment to work satisfaction.

Misunderstandings in Communication

Medical treatment usually begins with a dialogue. As is the case in any face-to-face situation, the effectiveness of doctor–patient interaction depends upon the ability of the participants to understand each other. However, a major barrier to effective communication lies in the differences between physicians and their patients with

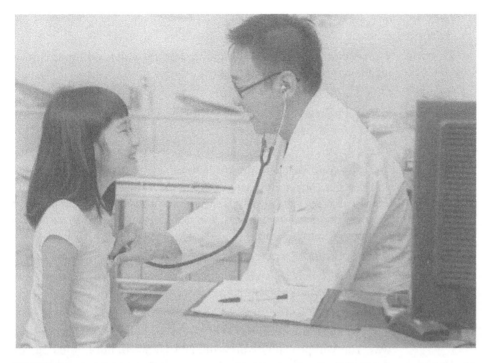

PHOTO 9.2 A physician reassures a young girl about her health. Parsons's concept of the sick role emphasizes a traditional one-to-one relationship between the doctor and the patient.

respect to status, education, professional training, and authority. Several sources report that a failure to explain a patient's condition to the patient in terms easily understood is a serious problem in medical encounters (Rier 2000; Waitzkin 2000; Weitz 1999). Physicians, in turn, state that an inability to understand the potentially negative effect of threatening information are the two most common reasons for not communicating fully with their patients (Davis 1972; Howard and Strauss 1975). Consequently, as Fred Davis (1972) found in a study of the interaction between the parents of children who were victims of paralytic poliomyelitis and their doctors, the most common form of communication was evasion. The doctors tended to answer the questions of parents in terms that were either evasive or unintelligibly technical. Yet, some doctors are effective communicators and, as Eric Cassell (1985) explains, information can be an important therapeutic tool in medical situations if it meets three tests: (1) reduces uncertainty, (2) provides a basis for action, and (3) strengthens the physician–patient relationship. An example of what Cassell suggests is seen in the following dialogue between a physician and a female patient:

DOCTOR   First I want you to listen very carefully to what I have to say. Everything is all right. You can believe that. But there is one small problem on your X-ray that I will show to you. Here, look at this spot where the pituitary gland is—right here.

PATIENT   OK.

DOCTOR	It is larger than it should be.
PATIENT	Humm.
DOCTOR	The pituitary gland is small and makes hormones telling the other glands of your body what to do.
PATIENT	OK.
DOCTOR	When it's large, like it shows, it likely has a tumor. This kind of tumor is not cancer, however.
PATIENT	That's good.
DOCTOR	Yes, it is good that you do not have cancer, but the tumor can give you the headaches that you complain about. Tumors cause headaches and grow very slowly. They are not cancer. What you have is a tumor of the pituitary gland. It is called chromophobe adenoma, but its name is unimportant.
PATIENT	What does all of this mean?
DOCTOR	What it means is that you are going to be operated on, so we can remove the tumor and fix your headache problem.
PATIENT	So will I be all right?
DOCTOR	Yes, this does not mean you will not be anxious or scared along the way. You will probably worry and be frightened, but I'm telling you the truth. You will come out of this is in good shape.
PATIENT	Well. . . . That is reassuring.
DOCTOR	You know? Look, you will be able to exercise, work, have sex, fix meals, yell at your children, and grow to be a feisty old lady just like your mother, but with a better disposition.
PATIENT	That sounds good.

Other doctors do poorly when it comes to communicating with patients. Cassell provides further examples of physicians telling their patients they were not going to explain a disease because they would not understand what they were told, or being vague and ultimately frightening the patient. In the following example from a British study, a woman with a neck problem resulting from a car accident sought reassurance that no serious difficulties existed. However, she was clearly not reassured, as shown in this conversation with her doctor:

PATIENT	Could you tell me Doctor X, is it all right that my neck clicks now and then?
DOCTOR	Yes.
PATIENT	Is that all right?
DOCTOR	Yes, it may do. Yes.
PATIENT	Fine. Thanks.

She continued to express her concern to the interviewer. "The doctor just asked if my neck was all right and dismissed it, although I would like to have discussed it—the pain I'm having. I mean, I don't know if it's all right." (Fitton and Acheson 1979:75)

Another example of poor communication by physicians is found in the Weitz (1999) study on the refusal of ICU doctors to share decision making about treatments for Brian, her fatally burned brother-in-law. Lisa, Brian's wife, reported that "when I would try to get more info [from the doctors], their reactions ranged from 'this does not compute'—as if they had never heard questions like these before—to almost animosity" (Weitz 1999:214). The social workers, pastoral counselors, and psychologists on the hospital staff were not helpful in getting information but seemed focused instead on "cooling out" or calming down the family. The doctors did agree to have a weekly family meeting but were not helpful. The nurses were more forthcoming about how bad Brian really was, showing how his breathing was too shallow and infrequent to sustain his life. This, of course, is the type of situation that promotes misunderstandings between doctors and patients and leaves patients dissatisfied with the relationship. The two groups in society, however, who have been identified as generally having the most communication problems with physicians are the lower class and women.

Communication and Class Background

It has been found, for example, that poorly educated persons are the most likely to have their questions ignored and to be treated impersonally; upper- and upper-middle-class persons, on the other hand, tend to receive more personalized service from physicians (Peck and Conner 2011; Taira et al. 1997). They are also more active in presenting their ideas to a doctor and seeking further explanation of their condition (Boulton et al. 1986; Weitz 1999).

Howard Waitzkin (1991, 2001), a physician and medical sociologist, studied information given in medical care and found that social class differences were the most important factors in physician–patient communication. Noting that information often provides a basis for power by those who have it in relation to those who do not, Waitzkin determined that doctors did not usually withhold information to exercise control over their patients. Rather, doctors from upper-middle-class backgrounds tended to communicate more information to their patients generally than doctors with lower-middle- or working-class origins. Moreover, patients from a higher class position or educational level usually received more information. Socioeconomic status thus emerged as a determining factor in both providing and receiving medical information.

According to British medical sociologist Paul Atkinson (1995), a major characteristic of the clinical consultation is the physician's dominant role in the encounter. Atkinson notes that a key feature of the consultation is the assertion of control in which the physician takes over the patient's problem and sets about controlling or guiding what should be done. The focus is typically limited by the doctor to medical issues, and social situations are relegated to marginal topics of conversation (Waitzkin, Britt, and Williams 1994). The doctor's emphasis is on finding out what is medically wrong and doing something about it, so he or she can move on to the next patient. In this circumstance, lower-class patients in particular have difficulty holding the doctor's interest to anything other than brief comments about their specific health problem.

Mary Boulton and her colleagues (Boulton et al. 1986:328) explain that the influence of social class on the doctor–patient relationship is best understood in terms of social distance. Those patients who are similar to physicians in social class are more likely to share their communication style and communicate effectively with them. Those with dissimilar class backgrounds are likely to find communication more difficult because their communication style differs from that of the doctor and they lack the social skills to negotiate the medical encounter effectively. The effects of social distance apply not only to class differences but also to race as patient satisfaction is greatest when both doctor and patient are of the same race (LaVeist and Nuru-Jeter 2002; Malat 2001; Malat and Hamilton 2006; Stepanikova 2012). However, the physician's behavior toward the patient—regardless of either person's race or ethnicity—is the most important factor engendering trust in the doctor–patient relationship (Stepanikova et al. 2006).

Male Physicians and Women Patients

The lack of male sensitivity to women patients was a major factor in the formation of the women's health movement to combat sexual discrimination in medicine. As part of this movement, feminist health organizations have evolved that advocate natural childbirth, midwifery, home childbirth, self-help, abortion rights, funding for breast cancer, and recognition of the rights and intelligence of patients (Clarke and Olesen 1999; Joffe, Weitz, and Stacey 2004; Kolker 2004). A particular focus has been on the manner in which some male physicians exhibit sexist attitudes and behavior toward women patients and health workers or fail to be sensitive to the needs and complaints of women seeking care.

An example of the latter is seen in research conducted in the mid-1980s by Sue Fisher (1984:1–2) on doctor–patient communication in a family practice clinic in a small southeastern American city staffed by white middle-class men. She found that many women patients were not satisfied with the explanations given to them by their doctors. Fisher claimed that treatment decisions for women were not always in their best interest. She provided the example of a female graduate student whose doctor recommended a hysterectomy for a pelvic inflammatory condition after treatment with antibiotics had failed. Fisher advised the student to inform her doctor that she was engaged to be married to a doctor and ask if there was another form of treatment. After learning about the forthcoming marriage, the doctor suggested another course of antibiotics that cleared up the infection, thereby avoiding having surgery. Repeatedly, Fisher saw physicians recommend treatments and patients accept them, usually without question. Often women patients would come to her for advice since they did not understand or have enough information to make an informed decision and in some cases did not trust the doctors who were supposedly looking out for their best interests, especially when it came to concerns about medical problems related to reproduction.

Fisher's basic message is to call for greater insight on the part of male doctors in dealing with female patients and their complaints. One example of male physician misperceptions about female patients is a tendency to misdiagnose heart attacks as stomach or anxiety problems, even when a woman has signs of a heart attack (e.g., chest pain, numbness on left side, sweating, nausea). Estrogen is believed to protect women from heart attacks until after menopause when estrogen levels drop. Consequently, heart disease is often overlooked or undetected in premenopausal women (McKinlay 1996). An example of this situation was reported by Robin Henig (1993:58) about a 36-year-old woman whose heart condition was not diagnosed until after her third visit the same day to an emergency room, which included three separate electrocardiograms. The woman was finally hospitalized at her insistence with a diagnosed stomach ailment. The correct diagnosis was not made until the following day when a cardiologist, not paying attention to gender, was reviewing the previous day's electrocardiograms and asked who was the 36-year-old with the massive heart attack?

In research conducted in Great Britain and the United States, Ann Adams and her colleagues (2008) explored the problem of gender bias and uncertainty in primary care doctors' diagnostic decisions about coronary heart disease. They found that female doctors were more attentive to patient's comments and medical histories, especially those of women. Male doctors were less influenced by a patient's gender in making a diagnosis, but both male and female physicians paid particular attention to a male patient's age and considered more age-related diseases for men than women. This study did not find that women receive better quality care from female doctors for coronary heart disease. However, it did determine that the diagnostic model of coronary heart disease held by physicians generally fits male symptoms better than females whose heart attacks—especially if they are relatively young and considered unlikely for such a diagnosis—can be masked by upset stomachs or anxiety symptoms not commonly seen in men with heart problems. This research highlighted the need for better diagnostic models of coronary heart disease for women, particularly with respect to age.

Women Physicians

Sometimes, for women doctors in a work situation, being a woman is a more meaningful status than being a physician. Candace West (1984) reports that some patients may perceive women physicians as less of an authority figure than male physicians. In one instance, West (1984:99) notes that a male hospital patient was asked by a woman physician whether he was having difficulty passing urine and the patient replied, "You know, the *doctor* asked me that." In this case, indicates West, it was difficult to tell who the patient thought "the doctor" was because the doctor was evidently not the female physician who was treating him. A similar account comes from a frustrated female surgeon:

> I don't know how many times—especially in the first years of course—when I've seen patients on the round twice a day, 75 percent of whom by myself. I've admitted them, operated on them, discharged them, written prescriptions for them, signed taxi receipts and sick leave forms, explained things to them and then asked if there is anything else they've wondered about and they say, "When is the doctor coming?" (Davies 2003:734)

Judith Hammond (1980) suggests that women medical students deliberately develop personal biographies about themselves that show them as being no different than any other medical student. They do so to gain acceptance as colleagues from male students who question their motivation, skills, and potential for medicine. As one female medical student described the attitude of a male counterpart:

> This guy had this theory . . . if you're a woman, obviously you're going to be the one to bring up the kids . . . You know, maternal instinct and all that? Like you shouldn't spend all your time being a doctor. You can't do *both*. Well, that's what most of them think: you can't do both. (Hammond 1980:39)

There is evidence, however, that adverse attitudes and stereotypes about women are beginning to be modified among members of the medical profession. Visible changes are occurring in the approaches of some physicians and hospitals toward treating women. A particularly significant source of change is found in the increasing numbers of women physicians. The first female to graduate from medical school was Elizabeth Blackwell in 1849, but her experience was atypical. Women have historically been underrepresented in medical school classes until relatively recently. Differences in the socialization experiences of boys and girls and a greater degree of persistence among males whose academic records were marginal contributed to this situation (Cole 1986; Fiorentine 1987). It was not until the 1970s that women accounted for at least 10 percent of all first-year medical students. But in 2011–2012, 47.2 percent of all students entering medical schools were women.

This is not to claim that sexism in medicine is no longer significant because several accounts of women medical students and physicians detail the problems women have in being recognized as equal colleagues by male physicians and as "real" doctors by male patients (Hammond 1980; Lorber 1984, 1993, 1997; Riska 2010; Riska and Wegar 1993; West 1984). Most of these studies, however, are dated and the extent to which sexist attitudes toward women physicians currently exist is not fully known. It may be that such attitudes are lessening considerably as more and more women graduate from medical school, enter medical practice, and have patients who appreciate their skills. Conversely, there is still evidence of the sexual harassment of female medical students by male patients involving flirting and sexual inferences and unprofessional treatment by some male doctors in the form of sexual comments, inappropriate touching, and solicitations (Babaria et al. 2012).

Sexism may also be evident in the top posts in academic medicine where women physicians are rare. Women doctors can be hindered in combining a demanding career with motherhood—especially if they have young children. Usually one or the other suffers, unless the mother as doctor can find a position with flexible hours or fewer hours on the job. The pay is lower, but fewer hours allow time for a family life. Susan Hinze (1999) investigated the prestige hierarchy in medicine from the standpoint of gender and found that the top specialties such as surgery and internal medicine were characterized as masculine, with traits like "toughness," "macho," and "demanding," while those at the bottom like family practice, pediatrics, and psychiatry were considered "soft." The top specialties were open to women, but women moving into these fields tended to take on masculine traits, such as being assertive, highly professional, and not expressing warmth, to be successful.

Another female doctor described "how horrified her peers were when she turned down an extremely high status specialty—neurosurgery—for the lower status specialty of obstetrics-gynecology because, to paraphrase, she loved the daily miracle of birth" (Hinze 1999:236). This doctor admitted that she had some difficulty accepting a "girl" specialty because she was one of the top students in her class and could have specialized in anything she wanted. Regardless of the choices women doctors make concerning their career in medicine, it is obvious that they will comprise half of all physicians in numbers in the future and that their impact on the doctor–patient relationship will be significant. For example, Judith Lorber (1984) found that when male doctors assessed their accomplishments, they tended to speak only of their technical skills and choices of appropriate treatment. The personal side of the physician–patient relationship was rarely mentioned. Women doctors, on the other hand, stressed their value to patients and did so using words like "help" and "care." Steven Martin and his associates (Martin, Arnold, and Parker 1988) determined that men and women physicians have similar diagnostic and therapeutic skills, but there appear to be differences in their communication styles: Female physicians tend to be more empathic and egalitarian in their relationships with patients, more respectful of their concerns, and more responsive to patients' psychosocial difficulties. Other research shows that patients feel more of a partnership with a doctor when the doctor is a woman, most likely because of better communication skills on the part of the physician (Cooper-Patrick et al. 1999).

Today, women physicians are entering not only specialties that have traditionally attracted them—namely, pediatrics, obstetrics-gynecology, and general practice—but also increasingly in male-dominated specialties such as surgery, urology, and orthopedics. Thus, women physicians are adopting more specialties than before and are now entering areas of medicine where they deal with a wider range of patients. Consequently, we have the beginnings of a new trend in medicine that may not only affect the physician–patient relationship (in terms of improved communication and willingness to relate to patients as people) but likely to also have an impact on the general image of women held by the medical profession.

Cultural Differences in Communication

Physician–patient interaction can also be influenced by cultural differences in communication. A major study in this area is Irving Zola's (1966) comparison of Irish and Italian American patients in the presentation of symptoms at an eye, ear, nose, and throat clinic. Zola found that Irish patients tended to understate their symptoms, whereas Italian patients tended to overstate them. That is, the Irish made short, concise statements ("I can't see across the street"), while Italians provided far greater detail ("my eyes seem very burny, especially the right eye. . . . Two or three months ago I woke up with my eyes swollen. I bathed it and it did go away but there was still the burny sensation")—for the exact same eye problem. The doctors were required to sort the differences in communication styles to help them arrive at the appropriate diagnosis.

In contemporary American society, a particular problem in medical interviews is found among low-income and poorly educated Hispanics who speak little or no English, feel uncomfortable in impersonal social relationships, have no regular source of care, and find it difficult to negotiate their way through an Anglo health

BOX 9.1

Will Medicine Remain a Masculine-Dominated Profession?

Finnish medical sociologist Elianne Riska (2010) asks whether medicine will remain a masculine-dominated profession, given the increasing number of women entering its ranks. This is a question that women's health advocates and others have also raised in the past few years. At present, the answer, according to Riska, is that change is unlikely. While there are more women doctors than ever before in Western societies, men still fill the vast majority of leadership positions, and this has changed little. Moreover, there is a highly conspicuous segregation of medical work by gender in the United States, Great Britain, and the Nordic countries. That is, women physicians tend to practice in medical specialties consistent with the female gender role, namely primary care, and those specialties concerned with children and the elderly— such as pediatrics and geriatrics. Male doctors, in contrast, favor male-dominated and heroic fields such as surgery, sports medicine, and internal medicine. Female physicians may be entering these specialties, but they are much fewer in numbers and also less likely to occupy the most powerful positions.

Riska explains that two explanations have been given for gender segregation in medical practice: structural and voluntaristic. The structural explanation holds that barriers, such as a lack of mentors, keep women from advancing to top positions in medicine. Men already in the top positions tend to mentor other men who wish to follow in their footsteps, not women. The voluntaristic view is that women are socialized to follow stereotypical gender expectations and consequently tend to make occupational choices that fit those expectations. They choose specialties that allow them to practice the type of medicine they prefer and are best able to use their gender-specific skills. Riska therefore suggests that the most immediate effect of the large number of women entering the medical profession will be to change the culture of the profession as a whole and soften its masculine image, rather than make medicine a feminine field of work.

However, if the number of female medical students expands beyond the current 50–50 split now seen in entering medical school classes in the United States, the medical profession may well become heavily feminized. This will especially be the case as today's large number of female doctors replace men in future medical leadership positions. "The term *feminization*," says Riska (2010:348), "has been used to indicate a female majority in medicine and as a term that signals the gradual decline of the status and autonomy of medical work when women enter a profession." Therefore, while helping people still makes medicine attractive for both males and females, managed care limitations on income and authority, increasing workloads and paperwork, declining public status, and greater feminization may encourage males to opt out of considering medicine as a career. Being a health care "provider" may not be a title they aspire to have. Some male doctors feel reduced in status by being referred to as health care "providers" instead of physicians. "We didn't go to provider school," says a male doctor who now works full time in a venture capital firm (Williams 2008:9). The most exciting opportunities for top university graduates may instead be in investment banking, hedge funds, private equity firms, and other entrepreneurial businesses where financial opportunities are skyrocketing past the old professions of medicine and law (which is also experiencing feminization). As Alex Williams (2008:8) explains:

> In a culture that prizes risk and outsize reward— where professional heroes are college dropouts with billion-dollar Web sites—some doctors and lawyers feel they have slipped a notch in social status, drifting toward the safe and staid realm of dentists and accountants. It's not just because the professions have changed, but also because the standards of what makes a prestigious career have changed. . . . Especially among young people, professional status is now inexplicably linked to ideas of flexibility and creativity, concepts alien to seemingly everyone but art students even a generation ago.

care delivery system. This is also the case for Chinese, Korean, and other immigrants with limited English proficiency.

William Madsen (1973) provides an example of cultural misunderstandings when a Mexican American man took his wife to see a physician in south Texas several years ago. The doctor told the man his superstitions, concerning evil spirits and the like, were nonsense and laughed at him, saying he found it hard to accept that a grown man would believe such things. The doctor then asked the husband to go to the waiting room and the wife to disrobe for an examination. The husband refused to let his wife be examined in this manner and took her away—never to return. Madsen reported that increasing reliance on physicians had eased some social barriers as a few doctors explained illnesses in simple terms and treated their patients with respect. But others remained disrespectful of them and the culture surrounding folk medicine.

Other lower-class minorities can have communication problems with doctors as well. Beverly Robinson (1990:211) reports on one black woman who, when asked how she was feeling, told her doctor that "the pain gone." The physician thought the woman was recovering until someone else informed the doctor that the woman meant the pain had only left temporarily. The woman's use of English was influenced by an African dialect in which "gone" meant a temporary absence; "done gone" and "done been gone" meant something had indeed left but could return, and "gone gone" meant a complete absence. In another study of physician–patient consultations, following coronary angiography (insertion of a catheter and injection of material allowing radiographic visualization of coronary arteries) in a large Veterans' medical center in Houston, Howard Gordon and his colleagues (2005) found a tendency on the part of physicians to give less information to black patients and for black patients to request less information than non-Hispanic white patients. The pattern indicated a cycle of passivity in which certain patients would receive less information and, in turn, fail to request that doctors provide more.

Modern-day medical practice is provided within the context of middle-class norms and values emphasizing scientific beliefs, the application of sophisticated technology, and cooperation with physicians. For patients with a different cultural perspective, interaction with doctors can be difficult and subject to misunderstanding on both sides.

Patient Compliance

Another important aspect of physician–patient interaction is patient compliance with medical regimens (Lutfey 2005). Physicians prescribe medications, diets, and other interventions and expect patients to follow them faithfully. Perhaps most patients comply with a physician's instructions, but some patients do not. In fact, some patients may pay little attention to a doctor's guidance, and this is especially the case when they begin to feel better or when their symptoms are not obvious.

For example, in a study in Scotland, Mildred Blaxter and Richard Cyster (1984) found that a majority of patients with liver problems caused by alcoholism in an outpatient clinic continued to drink—despite being advised by their physicians to reduce or give up alcohol intake. Either the physicians had not adequately communicated the danger associated with continued drinking, or the patients had misunderstood. One male patient had been told to drink no more than two glasses of sherry a day as an example of how large a quantity of alcohol he could drink. However, since he drank whiskey, not sherry, he was happy to give up sherry altogether and proceeded to drink as much whiskey as he wanted. Other patients refused to believe their doctors or simply did not want to change their drinking habits, since it meant changing a preferred lifestyle.

Compliance requires comprehension by the patient, and communication is the key for avoiding noncompliance. The motivation to be healthy, a perceived vulnerability to an illness, the potential for negative consequences, effectiveness of the treatment, sense of personal control, and effective communication are the strongest influences on compliance.

The Future of Doctor–Patient Relations

Edward Shorter (1991) traced the social history of the doctor–patient relationship. First, he explains how the medical profession evolved from being a relatively low-status occupation to a highly respected scientific field. The image of the ideal doctor–patient relationship—the caring physician and the trusting patient—was not lasting. It had ended, in Shorter's view, by the 1960s. Doctors had become increasingly distant in interacting with patients, while patients, in turn, had evolved from being willingly passive to active, informed clients who wanted to participate more equally in their care. The high cost of care, high salaries of many doctors, and superior attitudes on the part of some, along with organized opposition to health reform, caused certain patients to become disillusioned with the medical profession. Doctors, on their part, became resentful about patients and others who questioned their commitment. As a result, Shorter concludes that doctor–patient relationships in the United States have seriously eroded in recent years.

Not all patients, however, are dissatisfied to the same degree and, as previously noted, social class differences appear to be the key variable in this situation. According to Freidson (1989:13), those of lower socioeconomic status, who lack education, do not have access to Internet and other sources of information, and who are not asked to make calculated choices are not likely to be difficult patients. Conversely, patients who consider themselves to be of equal or higher status than the doctor, are well informed about the treatments for their particular health problem, and are experienced in handling bureaucratic procedures have the potential to seriously challenge a physician's management of their affliction.

Therefore, as Cassell (1986) explains, the belief among laypersons that the "doctor knows best" is no longer virtually accepted. Americans have become more knowledgeable about medicine and while they do not believe they are doctors, they do believe that they can understand and perhaps apply a piece of knowledge that is the same as the doctor's in their own health situation. Yet, Cassell observes that simply having some knowledge about medicine is not enough to displace physicians from their previous preeminent status. Rather, he notes that during the 1960s, with the social turbulence associated with the civil rights movement and the Vietnam War, the relationship of individuals to authority began to change in the United States. Americans became more individualistic and questioning about the motives of those in authority, including physicians. Cassell finds that instead of being relatively passive in the doctor–patient relationship, patients now frequently believe themselves to be active partners in their care. They want to take part in decision-making that was once exclusive to the doctor.

Consequently, when it comes to health care, an identifiable pattern among many Americans is one of consumerism, in which the consumer wants to make informed choices about the services available and not be treated as inferior. The shift toward consumerism in health care means patients have more status in the doctor–patient relationship. However, this relationship is significantly affected by an external influence—third-party payers. This influence has led Sharyn Potter and John McKinley (2005) to question whether the doctor–patient relationship in the twenty-first century is a relationship at all. Potter and McKinlay argue that while patients need to use their time efficiently and effectively with doctors, and doctors need to improve their communication skills with patients, what needs to change the most is the organizational context within which the doctor–patient encounter takes place. They suggest that the idealized long-term relationship, in which the physician knows the patient and his or her family and lives in the same community, is unusual for many patients. In fact, they ask whether a patient's last visit to a doctor was similar to his or her last encounter with a cab driver or the person who sold that individual his or her last pair of shoes and conclude that it is evolving in this direction.

What has happened to the traditional doctor–patient relationship is that it has been intruded on by third-party payers—namely, the government in the case of Medicare and Medicaid, private health insurance companies, and managed care programs. These entities monitor the number of patients seen by physicians and the amount of time spent with them, as well as micro managing physician clinical decisions. Since third-party payers decide whether or not they will reimburse a physician for his or her services, and how much they will pay, they are influential in the doctor–patient relationship. Other relevant factors noted by Potter and McKinlay include (1) the shift in the state's role from protecting the medical profession to protecting corporate health care interests to reduce costs, a measure that reduces power of organized medicine; (2) the proliferation of commercial products for the body that the patient can use independent of the physician; and (3) the rise of chronic disease, which promotes the demand for a long-term doctor–patient alliance. The latter is a countercurrent that should invigorate the doctor–patient relationship, but Potter and McKinlay find the other factors reduce the strength of the interaction. It is unlikely that going to the doctor will ever be the same as buying a pair of shoes, because of the importance of the interaction. But it is clear that outside sources can impact on the relationship in the future and possibly induce further change.

Doctor–Patient Relations and New Technology

An important factor having profound implications for the doctor–patient relationship is new medical technology. The development of computerized information highways connecting a patient's personal home computer to those of doctors, hospitals, drug companies, medical suppliers, health insurers, and medical databases will allow patients to obtain health information directly from their own computer rather than visiting a physician. Electronic monitoring devices will allow the patient to keep track of his or her physical and mental state and report these to physicians or databases by computer. Physicians may be consulted by means of home computers, electronic mail, Skype, or teleconferencing, rather than in person. A computer can be used to diagnose the patient's ills and determine treatment. Prescription drugs may be ordered electronically and delivered to the patient. Moreover, physicians themselves can obtain current online clinical information, including new procedures and data on drugs, which can be used to improve patient care. Questions by patients can also be answered. Consequently, we see medicine adopting many features of information technology, as it generates vast electronic libraries of health knowledge for those that seek it.

Medical practice in advanced societies has therefore become more and more dependent on increasingly sophisticated technologies from other fields, such as computer science and bioengineering (Webster 2002). This expanding reliance on new technologies has promoted a shift away from "biographical medicine," with its focus on the patient's oral account of his or her medical history. Instead, "techno-medicine," involving the extensive use of advanced technology for testing, diagnosis, and the scientific determination of treatment in a more differentiated world of health care delivery, is becoming more common (Casper and Morrison 2010; Pinkstone 2000).

Internet Medicine

As noted the Internet has become a major source of medical information for many people. Millions of Americans go online to search for material on health and medical matters (Barker 2008). However, connecting to the Internet with desktop and laptop computers is no longer the only way to get access to health information. Today, there are a large number of apps for smartphones and tablet computers intended to help people cope with their medical problems and improve their health (Lupton 2012). Consequently, we see the spread of health and medical information expanding into the rapidly burgeoning social media by way of Facebook, Twitter, YouTube, blogs, and other sources through computerized technologies.

According to the Pew Research Internet Project (2013), some 85 percent of all adult Americans use the Internet and 72 percent have looked online for health or medical information. Typically they investigate whether they or someone else has a disease or health problem, search for treatment options, seek information about health care providers, and look for tips on staying healthy. Some 91 percent of all Americans own a cell phone and 56 percent have a smartphone. About 31 percent of cell phone owners and 52 percent of smartphone users have looked up health and medical information on their phones, and some 19 percent have apps to track their own health. What is clearly evolving is not just e-health (electronic health), but m-health (mobile health) as people use their mobile devices to acquire information that was formerly obtained from health care providers in face-to-face or telephone conversations.

Although the information varies in terms of quality and expertise, currently there are about 10,000 websites on health problems, ranging from minor ailments to life-threatening afflictions. Articles published in leading medical journals are included as well. This information is available to anyone who has a device with an Internet connection. As Michael Hardey (1999) points out, this development changes the doctor–patient relationship as patients acquire access to information that was previously limited to doctors and nurses. Hardey studied households in Britain, who used the Internet as a source of medical knowledge. He found that it is the *users* of the Internet, not physicians, who decided what information is accessed and used, as they educated themselves about various ailments and the drugs and procedures considered effective. Many of them negotiated with their physicians about treatment for themselves or children as a result of what they found on the Internet.

Shu-Fen Tseng and Liang-Ming Chang (1999) compared doctor–patient relationships in Taiwan on the Internet and in face-to-face visits in a community hospital. For both groups of patients, mutual participation was the most common form of interaction with physicians. However, those patients who visited doctors in person expressed more confidence in physicians and relied on doctors more to treat their ailments than online users. The online users, in contrast, showed less confidence in doctors, less compliance with a physician's instructions, and a greater willingness to use alternative medicine. Online users also indicated a strong preference for continued use of the Internet for physician consultations and medical information. However, online users did not rely exclusively on the Internet but visited physicians when necessary. The Internet often served as a "second opinion" on their health problems.

In a survey of women in three southern New Jersey counties in the United States, Sanjay Pandey and his colleagues (Pandey, Hart, and Tiwary 2003) found that the Internet had become a major source of health information for the study's participants. There was evidence of the so-called digital divide, where women with high incomes and education were more likely to use the Internet for health information than those at the lower end of the social scale who lacked Internet access. However, those with access actively used the Internet, primarily to supplement information provided by physicians. For this group, the availability of health information had changed dramatically and empowered the women to interact more knowledgeably with their doctors. Other research in California shows that people who are too embarrassed to see a doctor, because of the stigma associated with their illnesses (e.g., anxiety, herpes, and urinary problems), turn to the Internet for information (Berger, Wagner, and Baker 2005) and that adolescents in the United States and Great Britain use the Internet for health information because it is confidential and convenient (Gray et al. 2005).

Not only is the Internet providing individuals with an abundance of health information, but also electronic support groups (ESGs) are forming among people with similar health needs who wish to share their experiences online and develop greater expertise. Research in the United States on parents seeking information about pediatric cancer found that they preferred to receive information directly from trusted health care providers in times of crisis rather than the Internet since it was sometimes unreliable, but they turned to the Internet to connect with ESGs (Gage and Panagakis 2012). Kristin Barker (2008) studied an ESG for fibromyalgia syndrome, a controversial pain disorder for which no specific biomedical cause is known. Nevertheless, people with this problem formed a cybercommunity that traded information online about the way in which physicians treated them and their experiences with their affliction. Barker (2008:21) says: "As a result, the process of understanding one's embodied distress has been transformed from an essentially private affair between doctor and patient to an increasingly public accomplishment among sufferers in cyberspace."

In another study, Patricia Drentea and Jennifer Moren-Cross (2005) investigated an ESG for young mothers. They observed that with the greater employment of women outside the home, there are fewer children and mothers in neighborhoods to form the child-friendly social networks of support and advice that existed in the past. This function had been taken over by physicians and other—usually masculine—formal "experts." However, these researchers found Internet sites for mothers were popular for sharing information about child rearing and establishing links with other mothers like themselves, which, in the process, were creating female cyberspace communities. As increasingly more people with chronic diseases turn to the Internet, ESG websites are flourishing as a vital link providing online connections and blogs with similarly afflicted persons and information about treatments, drugs, health insurance, and other relevant topics. One website for diabetics, Diabetic Connect, saw its registered membership increase from 140,000 persons in 2010 to 688,000 in 2012. The Internet has become a huge repository of health and medical information, as well as an important source of social support for people with health problems. It now has a major role in health care delivery.

Other Developments

Not only is computer technology emerging as a major educational tool for laypersons and thereby changing the manner in which many persons interact with physicians, but medications are also likely to be different as various drugs become available in a variety of forms—pills, injections, patches, and nasal sprays or inhalers. And treatments normally available only in hospitals, such as chemotherapy, may be reconfigured into pills and taken at home. Other measures, such as the use of robotics and computer-guided imagery, may increase efficiency and precision in surgery and reduce the need for extensive hospitalization. Doctors may have little direct involvement in certain surgeries, as robots and teams of surgically trained nurses handle most of the tasks.

Moreover, it may be the patient who discovers the requirement for treatment through self-monitoring and computer-assisted analysis of his or her medical history and symptoms. This situation also significantly changes the traditional doctor–patient relationship because patients, not doctors, will cause health care to take place. Doctors will be responding to what patients themselves decide they need, rather than the other way around. Doctors and patients will still have contact, but much of that contact may be through computers. Thus, new technology is changing care-giving relationships, as providers and consumers of health care obtain diagnostic precision and treatment options that previously have not existed (Timmermans 2000).

The New Genetics

The rapid progress in genetics following completion of the Human Genome Project has attracted considerable attention from medical sociologists (Conrad and Gabe 1999; Dingwall 2007; Martin 2008; Martin and Dingwall 2010; Pescosolido et al. 2008; Pilnick 2002; Shostak, Conrad, and Horwitz 2008; Williams 2010). This is because breakthroughs in genetics have significant social consequences. This advance forecasts a potential change in doctor–patient interaction, as patients learn through genetic screening what diseases they are likely to get and what measures are needed to treat them. There is already new computer technology and software available for use in doctor's offices and local laboratories that can sequence (put in order) an individual's genome that can be used to determine that person's genetic probabilities for cancer, rare diseases, and responses to drugs. Not only will such screening anticipate an individual's susceptibility to various diseases, but gene therapy also has the potential to eliminate many afflictions before they happen. The idea behind gene therapy is simple: to treat or cure disease by giving patients healthy genes to replace defective ones.

Genetic or genomic information may also furnish the basis for "designer" drugs tailored to match the DNA (deoxyribonucleic acid) of a particular individual and provide more precise healing with fewer side effects. This approach is leading to the establishment of personalized health care or personalized medicine programs that are intended to provide care customized to meet the specific needs of individuals. This method has the potential to revolutionize the management of many illnesses (Salari 2009). The potential of gene therapy and genetically based drugs has yet to be realized, but the results of the Human Genome Project provide researchers with a map of the human genetic code. This development is likely to bring about an age of new genetics, in which genetic testing is the basis of a considerable portion of medical practice. At first, genetic testing will probably be used to refine drugs for common problems such as migraine headaches and heart disease, but at some point gene therapy is likely to become commonplace for many afflictions. Already there is research in sociology on gene-environment interaction, as discussed in Chapter 5, investigating the relationship between genes and the social environment in relation to stress, smoking, alcohol use, and mental health (Boardman, Blalock, and Pampel 2010; Boardman, Daw, and Freese 2013; Daw et al. 2013; Pescosolido et al. 2008; Schnittker 2010).

The study of gene-environment interaction, along with research on the social use, privacy and control of genetic information, risks, and ethics of genetic research has promoted the birth of a new field in medical sociology: the sociology of genetics (Boardman et al. 2013; Conrad 1999, 2000; Conrad and Gabe 1999; Cox and

McKellin 1999; Cunningham-Burley and Kerr 1999; Daw et al. 2013; Ettorre 1999; Freese 2008; Hallowell 1999; Kerr 2004; Martin 1999; Martin and Dingwall 2010; Pilnick 2002; Williams 2010). The interest of medical sociologists in genetics is in its infancy, but questions with serious social implications are already being examined. For example, can genetic testing become a form of social control, and if so, what are the consequences for the individual and society? Currently there is no answer. But such testing could lead to new forms of stigma and discrimination, as people are classified according to their genetic traits and potential for a healthy life.

Privacy and Gene Ownership

Important social disputes about genetic research also include issues of privacy and gene ownership. As Margaret Everett (2003) explains, genetic testing makes it possible to learn about someone's likely health future that even that person may not know. Genetic information therefore has unique implications for families and groups, and this information is potentially valuable to employers, insurance companies, researchers, and pharmaceutical firms who would use it for their own purposes. This situation opens the possibility of discrimination with respect to employment and insurance, and many states in the United States prohibit discrimination in health insurance based on genetic testing and have similar laws regarding discrimination in employment.

Given the potential for the commercialization of information about an individual's DNA, informed consent also takes on an especially high level of importance. Everett reports, for example, about a situation in Miami, Florida, where families affected by Canavan's disease (a fatal and rare recessive gene disorder) allowed their children's tissue samples to be used by hospital researchers to develop a prenatal diagnostic test and new treatment for the disease. The families were outraged when the test was developed and the hospital charged them a fee for administering it. The hospital argued that it needed to recover the costs of its research, while the families claimed that they had not given informed consent in writing, not been informed that hospital would get a patent on the test and limit its availability, and charge them a fee if they needed to be tested.

Meanwhile, in 2010, Arizona State University settled out of court with the Havasupai Indians after researchers from the school were found to have used DNA samples given by the tribe for diabetes research in other projects. The diabetes study was abandoned after poor results, but the samples were stored in a refrigerator and used by faculty and graduate students for several years. The continued utilization was discovered when a Havasupai student was invited by a faculty member to attend a dissertation defense featuring a graduate student's use of the sample. The Havasupai asked the grad student about permission to use the DNA from the tribe, and found there was none. Subsequent investigation by the university showed several published papers had been based on the sample that had nothing to do with diabetes. The tribal members had signed a vague consent form giving permission for use of their blood in medical or behavioral research, but both the spirit and intent of the agreement had been violated from the tribe's point of view. One research paper, for example, used the DNA to locate the origin of the tribe in Asia, when the tribe's ancient folklore placed its origin in the Grand Canyon as the canyon's guardians. This finding could have jeopardized the tribe's rights to its land. The university recognized its error and made restitution.

The question thus arises as to whether or not genes are commodities and have property rights. If so, do they belong to the individual or to others who would use them for research and/or commercial purposes? Or what if others use a person's genetic tests without permission to deny insurance or employment or cause harm in other situations? Oregon is one of the few states that has examined the legal aspects of this question and assigned property rights to the individual.

The general rule of law that has recently emerged is that genes are naturally occurring organic matter, not something invented by humans, and therefore cannot be patented. A patent would assign exclusive rights to a gene or genetic material for 20 years to the patent-holder, and no one else could use it for research or anything else without permission until the patent expires. In a 2010 district court case in New York City that had far-reaching consequences, a federal judge invalidated patents belonging to Myriad Genetics of Utah for two genes (BRCA1 and BRCA2) linked to ovarian and breast cancer. Myriad had patented a $3,000 test for these genes that showed whether or not a woman was at high risk of ovarian or breast cancer. These patents prevented other laboratories from doing research on the genes and developing similar tests.

The New York court held that genes are "products of nature" and fall outside the boundaries of objects that can be patented. The defendants claimed in rebuttal that isolating DNA from the body transforms it into a chemical that makes it possible to be patented. But the court disagreed, saying DNA's conveyance of the genetic code is its principal feature, which is not markedly different from that found in nature. This landmark decision placed gene patents in jeopardy. The controversy intensified when a federal appeals court in Washington, D.C. overturned the ruling in 2012 in favor of Myriad. This court held, in a split decision, that the isolated DNA molecules are not found in nature, but were obtained in a laboratory and could therefore be considered man-made and eligible to be patented as a product of human ingenuity. The case was then appealed to the U. S. Supreme Court that reversed the decision and unanimously ruled in 2013 that human genes cannot be patented. The court held that Myriad did not create anything, and separating a gene from its surrounding genetic material is not an invention. However, while isolated DNA cannot be patented, the court also held that synthetic DNA created in the laboratory, what is known as complementary DNA or cDNA, is protected under patent laws.

Prenatal Genetic Screening

Another major area of controversy is that of prenatal genetic screening with the option of abortions available for fetuses identified with gene defects. A study in Finland found considerable tension between the medical staff and the mothers of the unborn children with such defects (Jallinoja 2001). The staff expected the mothers to behave in responsible and health-conscious ways, with the goal of preventing genetic diseases by volunteering to have abortions. The mothers, however, refused, and the screening program was eventually terminated. The mothers felt that a life with genetic disabilities was better than no life at all and opted against having abortions. Research in the United States shows that public attitudes toward abortion—in the case of genetic defects—has become increasingly negative (Singer, Corning, and Antonucci 1999). The negative attitudes appeared to be primarily related to the abortion question, rather than the genetic testing itself, although racial minority persons were more pessimistic about such testing, which was possibly because of fears that the tests could be used as a basis of discrimination.

Human Cloning

Another major controversy is that of cloning. Cloning refers to making a precise genetic copy of a molecule, cell, plant, or animal. Cloning techniques have been used successfully in agriculture in the selective breeding of crops and less successfully in the cloning of animals, whose death rates are twice as high as animals conceived through sexual reproduction (Pilnick 2002). The cloning of a human has—to date—not been achieved, although some researchers claim it will happen some day. Human cloning is characterized as either *therapeutic* (the cloning of human organs for transplantation in sick people) or *reproductive* (the cloning of people themselves). As Alison Pilnick (2002) reports, reproductive cloning has been widely criticized as immoral and unnatural and made illegal in some countries such as the United States. Elsewhere, experiments in human cloning are nevertheless taking place, as reported sometimes in the media. Pilnick observes that the creation of life in the laboratory represents the ultimate scientific power and potentially offers more control over populations than any previous technology, as clones would be expected to display particular characteristics as a result of their genetic makeup. At this point in time, the extent to which human cloning is possible and the ways in which it could be successful are unknown. However, as Peter Conrad and Jonathan Gabe (1999:514) point out, "issues around genetics are not limited to those with genetic disorders or identified genetic susceptibilities, but rather the new genetics is likely to affect us all."

Summary

This chapter has examined the various social factors that affect doctor–patient interaction. The most likely model of interaction in future medical encounters is the mutual participation model suggested by Szasz and Hollender (1956). This model depicts the doctor and patient working together as more of a team than the patient simply following the doctor's orders in a more or less automatic fashion. However, it was found that a particularly significant barrier to effective interaction is differences in social class. Doctors from upper- and upper-middle-class backgrounds are likely to be better communicators than doctors from lower-middle- and working-class backgrounds, while patients from higher socioeconomic levels are more likely to demand and receive adequate information about their condition than patients with a lower status.

Two groups in society are the most likely to have communication problems in medical encounters. One group is the lower class and the other is women, who sometimes do not receive what they consider to be adequate information from male doctors. Cultural differences can also affect doctor–patient interaction and, in the United States, differences between Hispanic patients and non-Hispanic health care providers have been cited as a negative circumstance. Finally, patient compliance with a physician's directions is not always automatic, and some patients fail to comply because of poor communication or other reasons. The doctor–patient relationship typically begins with dialogue, and the quality of that dialogue is often affected by social factors. New technology is undoubtedly bringing additional changes in the relationship as well; the so-called new genetics in which issues like privacy, use of genetic information, the control and ownership of genes, and cloning are becoming increasingly important.

Critical Thinking Questions

1. Communication problems between doctors and patients are a common cause of a breakdown in the doctor–patient relationship. What are some causes of communication failure in this relationship?
2. How has the development of the Internet changed the face of medicine?
3. How can the new interest in genetics by social scientists affect medical sociology?

Suggested Readings

Andrew Webster (2007) *Health, Technology and Society*. New York: Palgrave Macmillan. A sociological analysis of the role of technology in relation to health and illness.

References

Adams, Ann, Christopher D. Buckingham, Antje Lindenmeyer, John B. McKinley, Carol Link, Lisa Marceau, and Sara Arber (2008) "The influence of patient and doctor gender on diagnosing coronary heart disease." *Sociology of Health & Illness* 30: 1–18.

Atkinson, Paul (1995) *Medical talk and medical work*. London: Sage.

Babaria, Palav, Sakena Abedin, David Berg, and Marcella Nunez-Smith (2012) "'I'm used to it': A longitudinal qualitative study of third year female medical students' experiences of gendered encounters in medical education." *Social Science and Medicine* 74: 1013–20.

Barker, Kristin K. (2008) "Electronic support groups, patient-consumers, and medicalization: The case of contested illness." *Journal of Health and Social Behavior* 49: 20–38.

Berger, Magdalena, Todd H. Wagner, and Laurence C. Baker (2005) "Internet use and stigmatized illness." *Social Science and Medicine* 61: 1821–27.

Blaxter, Mildred, and Richard Cyster (1984) "Compliance and risk-taking: The case of alcohol liver disease." *Sociology of Health & Illness* 6: 290–310.

Boardman, Jason D., Casey L. Blalock, and Fred C. Pampel (2010) "Trends in the genetic influences on smoking." *Journal of Health and Social Behavior* 51:108–23.

Boardman, Jason D., Jonathan Daw, and Jeremy Freese (2013) "Defining the environment in gene-environment research: Lessons from social epidemiology." *American Journal of Public Health* 103: S61–S72.

Boulton, Mary, David Tuckett, Coral Olson, and Anthony Williams (1986) "Social class and the general practice consultation." *Sociology of Health & Illness* 8: 325–50.

Boyer, Carol A., and Karen E. Lutfey (2010) "Examining critical health policy issues within and beyond the clinical encounter: Patient-provider relationships and help-seeking behaviors." *Journal of Health and Social Behavior* 51: S80–93.

Casper, Monica J., and Daniel R. Morrison (2010) "Medical sociology and technology: Critical engagements." *Journal of Health and Social Behavior* 51: S120–32.

Cassell, Eric J. (1985) *Talking with patients*, Vol. 2. Cambridge, MA: MIT Press.

—— (1986) "The changing concept of the ideal physician." *Daedalus* 115: 185–208.

Clarke, Adele E., and Virginia L. Olesen (1999) *Revisioning women, health, and healing*. London: Routledge.

Cockerham, William C., Guenther Lueschen, Gerhard Kunz, and Joe L. Spaeth (1986) "Social stratification and self-management of health." *Journal of Health and Social Behavior* 27: 1–14.

Cole, Stephen (1986) "Sex discrimination and admission to medical school, 1929–1984." *American Journal of Sociology* 92: 529–67.

Conrad, Peter (1999) "A mirage of genes." *Sociology of Health & Illness* 21: 228–41.

—— (2000) "Medicalization, genetics, and human problems," pp. 322–34 in Handbook of medical sociology, 5th ed., C. Bird, P. Conrad, and A. Fremont (eds). Upper Saddle River, NJ: Prentice Hall.

Conrad, Peter, and Jonathan Gabe (1999) "Introduction: Sociological perspectives on the new genetics: An overview." *Sociology of Health & Illness* 21: 505–16.

Conrad, Peter, and Kristin K. Barker (2010) "The social construction of illness: Key insights and policy implications." *Journal of Health and Social Behavior* 51: S67–79.

Cooper-Patrick, Lisa, Joseph J. Gallo, J. J. Gonzales, Hong Thi Vu, Neil R. Powe, Christine Nelson, and Daniel E. Ford (1999) "Race, gender, and partnership in the patient–physician relation." *JAMA* 282: 583–89.

Cox, Susan M., and William McKellin (1999) " 'There's this thing in our family': Predictive testing and the construction of risk for Huntington Disease." *Sociology of Health & Illness* 21: 622–46.

Cunningham-Burley, Sarah, and Anne Kerr (1999) "Defining the 'social': Towards an understanding of scientific and medical discourses on the social aspects of the new genetics." *Sociology of Health & Illness* 21: 647–68.

Davies, Karen (2003) "The body and doing gender: The relations between doctors and nurses in hospital work." *Sociology of Health & Illness* 25: 720–42.

Davis, Fred (1972) *Illness, interaction, and the self*. Belmont, CA: Wadsworth.

Daw, Jonathan, Michael Shanahan, Kathleen Mullan Harris, Andrew Smolen, Brett Haberstick, and Jason D. Boardman (2013) "Genetic sensitivity to peer behaviors: 5HTTLPR, smoking, and alcohol consumption." *Journal of Health and Social Behavior* 54: 92–108.

Dingwall, Robert (2007) "Medical sociology and genetics," pp. 2937–41 in *The Blackwell encyclopedia of sociology*, G. Ritzer (ed.). Oxford, UK: Blackwell.

Drentea, Patricia, and Jennifer L. Moren-Cross (2005) "Social capital and social support on the web: The case of an Internet mother site." *Sociology of Health & Illness* 27: 920–43.

Ettorre, Elizabeth (1999) "Experts as 'storytellers' in reproductive genetics: Exploring key issues." *Sociology of Health & Illness* 21: 539–59.

Everett, Margaret (2003) "The social life of genes: Privacy, property and the new genetics." *Social Science and Medicine* 56: 53–65.

Fiorentine, Robert (1987) "Men, women, and the premed persistence: A normative alternatives approach." *American Journal of Sociology* 92: 1118–39.

Fisher, Sue (1984) "Doctor–patient communication: A social and micro-political performance." *Sociology of Health & Illness* 6: 1–27.

Fitton, Freda, and H. W. K. Acheson (1979) *The doctor/patient relationship: A study in general practice.* London: Department of Health and Social Security.

Frank, Arthur W. (1991) *At the will of the body: Reflections on illness.* Boston: Houghton Mifflin.

Freese, Jeremy (2008) "Genetics and the social science explanation of individual outcomes." *American Journal of Sociology* 114: S1–35.

Freidson, Eliot (1970) *Profession of medicine.* New York: Dodd, Mead.

——— (1989) *Medical work in America: Essays on health care.* New Haven, CT: Yale University Press.

Gage, Elizabeth A., and Christina Panagakis (2012) "The devil you know: Parents seeking information online about paediatric cancer." *Sociology of Health & Illness* 34: 444–58.

Gordon, Howard S., Richard L. Street, Jr., P. Adam Kelly, Julianne Souchek, and Nelda P. Wray (2005) "Physician-patient communication following invasive procedures: An analysis of post-angiogram consultations." *Social Science and Medicine* 61: 1015–25.

Gray, Nicola J., Jonathan D. Klein, Peter R. Noyce, Tracy S. Sesselberg, and Judith A. Cantrill (2005) "Health information-seeking behaviour in adolescence: The place of the Internet." *Social Science and Medicine* 60: 1467–78.

Hallowell, Nina (1999) "Doing the right thing: Genetic risk and responsibility." *Sociology of Health & Illness* 21: 597–621.

Hammond, Judith (1980) "Biography building to insure the future: Women's negotiation of gender relevancy in medical school." *Symbolic Interaction* 3: 35–49.

Hardey, Michael (1999) "Doctor in the house: The Internet as a source of lay health knowledge and the challenge to expertise." *Sociology of Health & Illness* 21: 820–35.

Haug, Marie, and Bebe Lavin (1981) "Practitioner or patient—Who's in charge?" *Journal of Health and Social Behavior* 22: 212–29.

——— (1983) *Consumerism in medicine.* Beverly Hills, CA: Sage.

Hayes-Bautista, David E. (1976a) "Modifying the treatment: Patient compliance, patient control, and medical care." *Social Science and Medicine* 10: 233–38.

——— (1976b) "Termination of the patient-practitioner relationship: Divorce, patient style." *Journal of Health and Social Behavior* 17: 12–21.

Henig, Robin W. (1993) "Are women's hearts different?" *New York Times* 58 (October 3): 58–61.

Hinze, Susan W. (1999) "Gender and the body of medicine or at least some body parts: (Re) constructing the prestige hierarchy of medical specialties." *Sociological Quarterly* 40: 217–40.

Howard, Jan, and Anselm Strauss (eds.) (1975) *Humanizing health care.* New York: Wiley-Interscience.

Jallinoja, Piia (2001) "Genetic screening in maternity care: Preventive aims and voluntary choices." *Sociology of Health & Illness* 23: 286–307.

Joffe, C. E., T. A. Weitz, and C. L. Stacey (2004) "Uneasy allies: Pro-choices physicians, feminist health activists and the struggle for abortion rights." *Sociology of Health & Illness* 26: 775–96.

Katz, Pearl (1999) The scalpel's edge: The culture of surgeons. Boston: Allyn and Bacon.

Kerr, Anne (2004) *Genetics and society: A sociology of disease.* London: Routledge.

Kolker, Emily S. (2004) "Framing as a cultural resource in health social movements: Funding activitism and the breast cancer movement in the US 1990–1993." *Sociology of Health & Illness* 26: 820–44.

Laveist, Thomas A., and Amani Nuru-Jeter (2002) "Is doctor–patient race concordance associated with greater satisfaction with care?" *Journal of Health and Social Behavior* 43: 296–306.

Lorber, Judith (1975) "Good patients and problem patients: Conformity and deviance in a general hospital." *Journal of Health and Social Behavior* 16: 213–25.

———— (1984) *Women physicians: Careers, status, and power.* New York: Tavistock.

———— (1993) "Why women physicians will never be true equals in the American medical profession," pp. 62–76 in *Gender, work, and medicine*, E. Riska and K. Wegar (eds.). London: Sage.

———— (1997) *Gender and the social construction of illness.* Thousand Oaks, CA: Sage.

Lupton, Deborah (2012) "M-health and health promotion: The digital cyborg and surveillance society." *Social Theory & Health* 10: 229–44.

Lutfey, Karen (2005) "On practices of 'good doctoring': Reconsidering the relationship between provider roles and patient adherence." *Sociology of Health & Illness* 4: 421–47.

Madsen, William (1973) *The Mexican-Americans of South Texas*, 2nd ed. New York: Holt, Rinehart & Winston.

Malat, Jennifer (2001) "Social distance and patients' rating of healthcare providers." *Journal of Health and Social Behavior* 42: 360–72.

Malat, Jennifer, and Mary Ann Hamilton (2006) "Preference for same-race health care providers and perceptions of interpersonal discrimination in health care." *Journal of Health and Social Behavior* 47: 173–87.

Martin, Molly A. (2008) "The intergenerational correlation in weight: How genetics resemblance reveals the social role of families." *American Journal of Sociology* 114: S67–105.

Martin, Paul A. (1999) "Genes as drugs: The social shaping of gene therapy and the reconstruction of genetic disease." *Sociology of Health & Illness* 21: 517–38.

Martin, Paul A., and Robert Dingwall (2010) "Medical sociology and genetics," pp. 511–29 in *The new Blackwell companion to medical sociology*, W. Cockerham (ed.). Oxford, UK: Wiley-Blackwell.

Martin, Steven C., Robert M. Arnold, and Ruth M. Parker (1988) "Gender and medical socialization." *Journal of Health and Social Behavior* 29: 333–43.

McKinlay, John B. (1996) "Some contributions from the social system to gender inequalities in heart disease." *Journal of Health and Social Behavior* 37: 1–26.

Pandey, Sanjay K., John J. Hart, and Sheela Tiwary (2003) "Women's health and the Internet: Understanding emerging trends and issues." *Social Science and Medicine* 56: 179–91.

Parsons, Talcott (1951) *The social system.* Glencoe, IL: The Free Press.

Peck, B. Mitchell, and Sonya Connor (2011) "Talking with me or talking about me? The impact of status characteristics on doctor-patient interaction." *Sociological Perspectives* 54: 547–67.

Pescosolido, Bernice A., Brea L. Perry, J. Scott Long, Jack K. Martin, John I. Nurnberger, Jr., and Victor Hesselbrock (2008) "Under the influence of genetics: How transdisciplinarity leads us to rethink social pathways to illness." *American Journal of Sociology* 114: S171–202.

Pew Research Internet Project (2013) *Health fact sheet* (December 16): http://www.pewinternet.org/fact-sheets/health-fact-sheet/

Pilnick, Alison (2002) *Genetics and society: An introduction.* Buckingham, UK: Open University Press.

Pinkstone, J. (2000) *Ways of knowing: A new science, technology and medicine.* Manchester, UK: University of Manchester Press.

Potter, Sharyn J., and John B McKinlay (2005) "From a relationship to encounter: An examination of longitudinal and lateral dimensions in the doctor–patient relationship." *Social Science and Medicine* 61: 465–79.

Rier, David A. (2000) "The missing voice of the critically ill: A medical sociologist's first-person account." *Sociology of Health & Illness* 22: 68–93.

Riska, Elianne (2010) "Health professions and occupations," pp. 337–54 in *The new Blackwell companion to medical sociology*, W. Cockerham (ed.). Oxford, UK: Blackwell.

Riska, Elianne, and Katarina Wegar (1993) "Women physicians: A new force in medicine?" pp. 77–93 in *Gender, work and medicine*, E. Riska and K. Wegar (eds.). London: Sage.

Robinson, Beverly J. (1990) "Africanisms and the study of folklore," pp. 211–24 in *Africanisms in American culture*, J. Holloway (ed.). Bloomington: Indiana University Press.

Salari, Keyan (2009) "The dawning era of personalized medicine exposes a gap in medical education." *PLoS Medicine* 6: e1000138.

Scheff, Thomas J. (1966) *Being mentally ill.* Chicago: Aldine.

Schnittker, Jason (2010) "Gene-environment correlations in the stress-depression relationship." *Journal of Health and Social Behavior* 51: 229–43.

Shorter, Edward (1991) *Doctors and their patients.* New Brunswick, NJ: Transaction.

Shostak, Sara, Peter Conrad, and Allan V. Horwitz (2008) "Sequencing and its consequences: path dependence and the relationships between genetics and medicalization." *American Journal of Sociology* 114: S287–316.

Singer, Eleanor, Amy D. Corning, and Toni Antonucci (1999) "Attitudes toward genetic testing and fetal diagnosis." *Journal of Health and Social Behavior* 40: 429–45.

Stepanikova, Irena (2012) "Racial-ethnic biases, time pressure, and medical decisions." *Journal of Health and Social* 54: 329–43.

Stepanikova, Irena, Stefanie Mollborn, Karen S. Cook, David H. Thom, and Roderick M. Kramer (2006) "Patients' race, ethnicity, language, and trust in a physician." *Journal of Health and Social Behavior* 47: 390–405.

Szasz, Thomas, and Marc Hollender (1956) "A contribution to the philosophy of medicine: The basic models of the doctor–patient relationship." *JAMA* 97: 585–92.

Taira, Deborah, Dana Gelb Safran, Todd B. Seto, William H. Rogers, and Alvin R. Tarlov (1997) "The relationship between patient income and physician discussion of health risk behaviors." *JAMA* 278: 1412–17.

Timmermans, Stefan (2000) "Technology and medical practice," pp. 309–21 in *Handbook of medical sociology*, 5th ed., C. Bird, P. Conrad, and A. Fremont (eds.). Upper Saddle River, NJ: Prentice Hall.

Tseng, Shu-Fen, and Liang-Ming Chang (1999) "Virtual and reality: A comparison of doctor–patient relationship to the Internet and face-to-face medical encounter." Paper presented to the International Conference on Socio-cultural and Policy Dimensions of Health Care, Singapore (November).

Waitzkin, Howard (1991) *The politics of medical encounters.* New Haven, CT: Yale University Press.

——— (2000) "Changing patient–physician relationships in the changing health-policy environment," pp. 271–83 in *Handbook of medical sociology*, 5th ed., C. Bird, P. Conrad, and A. Fremont (eds.). Upper Saddle River, NJ: Prentice Hall.

——— (2001) *At the front lines of medicine: How the medical care system alienates doctors and mistreats patients . . . and what we can do about it.* Lanham, MD: Rowman & Littlefield.

Waitzkin, Howard, Theron Britt, and Constance Williams (1994) "Narratives of aging and social problems in medical encounters with older persons." *Journal of Health and Social Behavior* 35: 322–48.

Warren, Mary Guptill, Rose Weitz, and Stephen Kulis (1998) "Physician satisfaction in a changing health care environment: The impact of challenges to professional autonomy, authority, and dominance." *Journal of Health and Social Behavior* 39: 356–67.

Webster, Andrew (2002) "Innovative health technologies and the social: Redefining health, medicine, and the body." *Current Sociology* 50: 443–57.

Weitz, Rose (1999) "Watching Brian die: The rhetoric and reality of informed consent." *Health* 3: 209–27.

West, Candace (1984) "When the doctor is a 'lady': Power, status and gender in physician-patient encounters." *Symbolic Interaction* 7: 87–106.

Williams, Alex (2008) "The falling-down professions." *New York Times Sunday Styles* (January 6): 2, 8.

Williams, Simon J. (2010) "New developments in neuroscience and medical sociology," pp. 530–51 in *The new Blackwell companion to medical sociology*, W. Cockerham (ed.). Oxford, UK: Wiley-Blackwell.

Zola, Irving K. (1966) "Culture and symptoms: An analysis of patients' presenting complaints." *American Sociological Review* 31: 615–30.

PART 4

Providing Health Care

CHAPTER 10

Physicians

LEARNING OBJECTIVES

- Describe the development of medicine as a profession.

- Evaluate the socialization of medical students into the medical profession.

- Identify the power structure of hospitals.

In 2010, there were 794,862 doctors actively practicing medicine in the United States (National Center for Health Statistics 2013). Physicians constitute less than 10 percent of the total medical workforce, yet the entire U.S. health care industry is usually subordinate to their professional authority in clinical matters. Medical doctors generally control clinical work and the efforts of most other people who provide health care directly to patients. Consequently, the status and prestige accorded to the physician is recognition of the physician's expertise concerning one of society's most essential functions—the definition and treatment of health problems. As shown in comparisons of countries in North and South America, Europe, and Asia, as well as Australia, the medical profession is prestigious throughout most of the world (Quah 1989).

The Professionalization of the Physician

The social importance of the medical function and the limited number of people with the training to perform as physicians are not the only criteria explaining their professional status. A particularly important factor is the organization of the medical profession itself. William Goode (1957, 1960) noted that two basic characteristics are sociologically relevant in explaining professionalism: (1) prolonged training in a body of specialized and abstract knowledge and (2) an orientation toward providing a service.

Moreover, once a professional group becomes established, Goode indicates that it begins to further consolidate its power by formalizing social relationships that govern the interaction of the professionals with their clients, colleagues, and official agencies outside the profession. Recognition on the part of clients, outside agencies, and the wider society of the profession's claim to competence, as well as the profession's ability to control its own membership, is necessary if professional decisions are not to be reviewed by outside authorities. Once this situation (public acceptance of claims to competence and the profession's control of its membership) occurs, Goode (1960:903) believes that additional features of the profession can be established:

1. The profession determines its own standards of education and training.
2. The student professional goes through a more stringent socialization experience than the learner in other occupations.
3. Professional practice is often legally recognized by some form of licensure.

4. Licensing and admission boards are staffed by members of the profession.
5. Most legislation concerned with the profession is shaped by that profession.
6. As the occupation gains income, power, and prestige, it can demand high-caliber students.
7. The practitioner is relatively free of lay evaluation and control.
8. Members are strongly identified by their profession.

What Goode has accomplished, for our purposes, is the development of guidelines for analyzing the development of the medical profession in American society. While physicians in the United States have traditionally shared a basic service orientation, the second requirement, that of lengthy training in a specialized and abstract body of knowledge, was initially lacking. Most American medical practitioners in the period before the American Revolution were ships' surgeons, apothecaries, or clergy who had obtained a familiarity with medical knowledge in Europe. Few practitioners had been educated in either a university setting or a medical school. Anyone who wanted to practice medicine could do so and could claim the title of "doctor," which in Europe was reserved exclusively for persons educated at a university. The most distinguished early American physicians were those trained at the University of Edinburgh in Scotland, Great Britain's foremost medical school in that era. From this small group of British-trained physicians came the impetus for establishment of the first American medical school in 1765, at the College of Philadelphia. This later became part of the University of Pennsylvania and was subsequently joined in the years prior to 1800 by the organization of other medical schools at King's College (Columbia), Harvard, and Dartmouth.

After 1800, American medical schools mushroomed, as school after school was established. But the quality of medical education in the United States remained low, and physicians themselves had little prestige as late as 1850. Not only did the doctors of the day offer little hope in curing disease, but sometimes their methods were either unpleasant or fatal. Often patients were bled, a practice that tended to weaken their condition, or they were administered purgatives, which caused them to vomit. By the middle of the nineteenth century, states historian E. Richard Brown (1979:62–63), "cholera victims were given an even chance of being done in by the disease or by the doctor."

The best medical training at this time was in Europe, especially in France and Germany, where medical research was flourishing. In France, Louis Pasteur's germ theory of disease advanced during the mid-1800s, revolutionized medicine, and provided the foundation for the discovery, classification, and treatment of numerous diseases. By the last quarter of that century, however, Germany assumed the leading role in the scientific development of medicine. Medical scientists in Germany such as Rudolf Virchow, who unveiled a general concept of disease based on cellular pathology (1858), and Robert Koch, whose work in bacteriology led to the discovery of the bacillus for anthrax (1876), tuberculosis (1882), and cholera (1883), became important figures in medicine. Their work, and the work of their colleagues, stimulated the growth of clinics and university-affiliated laboratories and promoted high standards of admission for medical training in Germany and Austria. Beginning in 1870, large numbers of American students flocked to the famous clinics and laboratories of German and Austrian universities. First Vienna and then Berlin became *the* centers of medical knowledge. It is estimated that between 1870 and 1914, approximately 15,000 American doctors received at least part of their training in German-speaking universities (Stevens 1971). Most of these doctors returned to the United States to set up lucrative private practices by introducing into their work the latest scientific techniques. These procedures, as Brown (1979:73) explains, "at least *seemed* effective in reducing suffering and ameliorating the symptoms of disease." Brown (1979:73) describes the situation as follows:

> Physicians who had the money to take an extra year's study in Europe were able to build more prestigious practices than the ordinary American-trained doctor. Usually they would take themselves out of direct competition with the majority of physicians by specializing in gynecology, surgery, ophthalmology, or one of the other new branches of medicine. They quickly formed a new elite in the profession with reputations that brought the middle and wealthy classes to their doors.

Other European-trained physicians returned to develop medical laboratories and pursue the scientific investigation of disease. Henry Bowditch, for example, founded the first experimental physiology laboratory in the United States at Harvard University in 1871, while William Welch, who discovered staphylococcus in 1892, began the first pathology laboratory in America at Bellevue Hospital medical school in New York City in 1878. By 1900, the entire medical school faculties of Harvard, Johns Hopkins, Yale, and Michigan had been trained in Germany.

In the meantime, medical science continued to record impressive technical achievements. During the 1800s, these achievements included René Laennec's (1816) invention of the stethoscope; the work of Crawford Long (1842), Robert Liston (1846), and William Morton (1846) on ether as an anesthetic; Claude Bernard's (1849) discovery of glycogen and the development of a theory of hormonal secretions providing the basis for endocrinology; Joseph Lister's (1866) use of antiseptic procedures in surgery; William Welch's discovery of staphylococcus (1892); Wilhelm Roentgen's (1895) development of the X-ray; and Ronald Ross's (1895) research on the cause of malaria. Thus, by the beginning of the twentieth century, American medical doctors were clearly able to claim the two core characteristics of a profession as outlined by Goode—a service orientation and a body of specialized knowledge.

At the beginning of the twentieth century, medical research in the United States began to surpass that of Europe. American medicine had been influenced by the British until 1820, the French until the American Civil War, and then the Austrians and the Germans. By 1895, the Americans were ready to forge ahead thanks to the vast sums of money poured into medical research by private American philanthropic foundations, such as those funded by the Carnegie and Rockefeller families. According to Brown, physicians in America strongly supported the rise of scientific medicine because it gave them greater effectiveness in a rapidly industrialized society and provided them with higher status, prestige, and income. Wealthy industrialists supported scientific medicine because it appeared to be a good investment in maintaining the moral, social, and economic order of corporate capitalism. Nevertheless, the result was, to quote Rosemary Stevens (1971:135), that "under the impact of new knowledge, the rapid improvement of medical schools, and the proliferation of hospitals and clinics which in turn generated new information, medicine was becoming vastly more efficient."

The American Medical Association

Another important step was necessary before American physicians could take advantage of their evolving professional status—the organization of physicians into a professionally identifiable group. With the founding of the American Medical Association (AMA) in Philadelphia in 1847, physicians could mark the beginning of a new era in medicine. Dues were $3 a year, and immediately 426 physicians joined. Weak and ineffectual in the beginning, the AMA gradually extended its authority to become the single greatest influence on the organization and practice of medicine in the United States.

Two internal organizational measures were highly significant in this process. First, in 1883, the *Journal of the American Medical Association* (*JAMA*) appeared. This journal not only disseminated the latest medical knowledge and contributed to the prestige of the association but also developed awareness among the members of the AMA of their allegiance to the medical profession. Second, in 1902, an important reorganization took place when the AMA was divided into component societies on the local level (district or county medical societies), constituent societies (state or territorial medical associations), a national House of Delegates, a Board of Trustees, and national officers.

As a result of this reorganization, the basic unit of the AMA had become the local society. Most important, it had the authority to set its own qualifications for membership. In theory, all "reputable and ethical" licensed physicians were eligible to join the local society, but final approval of membership was dependent upon the local society's arbitrary discretion. The power of the local society was further enhanced because AMA's organizational structure permits no formal right to a hearing or right to appeal the local society's decisions. Thus, threats of denial of membership or of expulsion from the local society represented powerful sanctions because there is no alternative medical association and AMA membership may be important to a physician's career. Often such membership in the past influenced patient referrals, consultations, specialty ratings, and other professional and social contacts important to a highly successful medical practice.

In 2011, the AMA had a membership of less than 216,000 medical students, residents, research fellows, and physicians. About 15 percent of all fully qualified doctors are members. Nonmembers include those who have retired or are employed by the government, the armed forces, research agencies, or universities, and thus, they do not need the benefits of membership. Other physicians may not belong because such membership is simply not important to them, for some reason they are unacceptable, they disapprove of the AMA's policies, or feel the dues are too high in relation to the benefits provided. Less than one-fifth of all women doctors belong to the AMA, suggesting a lack of appeal by the organization for female practitioners. Women doctors also have their own professional organization—the American Medical Women's Association—which addresses issues of interest to them. Specialty societies, in contrast to the AMA, such as the American College of Physicians, the American College of Surgeons, and the American Academy of Family Physicians, have experienced significant growth, largely because of their role in providing continuing medical education and board certification (Collier 2011).

There is little dispute within the AMA concerning its national objectives. As Eliot Freidson (1970) and others (Collier 2011) have pointed out, the actual exercise of power in the AMA is concentrated in the hands of a relatively limited number of physicians. Many members either have not been interested in the association's internal politics or have been too busy with their own medical practices or research to devote time to professional issues. The vast majority has usually been content to let the AMA represent the medical profession with Congress and other governmental agencies. The association, in turn, keeps its membership informed about significant medical and health legislation on both state and national levels.

Additionally, there is no forum for effective dissent within the AMA, because public debates are disapproved of in order to project an image of a united profession in the association's interaction with outside agencies. Dissenting issues within the AMA must first win major support at the local level; otherwise, they are not considered further. Opposition groups within the AMA find it difficult to gain power because of the indirect system of elections for national officers. Only the House of Delegates, which consists of representatives from each state, elects members to the top offices and to the Board of Trustees, which exercises day-to-day control over the association. Many influential appointments to AMA councils and committees are made directly by the Board of Trustees and are not voted upon by either the general membership or the House of Delegates. "This ingenious design," states Donald Light (2004:6), "transformed the AMA into a pyramid of power and control."

One of the most significant guiding principles of the AMA had been its view of the physician as an independent practitioner, largely free of public control, who engages in private medical practice on a fee-for-service basis. Since the 1920s, a considerable portion of the AMA's energies has gone toward maintaining this situation. One major result is that the public image of the AMA has become that of a protective trade association, seeking to ensure that the position of the physician as an individual entrepreneur of health services is not undermined. Yet, the AMA's claim that it speaks for the majority of medical doctors is misleading. In 1963, 79 percent of all qualified doctors belonged to the AMA; so the figure of 15 percent in 2011 obviously represents a substantial decrease.

The reputation of the AMA as a powerful lobby in Washington, D.C. may now be spurious. David Mechanic (1972:28) suggested a weaker AMA decades ago when he explains that the idea of any particular political group being able to dominate health policy is not consistent with the history of social legislation in health care. Although the AMA opposed both Medicare and other federal medical programs, these programs became law. The AMA was also excluded from direct participation in the planning of health reform by the Clinton Administration in 1994, with President Bill Clinton referring to the AMA as just another "special interest group" (Hafferty and Light 1995:138). "Long accustomed to a privileged seat at the policy table," state Frederic Hafferty and Donald Light (1995:138), "the AMA and other major physician organizations found themselves unexpectedly, purposefully, and pointedly excluded from direct task force participation," and the AMA was warned by then Vice President Al Gore "that it would no longer dominate health reform."

Although the AMA was not directly involved in the design of President Barak Obama's Patient Protection and Affordable Care Act (ACA) in 2010, it nonetheless supported the enactment of the legislation intended to expand health insurance coverage to the uninsured. As noted, the AMA usually opposed government-sponsored insurance programs because of concern they would decrease physician incomes and reduce autonomy (Laugesen 2011). The AMA's approval was not unequivocal in that it opposed some aspects of the Affordable Care Act, namely, stipulations that affected physician incomes. This included opposition to restrictions on the participation of physician-owned hospitals, financial penalties on physicians not complying with the Physician Quality Reporting Initiative that measures the quality of services provided to Medicare patients, reductions in Medicare payments, and enrollment fees paid by physicians to be health care providers for Medicare patients.

Nevertheless, this marked the first time in history that the AMA officially supported a health care reform measure (Laugesen 2011). The support came at a cost, however, as some AMA members who opposed the legislation resigned or did not renew their membership. Regardless of the reason, the AMA had about 9,000 fewer members in 2011 compared to 2010. If the AMA had opposed the Affordable Care Act, could it have prevented it from becoming law? Not likely.

With its organization, financing, and claims to expertise, the AMA still makes policy recommendations and tries to guide the medical profession on public issues. Thus, it cannot be claimed that the AMA no longer yields influence in health matters. However, its traditional role in maintaining the best possible policy and financial outcomes for medical doctors—regardless of whether or not it is in the public's interest—seems to have eroded much of its credibility with lawmakers and the public (Light 2004; Pescosolido, Tuch, and Martin 2001; Potter and McKinlay 2005). When the AMA purports to speak in the public's interest, the public tends to be skeptical. Therefore, as Hafferty and Light (1995:138) summarize, the AMA's "ability to exert its influence in an increasingly crowded policy environment appears greatly diminished."

The Control of Medical Education

The professionalization of medicine would not have been possible without the control over the standards for medical education (Ludmerer 1999). At the beginning of the nineteenth century, the United States had seen the emergence of a vast number of proprietary medical schools. These schools, in the absence of any educational controls, were designed to offer medical degrees as a profit-making venture. It is estimated that about 400 proprietary medical schools existed during the 1800s. Generally, they had low standards of instruction and poor facilities and admitted any student who could pay the required tuition. Because proprietary schools competed with other schools of this type and with schools affiliated with universities, they attempted to make their programs as attractive as possible. One school, for example, gave free trips to Europe upon graduation to any students who paid fees regularly and in cash for three years (Stevens 1971). Anyone who had the financial resources could obtain a medical degree and practice medicine, especially in the developing American West.

In 1904, the AMA established the Council on Medical Education to originate suggestions for the improvement of education and to become the association's agency for implementing educational change. The council eventually became an important regulating agency that operated both to establish high standards in medical schools and to strengthen the AMA's influence in medical education. The subsequent success of this effort was stimulated by one of the most important events in the history of medical education—the Flexner Report.

Sponsored by the Carnegie Foundation for the Advancement of Teaching, Abraham Flexner visited every medical school in the country and issued his famous report in 1910. Hoping to obtain funds from the prestigious Carnegie Foundation,

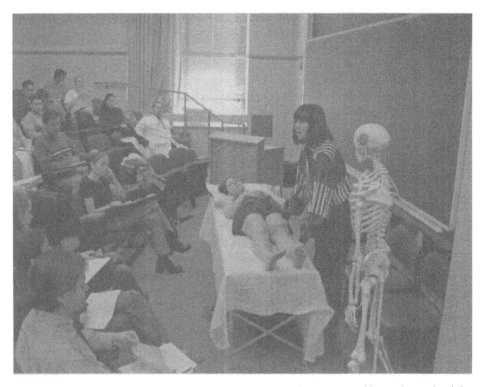

PHOTO 10.2 The medical profession is a service occupation supported by prolonged training in a specialized body of knowledge and determines its own standards of education and training.

most medical schools were anxious to discuss their problems and shortcomings while extending their full cooperation to Flexner in assessing their particular situation. The Flexner Report came out as a devastating indictment of the lack of quality medical education in the United States. Only three medical schools—Harvard, Western Reserve, and Johns Hopkins—were given full approval. Many other schools were characterized by Flexner as "plague spots," "utterly wretched," "out-and-out commercial enterprises," "wholly inadequate," and so forth (Stevens 1971:67).

Flexner strongly recommended that medical schools consist of a full-time faculty and that both laboratory and hospital facilities be made available to medical students. He also urged that standards concerning the admission of students to medical schools be established and that the qualifications of medical school faculty be raised significantly. He likewise believed that medical education should be conducted by universities on a graduate level and that teaching and research functions be integrated within the institution offering the instruction. The example of a model medical school was Johns Hopkins University, with its medical education system containing a medical school, a nursing school, and a university hospital. Johns Hopkins required the bachelor's degree or its equivalent for admission, as well as specific premedical college-level courses. According to historian Roy Porter (1997:530–31), Flexner wanted medical schools to be part of universities where medical students could receive a strong education in the natural sciences, such as biology and chemistry, and have its own biomedical departments for research, a teaching hospital, difficult entrance requirements, and a doctoral degree for graduates.

Although widespread protests arose from the affected schools, the Flexner Report induced considerable improvement in medical education. The better schools improved their programs, and the lesser schools eventually closed because of the bad publicity, financial adversity, and failure to meet the requirements of state licensing boards. Many states refused to certify the graduates of inferior medical schools, and money from various foundations was usually channeled only into those schools with good reputations. Women's medical schools closed, mistakenly thinking that women would be admitted to the newly reorganized mainstream schools, and six of the eight traditionally African American medical schools closed as well (Light 2004; Weiss and Miller 2010). Because the sole source of medical school ratings continued to be the AMA's Council on Medical Education, the medical profession was able to retain an effective monopoly over educational regulation.

As Light (2004:8) explains, what the Council on Medical Education accomplished with the help of Flexner and the Carnegie and Rockefeller Foundations "was to redefine professional education so that all the small, marginal, and for-profit medical schools had to close, and medical schools could only survive if they towed the line and thus received philanthropy from foundations dedicated to implementing the Council's new vision of professionalism." Between 1911 and 1938, the Carnegie and Rockefeller Foundations alone donated a total of $154 million—a staggering amount at the time—to a small circle of medical schools that agreed to install the new, costly curriculum recommended by Flexner. Another $600 million, according to Light, was provided by other industrialists.

In summary, by the mid-1920s, the medical profession had consolidated its professional position to the point that it clearly had become both the model of professionalism and a powerful profession. According to Goode's analysis of the characteristics of a profession, the medical profession had met the basic criteria of being a service occupation supported by prolonged training in a specialized knowledge. Furthermore, it had determined its own standards of education and training, had successfully demanded high-caliber students, had staffed its own licensing and admission boards, had shaped legislation in its own interests, had developed stringent professional sanctions, had become a terminal occupation, and was free of formal lay evaluation and control. Although threatened by social legislation advocating reforms in health care, physicians still constitute the dominant professional group in the rendering of medical services in the United States.

The Socialization of the Physician

To understand the perspectives of physicians as a professional group, it is important to also consider the manner in which physicians are selected and trained as medical professionals. In 2013, 20,055 students were selected out of 48,014 applicants to begin training at 141 accredited medical schools in the United States. The number of applicants to medical schools declined from 36,727 in 1981 to 26,721 in 1988. However, applications shot up dramatically as 45,365 students applied in 1994, only to drop to around 35,000 by 2000 and most recently reached approximately

48,000 in 2013. Some 52 percent of first-year students in 2012–2013 were male, the remaining 48 percent representing a significant increase for females. In the 1970s, only about 10 percent of all first-year medical students were female. There has also been an increase in the percentage of non-white students from 3 percent in 1969 to around 42 percent in 2011.

Typically, first-year medical students will be between the ages of 21 and 23 and will have a bachelor's degree with at least 3.6 (on a 4.0 scale) premedical grade point average or higher. Most likely the undergraduate college major will be in biology, chemistry, zoology, premedical, or psychology. Because these students are motivated and committed to a well-defined, terminal career goal, they have a high probability of successfully completing medical school once accepted—most entering medical students attain the M.D. degree.

Past studies on the social origins of American medical students show that most are from upper- and upper-middle-class families. Although increasing numbers of lower-middle- and lower-class students are entering medical school, most medical students are homogeneous in terms of social class affiliation. Howard Becker and his associates (1961) conducted what has become a classic study in medical sociology of students at the University of Kansas Medical School in the late 1950s using participant observation. They found that lower-class medical students, by virtue of their undergraduate education and commitment to becoming successful physicians, assimilated middle-class norms and values.

Oswald Hall (1948) pointed out several decades ago that the decision to study medicine is largely social in character; that is, it originates in a social group that is able to generate and nurture the medical ambition. Family influence is an especially important variable in encouraging and reinforcing the ambitions of the future recruit to the medical profession. Having a parent, close relative, or family friend who is a physician also seems to be a distinct advantage in promoting the desire to be a doctor.

The reason given by many medical students for choosing a career in medicine has been generally that of wanting "to help people." Becker and his associates, for example, found that first-year medical students had idealistic long-range perspectives about why they selected medicine as a career. These perspectives were summarized as follows (Becker et al. 1961:72):

1. Medicine is the best of all professions.
2. When we begin to practice, we want to help people, have enjoyable, satisfying work while upholding medical ideas. We want to earn enough money to lead comfortable lives, but this is not our primary concern.

Some medical students may enter medical school in order to make money or for the prestige of the M.D. degree, or both. According to John Columbotos (1969), physicians from a lower-class social origin were more likely than upper-class doctors to emphasize success values as reasons for going into medicine. But once in medical practice, social class background became less significant. Those physicians who were initially success oriented became less so after commencing their practices, while the reverse occurred with those who were less success oriented. Columbotos suggested this trend was most likely because of socialization by colleagues. Success-oriented physicians were probably encouraged to be less obvious about their ambitions, and the less-success oriented were encouraged to strive for the level of status indicative of their professional group. Becker and his associates noted that most of those entering medical students *assumed* they would be well paid. Hence, making money was apparently secondary to helping patients. Many resented the notion that they were solely out to make money. And there is evidence that many practicing physicians do indeed have a humanitarian orientation and believe in serving the sick (Chirayath 2006).

Once the medical student begins training, he or she is expected to acquire a foundation of knowledge in the basic medical sciences and the techniques employed in the actual practice of medicine. Included in this process is the internalization of ethical and moral principles that are essential if the physician is to be trusted by patients, colleagues, and the community and is to maintain his or her professional status. Most courses of study range from 32 to 45 months, and the educational experience is usually divided into basic medical science studies and clinical studies. Basic medical science studies consist of courses in anatomy, biochemistry, physiology, pathology, pharmacology, microbiology, physical diagnosis, clinical laboratory procedures, and behavioral science. The clinical programs consist of learning to use basic medical science to solve clinical problems, by working with patients under the supervision of the faculty. The students also rotate through clerkships in various medical services, such as internal medicine, surgery, pediatrics, obstetrics-gynecology, psychiatry, and other specialties.

Much of the sociological research concerning medical education has focused on the consequences of that experience, other than mastery of medical knowledge. Among the major studies, Renée Fox (1957) found that medical students at Cornell Medical School acquired basically two traits as a result of their medical training: ability to be emotionally detached from the patient and to tolerate uncertainty. Fox, whose work was part of an extensive study of student physicians (Merton, Reader, and Kendall 1957), noted that the medical student experienced three types of uncertainty. First, there was uncertainty resulting from an awareness of not being able to learn everything about medicine. Second, there was the realization that limitations existed in current medical knowledge and techniques. The first two uncertainties led to a third type of uncertainty, in which medical students had problems distinguishing between personal ignorance and the limits of available knowledge. However, Fox observed that as the student acquired medical knowledge and gained experience, along with a sense of personal adequacy in medicine, he or she learned to cope with the uncertainty and to assess conflicting evidence objectively in arriving at a diagnosis. This process was assisted by the realization that other medical students were coping with the same problems and that the faculty also experienced uncertainty in their everyday work.

One method medical schools have employed, to reduce uncertainty among students in the application of medical knowledge, is an emphasis upon a technique known as *evidence-based medicine* (EBM). EBM utilizes clinical practice guidelines, providing highly detailed step-by-step instructions on medical care that the students can refer to in clinical situations. These instructions are based on "proven" (supported by research and clinical trials) diagnostic and therapeutic procedures. Stefan Timmermans and Alison Angell (2001) investigated the use of EBM among physicians undergoing residency training in pediatrics at Brandeis University Medical School. They found that, while EBM is a major improvement in reducing uncertainty,

uncertainty is still attached to many aspects of medical practice. Timmermans and Angell suggest that the strength of a doctor's clinical judgment depends on how well he or she confronts the uncertainties that persist in medical knowledge. Timmermans and Neetu Chawla (2009) point out that while EBM addresses uncertainty and provides guidance on how to address many clinical questions, it causes another uncertainty because it requires applying evidence from large population-based studies and clinical trials to individual patients, and the best scientific evidence may not uniformly fit the needs of all patients. Timmermans and Chawla (2009:152) therefore conclude that the "effect of EBM on medical education" has been "subtle rather than revolutionary."

At the University of Kansas Medical School, Becker and his colleagues (1961) determined that the students developed a strong appreciation of clinical experience (actually working with patients rather than reading about disease and studying it in the laboratory) and that they acquired a sense of responsibility about patients. They also learned to view disease and death as medical problems rather than as emotional issues. The focal point of their passage through medical school was to graduate. Because they could not learn everything they needed to know to practice medicine, they directed their efforts toward finding the most economical ways of learning. Generally, they tried to guess what the faculty wanted them to know and then they studied this material for the examinations. Even so, they found that they put in an eight-hour day of classes and laboratories. They also studied four to five hours on weeknights and continued studying on the weekends.

One aspect of medical training that appears in several studies of medical students is the finding that the experience tends to promote emotional detachment from patients (Baker, Yoels, and Clair 1996; Hafferty 1991, 2000). Robert Coombs (1978), for example, found that in a California medical school, the faculty gave little real guidance in how to manage patients, except to serve as role models for emotional control and a businesslike demeanor. In Canada, Jack Haas and William Shaffir (1977) found the students to be initially dismayed by how the teaching faculty and other hospital staff members treated patients.

In trying to cope with the situation, the students began to rationalize that the large number of patients seen by the physicians precluded them from doing anything more than attending to the patient's medical condition. There were just too many patients and not enough time to be sociable. In fact, in their own work, the students found themselves depersonalizing patients so they could concentrate on learning what was medically important. A student described the situation this way:

> I think you realize that there is a structural problem, and there are a lot of demands made on you and you are forced to act in certain ways just to accomplish your work. But right now in the training phase, I find if the clinical preceptor takes me around to listen to six patients with heart murmurs and I only have five minutes with each patient, I don't get concerned that I'm not getting it on with the patient, because I'm trying to learn about heart murmurs. (Haas and Shaffir 1977:71)

Not having time to spend with patients is not just a problem for students but also for recent graduates serving medical residencies in hospitals to complete their qualifications. A study of resident doctors in a teaching hospital found they spent little time asking patients about the impact of their illness on their lives, counseling patients about their health behavior, explaining why they were having certain tests done, or the meaning of their diagnosis (Jagsi and Surender 2004). Many felt they were unable to provide good psychological support for their patients. As one hospital resident said:

> When I am running and trying to listen to their heart and lungs and they are trying to tell me something, or they are sad and they are crying, I am like, "I have got 5 minutes to spend . . . on you, and you have just taken it, and I have got to go." (Jagsi and Surender 2004:2184)

Previously, the Becker study had attempted to assess the general impact of such attitudes by exploring the charge that medical students become cynical as a result of their medical education. In reply, Becker and his colleagues noted that medical students did appear to enter medical school openly idealistic, but once in medical school, their idealism was replaced with a concern for getting through. Becker observed that medical students may in fact become cynical while in school, but he also pointed out that attitudes are often situational. Thus, when graduation approached, idealism seemed to return as the students could set aside the immediate problem of completing their program of study. What had happened was that medical students had been isolated in an institutional setting and forced to adjust to the demands of that setting. But once the medical student was ready to return to the mainstream of society, the student again became concerned about service to humanity. In an earlier article, Becker and Blanche Greer (1958) had argued that cynicism on the part of medical students represented growth toward a more realistic perspective. What appeared as a harmful change of attitude was actually part of a functional learning process fitted to the physician's role of maintaining an objective perspective of health and disease. The Coombs (1978) study likewise found that medical students' cynicism did not develop into a generalized personality trait. The students in this study learned to balance emotional attitudes with sensitivity toward patients.

For some physicians, the possibility still remains that medical training has focused their attention more on technical procedures than on dealing with patients as people. As Light (1979) pointed out, in emphasizing clinical judgments and techniques, physicians run the danger of becoming insensitive to complexities in diagnosis, treatment, and relations with patients. The result can be errors and malpractice suits. Light (1979:320) explains: "Their emphasis on techniques can make them oblivious to the needs of clients as *clients* define them; yet it is clients' trust that professionals will solve their complex problems which provides the foundation of professional power."

While much of the older literature on socialization in medical schools finds tendencies on the part of students to depersonalize patients, some accounts of medical training show a different situation. Ellen Lerner Rothman (1999) reported on her experiences as a student at Harvard Medical School and found numerous situations where she and her fellow students, as well as staff physicians, developed serious personal concerns about the well-being of their patients and worked hard to help them. She comments on a classmate who was initially annoyed by a 65-year-old man who kept complaining about abdominal pain despite a lack of evidence for a cause of the pain. However, after further tests, it was determined the man had widespread cancer. The classmate felt awful and that somehow her team of doctors

BOX 10.1

The Hidden Curriculum

All professions, including medicine and law, as well as sociology and psychology, have a "hidden curriculum" in which those learning to perform the work of the profession are informally socialized at the same time into adopting a particular professional identity and outlook. As Barret Michalec and Frederic Hafferty (2013:391) explain, the hidden curriculum refers to an "undercurrent" of norms, values, and viewpoints that are embedded in the training process and adopted by students as they are integrated into the profession. This is one of the most important methods by which a profession transmits its underlying norms and values to a novice and influences that individual to adopt them as his or her own.

This type of learning comes during a student's immersion in the interaction that takes place in academic health centers with faculty, fellow students, other health care workers, and patients and their families (Karneili-Miller et al. 2010). That is, the hidden curriculum imparts a professional outlook to its recruits as an informal part of the training process. According to Michalec and Hafferty (2013), the hidden curriculum of the medical school instills a sense of professional authority and autonomy in the future

physician. Often transmitted through faculty role models, medical students derive a sense of professional autonomy through the control of physicians over patients and the work of supporting occupations in health care. Feelings of authority emerge from mastering medical knowledge unavailable to most people. Autonomy comes from authority, thus the two professional characteristics are inter-related.

Michalec and Hafferty find that autonomy and authority are the key pillars in medicine's view of itself as a profession, but these characteristics also promote an unequal system of stratification within the social organization of health care delivery—with physicians entrenched at the top. They argue, however, that when the hidden medical curriculum takes a more team-oriented approach to health care, showing how all patient care disciplines contribute as a team, overall patient outcomes can be improved. Yet they also conclude that the effect of the current hidden curriculum in medicine remains a potent and durable influence in medical education. As Thomas Farrell and Porter Lillis (2013:336) point out, for physicians the preservation of their position of authority is integral to their continuation as a profession as we now know it.

was responsible. "I mean," stated the classmate (Rothman 1999:155), "he came in a healthy man, and if we hadn't gone mucking around, we never would have found the cancer in the first place." The classmate was determined to do as much as she could for the man. Rothman herself told of how much joy and excitement she felt when her trauma team saved a man's life on the operating table. "For the first time," states Rothman (1999:167), "I understood what it was like to care for hospitalized patients and become emotionally invested in their care."

As medical education enters the twenty-first century, significant changes are taking place. The number of male applicants has declined almost 50 percent since 1975, and medical school classes are no longer composed almost entirely of white males. Females and racial minority students have taken their place, indicating that the image of the medical profession as white and male is changing toward one of greater diversity. Admissions criteria also have been broadened to include a greater mix of students, not just women and racial minorities but students whose background and undergraduate experiences suggest they are personable and will likely take a humanistic approach in dealing with patients.

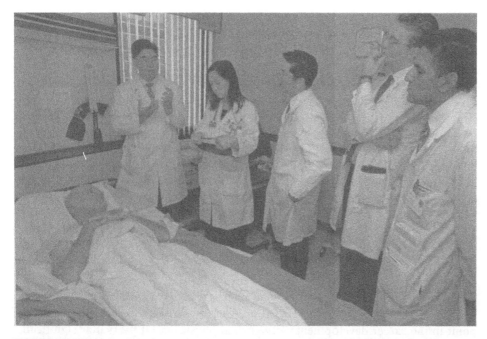

PHOTO 10.3 Medical students develop a strong appreciation for clinical experience that comes with working with patients instead of just reading about disease or learning about it in a laboratory or lecture hall.

Furthermore, as Light (1988) and others (Brosnan and Turner 2009; Hafferty 2000) indicate, medical education is having to adjust to new realities in medical practice. These realities, as Light points out, include the transition in American health care delivery from (1) a system run by doctors to one shaped by the purchasers of care and the competition for profits; (2) a decline in the public's trust in doctors to greater questioning and even distrust; (3) a change in emphasis on specialization and subspecialization to primary care and prevention; (4) less hospital care to more outpatient care in homes and doctors' offices; and (5) less payment of costs incurred by doctors' decisions to fixed prepayments, with demands for detailed accounts of decisions and their effectiveness. Even though the medical profession and medical schools have a long tradition of conservatism, medical education is adjusting to the realities of medical practice, in order to better prepare medical students for the changing environment they will face in the twenty-first century, including medical practice in managed care systems where physicians are employees (Hafferty 2000; Ludmerer 1999).

From a sociological perspective, medical schools can be viewed as recipients rather than catalysts of change (Cockerham 2009). Not only have they had to adjust to the practice realities of managed care, but medical schools also act as conduits to changes taking place in the wider society. The best example of this process is the significant increase in the gender and racial diversity of medical students fostered by societal change that is having a profound effect on the composition of the medical profession. Over time, as these more diversified cohorts of graduates move deeper into the medical profession, whether or not a physician is a man or a woman, or a racial minority, is less likely to be meaningful as the era of white-male dominance in medicine is already passing into history.

The Power Structure of American Medicine

Like any other profession, medicine has its own power structure. Such a power structure would be most common in large cities and have less relevance for small towns and rural settings. One of the early, but still relevant, studies concerning the power structure of the medical profession was conducted by Oswald Hall (1946, 1948) in an eastern American city. Hall identified three factors important in establishing prestige within the medical profession: (1) hospital affiliation, (2) clientele, and (3) the inner fraternity.

The Hospital

A significant factor in a successful urban medical career, according to Hall, was affiliation with a prestigious hospital because the more important hospital positions were usually associated with the more financially rewarding medical practices. Therefore, gaining an appointment at a prestigious hospital represented a crucial point in the career development of the urban physician. Of particular significance was the initial appointment as a resident because, as Hall (1948:330) explains, the hospital residency "that a doctor has served is a distinctive badge; it is one of the most enduring criteria in the evaluation of his [or her] status." In a study of the Harvard Medical Unit at Boston City Hospital, Stephen Miller (2010) determined that the "best" residency was not necessarily determined by the quality of teaching, the type of patient, or the range of responsibility residents were allowed to assume, though these factors were important. The "best" referred to the reputation of the program and its location.

For those physicians wishing to become general practitioners, the optimal setting for an internship would be in communities where they hoped to build a medical practice. Even at the local level, the initial hospital appointment was important in that it facilitated the formation of friendships and professional relationships that could help to enhance a career. Usually, the location of a residency determines the system of medical institutions and group of physicians the new doctor will be associated with in the future.

The Clientele

The next stage described by Hall is that of acquiring a clientele and retaining and improving it. Hall likened this process to that of a commercial enterprise, in that the physician needed to play the role of a promoter. In other words, the physician was required to interact with patients so as to secure their approval of the services provided. Freidson (1960) has pointed out that the lay-referral system not only channels the patient to certain doctors but also helps the patient to make a decision about returning. Freidson notes that the first visit to a doctor is often tentative, especially in a community large enough to support more than one doctor. Freidson

(1960:378) states: "Whether the physician's prescription will be followed or not, and whether the patient will come back, seems to rest at least partly on his [or her] retrospective assessment of the professional consultation." Thus, the patient passes through the lay-referral system not only on the way to the physician but also on the way back by discussing the doctor's behavior, diagnosis, and drug prescription with family and friends. In a given community, certain doctors are often chosen more frequently than others, because they have a good reputation and are fashionable or popular. Most physicians become aware of lay expectations and learn to deal with them if they expect patients to return.

The best medical practice in Hall's study was the specialized practice because he believed that the specialist was accorded superior status by others in the medical profession. There is a status hierarchy among specialties as well, with neurosurgery, thoracic surgery, and cardiology ranking highest, while geriatrics, dermatology, and psychiatry rank lowest (Album and Westin 2008). A specialized practice is dependent on having a group of colleagues who refer patients to the specialist and also requires access to hospital facilities. Hospital connections in themselves facilitate the development of referral relationships between physicians. However, referral systems are changing for many doctors (Anthony 2003). Whereas in the past, a physician typically referred his or her patients within an open-ended system to any doctor they wished, contractual arrangements in managed care practices require primary care providers to refer patients to a restricted list of doctors. This list includes only the doctors who are affiliated or employed by the managed care organization. Thus, referral networks have become considerably smaller for many physicians.

The "Inner Fraternity"

Hall's study pointed toward the existence of an "inner fraternity" in medicine that operated to recruit new members, allocate these new members to positions in the various medical institutions, and help them secure patients through referrals. Hall believed that the urban power structure of the medical profession consisted of four major groups of physicians. The first group was the "inner core," which he described as the specialists who have control of the major hospital positions. Immediately outside this inner core were the new recruits at various stages of their careers, who were likely to inherit positions in the inner core at some time in the future. Next were the general practitioners, who were linked to the inner core by the referral system. Women physicians tend to fall into this second group of "friendly outsiders"—that is, not members of the inner core (Lorber 1993). But with increasing numbers of women doctors, this is likely to change over time with women filling leadership positions in the future and moving into the inner core. The fourth group was the marginal physicians, whose practices were less successful and would remain on the fringes of the system.

What Hall's analysis has provided in terms of understanding the power structure of the medical profession is the realization that a doctor's career takes place in a system of formal and informal relationships with colleagues. Formal relationships develop as a result of a physician's position within the prevailing medical institutions in a particular community. The control of the dominant posts within these institutions is the critical variable that distinguishes influential from noninfluential doctors.

For example, in large regional medical centers anchored by university medical schools, the most powerful figures are the professors who chair the major medical school departments and act as chiefs of medicine, surgery, psychiatry, obstetrics-gynecology, pediatrics, and other services in the teaching hospitals (Starr 1982). They were the ones who controlled policy-making boards and determined the careers of residents. As one administrator put it, "It is inconceivable that the university would try to carry out a policy contrary to the wishes of the department chairmen of the Medical School and damned difficult for the hospital to carry out a policy contrary to the wishes of the chiefs" (Duff and Hollingshead 1968:46). Such a situation, as Starr observes, is practically a textbook definition of power.

Informal relationships also develop over time, as physicians interact with one another frequently and arrive at definitions of the quality of each other's work and personal characteristics. Thus, claims to position, status, and power become recognized and are perpetuated within the profession, and mechanisms for recruitment into the inner core become established in both formal and informal ways. The inner core is divided into two major groups: a knowledge elite (physician-researchers) and an administrative elite (physician-administrators). The knowledge elite, according to Freidson (1989), exercises influence over medical work through its research productivity. Rather than focus on individual diagnosis and treatment, the knowledge elite has shifted much of its attention to conducting clinical trials and assessing entire systems of health care (Hafferty and Light 1995). Members of the administrative elite, in turn, have established themselves on a long-term basis in major bureaucratic posts in medical centers, such as deans of medical schools, department chairs, or heads of clinics and hospitals. They wield considerable power over budgets and staff appointments.

Hafferty and Light (1995) predict that, as the physician-researchers and physician-administrators establish power and influence, they will move away from the everyday concerns of rank-and-file physicians. They will be more concerned with important research topics or institutional issues. Not only will there be increased professional distance from physicians outside the inner core, but there will also be greater separation between the two elite groups as they go in different directions in pursuit of their particular interests. "Rather, these new elites," state Hafferty and Light (1995:141), "will not only fail to identify with the rank-and-file or with broader professional values but they themselves will evolve in disparate directions, with the administrative elite becoming the more dominant of the two as it develops closer working and ideological ties with corporate interests and bureaucratic structures."

The most significant variable to emerge from this discussion of the power structure of the American medical profession is that of institutional position. The medical profession is based upon a variety of institutions—hospitals, medical centers, medical schools, the AMA, and so on. The policies and practices of these institutions are determined by those individuals who occupy decision-making positions within them. Power and influence among physicians (as in any other professional group) derive from being in a position to direct or at least share in decision making at the highest organizational levels.

Summary

This chapter has examined the professional development of physicians by high-lighting the manner in which an initial service orientation and development of a specialized body of knowledge resulted in power and status in American society. Instrumental in this evolution was the organization of the AMA, which expanded and protected the rights and privileges of doctors. However, in recent years, the AMA has often been perceived as a protective trade association for physicians rather than having public welfare as its central interest. Although still influential, the AMA has lost power and membership. There are increasing signs of changed attitudes toward their professional position on the part of many physicians, which suggest that greater attention to the needs of society may be ahead. The power structure of American medicine was also discussed from the standpoint of hospitals, clientele, and the "inner fraternity." The most powerful positions in medicine are those associated with prestigious academic appointments in the university medical centers of large urban areas.

Critical Thinking Questions

1. Describe the evolution of the medical profession.
2. Explain how the American Medical Association contributed to the professionalization of medicine.
3. How did the Flexner Report change medical education?
4. How could the changing demographics of new medical school students affect the profession?

Suggested Readings

Brosnan, Caragh Brosnan, and Bryan S. Turner (eds.) (2009) *Handbook of the sociology of medical education*. London: Routledge.
Collection of essays by leading medical sociologists in North America and Europe on medical education.

References

Album, Dag, and Steinar Westin (2008) "Do diseases have a prestige hierarchy? A survey among physicians and medical students." *Social Science and Medicine* 66: 182–88.
Anthony, Denise (2003) "Changing the nature of physician referral relationships in the US: The impact of managed care." *Social Science and Medicine* 56: 2033–44.
Baker, Patricia S., William C. Yoels, and Jeffrey M. Clair (1996) "Emotional processes during medical encounters: Social disease and the medical gaze," pp. 173–99 in *Health and the sociology of emotions*, V. James and J. Gabe (eds.). Oxford, UK: Blackwell.
Becker, Howard S., and Blanche Greer (1958) "The fate of idealism in medical school." *American Sociological Review* 23: 50–56.
Becker, Howard S., Blanche Greer, Everett C. Hughes, and Anselm Strauss (1961) *Boys in white: Student culture in medical school*. Chicago: University of Chicago Press.
Brosnan, Caragh, and Bryan S. Turner (eds.) (2009) *Handbook of the sociology of medical education*. London: Routledge.

Brown, E. Richard (1979) *Rockefeller medicine men: Medicine and capitalism in America.* Berkeley: University of California Press.

Chirayath, Heidi Taylor (2006) "Who serves the underserved? Predictors of physician care to medically indigent patients." *Health* 10: 259–82.

Cockerham, William C. (2009) "Medical education and the American healthcare system," pp. 228–41 in *Handbook of the sociology of medical education,* C. Brosnan and B. Turner (eds). London: Routledge.

Collier, Roger (2011) "American Medical Association woes continue." *Canadian Medical Association Journal* 183: E713–14.

Columbotos, John (1969) "Social origins and ideology of physicians: A study of the effects of early socialization." *Journal of Health and Social Behavior* 10: 16–29.

Coombs, Robert H. (1978) *Mastering medicine: Professional socialization in medical school.* New York: The Free Press.

Duff, Raymond S., and August B. Hollingshead (1968) *Sickness and society.* New York: Harper & Row.

Farrell, Thomas C., and Porter J. Lillis (2013) "An adaptation to Michel Foucault's medical authority: The lucid succor of the informal care giver." *Social Theory and Health* 11: 327–43.

Fox, Rene'e (1957) "Training for uncertainty," pp. 207–41 in *The student-physician,* R. K. Merton, G. Reader, and P. L. Kendall (eds.). Cambridge, MA: Harvard University Press.

Freidson, Eliot (1960) "Client control and medical practice." *American Journal of Sociology* 65: 374–82.

—— (1970) *Profession of medicine.* New York: Dodd, Mead.

—— (1989) *Medical work in America: Essays on health care.* New Haven, CT: Yale University Press.

Goode, William J. (1957) "Community within a community." *American Sociological Review* 22: 194–200.

—— (1960) "Encroachment, charlatanism, and the emerging profession: Psychology, sociology, and medicine." *American Sociological Review* 25: 902–14.

Haas, Jack, and William Shaffir (1977) "The professionalization of medical students: Developing competence and a cloak of competence." *Symbolic Interaction* 1: 71–88.

Hafferty, Frederic (1991) *Into the valley: Death and the socialization of medical students.* New Haven, CT: Yale University Press.

—— (2000) "Reconfiguring the sociology of medical education: Emerging topics and pressing issues," pp. 238–57 in *Handbook of medical sociology,* 5th ed., C. Bird, P. Conrad, and A. Fremont (eds.). Upper Saddle River, NJ: Prentice Hall.

Hafferty, Frederic W., and Donald W. Light (1995) "Professional dynamics and the changing nature of medical work." *Journal of Health and Social Behavior* 36(Extra issue): 132–53.

Hall, Oswald (1946) "The informal organization of the medical profession." *Canadian Journal of Economics and Political Science* 12: 30–44.

—— (1948) "The stages of a medical career." *American Journal of Sociology* 53: 327–36.

Jagsi, Reshma, and Rebecca Surender (2004) "Regulation of junior doctors' work hours: An analysis of British and American doctors' experiences and attitudes." *Social Science and Medicine* 58: 281–91.

Karneili-Miller, Orit, T. Robert Vu, Matthew C, Holtman, Stephen G. Clyman, and Thomas S. Inui (2010) "Medical students' professionalism narratives: A window on the informal and hid-den curriculum." *Academic Medicine* 85: 124–33.

Laugesen, Miriam J. (2011) "Civilized medicine: Physicians and health care reform." *Journal of Health Politics, Policy and Law* 36: 507–12.

Light, Donald W. (1979) "Uncertainty and control in professional training." *Journal of Health and Social Behavior* 20: 310–22.

—— (1988) "Toward a new sociology of medical education." *Journal of Health and Social Behavior* 29: 307–22.

—— (2004) "Introduction: Ironies of success—A new history of the American health care 'system.' " *Journal of Health and Social Behavior* 45(Extra issue): 1–24.

Lorber, Judith (1993) "Why women physicians will never be true equals in the American medical profession," pp. 62–76 in *Gender, work, and medicine*, E. Riska and K. Wegar (eds.). London: Sage.

Ludmerer, Kenneth (1999) *Time to heal.* New York: Oxford University Press.

Mechanic, David (1972) *Public expectations and health care.* New York: Wiley-Interscience.

Merton, Robert K., George G. Reader, and Patricia Kendall (1957) *The student-physician.* Cambridge, MA: Harvard University Press.

Michalec, Barret, and Frederic W. Hafferty (2013) "Stunting professionalism: The potency and durability of the hidden curriculum within medical education." *Social Theory and Health* 11: 388–406.

Miller, Stephen J. (2010) *Prescription for leadership: Training for the medical elite.* New Brunswick, NJ: Transaction.

National Center for Health Statistics (2013) *Health United States, 2012.* Washington, DC: U.S. Government Printing Office.

Pescosolido, Bernice A., Steven A. Tuch, and Jack K. Martin (2001) "The profession of medicine and the public: Examining Americans' changing confidence in physician authority from the beginning of the 'health care crisis' to the era of health care reform." *Journal of Health and Social Behavior* 42: 1–16.

Porter, Roy (1997) *The greatest benefit to mankind: A medical history of humanity.* New York: W. W. Norton.

Potter, Sharyn J., and John B McKinlay (2005) "From a relationship to encounter: An examination of longitudinal and lateral dimensions in the doctor–patient relationship." *Social Science and Medicine* 61: 465–79.

Quah, Stella R. (1989) "The social position and internal organization of the medical profession in the third world: The case of Singapore." *Journal of Health and Social Behavior* 30: 450–66.

Rothman, Ellen Lerner (1999) *White coat: Becoming a doctor at Harvard Medical School.* New York: HarperCollins.

Starr, Paul (1982) *The social transformation of American medicine.* New York: Basic Books.

Stevens, Rosemary (1971) *American medicine and the public interest.* New Haven, CT: Yale University Press.

Timmermans, Stefan, and Alison Angell (2001) "Evidence-based medicine, clinical uncertainty, and learning to doctor." *Journal of Health and Social Behavior* 42: 342–59.

Timmermans, Stefan, and Neetu Chawla (2009) "Evidence-based medicine and medical education," pp. 139–55 in *Handbook of the sociology of medical education*, C. Brosnan and B. Turner (eds.). London: Routledge.

Weiss, Richard M., and Lynn E. Miller (2010) "The social transformation of American medical education: Class, status, and party influences on occupational closure, 1902–1919." *Sociological Quarterly* 51: 550–75.

CHAPTER 11

The Physician in a Changing Society

Public attitudes toward the medical profession have shifted away from the unquestioning acceptance of physician authority as seen in the mid-twentieth century to a more questioning and critical view of doctors today (Light 2004; Mechanic 2004; Pescosolido 2013; Pescosolido, Tuch, and Martin 2001; Potter and McKinlay 2005; Timmermans and Oh 2010; Vanderminden and Potter 2010). In a nationwide survey, Bernice Pescocolido and her colleagues (Pescosolido et al. 2001:13) found that while Americans still have high regard for medicine as a social institution, "the movement of public opinion has been toward less confidence in physician authority."

Public dissatisfaction with the medical profession and its provision of health care in the United States is generally viewed as having largely economic and social origins. The specific issues usually cited are those of the rising financial costs of services and the failure to provide quality care for all Americans, despite the medical profession's claims of excellence and technological achievement. Both of these issues are based on the organization of medical practice around the concept of financial profit in a free enterprise system. Advocates of this system claim that the profit motive leads to enhanced efficiency in providing services, increased incentive for research and development, and greater responsiveness to patients. Opponents argue, in rebuttal, that the present system should be changed because the profit motive discriminates against those unable to pay, fosters the unnecessary duplication of services (thereby increasing costs), and introduces a dehumanizing connotation to a service intended to relieve human suffering. Nevertheless, economic considerations have become a primary motivation among physicians, hospitals, and private health insurance companies (Potter and McKinlay 2005; Timmermans and Oh 2010; Waitzkin 2000, 2001). The profit motive, in turn, has bred increasing resentment among consumers and demands that the professional power of doctors be reduced.

Part of the blame for this situation may lie in medicine's development as a profession. The model of professionalism followed by the medical profession is based upon the image of medical practice in the nineteenth and early twentieth centuries, when the majority of physicians worked on a solo basis as an independent, fee-for-service, private practitioner. By the beginning of the twenty-first century, this situation had changed radically as many doctors work as employees in hospitals and managed care practices of one type or another. Moreover, the highly rigid stratification system that promoted an increasingly large gap in status between physicians and nonphysician medical personnel has seriously eroded. Currently, nurses, pharmacists, nutritionists, physical therapists, and others may also hold doctorates in their fields, so that the

═══════════════ **BOX 11.1** ═══════════════

The Aims of Medicine?

British social historian Roy Porter (1997:717) asks if the aims of medicine have become muddled, after doing so much good. "What are its aims?" he asks. Is its primary duty to keep people alive, regardless of the circumstances? Is it to require people to live healthy lives? Or is it a service industry to fulfill whatever fantasies people may have for themselves, such as designer bodies or the wishes of postmenopausal women to have babies? Who is going to decide? The questions await an answer. Yet in the meantime, Porter finds that the healthier Western society becomes, the more medicine it craves and the greater the tendency on the part of the public to demand maximum access to it. Medicine, in turn, faced with a healthier population, expands its jurisdiction to include medicalizing even normal events such as menopause. The root of the problem is structural, says Porter, in that the public demands more medicine and medicine feels pressured to respond—even if the response means over-doctoring, unnecessary lab

tests, more extensive and expensive treatments, and treatments for trivial complaints. In many ways, Porter concludes, medicine has become a prisoner of its own success and needs to define its limits.

However, Peter Conrad (2007, 2013) says that medicalization—the process of turning human conditions commonly regarded as normal into medical ailments—is far from being a case of medical imperialism. That is, it is not just a situation where medicine is driving itself to expand its jurisdiction and control over more human problems. Rather, as Conrad points out, medicalization is a form of collective action in that patients may actively seek medicalization of their problems. In fact, social movements have evolved to advocate more medical intervention as seen for AIDS, posttraumatic stress in war veterans, and premenstrual syndrome in women. Consequently, it may not be possible for medicine to always define its limits when outside groups seek its expansion.

medical doctor may be just one type of doctor among many on a health care team. Although the physician remains in charge, the idea of a "super-physician" towering high above all other personnel on a health care team becomes unrealistic when other members of the team know more about their specialties than the physician. This is especially the case if they hold doctorates in their field as well.

Social Control of Medical Practice

The social control of medical practice has traditionally presented special problems for American society. It has been argued that because physicians themselves have established the medical standards enforced by governmental regulating agencies and because laypersons are generally unable to judge technical performance, the two most common forms of social control in advanced society—bureaucratic supervision and judgment by the recipient of services—are lacking (Rueschmeyer 1972). However, the argument continues that the problem of controlling organized medicine is solved by the medical profession's emphasis on the strong self-control of the individual physician, an ethical stance reinforced by both the formal and informal sanctions of a community of colleagues. Society is thus justified in granting the physician professional autonomy because he or she is a member of a self-controlled collectivity performing a vital function for society's general good. This argument contains three serious defects.

First, it is important to note that laypersons do judge technical performance, regardless of whether they are competent to do so. Eliot Freidson's (1960, 1989) discussion of the lay-referral system made it clear that lay avenues of influence and authority exist independently of the physician and operate to guide the patient either toward or away from the services of a particular physician. This activity may not only determine the physician's success in attracting patients, but it also affects the physician's mode of medical practice. As Freidson (1960:379) has stated, "in being *relatively* free, the medical profession should not be mistaken for being *absolutely* free from control by patients." The choices of clients act as a form of social control over professionals and can mitigate against the survival of a group as a profession or the career success of particular professionals (Goode 1957:198).

Several studies show that patients do terminate their relationships with physicians and actively shop around for other doctors who are more able to meet their expectations (Hayes-Bautista 1976; Kasteler, Kane, Olsen, and Thetford 1976). Besides lack of confidence in a physician's technical competence, other factors commonly identified as influencing patients to change doctors include the unwillingness of doctors to spend time talking to them, the high cost of services, the possible inconvenience of a particular doctor's office location and hours, long waiting times, and unfavorable assessments of the doctor's personality. High levels of trust, satisfaction, and participation in decision making are important features of a positive relationship for patients with their physicians (Stepanikova et al. 2006).

A second major defect in the argument legitimizing the medical profession's autonomy relates to physicians' efforts at peer regulation. In a study of a medical group practice, Freidson (1975, 1989) found that rules and standards existed to define the limits of acceptable performance by physicians associated with the group. However, norms governing colleague relations, essentially *rules of etiquette,* restricted the evaluation of work and discouraged the expression of criticism. Etiquette was a more important norm than accountability undermining attempts at critical evaluation and control by overlooking fault in order to maintain group harmony. Confrontation with a colleague was considered distasteful, even in private and was unthinkable in public. In this medical practice setting, the norms of etiquette had not only seriously limited the exercise of professional control but had also reduced the scope of procedures that colleagues were willing to review.

Marcia Millman (1977a, 1977b) noted a similar situation in her study of three private university–affiliated hospitals. Many doctors in this study were willing to criticize their colleagues for errors in small group discussions and behind the other's back. But they were strongly reluctant to criticize another doctor's mistakes at any official meeting, because of what Millman termed "a fear of reprisal" and "a recognition of common interests." Millman's examination of medical mortality and morbidity conferences, in which patient deaths were reviewed as a regular hospital procedure, was particularly illustrative of the collective rationalization of mistakes. The atmosphere of these conferences was likened to such social events as weddings or funerals, in which the participants were expected to show tact and restraint in order to remain on friendly terms. Restricted to members of the hospital's medical staff, the conferences were intended to be educational, not punitive. Only certain cases (conspicuous was the absence of cases involving patient deaths by gross medical mismanagement) were picked for review because, as one hospital chief of medicine stated, "it's got to be a cordial affair." Millman (1977a) described the meeting at one hospital in which different members of the staff related their role in contributing to a mistaken diagnosis and, as in a good detective story, the case was reviewed in detail to show there was evidence that had led them to the wrong diagnosis. The patient even received some blame for being uncooperative. In taking this overall approach, the physicians showed they were nonetheless careful and methodical in how they had dealt with the patient's complaint, although it had caused them as team to come to the wrong conclusion.

Millman contended that a "gentlemen's agreement" existed among the hospital physicians to overlook each other's mistakes. According to Charles Bosk (1979), in a study of physicians in a surgical training program at a major university medical center, there was a general recognition that honest errors exist and all physicians make them. Technical errors, if they were made in "good faith," were less serious than moral errors. A moral error was making the mistake of being unreliable, being uncooperative, lacking in responsibility to patients, and failing to acknowledge subordination to superiors on the staff. Technical errors, on the other hand, could be forgiven and often had the result of motivating the offending physician to work harder, spend more time with patients, double-check procedures, and learn from the mistake. By admitting mistakes and trying to make up for them, the physician remained a good colleague. Moral errors, conversely, resulted in unfavorable letters of recommendation for those seeking jobs and social isolation from other physicians in the hospital.

PHOTO 11.2 Hospital staff attending a meeting to review procedures and determine causes of problems.

The lack of physician peer control described by Freidson and Millman and the rather weak control studied by Bosk may still be typical of most medical practice settings. If lawsuits for malpractice can be regarded as any kind of valid indicator, it would appear that errors in medicine, or at least a greater public awareness of medical malpractice, are common. Malpractice suits rose dramatically from a few hundred in the 1950s to more than 10,000 a year in the 1980s, and continued to rise until 1988 when claims began to decline significantly. There is evidence that doctors have adopted improved standards to reduce patient injuries, as well as develop better rapport with patients, share decision making, persuade patients to take more responsibility for their health, and physicians have become more careful in dealing with patients. (Bergen and Stivers 2013; Boyer and Lutfey 2010). Rates for malpractice insurance have also declined as states have set limits on the amount of money awarded in malpractice lawsuits.

This is not to say that there are no incompetent or dishonest doctors. A national data bank was established in 1989, to identify incompetent physicians, dentists, and other licensed health practitioners. The data stored consist of suspensions and other serious disciplinary actions and malpractice settlements or judgments. The action to establish the data bank represents one of the most important efforts by the federal government to discipline doctors. Hospitals can be fined or subjected to lawsuits for failing to report disciplinary actions, while other information comes from court decisions, insurance companies, and medical societies. In addition to malpractice, another sign of ineffective control over medical practice is the high cost to the government of Medicare and Medicaid fraud because of physician corruption. Some physicians have been arrested and sentenced to prison for misrepresenting care they claimed they gave to Medicare and Medicaid patients.

There are also cases of iatrogenic (medically induced) illnesses or deaths in which medical personnel do something that makes patients sick or kills them through unsafe procedures, carelessness, inadvertently transmitting infections from one patient to another, and overprescribing or wrongful prescribing of drugs. For example, in 2007–2008, several patients in an Alabama community died from taking combinations of pain-killers and sleep medication liberally prescribed by a local doctor, after which the doctor lost his license to practice medicine. A young, famous movie actor (Heath Ledger) died the same way about the same time in New York City. Other examples include giving patients vaccinations or drugs that make them sick or aggravate preexisting conditions, leaving sponges or surgical instruments inside a patient's body after an operation, amputating the wrong leg or breast, and so on. Surgeons at one Rhode Island hospital in 2007 operated on the wrong side of the head of three different patients. One died. In 2008, the lives of twin newborns of the actor Dennis Quaid and his wife were put in jeopardy when they were twice injected with huge adult-size overdoses of the drug Heparin in a Los Angeles hospital. In all of these cases, human errors overcame procedural safeguards. The biggest health malpractice notification effort in U.S. history took place in 2008 when some 40,000 patients treated at a surgical center and its affiliated clinics in Las Vegas were notified they needed to be tested for HIV and hepatitis B and C. At least six acute cases of hepatitis C had been discovered among patients treated at these facilities. The clinics had been found to reuse syringes and vials of medication in which these viruses could be transmitted from infected patients to uninfected ones.

This discussion is not intended to convey the impression that physicians are generally untrustworthy or careless. It should be pointed out that physicians can also be the victims of malpractice suits that have no merit. Freidson (1975) argues that it can be *assumed* that physicians are dedicated to their patients. In an account of his cardiology residency in a New York City hospital, Sandeep Jauhar (2008) notes occasional but unintentional mistakes and doctors who sometimes acted indifferently toward patients or minimized their time with those who were foul smelling and inarticulate. But he finds that most doctors are good people trying to do good every day. Moreover, medical societies do cooperate with state licensing agencies to remove the medical licenses of demonstrably incompetent physicians, thus preventing them from legally practicing medicine. Furthermore, professional standards review organizations (PSROs) were established in 1970 in conjunction with Medicaid and Medicare, to review and evaluate the medical care given to patients eligible to use these services. PSROs are composed of licensed physicians and osteopaths who determine if the services rendered are medically necessary, meet professional standards of quality, and are provided as efficiently and effectively as possible. Although some latitude in the interpretation of standards occurs in any diagnostic category, Freidson (1975:251) points out that a consensus of opinion will at least exclude "the blatant, gross, or obvious deviations from common knowledge and practice."

Nevertheless, medical standards and practices continue to be regulated by the practitioners themselves. Thus, it is generally difficult to find a physician who will be openly critical of another physician or who will publicly testify against a colleague. Mistakes and errors in medical practice, through neglect or ignorance, can sometimes be defended as "a difference of opinion." Millman (1977a) suggests that possibly all doctors have at some time made a mistake in their careers and realize that they may do so again. Therefore, in matters of peer regulation, they tend to follow the golden rule: "Do unto others as you would have them do unto you."

The third major defect in the professional autonomy argument arises from the fact that the autonomy granted to the medical profession is granted *conditionally*, on the assumption that it will resolve significant issues in favor of the public interest. However, traditional AMA resistance to cost controls that threaten the income of physicians has been cited as an example of greater professional concern with matters of self-interest than with public welfare (Timmermans and Oh 2010). This situation has reduced public confidence in medicine more than did any other single issue, because physicians as professionals have sometimes been viewed as placing the desire for financial gain ahead of the desire to help people (Light 2000). In 1984, the AMA sued the federal government for its cost-containment measures for Medicare, claiming that the government did not have the authority to impose limits on physicians' fees and that such action interfered with the right to contract for services. This legal challenge was unsuccessful, but it underscored the AMA's historic opposition to cost controls in a losing battle. By 2010, however, the AMA has

begun embracing more of a public welfare agenda by emphasizing support for senior citizen groups opposed to budget cuts in Medicare services, looking for ways to
reduce health disparities such as promoting antismoking measures, and supporting
President Obama's Affordable Care Act.

Countervailing Power

By the mid-twentieth century, the medical profession in the United States stood at
the height of its professional power and prestige, enjoying great public trust. This
was a time that John McKinlay (1999) refers to as the "golden age" of doctoring, and Eliot Freidson (1970b) formulated his "professional dominance" theory to
account for an unprecedented level of professional control by doctors over health
care delivery that no longer exists. It was also a time of escalating prices and over-
charging to a degree previously unknown; a proliferation of unnecessary tests, hospitalizations, prescriptions, and surgical operations; provider-structured insurance
that paid for almost any mistakes; poor investments in technology or facilities; and
neglect of the poor in the name of "autonomy" (Light 2000:202). Donald Light
(2004:15) refers to the "Golden Age of Medicine" as the "Age of Gold" for professional medicine.

Porter (1997:658) observes that health had become one of the major growth
industries in America. It encompassed the pharmaceutical industry and manufacturers of sophisticated and costly diagnostic apparatus, laboratory instruments, and
therapeutic devices. This was in addition to the large number of medical personnel,
hospitals, and various lawyers, accountants, and insurers. Porter adds that health
expenditures were approaching 15 percent of the GDP in 1966. Such costs were
generally unchecked as insurers boosted them as high as the market could bear,
physician incomes were seven times higher than the national average, and hospitals
added costly technology that was often duplicated in nearby facilities.

The problem with a professional dominance thesis is that it does not allow for
decline. Instead, dominance brings greater dominance, making a profession even
more powerful over time without taking into account that it could become less
powerful (Light 2000). At the beginning of the twenty-first century, however, we
are witnessing a profession in decline, and professional dominance is no longer an
adequate theory (McKinlay 1999). Light (2000) and Light and Hafferty (1993) used
the term *countervailing power* to show how the medical profession was but one of
many powerful groups in society—the state, employers paying for health insurance
for their employees, patients as consumers of health care, and the medical-industrial
complex as producers of products and services for profit—maneuvering to fulfill
its interests in health care. Health insurance companies are also a major power in
health care delivery, as they determine who gets insurance coverage and what health
conditions are covered (Light 1992, 1994). Over time, the medical profession's
control over its market faltered as these countervailing powers established powerful positions as well and ended the profession's monopoly. "Dominance," states
Light (2000:204), "slowly produces imbalances, excesses, and neglects that offend
or threaten other countervailing powers and alienate the larger public." And this
process is exactly what happened.

Internally, the medical profession has been weakened through an oversupply of doctors and the fragmentation and lack of success in resisting government controls of its labor union, the AMA (McKinlay 1999). However, the greatest impact on the autonomy of the medical profession is external and largely because of the countervailing power of four sources: (1) government regulation; (2) the managed care system; (3) corporations in the health care business; and (4) changes in the traditional doctor–patient relationship. McKinlay (1999:1) points out, "A future sociology of the professions can no longer overlook pervasive macrostructural influences on provider behavior." This is indeed the case, as Sharyn Potter and McKinlay (2005) subsequently described how third-party payers (the government and private insurance companies) have intruded on the doctor–patient relationship, in order to control the cost of care by limiting physician prerogatives.

Government Regulation

Rising costs of health care result in increased public demands for government intervention (Timmermans and Oh 2010). The response of the federal government to these demands has been to support improvements in health care delivery for all segments of the population, exert limited controls over physicians, and initiate efforts to reform the health care delivery system. The passage of legislation establishing Medicare and Medicaid public health insurance in the 1960s, to provide for the medical needs of the elderly and the poor, was accomplished despite the opposition of the AMA.

Other legislation (also initially opposed by the AMA) followed in the 1970s. Professional standards review organizations, as previously discussed, were established to evaluate the care given to Medicare and Medicaid patients. Even though PSROs were controlled by doctors, their function was a signal that the government wanted to ensure a standard of quality care. Support through planning grants and loan guarantees was also provided to encourage the development of health maintenance organizations (HMOs)—a form of prepaid group practice emphasizing preventive care. Half of the funds earmarked for HMOs were allocated to areas that were medically underserved. Although doctors and hospitals still controlled the efforts of PSROs, the sum total of regulatory efforts (Paul Starr 1982:403–04) went far beyond what physicians and hospitals wanted. Planning was aimed not at expansion but at containment and was formally linked for the first time with regulation.

Further regulation came in the early 1980s with the establishment of diagnostic related groups (DRGs) by the federal government. DRGs are schedules of fees placing a ceiling on how much the government will pay for specific services rendered to Medicare patients by hospitals and doctors. This action continued the government's attempts to meet public demands to control the cost of health care, even though it was bitterly contested by hospitals and the AMA.

Clearly the medical profession was losing its partisan support from the government. As McKinlay (1999) explains, an important role of the state (local, state, and national governments) has been to sponsor medical professionalism. Medical doctors in particular were helped by the state regulating its competitors and allowing them favorable outcomes in health legislation. That situation has now changed. McKinlay observes that during the last decades of the twentieth century, the state shifted its primary allegiance from professional interests to private interests, especially those intended to better the health of the general public and contain costs. The medical profession, through the AMA, was a dominant institutional force in the corridors of government, but that is no longer the case, as organized medicine has lost the power to determine health policy. A key factor in this situation is the loss of public trust that began during medicine's "golden age of fee-for-service" in the mid-twentieth century, when profits in health care soared (Light 2000:212).

Managed Care

One of the most extensive changes in health care delivery, reducing the authority of physicians, has been the introduction of managed care. The failed health plan of the Clinton administration in 1994 featured a reorganization of health care delivery in the United States into systems of managed care, but those systems emerged in the private sector anyway, in response to market conditions and anticipated government controls. Managed care refers to health care organizations—health maintenance organizations or preferred provider organizations—that "manage" or control the cost of health care by monitoring how doctors treat specific illnesses, limit referrals to specialists, and require authorization prior to hospitalization, among other measures. As providers in managed care plans, doctors have to work in accordance with the regulations and fee structure set by the plan that employs them.

At their best, managed care organizations organize and improve health care in a stable, reliable, and less costly manner and combine prevention with patient education. At their worst, such organizations disrupt doctor–patient relationships, take deep discounts out of doctor and hospital fees, and produce large profits without developing good managed clinical care (Light 2000; Wholey and Burns 2000). In managed care systems, patients pay a set fee on a per capita basis every month and in return are entitled to whatever health care they require. Primary care physicians, on their part, function as both "double agents" and "gatekeepers" (Waitzkin 2000, 2001). They are "double agents" because they look out for the interests of the patient as well as for the interests of the managed care organization. Primary care physicians have to consider the interests of both in the treatment they provide. Patients are required to consult with them first, because they serve as "gatekeepers" to more expensive medical procedures and care by specialists. Primary-care practitioners are relied on to keep the "gates" closed unless it is absolutely necessary. "That is how physicians and their bosses keep enough of patients' capitation payments to break even," states Howard Waitzkin (2000:272), "or maybe come out a little ahead." Doctors in managed care systems are expected to generate a certain level of income for the organization, and if they fail to do so, they can be fired.

Furthermore, primary care physicians are forced to spend time as "patient advocates," convincing various bureaucrats that more specialized and expensive care is warranted, because they must secure the permission that patients need to receive the care. This process takes time and energy and is often frustrating (Waitzkin 2000). Light (2000) complains that most managed care corporations do a better job of managing contracts and costs through discounts than managing the complex tasks of patient care. On balance, the managed care concept has reduced costs, and some managed care organizations have moved to less rigid controls on the delivery of medical treatment (Wholey and Burns 2000). Yet, for doctors, managed care also means a significant reduction in the authority to make referrals and choose modes of treatment.

The gatekeeper function by primary care physicians also affects the patient's experience, as he or she is structurally constrained from simply going directly or being referred to a specialist. In some cases, patients have not been granted access to more expensive treatments or have experienced delays in obtaining such treatment while their health worsened, or in a few instances they died. Not surprisingly, many patients have voiced considerable dissatisfaction with managed care. This patient backlash, led by the middle class who strongly objected to the rationing of care, along with the complaints by physicians, has been successful in diluting many of the cost control measures inherent in managed care (Mechanic 2004). This includes removing constraints on the patient's ability to bypass primary care doctors and go directly to specialists. Consequently, the managed care concept is in a state of transition whose future form has yet to be determined (Casalino 2004).

The Coming of the Corporation

The "Coming of the Corporation" is the title of a chapter in Paul Starr's influential book *The Social Transformation of American Medicine* (1982). In this chapter, Starr describes how America was on its way to a major change in its system of health care delivery through the intervention of large health care conglomerates. Starr (1982:428) found that once government financing for Medicare and Medicaid showed health care could be financially rewarding for providers, large for-profit corporations moved into the health field and established a foothold in the market by buying privately owned hospitals and nursing homes.

Next came a virtual wave of mergers, acquisitions, and diversifications by the health care corporations, in which not only hospitals and nursing homes were acquired but also emergency-care centers, hospital supply companies, hospital restaurants, medical office buildings, alcohol and drug abuse centers, health maintenance organizations, health spas, psychiatric hospitals, home health care services, and hospital management systems. For the first time in the United States, health care became regarded as a major business arena. Profit-making corporations expanded either into markets that were underserved or into areas where their services could successfully compete with existing nonprofit-seeking institutions. For example, the profit-seeking hospital chains would provide attractively furnished rooms, good food, a friendly staff, and more efficient services. With health insurance paying the majority of the cost for hospital care, some patients evidently prefer the surroundings and more expensive services of the for-profit hospital. In the context of corporate health care, the physician is an employee rather than an independent practitioner. The doctor is bound by the rules and regulations of the corporation that, in all probability, is managed by people trained in business, not medicine.

At present, about 18 percent of all U.S. hospitals are owned by profit-making organizations. What attracted corporations to health care delivery, as noted, is the potential for financial profit. The federal government, through Medicare and Medicaid, has poured billions of dollars into health care since the mid-1960s. Much of this money went to pay for doctor and hospital services. The corporations, however, have not been as interested in this public money as they have in the private health insurance companies. Private insurance companies reduce the risk of nonpaying patients through the coverage they provide. Medicare and Medicaid spending limits have been set by the government on how much they would pay for specific health services. So the goal of the health care corporations is to attract patients with private health insurance that will cover the relatively higher charges of the profit-making hospitals.

Another development has been the expansion of free-standing emergency centers that take business away from hospitals. Sometimes referred to as "Docs-in-a-Box" or "7-Eleven Medicine," these centers (called free-standing because they are not affiliated with a hospital) are typically open 7 days a week, 18–24 hours a day, and try to attend to their patients with a minimum of waiting time. They treat the cuts, broken bones, bruises, and minor ailments usually treated in doctors' offices or hospital emergency rooms. Sometimes these facilities are located in shopping centers or other convenient locations. They are generally open for business, accessible, reasonably priced, and provide fast service.

In an era of cost containment, cost-efficient innovations, such as the free-standing emergency centers and the multihospital corporate systems, may have an advantage in attracting privately insured patients. They can offer quick and efficient service. In addition, the large multihospital systems can consolidate their resources and not duplicate services available elsewhere in the system, thereby saving them money. As not-for-profit hospitals find it increasingly difficult to contend with rising costs and limits on reimbursements from public health insurance, Starr suggests that there will be more pressure to sell out to the corporations with greater financial resources. There are, however, some limits to growth. Starr indicates that the large for-profit hospital chains avoid owning hospitals in depressed areas with high numbers of Medicaid patients, nor do they seek to own teaching hospitals. The market for these chains is considered to be in the more attractive neighborhoods where the hospitals serve relatively affluent patients. What this means is that the poor will not generally benefit because the for-profit hospitals, with their higher prices, try to attract those who can afford their services. As Starr (1982:436) notes, "The for-profit chains have an undisguised preference for privately insured patients."

Physicians have not shown strong objections to being employed by corporations or sending their patients to for-profit hospitals. There are two major reasons for this development. One is the availability of doctors for such jobs. Second, health care corporations provide jobs, offices, staffs, equipment, hospital privileges, and perhaps even a salary guarantee. Starr points out that because of their dependence on doctors, the corporations will be generous in granting them rewards, including more autonomy than they give to most corporate employees. More part-time and intermittent employment is also available, especially for women doctors who wish to spend time with their children. Starr found that the medical profession was no longer opposed to the expansion of corporate medicine in that such organizations provided regular hours and time for a private life that a solo practice could not offer, a situation that was particularly attractive to new physicians. "Young doctors," states

Starr (1982:446), "may be more interested in freedom *from* the job than freedom *in* the job." Consequently, a major shift in American health care today is the movement of physicians away from fee-for-service practices into salaried jobs. In 2014, about 60 percent of all family doctors and pediatricians, 50 percent of surgeons and 25 percent of doctors practicing surgical subspecialties, such as ophthalmologists and ear, nose, and throat surgeons, were employees rather than independent practitioners (AMA 2014).

Nevertheless, there is a loss in autonomy for those physicians who do corporate work. Starr explains that doctors will no longer control such basic issues as time of retirement and there will probably be more regulation of the pace and routines of work. There will also be standards of performance, in which doctors will be evaluated and paid on the basis of the amount of revenues that they generate or number of patients treated per hour. Physicians who do not meet corporate standards are in danger of losing their jobs. Moreover, there is likely to be a close scrutiny of mistakes, in order not only to ensure quality medical care but also to avoid corporate liability for malpractice. Corporate management, utilizing data supplied by statisticians monitoring quality-of-care programs, will probably not be particularly concerned about professional norms of etiquette when it comes to dealing with doctors who are careless or incompetent. The locus of control will be outside the immediate health care facility and in the hands of a management system that is primarily business oriented. In corporations, doctors are not as likely to dominate decision making on policy, hospital budgets, capital investments, personnel appointments, salaries, and promotions.

To what extent the large health care corporations will be able to extend their control over the medical marketplace is not known. But it seems apparent that those doctors who practice corporate medicine will constitute a physician group with less control over the conditions of their practice than American physicians in the past. In successfully avoiding government regulation of their work, physicians may have established the circumstances for corporations to move in and dominate an unregulated area of the economy. This process is materially aided by a growing surplus of physicians desiring the benefits and work schedule a corporate practice can provide. As Starr (1982:445) explains, "The great irony is that the opposition of doctors and hospitals to public control of public programs set in motion entrepreneurial forces that may end up depriving both private doctors and voluntary hospitals of their traditional autonomy." Future studies of physicians may have to distinguish between owning, managing, employed, and independent physicians. Physicians who own hospitals and clinics, or who are in independent private practice, will have considerably more autonomy than physician managers of corporate facilities and doctors employed as practitioners by a corporation. Nevertheless, more physicians, both older and younger, are accepting salaries at hospitals and large health care systems and abandoning private practice. In 2005, about 67 percent of all medical practices were owned by physicians; by 2013, less than 50 percent were physician owned.

The Changing Physician–Patient Relationship

Leo G. Reeder (1972) was among the first to show the changing relationship between physicians and their patients. He identifies three significant trends in contemporary society. One is the *shift in medicine away from the treatment of acute diseases toward preventive health services* intended to offset the effects of chronic disorders. Because the control of acute diseases has largely been accomplished, it is no longer the most important task for modern medical practice. Reeder finds that physicians have to resort to persuasion to convince patients to engage in preventive care, rather than excise direct authority by issuing patients orders. Patients may have to be convinced to give up smoking, to exercise, stop eating fatty and sugary foods, and the like in order to protect their health from chronic disease.

The other two features of societal change noted by Reeder are the *growing sophistication of the general public with bureaucracy* and the *development of consumerism.* Reeder claims that the increased development of large-scale bureaucratic industrial systems has ensured a similarity of experiences and attitudes in contemporary society, and this has tended to "level" or make more familiar the bureaucratic aspects of modern medicine. Also highly significant is the development of consumerism. Reeder states that during the 1960s, the concept of the person as a "consumer" rather than a patient became established. Doctors were regarded as "health providers," so a new provider–consumer relationship emerged in direct opposition to the old physician–patient relationship with its emphasis upon patient dependency. The new concept places the consumer on a more equal basis with the physician in the health care interaction. It also provides the philosophy behind the increased consumer involvement in health legislation and other matters such as consumer interest health care groups.

In an age of consumerism, the social role of the physician and the overall physician–patient relationship can hardly escape modification. In general, this modification takes the form of physician and patient interacting on a more equal footing in terms of decision making and responsibility for outcome. There is evidence that the physician–patient relationship has turned into more of a provider–consumer relationship among patients who are relatively well educated and have middle- and upper-class social backgrounds (Cockerham 2000, 2013; McKinlay 1999). Ample health information on the Internet and the increase in direct-to-consumer advertising are also important factors changing the knowledge base of patients and influencing the interaction between doctors and patients, including challenges to physician authority (Timmermans and Chawla 2009). Some medical sociologists now describe the interaction between a doctor and patient as more of an "association" than a "relationship" because it often consists of more than two people and the personal closeness of the individuals involved has weakened (Potter and McKinlay 2005; Vanderminden and Potter 2010).

The Deprofessionalization of Physicians

Increased consumerism on the part of patients and greater government and corporate control over medical practice have resulted in the decline of the professional status of physicians. That is, doctors are moving from being the absolute authority in medical matters toward having lessened authority. With many patients insisting on greater equality in the doctor–patient relationship and corporate health organizations that employ doctors seeking to control costs, maximize profits, and provide efficient services that are responsive to market demand, physicians are caught in the middle.

George Ritzer and David Walczak (1988) indicate that medical doctors are experiencing a process of deprofessionalization. Ritzer and Walczak (1988:6) define deprofessionalization as "a decline in power which results in a decline in the degree to which professions possess, or are perceived to possess, a constellation of characteristics denoting a profession." Deprofessionalization essentially means a decline in a profession's autonomy and control over clients. In the case of physicians, they still retain the greatest authority in medical affairs but that authority is no longer absolute, and medical work is subject to greater scrutiny by patients, health care organizations, and government agencies. As Donald Light (1989:470) notes, buyers of health care "want to know what they are getting for their money," and it did "not take long for them to demand detailed accounts of what services are being rendered at what cost." This situation has led to greater control and monitoring systems by the government seeking to control costs, businesses attempting to constrain the expenses of employee health care, and insurance companies and profit-seeking health care corporations looking to maximize income.

Ritzer and Walczak argue that government policies emphasizing greater control over health care and the rise of the profit orientation in medicine identify a trend in medical practice away from substantive rationality (stressing ideals like serving the patient) toward greater formal rationality (stressing efficiency) in medical practice leading to greater profit. Formal rationality is defined by Max Weber (1978) as the purposeful calculation of the most efficient means to reach goals, while substantive rationality is an emphasis on ideal values. Ritzer and Walczak claim that formal rationality has become dominant in medical practice. The decline of the substantive element signaled a loss of public support and an invitation to countervailing powers to enter into an unregulated market that the medical profession had previously kept for itself. A quest for a share of the medical market by health care corporations and the public's demands for cost controls led to greater external control over the work of physicians by business corporations and the government. This is seen in research on the use of electronic medical record-keeping that makes review of doctors' work easier for employers with respect to the number of patients seen, the treatment rendered, and tests ordered, which also puts pressure on them to conform to the organization's evidence-based practice standards (Reich 2012).

Hence, pressure on physicians from below (consumers) and above (government and business corporations in the health field) resulted in a decline in their professional dominance. Doctors are still powerful in health matters but not to the extent that they were in the 1950s and 1960s, which has been described as a "golden age" of medical power and prestige (Hafferty and Light 1995; Pescosolido 2013; Timmermans and Oh 2010). Government policies, market forces, and consumerism have required greater accountability and placed constraints on the exercise of professional power in an ever-increasing manner. Frederic Hafferty and Donald Light (1995:138) note that "the basic overall thrust of professionalism is toward a loss and not a continuation or strengthening of medicine's control over its own work." According to historian Charles Rosenberg (2007:1):

> These are difficult times in which to practice medicine. These are the best of times, and these are the worst of times for American clinicians. . . . Never have physicians been able to intervene more effectively in the body, never have practitioners felt themselves more—constrained—by bureaucratic guidelines and intrusive administrative oversight. Increasing technical capacity seems wedded to diminishing autonomy, an odd situation indeed.

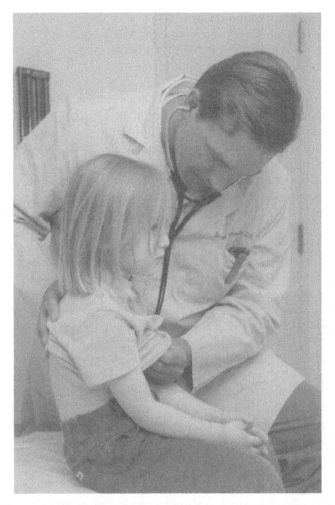

PHOTO 11.3 Some sources predict that the majority of physicians will be employees—rather than self-employed practitioners—in the near future.

The Evolution of the Organization of Medical Practice

All of these factors—government regulation, corporate medicine, the contemporary physician–patient relationship, and deprofessionalization—forecast change in the manner in which health care is organized and delivered in the United States. Phillip Kletke et al. (1996) examined trends in the organization of medical practice and predicted that the majority of physicians will be employees in the future. This trend, which Kletke and his colleagues found was evident in virtually every segment of the patient care physician population, was especially characteristic of young physicians. However, the shift toward practicing medicine as an employee is not limited to younger doctors but is evident among physicians at all stages of their careers. The trend is also seen among both male and female doctors, and in all medical specialties and regions of the country. This development, as previously noted, has already happened among family doctors and pediatricians, with surgeons not far behind (AMA 2014). Thus, the dominant pattern of medical practice in the United States is becoming one in which many, perhaps most, doctors will be employees.

What is promoting the trend away from self-employment, according to Kletke and his associates, is a general evolution in the health care delivery system toward greater size and complexity. The loss in autonomy, government and insurance regulations, cost controls, the growth of managed care, competition in the medical marketplace, the attraction of regular hours and guaranteed salaries, and the possibility of higher earnings than solo physicians anchored outside of large health care systems play an important role in this development. Whereas solo physicians are thought of as having greater clinical autonomy, Kletke and his associates note that such autonomy has declined for all doctors—not just those who are employees. Consequently, the opportunity for exercising autonomy in patient care is not overwhelmingly on the side of the self-employed.

Evidence from several sources shows that the dominance of the medical profession is weakening. In medical sociology, several studies find that medicine is no longer able to exercise exclusive control over the context of its work (Casalino 2004; Freidson 1993; Hafferty and Light 1995; Hafferty and McKinlay 1993; Light 1993, 2000; McKinlay 1999). Therefore, in comparison to physicians in the past, current and future generations of doctors are likely to have much lower levels of clinical autonomy and professional control. "Many of these physicians," state Kletke and colleagues (1996:560), "will be in the employ of what has been called the 'new medical-industrial complex,' with their practices subject to an increasing degree of bureaucratic rationalization." This situation represents a major shift in the organization of American health care delivery because solo, self-employed, fee-for-service doctors have been the nation's traditional model of medical practitioner. However, this does not mean that medicine is no longer a high status profession. Although it has lost considerable authority over the context (the setting and practice) of its work, it still maintains control over the content (medical knowledge) that comprises the work and continues medicine's professional character (Pescosolido 2013b).

Summary

There are increasing signs of influences outside the medical profession that the professional dominance of the physician is weakening. This change originates from four directions. First, there are signs of increasing government regulation. Second, managed care is reducing the authority of doctors. Third, corporations are taking over more of the medical market and hiring physicians as employees to provide medical services. In this situation, decision making is vested in the hands of corporate management and not physician practitioners. Just what type of role doctors will play in a corporate system of health care delivery is not fully established, but it seems likely that physicians will lose some of their autonomy. Last, more affluent and educated persons appear to be increasingly consumer oriented toward health care. That is, they are making decisions on their own about which steps are most appropriate for them in dealing with their health. In doing so, they are becoming less dependent on physicians and changing the traditional physician–patient relationship to one of provider–consumer relationship. If current trends continue, most doctors in the near future will be employees, rather than self-employed practitioners.

Critical Thinking Questions

1. How does society influence the work of the medical profession?
2. When it comes to control over medical work, what countervailing powers have reduced the power of physicians?
3. What are some of the social conditions that have led to the deprofessionalization of the medicine?
4. How is the deprofessionalization of the medicine affecting the way doctors interact with patients?

Suggested Readings

Pescosolido, Bernice (2013) "Theories and the rise and fall of the medical profession," pp. 173–94 in *Medical Sociology on the Move: New directions in theory*, W. Cockerham (ed.). Dordrecht: Springer.
Excellent sociological analysis of the evolution of the medical profession.
Rosenberg, Charles E. (2007) *Our present complaint: American medicine then and now.* Baltimore: Johns Hopkins University Press.
An historical view of where American medicine was headed before the health care reforms in 2010.

References

American Medical Association (2014) *Physician characteristics and distribution in the U.S.* Chicago: AMA.
Bergen, Clara, and Tanya Stivers (2013) "Patient disclosure of medical misdeeds." *Journal of Health and Social Behavior* 54: 221–40.
Bosk, Charles L. (1979) *Forgive and remember: Managing medical failure.* Chicago: University of Chicago Press.
Boyer, Carol A., and Karen E. Lutfey (2010) "Examining critical health policy issues within and beyond the clinical encounter: Patient-provider relationships and help-seeking behaviors." *Journal of Health and Social Behavior* 51: S80–93.
Brown, E. Richard (1979) *Rockefeller medicine men: Medicine and capitalism in America.* Berkeley: University of California Press.
Casalino, Larry (2004) "Unfamiliar tasks, contested jurisdictions." *Journal of Health and Social Behavior* 45(Extra issue): 59–75.
Cockerham, William C. (2000) "The sociology of health behavior and health lifestyles," pp. 159–72 in *Handbook of medical sociology*, 5th ed., C. Bird, P. Conrad, and A. Fremont (eds.). Upper Saddle River, NJ: Prentice Hall.
—— (2013) *Social causes of health and disease,* 2nd ed. Cambridge, UK: Polity.
Collier, Roger (2011) "American Medical Association woes continue." *Canadian Medical Association Journal* 183: E713–14.

Conrad, Peter (2000) "Medicalization, genetics, and human problems," pp. 322–34 in *Handbook of medical sociology*, 5th ed., C. Bird, P. Conrad, and A. Fremont (eds.). Upper Saddle River, NJ: Prentice Hall.

—— (2007) *The medicalization of society: On the transformation of human conditions into treatable disorders*. Baltimore: Johns Hopkins University Press.

—— (2013) "Medicalization: Changing contours, characteristics, and contexts," pp. 195-214 in *Medical sociology on the move: New directions in theory*, W. Cockerham (ed.). Dordrecht: Springer.

Freidson, Eliot (1960) "Client control and medical practice." *American Journal of Sociology* 65: 374–82.

—— (1970a) *Profession of medicine*. New York: Dodd, Mead.

—— (1970b) *Professional dominance*. Chicago: Aldine.

—— (1975) *Doctoring together*. New York: Elsevier North-Holland.

—— (1989) *Medical work in America: Essays on health care*. New Haven, CT: Yale University Press.

—— (1993) "How dominant are the professions?" pp. 54–66 in *The changing medical profession: An international perspective*, F. Hafferty and J. McKinley (eds.). New York: Oxford University Press.

Goode, William J. (1957) "Community within a community." *American Sociological Review* 22: 194–200.

—— (1960) "Encroachment, charlatanism, and the emerging profession: Psychology, sociology, and medicine." *American Sociological Review* 25: 902–14.

Hafferty, Frederic W., and John B. McKinley (1993) *The changing medical profession: An international perspective*. New York: Oxford University Press.

Hafferty, Frederic W., and Donald W. Light (1995) "Professional dynamics and the changing nature of medical work." *Journal of Health and Social Behavior* 36(Extra issue): 132–53.

Hayes-Bautista, David E. (1976) "Termination of the patient-practitioner relationship: Divorce, patient style." *Journal of Health and Social Behavior* 17: 12–21.

Jauhar, Sandeep (2008) *A doctor's initiation*. New York: Farrar, Straus & Giroux.

Kasteler, Josephine, Robert L. Kane, Donna M. Olsen, and Constance Thetford (1976) "Issues underlying prevalence of 'doctor-shopping' behavior." *Journal of Health and Social Behavior* 17: 328–39.

Kletke, Phillip R., David W. Emmons, and Kurt D. Gillis (1996) "Current trends in physicians' practice arrangements." *JAMA* 276: 555–60.

Light, Donald W. (1989) "Social control and the American health care system," pp. 456–74 in *Handbook of medical sociology*, 4th ed., H. Freeman and S. Levine (eds). Englewood Cliffs, NJ: Prentice Hall.

—— (1992) "The practice and ethics of risk-related health insurance." *JAMA* 267: 2503–8.

—— (1993) "Countervailing power: The changing character of the medical profession in the United States," pp. 69–79 in *The changing medical profession: An international perspective*, F. Hafferty and J. McKinley (eds.). New York: Oxford University Press.

—— (1994) "Life, death, and the insurance companies." *New England Journal of Medicine* 330: 498–500.

—— (2000) "The medical profession and organizational change: From professional dominance to contervailing power," pp. 201–16 in *Handbook of medical sociology*, 5th ed., C. Bird, P. Conrad, and A. Fremont (eds.). Upper Saddle River, NJ: Prentice Hall.

—— (2004) "Introduction: Ironies of success—A new history of the American health care 'system.' " *Journal of Health and Social Behavior* 45(Extra issue): 1–24.

Light, Donald W., and Frederic W. Hafferty (eds) (1993) *The changing medical profession: An international perspective*. New York: Oxford University Press.

McKinlay, John B. (1999) "The end of the golden age of doctoring." *New England Research Institutes Newsletter* (Summer): 1, 3.

Mechanic, David (2004) "The rise and fall of managed care." *Journal of Health and Social Behavior* 45(Extra issue): 76–86.

Millman, Marcia (1977a) "Masking doctors' errors." *Human Behavior* 6: 16–23.

—— (1977b) *The unkindest cut*. New York: Morrow.

National Center for Health Statistics (2013) *Health United States, 2012*. Washington, DC: U.S. Government Printing Office.

Pescosolido, Bernice A. (2013) "Theories and the rise and fall of the medical profession," pp. 173–94 in *Medical Sociology on the Move: New directions in theory*, W. Cockerham (ed.). Dordrecht: Springer.

Pescosolido, Bernice A., Steven A. Tuch, and Jack K. Martin (2001) "The profession of medicine and the public: Examining Americans' changing confidence in physician authority from the beginning of the 'health care crisis' to the era of health care reform." *Journal of Health and Social Behavior* 42: 1–16.

Porter, Roy (1997) *The greatest benefit to mankind: A medical history of humanity*. New York: W. W. Norton.

Potter, Sharyn J., and John B. McKinley (2005) "From a relationship to encounter: An examination of longitudinal and lateral dimensions in the doctor-patient relationship." *Social Science and Medicine* 61: 465–79.

Quah, Stella R. (1989) "The social position and internal organization of the medical profession in the third world: The case of Singapore." *Journal of Health and Social Behavior* 30: 450–66.

Reeder, Leo G. (1972) "The patient-client as a consumer: Some observations on the changing professional-client relationship." *Journal of Health and Social Behavior* 13: 406–12.

Reich, Adam (2012) "Disciplined doctors: The electronic medical record and physicians' changing relationship to medical knowledge." *Social Science and Medicine* 74: 1021–28.

Ritzer, George, and David Walczak (1988) "Rationalization and the deprofessionalization of physicians." *Social Forces* 67: 1–22.

Rosenberg, Charles E. (2007) *Our present compliant: American medicine, then and now*. Baltimore: Johns Hopkins University Press.

Rueschmeyer, Dietrich (1972) "Doctors and lawyers: A comment on the theory of professions," pp. 5–19 in *Medical men and their work*, E. Freidson and J. Lorber (eds.). Chicago: Aldine.

Starr, Paul (1982) *The social transformation of American medicine*. New York: Basic Books.

Stepanikova, Irena, Stefanie Mollborn, Karen S. Cook, David H. Thom, and Roderick M. Kramer (2006) "Patients' race, ethnicity, language, and trust in a physician." *Journal of Health and Social Behavior* 47: 390–405.

Stevens, Rosemary (1971) *American medicine and the public interest*. New Haven, CT: Yale University Press.

Timmermans, Stefan, and Hyeyoung Oh (2010) "The continued transformation of the medical profession." *Journal of Health and Social Behavior* 51: S94–106.

Timmermans, Stefan, and Neetu Chawla (2009) "Evidence-based medicine and medical education," pp. 139–55 in *Handbook of the sociology of medical education*, C. Brosnan and B. Turner (eds.). London: Routledge.

Vanderminden, Jennifer, and Sharyn J. Potter (2010) "Challenges to the doctor–patient relationship in the twenty-first century," pp. 355–72 in *The new Blackwell companion to medical sociology*, W. Cockerham (ed.). Oxford, UK: Wiley-Blackwell.

Waitzkin, Howard (2000) "Changing patient–physician relationships in the changing health-policy environment," pp. 271–83 in *Handbook of medical sociology*, 5th ed., C. Bird, P. Conrad, and A. Fremont (eds.). Upper Saddle River, NJ: Prentice Hall.

—— (2001) *At the front lines of medicine: How the medical care system alienates doctors and mistreats patients . . . and what we can do about it.* Lanham, MD: Rowman & Littlefield.

Weber, Max (1978) *Economy and society*, 2 vols, G. Roth and C. Wittich (eds.). Berkeley: University of California Press.

Wholey, Douglas R., and Lawton R. Burns (2000) "Tides of change: The evolution of managed care," pp. 217–37 in *Handbook of medical sociology*, 5th ed., C. Bird, P. Conrad, and A. Fremont (eds.). Upper Saddle River, NJ: Prentice Hall.

CHAPTER 12

Nurses, Physician Assistants, Pharmacists, and Midwives

Although the dominant form of social interaction in the health care relationship has traditionally been that of the one-to-one encounter between the physician and the patient, the technical complexity and range of contemporary medical care have evolved well beyond this exclusive two-person dyadic social system. Modern medicine features a team approach involving a variety of health personnel who specialize in treatment, medications, laboratory tests, therapy, rehabilitation, and administration. More than four million people in the United States are currently employed in nonphysician health care tasks.

Other than a few consulting professions such as clinical psychology, the occupations performing tasks of patient care are organized around the work of the physician and are usually under the physician's direct control. Eliot Freidson (1970a:49) claims that these occupations—such as nurse, pharmacist, laboratory technician, and physical therapist—reflect four characteristic features that account for their subordinate position in the practice of medicine. First of all, Freidson notes that the technical knowledge employed in health occupations needs to be approved by physicians. Second, these workers usually assist physicians in their work rather than replace the skills of diagnosis and treatment—although nurse practitioners and physician assistants are moving into these areas with respect to many health problems. Third, such workers are subordinate to the physician because their work largely occurs at the "request of" the physician; that is, the "doctor's orders" provide them with their work requirements. And fourth, among the various occupational roles in the health field, physicians have the greatest prestige.

However, just as the physician–patient relationship appears to be moving toward less dependency and increased equality for the patient, a similar trend is developing in the relationship between physicians and certain other health care occupations, as nurse practitioners and physician assistants can make treatment decisions independently of doctors in some states and prescribe drugs. So inroads are being made on the authority once exclusively held by physicians.

Nursing: Past and Present

Nursing represents the largest single group of health workers in the United States, with some three million people employed as licensed registered nurses in 2012. Another 725,000 people were employed as licensed practical nurses that same year. About 70 percent of all licensed registered and practical nurses in the United

States work in hospitals and nursing homes, while the remainder are employed in doctors' offices, public health agencies, schools, industrial plants, programs of nursing education, or as private duty nurses.

Registered nurses (RNs) are responsible for the nature and quality of all nursing care patients receive, as well as for following the instructions of physicians regarding patients. In addition, they supervise practical nurses and other health personnel involved in providing patient care. The primary task of licensed practical nurses is the bedside care of patients. They may also assist in the supervision of auxiliary nursing workers, such as certified nurse's aides (CNAs), orderlies, and attendants. These auxiliary nursing personnel, who number about 1.4 million in the United States, assist registered and practical nurses by performing less skilled medical care tasks and by providing many services designed for the overall personal comfort and welfare of patients.

While the licensed registered and practical nurses and nurses' aides are generally women, orderlies and attendants are usually men employed to care for male patients and perform whatever heavy duties are required in nursing care. Nursing tasks occur in a system of social relationships that were historically stratified by sex. The registered nurse, who has the most advanced training and professional qualifications of any of the nursing workers, is generally a female who is matched occupationally with a physician, whose role is dominant and who, in the past, was likely to be a male although this distinction is rapidly changing. The registered nurse, in turn, supervises lesser-trained females (practical nurses and nurses' aides) and lesser-trained males (orderlies and attendants). Thus emerges the traditional stereotype of the physician as father figure and the nurse as mother figure. However, this stereotype is now being altered with respect to physicians, because of the increasing number of female doctors, yet still persists with respect to nurses.

The Early Development of Nursing as an Occupation

While males perform nursing tasks, the social role of the nurse has been profoundly affected by its identification with traditionally feminine functions (Davies 2003; Freidson 1970a, 1970b; Porter 1992). For instance, in many European languages, the word *sister* not only refers to nuns but also generically identifies the nurse. In the English language, the word *nurse* carries with it a connotation of the mother's relationship to her child. Another name for a mother breast-feeding a baby, for example, is "nursing" the baby. Accordingly, a popular public image of the nurse in Western society was that of a "mother-surrogate," in which nursing was equated with the mothering function. Only in this case, the function is to help heal the sick.

Following the rise of Christianity in the Western world, the practice of nursing as a formal occupation was significantly influenced by the presence of large numbers of nuns who performed nursing services under the auspices of the Roman Catholic Church. Prior to the late nineteenth century, hospitals were generally defined as places for the poor and lower social classes, often little more than "flophouses." Anyone who could afford it was usually cared for at home. Nursing activities in hospitals were viewed as acts of charity because they were usually carried out under difficult and unpleasant circumstances, as nurses served the personal needs of patients who were usually dirty and illiterate as well as diseased. Nursing under these conditions was regarded by the church as a means by which those persons providing the services could attain spiritual salvation by helping those less fortunate. Hence, the original concept of nursing was not as a formal occupation with its own body of knowledge and specialized training procedures. Rather, its primary focus as religious activity was in spiritual considerations. Nuns were not under the authority of doctors, and they could refuse any orders they did not believe appropriate for themselves or their patients. Nuns were also reported to have refused to treat certain categories of patients, such as unwed mothers or persons with venereal disease (Freidson 1970a).

Besides nuns, there were secular nurses working in public hospitals. But these women were characterized as "women off the streets" or "of bad character," who were considered little or no better than the low class of patients for whom they provided their services. Well into the nineteenth century, nursing could be described as an activity for women who lacked specialized training in medical care, a supportive work role that was not officially incorporated into the formal structure of medical services. Moreover, nursing was not an occupation held in high regard by the general public.

Florence Nightingale

The role of nursing in Western society was changed in the middle of the nineteenth century, through the insight and effort of Florence Nightingale. An English Protestant from a respectable middle-class family, she believed that God had called her to the service of Christianity as a result of a vision she had experienced in 1837. There was some confusion on Nightingale's part as to exactly what service she was expected to render. Being a Protestant, she could not choose to become a Catholic nun. She solved her dilemma by deciding to become a nurse. Despite the strong objections of her family and after a delay of several years, she was finally able to secure training as a nurse from a Protestant minister in Germany.

Returning to England in 1853, Nightingale established a hospital for "Sick Gentlewomen in Distressed Circumstances" and staffed it with trained nurses from good families. She insisted that nursing was intended to become an honorable and respected occupation, and she sought to achieve this purpose through a formal training program with recruits from upper- and middle-class social backgrounds. Good intentions notwithstanding, Nightingale's hospital was not entirely successful because of the role conflict between the duties of the nurse and the prevailing standards of proper behavior for "ladies." Some of her nurses, for example, were reluctant to view nudity or to be present at physical examinations (Freidson 1970a).

In 1854, the Crimean War afforded Nightingale a much better opportunity to establish nursing as a formal occupation. She organized a contingent of nurses and, assisted by money raised by public subscription, she and her group sailed for the Crimea, where Great Britain, France, and Turkey were involved in war with Russia. Once there, Nightingale offered to the British military authorities the nursing services of her women for sick and wounded troops.

At first, the military refused to employ her nurses, and she retaliated by refusing to allow any of the nurses to provide patient care on their own initiative. Instead, the nurses worked only when their assistance was specifically requested by physicians. Eventually such requests were forthcoming and Nightingale's nurses received considerable publicity in the British press as "angels of mercy." In fact, Nightingale's nurses had captured the imagination of the British public, and when Nightingale returned to England after the war, she found herself hailed as a heroine. Capitalizing upon her fame and popularity, she instigated a successful fund-raising effort that generated enough money to organize a nursing school at St. Thomas Hospital in London. Other schools were also established, and within a few years, the "Nightingale system" became the model for nursing education.

Nightingale's approach to nursing training emphasized a code of behavior that idealized nurses as being responsible, clean, self-sacrificing, courageous, cool headed, hardworking, and obedient to the physician and possessing the tender qualities of the mother. This idealized portrayal of nurses saw them as nothing less than "disciplined angels" (Strauss 1966). In reality, Nightingale had incorporated the best attributes of the mother and the housekeeper into her ideal nurse. This image did little to establish the view of nurses as having the qualities of leadership and independence necessary for true professional status. Although Nightingale had been able to establish nursing as a distinct and honorable occupation, her philosophy perpetuated the traditional social role of the nurse as a female supervised and controlled by a male physician. Perhaps in her time there was no other way to gain access to an official position within the male-dominated field of medicine, but the overall effect of subordination to the physician's orders weakened nursing's efforts in its struggle to achieve professionalization.

Nursing Education

Florence Nightingale's ideas formed the basis for establishing the first accredited schools of nursing in the United States. These schools, founded in 1873, were located at Bellevue Hospital in New York City, the Connecticut Training School in New Haven, and the Boston Training School. Although they were intended to be separately administered, the new nursing schools were affiliated with hospitals that provided financial support and required, in turn, that the students furnish much of the nursing services on the hospital wards. During the late nineteenth and early twentieth centuries, the number of hospitals and hospital nursing schools grew rapidly. At the same time, increasing numbers of women entered the labor market as a result of immigration from abroad or migration from rural to urban areas. Nursing was an attractive occupation for many of these women, because it afforded an opportunity for a woman to make a living and also to have a respectable position in the community.

But many of the students in these early nursing schools did not receive the training that the Nightingale system required. Because only a few trained nurses were available and money was often in short supply, many hospital administrators and physicians, perhaps also unaware of Nightingale's techniques for training nurses, used nursing students as inexpensive and exploitable sources of hospital labor. As a result, much of the effort of nursing educators during the first decades of the twentieth century was directed at securing less hospital service and more education for nursing students in hospital schools. They also sought a university-based nursing school, with the first one being formed at the University of Minnesota in 1909.

While nursing educators were able to improve the standards of education for their students, they failed to obtain centralized control over educational programs. Unlike medical schools, which follow a prescribed and generally similar program of education leading to the M.D., nursing has been characterized by different types of educational experiences—all of which can qualify the student as a registered nurse (RN). For example, there are currently three types of programs available for RNs: (1) two-year associate degree programs usually located in junior or community colleges; (2) hospital-based diploma schools requiring two and one-half to three years of study; and (3) four-year and five-year university baccalaureate programs.

The most prestigious of the nursing education programs is the baccalaureate program, which is intended not only to provide training in nursing skills and theory but also to provide the background for becoming a nursing educator or leader. The major source of nurses in the United States had traditionally been the hospital-based diploma school. However, college-based programs, with their combination of occupational training and liberal arts education, have become more popular with nursing students. In 1961, diploma schools accounted for more than 80 percent of all nursing graduates, but by 1970, this percentage had declined to 52 percent. The period between 1970 and 2012 witnessed an even sharper decline to less than 3 percent, moving diploma schools to the edge of disappearance. The primary beneficiary of declining numbers of diploma graduates initially had been the associate degree (A.D.) programs. With only 3 percent of the total number of nursing graduates in 1961, A.D. programs produced 60 percent of the total by 1995–1996 only to decline somewhat to 55 percent in 2007. However, baccalaureate programs have shown steady gains from 13 percent of all nursing graduates in 1961 to 45 percent in 2012. Currently, there are about 710 baccalaureate programs in nursing.

The A.D. programs are relatively inexpensive, require only two years of training, and yet place their graduates on the same career track as graduates of diploma and baccalaureate degree schools. Originally conceived as a middle-range level of nursing education, somewhere between the training required to perform simple or assisting nursing tasks and that required for complex tasks, the work role of the A.D. graduate has expanded into supervisory and management functions. Some controversy has arisen over this trend, because it requires A.D. nurses to function beyond their intended level of training. Although problems regarding the work role persist, A.D. programs have become the largest single source of nurses in the United States.

Despite the remarkable growth of the A.D. programs and the growing acceptance of their graduates in nursing, their appearance has presented a special problem in terms of nursing's claims of professional status. This has arisen because the A.D. programs are essentially vocational rather than professional. A strategy to avoid this situation was to designate A.D. nurses as "technical" nurses and baccalaureate degree nurses as "professional" nurses, while advocating that all nurses be graduates of college programs at some time in the future. Although this became the official position of the American Nurses' Association in 1965, it was not accepted by the majority of its membership, who at that time had graduated from diploma schools. The result initially was that among RNs, the baccalaureate nurses were regarded as the *most* professional, yet associate degree and diploma nurses considered themselves to also be professionals. As this perception continued, many hospitals began requiring their nurses to have bachelor's degrees to be hired or keep their jobs. This development sent many A.D. nurses (about 90,000 in 2012) back for more education to the approximately 600 university-based nursing schools that now offer "Registered Nurse to Bachelor of Science Nurse (R.N. to B.S.N.)" programs. The clear trend today is toward all registered nurses having a bachelor's degree.

In the late 1980s, nursing received a considerable boost in status and income with the development of a severe nursing shortage in American hospitals. The number of available nursing school graduates had declined significantly. Long hours, stress, and low pay had reduced the attractiveness of nursing as a career field. However, enrollment in nursing schools has increased dramatically along with higher salaries. As salaries and demand for nurses rose, nursing school enrollments increased. Although the nursing shortage has yet to ease, the image of nursing as a career has been enhanced, especially as the passage of the Affordable Care Act should facilitate the entrance of millions of additional patients into the nation's health care system on a regular basis.

Nursing Students

In 2012, some 1,500 schools of nursing in various types of institutions offered programs leading to the RN. Nursing students have traditionally been characterized as having lower-middle-class and working-class social origins, often from small towns or rural areas, who are attracted to nursing as a means of upward social mobility. However, there have been increasing numbers of students from upper-middle-class families and urban areas entering nursing schools, with the result that nursing, like teaching, is ranked by sociologists as a distinctly middle-class occupation.

Sociological studies of nursing students have significantly declined since the 1970s, as medical sociologists have focused less on their training and more on the professional role of nurses. For example, in a major study of nursing students in California many years ago, Fred Davis (1972) observed six distinct stages of socialization. First was the stage of *initial innocence*, which consisted of the nursing students wanting to do things for patients within what he called a secularized Christian-humanitarian ethic of care and kindness, consistent with the lay (mother-surrogate) image of nursing. This stage was characterized, however, by feelings of inadequacy, worry, and frustration, as the nursing instructors failed to support the lay image of the nurse. Nursing faculties have tended to insist on students viewing their patients objectively, and this tendency has operated to de-emphasize an intimate nurse–patient relationship. Instead, the students were directed toward seemingly inconsequential tasks of patient care, such as making beds and giving baths. These feelings of frustration, which usually came during the first semester of training, generated the second stage, which Davis called *labeled recognition of incongruity*. In this stage, the nursing students began to collectively articulate their disappointment and openly question their choice of becoming a nurse. At this point, a number of students resigned from the school because they did not or could not adjust to the incongruity between pre-nursing expectations and actual training.

For those that remained, the third stage of *"psyching out"* began, in which the nursing students, like the medical students in the study by Howard Becker and his associates (1961), attempted to anticipate what their instructors wanted them to know and to concentrate upon satisfying these requirements: Although some students may have attempted to "psych out" the instructors from the very beginning, it now became a group phenomenon, with the entire class collectively participating in the process. The fourth stage, termed *role simulation,* was characterized by students performing so as to elicit favorable responses from the instructors. The approved mode of behavior was the exhibition of an objective and "professional" (detached) attitude toward patient care, which included an understanding of the principles behind nursing techniques as well as mastery of those techniques. Many of the students felt they were "playing at acting like a nurse," and they questioned their lack of conviction about the role. But Davis points out that the more successful they became at convincing others that their performance was authentic, the more they began to gain confidence in themselves as nurses. This stage usually came at the end of the first year. The last two years of their program were characterized as the fifth stage of *provisional internalization* and the sixth stage of *stable internalization*. During these final two stages, the nursing students took on a temporary self-identity as a "professional" nurse, as defined by the faculty, and settled into this identification by the time of their graduation.

The Davis (1972) study ranks, with that of Virginia Olesen and Elvi Whittaker (1968), as one of the two best-known sociological studies of nursing education. Some of the findings, however, may not reflect conditions today. Davis found that, unlike medical students who desire a medical education as a terminal career, not all nursing students, perhaps not even a majority, view a career in nursing as their primary life goal. Davis, along with Olesen (Davis 1972; Davis and Olesen 1963), observed that several nursing students did not, either upon entry into nursing school or upon graduation, see themselves as being fully committed to a career in nursing. Their major life goal was that of marriage and family. They held such views, despite the influence of the women's movement and the encouragement of the nursing faculty to view nursing as a lifelong career. Davis (1972:46) found that the majority of students sought nursing training "as a kind of life insurance," should marriage and having a family not occur or should the marriage be less than ideal and result in "childlessness, divorce, premature widowhood, excessive financial burdens, or boredom with the home."

Therefore, the contingency of marriage became the decisive factor upon which all other decisions were based. Davis noted that a student's announcement of an engagement to be married was a great occasion for both the student and her classmates. Not only did it indicate that the major concern was resolved in a positive manner for the engaged student, but it also served to remind those not engaged of their less positive circumstances. Davis (1972:46) found that during the senior year, there was "a veritable marital sweepstakes," in which the announcements of some engagements acquired the "theatrical overtones of a last minute rescue."

The overall image of nursing projected by such studies is that of an occupation dominated by a small group of older, career-oriented RNs who serve as leaders, policy makers, and educators for a large and transient mass of younger nurses, whose career aspirations are often affected by outside influences such as marriage (Freidson 1970b).

However, research by Sam Porter (1992) in Northern Ireland presents a different view. Porter, who worked as a nurse, conducted a participant observation study of the nursing staff at a large urban hospital in Belfast. He finds that, contrary to the conclusions of previous studies, many nurses now regard their employment as a career. "A number of nurses," comments Porter (1992:523), "explicitly stated that, notwithstanding their desire to marry, they saw their job as a career which they expected to follow throughout their working lives." He concludes that with the increasing perception of nursing as a career in itself, the notion that nurses regard their first priority as finding a spouse is out of date.

Change has undoubtedly taken place in the career aspirations of registered nurses and the physician–registered nurse relationship. This change comes in the form of greater stability in nursing ranks as increasing numbers of nurses make it a career and in more autonomy for nurses in their work role along with a higher level of colleagueship with physicians. As Robert Brannon (1994a, 1994b) points out, physicians continue to control the critical decisions of admitting and discharging hospital patients, diagnosing a patient's ills, and conceptualizing the overall treatment plan. Registered nurses do not decide on the medical problems to be addressed or the means of doing so. "Their observations, discretion, and continuous presence on [a] hospital's wards," states Brannon (1994b:170), "[are] essential to meeting a physician's medical objectives, but RNs [are] more likely to facilitate the production of care than to define what that care should be."

Gender and "The Doctor–Nurse Game"

As Porter (1992) observes, issues of gender have been of considerable importance in explaining the role of nurses. Nursing has traditionally been one of the world's major occupations for women. But unlike other jobs dominated numerically by women—elementary school teachers, librarians, and secretaries—nursing is paired with a powerful male-dominated profession. Sociologists have long recognized that nursing, as a historically subordinated occupation, has been constrained in its development by the medical profession (Freidson 1970b). However, there are signs that gender inequality is losing some of its power in nurse–doctor relationships. The changes appear to be the result of three developments: (1) greater assertiveness by nurses, (2) increased numbers of male nurses, and (3) the growing numbers of female doctors.

The formal lines of authority that exist in the medical setting operate to place nurses at a disadvantage in acting upon their judgments regarding medical treatment. Yet, there are times when nurses do go ahead and exercise their own judgment in opposition to the orders of physicians. An example of this situation is found in the experiment conducted by Steven Rank and Cardell Jacobson (1977) in two hospitals in a large Midwestern city. The experiment consisted of having an assistant, using the name of a little known staff surgeon at the hospital who had given permission to use his name, telephone 18 nurses who were on duty and order them to administer a nonlethal overdose of Valium to appropriate patients. The call was made in a self-confident manner, using medical terminology and familiarity with hospital routine. None of the nurses questioned the telephone request, and all but one suspicious nurse entered the request on a medication chart. One of the experimenters, posing as a contractor working on a bid to install some new equipment on the ward, was present at the time of the call with the duty of terminating the experiment should the nurse actually proceed to administer the drug, refuse to comply, fail to take action after 15 minutes, or try to call the "doctor" back.

As a further safeguard, nursing supervisors were stationed in each of the patients' rooms to prevent the medication from being administered. Sixteen out of eighteen nurses decided on their own not to administer the Valium. One nurse (Rank and Jacobson 1977:191) said, "Whew! 30 mg—he [the doctor] doesn't want to sedate her [the patient]—he wants to knock her out." Twelve of these nurses tried to recontact the doctor, and only two appeared ready to comply with the order. Rank and Jacobson suggest that the high rate of noncompliance was because of an increased willingness among hospital personnel to challenge a doctor's orders in contemporary medical practice (a 1966 study had 21 out of 22 nurses willing to give an overdose), rising self-esteem among nurses, and a fear of lawsuits for malpractice.

However, rather than challenge physicians' orders directly, which can have unpleasant consequences for the nurse (being "chewed out," fired), most nurses have been able to develop an extremely effective informal interactional style with physicians.

This interaction has been described by Leonard Stein (1967) as the "doctor–nurse game" because it has all the features of a game—an object, rules, and scores. The object of the game is for the nurse to be bold, show initiative, and make significant recommendations to the doctor in a manner that appears passive and totally supportive of the "super-physician." The central rule of the game is to avoid open disagreement between the players. This requires the nurse to communicate a recommendation without appearing to do so, while the physician, in seeking a recommendation, must appear not to be asking for it. Stein notes that the greater the significance of the recommendation, the more subtly it must be conveyed. Both participants must therefore be aware of each other's nonverbal and verbal styles of communication.

Stein illustrates the doctor–nurse game with an example of a nurse telephoning and awakening a hospital staff physician who is on call, with a report about a female patient unknown to the doctor. The nurse informs the doctor that the patient is unable to sleep and had just been informed that day about the death of her father. What the nurse is actually telling the doctor is that the patient is upset and needs a sedative to sleep. Because the doctor is not familiar with the patient, the doctor asks the nurse what sleeping medication has been helpful to the patient in the past. What the doctor is actually doing is asking the nurse for a recommendation. However, the sentence is phrased in such a way that it appears to be a question rather than a request for a recommendation. The nurse replies that phenobarbital 100 mg has been effective for this particular patient, which Stein interprets as a disguised recommendation statement. The doctor then orders the nurse to administer phenobarbital 100 mg as needed, and the nurse concludes the interaction by thanking the doctor for the order. The nurse has been successful in making a recommendation without appearing to do so, and the doctor has been successful in asking for a recommendation without appearing to do so.

While all this may seem silly to persons unfamiliar with the physician–nurse relationship, it nonetheless represents a significant social mechanism by which the physician is able to utilize the nurse as a consultant and the nurse is able to gain self-esteem and professional satisfaction from her work. A successful game creates a doctor–nurse alliance and allows the doctor to have a good "score" by gaining the respect and admiration of the nursing staff. The nurse, in turn, scores by being identified by the physician as "a damn good nurse." If the doctor fails to play the game well, pleasant working relationships with the nurses may become difficult, and the doctor may have problems of a trivial yet annoying nature when it comes to getting his work done. Nurses who do not play the game well (are outspoken in making recommendations) either are terminated from employment if they also lack intelligence or are tolerated but not liked if they are bright. Nurses who do not play the game at all, according to Stein, are defined as dull and are relegated to the background in the social life of the hospital. The essence of the doctor–nurse game is that physicians and nurses agree that the physician is superior and this hierarchical structure must be maintained. However, nurses may make recommendations to doctors as long as they *appear* to be initiated by the physician and disagreement is avoided.

Stein, Watts, and Howell (1990) reexamined the doctor–nurse game several years later and determined that a different situation now exists. Stein and his colleagues and others (Allen 1997; Davies 2003; Porter 1992; Svensson 1996; Weiss and Lonnquist 2012) find that many nurses are no longer willing to be treated as mere subordinates by physicians. Several reasons are offered for this change. First is declining public esteem for doctors because of widespread questioning of the profit motive in medical practice and greater recognition that physicians make mistakes. Second is the increased number of women doctors. When female doctors and nurses interact, the stereotypical roles of male domination and female submission are missing. Third, the nursing shortage has emphasized to doctors the value of highly trained, competent nurses. Fourth, most nurses today are educated in academic settings. Nurses are recognizing that academic qualifications—as opposed to practical on-the-job training—mean enhanced skills and status. Fifth, the women's movement may be encouraging nurses to define their own roles with greater autonomy. Instead of trying to professionalize the entire occupation of nursing, nurses are turning to "clinical nursing" as an exclusive specialty within general nursing, which emphasizes specific nursing procedures, management of basic-skill nurses, and the central role of the nurse as the responsible worker for groups of patients.

Besides more assertiveness by female nurses, nursing has attracted larger numbers of males in recent years with increasing pay. Men comprise about 6 percent of all registered nurses. Male nurses tend to disrupt the traditional gender role of submission for nurses, because they are not as likely to play the doctor–nurse game. Liliane Floge and Deborah Merrill (1986) found that while female nurses were supposed to appear passive in making recommendations to physicians, this did not seem to be the case for male nurses. Male nurses were more likely to express their opinion and have it accepted by male doctors. One male nurse, for example, was thanked for pointing out a mistake by a physician, while a female nurse was called a derogatory name earlier by the same doctor for pointing out the same mistake.

While male physicians tended to regard male nurses as more competent than female nurses and to treat them accordingly, Floge and Merrill (1986) found that female physicians were not as likely to play the doctor–nurse game with either male or female nurses. But female physicians were also more likely than male

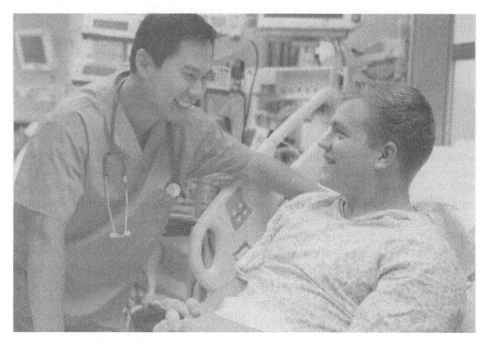

PHOTO 12.2 The percentage of male nurses has increased in recent years.

physicians to have their actions questioned by nurses. Consequently, when it comes to physician–nurse relationships, gender still plays a significant role in shaping the nature of the interaction.

While it might be inferred that gender issues have promoted poor relationships between physicians and nurses, this does not appear to be the case. Extensive research shows considerable satisfaction among both groups and generally positive working relations (Prescott and Bowen 1985). Nurses valued trust and respect on the part of doctors and being regarded as intelligent participants in patient care. Doctors, on their part, appreciated nurses who were competent and helpful and had good communication skills.

Nursing: Future Trends

Nurses have achieved status through their high standards and professional orientation toward their work role and the extension of nursing tasks beyond bedside care. Typically, lower-echelon workers such as nurses' aides provide the majority of bedside care under the supervision of an RN. RNs, especially those with baccalaureate degrees, have expanded their range of services to include hospital administration, primary-care healing, nurse anesthetists, cardiovascular nurse specialists, and other areas of specialization in nursing. Nurse specialists, like those in AIDS units, have enhanced status and greater autonomy in patient care than do nonspecialists. According to Linda Aiken and Douglas Sloane (1997:218), who studied the effects of specialization on nurses providing care for AIDS patients, "Nurse specialization allows nurses to develop, demonstrate, and communicate to physicians their superiority in certain important spheres of patient care." This situation is promoted by the fact that nursing skills are critically important to AIDS patients for symptom control and comfort. Aiken and Sloane also found that the willingness of nurses in AIDS units to accept responsibility for patients with a stigmatized, fatal, and communicable disease enhanced their social standing in the hospital.

Hospital Administration

One significant change in the work role of nursing has been the evolution of the RN into an administrative role. Competent nurses cannot be rewarded by promotion to the higher rungs of the medical profession. To reach the top of the medical hierarchy, the nurse is forced to leave nursing altogether and become a doctor. Because this is usually impractical, many nurses have sought a career in hospital administration. From the perspective of hospital administrators, registered nurses can be used more economically in managerial and supervisory positions, because lower-paid personnel are available for bedside tasks.

The paradox in this development is that while it allows the nurse to gain a somewhat more secure claim of professional status, it greatly reduces or eliminates the contact with patients for which nursing was organized in the first place. Yet, patients usually cannot tell one type of nurse from another, and it may be uncommon to overtly request emotional support. Instead, patients typically request simple tasks—such as medications to ease pain, bedpans, or assistance in moving to a more comfortable body position—that can be accomplished by less-qualified nursing aides. As Sam Schulman (1972:236) points out, in hospitals "mother-surrogateness is seldom encountered: in large measure, it is not asked for by patients nor is it given by nurses." Schulman concludes that, in an indirect sense, patients are supportive of the removal of most professional nurses from their bedsides, because they want the most professional persons in charge of their care. Whether patients do approve of removing the best-qualified nurses from their bedside is an arguable point; nevertheless, it is happening.

The Nurse Practitioner/Clinician

An important change in nursing has been the emergence of another kind of nurse—the nurse practitioner or nurse clinician. This change is not intended to create a completely new type of health worker, but instead to use more fully the skills and capabilities of the well-trained nurse. The nurse practitioner is intended to occupy a work position similar to that of the physician assistant role. The nurse practitioner is a registered nurse trained in the diagnosis and management of common ailments needing medical attention. They provide some of the same care as physicians, but are limited in the types of treatment they can provide to patients. Usually the work of nurse practitioners is supervised by a physician who can be called up to assist them if necessary. This role for the nurse practitioner frees physicians from routine forms of medical care and, in theory, allows doctors to concentrate on more complex medical problems. In 2014, there were over 180,000 nurse practitioners in the United States with an average annual salary of $95,000.

Hence, a formal role for nurses who practice medicine as well as nursing is developing within the context of patient care. In the future, nurse practitioners may provide much of the primary care for patients. This is thought to be especially the case with the passage of the Affordable Care Act scheduled to be fully implemented in 2014 that is expected to increase the number of patients with health insurance coverage. Another development is the establishment of primary care centers in retail stores such as Walmart and CVS offering services for minor health problems and injuries, frequent illnesses like the flu, and in some instances, more advanced care such as management of chronic diseases. These primary care centers are largely staffed by nurse practitioners, with a physician in a supervisory role but not necessarily on site.

Although the emergence of the nurse practitioner does not change nursing's subordinate work role, it allows the practitioners a greater degree of decision making. A major concern by nurses, however, with this projection of an expanded role is that the nurse practitioner may simply be "consumed" by the medical profession as a "lesser" doctor or be simply a nurse given a more complex form of tasks delegated by the physician. Current trends suggest, however, that nurse practitioners in the United States are playing an expanded role in medicine through increased decision making and direct responsibility for their decisions. All 50 states and the District of Columbia in the United States allow nurse practitioners to prescribe medications, 46 states allow them to prescribe controlled substances, and 12 states allow them to prescribe independently of physicians.

A recent development moving nurses even closer to doctors in professional status is the new Doctor of Nursing Practice (DNP) degree. This program, which is in its infancy, is for advanced nurses with master's degrees, such as nurse practitioners, and other nurses working as anesthetists, midwives, educators, and executives to acquire doctoral qualification. The nursing doctoral students are taught advanced clinical skills, collaboration with other health professionals to solve complex clinical problems, leadership, statistics, epidemiology, health economics, and other topics. The goal is to train nurses to work at the highest professional levels.

With nurses holding clinical doctorates, along with doctorates for pharmacists (required since 2004) and physical therapists (required beginning in 2015), there is likely to be further erosion of the power and authority of medical doctors in health care situations. It will also mean a higher level of professionalism on health care teams in which the medical doctor may be first among equals—as other team members hold doctorates in their fields. There is concern, however, on the part of some physicians, that the title "doctor" could lose its meaning in a clinical setting and confuse patients as to whom *the* "doctor" really is, namely the physician (Harris 2011). There is also some concern by physicians that patients may first visit these other "doctors" instead of coming to them directly for health care. Nevertheless, by 2015, new nurse practitioners are expected to hold doctorates qualifying them for the title "doctor." Some 14,699 students were enrolled in 241 nursing schools that offered the DNP in 2013.

Physician Assistants

While the nurse practitioner emerged from the expansion of nursing, a traditional occupation, that of physician assistant (PA) represents another form of paramedical practitioner. Physician assistants typically have a bachelor's degree, previous experience in health care as a nurse or paramedic, and become qualified after completing a PA training program of approximately 26 months that is equivalent to a master's degree. There are currently more than 168 accredited PA programs in the United States. Physician assistants are licensed to practice medicine under the supervision of a physician and are trained to handle routine medical problems. A general job description of the PA would be to provide a level of primary patient care similar to or higher than that of nurse practitioners.

By 2013, there were 84,064 licensed PAs in the United States, of whom 75 percent were women. The first physician assistant program was established at Duke University in 1965 as a means for medics trained in the military to transition into the civilian workforce and use their skills to assist physicians. However, in the intervening years, as PA programs expanded, the occupation has undergone extensive feminization, changing from mostly all male in the beginning to a predominately female workforce (Hooker et al. 2013). The average annual salary for a PA in 2013 was $86,000. Their training was either in primary care or in specialties, especially cardiology, ophthalmology, and orthopedics. Typically, they work directly for physicians, either in private medical practices or in hospitals providing inpatient services. They spend the largest part of their workday providing direct patient care, divided about equally between those tasks directly supervised and those indirectly supervised by physicians. Considerably less time was spent in technical or laboratory work or in the supervision of other health workers.

The PA is becoming an established occupation within medicine (Cawley and Hooker 2013; Hooker et al. 2013). The District of Columbia and all states

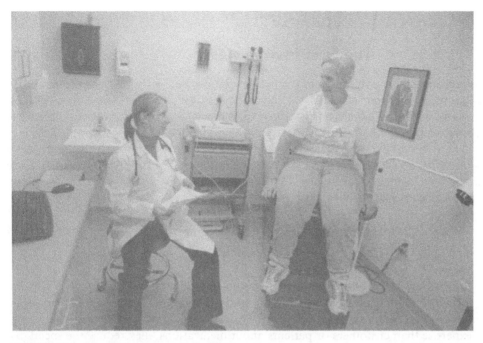

PHOTO 12.3 Some 75 percent of all physician assistants are women compared to the mid-1960s and 1970s when they were mostly men.

legally recognize PA practice. Forty-eight states and the District of Columbia now authorize PAs to prescribe medications, with Indiana and Ohio the only exceptions. Most important for patient care, the PA, in conjunction with the nurse practitioner, may be able to resolve the significant issue of providing more primary-care practitioners in the American system of health care delivery. The use of nurse practitioners and physician assistants is expanding, along with significant growth in their numbers. As long as they extend the medical functions of physicians without competing for or challenging the authority and autonomy of medical doctors, they are likely to become a highly integral part of health care delivery. If not, the professional boundaries of medicine will likely be severely tested.

Pharmacists

Pharmacy is another area of health care that expanded its role in the twenty-first century. Pharmacists no longer just prepare and dispense medication but also provide advice, information, and instructions about drug use (Pilnick 1999). Pharmacists, in fact, are the most accessible of all health care personnel as they practice in a wide range of settings, including community pharmacies, hospitals, and clinics, and also provide mail and telephone services. While pharmacists cannot dispense prescription drugs without authorization from a physician or other legally sanctioned practitioner, they explain the effects of prescription drugs and levels of doses primarily to patients and at times to practitioners—as well as provide instructions

BOX 12.1

The First Pharmacies

Arabs founded the first pharmacies. In fact, the word "drug" is of Arab origin, as are the words "alcohol," "sugar," and "syrup." Many drugs were introduced by the Arabs, including camphor, the painkiller laudanum, and medicinal alcohol. Roy Porter (1997:102) points out that since the time of the great Arab alchemist Jabir ibn Hayyan, in the tenth century, Arabs were developing the techniques of crystallization, filtration, and distillation in the making of drugs and investigating their properties. The value of this Arab contribution to medicine, Porter finds, was not the novelty of their drugs but the thoroughness with which they catalogued and preserved their knowledge. Latin translations of Arabic texts helped Western medicine revive after the Dark Ages and promoted the establishment of pharmacies in the West.

for their use. They also explain and recommend over-the-counter drugs to customers with common ailments. Most importantly, they are the key source of medication information for the general public. Although pharmacists have considerably more expertise than customers or patients about medications, they reduce the social distance between them by using terms that a layperson can understand.

In 2011, there were 272,320 pharmacists in the United States and 116 schools of pharmacy. Educational requirements have changed in that pharmacy schools will only award the doctor of pharmacy (Pharm.D.) degree for six years of study beyond high school. Previously, a five-year bachelor of science in pharmacy (B.S. Pharmacy) degree was available, but it has been phased out in favor of greater professional preparation. This development reinforces the position of pharmacists as the most knowledgeable health care specialist about medicines and their use. Although the role of pharmacists is expanding to assume greater patient counseling, they supplement rather than challenge the patient care tasks of physicians and health care practitioners.

Midwives

Midwives are women who assist a mother during childbirth. There are two types of midwives, nurse-midwives who assist to deliver babies under the supervision of a physician and lay midwives who assist births on their own. Midwifery is one of the earliest forms of care available to women. As Rose Weitz and Deborah Sullivan (1986) describe the history of midwifery, midwives attended practically all births in colonial America. In fact, as late as the eighteenth century it was considered undignified for male physicians to care for pregnant women and attend to the delivery of babies. That function was considered "women's work." What changed this situation was a growing belief in scientific progress among the general population and the development of obstetrics as a new medical specialty. Births attended by midwives began to drop rapidly, as physicians took over the responsibility for delivering babies. In the meantime, the medical profession developed strong opposition to midwifery, arguing that surgical skills and knowledge of drugs, as well as more sanitary conditions found in hospital delivery rooms, were far superior to any service midwives could provide. Weitz and Sullivan found that, by 1900, only about half of all births in the United States were attended by midwives. By 1950, midwifery ceased in all but remote areas.

However, midwifery has slowly made a comeback in American society, despite the opposition of the medical profession. Midwives have become available to women in some locales who wish to have a natural childbirth, featuring breathing and relaxation techniques and emotional support in the place of pain-killing drugs. Many physicians, in turn, now practice some of the same techniques as that of midwives for women who opt for natural childbirth. Lay midwives have remained in existence because they deliver babies in the home, something that physicians typically refuse to do, and they have disproportionately served racial/ethnic minorities and people in rural areas (Hartley 1999, 2002). Midwives also serve women whose religious beliefs prevent them from using doctors. While opposition to midwifery by the medical profession continues, today some 16 states license or register lay midwives, who number about a 1,000 practitioners.

Weitz and Sullivan (1986) studied the development of midwifery in Arizona. They found that to become a midwife, a woman had to show evidence of formal training in midwifery, observations of live births, and supervised experience, as well as pass oral, written, and clinical examinations developed by a nurse-midwife in consultation with physicians. These rules were developed in Arizona in the late 1970s, after controversy emerged over the legal requirements for licensing. Earlier requirements had not been stringent, but when the number of midwives in the state increased and began serving middle-class clients, physicians objected. The new rules, as Weitz and Sullivan point out, gave the medical establishment substantial control of the licensure process, but midwives are able to practice. Weitz and Sullivan characterize the conflict with doctors as a struggle for women's rights and note continued problems with physician acceptance of midwives.

Nurse-midwives, however, are registered nurses trained to deliver babies, often without a doctor's direct supervision (but legal arrangements to have a physician on call are required). Nurse-midwives are legally authorized to work in all 50 states and the District of Columbia. Approximately 13,000 certified nurse-midwives were practicing in the United States in 2012. According to Heather Hartley (1999, 2002), the use of nurse–midwives is increasing in urban managed care systems to meet the demands of consumers desiring a natural childbirth and reducing costs. Hartley suggests that the number of nurse–midwives will increase as the college-educated population continues to show a growing preference for less technology-oriented births.

Summary

Nursing as an occupation has evolved from being an informal exercise of charity ("sisterhood") into a formal occupational role subordinate to the authority and control of the physician. Many social factors have contributed to the maintenance of this situation, especially the stereotype of the mother-surrogate. It has also been noted that in some cases, nurse's training is not always viewed by nursing students as a means to a career but as a kind of "life insurance" should they be disappointed in their primary goals of marriage and family. Nevertheless, nurses have continually struggled to achieve formal colleagueship with physicians, and they have achieved professional-like status, especially through their roles in hospital administration and as nurse practitioners.

The role of nurse practitioner seems particularly promising because it enables nurses to gain some autonomy over what they do and to share more fully in medicine's specialized body of knowledge. Both the nurse practitioner and the physician assistant roles result from a trend toward physician specialization that has made doctors less accessible to patients with minor and generalized ailments who nonetheless require attention. These relatively new roles represent evidence that some health workers are displacing physicians. Pharmacists are not competing with physicians, but their role has expanded as well with greater involvement in discourse with laypersons about the use and effects of medications. Midwives, however, find their services constrained by doctors and their occupation relegated to a marginal role in medicine.

Critical Thinking Questions

1. How has gender played a role in the doctor–nurse relationship?
2. Has the professional relationship between nurses, physician assistants, and doctors changed in recent years?
3. How has the medical profession responded to the resurgence of midwifery?

Suggested Readings

Gordon, Suzanna (2005) "Nursing against all odds: How health care cost cutting, media stereotypes, and medical hubris undermine nurses and patient care." *JAMA*, 294:848–49.
An engaging account of problems nurses still face.

References

Aiken, Linda H., and Douglas M. Sloane (1997) "Effects of specialization and client differentiation on the status of nurses: The case of AIDS." *Journal of Health and Social Behavior* 38: 203–22.
Allen, Davina (1997) "The nursing-medical boundary: A negotiated order?" *Sociology of Health & Illness* 19: 398–498.
Becker, Howard S., Blanche Greer, Everett C. Hughes, and Anselm Strauss (1961) *Boys in white: Student culture in medical school.* Chicago: University of Chicago Press.
Brannon, Robert L. (1994a) *Intensifying care: The hospital industry, professionalization, and the reorganization of the nursing labor process.* Amityville, NY: Baywood.
—— (1994b) "Professionalization and work intensification." *Work and Occupations* 21: 157–78.
Cawley, James F., and Roderick S. Hooker (2013) "Physician assistants in American medicine." *American Journal of Managed Care* 19: e333–41.
Davies, Karen (2003) "The body and doing gender: The relations between doctors and nurses in hospital work." *Sociology of Health & Illness* 25: 720–42.
Davis, Fred (1972) *Illness, interaction, and the self.* Belmont, CA: Wadsworth.

Davis, Fred, and Virginia Olesen (1963) "Initiation into a women's profession: Identity problems in the status transition of coed to student nurse." *Sociometry* 26: 89–101.

Floge, Liliane, and Deborah M. Merrill (1986) "Tokenism reconsidered: Male nurses and female physicians in a hospital setting." *Social Forces* 64: 925–47.

Freidson, Eliot (1970a) *Profession of medicine.* New York: Dodd, Mead.

——— (1970b) *Professional dominance.* Chicago: Aldine.

Harris, Gardiner (2011) "When the nurse wants to be called 'Doctor'." *New York Times* (October 2): A1.

Hartley, Heather (1999) "The influence of managed care on supply of certified nurse-midwives: An evaluation of the physician dominance thesis." *Journal of Health and Social Behavior* 40: 87–101.

——— (2002) "The system of alignments challenging physician professional dominance: An elaborated theory of countervailing powers." *Sociology of Health & Illness* 24: 178–207.

Hooker, Roderick S., Stephen P. Robie, Jennifer M. Coombs, and James F. Cawley (2013) "The changing physician assistant profession: A gender shift." *Journal of the American Academy of Physician Assistants* 26: 36–44.

Olesen, Virginia L., and Elvi W. Whittaker (1968) *The silent dialogue.* San Francisco: Jossey Press.

Pilnick, Alison (1999) " 'Patient counseling' by pharmacists: Advice, information, or instruction?" *Sociological Quarterly* 40: 587–612.

Porter, Roy (1997) *The greatest benefit to mankind: A medical history of humanity.* New York: W. W. Norton.

Porter, Sam (1992) "Women in a women's job: The gendered experience of nurses." *Sociology of Health & Illness* 14: 510–27.

Prescott, Patricia A., and Sally A. Bowen (1985) "Physician–nurse relationships." *Annals of Internal Medicine* 103: 127–33.

Rank, Steven G., and Cardell K. Jacobson (1977) "Hospital nurses' compliance with medication overdose orders: A failure to replicate." *Journal of Health and Social Behavior* 18: 188–93.

Schulman, Sam (1972) "Mother surrogate—After a decade," pp. 233–39 in *Patients, physicians and illness*, E. Jaco (ed.). New York: The Free Press.

Stein, Leonard I. (1967) "The doctor–nurse game." *Archives of General Psychiatry* 16: 699–703.

Stein, Leonard I., David T. Watts, and Timothy Howell (1990) "The doctor–nurse game revisited." *New England Journal of Medicine* 322: 546–49.

Strauss, Anselm (1966) "Structure and ideology of the nursing profession," pp. 60–104 in *The nursing profession*, F. Davis (ed.). New York: John Wiley.

Svensson, Roland (1996) "The interplay between doctors and nurses—A negotiated order perspective." *Sociology of Health & Illness* 18: 379–98.

Weiss, Gregory L., and Lynne E. Lonnquist (2012) *The sociology of health, healing, and disease*, 7th ed. Upper Saddle River, NJ: Pearson-Prentice-Hall.

Weitz, Rose, and Deborah Sullivan (1986) "The politics of childbirth: The reemergence of midwifery in Arizona." *Social Problems* 33: 163–75.

CHAPTER 13

Healing Options

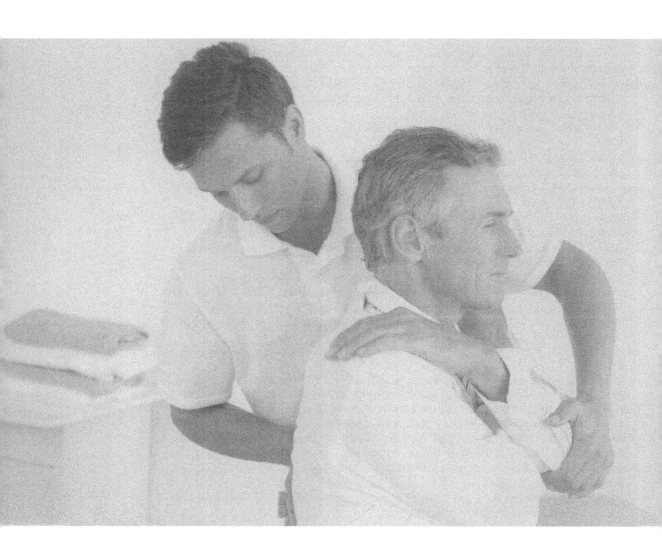

- Describe CAM and the social classes most likely to use this form of treatment.

- Compare osteopaths and chiropractors.

- Identify the types of religious healing.

- Explain the persistence of folk healing.

Most people turn to medical doctors for help when they are sick or injured. Other people seek treatment elsewhere. This may be for reasons that are religious, finan-cial, or cultural, or simply because no doctors are available or because modern medicine may not meet their needs. To complete our discussion of help seeking, this chapter examines healing options in the United States. These healers exist be-cause they provide a service to their clients. What these services are and why they are sought is our focus. First, we will discuss the osteopath, *who is a physician. Next, we will expand our discussion to include a consideration of* complementary and alternative medicine *(CAM), chiropractors, faith healers,* and folk healers.

Osteopaths

For many years, osteopathy was viewed by the medical profession as a form of quackery. But gradually professional respectability was achieved by moving away from an exclusive focus on spinal manipulation techniques to treat general health problems. Today, osteopaths are part of mainstream medicine, and they work as physicians with the added skill of training in spinal procedures. Osteopathy began in the 1860s in Kirksville, Missouri (Baer 2001; Lesho 1999). Its founder, Andrew Taylor Still, a physician, believed that illness was caused by a dislocation of one or more bones in the spinal column and that a pathological condition in one of the body's organs affects other organs. Because of the close relationship between the spinal vertebrae and the autonomic nervous system, the neuromuscular sys-tem is considered to play a vital role in the healthy functioning of the body. By the mid-twentieth century, osteopaths were receiving scientific medical training in such areas as surgery and pharmacology. Training for osteopaths takes place at 19 osteopathic colleges in the United States, whose graduates are awarded the Doctor of Osteopathy degree (D.O.). Further training as an intern and resident is required. Osteopaths have also formed their own professional organization, the American Osteopathic Association (AOA), which serves to promote professionalism.

In 1953, the American Medical Association (AMA) recognized osteopaths as a medical specialty, and they now enjoy the rights and privileges of medical doctors. To date, osteopaths have been able to maintain their separate identity, yet the trend is toward absorption into medicine. Osteopaths, for example, can specialize in surgery, anesthesiology, psychiatry, pediatrics, radiology, and other medical specialties. A hotly debated question in osteopathy is whether "classical" osteopathy has given itself over totally to medicine as practiced by medical doctors. This argument remains unresolved as the osteopathic profession continues to resist complete assimilation into traditional medicine. Because osteopaths are trained to practice manipulation of the musculoskeletal system, they see themselves as able to provide this service as an added dimension of health care. However, some observers find that the therapeutic practices that originally distinguished osteopathy from traditional medicine have become less and less important to the majority of its practitioners (Baer 2001). In 2013, there were approximately 82,000 osteopaths licensed in the United States.

Complementary and Alternative Medicine (CAM)

Complementary and alternative medicine (CAM) is the use of treatments that are not commonly practiced by the medical profession. CAM includes visits to chiropractors, faith healers, and folk healers, as well as to acupuncturists, homeopaths, and naturopaths, and the use of dietary supplements to prevent or cure disease. Acupuncture is an ancient Chinese technique of inserting fine needles into specific points in the body to ease pain and stimulate bodily functions, while homeopathy is the use of microdoses of natural substances to bolster immunity. In large amounts, these substances could cause an illness, but tiny doses are intended to promote prevention or provide a cure by stimulating the body's defenses. Naturopathy is based on the idea that disease arises from blockages in a person's life force in the body, and treatments such as acupuncture and homeopathy are needed to restore the energy flow.

Other types of therapists may provide aromatherapy (the use of aromatic oils for relaxation), ayurveda (a centuries-old Indian technique of using oils and massage to treat insomnia, hypertension, and digestive problems), shiatsu (Japanese therapeutic

PHOTO 13.2 Women participating in a meditation and relaxation therapy session.

massage), crystal healing (based on the idea that healing energy can be obtained from quartz and other minerals), and biofeedback (the use of machines to train people to control involuntary bodily functions). CAM also includes the use of dietary supplements such as algae to enhance alertness, shark cartilage to cure cancer, fish oil capsules to reduce the threat of heart attacks, garlic to prevent blood clots, and the consumption of megadoses of vitamins and herbs to ward off or treat illnesses.

Up to now it is not clear whether many of the techniques actually work, cause harm, or are useless. Some procedures such as acupuncture appear effective and show some possibility of being considered by mainstream medicine (Baer 2001, 2010; Baer et al. 1998; Jackson and Scambler 2007). However, most evidence supporting the various types of alternative medicine is based upon personal observations or testimonials from satisfied patients, not scientific testing. The lack of scientific evidence, especially from randomized controlled clinical trials, has led critics to argue that CAM is no more effective than a placebo (Segar 2011). The Office of Alternative Medicine, now the National Center for Complementary and Alternative Medicine, was created in 1992 by Congress as part of the National Institutes of Health. The mission of the Center is to facilitate research and evaluation of CAM techniques and make this information readily available to practitioners and the public.

Despite the lack of scientific research, the rise in the number of CAM practitioners has been accompanied by surprisingly broad acceptance of many of their therapies by the general public (Ayers and Kronenfeld 2010; Baer 2010; Foote-Ardah 2003; Goldner 2004; Goldstein 2000; Grzywacz et al. 2007; Kelner, Wellman, Pescosolido, and Saks 2000; Leiser 2003; Saks 2003). Some CAM practitioners are even allowed to provide their services in hospitals and clinics but are typically not part of the regular staff and occupy only a marginal position in relation to the other practitioners (Leiser 2003; Shuval, Mizrachi, and Smetannikov 2002). However, the acceptance of CAM therapies by the general public is so extensive that it is estimated that Americans spend more than $27 billion annually on its services and products (Kelner et al. 2000). The dietary supplement industry alone has sales of over one billion dollars annually. This business has flourished since the passage of the Dietary Supplement Health and Education Act by Congress in 1994. This legislation allows food products to be sold as cures for disease as long as claims that they can actually enhance health are not on the label. Such claims, however, can be displayed in books, pamphlets, and store signs where the products are sold.

While little sociological research has been conducted on these phenomena, it appears that many persons who use some form of alternative or "new age" medicine have middle- or working-class social backgrounds (Schneirov and Geczik 1996) and are typically middle age or younger adults (Grzywacz et al. 2007). They also consult regularly with medical doctors. The stereotypical CAM user is that of a white, middle-class or working-class person seeking alternate sources of healing. CAM techniques have been underutilized by African Americans, although recently blacks have been found to use CAM as a strategy to adapt to discriminatory practices in professional health care settings (Shippee, Schafer, and Ferraro 2012). Women are more likely to use CAM than men and some accounts highlight its practices as a form of female empowerment, yet men also utilize it and do so along lines they consider masculine by generally emphasizing a scientific and rational approach to its practices (Brenton and Elliot 2014).

People use CAM techniques for a variety of reasons, such as being dissatisfied with physician care or wishing to supplement it or they dislike haggling with insurance providers, want to be in control of their own health, enjoy the experience, and believe it can actually help them be healthier and live longer. Other people, those who use faith and folk healers, typically come from a lower-class background and use these practitioners because they are inexpensive and culturally similar. What both groups have in common is dissatisfaction with professional medicine.

Chiropractors

The chiropractic approach to healing also involves manipulation of bones in the spinal column. This type of treatment originated with Daniel Palmer in Davenport, Iowa, in 1895. It is based on the idea that manipulation of the spine can relieve pressure on the nerves and thereby alleviate illness and pain. While there is some dispute over whether the osteopathic and the chiropractic approaches evolved independently of each other in terms of initial conceptualization, chiropractors today are restricted solely to nonmedical techniques. There are 17 chiropractic colleges in the United States and others in Canada, England, and Australia. Training is four years in duration, three in the classroom and one in practice at the college. There are no internships or residencies to serve.

While there is evidence that chiropractic techniques can help patients with back, shoulder, and neck pain, the medical profession has traditionally opposed the extension of professional status to chiropractors (Baer 2001; Theberge 2008). This opposition is based on the assertion that chiropractic methods are derived from inaccurate theories, chiropractic educational standards are low, and the techniques are of little or no therapeutic value to patients. Rather than attempt to absorb the chiropractor into medicine, some physicians have preferred to eliminate the field altogether. In 1987, a federal court ruled that the American Medical Association (AMA) had conspired to destroy chiropractic medicine in violation of antitrust statutes. The AMA was ordered to cease undermining the public's confidence in chiropractic procedures.

Chiropractors are licensed to practice in all 50 states, are authorized to receive Medicare payments for treatments rendered to patients over the age of 65, and provide services covered by major private insurance carriers. There are over 74,000 chiropractors nationwide providing services to their clients. Chiropractors may be favored by some patients because they have a reputation for charging less than physicians, being friendly, giving more time to patients and using words easily understood, as well as being able to help with back problems.

However, chiropractors have been hampered in their attempts at professionalization, not only by physicians but also because of conflicts among themselves. Some chiropractors favor a more expanded role, using a variety of techniques, in which a wider range of health problems would be treated. Others prefer a more "pure" approach, in which chiropractors would limit themselves to spinal manipulation. Chiropractors must often strongly compete among one another for patients and have little control over who should be licensed to practice.

Physicians rarely refer patients to chiropractors. Yet, most people who visit chiropractors also visit a physician for treatment. Therefore, it appears that the majority of people who use chiropractic services do not depend entirely on this method of care. Instead, they use chiropractors and physicians in a complementary manner, rather than use chiropractors as an alternative to medical doctors (Davis et al. 2012). Because physicians do not typically refer their patients to chiropractors, it must be assumed that most people visit chiropractors on their own initiative. Many people go to chiropractors for treatment in addition to that received from physicians, but some seek help from both chiropractors and physicians for the same conditions. Chiropractors are the second largest category of primary health care practitioners in the United States, just after medical doctors, when the number of providers and patients treated is taken into account. Nevertheless, chiropractors remain outside mainstream medicine.

Faith Healing and Religion

Faith healers are people who use the power of suggestion, prayer, and faith in God to promote healing. According to John Denton (1978), two basic beliefs are prevalent in religious healing. One form of belief supports the idea that healing occurs primarily through psychological processes and is effective only with psychophysiological disorders. The other belief is that healing is accomplished through the intervention of God and constitutes a present-day miracle. Denton offers five general categories of faith healing: (1) self-treatment through prayer; (2) treatment by a layperson thought to be able to communicate with God; (3) treatment by an official church leader, for whom healing is only one of many tasks; (4) healing obtained from a person or group of persons who practice healing full time without an affiliation with a major religious organization; and (5) healing obtained from religious healers who practice full time and are affiliated with a major religious group, such as Christian Science healers. A common theme running through each of these categories is an appeal to God to change a person's physical or mental condition for the better.

An example of faith healing is found in the study conducted by Gillian Allen and Roy Wallis (1976) of members of a small congregation of a Pentecostal church, the Assemblies of God, in a city in Scotland. Members of the church subscribed to a belief that the devil caused illness and that even for such afflictions as mental illness, blindness, dumbness, and epilepsy, a person could be possessed by evil spirits. Accepting the Bible as the literal truth, the Assemblies of God officially support the idea of *divine healing* based upon Biblical passages indicating that (1) some people have the power to transmit the healing forces of the Holy Spirit or to exorcise demons and (2) healing can be obtained through faith the same way as salvation from sin. The healing procedure was a prayer at the end of service consisting of the pastor and elders laying hands on the person, sprinkling holy oil on the individual, and praying for the removal of demons or whatever was causing the affliction.

Although the Pentecostal church used divine healing as a central aspect of church dogma, it did not prohibit members from seeking professional medical care. Use of divine healing, however, was preferred because it offered the advantage of providing both spiritual and physical healing. It was also believed to work in many cases where orthodox medical practices failed. The members had a fund of knowledge attesting to spectacular cures, either through the specific effect of the emotional healing services or through the power of prayer in general. Yet, because church members also believed that "God's methods are sometimes through humans" and that "God put doctors in the world and gave them their skills," it was permissible to seek physician assistance. For serious illnesses in particular, divine healing was used in conjunction with professional medicine. Hence, church members simultaneously held religious and scientific beliefs about the causation and treatment of illness, without any apparent conflict. "In serious illnesses," state Allen and Wallis (1976:134–35), "members were not faced with the choice between breaking their religious principles by fetching the doctor and refusing medical treatment altogether." Consequently, Pentecostalists were usually able to avoid the dilemma of whether to use *either* a religious *or* a medical curing process.

Deborah Glik (1990) interviewed several people who participated in spiritual healing groups in Baltimore, Maryland. The majority of respondents claimed they had experienced some type of healing and attributed it to their participation and belief in spiritual healing. Rather than cures, however, the most common form of healing was alleviation of symptoms. This was followed by relief from psychological distress, acceptance of one's health or life situation, or adoption of another perspective about one's situation. In some cases, people redefined what was wrong with them to better fit the outcome of their healing experience; that is, they redefined their ailments as less serious and less medical after religious healing. "While few persons claimed their healing had been complete," states Glik (1990:161), "most cited improvements in some health or life situation." Glik's data suggest that the benefits of religious healing primarily lay in relief from stress, enhanced feelings of support from God, and the adoption of a different viewpoint about the meaning of their health problem in their lives. For example, as two of the respondents in the Glik (1990:157) study reported:

> A 61-year-old female teacher going through a divorce and dealing with depression and arthritis said: "Faith and belief has made me accepting of problems. I have been able to fill up with God, and He will not let my problems get to me."
>
> A 34-year-old male real estate broker suffering from stress and lower back pain noted, "I am now relaxed. I have learned to let go and let God be alive in my body, mind and all my affairs. Life has changed dramatically for the good."

Some faith healers hold services in a church or in their homes. Others travel from city to city, often in rural areas, holding meetings (perhaps in tents), and some appear on television or radio. The number of people who frequent such healing services and who are actually helped by this method is not known. But faith healers tend to be readily available, and such healers visit cities and towns across the country at least once a year.

In the United States, most religious groups favor a combination of religious practices and professional medical care in treating health problems. However, the doctrines of a few religious groups prohibit their members from seeking modern medical treatment. These groups utilize faith healing, laying on of hands, and individual and communal prayers in treating illnesses. Sometimes there are accounts of "miracle" cures in which a deadly affliction such as cancer is overcome. On other occasions, there are tragic cases in which children die unnecessarily because their parents refuse to obtain medical care because of their religious beliefs.

The most prominent group in American society advocating a preference for religious healing is the Christian Science Church. Founded in 1866 in Boston by Mary Baker Eddy, the Christian Science Church maintains that sickness and pain are an illusion. Disease is not God given but is believed to be produced by a distorted view people have of their spiritual nature. All forms of disease are considered symptomatic of an underlying spiritual condition that can be healed only through prayer. The key to life and health is thus obtained through spiritual discovery. Christian

Scientists are believed to possess the capacity to heal themselves, although the assistance of self-employed Christian Science practitioners, licensed by the church, are also available. Christian Science practitioners are not considered to be the equal of medical doctors but are intended to help the sick person find a cure through prayer and are paid for their services. Healing consists of prayers meant to convey to individuals a deeper understanding of their spiritual being. This understanding is held to be the crucial factor in eliminating the mental attitudes from which all diseases are thought to originate. There are certain medical problems that are considered more mechanical than spiritual, such as broken bones or a need for surgery that can be legitimately treated by a doctor. But Christian Science healing is considered to be the first choice of treatment for most afflictions.

In the late 1980s, four court cases resulted in convictions of manslaughter or neglect for Christian Science parents in the deaths of their children because of a failure to seek conventional medical care. One case involved the death of a two-year-old boy from a bowel obstruction in Boston, when the parents relied exclusively on prayer to help the child find relief. In another case in Florida, a judge rejected a charge of manslaughter against a Christian Science couple after a jury found them guilty of allowing their seven-year-old daughter to die from diabetes. Instead, the judge accepted the more stringent conviction of third-degree murder, along with child abuse, and sentenced the parents to suspended four-year prison terms and 15 years of probation and ordered them to provide medical treatment for their surviving children. A Florida appeals court upheld the sentence in 1990 and stated that the right to practice religion freely does not include the liberty to expose a child to ill health or death and added that while parents may be free to become martyrs themselves, they are not free to make martyrs of their children.

The legal issues in cases such as these are clear. On one side is the issue of religious freedom and parental autonomy and on the other is the state's right to protect children. The current trend in court decisions in this matter appears in a 1991 finding by the State Supreme Court in Massachusetts involving Jehovah's Witnesses who refused blood transfusions for their children in two separate cases, one where the child had leukemia and the other hemorrhage of an ulcer. The court held that while adults have the right to refuse medical care, parents can be required to have their children treated for life-threatening illnesses. More recently, in 2009, Christian Science changed its position to allow believers to seek conventional medical care if necessary and suggested that it can be a supplement to such care, possibly even qualifying its healers for health insurance payments. This measure has yet to be approved by any private insurers, states, or the federal government. In 1950, there were about 11,000 Christian Science healers in the United States alone. By the late 1990s, there were fewer than 2,000 worldwide because of legal and other problems, and this number is thought to have dropped even further to around 1,400 by 2010 (Fraser 1999; Vitello 2010).

When it comes to faith healing, however, there is considerable controversy about whether it actually works. Moreover, questionable ethics on the part of some once prominent television evangelists in past years, including sex scandals, cannot have helped the overall image of faith healing among the general public. Moreover, the medical profession does not hold faith healing in high esteem nor do large segments of society (Baer 2001). The future of this mode of health care delivery in the United States is uncertain—at least with respect to its electronic version.

Nevertheless, the relationship between health and religion is an important area that needs to be studied in greater detail. Such studies should not be limited to faith healing but should include the manner in which religious beliefs have an impact generally on health and medical care. It is clear, for example, that an appeal to a spiritual or divine being promotes a sense of psychological well-being in the individual (Abrums 2000; Idler 2010; Musick, House, and Williams 2004). Among the existing studies is that of Ellen Idler (1987), who investigated the health and degree of religious involvement among a sample of elderly persons living in New Haven, Connecticut. Idler found that those persons with the highest levels of religious involvement showed the least depression and physical disability. In a subsequent study, Idler (1995) noted that religiousness could also be associated with poor health, as sick people use their religion to help them cope with their illness. Some patients feel prayer should be classified as a new domain of complementary and alternative medicine (Ayers and Kronenfeld 2010).

Most studies find that religion is associated with positive levels of health and lower mortality (Idler 2010; Scheitle and Adamczyk 2010; Sternthal et al. 2010). This may be because of its influence on health risk behaviors. According to Idler (2010:138–39): "Although most religious groups do not have specific teachings regarding many of the behavioral risk factors implicated in leading risk-factors for cardiovascular disease, cancer, and diabetes, an increasing number of large, representative, population-based studies show a consistent pattern of higher levels of religious participation being associated with lower levels of a number of risk behaviors, including smoking, alcohol and drug use, lack of physical activity, risky sexual practices, and high-fat diet." Thus religion likely promotes good health through encouraging positive health lifestyles practices and discouraging harmful habits like drinking and smoking, as well as providing comfort and social support in times of stress.

BOX 13.1

The Storefront Church

Mary Abrums (2000) interviewed a group of poor and working-class black women belonging to a storefront church in a rundown neighborhood in Seattle, Washington. She found these women were skeptical about their encounters with the health care system. For example, some of them had been paid to participate in clinical trials to test new drugs and medical procedures, but they rarely felt the research was for their benefit. Nevertheless, they developed an attitude that enabled them to better understand their experiences with physicians and feel in control over their own healing. They believed that the body was a gift from God and that only God, not doctors, had the ultimate authority over what happened to their health. They knew who was *really* in charge and that belief made them more comfortable with their illnesses and doctors. As one woman (Abrums 2000:104) reported:

> I admire doctors but they don't know it all. Doctors don't accept nothing they don't understand! Doctor said he was ready to sign my death certificate [the woman had a body temperature of 60 degrees], but I said, "Doctor, you don't know, because I'm not yours!"

The woman obviously survived and clearly her religion was a major resource in coping with her health problems.

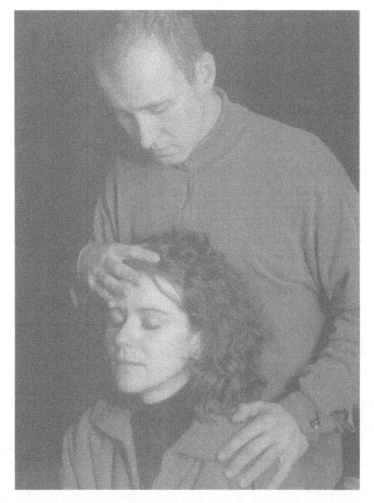

PHOTO 13.3 Some faith healers practice a type of touch healing known as the laying on of hands. It involves the healer attempting to direct healing energy into the person to cure imbalances believed to cause physical or mental illness or spiritual distress.

Folk Healing

Folk healers are not used to any significant extent in the United States except by some low-income persons usually belonging to racial and ethnic minority groups. Apparently, few non-Hispanic whites go to folk healers, although some elderly persons living in poverty and rural areas may be prone to use "folk remedies" in treating ailments. Common ingredients in folk remedies are such substances as ginger tea, whiskey, honey, sugar, lemon juice, baking soda, aspirin, peppers, garlic, kerosene, salt, butter, mustard, and sassafras (Baer 2001). Practicing folk healers are most likely to be found among African Americans, Hispanics, and American Indians.

Folk medicine is often regarded as a residue of health measures left over from prescientific historical periods (Bakx 1991). Yet, folk practices have persisted in modern societies, and the major reason appears to be dissatisfaction with professional medicine and a cultural gap between biomedical practitioners and particular patients (Baer 2001; Bakx 1991). These patients, typically low-income persons, may view folk medicine as a resource because it represents a body of knowledge about how to treat illness that has grown out of the historical experiences of their family and ethnic group.

African American Folk Healers

The tendency of some low-income black people to seek the services of lay practitioners rather than physicians is illustrated in the work of Loudell Snow (1978), who studied black folk healers in Chicago many years ago. Although this study is dated, it remains the most authoritative account of urban African American folk healers. Such healers and their patients, according to Snow, subscribe to a belief system that—unlike modern medicine—does not differentiate between science and religion. All life events, including illness, are viewed in relation to the total environment as either natural or unnatural, good or evil. Being healthy is an instance of good fortune, such as having a good job or a faithful spouse. Being sick is an example of misfortune, such as unemployment and marital strife. Thus, life is *generally* good or bad, and the cure for *one* problem, says Snow, might cure *all* problems.

Additionally, Snow notes that folk diagnosis of a health problem emphasizes the *cause* of the problem, not the symptoms. Having a body rash might initially be seen as stemming from a lack of cleanliness but comes to be defined as the result of black magic. In this belief system, what is important is not the rash, but what or who brought on the rash. Snow gives the example of a woman who died from bacterial meningitis, but her family viewed the ultimate cause of her death as punishment for her father's drinking and chasing after women.

Another prominent belief is that all illnesses can be cured, if not by medicine, then by magic. This belief is supported by the idea that illnesses are either natural or unnatural. Natural illnesses are those maladies caused by abusing the natural environment (e.g., staying out too late, eating too much, failing to wear warm clothing) or brought on as a punishment by God for sin or for not living up to the Lord's expectations. Thus, in the case of divine punishment, the afflicted person must make contact with God either directly or indirectly through an intermediary such as a faith healer. Praying and repenting, not taking antibiotics, is considered the cure for sin (Snow 1978:73).

Unnatural illnesses are outside of "God's plan" and beyond self-treatment or treatment prescribed by friends and relatives. And if the mind is affected, unnatural illnesses are thought to be beyond the capabilities of physicians, who are usually associated only with the treatment of natural illnesses that have obvious physical symptoms. The cause of an unnatural illness can be worry or stress, but often the etiology is ascribed to evil influences or acts of sorcery. When black magic is suspected, it is necessary to find a healer with unusual magic or religious powers, who can successfully intervene for the victim.

Snow observed that the term *healer* in Chicago's black community included a bewildering array of persons performing different healing roles. The variety of healers is reflected in the number of names used to describe them, such as healer, root doctor or root worker, reader, adviser, spiritualist, or conjure man or woman. If voodoo is practiced, a male healer may be called *houngan* or *papaloi,* and a female healer would be a *mambo* or *maraloi.* Few of them refer to themselves as "doctor," because healing is only part of their services. Instead, their given name is likely to be prefaced by a kinship, religious, or political title, such as Sister, Brother, Mother, Reverend, Bishop, Prophet, Evangelist, or Madam. These healers depend on word of mouth for patient referrals, or they may advertise by newspaper or leaflet. They claim to have received their ability to heal (1) as a result of learning (which confers little status because almost anyone can be expected to learn); (2) during an altered state of consciousness, such as a profound religious experience or a divine "call" to healing; or (3) at birth. Snow states (1978:79), "they will probably have in common only the assertion that the abilities are a gift from God."

Many folk healers do not require direct personal contact with the recipient of services but will conduct business over the telephone or by mail. If the individual's complaint involves sorcery, the use of some substance (such as oils, potions, or perfumes) will be required and may need to be purchased; if witchcraft is at work, a thought, prayer, or verbal spell is necessary. In the case of witchcraft, it might be necessary to purchase candles to assist the healer in effecting a solution. For example, when Snow (1978:99) complained in a letter to "Sister Marina" that she had problems sleeping and eating, was losing weight, and did not seem to enjoy life any more, Sister Marina replied in writing that Snow needed to contact her by telephone so she could better explain to her that her problem was "unnatural." Snow wrote back asking if Sister Marina could help her by mail and she received a warning by return mail that if she did not hurry it might be too late to save her. Sister Marina had written that she had to burn nine candles for Snow at a cost of $10 each for a total of $90 that must be received by her within the next eleven days or no one would be able to help.

How effective black folk healers like Marina are in treating their clients is not known. Some of these healers are likely to be frauds. Yet, the advantage they offer to their clients is that they are readily available, results are usually quick and sometimes guaranteed, and they claim to be able to solve any problem. Their abilities are supposed to be derived from divine authority and, if they fail, they can attribute the failure to the will of God. In essence, what black folk healers appear to accomplish is to reduce the anxieties of their clients, and they are most effective in dealing with health problems that have some emotional basis. What distinguishes their practice and is particularly significant in the reduction of anxiety is the recognition that health problems are an integral part of other problems of daily life (i.e., lack of money, a strayed spouse, loss of a job, or envious relatives or neighbors). Consequently, black folk healers treat the whole person, not just a single symptom, which is often the case with a physician. Moreover, physicians tend to charge significantly higher prices for their services, are not as readily available in low-income areas, and may be unable to show quick results because of the patient's delay in seeking treatment or the severity of the disorder, or both.

While the Snow study dealt with low-income black Americans living in an urban area, other data on similar blacks living in a rural setting point toward the same kind of pattern. Julian Roebuck and Robert Quan (1976) compared the health practices of 50 black and 50 white lower-class households in a small town in Mississippi. Although the white households tended to have a slightly higher average income, practically all of the households received supplemental income from public assistance and welfare programs. Overall educational levels for both black and white households were between the fifth and sixth grades, and those household members who were employed held jobs that were either semiskilled or unskilled. However, there were important differences when it came to seeking treatment for health problems. More white (68 percent) than black (48 percent) households sought health care only from physicians. More black (42 percent) than white (24 percent) households obtained care from a combination of practitioners—physicians, marginal healers (defined as chiropractors, pharmacists, podiatrists, and nurse-midwives) and illegal healers (defined as folk practitioners, spiritualists, and sorcerers). Somewhat more whites (8 percent) than blacks (4 percent) went to marginal healers only. As for illegal healers, 6 percent of the black households used this source only, compared to none of the white households.

In general, Roebuck and Quan found that lower-class blacks usually waited longer than lower-class whites before seeking the services of a healer when sick. Blacks were less oriented toward scientific medicine than whites and believed more in the effectiveness of illegal healers (who were sometimes used along with physicians). One black respondent, for example, stated: "The doctor thought I had a stroke because I couldn't move, but the hoodoo man said someone had placed stumbling blocks in front of me and he chased it away" (Roebuck and Quan 1976:157). Another black respondent said: "I saw Sister Cherokee [spiritualist] and she rubbed some olive oil on the back of my neck and told me I was suffering from high blood—exactly what the doctor told me!" (Roebuck and Quan 1976:157). Many of the blacks not only believed in the effectiveness of the illegal healers but had a corresponding lack of faith in physicians as well. None of the whites used the illegal healers in any capacity nor expressed confidence in their methods.

Other research conducted by Snow (1977, 1993) among lower-class blacks in a community in the southwest United States showed health practices similar to those found by Snow in Chicago and Roebuck and Quan in Mississippi. Sick people were typically channeled through a lay-referral system of family and neighbors to a source of medical treatment, which in many cases was not a physician. Sometimes physicians were consulted only as a last resort. Health in low-income African American communities was seen as the "ability to 'keep on keeping' on" (Snow 1993:73).

There are two distinct types of black folk healing in the United States: traditional and Caribbean. The traditional form has been discussed in this section. The Caribbean form consists of several variations, such as *Voodoo* (Haiti), *Santeria* (Cuba), and *Obeah* (West Indies). What each of these Caribbean approaches to folk healing have in common is that they are based on native African beliefs and are part of the Caribbean's past slave culture. Each uses rituals, charms, herbs, concoctions, and prayer to prevent or cure illness by healing the mind and spirit, along with the body (Baer 2001, 2010). These healing practices are all part of a larger system of religious and spiritual beliefs that are limited in the United States to small numbers of black Americans with ties to the Caribbean. Miami, New Orleans, Chicago, Philadelphia, and New York show the largest concentrations of these practitioners.

Curanderismo Healing

Male Mexican American folk healers are known as *curanderos* and females as *curanderas*. Like black folk healers, curanderos and curanderas blend religion and folk medicine into a single therapeutic approach. They likewise classify illnesses primarily on the basis of *what* causes the disorder rather than the symptoms, and they do not separate the natural from the supernatural when it comes to diagnosis and treatment. Most of their patients belong to the lower class. Unlike black folk healers, they do not charge for their services, or they charge very little. They may ask for a small donation (perhaps a dollar or two) for expenses, or they may accept a small gift such as vegetables or a chicken.

Curanderos and curanderas also emphasize religion to a much greater extent than most healers. There is a lack of current research, but in an older study Ari Kiev (1968) points out that religion, based upon a Spanish Catholic tradition, is central to the healing practices of the curandero. They believe life is ordained by the divinity, and good health and happiness can be achieved only by those who keep God's commandments. A patient who suffers, therefore, is seen as helping God's plan for the universe because it is believed that God allows people to suffer to learn. The example of Christ suffering on the cross is often used to illustrate that suffering and illness can be a worthwhile experience. Thus, the curandero views helping the patient accept suffering as a major task. In this context, suffering is explained as being part of the patient's burden for the world's sin and ignorance and a necessary role in God's plan for the universe. The more religious the curandero appears to be and the more convincing he or she is in influencing others to accept the will of God, the more highly regarded the curandero is as a healer. One effect the curandero uses to help accomplish this task is to establish a work setting that supports his or her image as a healer whose powers come from God, there is a special place in the home with religious objects, candles, and an altar. The setting is intended to represent the authority of the healer and increase the expectation of a cure.

Besides prayer and religious counseling, the curandero or curandera employs a variety of folk drugs and herbs to produce a cure (rattlesnake oil, mineral water, garlic, sweet basil, wild pitplant, licorice, camphor, etc.). To a large extent, this approach is based on sixteenth-century Spanish medicine, derived largely from Greek and Arabic sources and influenced by beliefs of the Mayans and Aztecs. Prevalent in this view is the Hippocratic notion of bodily equilibrium. Hippocrates, the famous physician of ancient Greece, believed that good health resulted from the equilibrium within the body of four humors: blood, phlegm, black bile, and yellow bile. Important, too, was the harmony of the body with living habits and the environment. As long as the four humors were in balance, the body was healthy. If an imbalance occurred and more of one type of humor than another was present, a person was sick. Because the body is perceived as being a mix of cold and hot conditions, curanderos and curanderas use "hot" foods and medicines to treat "cold" conditions (e.g., drowsiness, chills) and "cold" foods and medicines to treat "hot" conditions (e.g., fever, hypersexuality).

The most dreaded form of disorder, either physical or mental, is that caused by witchcraft. Witches, or *brujas,* are evil persons who supposedly have made pacts with the devil and use supernatural powers in the form of curses, magic, herbs, or ghosts to harm other people. According to William Madsen (1973), who studied Mexican Americans living in south Texas, conservative lower-class Mexican Americans showed an almost universal acceptance of the existence of witchcraft, even though belief in witchcraft is more strongly denounced than other folk theories of disease by the churches and in newspapers and schools. Hence, curanderos were needed to provide "good" power to offset "evil" influences.

Kiev (1968) points out that curanderismo persists in the American Southwest because it works in many cases. The advantage the curandero brings to the treatment setting is that he or she works in a subculture supportive of beliefs in the effectiveness of the curandero's methods. Especially important is the anxiety-reducing approach of the curandero, carried out within the context of family and friends that defines the treatment as therapeutic and positive according to the norms and values of the Mexican American community. While Anglos may view illness as impersonal and unemotional in origin and caused by germs, lower-class Mexican Americans may see illness as related to one's interpersonal relationships, community life, and religion.

American Indian Healing: The Navajos and the Cree

There are few studies of American Indian healers. Exceptions are Jerrold Levy's (1983) research on Navajo health beliefs and practices in Arizona and that of Janice Morse, David Young, and Lise Swartz (1991) among the Cree in Canada. Levy notes that the rituals associated with traditional Navajo religion are predominantly health-oriented and stem from an emphasis upon enhancing the well-being of the hunter. The principal figure in these rituals is the *singer,* whose knowledge of ceremonies is obtained through several years of apprenticeship with another practitioner. The singer, who is the most prestigious person among Navajo healers, is the ceremonial leader in rituals that may last several days and are intended to drive out of the body whatever is causing the illness. Diseases, according to traditional beliefs, are thought to be caused by soul loss, witchcraft, spirit possession, or improper behavior such as violating a tribal taboo. The singer is assisted by the *diviner* (or the singer may fill both functions), whose role is to diagnose illness and whose ability is believed to be a special gift. Upon making a diagnosis, the diviner may refer the patient to the singer, who performs the ceremony appropriate for the diagnosis. There are also *herbalists* and *bone setters* in Navajo communities who have knowledge of a practical nature about how to treat various common ailments and injuries.

Levy found that the number of singers has been declining over the years because fewer men (healers are males) are able to devote their time to learning the chants because they also must earn a living. In Levy's view, the demands of a wage work economy and education about modern health practices may cause traditional healing to disappear. Furthermore, the large traditional healing ceremonies last from five to nine nights and involve many guests, so the practice is expensive for families with limited incomes. Some Navajos have substituted the peyote rituals of the Native American church for traditional ceremonies because these rituals serve the same purpose, last only one night, are more economical, and are consistent with basic Navajo beliefs about harmony with nature and the supernatural.

Similar to black folk healers and curanderos, Navajo healers are primarily concerned with the cause of an illness rather than its symptoms. In fact, Levy found it difficult to determine precisely what role symptoms play in diagnosis. Levy (1983:132) states:

> No Navajo disease is known by the symptoms it produces or by the part of the body it is thought to affect. Rather, there is bear sickness and porcupine sickness, named for the agents thought to cause them; or there is "that which is treated by the Shooting Chant," so named by the ceremonials used to cure it. Because the traditional health culture does not rely upon knowledge of symptoms in the diagnostic process, Navajo patients often have difficulty understanding the purpose of history taking and physical examination, a circumstance that often leads to misunderstanding in the clinical setting.

Nevertheless, Navajos do recognize illness by personal discomfort, and some symptoms have meaning for them. Also certain types of healing ceremonies are associated with certain symptoms and not others, as some ceremonies are used to treat a broad range of symptoms. So knowledge and logic linking causes to solutions are an inherent feature of Navajo medicine, and symptoms play a part in deciding which ritual to use.

Levy indicates that Navajos will often use both native healers and physicians because of the belief that modern medicine will remove symptoms and Navajo medicine will remove the cause of the illness. Among Christian Navajos, the tendency is to combine modern medicine with prayer and not go to native healers. Levy suggests that about half of the Navajo population uses physicians exclusively, about 40 percent use a combination of native healers and physicians, and 10 percent use native practitioners only. Fractures, cuts, and childbirth were treated most often by doctors, while fainting, vague symptoms, or culturally defined illnesses without symptoms were never treated by physicians alone. Because the use of native healers conjointly with physicians was common, it was difficult to determine the effectiveness of traditional medicine, but Levy maintained that utilization of native healers was due more to a lack of access to medical facilities and poor communication with doctors than to adherence to native beliefs. The major factor affecting frequency of hospital use, for example, was distance from the hospital on a reservation the size of West Virginia. The declining number of singers, the growing tendency to shorten traditional ceremonies, the gradual replacement of herbalists by physicians among the population, and health education in the schools all point toward a demise in native healing for the Navajos.

In Canada, Morse and her colleagues (1991) identified five phases in the healing ceremony of the Cree tribe. First was an initial ritual in which the healer, other people serving as the healer's spiritual helpers, and the patient participated. A ceremonial pipe was passed around three times to all who were present, and smoke from a smoldering fungus, sage, or sweetgrass was carried around the room four times in a clockwise direction. This activity was a process of purification intended to open channels of communication to the spirit world and to attract the attention of the Great Spirit. Purification is intended to foster a receptive attitude among the participants and place the healer in a position of control. All movements by the healer are clockwise, and like rituals in other Native American tribes (Avery 1991; Baer 2001) are oriented toward maintaining harmony with nature. Second came a contract phase in which the patient formally requests healing, and the healer agrees to mediate with the Great Spirit on behalf of the patient.

Third was the treatment component. This phase consisted of the patient drinking herbal tea and having a herbal solution applied to his or her skin. Throughout this stage, the healer provides vivid descriptions of what the medicine is doing to the cause of the disease, thereby providing visual imagery intended to facilitate the healing process in the patient's mind. Furthermore, the healer constantly offers reassurance to the patient that the treatment is effective and many people in worse condition have been healed in the past. The final treatment consists of a sweat-lodge ceremony in which the patient sits in the dark around a pit of heated rocks and absorbs steam from herbally medicated water that is sprinkled on the stones. The healer sings and occasionally conveys messages to the patient from the spirit world. The fourth phase, which Morse and her colleagues call didactic, consists of the healer educating the patient about the healing process and the effectiveness of the treatment. And, finally, in the fifth phase, closure, the healer ends the healing but assures the patient of the continued healing and support of the Great Spirit.

Cree healing, like folk healing generally, treats the whole person, not just particular symptoms. It is probably effective at reducing anxiety, as the methods are consistent with Cree cultural beliefs. Moreover, the sweat-lodge ceremony may be especially helpful for some respiratory ailments. Morse and her colleagues found, however, that the Cree have low rates of physician utilization and relatively poor health.

Summary

This chapter has examined the role and function of alternative healers and alternative medicine in American society. Apart from osteopaths, such healers continue to maintain themselves because there is a demand for their services. Chiropractors, in fact, represent the second largest category (behind medical doctors) of primary health care practitioners in the United States, but they are not generally accepted by the medical profession. Folk healers work generally among persons from low-income backgrounds and racial minority group status. They provide a service consistent with the cultural beliefs of the people who go to them. Many people combine medicine with prayer, but faith healers actively work to achieve recovery from illness and injury through spiritual means. Some religious groups believe in working with doctors, while a few reject medical treatment as incompatible with their beliefs. Excluding osteopaths, the role and function of alternative healers are to meet the health needs of those persons not helped by professional medicine. Generally, these are persons who are not affluent or well educated, with the exception of middle- and upper-class individuals who utilize so-called "new age" therapies and diet supplements.

Critical Thinking Questions

1. What social classes are more likely to use various forms of complementary and alternative medicine and why?
2. Explain how religiosity influences health.
3. Why is CAM often not accepted by the medical profession and how has the profession reacted to its increased popularity?

Suggested Readings

Idler, Ellen L. (2010) "Health and Religion," pp. 159–183 in *The New Blackwell Companion to Medical Sociology*, William Cockerham (ed.). Oxford, UK: Wiley-Blackwell.
Excellent discussion of the relationship between religion and health from a sociological perspective.

References

Abrums, Mary (2000) "Jesus will fix it after a while: Meanings and health." *Social Science and Medicine* 50: 89–105.

Allen, Gillian, and Roy Wallis (1976) "Pentecostalists as a medical minority," pp. 110–37 in *Marginal medicine*, R. Wallis and P. Morley (eds.). New York: The Free Press.

Avery, Charlene (1991) "Native American medicine: Traditional healing." *JAMA* 265: 2271, 2273.

Ayers, Stephanie L., and Jennie J. Kronenfeld (2010) "Using factor analysis to create complementary and alternative medicine domains: An examination of patterns of use." *Health* 14: 234–52.

Baer, Hans A. (2001) *Biomedicine and alternative healing systems in America: Issues of class, race, ethnicity, and gender.* Madison, WI: University of Wisconsin Press.

Baer, Hans A. (2010) "Complementary and alternative medicine: Processes of legitimation, professionalization, and cooption," pp. 373–90 in *The new Blackwell companion to medical sociology*, W. Cockerham (ed.). Oxford, UK: Wiley-Blackwell.

Baer, Hans A., Cindy Jen, Lucia M. Tanassi, Christopher Tsia, and Helen Wahbeh (1998) "The drive for professionalization in acupuncture: A preliminary view from the San Francisco Bay Area." *Social Science and Medicine* 46: 537–53.

Bakx, Keith (1991) "The 'eclipse' of folk medicine in western society." *Sociology of Health & Illness* 13: 20–38.

Brenton, Joslyn, and Sinikka Elliott (2014) "Undoing gender? The case of complementary and alternative medicine." *Sociology of Health & Illness* 36: 91–107.

Davis, Matthew A., Todd A. McKenzie, Ian D. Coulter, James M. Whedon, and William B. Weeks (2012) "The United States chiropractic workforce: An alternative or complement to primary care." *Chiropractic & Manual Therapies* 20:35.

Denton, John A. (1978) *Medical sociology.* Boston: Houghton Mifflin.

Foote-Ardah, Carrie E. (2003) "The meaning of complementary and alternative medicine practices among people with HIV in the United States: Strategies for managing everyday life." *Sociology of Health & Illness* 25: 481–500.

Fraser, Caroline (1999) *God's perfect child: Living and dying in the Christian Science Church.* New York: Metropolitan Books/Henry Holt.

Glik, Deborah C. (1990) "The redefinition of the situation: The social construction of spiritual healing experiences." *Sociology of Health & Illness* 12: 151–68.

Goldner, Melinda (2004) "The dynamic interplay between Western medicine and the complementary and alternative medicine movement: How activists perceive a range of responses from physicians and hospitals." *Sociology of Health & Illness* 26: 710–36.

Goldstein, Michael S. (2000) "The growing acceptance of complementary and alternative medicine," pp. 284–97 in *Handbook of medical sociology*, 5th ed., C. Bird, P. Conrad, and A. Fremont (eds.). Upper Saddle River, NJ: Prentice Hall.

Grzywacz, Joseph G., Cynthia K. Suerken, Rebecca H. Neiberg, Wei Lang, Ronny A. Bell, Sara A. Quandt, and Thomas A. Arcury (2007) "Age, ethnicity, and use of complementary and alternative medicine in health self-management." *Journal of Health and Social Behavior* 48: 84–98.

Idler, Ellen L. (1987) "Religious involvement and the health of the elderly: Some hypotheses and an initial test." *Social Forces* 66: 226–38.

—— (1995) "Religion, health, and nonphysical senses of self." *Social Forces* 74: 683–704.

Jackson, Sue, and Graham Scambler (2007) "Perceptions of evidence-based medicine: Traditional acupuncturists in the UK and resistance to biomedical modes of evaluation." *Sociology of Health & Illness* 29: 412–29.

Kelner, Merrijoy, Beverly Wellman, Bernice Pescosolido, and Mike Saks (2000) *Complementary and alternative medicine: Challenge and change.* Amsterdam: Harwood.

Kiev, Ari (1968) *Curanderismo: Mexican-American folk psychiatry.* New York: The Free Press.

Leiser, David (2003) "Support for non-conventional medicine in Israel: Cognitive and sociological coherence." *Sociology of Health & Illness* 25: 457–80.

Lesho, Emil P. (1999) "An overview of osteopathic medicine." *Archives of Family Medicine* 8: 477–84.

Levy, Jerrold E. (1983) "Traditional Navajo health beliefs and practices," pp. 118–78 in *Disease change and the role of medicine: The Navajo experience*, J. Kunitz (ed.). Berkeley: University of California Press.

Madsen, William (1973) *The Mexian-Americans of south Texas*, 2nd ed. New York: Holt, Rinehart & Winston.

Morse, Janice M., David E. Young, and Lise Swartz (1991) "Cree Indian healing practices and Western health care: A comparative analysis." *Social Science and Medicine* 32: 1361–66.

Musick, Marc A., James S. House, and David R. Williams (2004) "Attendance at religious services and mortality in a national sample." *Journal of Health and Social Behavior* 45: 198–213.

Roebuck, Julian, and Robert Quan (1976) "Health-care practices in the American Deep South," pp. 141–61 in *Marginal medicine*, R. Wallis and P. Morely (eds.). New York: The Free Press.

Saks, Mike (2003) *Orthodox and alternative medicine.* London: Sage.

Scheitle, Christopher P., and Amy Adamczyk (2010) "High-cost religion, religious switching, and health." *Journal of Health and Social Behavior* 51: 325–42.

Schneirov, Matthew, and Jonathan David Geczik (1996) "A diagnosis for our times: Alternative health's submerged networks and the transformation of identities." *Sociological Quarterly* 37: 627–44.

Segar, Julia (2011) "Complementary and alternative medicine: Exploring the gap between evidence and usage." *Health* 16: 366–81.

Shippee, Tetyana Pylypiv, Markus H. Schafer, and Kenneth F. Ferraro (2012) "Beyond the barriers: Racial discrimination and use of complementary and alternative medicine among Black Americans." *Social Science and Medicine* 74: 1155–62.

Shuval, Judith T., Nissim Mizrachi, and Emma Smetannikov (2002) "Entering the well-guarded fortress: Alternative practitioners in hospital settings." *Social Science and Medicine* 55: 1745–55.

Snow, Loudell F. (1978) "Sorcerers, saints and charlatans: Black folk healers in urban America." *Culture, Medicine, and Psychiatry* 2: 69–106.

——— (1993) *Walkin' over medicine.* Boulder, CO: Westview Press.

Sternthal, Michelle J., David R. Williams, Marc A. Musick, and Anna C. Buck (2010) "Depression, anxiety, and religious life: A search for mediators." *Journal of Health and Social Behavior* 51: 343–59.

Theberge, Nancy (2008) "The integration of chiropractors into healthcare teams: A case study from sports medicine." *Sociology of Health & Illness* 30: 19–34.

Vitello, Paul (2010) "Christian Science Church seeks truce with modern medicine." *New York Times* (March 23): A20.

PART 5

Health Care Delivery Systems

CHAPTER 14

The Hospital in Society

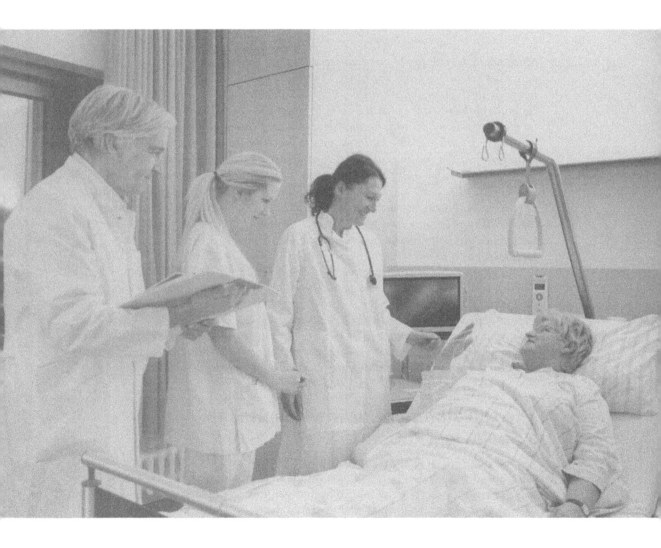

- Trace the development of the hospital as a social institution.

- Evaluate the dual authority system of hospitals.

- Compare the hospital patient role to the sick role.

Since many health problems require a level of medical treatment and personal care that extends beyond the range of services normally available in the patient's home or in the physician's office, modern society has developed formal institutions for patient care intended to help meet the more complex health needs of its members. The hospital, the major social institution for the delivery of health care, offers considerable advantages to both patient and society.[1] From the standpoint of the individual, the sick or injured person has access to centralized medical knowledge and the greatest array of technology in hospitals. From the standpoint of society, as Talcott Parsons and Renée Fox (1952) suggest, hospitalization both protects the family from many of the disruptive effects of caring for the ill in the home and operates as a means of guiding the sick and injured into medically supervised institutions where their problems are less disruptive for society as a whole.

The purpose of this chapter is to consider the social role of the hospital. Besides serving the prescribed social function of providing medical treatment, hospitals can be viewed from the perspective of a functionally specific world. This chapter will examine the organizational aspects of that world in the following order: (1) development of the hospital as a social institution; (2) the hospital system in the United States; (3) social organization of hospital work, including its effect on the patient role; and (4) the rising cost of hospital services.

The Development of the Hospital as a Social Institution

The development of hospitals as institutions providing medical services for the general public proceeded in pace with prevailing needs, beliefs, values, and attitudes of the societies they served. This is seen in the evolution of the hospital's role in society over time. Historically, hospitals have passed through four distinct phases of development: (1) as centers of religious practice; (2) as poorhouses; (3) as deathhouses; and (4) as centers of medical technology.

---

[1]A hospital is defined as a facility with at least six beds that is licensed by the state as a hospital or that is operated as a hospital by a federal or a state agency.

Hospitals as Centers of Religious Practice

Although the Romans were the first to establish separate medical facilities (for economic and military reasons) that have been described as hospitals, the origin of the institution we know today as the hospital has usually been associated with the rise of Christianity. Christian theology emphasized that human beings were duty bound to provide assistance to the sick and needy. This belief was reinforced by the notion that spiritual salvation could be obtained by whoever provided such a service. Consequently, the Roman Catholic Church encouraged its clergy to found hospitals, located near churches as an integral feature of Christian religious endeavor. Furthermore, during the period of the Crusades (between 1096 and 1291), many hospitals were established along the routes to the Holy Land followed by the Christian armies. Secular benefactors, such as kings, queens, and other members of the nobility, wealthy merchants, artisan and craftsmen's guilds, and municipalities also founded hospitals. By the end of the fifteenth century, an extensive network of hospitals existed throughout Western Europe.

The medieval hospital, however, was not a hospital by any modern standard. True, these hospitals were community centers for the care of the lower-class sick. The medical care, supervised and largely performed by clergy and nuns, consisted primarily of a rudimentary form of nursing. The primary functions of the medieval hospital were the exercise of religious practices and the extension of charity and welfare services to the poor, including both the able-bodied and the sick. These early hospitals, therefore, provided a wide spectrum of social tasks for the benefit of the lower classes, especially the provision of food, shelter, sanctuary, and prayer as well as nursing.

During the Renaissance and the Reformation, the religious character of the hospital began to disappear, as increasing numbers of hospitals were placed under the jurisdiction of secular authorities. Nevertheless, as Rodney Coe (1978) has observed, three basic features of the modern hospital are derived from the influence of the Church. First, the concept of being service oriented toward helping others has become a guiding principle for the manner in which hospital personnel are required to approach their work. Second, hospitals are supposed to have a "universalistic" approach—that is, to accept for treatment all people who may be sick or injured. And third, the custodial nature of hospital care has been facilitated by housing patients within the confines of a single location.

Hospitals as Poorhouses

The secular control of hospitals marked a period of decline for the development of Europe's hospital system. Even though monks and nuns continued to work in hospitals, the removal of the centralized authority of the Church left hospitals under many separate administrations, usually those of municipal governments. Without general regulations pertaining to hospital administration, individual hospitals were free to pursue any course of action they desired. This situation encouraged abuse, particularly in regard to neglect of facilities, misappropriation of funds, and the lowering of prevailing standards of patient care. In England, the suppression of the monastery system in the mid-1500s led to the collapse of the English hospital system as many hospitals, left without personnel or money, were forced to close. The few remaining hospitals limited their services to people who were actually sick and who could be cured. While this policy relegated the poor, both the incurably ill and the able-bodied, to poorhouses or to the streets for their support, it marked the beginning of a new definition of hospitals as institutions active in treating the sick and injured so that they could return to society.

However, by the end of the sixteenth century, the economic and social conditions of the poor worsened to a considerable degree. Unemployment, higher prices, and the loss of land created a serious problem of vagrancy throughout Europe. Many vagrants claimed to be sick or crippled, and they crowded whatever hospital facilities were available. In accordance with the new definition of social welfare as a community rather than a church responsibility, measures were eventually taken by city and national authorities to provide public assistance. Many hospitals were reopened, but they soon acquired the characteristics of boarding houses, because they offered food and shelter to the poor, regardless of whether they were sick or healthy. Those persons living in hospitals who could work were required to pay for their lodging, while hospitals received further financial support through public taxation. Hospitals became little more than social "warehouses," where invalids, the aged, orphans, and the mentally defective could be sent and thus removed from the mainstream of society. Even today in the United States, people with chronic health problems requiring long-term hospitalization—the insane, the incurable, and individuals suffering from highly infectious diseases—tend to be sent to public institutions, whereas private hospitals tend to accept patients with acute disorders. And some hospitals, such as Cook County in Chicago, Philadelphia General, Bellevue and Kings County in New York, and San Francisco General, were established as institutions for the poor.

Hospitals as Deathhouses

Following the Renaissance and the Reformation, the outward character of hospitals appeared to change little from that of public institutions, whose purpose was to provide welfare services for the lower social classes on behalf of the communities in which they were located. Nonetheless, changes were taking place as physicians discovered that hospitals contained large numbers of sick and injured (and also generally powerless) people whose health problems could be studied and upon whom the various evolving techniques of medical treatment could be practiced.

Physicians had first begun to associate themselves with hospitals during the fourteenth century. Initially, they had little influence because they were not members of the hospital staff and provided their services on a purely voluntary basis. By the seventeenth century, however, physicians acquired a virtual monopoly over the existing body of medical knowledge that placed them in the position of first advising and eventually directing all patient care within the hospital. As physicians became increasingly influential, nonmedical hospital tasks gradually disappeared. By the early nineteenth century, hospitals had clearly assumed their present-day role as institutions for medical care, for medical research, and for the education of medical students.

Although medical treatment was recognized as the primary function of the hospital in the eighteenth century, the primitive level of that treatment produced few cures. Trained physicians were unable to achieve consistent results with their techniques, and accordingly, neither they nor hospitals were held in high esteem by the general population. Because so few patients survived treatment, despite occasional heroic efforts, hospitals acquired an image as places where the poor went to die.

According to Coe (1978), the high death rate in hospitals was also related to the appalling living conditions provided for patients. Typically, hospitals were dirty, poorly ventilated, and filled to capacity. Often, more than one patient was placed in a single bed, regardless of the patient's disorder, and treatment was usually carried out publicly on the ward itself. Surgery, which Coe points out was limited at that time mostly to amputations and childbirth, plus the purging of fevers with various potions, bloodletting to eliminate "excess" blood, and the removal of the dead, all occurred in the same general area where patients ate and slept. Nor did the attending physicians and surgeons practice even the most rudimentary standards of sanitation, moving from bed to bed and treating a great variety of diseases, including those that were infectious, without washing their hands or changing their clothes. Thus, it is not surprising that hospitals were regarded by most people as places where only the lower social classes went to die.

Hospitals as Centers of Medical Technology

Since the end of the nineteenth century, a new image of hospitals evolved as institutions where patients of all social classes could generally expect to find the highest quality medical care and could reasonably expect to be cured of their disorders. Three major factors were responsible for this change. First was the fact that medicine had indeed become a science in terms of employing the scientific method to seek out accurate medical knowledge and to develop successful techniques that could be employed in a consistent manner. Of particular importance were increased knowledge about human physiology and the development of the science of bacteriology. Also important was the perfection of ether as an anesthetic, which allowed surgery to be performed in a relatively painless fashion. Because the new medical technology required extensive and often expensive facilities, these facilities were centralized in hospitals so that they could be available to most physicians. Hospitals eventually became places where physicians also referred their upper- and middle-class patients, since the most advanced medical technology was located there. While the poor generally remained in a charity status as hospital patients, a new type of patient came into being—the private patient—who required private accommodation, who usually had a private physician, and who paid for hospital services.

A second important factor, concomitant with the development of medical technology, was the discovery and use of antiseptic measures in the hospital to help curtail infection. Hospitals were not only properly cleaned and ventilated but also patients with infectious diseases were isolated in special areas of the hospital, and hospital staffs were required to wash their hands and change their clothing after working with these patients. The use of such items as surgical masks, rubber gloves, and sterilized surgical instruments became commonplace. These procedures not only reduced the number of deaths among hospital patients but also reduced the amount of time required for patient recovery.

Third, there was a significant improvement in the quality of hospital personnel. Especially important was the entry on to the scene of the trained nurse and the laboratory technician, whose specialized skills were able to support the physician in his or her primary role of diagnostician and practitioner. As Charles Rosenberg (1987) pointed out, in his historical analysis of the development of American hospitals, no single change has transformed the day-to-day work in a hospital more than trained nurses. In the twentieth century, the hospital has become the major institutional resource available to society for coping with problems of health and illness.

Hospitals in the United States

The first hospitals were founded in the United States more than 250 years ago. Generally, their development paralleled that of Western European institutions in the 1700s. The first such hospital was established by William Penn in Philadelphia in 1713, with the care of the sick being incidental to the main purpose of providing shelter for the poor. Charity Hospital in New Orleans was founded by the Catholic Church in 1737, for similar reasons. The first hospital to be established in the United States solely for the purpose of treating the sick was the Pennsylvania Hospital, founded by Benjamin Franklin and a group of interested citizens in 1751. These early hospitals were not governmental undertakings but were largely based on voluntary initiative by private citizens who wanted medical care available on a nonprofit basis. They were generally intended to provide treatment for patients who had curable disorders.

Federal government participation in health care did not actually begin until 1798, with the U.S. Public Health Service hospital program for merchant seamen. State governments did not enter into health care delivery until the 1800s, and their efforts were largely confined to the establishment of state mental institutions. By 1873, there were only 178 hospitals of all types in the United States—in 2011, the number of hospitals was 5,724.

Hospital Ownership

The ownership of hospitals in the United States may be classified into three major types: (1) nonprofit, (2) for profit, or (3) government (local, state, or federal). Table 14.1 shows the number of hospitals for the years 1975–2011. The figures

PHOTO 14.2 Founded in 1751, Philadelphia's Pennsylvania Hospital was the first general hospital in America.

in Table 14.1 show that the total number of hospitals has fallen from 7,156 in 1975 to 5,724 in 2011. Table 14.1 indicates that 208 (less than 4 percent) of the hospitals were owned by the federal government, while 5,516 (more than 96 percent) were nonfederal. Table 14.1 also shows that 4,913 or 86 percent of all hospitals are classified as community or short-stay hospitals, in which patients are expected to stay only for a few days or weeks. The most common type of hospital in the United States is the nonfederal and nonprofit community hospital. Nonprofit hospitals numbered 2,903 in 2011, representing 51 percent of all American hospitals.

Controlled by a board of trustees, nonprofit hospitals are exempt from federal income taxes and many other forms of state and local taxes. These hospitals have generally been characterized as emphasizing high-quality care for all social classes. Nonprofit hospitals are highly dependent on community physicians for membership on their staffs and for the referral of patients. Large nonprofit hospitals, however, are less dependent than smaller hospitals on local physicians, because of more extensive facilities and a higher ratio of staff positions for doctors.

Table 14.1 shows that 1,025 community hospitals (18 percent of the total) were classified in 2011, as for profit. Preliminary figures for 2014, not shown in Table 14.1, indicate that the number of for-profit hospitals increased even further that year to 1,068, making the for-profit sector the most significant category of community hospital expansion in 2010–14. In the past, these hospitals have usually been small and highly dependent on local physicians for staff membership and patient referrals, but this has changed. Paul Starr's (1982) research demonstrated that the trend for profit-making hospitals is to merge into a multihospital chain owned by a large corporation. In this situation, physicians on the hospital staff are generally employees of the corporation, but doctors outside the hospital are encouraged to also place their patients in the profit-making hospitals through incentives such as hospital staff privileges and higher-quality care for their patients by the hospital staff. The usual source of income for profit-making hospitals is internal and generated from patient care, especially payments from private insurance companies.

TABLE 14.1 Types of Hospitals, United States, 1975–2011

Type of Ownership	Number				
	1975	1980	1990	2000	2011
Total	7,156	6,965	6,649	5,810	5,724
Federal	382	359	337	245	208
Nonfederal	6,774	6,606	6,312	5,565	5,516
Community	5,875	5,830	5,384	4,9359	4,913
Nonprofit	3,339	3,322	3,191	3,003	2,903
For profit	775	730	749	749	1,025
State-local government	1,761	1,778	1,444	1,063	1,045

Source: National Center for Health Statistics, 2014.

The number of state and local government-owned community hospitals in Table 14.1 for 2011 is 1,045, which is about 19 percent of the total. Government hospitals tend to lack prestige in comparison to other hospitals. They are the major source of health care for people with low incomes, particularly in urban areas. Government hospitals place their emphasis on public access to their facilities. Yet, the increased affiliation of government hospitals with medical schools portends a shift in emphasis toward quality care and modern facilities. Nevertheless, America's hospital system remains a two-class system of medical care—one primarily for the relatively affluent and the other generally serving the less affluent in state and local government hospitals.

The Organization of the Nonprofit Community Hospital

Certainly not all hospitals are alike in their organization of services, but nonprofit community hospitals, as the most common single type of hospital in the United States, exhibit the organizational features of many hospitals. Figure 14.1 shows an example of an organizational chart for a large nonprofit community hospital. The organization chart depicted in Figure 14.1 is the basic framework for this type of hospital. Many such hospitals today also have satellite outpatient clinics, affiliated group practices, smaller hospitals, and management organizations providing administrative services to physicians, and they employ primary care doctors as part of their physician network (Rundall, Shortell, and Alexander 2004; Wright and Perry 2010). Such hospitals have been described as "multipurpose institutions," in that they provide a variety of health-related functions such as: (1) treating patients; (2) providing laboratories and other medical facilities to the community; (3) training health practitioners; (4) conducting medical research; and (5) sponsoring health education and preventive medicine programs for the general public. The *primary* goal of the hospital, however, is that of providing medical treatment to its patients within the limits of contemporary medical knowledge and technology and the hospital's available resources.

To accomplish its tasks and coordinate its various activities, the hospital relies on a prescribed hierarchy of authority (Figure 14.1), which is operationalized through formal rules, regulations, and administrative procedures. The key to hospital efficiency and overall effectiveness is coordination of the various departments and individuals. They represent a complex and highly specialized division of labor that is both interlocking and interdependent.

Consider what happens when a staff doctor prescribes medication for a patient. The doctor's order for medication is written in the patient's medical records by the doctor, a nurse or floor clerk and sent to the pharmacy. When the medication is provided by the pharmacy, it is most likely administered by a nurse. A record is then forwarded to the accounting office so that the charges for the drug can be entered on the patient's bill; another written order might be sent from the pharmacy to purchasing (through the appropriate administrative channels) to reorder the medication and replace it for future use by another patient. So the rather routine activity

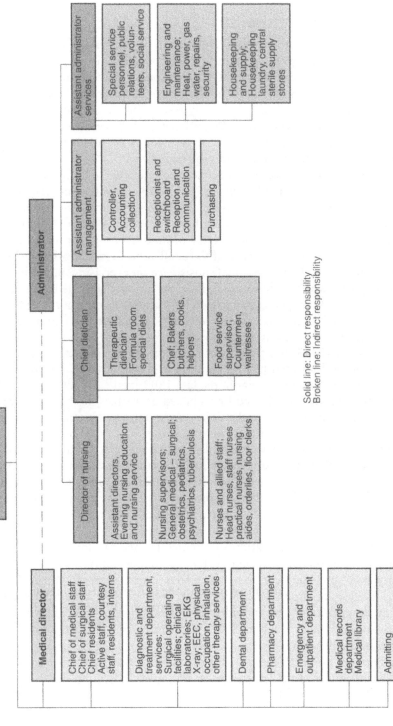

FIGURE 14.1

Typical Large Nonprofit Community Hospital Organized into Five Divisions.

Source: Technology and Manpower in the Health Service Industry (1967).

of one particular member of the hospital staff (in this case a doctor) initiates a chain of events that affects the work of several other hospital employees.

The Hospital: Dual Authority

According to Figure 14.1, the overall supervision of the general hospital comes under the auspices of its governing body. In most nonfederal hospitals, that governing body is a board of trustees. Figure 14.1 also shows that although the medical director and the hospital administrator are linked to the governing body by a direct line of responsibility, they are only indirectly responsible to each other. What this type of arrangement indicates is that the authority system of the general hospital operates on a dual level. This system is an outgrowth of the organizational conflict in the hospital between bureaucracy and professionalism.

It has been noted that Max Weber's concept of bureaucracy is not totally compatible with the norms of hospital authority (Hillier 1987). Weber described bureaucracy as a rational and impersonal division of labor characterized by the principles of *office hierarchy* and levels of graded authority (lower offices are supervised by higher ones) and by *fixed and official areas of jurisdiction* governed by laws or administrative regulations. The essence of the conflict between bureaucracy and the professional consists of the professional's insistence on exercising an autonomous individual judgment, while the bureaucrat (here, the hospital administrator) seeks to follow a rationalistic management approach that favors the efficient coordination of the hospital's activities through formal rules and impersonal regulations applicable to all persons in all situations.

Charles Perrow (1963) has traced the evolution of this conflict in his study of one voluntary general hospital he believes to be representative of most other hospitals of this type. Perrow noted that in the late 1800s and early 1900s, the voluntary general hospital was dominated by its board of trustees, because this was an era when securing capital funds and gaining community recognition were critical hospital goals. Because community involvement was the pivotal factor, individual members of boards of trustees were usually laypersons selected at large from the community. Legally they were responsible for protecting the community's interests, but they also sought to incorporate hospital services into the general pattern of community life. Perrow believes this approach ultimately derives from seventeenth-century attitudes toward hospitals as state institutions operated on public funds, that is, as community welfare agencies and poorhouses.

In the 1930s, trustee domination succumbed to medical domination. Perrow cites three major reasons for this change: First, the emphasis on free care declined significantly as hospital services became oriented toward patients who could pay; second, the facilities to support a complex system of medical technology were developed, and the quality of care provided to patients was improved; and third, the hospital sought prestige through medical research in terms defined by physicians. Hence, medical domination went hand in hand with increasing medical knowledge. During this period, however, Perrow also noted the appearance of several abuses that could be attributed to the great personal power of the medical director and department heads. Especially deficient was the outpatient care afforded to people with low incomes. Also conspicuous was the favoritism shown toward certain physicians in the use of hospital facilities and staff promotions.

What was needed, said Perrow, was a system to limit these powers, to establish objective criteria for promotion and to provide for more effective representation of patient and organizational interests. This system gradually emerged during the 1940s and 1950s, as the role of hospital administrator gained in importance. Through a constitutional system, the administration was able to define limits on the medical staff's power, standardize the hospital's administrative procedures, and establish a level of quality for the hospital's medical services. These early administrators were often physicians who could be expected to further the interests of the medical staff, but in doing so began to curtail their power. As authority became centralized in the administrator's office, there often developed a blockage of communication between the staff and the board of trustees. This period, according to Perrow, was characterized by a complex power struggle that eventually led, in the 1950s, to a system of multiple leadership common among general hospitals today, with some modification. The modification is the decline in control (since the 1980s) over the work of the hospital by doctors, as they are subjected to the hospital's fiscal policies and cost control measures, government regulations, and corporate procedures (in the case of corporate-owned facilities where the physician is an employee).

Multiple leadership, at least in its hospital version, is actually a system of dual authority, one administrative and the other medical. The separate billing of hospitalized patients by the hospital and the doctor reflects this duality. Perrow notes the high probability of such a system developing in the hospital, because goals are generally multiple (trustees, administration, and medical staff often have diverse interests), the criteria for achieving them are broad, and the power of each group to protect its interests is considerable. Because the physician's professional norms can set specific limits on the hospital administrator's authority and vice versa, the result has been to reconcile the physician–professional with the administrator–bureaucrat, by establishing a system of dual authority.

The board of trustees still remains the nominal center of authority in the general hospital. It usually meets on a periodic basis, weekly or monthly, to review the hospital's operations act upon matters brought to its attention and plan for the future (Alexander, Lee, Weiner, and Ye 2006). Generally, the trustees themselves are people who are influential in the wider community. But despite their position as the hospital's ultimate source of authority, the trustees have only limited de facto authority over the medical staff, who usually make all health-related decisions. The board of trustees typically concerns itself with administrative matters and public relations while working closely with the hospital administrator, who acts as their agent in exercising authority and supervising the day-to-day routine of the hospital.

The occupational groups in the hospital most affected by its system of dual authority are the nurses and auxiliary nursing workers who perform health care tasks on the hospital's wards. Nurses are responsible to the physician for carrying out the physician's orders, but they are also responsible to the nursing supervisors and the upper echelons of the hospital's administration. Even though the communication and allegiance of ward personnel tend to be channeled along occupational lines within and toward the "administrative channel of command," medical authority can and does cut across these lines. While this system can at times cause stress, inconsistency, overlapping of responsibility, and inadequate coordination, it also allows ward personnel to pit one authority against the other, if one appears unreasonable and acts to reduce organizational inflexibility and authoritarianism. Given the high degree of functional specialization and professionalism, the hospital's system of dual authority may well be necessary. Hospital personnel share a common goal of providing quality patient care through competency, devotion to duty, and hard work, qualities that have the effect of producing common norms, values, and complementary expectations. The hospital's normative system underlies its administrative structure and

> . . . enables the hospital to attain a level of coordination and integration that could never be accomplished through administrative edict, through hierarchical directives, or through explicitly formulated and carefully specified organizational plans and impersonal rules, regulations, and procedures. (Georgopoulos and Mann 1972:308)

In a separate study of a psychiatric hospital, Anselm Strauss and his associates (1963) noted a similar process in which the hospital rules governing the actions of the professionals who worked within its setting were far from extensive, clearly stated, or clearly binding. These researchers contended that the social order of the hospital was not fixed or automatically maintained, but was the result of continual negotiation between the administration, the medical staff, other hospital employees, and patients. The individuals involved had varying degrees of prestige and power, were at different stages in their careers, and had their own particular goals, reference groups, and occupational ideologies. In addition, hospital rules governing physicians' conduct were not clearly stated, extensive, or binding. The hospital administration tended to take a tolerant position toward institutional rules, in the belief that good patient care required a minimum of "hard and fast" regulations and a maximum of "innovation and improvisation." Thus, there was continual negotiation of the medical rules—what they were and whether they applied in a particular situation. What held the hospital staff together was the sharing of a common goal to return their patients to the outside world in a better condition than when they entered the hospital. Strauss and associates (1963:154) explained:

> This goal is the symbolic cement that, metaphorically speaking, holds the organization together: the symbol to which all personnel can comfortably, and frequently point—with the assurance that *at least* about this matter everyone can agree! Although this symbol . . . masks a considerable measure of disagreement and discrepant purpose, it represents a generalized mandate under which the hospital can be run—the public flag under which all may work in concert.

Although it might appear from the Strauss study that the hospital was in a state of chaos, held together by only a single, idealistic agreement, actually the process of negotiation was observed to have a definite pattern. In following their own particular approach to their work, the physicians were able to originate relatively stable understandings with the nurses and other hospital employees. This process resulted in efficient and standardized forms of behavior not dependent on special instructions for all contingencies. Consequently, the process of negotiation not only

PHOTO 14.3 Hospital administrators having a meeting. Hospitals have a dual system of authority—one system is administrative and the other is medical.

created new meanings but also reinforced the significance of the more formalized rules through a process of periodic appraisal. Such negotiation appears less likely in the present era than earlier when Strauss did his research, but the overall orientation of hospital staffs toward quality patient care remains the norm (Carey 2005).

In summary, the hospital's organization consists of a varied group of professionals and allied health workers with different functions, training, and occupational values. To make this social organization function effectively, it has been necessary to construct a decentralized system of authority organized around the central objective of service to the patient. While the administrator directs and supervises hospital policy, the medical staff retains control over medical decisions. Yet, hospitals can be held legally responsible for what happens within its premises. Thus, hospitals have a responsibility for the care of its patient separate from that of physicians.

Therefore, if the hospital is going to be held liable for professional medical decisions, administrators are likely to exercise greater control over the practice of medicine within its facilities. Liability for patient care will result in the hospital imposing more of its rules and regulations on the physicians, raising the standards of qualification required for staff privileges, and generally reducing the amount of professional discretion and autonomy physicians have traditionally been allowed to exercise. This is especially the case in corporate-owned profit-making hospitals. Thus, control by hospital administrators may affect not only professional discretion but also professional effectiveness, as the practitioners within the hospital are provided with better coordination of services and staff support. Enhanced coordination and control of services are already being provided to hospital administrators through the information systems made available by modern computer technology. In all probability, the hospital administration in both nonprofit and profit-making hospitals will have increased control over the staff in the future, through computerization of information used as a basis for decision making.

The Hospital–Patient Role

While hospital services are oriented toward a supportive notion of patient welfare, hospital rules and regulations are generally designed for the benefit of hospital personnel, so that the work of treating large numbers of patients can be more efficient and easier to perform. Consequently, the sick and the injured are organized into various patient categories (e.g., maternity-obstetrics, neurology, orthopedics, urology, pediatrics, psychiatry) that reflect the medical staff's definition of their problem and are then usually subject to standardized, staff-approved medical treatment and administrative procedures.

While it can be argued that standardizing patient care results in increased organizational efficiency—and ultimately serves the best interest of the patient—a prominent theme of the hospitalization experience noted by medical sociologists has been that of depersonalization. Erving Goffman (1961) describes the status of mental hospital patients as akin to being "nonpersons," while Coe (1978) believes that patients in general tend to be devalued by hospital personnel because they are sick and dependent. H. Jack Geiger (1975), an MD, illustrates the feelings of depersonalization in hospital care during his own experience as a patient when he went from being a technically skilled, authoritative physician to a state of dependence and loss of status.

Geiger was subsequently placed in the ward's only private room, which he believed was more for the benefit of the staff than for himself. He felt that had he been placed among the other patients, lending objective credence to physician "mortality," the patients might have used the situation to reduce status and role barriers between themselves and the staff. Furthermore, Geiger learned what he now believes is the major reason why physicians make such "notoriously terrible patients." It was not because their technical knowledge caused them to be more fearful of the consequences of their disorder or more critical of the way it was treated. Instead, it was the loss of their professional role and authority in the medical setting that Geiger surmises is an integral part of their self-concept.

The same situation is seen in a study by Christopher McKevitt and Myfanwy Morgan (1997), of doctors in Great Britain who had recently been ill. Being a patient was described as "difficult" and "embarrassing," and many resisted the idea of admitting they were ill. Physicians seemed to minimize their symptoms and those of other doctors. A doctor in a group practice said he was amazed that his colleagues did not take more notice that he was having trouble breathing. He told one doctor that he had a pain in his chest when he took a deep breath. The other doctor replied, "Don't take a deep breath" (McKevitt and Morgan 1997:649). Being so ill as being unable to cope with one's daily tasks was considered something to be avoided at all costs, especially if it led to hospitalization. As one female psychiatrist, admitted to a hospital with a psychiatric disorder, put it:

I was horrified, just horrified. I was working on the day I went into hospital. I was like, working in the bin—to being part of the bin! I found it hard to mix with other patients because, you know—these are *patients*. It was hard to say "I'm a patient. I'm part of this group." Accepting that was like going lower and lower. (McKevitt and Morgan 1997:650)

Another example comes from a woman who was a nonclinical employee in a California hospital, where she broke her kneecap rushing to a meeting. A member of her staff got a wheelchair and took her to the employee health department. A nurse practitioner she had known for years began arranging her care with the person pushing her wheelchair, not her. The injured woman reported:

"It was crazy", she said. "Here I am in my own hospital, hurt but perfectly capable, and she's [the nurse practitioner] talking over my head as if I were a child. And we worked together. She knew me!" (Carey 2005:A12)

Personnel in hospitals do not have the express goal of making their patients feel depersonalized, but the organization of the hospital's work does favor rules and regulations that reduce patient autonomy and encourage patient receptivity of the hospital routine. The hospital building itself can be drab, disorienting, and the locations of wards and clinics confusing to patients. Yet, it should be noted that the process of depersonalization is not just a result of the manner in which large numbers of patients are managed or the work conditions, but it is also related to the patient's subjective experience of feeling sick. Howard Leventhal (1975) has explained that most reports of depersonalization commonly cite the experience of one's self as a physical object or thing. A second common experience is the feeling that one's own psychological self is isolated from other psychological selves (other people). Furthermore, Leventhal suggests that bodily symptoms such as pain can create a sense of separation within the individual of the physical self from the conscious psychological self. This inner alienation, in addition to the feeling of isolation from others, compounded by the doubt, uncertainty, and confusion that often accompany feelings of illness, can create for patients a sense of inadequacy and inability to control their lives.

Leventhal's argument is that this attitude of incompetency is further intensified by the patient's having to assume an institutional role like the sick role, in which he or she is officially dependent and excluded from decision making. The process of depersonalization is undoubtedly enhanced by the need of the physician or nurse to have access to the patient's body. However legitimate this may be, Coe (1978) points out that the exposure and giving over of one's body to strangers can be a degrading and humiliating experience, even though it is intended to be therapeutic.

Stripping, Control of Resources, and Restriction of Mobility

Coe (1978) states that patients are alienated from their usual lives and reduced to a largely impersonal status in the hospital through three basic mechanisms of hospital processing: (1) stripping; (2) control of resources; and (3) restriction of mobility. Coe explains that when patients present themselves for treatment in a hospital, they bring with them a particular social identity, what Goffman refers to as a "face"(Chapter 5); this represents their attitudes, beliefs, values, concept of self, and social status, all of which form the basis for their manner of presenting themselves to the world. *Stripping* occurs when the hospital systematically divests the person of these past representations of self. The patient's clothes are taken away and replaced with a set of pajamas. This is regardless of whether the pajamas are the property of the hospital or the patient. The simple fact of wearing pajamas serves as a uniform that identifies that person as sick and restricts movement to those areas of the hospital in which pajamas (patient dress) are authorized. Personal belongings of value are taken away and locked up for safekeeping by the staff. Visiting regulations control not only when patients are allowed to have visitors but also who is allowed to visit (children under age 14 are typically excluded). In addition, the staff supervises the patient's diet, decides when the patient should be asleep or awake, and in essence controls the general conduct of the patient's social life in the hospital. The hospital routine for one patient is very similar to the routine of others who have the same or similar health problems.

Another important feature of hospitalization is the *control of resources* by the staff. Coe includes under the control of resources not only physical items, such as bedclothes and toilet paper, but also the control of information about the patient's medical condition. Patients are normally not aware of their prognosis or the results of laboratory tests and X-rays, unless the physician decides to inform them.

The third aspect of depersonalization outlined by Coe is the *restriction of mobility*. In most hospitals, patients are not allowed to leave their wards without the permission of the head nurse, who is usually required to know the location of all patients at all times. When patients do leave the ward to travel to another area of the hospital, they are generally accompanied by a nurse, nurse's aide, or orderly. When patients are admitted to the hospital and also when discharged, they are taken in a wheelchair between the ward and the hospital entrance, regardless of their ability to walk, because the hospital is "responsible" for them whenever they are inside its walls. The result is that even the ability of patients to move about is supervised and controlled.

Conforming Attitudes

Some patients may be so seriously ill that feelings of depersonalization do not enter the picture. All they desire is to get well, and they are happy to do or experience whatever is necessary to accomplish that goal. That is, they are quite willing to conform to the situation.

Yet, this assumption may not be entirely correct. In a study of hospital patients in New York City, Judith Lorber (1975) found that conforming attitudes were common among cancer patients but not among patients hospitalized for very serious surgery. Lorber suggests that the cancer patients may have been scared by the ambiguities of the information they received. One woman, for example, refused to believe her doctor was telling her the truth after she had a tumor removed and it was found to be benign. Serious surgery patients, however, were much better informed about their illnesses, yet they behaved more "deviantly" (i.e., were troublesome, uncooperative, and complaining) than the cancer patients. Their somewhat lengthy stays in the hospital had not generally resulted in their complete acceptance of the staff's model of the "good" (obedient) patient. Thus, seriousness of a patient's illness was not a good predictor of whether a patient would conform to hospital routine.

The best attitude predictors, according to Lorber, were age and education. The younger and better educated the patient, the less likely was the patient to express highly conforming attitudes. Conversely, the older and more poorly educated patients were the least likely to express deviant attitudes. Lorber (1975:220) also examined the attitudes of the doctors and nurses toward the patients, and her analysis of staff evaluations suggested the important finding that patients were labeled good or bad depending on how easy they were to manage and whether or not their demands for attention were warranted. The less time the patient took, the better the patient was rated. Patients who had a tendency to complain or be uncooperative or overemotional were generally considered to be a problem only by the particular staff member who had cause to interact with them. The key variable, therefore, in how the doctors and nurses defined the patients, was the amount of time from the staff that the patient demanded. Interestingly enough, Lorber reported that some staff members labeled certain patients as "good" if they couldn't remember them very well.

A question remains as to what actions physicians and nurses take to deal with troublesome hospital patients. Some studies suggest that staff members tend to avoid patients who are not liked or who are uncooperative. Sometimes particularly bothersome patients will be reprimanded or scolded (Green and Platt 1997). Lorber found that the usual method of handling difficult patients in a New York City hospital was to prescribe tranquilizers or sedatives. If drugs did not accomplish the desired cooperation, then disruptive patients might on occasion be sent home or transferred to a convalescent center with trained psychiatric nurses. Lorber's general impression was that the hospital staff tended to treat the short-term, paying patients in a permissive fashion and put up with the problems they caused. It remains to be seen if the staff would have been as tolerant had the patients been hospitalized on a long-term, charity basis.

The Sick Role for Hospital Patients

To Parsons's (1951) concept of the sick role, which emphasizes patient cooperation and striving to get well, we may now add that of the hospitalized sick role, which apparently includes an obligation to accept hospital routine without protest. Lorber (1975:214) notes the similarities between Parsons's sick role and the role of the hospital patient. Both are universalistic, affectively neutral, functionally specific, and collectivity oriented. However, a major difference between them, Lorber observes, is that the idea of voluntary cooperation, one-to-one intimacy, and conditional permissiveness (being temporarily excused from normal social activities on the condition of seeking medical advice and care) applies primarily to the relationship between an outpatient and a private physician. Inpatient care subjects the hospital patient to a role additionally characterized by submission to authority, enforced cooperation, and depersonalized status.

Coe (1978) has suggested that acquiescence is the most common form of patient adjustment to hospital routine and the most successful for short-stay patients in terms of the quality of their interaction with the hospital staff. Basically, all the attitudes of the hospitalized sick role are results of the necessity for a well-established work routine for hospital staff. In meeting the medical needs of patients, the hospital demands that its patients give up substantial rationality about the direction and nature of their personal activities in favor of the functional rationality of organizational life (Coser 1956). In essence, this philosophy requires the patient to submit to the constraints of hospital procedures.

The Rising Cost of Hospitalization

Any discussion of American hospitals would be incomplete without considering the financial cost of hospitalization, which has risen more sharply in recent years than any other aspect of medical care. For purposes of comparison, John Knowles (1973) indicates that in 1925 the cost of one day's stay at the Massachusetts General Hospital in Boston was $3.00 ($41.40 in today's dollars), and the bill was paid entirely by the patient. By 2011, however, the average one-day cost of hospitalization had risen to $1,960, with most of the expense paid by a third party, such as a private health insurance company—Blue Cross, Blue Shield, or some other hospital-medical plan—or Medicare, Medicaid, or a state welfare agency. Not only did costs increase significantly, but the manner of payment has also changed, as about 90 percent of all expenses for hospital services are now paid by third-party sources. In some cases, third-party coverage has led to increased hospital admission rates because health needs that are met in the physician's office may not always be covered by insurance. Hospitalization can therefore reduce the patient's direct cost of health care. But this does not mean that patients escape paying hospital bills. Government expenditures are paid out of tax revenues, while private health insurance costs must also be covered and private companies are set up to make a profit.

Overall health expenditures in the United States in 2012 amounted to $2.8 trillion, of which $882 billion was spent on hospital care. Thus, over 31 percent of all the money spent on health in the United States that year was spent on hospital services. What does the hospital do with its income? Knowles explains that hospital expenses are categorized as either routine or ancillary costs. Routine costs are those expenses of providing room and board, including the following: the provision of several different diets of three meals a day served in bed; the cost of nonmedical supplies and equipment; the salaries of all members of the hospital's nonmedical staff; and the salaries of medical technicians, nurses, auxiliary nursing workers, and residents who are available to patients on a 24-hour basis, seven days a week. Ancillary expenses include the cost of laboratories, the pharmacy, operating rooms, X-ray rooms, cast rooms, and other specialized hospital facilities; plus the cost of all medical supplies. Even though patients do not get to see or even use all of a hospital's facilities, the cost of maintaining and operating these facilities for those patients who do use them continues regardless.

The most expensive hospitals in the United States are located in New England and on the Pacific Coast, while the least expensive are found in the South and in some of the Rocky Mountain states. Supposedly, regional differences in the cost of hospitalization are related to regional differences in the overall cost of living. Other factors that have been found to be important in determining hospital costs are the ratio of personnel to total expenses (the cost of labor is higher in high-cost hospitals) and the patient occupancy rate (low-cost hospitals tend to have relatively high occupancy rates). Hospital costs also rise from increased costs for labor, medical equipment, supplies, and new construction.

However, the cost of paperwork is also significant. Steffie Woolhandler and associates (Woolhandler, Himmelstein, and Lewontin 1993) suggested years ago that hospitals in the United States could save $50 billion annually at that time if they required less paperwork and utilized one form for all health insurance claims, as is done in Canada. For example, a hospital in the Canadian province of British Columbia employed one clerk to process insurance claims. A few miles away in an American hospital of the same size in the state of Washington, 45 clerks were employed full-time to handle insurance claims. Canada, with its system of national health insurance, uses a single claim form. Yet, the United States—with government-sponsored Medicare and Medicaid health insurance programs and numerous private health insurance companies requiring various deductions and copayments and providing different levels of coverage—has a complex and administratively burdensome approach to filing claims.

Technological innovations have also been identified as an important cause of rising hospital costs. However, innovations in technology are not always translated into higher hospital costs. New technology increases hospital costs when the innovations are used by only a few patients and require the training and employment of increased numbers of personnel to operate the technology. Furthermore, physicians are often dependent upon the technology based in hospitals, and the technology needs to be available for the hospital to support its relationships with doctors. Consequently, public expectations, the nature of hospital services, and physician–hospital relationships all combine to encourage a hospital to have the most recent innovations, regardless of whether such innovations are cost effective.

What can be done about controlling hospital costs? One improvement would be a single uniform insurance claim form that would reduce the amount of paperwork and the need for armies of clerks to process claims. Another improvement would be basic health insurance coverage for everyone. If all patients carried a basic coverage, hospitals could rely on a steady stream of income and not suffer serious financial losses for treating the uninsured. Many of America's uninsured rely on hospital emergency rooms for primary care. Inappropriate use of costly emergency services contributes to the rising cost of health care—especially when the cost of care cannot be recovered. Federal law requires hospitals to accept patients in emergency rooms and prevents them from turning away emergency patients who cannot pay until their condition is stabilized. This requirement forces hospitals to accept acutely ill or injured patients through their emergency rooms, regardless of insurance status. It also encourages the uninsured to use emergency rooms for primary care, because they know it is difficult or impossible to be treated at a private doctor's office without adequate funds or insurance coverage. With universal coverage, everyone could visit doctor's offices or use less expensive hospital facilities during normal working hours.

One measure, instituted in 1983, is federal legislation that establishes a fixed rate for each procedure [according to which diagnostic related group (DRG) the procedure falls under], that the government will pay hospitals for patients insured by Medicare. In the past, Medicare, which covers the elderly, paid hospitals for whatever it reasonably cost them to treat Medicare patients. The more hospitals spent, the more the government paid. If the spending had continued unchecked, the Medicare hospital insurance trust fund might have been depleted in a few years. Some states passed legislation aimed at regulating hospital rates, limiting construction of hospitals and nursing homes, and encouraging doctors to lower their fees. Private insurance companies also took steps to set fixed rates, so that hospital expenses for publicly insured patients would not be passed on to them.

Hospitals responded by expanding services and controlling costs in ways that ensured their survival (Potter 2001). Some hospitals in the early twenty-first century had not only made special arrangements with local doctors for patient referrals,

BOX 14.1

Mental Hospital Admissions

A legacy of the hospitals as poorhouses is that of mental hospitals, the majority of which are operated by state or county governments. Mental hospital admissions are either voluntary or involuntary. Voluntary commitment results when individuals consent to be admitted, and about 70 percent of all resident patients in psychiatric facilities enter voluntarily (Cockerham 2014). Involuntary commitment results when a state uses its legal authority to confine an individual to a mental hospital. Involuntary commitment proceedings are of two types: those dealing with criminal offenses, in which insanity is claimed as a defense, and those that are civil (noncriminal) in nature.

In criminal cases, the claim of mental disorder is used as an excusing condition that relieves the individual of criminal responsibility for his or her crime. The model for an excusing condition in Anglo-American law is the accident, and it defines a class of persons who fall outside the boundaries of blame. The defendant takes the position that he or she is guilty but attempts to shift the responsibility to a mental disorder. The culprit then becomes the mental disorder because *it* kept the person from acting in a reasonable manner under the circumstances. A finding of insanity by a judge or jury, based upon the testimony of psychiatrists as expert witnesses, is a matter of opinion as there are no objective standards for ascertaining mental disorder. A verdict of insanity in favor of the defendant, however, does not usually release the individual to return immediately to society, but instead it commits the person involuntarily to a mental hospital for a time to be determined later by the hospital staff and the courts.

For involuntary civil commitment, the diagnosis of a mental disorder is not sufficient justification for the confinement of an individual to a mental hospital. There usually must also be a finding that the mental disorder is of such a degree or character that if the individual in question were allowed to remain at large, that person would constitute a danger to self, others, or property. Judges normally make decisions on a case-by-case basis, based on the opinion of psychiatrists who estimate the probability that the individual will commit a dangerous act. Actions ranging from murder to writing bad checks have been found to be sufficient evidence of dangerousness. To determine dangerousness, the courts look to the severity of the harm, the likelihood that the action will occur, and the past behavior of the person who provoked the prediction of dangerousness.

but also purchased or connected with neighborhood clinics and urgent care centers to form a provider network. While some hospitals have been more successful than others in this regard, Rosemary Stevens (1989:324) points out that hospitals reacted with an eye to maintaining their own income, expanding services rather than contracting, and maintaining their competitive position. Even not-for-profit hospitals have to buy new technology, replace worn equipment, and maintain or improve their physical plant—besides meeting rising labor and energy costs and dealing with inflation. Throughout the twentieth century, as Stevens observes, not-for-profit hospitals have been profit-maximizing enterprises, even though they viewed themselves as charities serving the community and still, to some extent, are charities in that they discount or write off some services for the poor. The same situation continues today. On balance, however, the record of American hospitals in meeting the health needs of the socially disadvantaged is not good, and Stevens explains that disparities in services between social classes is a major challenge to the ideals of hospital services today.

Whenever the prices of goods and services in general increase, the cost of health care and hospitalization can be expected to rise accordingly. The principal social policy issues today, with respect to American hospitals, are to limit costs in such a way that hospital care is kept within a reasonable relationship to the rest of the economy and that the needs of all Americans for hospitalization are met.

Summary

This chapter has reviewed the hospital's evolving role as a community institution intended to serve the needs of sick and injured people as a form of social responsibility. Passing through stages of being a center for religious practice, a poorhouse, and a deathhouse, the hospital has finally come to be a center for medical technology designed to handle the health problems of all members of society, not just the lower classes.

Today, in the United States, hospitals can be classified in terms of their type of ownership (voluntary or nonprofit, profit making, or government owned) and by their type of service (general medical-surgical or specialty). The largest single type of hospital in the United States is voluntary and general medical-surgical. These hospitals are nominally supervised by a governing body, such as a board of trustees, but actually exhibit a dual system of authority: administrative and medical. Although hospitals are supposedly oriented toward the welfare of the patient, a significant body of literature in medical sociology is concerned with the fact that treating large numbers of people has resulted in organizational procedures that tend to depersonalize the individual patient. The final section of the chapter dealt with the rising cost of hospitalization, which has become a major social issue.

Critical Thinking Questions

1. Trace the evolution of the hospital as a social institution.
2. Explain the dual authority common in many hospitals and why it is not compatible with Max Weber's concept of bureaucracy.
3. What is depersonalization and how does it happen to hospital patients?

4. How is the hospital patient sick role similar to that of Talcott Parson's sick role? How are the two concepts different?
5. Why are hospital costs rising in the United States? How have hospitals responded to efforts to control costs?

Suggested Readings

Scott, Richard W., Martin Ruef, Peter J. Mendel, and Carol A. Caronna (2000) *Institutional change and healthcare organizations: From professional dominance to managed care.* Chicago: University of Chicago Press.
Examines the effects of managed care on hospitals and other health care delivery organizations.

References

Alexander, Jeffrey A., Shoou-Yih Lee, Bryan J. Weiner, and Yining Ye (2006) "The effects of governing board configuration on profound organizational change in hospitals." *Journal of Health and Social Behavior* 47: 291–308.
Carey, Benedict (2005) "In the hospital, a degrading shift from person to patient." *New York Times* (August 16): A1, A12.
Cockerham, William C. (2014) *Sociology of mental disorder*, 9th ed. Upper Saddle River, NJ: Pearson Prentice Hall.
Coe, Rodney M. (1978) *Sociology of medicine*, 2nd ed. New York: McGraw-Hill.
Coser, Rose L. (1956) "A home away from home." *Social Problems* 4: 3–17.
Geiger, H. Jack (1975) "The causes of dehumanization in health care and prospects for humanization," pp. 11–36 in *Humanizing health care*, J. Howard and A. Strauss (eds.). New York: Wiley-Interscience.
Georgopoulos, Basil F., and Floyd C. Mann (1972) "The hospital as an organization," pp. 304–11 in *Patients, physicians and illness*, 2nd ed., E. Jaco (ed.). New York: Macmillan.
Goffman, Erving (1961) *Asylums*. New York: Anchor.
Green, Gill, and Stephen Platt (1997) "Fear and loathing in health care settings reported by people with HIV." *Sociology of Health & Illness* 19: 70–92.
Hillier, Sheila (1987) "Rationalism, bureaucracy, and the organization of the health services: Max Weber's contribution to understanding modern health care systems," pp. 194–220 in *Sociological theory and medical sociology*, G. Scambler (ed.). London: Tavistock.
Knowles, John H. (1973) "The hospital," pp. 91–102 in *Life and death and medicine*, San Francisco: W. H. Freeman & Company Publishers.
Leventhal, Howard (1975) "The consequences of personalization during illness and treatment: An information-processing model," pp. 119–62 in *Humanizing health care*, J. Howard and A. Strauss (eds.). New York: Wiley-Interscience.
Lorber, Judith (1975) "Good patients and problem patients: Conformity and deviance in a general hospital." *Journal of Health and Social Behavior* 16: 213–25.
McKevitt, Christopher, and Myfanwy Morgan (1997) "Anomalous patients: The experiences of doctors with an illness." *Sociology of Health & Illness* 19: 644–67.
National Center for Health Statistics (2014) *Health United States, 2013*. Washington, DC: U.S. Government Printing Office.
Parsons, Talcott (1951) *The social system*. Glencoe, IL: The Free Press.
Parsons, Talcott, and Reneʹe Fox (1952) "Illness, therapy and the modern urban American family." *Journal of Social Issues* 8: 31–44.

Perrow, Charles (1963) "Goals and power structures: A historical case study," pp. 112–46 in *The hospital in modern society*, E. Freidson (ed.). New York: The Free Press.

Potter, Sharyn J. (2001) "A longitudinal analysis of the distinction between for-profit and not-for-profit hospitals in America." *Journal of Health and Social Behavior* 42: 17–44.

Rosenberg, Charles E. (1987) *The care of strangers: The rise of America's hospital system.* New York: Basic Books.

Rundall, Thomas G., Stephen M. Shortell, and Jeffrey A. Alexander (2004) "A theory of physician-hospital integration: Contending institutional and market logics in the health care field." *Journal of Health and Social Behavior* 45(Extra issue): 102–17.

Starr, Paul (1982) *The social transformation of American medicine.* New York: Basic Books.

Stevens, Rosemary (1989) *In sickness and in wealth: American hospitals in the twentieth century.* New York: Basic Books.

Strauss, Anselm, Leonard Schatzman, Danuta Ehrlich, Rue Bucher, and Melvin Sabshin (1963) "The hospital and its negotiated order," pp. 147–69 in *The hospital in modern society*, E. Freidson (ed.). New York: The Free Press.

Weber, Max (1978) *Economy and society*, 2 vols, G. Roth and C. Wittich (eds.). Berkeley: University of California Press.

Woolhandler, Steffie, David U. Himmelstein, and James P. Lewontin (1993) "Administrative costs in U.S. hospitals." *New England Journal of Medicine* 329: 400–3.

Wright, Eric R., and Brea L. Perry (2010) "Medical sociology and health services research: Past accomplishments and future policy challenges." *Journal of Health and Social Behavior* 51: S107–19.

CHAPTER 15

Health Care Reform and Health Policy in the United States

The major issues in the public debate about health care delivery in the United States are those of (1) cost, (2) equity, and (3) the geographic distribution of services. The issue attracting the greatest amount of public attention is the rising cost of health care that diminishes the ability of some people in American society to obtain adequate health services because they cannot afford health insurance. This situation changed dramatically in 2010 when Congress passed the Patient Protection and Affordable Care Act (ACA), and President Barack Obama signed the measure into law. The full force of the legislation did not take effect until 2014, and by 2019, it is estimated that about 95 percent of all Americans will be covered by health insurance. Health care reform was supposed to allow an additional 32 million Americans to gain health insurance coverage, thereby reducing the percentage of the uninsured to around 5 percent—the lowest percentage ever. Whether this will actually happen at the time this book goes to press, is yet unknown. If so, this would be a major development as the proportion of persons without insurance has increased in recent years, with some 13.9 percent of the population under the age of 65 uninsured in 1990 compared to 18.2 percent in 2010.

People who already had health insurance were supposed to see little or no change, but this was not the case as many individuals and families saw their insurance costs rise substantially because of the basic level of benefits mandated by the law. Making health insurance affordable for many persons without coverage or help their employer to purchase it remains the goal, but many challenges continue that will be discussed later in this chapter.

This is an important policy measure nonetheless because not having health insurance drastically undermines the ability of people to obtain health care. Jill Quadagno (2005), for example, relates the experience of an uninsured Mexican immigrant house painter who fell off a ladder in Texas and injured his wrist. His employer sent him home to avoid paying any medical expenses. His family took him to a hospital emergency room that put a splint on his wrist and referred him to a local physician. The doctor refused to treat him because he did not have insurance. His wrist continued to bother him; so three weeks later he went to a public clinic and found he had a fracture. While this outcome was not serious, it nevertheless shows how people without health insurance have problems in obtaining medical care.

Sometimes not having health insurance can contribute to the death of a patient. A newspaper story in 2006 told of a young woman who failed to get regular treatment for lupus because she had no health insurance, refusing to even *go to a hospital emergency room. She was taken anyway after a seizure, and despite heroic efforts by the hospital to save her—she died later because of the advanced stage of the disease. A confirmed story told during the 2008 presidential campaign was about a young woman in Ohio who suffered complications from her pregnancy but was denied care at a local clinic because she had a large unpaid bill for her previous care as an uninsured patient. The clinic agreed to treat her again if she paid $100 per visit, which she was unable to do. She eventually sought care at a hospital 30 miles away that—contrary to initial reports—provided her medical care, yet it was too late, and both she and her baby subsequently died.*

These and similar reports that appeared in the news media illustrate the obvious fact that people without health insurance do not receive the care that those with insurance are provided and can suffer for it. This is seen in a nationwide study that found previously uninsured persons, especially those with cardiovascular disease and diabetes, had worse health and used more services when they became eligible for government-sponsored Medicare coverage at age 65 than those with prior health insurance (McWilliams, Meara, Zaslavsky, and Ayanian 2007). Once Medicare was obtained, the health of the previously uninsured people improved significantly. By age 70, health differences between the previously uninsured and insured were reduced by half, which shows the importance of having access to health care that insurance provides. A lack of insurance over time can have a strong negative cumulative effect on a person's health (McWilliams et al. 2007; Quesnel-Vallée 2004).

It is therefore true that people without health insurance are less likely to have their health problems treated or are more likely to hesitate before seeking treatment, even in emergencies, because of the expense. Solutions to this outcome for both policymakers and the uninsured have been complicated by the continually rising costs for such care, which make it ever more difficult to fund. Nevertheless, it has been clear for years that some type of reform was needed, and the only social institution having the power to enact decisive reform is the federal government. Before discussing the health care measures the government adopted in 2010 and the outcome, this chapter will first review the rising costs of such care that propelled it far beyond the capability of many people to purchase on their own.

Rising Costs

In 1980, an average of $1,100 per person was spent on health care in the United States, which was the highest in the world at that time. By 2012, this figure had risen to $8,900—the highest ever recorded anywhere. Also in 1980, Americans spent a total of $253.4 billion on health needs, as compared to expenditures of more than $2.8 trillion in 2012. Estimates for 2019, made before the Affordable Care Act, indicate that health costs could average $13,387 for every man, woman, and child in the country and that total health costs could reach $4.5 trillion as the price of care outstrips the growth of the entire economy. However, according to the Congressional Budget Office in 2010, health care reform measures are expected to result in significant savings in future decades, but it is too soon to know if this will actually be the case. The initial expenditure of funds to support reform will be significant and costly.

The rising cost of care is due not only to the aging of the population and the demand by growing numbers of elderly for health care but also because of the increases in hospital expenses and fees for doctors, dentists, and other professional health services. Other sources of greater costs are higher prices for health insurance, the wider availability of insurance under the Affordable Care Act to cover prescription drug costs, an increase in the number of prescriptions written by doctors, and a shift toward more use of new, high-price drugs. Advertising also drives up drug costs in that $1 out of every $4 paid for prescription drugs covers the cost of advertising and marketing that drug. In the past, prescription drugs were primarily advertised to physicians, but now there is direct-to-consumer marketing. Some drugs can reduce health spending by preventing heart disease and other health problems, thereby lowering the need for hospital care, but that is not the case for all drugs. Overall, prescription drug expenditures rose from $120.6 billion in 2000 to approximately $326 billion in 2013, with an expected increase of 3–5 percent in 2014 (Schumock et al. 2014).

An illustration of the increase and magnitude of the cost of health care in American society can be found in an examination of the U.S. consumer price index. As in most other nations of the world, the cost of goods and services has been steadily rising. Table 15.1, however, shows that between 1982–1984 and 2012, the cost of medical care increased more (414.9%) than any other major category of personal expense.

TABLE 15.1   Consumer Price Index, United States, Selected Years, 1950–2012

Year	All Items	Medical Care	Food	Apparel	Housing	Energy
1950	24.1	15.1	25.4	40.3	—	—
1955	26.8	18.2	27.8	42.9	—	—
1960	29.6	22.3	30.0	45.7	—	22.4
1965	31.5	25.2	32.2	47.8	—	22.9
1970	38.8	34.0	39.2	59.2	36.4	25.5
1975	53.8	47.5	59.8	72.5	50.7	42.1
1980	82.4	74.9	86.8	90.9	81.1	86.0
1985	107.6	113.5	105.6	105.0	107.7	101.6
1990	130.7	162.8	132.4	124.1	128.5	102.1
1995	152.4	220.5	148.4	132.0	148.5	105.2
2000	172.2	260.8	167.8	129.6	169.6	124.6
2005	195.3	323.2	190.7	119.5	195.7	177.1
2010	218.1	388.4	219.6	119.5	216.3	211.4
2012	229.6	414.9	233.8	126.3	222.7	246.1

Note: 1982–1984 = 100.
Source: U.S. Department of Labor, as quoted in National Center for Health Statistics, 2014.

Within the general category of medical care, Table 15.2 shows the increase in the costs of various subcategories of items. The greatest single increase between the period 1982–1984 and 2012 was the cost of hospital and related services (672.1%). Prescription drugs increased by 440.1 percent and physician services rose by 347.3 percent.

As shown in Table 15.1 and Table 15.2, the costs of health care have continued to soar since the 1980s. There were cost containment measures in a number of areas. In the public sector, the federal government instituted cost controls for services to Medicare patients by establishing set fees for diagnostic related groups (DRGs). DRGs-listed medical procedures and what the government would pay for patients receiving these procedures. The government was no longer inclined to accept charges set by health care providers, but instead instituted its own fee system.

TABLE 15.2 Consumer Price Index for All Items and Medical Care Components, United States, Selected Years, 1950–2012

Consumer Price Index

Item and Medical Care Component	1950	1960	1970	1980	1990	2000	2012
All items	24.1	29.6	33.8	82.4	130.7	172.2	229.6
All items less medical care	—	30.2	39.2	82.8	128.8	167.3	220.6
Services	16.9	24.1	35.0	77.9	139.2	195.3	271.4
Medical care services	12.8	19.5	32.3	74.8	162.7	266.0	440.3
Professional medical services	—	—	37.0	77.9	156.1	237.7	342.7
Physicians' services	15.7	21.9	34.5	76.5	160.8	244.7	347.3
Dental services	21.0	27.0	39.2	78.9	155.8	258.5	417.5
Eye care[1]	—	—	—	—	117.3	149.7	179.9
Services by other medical professionals[1]	—	—	—	—	120.2	161.9	219.6
Hospital and related services	—	—	—	69.2	178.0	317.3	672.1
Inpatient hospital services[2]	—	—	—	—	—	117.0	256.6
Outpatient hospital services[1]	—	—	—	—	138.7	263.8	574.0
Medical care commodities	39.7	46.9	46.5	75.4	163.4	238.1	333.6
Prescription drugs	43.4	54.0	47.4	72.5	181.7	285.4	440.1
Nonprescription drugs and medical supplies[1]	—	—	—	—	120.6	149.5	—
Internal and respiratory over-the-counter drugs	—	—	42.3	74.91	145.9	176.9	—
Nonprescription medical equipment and supplies	—	—	—	79.2	138.0	178.1	—

Note: 1982–1984 = 100, except where noted.
[1] December 1986 = 100.
[2] December 1996 = 100.
Source: U.S. Department of Labor, as quoted in National Center for Health Statistics, 2014.

In the private sector, insurance companies adopted DRGs to set limits on what they would pay as well. Also business corporations increasingly turned to lower-cost health maintenance organizations (HMOs) and preferred provider organizations (PPOs) to provide less expensive health care to their employees. Some corporations required second opinions from other doctors before surgery could be scheduled, and some required data from insurance carriers to enable them to evaluate the performance of doctors and hospitals serving their employees. Many firms also increased the amount that their employees had to pay out of their own pockets for health care. But costs continued to rise as over 18 percent of the population found by 2010 they could afford neither health care nor the insurance to pay for that care.

The Road to Health Care Reform

Initial Federal Efforts: Medicare and Medicaid

President Harry Truman had proposed a national health insurance program for all Americans in 1945, when health care costs consumed only 4 percent of GDP. But Truman's plan died in Congress after strong opposition from the American Medical Association and public concerns that such a program was a form of socialism. The medical profession in the United States had a consistent record of resistance to any social legislation seeking to reduce the authority, privileges, and income of physicians (Light 2004; Mechanic 2004; Quadagno 2004, 2005, 2010; Starr 1982). With the exception of some individual doctors, the medical profession as a group opposed workmen's compensation, social security, and voluntary health insurance in their initial stages, and strongly resisted any proposals for national health insurance through the AMA. Nevertheless, in 1974, Richard Nixon began pushing for a national health insurance scheme that was closely tied to the concept of HMOs, only to become politically crippled by the Watergate scandal that ultimately forced him to resign. Jimmy Carter suggested national health insurance was needed during his first term in office but lost reelection in 1980. Only Lyndon Johnson had success with his limited reforms that established Medicare and Medicaid in 1965.

Johnson: Medicare and Medicaid By the early 1960s, it was obvious to many people that private health insurance had not met the needs of the aged and the poor (Budrys 2001, 2003; Light 2004; Quesnel-Vallée and Jenkins 2010; Starr 1982). A considerable portion of the literature in medical sociology, during the 1950s and 1960s, documented the disadvantaged position of the elderly and the poor in obtaining adequate health care in American society. Several social and political factors thus combined to influence the drafting of laws to provide health insurance for these segments of the population: the commitments of Presidents John F. Kennedy and Lyndon B. Johnson; the changed composition of the U.S. Senate in 1962 and the U.S. House of Representatives in 1964; the lack of past effective health care legislation; the continuing increase in the cost of medical care; and perhaps the lessening credibility of the AMA, which claimed that "physicians cared for the elderly" and "knew their health needs better than anyone else" or that federal health insurance was incompatible with "good" medicine (Stevens 1971:438–39).

The resistance of the medical profession to Medicare brought home the point to the general public and lawmakers that the medical profession could not always be relied upon to place the public's interest ahead of that of the profession.

Despite the strong resistance of the medical profession, Congress passed the Medicare and Medicaid amendments of the Social Security Act in 1965. Although these amendments were a compromise between what was ideal and what was politically feasible, their passage marked a watershed in the history of medical politics in the United States, as Congress for the first time emerged as a dominant voice in health care delivery and demonstrated that the direction of medical practice was no longer the sole prerogative of organized medicine.

Medicare is a federally administered program providing hospital insurance (part A) and medical insurance (part B) for people aged 65 years or older, regardless of financial resources. It also includes disabled people under the age of 65 who receive cash benefits from Social Security or railroad retirement programs and certain victims of chronic kidney disease. There are specified deductible and coinsurance amounts for which the beneficiary is responsible, as well as limits to the benefits, but most of the cost is paid by the federal government. The hospital insurance is financed primarily through social security payroll deductions and does not require a monthly premium if the recipient paid Medicare taxes while working. The medical insurance plan, whose participation is voluntary, is financed by premiums paid by the enrollees whose cost depends upon the plan selected from those available in their home state and from federal funds.

As of 2006, prescription drug coverage is available to everyone with Medicare. There is a wide range of plans and options. There is a monthly fee that varies according to the plan the individual selects from those available in the state the person lives in, but virtually all drug plans must provide a minimum standard coverage. People living below the federal poverty line or just above do not have to pay these costs, while others with low incomes pay according to a sliding scale. The Medicare program is under the overall direction of the Secretary of Health and Human Services and is supervised by the Bureau of Health Insurance of the Social Security Administration (SSA). Most of the day-to-day operations of Medicare are performed by commercial insurance companies and Blue Cross/Blue Shield plans that review claims and make payments. Requests for payment are submitted by the provider of services. Reimbursement is made on the basis of reasonable charges, as determined by the private insurance companies who issue the payments. In 2012, a total of $573 billion in Medicare benefits was paid under coverage that extends to 50.7 million elderly and disabled people and covered 16 percent of the American population.

Medicaid is technically a welfare program. It provides for the federal government's sharing in the payments made by state welfare agencies to health care providers for services rendered to the poor. Medicaid gives the states federal matching funds ranging from 50 to 76 percent of expenditures, depending on the per capita income of the states involved. Each state is required to cover all needy persons receiving cash assistance. States are permitted to include not only the financially needy but also the medically needy, the aged, blind, and disabled poor as well as their dependent children and families. In 1986, Congress passed legislation extending Medicaid coverage to children under five years of age and pregnant women with incomes below the federal poverty level, which in 2014 was $23,850 annually for a family of four. Medicaid coverage was expanded under the 2010 Affordable Care Act to additionally cover low-income persons earning below 133 percent of the poverty line (about $31,000 for a family of four in 2014). However, the U.S. Supreme Court ruled in 2012 that states could opt out of the expansion and 27 states, as of 2014, have not yet agreed to participate.

In 2012, 57.5 million people or 18.3 percent of the population received Medicaid benefits. These benefits cost federal and state governments $428.5 billion. Medicaid was originally intended to cover people on welfare, but the extension of benefits to children and pregnant women from low-income families, who may or may not be on welfare, indicates that the insurance is also being used to cover people with medical expenses who have no other source of health insurance. When the percent of the U.S. population covered by Medicaid and Medicare is combined with the percentage insured by CHIP (Children's Health Insurance Program) that covers uninsured children and teenagers, some 37.9 percent of all Americans in 2012 had all or most of their health insurance needs paid for by federal and state governments.

What Medicare and Medicaid accomplished on a national scale are two highly important measures: First, these programs may have been expensive and may not have met all the needs of the aged and the poor for which they were intended, but they have provided needed health services for the old and those in poverty where these services were not previously available. Second, Medicare and Medicaid established the precedent of the federal government's involvement in the administration of health care, and this involvement is the key to any future health care planning and reorganization. The time has long passed in the United States when the question of whether the federal government should be involved in health matters is debated. As seen in the health care reform that was to come in 2010, federal government participation in health care is an important and substantial reality, and whatever happens in the organization and scope of health care services in the United States is dependent on its decisions.

Clinton The most recent attempt to provide health insurance for the entire country prior to 2010 was President Bill Clinton's effort in 1994. The problems of rising costs and increasing numbers of uninsured persons had pushed public demand for universal coverage to one of the top positions on the nation's political agenda. At the time, this plan or a modified version of it seemed likely to become reality because of its popularity. However, when the plan was delivered to Congress in October 1993, numerous interest groups lobbied legislators to adopt provisions favorable to them or to oppose it altogether (Quadagno 2004, 2005, 2010). Delays in bringing the health reform bill forward through various congressional committees gave vested interests more time to mobilize. The small business lobby was especially influential in opposing the plan, since it required even businesses with few employees to pay most of the costs (80 percent) of health insurance for their workers. The AMA opposed government control over health care delivery and losses in income for doctors; hospitals, drug companies, and insurance companies were opposed to price controls; labor unions and the elderly were against losses or caps on health benefits that they already had; and some consumer groups were dissatisfied with various aspects of the plan.

These anti-insurance lobbying efforts, lack of consensus between the Democrats and Republicans in Congress charged with drafting the legislation, and growing public uncertainty resulted in congressional inaction. In September 1994, the White House conceded there was no chance of passing national health insurance that year, but vowed to make it a priority in 1995, which it did not do as the Republicans had gained control of both the House and Senate. Weakened by a sex scandal, leading to an unsuccessful impeachment trial, President Clinton did not advance national health care legislation again as his term ended in early 2001.

The Clinton plan nevertheless had two major effects. First, it moved health to the forefront of domestic politics, with both Democrats and Republicans in Congress recognizing that changes need to be made. One legacy of this situation was the passage by Congress in 1996 of the Health Insurance Reform Act, whose major provisions guaranteed that workers in employer-sponsored health plans would be able to maintain their health insurance after changing or losing their jobs. Second, it stimulated movement toward the massive reorganization of American health care into a delivery system in which managed care is now the dominant approach in the private sector.

The Emergence of Managed Care

In the early to mid-1990s, private health care in the United States experienced a major reorganization into managed care plans. Changing from a largely office-based, fee-for-service system to an increasingly group or organization-based managed care system, American medical practice took on a dramatically different new structure (Pescosolido and Boyer 2010; Pescosolido, Tuch, and Martin 2001). Some of this restructuring was in response to the anticipated health reforms of the Clinton administration, and some was due to a "buyer's revolt" by business corporations and insurance companies seeking to control health care costs by controlling medical work (Budrys 2001, 2003; Pescosolido and Boyer 2010; Stevens 2010). The medical market was under considerable pressure to control costs, and managed care was considered the most effective means for doing so. Managed care, as noted in Chapter 11, refers to health organizations, such as HMOs and PPOs. These organizations "manage" or control the cost of health care by monitoring the work of doctors and hospitals, limiting visits to specialists within a particular managed care network and to all physicians outside it, and requiring prior authorization for hospitalization. Managed care has become the most common form of health care delivery in the United States, including a majority of persons with private health insurance and those covered by Medicare and Medicaid.

Managed care alters the patient–physician relationship, by introducing a third party—the case manager—to the decision-making process. The case manager represents the bill payer, usually an insurance company, who certifies that the care to be rendered is both effective and the least costly alternative. The case manager also authorizes hospitalization. Another feature of managed care is its reliance upon capitation financing. Capitation (per capita) financing is a fixed monthly sum paid by the subscriber and his or her employer that guarantees care to that person and the person's immediate family, with little or no additional cost. Health care providers, in turn, must provide necessary care and are not paid for any additional services. This measure discourages inefficient and unnecessary treatment.

BOX 15.1

The Argument for and Against Health Reform

Medical sociologist David Mechanic (2006:ix) says that he sometimes jokes that if we brought the country's most talented health experts together and asked them to design a health care system that gives as little value for money as possible, they would have trouble coming up with a system that does any better than the one we now have. He adds, however, that health care in the United States is not a joke. Rather, through no planned design or evil intent, it has evolved into a structure that fails to serve the needs of many people. In his view, having millions of people without health insurance in the richest country in the world is fundamentally wrong.

He points out that some Americans view health care as a commodity best improved through a competitive marketplace with minimal regulation. Although concerned about people without health insurance and supportive of programs to help them, they feel health care is not a "right." Rather, they favor employment opportunities that would allow the uninsured to purchase their own insurance. Mechanic suggests these Americans generally believe in individual responsibility, while supporting fee-for-service health care, and cost sharing on the part of the patient as a way to encourage prudent use of health services.

The opposing view is that health care is different from other goods and services, is a public obligation and an individual right, and should not be a form of service subject to profit making in an unregulated marketplace. Americans in this group support national health insurance, with the federal government having a significant role in financing and regulating health care. Mechanic (2006:22) sees these ideological differences as an unbridgeable divide that makes health reform difficult. However, in 2010, that divide was temporarily bridged, when Congress enacted health care reform despite the strong feelings of many who opposed it.

Patients are also allowed to see a specialist only after being screened by the primary care physician who routinely cares for them. Because specialist care is usually more costly, the primary care physician serves as a gatekeeper to the use of specialists and is usually rewarded by keeping referrals to a minimum. Finally, patients are required to use the physicians within the managed care network—unless the subscriber or a family member has a medical emergency outside the plan's geographical area.

The current cost containment effort in U.S. health care had its origins in the federal government's effort to control payments to providers of Medicare services by the introduction of DRGs. Hospitals, in turn, sought to shift some of their costs from government payers to private payers, primarily health insurance companies. The insurance companies responded by playing a more substantial role in the organization and management of the use of services through managed care programs. Managed care organizations emerged because corporate and government purchasers of health care faced a crisis of excess spending by the physician-dominated system, and a new concept was needed to control costs (Light 2004). These purchasers became stakeholders in the nation's system of health care delivery. As stakeholders, observes Donald Light (2004:19), "they sought to rein in the excesses, replace professional autonomy with accountable performance measures, and reorganize the center of health care from hospital-based acute intervention to community-based prevention and primary care." Light finds that a large new secondary industry arose in support of managed care organizations. These new businesses designed benefits, selected providers, managed services, defined outcomes, and established systems measuring quality and performance. The control of managed care was stripped away from physicians as the managed care model became a product of big business (Mechanic 2004). The attraction for business corporations was to keep costs down through greater efficiency that would nonetheless provide a pipeline into the huge profit potential of the health care market. No longer is managed care the alternative health care delivery model that it once was, rather it has become the dominant model (Pescosolido and Boyer 2010).

Some medical sociologists point out that the first "social contract" between professional medicine and American society for health care featuring fee-for-service reimbursement, physician dominance, and limited government intervention has been replaced by a second one (Light 2004; Pescosolido and Boyer 2010; Pescosolido, McLeod, and Alegría 2000). The second social contract involves third-party reimbursements, greater use of nonphysician providers, and direct government involvement in financing and regulation. According to Bernice Pescosolido and Carol Boyer (2010), the second social contract significantly altered the powerful position of physicians by making them more subject to limitations set by the government, insurance companies, and the demands of employers who purchased managed care plans. This situation led to a dramatic decline of their power in the private medical market in the United States (Caronna 2004; Casalino 2004; Light 2004).

Has managed care controlled costs? The answer appears to be that the system initially kept rising costs in check, but more lately it has faltered. Between 1993 and 1997, health care's portion of the GDP fluctuated around 13.5 percent. In 1995, the U.S. Department of Commerce estimated that national health expenditures would exceed 15 percent of the GDP. Yet, only 13.4 percent of the GDP was spent on health that year—the smallest increase in several years. By 1997, the percentage of the GDP had fallen to 13.1 percent. However, by 2007, the percentage of the GDP spent on health care rose to 16.2 percent, and the total amount of spending had soared to $1.97 trillion. And, as noted earlier in this chapter, health spending in the United States reached $2.8 trillion in 2012. Therefore, it is clear that health expenditures are generally rising, although health spending declined slightly from 17.3 percent of the GDP in 2011 to 17.2 percent in 2012.

According to David Mechanic (2004), some sources suggest that the managed care model is either "dead" or transformed into "managed care lite" as its controls on costs have weakened. Mechanic finds the central cause in managed care's decline is the repudiation of its rationing services by the middle class. He points out that Americans are accustomed to having choice and autonomy in their utilization of health services. The middle class in particular reacted negatively to restrictions. Pressure on managed care plans by physicians, the media, and politicians responding to patients also helped dilute cost controls, including the requirement to obtain approval from a primary care physician before seeing a specialist in many managed care programs. Employers and health care plans offering managed care health insurance retreated by allowing the relaxation of cost constraints. Managed care plans, in turn, adapted to the changing environment by devising new provisions and practice arrangements. The result was a return of upwardly spiraling costs for health care that is ultimately passed on to patients in the form of higher out-of-pocket costs and health insurance premiums. As for the managed care model, Mechanic forecasts that it will persevere by dispensing with gatekeepers and limited choices but institute other ways of forcing patients to be more frugal in their choices and reintroducing rationing.

State Efforts at Health Reform

In the meantime, some states took the lead in developing their own health coverage for the uninsured. Hawaii was the first to enact a health insurance program for its residents in 1974 that required all employers to contribute to an insurance program for their employees and provided financial assistance to small businesses in meeting the costs. The state plan, along with Medicare, Medicaid, and private insurance, eventually resulted in more than 90 percent of the population in Hawaii having health insurance.[1] In 1994, Tennessee committed itself to becoming the first state to give health insurance to every uninsured person by converting its Medicaid program into the TennCare managed care program. Unfortunately by 2004, TennCare was in jeopardy because of high costs and came to resemble a more conventional Medicaid program. Oregon, long a leader in health reform, also tried to insure all of its uninsured but could not do so because of state budget cuts. Its Medicaid program, known as the Oregon Health Plan, nevertheless used a lottery to select some people for coverage who lacked private health insurance and did not qualify for Medicaid or Medicare.

Vermont, however, provided health insurance to its poor for a nominal fee, while guaranteeing free medical and dental care to all residents under the age of 18 with family incomes of less than $50,000 annually. Massachusetts also enacted a new law beginning in 2006 requiring health insurance of its residents. Individuals are penalized on their state income taxes if they do not have it, state government subsidies help the working poor buy private health insurance, and businesses that employ ten or more workers that do not provide their employees with health insurance are assessed fines by the state. Since the law took effect, it is estimated that 96 percent of the population in Massachusetts has health insurance. Massachusetts was the only state providing the means for all its citizens to obtain health insurance. The death rate in Massachusetts decreased significantly (about 3% between 2006 and 2010) after it adopted mandatory health insurance coverage. The decline in mortality was greatest in counties with the highest proportion of poor and previously uninsured residents.

Enactment of the Affordable Care Act (ACA)

None of the state measures solved the problem of the uninsured nationwide. The solution was dependent upon the capacity of the federal government to act, which it did when President Obama took office in 2009. His election gave the Democrats both occupancy of the White House and a majority in the House and Senate, giving them the power to enact legislation regardless of opposition from Republicans.

---

[1]In 2012, states with 90 percent or more of the population having some type of health insurance were Massachusetts, Hawaii, Vermont, Connecticut, and Minnesota, along with the District of Columbia. States with the lowest percentage of insured were Texas, Nevada, Florida, and New Mexico.

PHOTO 15.2 President Barack Obama signing the Affordable Care Act in 2010.

Obama put health care reform at the top of the domestic agenda, despite the largest budget deficit in history exacerbated by a massive federal infusion of funds into the economy to counter a major recession brought on by widespread defaults on home mortgages and bank mismanagement, losses in savings plans and pensions, high unemployment, and wars in Iraq and Afghanistan. Opposition to health care reform was intense. Those opposed cited these concerns:

- prohibitive costs
- higher taxes
- cuts in Medicare benefits
- expanded federal funding for abortion services[2]
- government-controlled health care delivery would be too bureaucratic and unresponsive to individual needs.

Nevertheless, the health care reform bill (the Patient Protection and Affordable Care Act) was passed by Congress and signed into law in March, 2010.

---

[2]Since 1977, with the passage of the Hyde Amendment, federal law has banned the use of any federal funds for abortion, with the exception of pregnancies resulting from rape, incest, or if it is determined the woman's life is at risk. The Affordable Care Act continues the current Hyde Amendment restrictions. State Medicaid programs, however, have the option to cover abortions in other circumstances by using only state funds. The ACA also does not affect other state policies concerning abortion, such as requiring parental consent or notification, waiting periods, or any of the abortion limits or coverage requirements that states have authorized.

The provisions of the law stipulated that, as of 2014, (1) persons with preexisting medical conditions can no longer be denied coverage because of those conditions, (2) a minimum level of benefits to be set by the federal government must be provided in all health insurance plans, (3) state insurance exchanges will be established that will offer a range of competitive health care plans at affordable prices, (4) persons not covered by their employer will be able to purchase coverage through the state exchanges, (5) persons under the age of 65 who already have health insurance may also purchase plans from the exchanges and those who earn up to four times the federal poverty line will receive government subsidies to help pay the cost, (6) low-income persons under the age of 65 earning below 133 percent of the federal poverty line will be covered by an expanded Medicaid program, (7) small businesses can buy insurance for their employees through the exchanges and get tax credits, (8) children may remain on their parent's health insurance plan until age 26, and (9) most Americans would be required by law to purchase health insurance or pay a penalty added to their federal income tax (American Indians, people with extreme hardships, and religious objectors are exempt), while employers with more than 50 workers who do not provide coverage will also pay penalties. Penalties range from $95 to $11,000 for individuals, depending on income, and are scheduled to increase in future years. The minimum level of benefits mandated to be in *all* health insurance plans include coverage for:

- ambulatory (outpatient) services
- emergency room visits
- hospitalization
- maternity and newborn care
- mental health and substance use services
- prescription drugs
- rehabilitation services
- laboratory tests
- preventive and chronic disease care
- pediatric services.

The cost of health care reform was estimated by the Congressional Budget Office to be $1.1 trillion over the next decade. Some 49 percent of this amount is to be paid for by spending cuts and limits on Medicare payments and other savings, while the other 51 percent is planned to come from higher Medicare taxes, fees and new taxes on drug manufacturers and others, as well from penalties paid by businesses and uninsured individuals.

However, the Affordable Care Act had several initial problems. First, the website for signing up for the insurance worked poorly or not at all, and it was difficult in some states to arrange coverage until the site was functional. This was frustrating for many people. Those persons who had tried to enroll but were unable to complete the application before the deadline expired were given more time. Obama waived the tax penalties the first year without consulting Congress, causing Republicans in the House of Representatives to initiate a lawsuit charging he had changed a federal law without Congressional approval and did not have the authority to do so.

Next, despite President Obama's assurance that people who already had insurance could keep it, many individuals and families had their policies canceled and were required to pay higher prices for new ones. Some people paid less than previously, but others paid more. Policies that lacked all of the basic benefits were no longer viable under the law and new ones contained benefits that some people did not need, such as coverage for maternity and pediatric care. But such benefits were nonetheless required for everyone, including women past their childbearing years, and this added to the cost.

Obama, in response, allowed insurance companies to let people keep their old policies for another year, but in some states the insurance companies declined to do so because of the cost of issuing replacement policies with the old benefits. At the end of the first enrollment period in early 2014, eight million people had nonetheless obtained private health insurance through either federal or state-managed exchanges of whom it is estimated that about 3.5 million did not previously have coverage. About four million more people gained insurance in states that expanded their Medicaid programs.

Legal Challenges to the Affordable Care Act

There were several legal challenges to the Affordable Care Act concerning religious exemptions, the mandate for employers to provide health insurance, and the legality of paying subsidies and giving tax credits to low- and middle-income Americans. However, the major legal hurdle pertained to questions about its constitutionality. Some 26 states joined in a lawsuit to challenge the stipulation requiring Americans to have health insurance by claiming it is unconstitutional and unprecedented to compel people to buy any commercial good or service as a condition of lawful residence in the United States. Federal courts in Michigan and Virginia ruled in 2010 that the mandate to require health insurance was indeed constitutional, while another federal court in Virginia decided it was unconstitutional to require mandatory purchase of health insurance. The federal government argued two main points in the Virginia case. First, that the Commerce Clause of the Constitution allows Congress to regulate activities that substantially affect interstate commerce, which includes the health care market. Second, if the requirement to have such insurance is not protected by the Commerce Clause, it is nevertheless allowable under Congress's broad powers of taxation because noncompliance would result in an income tax penalty.

This case was appealed to the U.S. Supreme Court that ruled in a 5-4 vote in 2012, that the law requiring most Americans to obtain health insurance or pay a penalty *was* constitutional under Congress's power to levy taxes. The Supreme Court also ruled by a second 5-4 vote that the expansion of Medicaid was legal, but Congress had exceeded its authority to trying to coerce the states into participating by withholding existing federal Medicaid payments. The states, accordingly, were given the option to opt in or out of expanding their Medicaid programs.[3]

---

[3]As of early 2014, the states that had opted out of expanding Medicaid coverage were Alabama, Alaska, Florida, Georgia, Idaho, Indiana, Kansas, Louisiana, Maine, Michigan, Mississippi, Missouri, Montana, Nebraska, New Hampshire, North Carolina, Ohio, Oklahoma, Pennsylvania, South Carolina, South Dakota, Tennessee, Texas, Utah, Virginia, Wisconsin, and Wyoming. The federal government had agreed to pay for the first three years of expansion (2014–16) and 90 percent of added costs beginning in 2020. States that have opted out of providing expanded Medicaid coverage will not receive these funds.

The overall effect of the Supreme Court ruling, however, was to reaffirm the legal basis of the Affordable Care Act.

Two other court cases involving the Affordable Care Act in 2014 were resolved by the Supreme Court. Both addressed the requirement of employers to provide insurance coverage for contraceptive services. In one case, the Supreme Court granted an injunction to an order of Roman Catholic nuns preventing them from having to provide contraceptive devices to their employees at a convent because it violated their religious beliefs. In the second case, the Supreme Court ruled that family-owned corporations run on religious principles (Hobby Lobby and Conestoga Wood Specialties) likewise did not have to pay for contraceptive services as required by the Affordable Care Act. These rulings were consistent with the Religious Freedom Restoration Act passed in 1993 that maintains the government cannot "substantially burden" the exercise of religion unless it is able to satisfy a very demanding legal test.

The Affordable Care Act nevertheless seems likely to survive unless repealed in some yet-to-come Congressional legislation or some court case is able to overturn its major provisions. Past efforts all failed. The landscape of health care delivery in the United States has been significantly altered with the federal government taking increasing fiscal responsibility for the provision of services, as well as for regulation and even pricing of those services. All of these measures move the nation closer to a national health insurance system sometime in the future. These events also signal the end of the medical profession's once dominant role in setting health policy for Congress.

Equity in Health Services

The problem of equity with respect to health services has been lessened with health care reform but still remains a problem in American society. In a free-market system lacking national health insurance, those persons who are economically disadvantaged are also medically disadvantaged when it comes to obtaining quality services. As discussed in Chapter 7, the United States has a two-track system of health care delivery, divided into a private track and a public track. The public track is a system of welfare medicine supported by public health insurance, especially Medicaid but also Medicare for the elderly poor.

Public health insurance has provided access to the American health care delivery system for the poor, but the character of the services rendered—that of welfare medicine—has not changed significantly. The urban poor have historically been dependent on public hospitals and clinics rather than private hospitals and practitioners for providing patient care. That is still the case today for many of the poor and near poor, as physicians, pharmacists, and hospitals have joined banks, supermarkets, and department stores in migrating out of inner-city areas where the poor are concentrated. Such areas sometimes have "free" clinics funded by local communities that exist to serve patients left out of a city's usual health care delivery system (Weiss 2006). Typically the poor and, increasingly, the near poor have no regular relationship with a physician and are treated by the doctor on duty, who may not know them and is not the physician who treated them on their last visit.

The rural poor likewise have problems of access to health care, as medical facilities and health practitioners may not be available locally. And the rural poor (as other people living in rural areas) also may be more likely to be treated by foreign medical school graduates. This situation is brought on by the doctor shortage in these areas, caused by a reluctance of many American-trained physicians to work in small communities. Another segment of society particularly affected by problems of equity is the large number of Americans who currently do not have health insurance. This situation changes for the better with health care reform. True equity in health care has not been achieved, but the problem is not as acute as in the past if the Affordable Care Act achieves its goals.

Geographic Distribution of Services

Besides problems with rising costs and equity, the American system of health care delivery is not evenly distributed geographically, and primary care or family practitioners are underrepresented among physicians. A major factor in obtaining adequate medical care for some people is the numerical shortage of physicians serving patients in rural areas and urban slums. Physicians generally prefer to practice medicine in urbanized settings, where they are close to cultural, educational, and recreational facilities. Another advantage of an urban practice is its proximity to extensive technological resources in the form of well-equipped hospitals, clinics, and laboratories staffed by well-trained personnel. Also important are the relationships with colleagues, which tend to enhance professional life. These relationships are more readily available in urban areas where there are greater opportunities for professional recognition. Finally, it should be recognized that the more financially rewarding medical practices are those in large cities.

The maldistribution of physicians in the United States can be illustrated by comparing differences between predominantly urban and rural states. Differences within states are even greater. One out of every 20 counties in the United States does not have a single doctor, and more than half of all counties do not have a pediatrician. In some rural areas, nurse practitioners fill in for physicians. Even though small communities often advertise and try actively to recruit physicians, many doctors remain attracted to urban living.

The physician shortage is not limited to rural areas, however. It also extends into certain urban locales. Physicians in private practice are seldom found in neighborhoods characterized by large numbers of poor and nonwhite residents. Areas whose residents have relatively low levels of education and income tend to have proportionately fewer medical doctors in private practice. Consequently, shortages of physicians may exist in parts of New York City as well as in rural Alaska and Texas.

But there are a few signs that the distribution of physicians is beginning to improve. Part of this development is due to market conditions. Some areas have an oversupply of doctors, which encourages others to look elsewhere for establishing their practice. Also, some towns in rural areas advertise and try to attract doctors with special incentives to move to their locale and practice medicine there. Some states have programs to attract medical students to rural practices upon graduation by giving them scholarships or paying their tuition.

Another factor in the maldistribution of physicians is that of overspecialization, which has reduced the number of doctors engaged as general practitioners in primary care and family practice. The number of general and family practitioners declined substantially from 95,980 in 1949 to 60,049 in 1980; but by 2012, there were 110,050 doctors providing this service.

A major reason for the trend in specialization has to do with the complexities of modern medicine. Patricia Kendall and Hanan Selvin (1957) noted decades ago that as students progressed through medical school, more and more of them began to express a preference for specialized training. Kendall and Selvin found that the reason for the tendency to specialize was the students' desire to restrict themselves to a particular area of knowledge with which they could be highly skillful, rather than trying to deal with an insurmountable body of knowledge. In addition, a specialized and more manageable area of medicine may be less demanding of personal time, has more prestige, and provides a greater income. A particularly important factor for many younger doctors is having a controllable lifestyle and family time. This means more personal time away from the job and not having to deal with patients after their usual working hours.

Consequently, medical specialties such as dermatology, radiology, anesthesiology, and even emergency-room medicine became increasingly popular in recent years. For example, a dermatologist averaged $411,499 annually in 2013. Doctors in internal medicine averaged $226,833 a year and pediatricians $222,827. In comparison, general surgeons made $373,478 a year and orthopedic surgeons $525,000.

There are 24 specialty boards affiliated with the American Medical Association (AMA) that certify physicians to practice in as many as 145 medical specialties and subspecialties, such as internal medicine, pediatrics, anesthesiology, family practice, obstetrics, gynecology, dermatology, psychiatry, general surgery, orthopedic surgery, urology, ophthalmology, and neurology. While medical specialization has produced positive benefits by allowing physicians to concentrate their efforts upon treating certain parts of the body, it has produced negative side effects in that it makes it more difficult to find a physician to take on continuing responsibility for the "whole" patient.

The relatively low number and availability of primary care practitioners inhibit the access of patients to the health care delivery system in the United States. Hospital emergency rooms thus become centers of primary care because of the lack of general practitioners, the reluctance of physicians to make house calls, and the unavailability of private physicians in the urban inner city. Also relevant is the fact that hospital emergency rooms are accessible, have a minimum of administrative barriers, and have the resources of an entire hospital behind them. The people who tend to utilize emergency rooms for primary care are the underprivileged who have no other regular source of medical care. Patients who do not have true emergencies often wait for long periods before receiving care and are charged high fees.

Overview of Health Care Delivery

The existing health care delivery system in the United States is a conglomerate of health practitioners, agencies, and organizations, all of which operate more or less independently. The managed care model did not alter this patchwork system nor has health care reform yet to address it (Pescosolido and Boyer 2010). This system's current managerial controls and market mechanisms have configured it into an industry whose motivating values are efficiency and profit (Wright and Perry 2010). The greatest portion of all patient services is provided in offices and clinics by physicians who sell their services on a fee-for-service or per capita fee basis in a managed care network. About two-thirds of all active physicians involved in direct patient care work in an office- or clinic-based practice, while the remainder are mostly residents in training, full-time staff members of hospitals, administrators, or researchers.

The next most prominent form of health care delivery consists of services provided by hospitals. With the exception of tax-supported government institutions, hospitals, similar to physicians, charge patients according to a fee-for-service system. Nonprofit hospitals charge patients for hospital services from the standpoint of recovering the full cost of services provided and meeting the hospital's general expenses. Proprietary hospitals not only calculate the cost of services rendered but also function to realize a profit from those services. Nonprofit and profit-making hospitals rely heavily on third-party sources, either private health insurance or government agencies, to pay most or all of a patient's bill.

Besides office-based medical practices and hospitals, the other types of organizations involved in the delivery of health care to the American public are official agencies, voluntary agencies, HMOs, PPOs, and allied health enterprises in the business community.

Official agencies are public organizations supported by tax funds, such as the U.S. Department of Health and Human Services, the Centers for Disease Control and Prevention, the U.S. Public Health Service, and the Food and Drug Administration, which are intended to support and conduct research, develop educational materials, protect the nation's health, and provide services designed to minimize public health problems. Official agencies also have the responsibility for the direct medical care and health services required by special populations, such as reservation Indians, the mentally ill, lepers, tuberculosis patients, and others.

Voluntary agencies are charitable organizations, such as the Multiple Sclerosis Society, the American Cancer Society, and the March of Dimes, who solicit funds from the general public and use them to support medical research and to provide services for disease victims.

Health maintenance organizations (HMOs) are managed care prepaid group practices, in which a person pays a monthly premium for comprehensive health care services. HMOs are oriented toward preventive and ambulatory services intended to reduce hospitalization. Under this arrangement, HMOs derive greater income from keeping their patients healthy and not having to pay for their hospital expenses than they would if large numbers of their subscribers were hospitalized. There is evidence that HMOs and other managed care organizations reduce hospital use and produce lower overall medical costs than the traditional open-market fee-for-service pattern (Wholey and Burns 2000). Most of the savings are due to lower rates of hospitalization, but surgical rates and other fees may be lower for

HMO populations. Physicians participating in HMOs may be paid according to a fee-for-service schedule, but many are paid a salary or on a capitation (set amount per patient) basis. Membership entitles patients to receive physicians' services, hospitalization, laboratory tests, X-rays, and perhaps prescription drugs and other health needs at little or no additional cost. There are also *individual practice associations* (IPAs), which are solo practitioners or small groups of physicians who contract independently with HMOs to provide care to patients enrolled in their plans.

There are some disadvantages to HMOs, namely that patients (especially at night or on weekends) may be treated by whoever is on duty rather than their "own" doctors, and a patient may need a referral from his or her primary care practitioner to consult a specialist. HMOs have attracted considerable attention because of their cost control potential and emphasis on preventive care. The number of HMOs and their enrollment has been rapidly increasing in the last few years. In 1970, there were 37 HMOs serving 3 million people. In 2012, there were 545 HMOs enrolling over 73 million people.

Preferred provider organizations (PPOs) are managed care health organizations, in which employers who purchase group health insurance agree to send their employees to particular hospitals or doctors in return for discounts. PPOs have the advantage of being imposed on existing networks of hospitals and physicians, without having to build clinics or convert doctors into employees. Doctors and hospitals associated with a PPO are expected to provide their usual services to PPO members, but lower charges are assessed against the members' group health insurance. Thus, the health care providers obtain more patients and in return charge less to the buyer of group insurance.

Allied health enterprises are the manufacturers of pharmaceuticals and medical supplies and equipment, which play a major role in research, development, and distribution of medical goods.

The majority of Americans have health insurance benefits provided through their place of employment and paid for by contributions from both the employee and employer. In 1984, some 96 percent of all insured workers were enrolled in traditional health plans that allowed them to choose their own doctors and have most of their costs for physician and hospital services covered in an unmanaged fee-for-service arrangement. However, this situation changed because of soaring costs of health care and limitations being placed on the insurance benefits provided. By 2012, very few insured workers had unmanaged fee-for-service health plans, while the great majority had managed fee-for-service plans, in which utilization was monitored and prior approval for some benefits, such as hospitalization, was required. The day in which doctors and their patients decided just between themselves what care was needed without considering cost appears over, as financial concerns are increasingly influencing how patients are cared for and managed.

Some features of the health care delivery system in the United States remain unchanged. The system is still characterized by more than one major client—a substantial private sector, the elderly and the poor with government-sponsored health insurance, and a large but presumably shrinking uninsured population. There has also been widespread change, with the federal government, as noted, dominating health policy, as both the government and employers have become the major purchasers of health services and support managed care as the primary form of medical practice. This development means that more people with private health insurance are now limited in their use of health services to a particular managed care network, such as an HMO or PPO. Moreover, as Marsha Gold (1999:14) explains, "Physician practice is shifting away from its historical roots in self-employment toward group and salaried arrangements that are better positioned to meet the current demands on providers stemming from both the shift to managed care and growth of medical technology." Physician incomes are increasing less rapidly than in the past, and professional autonomy is declining as previously discussed.

Given the magnitude of these changes—the reorganization of medical practice into managed care, along with constraints on income and autonomy—it is not surprising, as Gold (1999:14) points out, that the satisfaction of physicians with their work situation has decreased. However, as Mary Warren and her associates (Warren, Weitz, and Kulis 1998:364) explain, "Whereas physicians 20 years ago may have been horrified at the prospect of managed care, physicians now accept it as the rules of the game—at least in areas in which high percentages of patients belong to such plans—and recognize that the price of refusing to play by those rules is bankruptcy." Thus, many physicians have had to make the adjustment to managed care, and the revenue, especially capitation fees, from this type of practice now constitutes a growing percentage of physician incomes.

Traditionally, doctors and hospitals have been paid on a fee-for-service basis. This method of payment is consistent with the principle of the open market, in which the consumers of health care, like the consumers of other products, are free to choose which health care providers offer the best services at prices they can afford. High-quality services and affordable prices are supposed to result from competition among providers. Theoretically, physicians who are incompetent or who charge excessive fees, and hospitals with lower-quality services, would be driven out of the market by more competent, reasonably priced, and more effective physicians and better hospitals. To eliminate or reduce free choice would supposedly undermine the incentive of physicians and hospitals to satisfy patients.

The unmanaged fee-for-service system is a highly attractive situation for doctors. It allows physicians to decide how much money they should charge for their services, how many patients they should have, how many hours they should work per week, and where they should practice medicine. The market, professional ethics, and sense of duty to their patients are supposed to block any desire to make as much money as possible. The reality of the fee-for-service system for doctors, however, is that their fees are typically set by fixed amounts or fee schedules (DRGs) based on what insurance companies or the government pay, and in managed care systems the flow of patients and work hours are scheduled by administrators.

Fee-for-service health care delivery is not a good example of a competitive marketplace. The fundamental law of the marketplace is supply and demand. When the supply of a product exceeds the demand for it, prices should drop. However, that law does not apply to medicine, because physicians define what patients need and provide their services at prices they, their employers, or the federal government set. Therefore, doctors and hospitals create their own demand in a market in which their services are essential. Organized medicine has traditionally opposed changing the fee-for-service system, because of the advantages it provides to the profession. Yet, fee-for-service discriminates against those people who are unable to pay the fees, making them dependent on welfare or charity. It also contributes to increased costs through high fees and the unnecessary duplication of technology and services by various providers and hospitals seeking to gain or maintain income. Rising costs and lack of universal access to quality care finally forced changes, beginning with Medicare and Medicaid in the 1960s and continuing today with the dominance of managed care systems charging a set capitation fee to patients each month and implementation of the Affordable Care Act.

However, as noted, managed care constraints have eroded leading to higher contributions for health insurance benefits on the part of both employers and employees as well as higher costs for the care itself. Light (2004) depicted the American health care delivery system before the introduction of health care reform as the most costly, inefficient, wasteful, and inequitable system of health care in the industrialized world. Mechanic (2004) described it as disorganized and irrational. "In the final analysis," states Mechanic (2004:83), "fault is in the failure of the United States to introduce a rational system of universal health care." While health care reform partially addresses the problem of equity, the organization of the current health care delivery system remains generally intact.

Health Care: A Right or a Privilege?

According to Bryan Turner (1988), one way to understand politics in modern democracies is to view issues from the standpoint of conflict theory. Conflict theory takes the position that social inequality leads to conflict, which leads to change. Its modern focus is not just on conflict between social classes, but also on competition between interest groups, as they maneuver for advantages in democratic political systems. Turner suggests that modern societies are characterized by conflict between democratic principles (which emphasize equality and universal rights) and the organization of economic services involving the production, exchange, and consumption of goods and services (which feature inequality). In other words, the ideology of advanced democracies promotes equality, but the reality of the capitalist economic system produces inequality. Conflict or tension arises, states Turner, as democracies try to resolve this contradiction and bring equality to an economic system that is inherently unequal. It is therefore possible, concludes Turner (1988:52), "to conceptualize modern politics in terms of struggles by interest blocs and communities for political recognition of their needs and interests." This outcome is seen in an analysis of diseases that have the most efficient advocacy organizations (e.g., AIDS, breast cancer) in the United States showing such interest groups have been able to reshape funding distributions by the federal government in their favor (Best 2012).

And this is also exactly what happened with respect to health care reform in the United States over the years, as various interest groups lobbied to secure their interests and were able to defeat measures for national health insurance. Also with the passage of time, some of the major players like the AMA became significantly weaker, and others, such as the federal government, became more assertive against special interests to the point that President Obama was successful with his Democratic allies in getting Congress to take action. He did not try to change the system of health care delivery by forcing a national health insurance program through Congress. This would have met greater resistance and perhaps failed. Instead, he opted for providing affordable health insurance for the uninsured, a measure that could be realized politically.

However, social scientists working in the tradition of conflict theory have long argued that Americans would best be served by adopting a national health insurance system similar to those found in Europe (Waitzkin 1991, 2001). This argument is a reaction to the traditional role of medical care as a commodity in the United States to be bought and sold. Mechanic (2006:ix) points out that most medical activity is motivated and sustained by good intentions but adds that "big money" has become dominant in health care matters. As Paul Starr (1994) explains, the best organized interests in health benefit from the present system, because the costs of health care equal incomes from health care. As Starr (1994:xxxvi–xxxvii) puts it:

> Rising costs have meant rising incomes; controlling costs means controlling incomes. The health care industry now represents a seventh [currently an eighth] of the U.S. economy, and the stakeholders in that industry—not just physicians, but hospitals, makers of medical equipment and pharmaceuticals, venture capitalists, and insurance companies—are not about to sit out a political battle that could so greatly affect their interests, in some cases their survival.

The quest for profits serves economic, political, and professional interests more so than patients and families, and health care reform efforts have to be realistic about such influences. Obtaining affordable health insurance for the uninsured is an historic change but is not likely to be the end of reform. In the final analysis, what health reform is really about is the issue of whether medical care is a *right* of all Americans or whether it is a *privilege*. As a commodity, medical care is a privilege. One argument is that such care is indeed a privilege, not a right, and if people want medical treatment, they should pay for it. The difficulty of the training and the high value of the skills required to become a physician, as well as the time and effort put into providing care, should entitle doctors to receive high incomes. Others in the health field should be appropriately reimbursed for their services, too. This argument should not necessarily be construed to mean that the poor are unworthy of receiving medical care. Behind this argument is a generalized opposition to the welfare state; it is felt that the best way to help the poor is to provide them with jobs so that they can *buy* medical care like everybody else. To give the poor the highest quality of medical care available without improving the conditions of poverty within which they live is thought to be an exercise in futility.

However, a more socially responsible argument is that medical care does represent a special case. More in the nature of an opportunity rather than a commodity, quality health care should be available as a right of all Americans, regardless of living conditions or financial status. As Jill Quadagno (2005) points out, the right to health care is recognized in international law and guaranteed in the constitutions of many nations. This is why virtually all Western countries—other than the United States—provide every citizen some type of national health insurance coverage. Although many of these countries also permit their citizens to purchase private health insurance to supplement or upgrade their government-provided benefits, all citizens are nonetheless guaranteed essential health services by the state. However, since the United States does not have national health insurance, people are adversely affected when the costs of care rise above what the average person can pay on their own and insurance to cover those costs is beyond their ability to purchase as well.

Even though people have the ability through their choice of lifestyles and preventive measures to influence their health status, many health problems are beyond their control. For example, a person's health can be adversely affected by genetics, the environment, or even chance in the case of accidents, exposure to disease, or an adverse class situation causing greater risk. While it seems reasonable for individuals to bear the responsibility for health outcomes based upon their informed and voluntary choice, people are not always fully informed about the consequences of their behavior, and some health problems arise that individuals are unable to contain on their own.

A society's commitment to health care reflects some of its most basic values about what it is to be a member of the human community. Therefore, it can be argued that society has an ethical obligation to ensure equitable access to health services by making that care a basic social right. This is because of health care's special importance to society in relieving suffering, preventing premature death, and restoring the ability to function to the people who live in it. The concept that the individual has a right to health care and society the ethical obligation to provide it has been accepted by those countries that have national health insurance coverage for its population.

Movement toward conceptualizing and establishing health care as a right in the capitalist economy of the United States is consistent with other measures associated with being a welfare state. The advent of the welfare state in Western society, as T. H. Marshall (1964) explained, is a culmination of processes that began in the eighteenth century. Marshall pointed out that the establishment of the welfare state is the latest phase in the evolution of citizens' rights in the West. To *civil* rights (gained in the eighteenth century), such as freedom of speech and equality before the law, and *political* rights (acquired in the late eighteenth and nineteenth centuries), such as the right to vote and participate in the exercise of government, were added *social* rights (achieved in the late nineteenth and twentieth centuries) of protection from economic insecurity and the provision of at least a marginal level of economic welfare.

The emergence of these various rights of citizenship, all promoting equality, states Marshall, is a paradox, because they came during the same historical period as the rise of capitalism, which essentially is a system of inequality. Inequality in the capitalist system stems from the fact that it is based on private ownership of property and the gearing of economic activity to profit in the marketplace. Individuals are not equal in the amount of property they own or acquire, their position in relation to the production of goods and services in the marketplace, and the amount of profits (or losses) they derive from their work. As John Myles (1984:30) comments, "This marriage between a protective state and a capitalist economy was a union of opposites, for it required an accommodation between two opposing logics of distribution—one that attached rights to the possession of *property* and another that attached rights to *persons* in their capacity as citizens."

Essentially, what had taken place, in Marshall's (1964) view, was conflict between the rights of citizenship considered inherent in a democratic society by the general populace and the capitalist social class system. In the modern welfare state, individual rights of citizenship, not ownership and control of property, emerged as the basis for political representation and entitlement to public programs. Current efforts at health care reform are an extension of the rights of citizenship to health care in the United States. Canada and the nations of the European Union have previously made health care a social right.

Summary

This chapter has examined health care reform in the United States and the issues surrounding the rising costs of health care, problems in equity, and the unequal distribution of health services. The road to health reform was reviewed, including the passage of Medicare and Medicaid that signified the emergence of public awareness that the medical profession's interests were not always those of the general public and Clinton's failed effort that nonetheless stimulated the rise of managed care. The focus was on the Obama administration's health care reform measures contained in the Affordable Care Act that were intended to make health insurance more affordable for the majority of uninsured. While this measure has not changed the system of health care delivery, it tries to resolve the deficiencies in equity by addressing the health problems of uninsured persons. This reform is also another step toward establishing health care as a social right consistent with the social policy of virtually all other Western welfare states.

Critical Thinking Questions

1. Why are health expenditures rising in the United States? What are some of the major efforts taken to contain costs?
2. What are some of the initial successes and failures of the Affordable Care Act? Explain why they happened and the outcome. Analyze its impact on health care delivery in the United States.
3. How has the rise of managed care changed the way people receive health care?
4. Is health care a right or a privilege? Defend your answer.

Suggested Readings

Buse, Kent, Nicholas Mays, and Gill Walt (2012) *Making health policy*, 2nd ed. New York: McGraw-Hill.
A textbook on how health policies are developed.
Pescosolido, Bernice A. and Carol A. Boyer (2010) "The American health care system: Beginning the twenty-first century with high risk, major challenges, and great opportunities," pp. 391–411 in *The New Blackwell Companion to Medical Sociology*, William Cockerham (ed.). Oxford, UK: Wiley-Blackwell.
A thorough and richly detailed account of the conditions leading to health care reform.
Quadagno, Jill (2010) "Institutions, interest groups, and ideology: An agenda for the sociology of health care reform." *Journal of Health and Social Behavior* 51: 125–36.
A sociological analysis of health care reform.

References

Best, Rachel Kahn (2012) "Disease politics and medical research funding: Three ways advocacy shapes policy." *American Sociological Research* 77: 780–803.

Budrys, Grace (2001) *Our unsystematic health care system*. Lanham, MD: Rowman & Littlefield.

——— (2003) *Unequal health*. Lanham, MD: Rowman & Littlefield.

Caronna, Carol (2004) "The mis-alignment of institutional 'pillars.' " *Journal of Health and Social Behavior* 45(Extra issue): 45–58.

Casalino, Larry (2004) "Unfamiliar tasks, contested jurisdictions." *Journal of Health and Social Behavior* 45(Extra issue): 59–75.

Gold, Marsha R. (1999) "The changing US health care system: Challenges for responsible public policy." *Milbank Quarterly* 77: 3–37.

Kendall, Patricia L., and Hanan C. Selvin (1957) "Tendencies toward specialization in medical training," pp. 153–74 in *The student-physician*, R. Merton, G. Reader, and P. Kendall (eds.). Cambridge, MA: Harvard University Press.

Light, Donald W. (2004) "Introduction: Ironies of success—A new history of the American health care 'system.' " *Journal of Health and Social Behavior* 45(Extra issue): 1–24.

Marshall, T. H. (1964) *Class, citizenship, and social development*. Chicago: University of Chicago Press.

McWilliams, J. Michael, Ellen Meara, Alan M. Zaslavsky, and John Ayanian (2007) "Health of previously uninsured adults after acquiring Medicare coverage." *JAMA* 298: 2886–94.

Mechanic, David (2004) "The rise and fall of managed care." *Journal of Health and Social Behavior* 45(Extra issue): 76–86.

——— (2006) *The truth about health care: Why reform is not working in America*. New Brunswick, NJ: Rutgers University Press.

Myles, John F. (1984) *Old age in the welfare state*. Boston: Little, Brown.

National Center For Health Statistics (2014) Health United States, 2013. Washington, DC: U.S. Government Printing Office.

Pescosolido, Bernice A., and Carol A. Boyer (2010) "The American health care system: Entering the twenty-first century with high risk, major challenges, and great opportunities," pp. 391–411 in *The new Blackwell companion to medical sociology*, W. Cockerham (ed.). Oxford, UK: Blackwell.

Pescosolido, Bernice A., Jane McLeod, and Margarita Alegría (2000) "Confronting the second social contract: The place of medical sociology in research and policy for the twenty-first century," pp. 411–26 in *Handbook of medical sociology*, 5th ed., C. Bird, P. Conrad, and A. Fremont (eds.). Upper Saddle River, NJ: Prentice-Hall.

Pescosolido, Bernice A., Steven A. Tuch, and Jack K. Martin (2001) "The profession of medicine and the public: Examining Americans' changing confidence in physician authority from the beginning of the 'health care crisis' to the era of health care reform." *Journal of Health and Social Behavior* 42: 1–16.

Quadagno, Jill (2004) "Why the United States has no national health insurance: Stakeholder mobilization against the welfare state, 1945–1996." *Journal of Health and Social Behavior* 45(Extra issue): 25–44.

——— (2005) *One nation, uninsured: Why the U.S. has no national health insurance*. New York: Oxford University Press.

——— (2010) "Institutions, interest groups, and ideology: An agenda for the sociology of health reform." *Journal of Health and Social Behavior* 51: 125–36.

Quesnel-Vallée, Amélie (2004) "Is it really worse to have public health insurance than to have no insurance at all? Health insurance and adult health in the United States." *Journal of Health and Social Behavior* 45: 376–92.

Quesnel-Vallée, Amélie, and Tania Jenkins (2010) "Social policies and health inequalities," pp. 455–83 in *The new Blackwell companion to medical sociology*, W. Cockerham (ed.). Oxford, UK: Wiley-Blackwell.

Schumock, Glen T., Edward C. Li, Katie J. Suda, Linda M. Matusiak, Robert J. Hunkler, Lee C. Vermeulen, and James M. Hoffman (2014) "National trends in prescription drug expenditures and projections for 2014." *American Journal of Health-System Pharmacists* 71: e6–23.

Starr, Paul (1982) *The social transformation of American medicine.* New York: Basic Books.

——— (1994) *The logic of health care reform*, rev. and enl. ed. New York: Penguin Books.

Stevens, Fred (2010) "The convergence and divergence of modern health care systems," pp. 434–54 in *The new Blackwell companion to medical sociology*, W. Cockerham (ed.). Oxford, UK: Blackwell.

Stevens, Rosemary (1971) *American medicine and the public interest.* New Haven, CT: Yale University Press.

Turner, Bryan S. (1988) *Status.* Milton Keynes, UK: Open University Press.

Waitzkin, Howard (1991) *The politics of medical encounters.* New Haven, CT: Yale University Press.

Warren, Mary Guptill, Rose Weitz, and Stephen Kulis (1998) "Physician satisfaction in a changing health care environment: The impact of challenges to professional autonomy, authority, and dominance." *Journal of Health and Social Behavior* 39: 356–67.

Weiss, Gregory L. (2006) *Grass roots medicine: The story of America's free health clinics.* Lanham, MD: Rowman & Littlefield.

Wholey, Douglas R., and Lawton R. Burns (2000) "Tides of change: The evolution of managed care," pp. 217–37 in *Handbook of medical sociology*, 5th ed., C. Bird, P. Conrad, and A. Fremont (eds.). Upper Saddle River, NJ: Prentice Hall.

Wright, Eric R., and Brea L. Perry (2010) "Medical sociology and health services research: Past accomplishments and future policy challenges." *Journal of Health and Social Behavior* 51: S107–19.

CHAPTER 16

Global Health Care

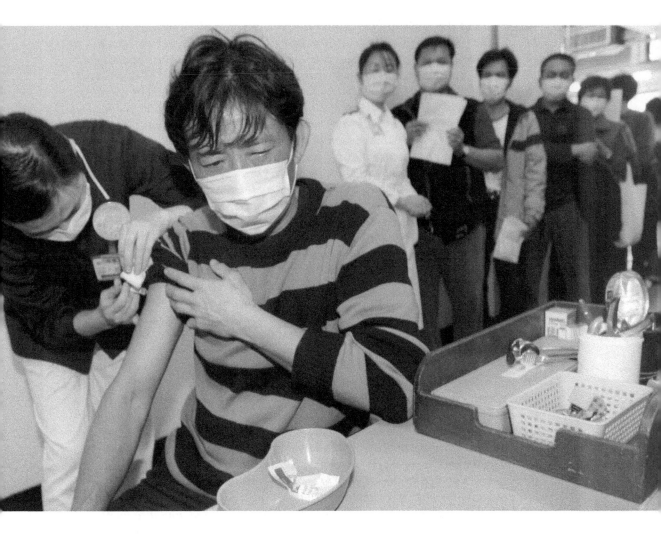

All nations of the world are faced with the pressure of public demands for quality health care and the rising costs of providing that care. Different approaches to these problems have led to renewed interest in comparative or transnational studies of health care systems in order to learn from the experiences of other countries (Amzat and Razum 2014; Kikuzawa, Olafsdottir, and Pescosolido 2008; Olafsdottir and Beckfield 2011; Quadagno 2010; Stevens 2010). In this chapter, the focus is on modern forms of socialized health care common to Canada, Great Britain, and Sweden, followed by an examination of decentralized national health programs in Japan, Germany, and Mexico and former socialist systems in Russia and China.

The value of studying the health care delivery systems of different countries is the insight provided into the norms, values, culture, and national outlook of those societies, as well as the lessons learned from their experiences. Health care delivery systems worldwide are faced with the same problem of rising costs, aging populations, and the requirement to meet their nation's health needs. However, they differ in the variety of their approach. Such systems do not evolve in a vacuum but reflect the social and political philosophy of the country in which they exist. Therefore, social and political values underlie the choices made, the institutions formed, and the levels of funding provided. A nation's approach to health care is based upon its historical experience, culture, economy, political ideology, social organization, level of education and standard of living, economic resources, and attitudes toward welfare and the role of the state.

In Europe, the provision of health services became an important component of government policy in the last half of the nineteenth century. Behind this development was the desire of various European governments for a healthy population whose productivity could be translated into economic and military power. In some countries, providing national health insurance was also a means to reduce political discontent and the threat of revolution from the working class. Compulsory health insurance was usually part of a larger program of social insurance intended to protect the income of workers when sick, disabled, unemployed, or elderly. Initially, protection was provided only to wage earners below a certain income level, but gradually benefits were extended to all or most of the population. Germany established the first national health insurance program in 1883, followed by Austria in 1888, and other European countries over the course of the twentieth century.

Entitlements based on citizenship are aimed at providing people with welfare and health benefits, regardless of their class position. The social welfare systems of Europe are more advanced in this direction than in the United States. Many Europeans receive comprehensive health insurance; protection of lost income due to illness, injury, or unemployment; and allowances to supplement family expenses for the maintenance of children, such as clothing and school lunches. These benefits are provided to all citizens, the affluent and the nonaffluent alike. The result is that European governments are typically responsible for the delivery of health care and most of its financing. For example, over 80 percent of all health costs in the European Union (EU) are financed from public sources, either through national health insurance programs or direct payments by the state.

It was not until 1965 and the passage of Medicare and Medicaid that the United States provided health care benefits for some Americans—the aged and the poor. When European governments were introducing social insurance programs, the U.S. government was not deeply involved in regulating either the economy or the health services. Although this has changed, Americans have historically been less committed to government welfare programs and more in favor of private enterprise in dealing with economic and social problems. However, except for the elderly, participation in the welfare system is still not considered normative in the United States, and those Americans under the age of 65 who do receive welfare benefits tend to be stigmatized and have low social status. In Europe, providing welfare and social security for the general population, not just the poor and elderly, is a normal feature of the state's role. This situation implies a fundamental difference in the social values of Americans and Europeans, with Americans stressing individualism and Europeans viewing government in a more paternalistic fashion.

The United States spends more on health than any other country in the world. Table 16.1 shows the total health expenditures as a percentage of gross domestic

TABLE 16.1	Total Health Expenditures as a Percentage of Gross Domestic Product: Selected Countries, Selected Years, 1960–2009									
Country	1960	1970	1975	1980	1985	1990	1995	2000	2005	2009
Australia	4.3	5.4	5.7	7.0	7.5	7.9	8.2	8.8	8.4	—
Austria	4.3	5.3	7.3	7.6	6.6	7.1	8.5	9.4	10.4	11.0
Belgium	3.4	4.0	5.8	6.4	7.2	7.4	8.7	8.6	10.1	10.9
Canada	5.4	7.0	7.3	7.1	8.3	9.0	9.3	8.9	9.8	11.4
Czech Republic	—	—	—	—	4.5	5.0	7.3	6.7	7.2	8.2
Denmark	3.6	6.1	6.5	9.1	8.7	8.5	8.2	8.5	9.8	11.5
Finland	3.9	5.6	6.3	6.4	7.2	7.9	7.5	6.7	8.4	9.2
France	4.1	5.7	6.8	7.4	8.3	8.6	9.6	9.2	11.1	11.8
Germany	4.7	6.3	7.8	8.8	9.3	8.7	10.2	10.3	10.7	11.6
Greece	3.1	5.6	—	6.5	—	—	8.9	9.9	9.6	—
Hungary	—	—	—	—	—	—	7.5	7.1	8.3	7.4
Iceland	3.3	4.9	5.9	6.1	7.2	7.9	8.2	9.2	9.4	9.7
Ireland	3.6	5.1	7.7	8.4	7.6	6.7	7.3	6.3	7.6	9.5
Italy	3.6	5.1	5.8	7.0	7.0	8.1	7.9	8.1	8.9	9.5
Japan	3.0	4.6	5.5	6.5	6.7	6.1	7.2	7.6	8.2	—
Mexico	—	—	—	—	—	4.4	5.6	5.6	5.9	6.4
Netherlands	3.9	6.0	7.7	8.0	7.8	8.5	8.9	7.9	9.8	12.0

(continued)

TABLE 16.1	Total Health Expenditures as a Percentage of Gross Domestic Product: Selected Countries, Selected Years, 1960–2009 (continued)									
Country	1960	1970	1975	1980	1985	1990	1995	2000	2005	2009
New Zealand	4.3	5.2	6.4	6.0	5.3	7.0	7.3	7.7	8.7	10.3
Norway	—	—	—	—	—	8.0	8.0	8.5	9.1	9.6
Poland	—	—	—	—	—	5.3	6.0	5.7	6.2	7.4
Portugal	—	—	6.4	5.6	6.1	6.2	7.6	9.4	10.4	—
Spain	1.5	3.6	5.1	5.4	5.4	6.6	7.0	7.2	8.3	9.5
Sweden	4.5	6.9	8.0	9.1	8.7	8.5	8.1	8.4	9.1	10.0
Switzerland	4.8	5.4	7.0	7.3	7.7	8.3	9.6	10.4	11.2	11.4
United Kingdom	3.9	4.5	5.5	5.6	5.9	6.0	6.9	7.3	8.2	9.8
United States	5.1	7.0	8.4	8.8	10.1	12.0	13.4	13.3	15.7	17.4

Source: National Center for Health Statistics, 2013.

product (GDP) for selected countries from 1960 to 2009. In 1960, the United States was second only to Canada in health spending but forged into a tie for first place in 1970 and has been first ever since—except in 1980 when Sweden spent a higher percentage of its GDP. Table 16.1 shows that for 2009 (the most recent year comparative data are available as this book is being published), the United States spent 17.4 percent of its GDP on health, followed by the Netherlands at 12.0 percent, and France at 11.8 percent. The country with the lowest percentage of health expenditures in 2009 among the countries shown in Table 16.1 is Mexico at 6.4 percent.

Another measure of health costs is per capita health expenditures. Table 16.2 indicates that the United States spent more per capita from 1960 to 2009 than any other country. For 2009, Table 16.2 shows the United States spent $7,960 per capita on health. Mexico was last with expenditures of $918. The United States clearly leads the world in health care spending because its costs for care are the most expensive anywhere. For example, in 2013, a hip replacement operation in the United States could cost $8,050 for three nights in a hospital room, $36,861 for the artificial hip implant, and $17,500 for the surgeon's fee for a total of $67,461; the same hip replacement in Belgium at that time would be $3,700 for the room, $4,200 for the implant, and $1,110 for the surgeon for a total of $9,010 (Rosenthal 2013). Americans or their insurance providers literally pay more for everything—doctors' fees, laboratory tests, childbirths, surgery, hospital charges, emergency room visits, prescription drugs, nursing care, and so on.

Yet, on the two most common measures of a country's overall level of health—infant mortality and life expectancy—the United States does not rank especially high. As shown in Table 16.3, Japan and Finland had the lowest infant mortality rate in the world at 2.3 per 1,000 live births in 2010. Sweden and Portugal were next with a rate of 2.5 infant deaths per 1,000 live births. The United States was twenty-sixth among the twenty-nine countries in Table 16.3, with an infant mortality in 2010 of

6.1 per 1,000 live births. Poland, Hungary, New Zealand, and the Slovak Republic all had lower rates of infant mortality than the United States.

As for life expectancy, perhaps the best overall single measure of a nation's health, Table 16.4 shows that Switzerland had the highest life expectancy for males at 80.3 years in 2010. Next are Israel, Japan, Australia, and Iceland. The United States ranked twenty-fifth in male life expectancy at 76.2 years among the countries

TABLE 16.2 Per Capita Health Expenditures: Selected Countries, Selected Years, 1960–2009

Country	1960	1970	1975	1980	1985	1990	1995	2000	2005	2009
Australia	$89	$212	$443	$663	$998	$1,318	$1,792	$2,398	$2,980	$3,946
Austria	64	159	377	663	816	1,205	1,834	2,667	3,472	4,363
Belgium	53	130	310	578	884	1,247	1,906	2,227	3,231	2,108
Canada	109	260	434	710	1,193	1,678	2,128	2,503	3,442	4,363
Czech Republic	—	—	—	—	—	576	901	980	1,475	2,108
Denmark	—	—	—	819	1,177	1,453	1,882	2,380	3,245	4,348
Finland	54	163	312	510	849	1,292	1,421	1,716	2,589	3,226
France	72	206	393	701	1,082	1,520	1,991	2,450	3,306	3,978
Germany	77	224	462	824	1,242	1,602	2,178	2,632	3,364	4,218
Greece	21	100	104	345	—	707	1,139	1,616	2,352	—
Hungary	—	—	—	—	—	—	678	856	1,411	1,511
Iceland	50	137	294	576	947	1,376	1,823	2,623	3,303	3,538
Ireland	35	98	233	455	592	796	796	1,809	2,959	3,781
Italy	49	154	286	579	831	1,327	1,589	2,083	2,516	3,137
Japan	26	130	260	523	818	1,082	1,632	1,967	2,491	—
Mexico	—	—	—	—	—	260	388	506	731	918
Netherlands	—	207	414	715	961	1,403	2,714	2,257	3,450	4,914
New Zealand	90	—	359	456	587	937	1,244	1,605	2,197	2,983
Norway	46	131	311	632	915	1,363	1,864	3,080	4,301	5,352
Poland	—	—	—	—	—	258	420	590	857	1,394
Portugal	—	45	154	260	381	614	1,050	1,624	2,212	—
Spain	14	82	190	325	454	815	1,068	1,520	2,269	3,067
Sweden	89	270	477	850	1,172	1,492	1,622	2,271	2,963	3,722
Switzerland	132	279	522	854	1,251	1,782	2,477	3,179	4,015	5,144
United Kingdom	74	144	277	444	669	968	1,301	1,858	2,735	3,487
United States	141	341	582	1,052	1,735	2,688	3,637	3,637	6,700	7,960

Source: National Center for Health Statistics (2013).

| | Infant Mortality Rate | |
| | 1990 | 2010 |
Country	Infant deaths per 1,000 live births	
Japan	4.6	2.3
Finland	5.6	2.3
Sweden	6.0	2.5
Portugal	10.9	2.5
Czech Republic	10.8	2.7
Norway	6.9	2.8
Spain	7.6	3.2
South Korea	—	3.2
Denmark	7.5	3.4
Germany	7.0	3.4
Italy	8.1	3.4
Belgium	8.0	3.6
France	7.3	3.6
Israel	9.9	3.7
Greece	9.7	3.8
Ireland	8.2	3.8
Netherlands	7.1	3.8
Switzerland	6.8	3.8
Austria	7.8	3.9
Australia	8.2	4.1
United Kingdom	7.9	4.2
Canada	6.8	4.9*
Poland	19.4	5.0
Hungary	14.8	5.3
New Zealand	8.4	5.5
Slovak Republic	12.0	5.2
United States	9.2	6.1
Chile	16.0	7.4
Turkey	51.5	7.8
Russia	26.9	10.3
China	50.2*	12.1*
Mexico	—	14.1

TABLE 18.3 Infant Mortality Rates: Selected Countries, 1990 and 2010

Source: National Center for Health Statistics (2014) and Statistics Canada (2013).
*Infant mortality rate for Canada is for 2009; infant mortality rates for China are for 1991 and 2011, respectively.

TABLE 16.4 Life Expectancy at Birth, According to Sex: Selected Countries, 2010

| | Males | | Females |
Country	Life Expectancy in Years	Country	Life Expectancy in Years
Switzerland	80.3	Japan	86.4
Israel	79.7	Spain	85.3
Japan	79.6	Switzerland	84.9
Australia	79.5	France	84.7
Iceland	79.5	Italy	84.6
Sweden	79.5	South Korea	84.1
Italy	79.4	Australia	84.0
New Zealand	79.1	Israel	83.6
Spain	79.1	Iceland	83.5
Norway	79.0	Sweden	83.5
Netherlands	78.8	Austria	83.5
Canada*	78.8	Finland	83.5
Ireland	78.7	Norway	83.3
United Kingdom	78.6	Canada*	83.3
Greece	78.4	Ireland	83.2
France	78.0	Belgium	83.0
Germany	78.0	Germany	83.0
Austria	77.9	Belgium	83.0
Belgium	77.6	New Zealand	82.8
Denmark	77.2	Greece	82.8
South Korea	77.2	Portugal	82.8
Finland	76.9	Netherlands	82.7
Portugal	76.7	Slovenia	82.7
Slovenia	76.3	United Kingdom	82.6
United States	76.2	Chile	82.0
Chile	75.9	Denmark	81.4
Czech Republic	74.5	United States	81.1
Mexico	73.1	Czech Republic	80.9
Poland	72.1	Poland	80.6
Turkey	71.8	Estonia	80.5
China*	71.8	Slovak Republic	78.8
Slovak Republic	71.6	Mexico	77.8
Estonia	70.5	Turkey	76.8
Hungary	70.5	China	75.2*
Russia	63.1	Russia	74.9

Source: National Center for Health Statistics (2013) and *Statistics Canada* (2013).
*Life expectancy in Canada is for 2009; life expectancy in China is for 2011.

listed. Table 16.4 indicates that males in Slovenia and Portugal lived longer on average than their American counterparts. For females, Table 16.4 shows Japan with the highest life expectancy at 86.4 years for 2010. Spain was next at 85.3 years, followed by Switzerland and France. The United States is shown in Table 16.4 to have a female life expectancy of 81.1 years, which is ranked twenty-sixth highest, behind Denmark and just ahead of the Czech Republic.

Socialized Medicine: Canada, Britain, and Sweden

A summary of the key features of fee-for-service, socialized medicine, decentralized national health, and socialist systems are shown in Table 16.5 (Field 1989). The fee-for-service model was examined in Chapter 15 on the United States. In this section, socialized medicine will be discussed. Socialized medicine refers to a system of health care delivery in which health care is provided in the form of a state-supported consumer service. That is, health care is purchased, but the buyer is the government, which makes the services available at little or no additional cost to the consumer. There are several different forms of socialized medicine, and the types that exist in Canada, Britain, and Sweden will be reviewed. Despite some differences between countries, what is common to all systems of socialized medicine, as shown in Table 16.5, is that the government (1) directly controls the financing and organization of health service in a capitalist economy; (2) directly pays providers; (3) owns most of the facilities (Canada is an exception); (4) guarantees equal access to the general population; and (5) allows some private care for patients willing to be responsible for their own expenses.

Canada

The Canadian system of health care delivery is of particular interest to Americans, because it is the system most often discussed as a future model for the United States (Dickinson and Bolaria 2005; Segall and Fries 2011). Like the United States, physicians in Canada are generally private, self-employed, fee-for-service practitioners. Unlike the

TABLE 16.5 The Role of Government and Types of Health Care Delivery Systems

Role of Government	Types of Systems			
	Fee-for-Service	Socialized Medicine	Decentralized National Health	Socialist Medicine
Regulation	Limited	Direct	Indirect	Direct
Payments to providers	Limited	Direct	Indirect	Direct
Ownership of facilities	Private and public	Private and public	Private and public	Public
Public access	Not guaranteed	Guaranteed	Guaranteed	Guaranteed
Private care	Dominant	Limited	Limited	Unavailable

United States, doctors' fees are paid by government-sponsored national health insurance, known as Medicare, according to a fee schedule negotiated between the provincial or territorial government and the medical association. Most hospitals also operate on a budget negotiated with government officials at the provincial or territorial level. Thus, Canada does not have a single health care delivery system, but instead ten provincial and three territorial ones. The federal government, however, influences health policy and the delivery of care through fiscal and budgetary mechanisms, so the Canadian system is not as decentralized as that of Germany or France, where central governments exercise little direct control over health matters. Canada essentially has a private system of health care delivery paid for almost entirely by public money.

The publicly financed health care system is supported by taxes and premiums collected by the federal and provincial/territorial governments. Responsibility for providing health care rests with each province or territory, with federal government supplementary funds. Virtually every Canadian has comprehensive insurance coverage for hospital and doctor expenses. Dental care, prescription drugs for persons under age 65, ambulance service, private hospital rooms, and eyeglasses are not covered.

Canada was late in adopting its version of socialized medicine. Universal hospital insurance was not provided until 1961, and coverage for physician fees was not passed until 1971, over the opposition of doctors. Prior to this period, Canadians paid their medical and hospital bills in a variety of ways—direct payments by patients, private health insurance, and municipal government payments. The health profile of Canadians with respect to infant mortality and life expectancy is better than for Americans. Table 16.3 shows that, in 2009, Canadians had a lower rate of infant mortality than Americans in 2010 (4.9 as compared to 6.1 deaths per 1,000 live births). Table 16.4 shows that Canadian males had a life expectancy of 78.8 years in 2009 compared to 76.2 years for American males in 2010. Canadian females had a life expectancy of 83.3 years in 2009 compared to 81.1 years in 2010 for American females. Like the United States and other countries, Canada has a social gradient in health and life expectancy, with Canadians at the bottom of the class structure being less healthy and living less longer lives than those at the top (Alter, Stukel, Chong, and Henry 2011; Kosteniuk and Dickinson 2003; Segall and Fries 2011). Universal health insurance coverage in Canada has reduced social disparities in health but not eliminated them (Alter et al. 2011).

The major problem facing Canada with respect to health care delivery is, as in most other major countries, one of rising costs. During the 1970s, Canada's expenditures for health remained constant at about 7 percent of GDP but rose to over 8 percent in the early 1980s. The federal government realized it had no control over spending and enacted Bill C-37 in 1977, which limited federal contributions to national health insurance and made them independent of provincial health spending. Federal income and corporate taxes were also reduced, thereby giving the provinces room to increase their taxes to balance spending without increasing the overall tax rate. Federal taxes went down, but provincial taxes went up, and taxation in general stayed at about the same level. Until 2004, the federal government paid about 24 percent of health care costs, the provinces/territories 44 percent, private spending 30 percent, local governments 1 percent, and worker's compensation 1 percent. At that time, these levels changed, with the federal government agreeing to send an additional $14 billion in federal money over the next six years to the provinces and territories for health care, with guarantees of additional 6 percent annual increases through to 2015. This agreement to increase federal contributions should help equalize the budget allotments for all levels of government by bringing more federal money into the health care system. In coming years, federal and provincial/territorial spending levels should be more similar. The new monies were necessary to offset the country's growing problems in the health sector, including an increasing shortage of doctors and nurses, lengthy waits for cancer care and surgery, and mounting costs for drugs for an aging population.

The private market for health is also growing in Canada, with the emergence of private clinics that accept both public and private health insurance. Canada's private health insurance, usually provided by employers, supplements public benefits with coverage for private or semiprivate hospital rooms, prescription drugs, dental and vision care, and other services. In 1984, the Canada Health Act was passed, reaffirming the principle of universal access to health care and imposed penalties on provinces that allowed physicians to charge patients fees above government limits. By 1987, all provinces had banned extra billing by doctors. However, while Canadian health care is essentially free at the point of service in that patients never see a bill, it is not free for the taxpayer. Canadians pay 15 to 20 percent more in income tax than Americans, with the result that some of the affluent pay over half of their income in taxes. Quebec, for example, has the highest income tax, and persons in the highest tax bracket pay 51.7 percent of their income in taxes. Canadians also pay a sales tax (value added tax) of about 15 percent on their purchases.

Canadian physicians, like their American counterparts, are a profession whose power is in decline (Dickinson and Bolaria 2005). In 1986, doctors in Ontario conducted a major strike in protest to the federal government's decision to curtail the extra billing of patients. The issue was over whether or not doctors could set their own fees. The medical profession in Ontario contended that the Canada Health Act changed their status from that of private practitioner to "public employee," since the government determined how much physicians could charge for their services. Many physicians supported the strike, but others did not, and the protest collapsed, leaving the government's position unchanged. Since the mid-1980s, there has been little or no conflict between the government and the medical profession. Most Canadian physicians today appear to have accepted the government's payment system. Virtually all Canadian doctors participate in provincial health plans and have no other major source of payment for most medical procedures.

Canadians appear to prefer their health care system—especially in contrast to the American model. Major reasons for the greater satisfaction of Canadians with their health care delivery system are its quality and lower cost. Canadian patients pay virtually nothing directly to doctors and hospitals. Rather, the provincial governments are the nation's purchaser of health services, paying a set fee to doctors for patient care and providing a set budget for operating costs to hospitals. Canadian hospitals, unlike American hospitals, cannot make more money by providing more services. The essential difference between the United States and Canada in health spending, as Robert Evans (1986) explained years ago, is that the Canadian system combines universal comprehensive coverage for the population combined with cost controls. "Universal coverage," as Evans (1986:597) points out, "is a necessary condition for government to engage in bilateral negotiations to exercise the leverage whereby cost escalation can be controlled." Since the government buys essentially all the care provided, it has the leverage to control the costs of that care. The largest drawback to the Canadian system is long waits for some medical procedures, such as certain types of surgery, cancer radiation, and some diagnostic tests. It may take up to 16 weeks after diagnosis, for example, for cancer radiation treatment. When such delays are serious for individual patients, sometimes they cross the border into the United States on their own to obtain private care or the government allows them to do so at government expense.

The most significant recent change in Canada's public health care delivery system occurred when the Supreme Court ruled in 2005 that Quebec's ban on private health insurance was unconstitutional. The court held that the prohibition on banning private health insurance is not constitutional when the public system fails to deliver reasonable services. Quebec is allowing patients to be treated in private hospitals when they cannot be treated within six months in the public system, while Alberta, British Columbia, and other provinces are encouraging the expansion of private health facilities and insurance. Yet problems remain. Canada's population is aging, so fewer people will be working and paying taxes to support the health care system. At the same time, demands on the system will be increasing because older people need more care. Canada faces major challenges in maintaining the quality of its health care in the twenty-first century.

Britain

Britain had inaugurated a national health insurance program between 1911 and 1913, but it provided limited benefits and covered only manual workers. In 1948 the British government went much further and formed the National Health Service (NHS) by nationalizing and taking over the responsibility for the country's health care. In such circumstances, the government becomes the employer for health workers, maintains facilities, and purchases supplies and new equipment through the use of funds collected largely by taxation and allocated by Parliament. Health services are provided at no cost to those who use them. The NHS is Britain's largest employer with 1.7 million employees in 2013. It is also the largest publicly funded health service in the world.

Although Germany was the first country to enact national health insurance, Britain established the first health care system in any Western society to offer free medical care to the entire population. Prior to 1948, the quality of care one received in Britain clearly depended on one's financial resources, with the poor suffering from a decidedly adverse situation. The Labor Party, which was in power after World War II, wanted to ensure that everyone would receive medical treatment free of charge. To accomplish this purpose, the government had to take over privately owned medical facilities. The National Health Service Act of 1948 reorganized health care delivery in the United Kingdom under the single umbrella of the NHS. This organizational structure changed in 2000 with the political separation of the NHS into separate semi-autonomous health services for England, Wales, Scotland, and Northern Ireland (Bury 2010; Hughes and Vincent-Jones 2008).

The first line of medical care in Britain remains that of the general practitioner (GP) who works from an office or clinic as part of either a solo or group practice. GPs are paid an annual capitation fee for each patient on their patient list, as part of a contractual arrangement with their NHS. The average number of patients on a GP's list is about 2,000. With special permission, a GP may have up to 3,500 patients on his or her list, if a solo practitioner. Group practices can have even larger patient lists, depending on the number of doctors involved. The GP is required to provide medical services free of charge. The patient (if over the age of 16) has the right to select his or her doctor, and the doctor is free to accept or reject anyone as a full-time patient. But if a potential patient is rejected from joining a doctor's list, the doctor must still provide treatment if the person is not on any other physician's list or if the person's physician is absent. A higher capitation fee is paid for patients who are 65 years of age or older, and additional sums are paid by the government to meet certain basic office expenses, to join a group practice, for additional training, for seniority, and for practicing medicine in areas that are underserved by physicians.

Except for emergencies, if treatment by a specialist (called "consultant" in the British system) or hospitalization is warranted, the GP must refer the patient to a specialist. Generally, specialists are the only physicians who treat patients in hospitals and are paid a salary by the government. About 11 percent of the total funds to support the NHS are derived from payroll deductions and employer's contributions, thus most of the revenue comes from general taxation. The average worker pays about 9 percent of his or her earnings for national health insurance, which is matched by employers.

Because of strong opposition from physicians when the NHS was first organized, physicians are also allowed to treat private patients, and a certain number of hospital beds ("pay" beds) are reserved for this type of patients. Private patients are responsible for paying their own bills, and most of them have health insurance from private insurance companies. The advantage of being a private patient is less time spent in waiting rooms and obtaining appointments and, of course, more privacy. In addition to the medical care provided by the NHS, the British have a sickness benefit fund to supplement income while a person is sick or injured, death benefits paid to survivors, and maternity benefits.

The British Medical Association (BMA) had initially opposed both the enactment of national health insurance between 1911 and 1913 and the formation of the NHS after World War II. However, each became law as the government was determined to institute the programs, and enough inducements were offered to physicians to reduce the strength of their opposition. In the face of strong government determination and skillful politics by the prime ministers of that time (Lloyd George in 1912 and Aneurin Bevan in 1946), the BMA was rendered ineffective. Both prime ministers managed to divide the loyalties of the BMA. Bevan, for example, refused to be drawn into lengthy negotiations with the BMA but provided concessions to teaching hospitals and consultants (specialists) and permitted the treatment of private patients in state hospitals to gain the support of many in the medical establishment. It also became increasingly clear to the medical profession that the government was going to turn the measure into law, either with or without the support of the BMA. In the end, the BMA became a partner with the government in instituting changes.

Initially, the NHS was marked by controversy and subjected to criticism. The mode of capitation payments to GPs meant that the more patients seen by a physician, the more money the physician was able to make. Hence, there was a serious concern and some evidence that medical care was being provided in quantity rather than quality. A measure was introduced to pay physicians less for treating more patients, but as the population increased, the doctors found it difficult to reduce their patient load. Also, the government and physicians have disputed the amount paid for capitation fees, with the physicians arguing that it is not enough. Disputes have likewise taken place between GPs and consultants (specialists). Consultants have higher prestige and draw higher incomes, and GPs have claimed that the NHS favors consultants, not only with regard to income but also to fringe benefits (vacations, retirement, and so on), while demanding that politicians and government administrators be more sensitive to their needs.

Consequently, conflict and problems concerning health care delivery in Britain are largely between health care providers and the government. There is little direct involvement by the general public. It is the state's role to act as the protector of patients' rights and interests, but only in the last few years have there been channels for the public to voice its concerns directly. The central problem faced by the NHS is its lack of financial resources. Although the British have a relatively high standard of living, there are large pockets of poverty. Moreover, the NHS has worked hard to hold down medical costs, but 9.8 percent of Britain's GDP was spent on health care in 2009. This is slightly more than the 2009 European Union average of 9.2 percent. Though relatively successful in combating rising expenses, this policy has had its drawbacks. British doctors and nurses, on average, are not paid exceptionally high salaries. Occasionally they go on strike to bargain for more pay. Many doctors, especially consultants, do a considerable amount of private practice to increase their income.

British patients became increasingly dissatisfied with waiting for long periods of time in doctors' offices and for appointments to see them. There were also long delays in obtaining elective surgery and criticism about low staffing levels in hospitals. To improve the situation, the British government, led by Prime Minister Margaret Thatcher, initiated reforms in the 1990s intended to create a competitive "internal market" within the nation's health care delivery system. Hospital trusts were established that allowed hospitals to be self-governing and to finance themselves by contracting directly with local health districts. Additionally, GPs in group practices were allowed to establish primary care trusts to purchase services from hospitals for their patients. This arrangement changed, however, in 2013 when Prime Minister David Cameron initiated new reforms in which primary care trusts were abolished and replaced with local foundation trusts and clinical commissioning groups (CCGs) to make decisions about patient services and how to pay for them. The Health and Social Care Act of 2012 authorized Healthwatch England with statutory powers in its jurisdiction to monitor the quality of health care on behalf of consumers. Additionally, the Equality Act of 2010 made it unlawful to discriminate within the NHS.

Furthermore, hospitals providing services to private patients are allowed to make a profit from those services instead of providing them at cost. Hospitals are also allowed to market their services to make them more attractive to private patients, and NHS patients can be admitted by their doctors to the best hospitals available—not just those in their district. These measures were intended by the government to improve efficiency, reduce delays in receiving treatment, and assist doctors and hospitals to increase their incomes by attracting more patients. Although these measures signified the application of free-market methods to a state-financed system, the principle of state-sponsored health care remained in place. In addition to reforming the health care marketplace, a *Patient's Charter* was provided that assured patients of ten basic rights, including the following: the right to receive care; be referred to a consultant, if necessary; be given a clear explanation of treatment; have access to health records, and have the confidentiality of those records maintained; receive detailed information on local health services; be guaranteed admission to treatment by a specific date; and have any complaints about the NHS investigated.

Although reforms have been found necessary, the NHS has accomplished what it set out to do—provide free comprehensive medical care to the residents of the United Kingdom. It has shown significant results. The general health profile of Britain is among the best in the world. Tables 16.3 and 16.4 show, for example, that the infant mortality rates for the United Kingdom are lower than in the United States, while life expectancy for males and females is higher. On balance, health care is of a high quality despite problems, and particular success has been achieved against heart disease. Yet significant inequalities in health remain between social classes (Bartley 2012; Bradby 2012; Bury 2010; Lahelma, Arber, Kivela, and Roos 2002; Marmot 2004;). Poor health among the lower classes in Britain, however, is due more to the unhealthy lifestyles and living environment associated with poverty, rather than a lack of access to quality health care (Jarvis and Wardle 1999; Shaw, Dorling, and Smith 1999).

Sweden

Sweden, along with Great Britain, has demonstrated that a socialized system of health care delivery can be effective in a capitalist country through the formation of a national health service. The Swedish National Health Service is financed through taxation. Taxes in Sweden have been the highest in the world. Tax reform in 1991 reduced the highest income tax rate from 72 to 51 percent, but the top tax bracket was increased to 56 percent in 1995 and Swedish tax rates in 2013 show it is possible to be taxed as much as 59 percent of one's income. Sweden is one of the world's most egalitarian countries when it comes to the provision of welfare benefits to the general population, and inequities in living conditions have been reduced to a level that is more equal than in most other countries. Universal health insurance, old-age pensions, unemployment insurance, and job-retraining programs protect employed Swedes and their families from serious concern about being pushed into poverty by poor health, old age, and unemployment. There are social class differences in health in Sweden, with the lower class showing a less-positive health profile than more affluent Swedes, but the difference is less pronounced than in most other countries (Burström 2012; Hemström 2005). Sweden, along with the other Nordic countries, has the lowest proportion of poor people in Europe.

On virtually every measure, the Swedes must be considered one of the world's healthiest populations overall. As shown in Table 16.3, Sweden has the third lowest infant mortality rate in the world (2.5 deaths per 1,000 live births) in 2010. Table 16.4

shows that Sweden has high life expectancy for males (79.4 years) and females (83.5 years). Sweden spent 10 percent of its GDP on health in 2009.

The Swedish National Health Service is the responsibility of the Ministry of Health and Social Affairs. Only particularly important health issues are decided by the ministry. Most decisions pertaining to health policy are made by the National Board of Health and Welfare. This board plans, supervises, and regulates the delivery of health services at the county level. Physicians are employed by county councils and are paid according to the number of hours worked rather than the number of patients treated. Physicians are obligated to work a fixed number of hours per week, usually about 40 to 42. It is generally left up to the doctor to decide what percentage of his or her time is to be spent on treating patients, doing research, or teaching. Physicians' salaries are standardized by specialty, place and region of work, and seniority.

A major characteristic of the NHS in Sweden is that general hospitals are owned by county and municipal governments. These local governments are responsible for maintaining and providing services. The state pays the general hospitals a relatively small amount of money from a health insurance fund, leaving the balance to be paid from local tax revenues. Enrollment in the government-sponsored health insurance program is mandatory for the entire population. Most of the money to support the insurance program comes from the contributions of employers and payroll deductions of employees. This insurance, a form of national health insurance, is used primarily to pay the salaries of physicians and other health workers. There are also some general practitioners in private practice whose fees are paid by the insurance fund and token payments from patients. Fees for all physicians, however, are set by the government and paid according to their schedule.

The Swedish health care system has some additional benefits other than generally free medical treatment. Beginning in 2010, Swedes were able to choose whether they wish to be treated in either a public or private medical facility at state expense. They can be treated almost anywhere in the country they wish. Sweden introduced a health guarantee in 2005 that patients would not have to wait more than seven days for a doctor's appointment or 90 days to see a specialist or have an operation. Excessive travel expenses to visit physicians and hospitals are paid by the government, and there is a cash sickness fund designed to protect a person's standard of living against losses of income because of illness or injury. Under this program, people may receive up to 80 percent of the income they would be earning if they were able to work at their job. Drugs are either free or inexpensive, and financial supplements are paid to each woman giving birth to a child and to families with children under the age of 16, regardless of the family's income.

Thus, it would be somewhat misleading to consider the funding of Sweden's health care delivery system as an example of national health insurance because most of the revenues come from county councils. The total health bill in Sweden is met by contributions of 71 percent from county taxes, 16 percent from the national government, 10 percent from the health insurance system and other sources, and 3 percent from patient fees. The county councils introduced a financial system of payments to hospitals in 1994 based on the actual number of patients treated, instead of a traditional fixed annual budget, and competition between hospitals was allowed with the goal of improving quality and lowering costs. Consequently, Sweden, like

BOX 16.1

National Health Insurance in Rwanda

The African country of Rwanda with a population of 11.5 million people is one of the poorest countries in the world, but it has national health insurance. The Rwandan health insurance program covers 92 percent of the population and originally cost $2 a year. As of 2011, the cost was $6 annually, with a $10 per visit co-pay. Since the insurance program was established in 1999, life expectancy has risen for the country as a whole from 48 years to 63.5 years in 2012, despite the AIDS epidemic. The plan provides basic coverage in a country where CT scans and kidney dialysis are usually unavailable, and there is only one neurosurgeon and three cardiologists (McNeil 2010). The six-dollar annual fee and co-payment can't really cover the cost of care, even in Rwanda, but over half of the cost is paid by foreign donors, especially the United States. The poorest of the poor have their premiums paid by organizations such as the Global Fund to Fight AIDS because many people cannot afford to pay even $6. A complaint, however, is that some people do not like to pay in advance for something they may not use and want their $6 refunded if they don't get sick.

the United Kingdom, has moved toward a purchaser–provider model within its own government-run health system and has maintained this approach.

Sweden remains committed to universal and equal access to health services paid by public funding. County councils have been directed by the national legislature to remain responsible for health care delivery but pass the responsibility for nursing homes to municipalities and transfer part of their budgets to local health districts. This measure will allow the districts to purchase services from different primary care centers and hospitals, a development intended to promote competition between providers and greater freedom of choice for patients. These changes in Sweden's health services are not extreme. Instead, they are intended to improve a highly successful system by introducing limited aspects of a free market.

Decentralized National Health Programs: Japan, Germany, and Mexico

Decentralized national health programs differ from systems of socialized medicine, in that government control and management of health care delivery is more indirect. The government acts primarily to regulate the system, not operate it. Often the government functions in the role of a third party, mediating and coordinating health care delivery between providers and the organizations involved in the financing of services. In decentralized national health programs, the government (1) indirectly controls the financing and organization of health services in a capitalist economy; (2) regulates payments to providers; (3) owns some of the facilities; (4) guarantees equal access to the general population; and (5) allows some private care for patients willing to be responsible for their own expenses. In this section, the decentralized national health care systems in Japan, Germany, and Mexico will be discussed.

Japan

Japan spends 8.5 percent of its GDP on health care (about half of that of the United States), but the Japanese have achieved striking results over the last 60 years. For example, in 1955, the average life expectancy of the Japanese was more than four years less than that of an American. By 1967, Japan's life expectancy had passed that of the United States and, as shown in Table 16.4, is the third highest in the world for males (79.6 years) and highest for females (86.4 years) as of 2010. Japanese rates for infant mortality (Table 16.3) are tied with Finland for the lowest in the world (2.3 per 1,000 live births in 2010).

Japan has a national health insurance plan, introduced in 1961, but its benefits are relatively low by Western standards. Japanese patients pay 30 percent of the cost of health services, with the national plan paying the remainder. However, patients are reimbursed by the plan for expenses over 60,000 yen (about $680) for medical care during any given month; low-income patients are reimbursed for amounts spent over 33,600 yen (about $381) monthly. People over 70 years of age have all of their costs covered. Patients are allowed to choose their own doctors and encouraged to visit them regularly, and these policies more than likely promote the longevity of the Japanese because health problems can be diagnosed during early stages. Under a national law effective in 2008, companies and local governments are required to have the waistlines measured of persons under their jurisdiction between the ages of 40 and 74 years during their annual physical. Persons exceeding Japanese government limits of 33.5 inch waists for men and 35.4 inches for women are given guidance for dieting and time periods for weight loss. Companies and local governments that fail to meet weight-reduction goals are required to pay fines to the national government.

About one-third of Japanese doctors are in private practice and are paid on a fee-for-service basis. All the rest are full-time, salaried employees of hospitals. Physicians not on a hospital staff cannot treat their patients once they are hospitalized. Physician fees for office visits and examinations are low because the government sets fees. Regardless of seniority or geographical area, all Japanese doctors in private practice are paid the same amount for the same procedures, according to the government's uniform fee schedule. Fee revisions are negotiated by the Central Social Medical Care Council in the Ministry of Health and Welfare, comprising eight providers (doctors, dentists, and a pharmacist); eight payers (four insurers, two from the government, and two from management and labor); and four who represent public interests (three economists and a lawyer). However, any changes in fees are ultimately decided by the Ministry of Finance because government subsidies must be kept within general budgetary limits. In effect, the government virtually determines fees for doctors and hospitals. Hospital costs tend to be low because the government refuses to pay high costs in that area as well.

The government fee schedule is the primary mechanism for cost containment. Providers are prohibited by law from charging more than the schedule allows. Japanese doctors do receive a substantial supplementary income from the drugs they prescribe (25 percent or more of the price of the drug). Not surprisingly, the Japanese have a high rate of prescription drug use. Private practitioners in Japan earn significantly more (about four times as much) than hospital-based doctors.

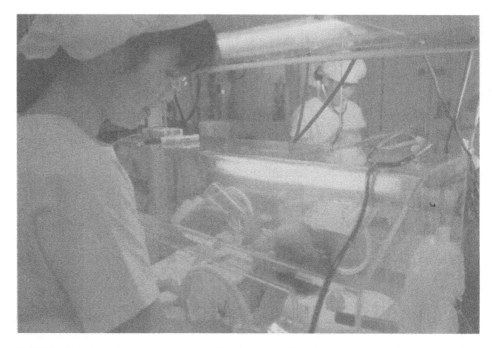

PHOTO 16.2 Prenatal Intensive Care Unit in Japan. The Japanese have the lowest infant mortality in the world.

The Japanese national health insurance plan does not cover all Japanese. Instead, the government encouraged private organizations to keep government involvement at a minimum by setting up their own welfare programs. Part of the normative structure of the Japanese business world is that companies are responsible for taking care of their own employees. In Japan, this responsibility includes providing retirement plans, helping retired employees find postretirement work, arranging vacations, offering low-cost loans for housing, and providing medical care. Consequently, there are separate programs of health services for employees of large companies, small and medium-sized companies, and public and quasi-public institutions. Some large companies employ doctors and own hospitals. There is also a program for citizens who are not covered under other plans. Consequently, the entire Japanese population is covered by some type of health insurance plan, and the average Japanese has a much greater measure of security concerning health care than the average American (Anesaki and Munakata 2005; Ikegami et al. 2011).

The concept of having a decentralized system of health care based largely on occupation is supported by Japanese businessmen, who generally provide more benefits than are required by law. Business leaders oppose a heavy welfare burden for the government, as they want to pay less in taxes and avoid the governmental administrative overhead required for a large public welfare system. The tax burdens in welfare states such as Sweden and Great Britain are undesirable as is the income-based welfare system in the United States. Also important is the desire of

Japanese businesses to provide security to their employees in exchange for employee loyalty and productivity. This policy gives large Japanese corporations an advantage in attracting workers because of the greater benefit packages they can offer. As a result, some Japanese have better health care benefits than others, although the overall provision of health benefits in Japan is highly equitable.

Japanese lifestyles and the country's high standard of living have undoubtedly contributed to the overall level of good health and longevity, while the provision of universal health insurance coverage without rationing care is a major achievement. While no health system can be perfect because demands can easily exceed resources, the Japanese have established one of the most efficient health care systems in the world: It is relatively low cost, effective, and equitable.

However, there are problems. Some 80 percent of all Japanese hospitals are privately owned by physicians, but many facilities are old and lack space. Because the Japanese government limits how much they can charge, Japanese hospitals are often required to admit more and more patients in order to meet their expenses. Overcrowding has therefore become common in most hospitals. The average length of hospitalization in Japan is also longer than in the West. Hospital administrators complain that it is difficult to finance updated facilities or hire additional personnel without increases in the amounts charged to patients.

There are typically long waits at doctors' offices and clinics as well, because Japanese physicians do not use an appointment system. Basically, it is a case of first come, first served, and some patients begin lining up outside the doctor's office before it opens. Furthermore, relationships between doctors and patients in Japan tend to be more impersonal than in the United States. Patients are told little about their diagnoses, the treatment prescribed, or types of drugs being administered. As Margaret Powell and Masahira Anesaki (1990:174) reported years ago: "Doctors tend to explain away the problem in soothing terms without necessarily providing precise information about what exactly the problem is." The doctor–patient relationship is based on trust and the traditional Japanese cultural value of deference to authority. A patient requesting information directly would be seen as questioning the physician's authority, judgment, and knowledge. Therefore, patients are to rely on what doctors tell them. The Japanese medical profession is highly self-regulated and adverse to public scrutiny.

There are also changes in disease patterns. Heart disease is on the rise and is now the second leading cause of death after cancer. Historically, Japan has had low mortality rates from heart disease in comparison to Western countries. This trend undoubtedly influences higher levels of life expectancy among the Japanese, especially among males. The traditional low-fat, low-protein, and high-carbohydrate Japanese diet of fish, rice, and green vegetables is a major factor in this situation (Cockerham, Hattori, and Yamori 2000; Powell and Anesaki 1990). Also, the stress-reducing aspects of Japanese culture, such as strong group solidarity and cooperation in dealing with problems and after-work socializing by males on a regular basis with close friends in bars or noodle shops, may be important. These drinking places are often designed to encourage relaxation and allow a temporary escape from the tensions of modern living. After-work socializing with coworkers seems to have become a routine activity in the lifestyles of many men in industrial Japan.

Nevertheless, a more Westernized lifestyle and increase in the consumption of animal fats and proteins—associated with Western diets—have promoted more heart disease, along with the stresses of living in a dynamic, hardworking, and densely populated society (Anesaki and Munakata 2005). Research examining socioeconomic differences in risk behavior for coronary heart disease in urban Japanese civil servants shows that persons with less education and lower status jobs smoke significantly more than those with a university education and higher status positions (Nishi, Makino, Fukuda, and Tatarra 2004). Alcohol consumption, however, was widespread at both the top and bottom of the social scale. The shift toward higher fat in Japanese diets has also contributed to a rise in colon and pancreatic cancers, and heavy smoking among Japanese males has led to an increase in mortality rates from lung cancer. The Japanese also have the highest rates of stomach cancer in the world. Increases in death rates from cancer and heart disease, as well as the highest mortality rates from stroke of any advanced country, suggest that increases in life expectancy for the Japanese may be slowing down and perhaps reaching a limit.

These changes, combined with the rapid growth of Japan's elderly population, are likely to place tremendous pressure on Japan's health care delivery system in the future. The proportion of people living to old age is increasing in Japanese society faster than in any other country in the world, and this situation is going to require a significant response from Japan's system of health care delivery.

Germany

The structure of health care delivery in the Federal Republic of Germany has not changed significantly since 1883 and the reforms instituted by Bismarck's administration in imperial Germany. The program established at that time was based on three principal components: (1) compulsory insurance; (2) free health services; and (3) sick benefits. Employees, self-employed, unemployed, old-age pensioners, and certain categories of domestic workers providing infant and child care, home help, and so on are all required to be insured by one of Germany's public health insurance organizations. There are about 1,300 public health insurance groups, and membership in a particular health plan was once determined by occupation or place of employment. Today, anyone can join any plan who can now advertise for members. Germany's largest public health insurance organization is the Allgemeine Ortskrankenkassen (AOK), which insures about half the population. The AOK originally insured only blue-collar workers but broadened its membership base to include the general population.

Bismarck's welfare measures in the late nineteenth century were both a response to democratization and an attempt to suppress it. That is, Bismarck wanted to defuse the demands for political rights from an increasingly well-organized and leftist-oriented working class by providing them with social rights that linked workers to the state, rather than to labor unions or socialist political parties. Included in Bismarck's plan was the first national health insurance program ever. Regardless of his political motives, Bismarck's health insurance scheme proved to be durable and effective.

Following Germany's defeat in World War II and the incorporation of its eastern lands into a separate communist state, West Germany became a multiparty republic in 1949. The Federal Republic's constitution, the Basic Law, guarantees the social welfare of its citizens, continues the comprehensive social welfare system developed by Bismarck, and now includes the East Germans after reunification in 1990. The program that currently exists includes health insurance, old-age pensions, sickness benefits for income lost to illness or injury, unemployment insurance, and family assistance in the form of allowances for children, rent (especially for the elderly), and public funds for the construction of low-income housing.

Approximately 90 percent of all Germans participate, involuntarily or voluntarily, in the nation's public health insurance program. The remainder consists mainly of civil servants, who have their own insurance, and high-income earners who can take out private insurance or pay for state-sponsored insurance. In the state plan, health care is free to the individual except for small copayments and covers medical and dental treatment, drugs and medicines, and hospital care as needed. In the event of illness, the employer must continue to pay the employee's full wages for six weeks, and then the health insurance fund provides the individual with his or her approximate take-home pay for up to 78 weeks. If the illness is more protracted, benefits are continued under a welfare plan unless the person is permanently incapacitated and is entitled to a disability pension. About 13.2 percent of a worker's monthly gross earnings is deducted for health insurance, with half paid by the employee and half by the employer.

Public health insurance plans are coordinated by the National Federation of Health Insurance. The insurance plan issues a medical certificate to members and their dependents periodically. This certificate is presented to a physician when services are rendered. The physician then submits the certificate to his or her association of registered doctors, which all physicians are required to join. Payment is made to the physician through the doctors' association, according to a fee schedule agreed upon by the association and the public health insurance plans. Hospital fees and payments are handled in the same manner. The Health Care Fund was introduced in 2009 that reallocates revenues to insurance plans according to a risk compensation formula in which funds with higher proportions of elderly, women, and sick persons can obtain additional money.

As the preceding discussion indicates, the German government does not play a major role in the financing of health services. The government's primary function is one of administration. The Federal Ministry of Labor and Social Affairs exercises general supervision of the health care delivery system through state ministries and local health boards. According to Donald Light (Light and Schuller 1986), this form of health service organization is one of corporatism and represents a unique contribution by Germany to the provision of health care. Corporatism in the German context consists of: (1) compulsory membership on the part of the population in a national health plan and (2) a set of institutions situated between the government and its citizens with the authority to manage health care under government auspices.

Approximately 42 percent of Germany's physicians are general practitioners, which is a high percentage compared to the United States where GPs are about 12 percent of all physicians. Most German doctors practice medicine in private offices or clinics on a solo basis. Few work in a group practice, but that may change as outpatient medical centers are being established throughout the country.

German physicians are well paid, earning somewhat more, on average, than American doctors. The Health Care Reform Act of 1989 helped limit costs by increasing the amounts paid by persons insured voluntarily in the public health plan, adding a small copayment for prescription drugs, establishing price ceilings for most drugs, and other measures. The Health Structure Act of 1993 mandated price cuts for drugs, lower incomes for doctors and dentists (along with compulsory retirement at age 68), increased copayments for patients, and limits on hospital budgets. Germans have been able to choose their own public health insurance plan since 1997. The 2007 Strengthening of Competition in Legal Health Insurance Law made having health insurance mandatory for all Germans and extended insurance options.

Since 1995, approximately 10 percent of the GDP has been spent on all health, and cost containment remains a major policy objective for the government. The German population is also aging, which signals higher expenses in the future. Some 26 percent (or one in four) of the German people were age 60 and over in 2010. This situation is complicated by the fact that Germany has the lowest birthrate in Europe at 8.3 births per 1,000 persons or 1.39 per woman in 2012. German death rates have exceeded birthrates since 1972 and, as a consequence, its population is shrinking and now stands at 80.3 million inhabitants despite immigration. The population declined 11 percent between 2000 and 2013, and if present trends continue, the number of people in Germany could fall to 60 million by 2060. Fewer younger adults of working age in relation to the number of elderly persons means fewer potential tax revenues to support health care and the social welfare system. To generate more income without raising taxes, health ordinances have increased copayments by patients for prescription drugs, hospitalization, physical therapy, and other services. Future changes in health policy are inevitable as Germany continues to provide generous benefits to its citizens and permanent residents.

The general level of health of the German population, however, is good. Table 16.3 shows that in 2010 Germany had a lower infant mortality rate than the United States. The U.S. infant mortality rate was 6.1 per 1,000 compared to 3.5 for Germany. Table 16.4 indicates that both German men and women had a higher life expectancy than Americans. For men, the Germans showed a life expectancy of 78.0 years in 2010 and American men were listed at 76.2 years. For women, the German figures were 83.0 years versus 81.1 years for Americans. Almost half of all deaths are due to diseases of the heart and circulatory system. The prevalence of heart disease in eastern Germany is higher than in the western lands, with eastern men showing higher levels of cigarette smoking, hypertension, cholesterol, and obesity (Knesebeck and Siegrist 2005; Nolte, Scholz, Shkolnikov, and McKee 2002). However, evidence shows that the change in the health care delivery and improved living conditions in eastern Germany is improving life expectancy. Recent data show, for example, that as of 2011, East German men had gained 6.2 years and women 4.2 years in life expectancy since reunification (Vogt 2014).

Mexico

Mexico has a decentralized national health system that now covers about 98 percent of the general population through a variety of programs that fall into one of three broad categories. First, there are the public social security organizations that provide both health insurance and old-age benefits for specific groups of private and government employees. Second is the health care provided through the government's Secretariat of Health and Welfare or Secretaria de Salubridad y Asistencia (SSA), which is the primary source of care for the majority of persons not covered by a social security organization—especially the urban poor. And third, there is the private health care system, which consists of various private practitioners, hospitals and clinics, and charitable organizations.

What allowed Mexico to have near universal health insurance coverage today was passage in 2003 of legislation establishing the System of Social Protection in Health (SSPH). The major feature of the SSPH is *Seguro Popular*, a public insurance program that offers comprehensive health benefits, including protection against being unable to afford coverage by guaranteeing health care as a right recognized by the Mexican Constitution of 1983 (Knaul et al. 2012). For low-income persons without employer contributions, health benefits are paid by federal and state governments out of taxes, with the state's responsible for 50 percent of the funding. About 50 million Mexicans, nearly half of the population, are insured by *Seguro Popular*. The next largest health plan in Mexico covers salaried workers in the private sector is administered by the Mexican Social Insurance Institute or Instituto Mexicano de Seguro Social (IMSS). The IMSS was established in 1943 as a compulsory government-sponsored social security program for salaried workers in Mexico City and surrounding areas, financed by contributions from workers, employers, and the state. The program was extended to other metropolitan areas during 1943–1945. Salaried agricultural workers were added in 1954; and, in 1973, legislation was enacted that provided for the extension of IMSS social insurance to everyone with jobs in the private sector. Despite efforts to expand into rural areas, most of the IMSS membership is urban.

Another health plan, which provides the most extensive and generous benefits of any social security program, was established in 1960 for government workers and is administered by the Social Insurance Institute of State Employees or Instituto de Seguridad y Servicios Sociales Para los Trabajadores del Estado (ISSSTE). Other social security programs with health insurance are available to members of the armed forces (ISSSFAM) and the state-run oil industry (PEMEX). Approximately 50 percent of Mexico's population is covered by the IMSS, ISSSTE, ISSSFAM, and PENEX.

Mexico has a serious maldistribution of services. More than 35 percent of all doctors are located in the Mexico City area, which has 20 percent of the population. Consequently, Mexico City has a surplus of physicians, while other parts of the country have a shortage. Even though health clinics are established throughout the country, rural areas are likely to be served by a nurse. For the country as a whole, there are approximately 80 physicians per 100,000 people, and most doctors are employed in some type of government-sponsored health program—although some have both a public and private practice. The remaining doctors are private fee-for-service practitioners. In border areas near the United States, affluent Mexicans and others covered by some type of U.S. health insurance visit American doctors. Some Americans, in turn, seek the services of less expensive Mexican physicians and buy drugs at cheaper prices in Mexican pharmacies. Many drugs in the United States requiring prescriptions, including some antibiotics and painkillers, are sold over the counter in Mexico. Crossing the U.S.–Mexico border from one side or the other to obtain health services is common for some people.

The overall health of the Mexican population is improving. Life expectancy in 2010 was 73 years for males and 77.8 years for females. Infant mortality was 14.7 deaths per 1,000 births in 2010 compared with 80 per 1,000 in 1965. Some 6.4 percent of Mexico's GDP was spent on health in 2009. Health care delivery in major urban centers in Mexico is often of high quality, especially in the national medical institutes in Mexico City. In rural areas, however, access to modern medicine is limited and difficult to obtain. When physicians, clinics, or nurses are not available locally, people turn to a variety of sources, such as nuns or folk healers, or they rely on self-treatment (Nigenda, Lockett, Manca, and Mora 2001). Overall, Mexico has established a generally effective national system of health care delivery, despite being a developing nation and having an often-troubled economy that has affected public spending on health care.

But significant problems remain. Mexican health care is oriented toward curative rather than preventive medicine. Hence, there has not been a large-scale effort to prevent illness through public health programs intended to improve nutrition, water, sewage systems, and training in hygiene. In addition, the various social health insurance plans differ in the levels of benefits provided, and the decentralized system of health care delivery promotes a lack of coordination, planning, and fiscal control in a country that lacks great national wealth. And, most importantly, as noted, a significant segment of the population in rural areas lacks access to modern health services.

However, health care coverage has at least been extended to large segments of the population, including both blue- and white-collar workers and low-income

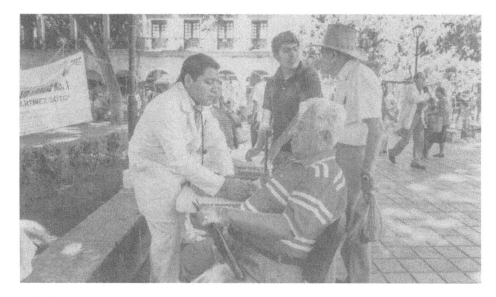

PHOTO 16.3 Mexican man having his blood pressure taken at a free public health clinic.

persons. Mexico's health policy emphasizes continued improvement in the health of the general population, with a particular focus on meeting the basic health needs of the underprivileged and extending health insurance coverage. Health care for the urban poor seems to be Mexico's highest priority at this point in the development of its health care delivery system, but rural residents have witnessed improvement as well (Knaul et al. 2012). According to Mexican medical sociologist Roberto Castro (2005), health conditions in Mexico have changed significantly since the last century, but health disparities remain across social classes and regions in the country.

Socialist Medicine: Alterations in Russia and China

The socialist model of health care delivery features central government ownership of all facilities, state employment of health workers, and free universal care paid out of the national budget. It has largely disappeared since 1989–1991, when communism ended in Eastern Europe and the former Soviet Union. Of the four remaining communist countries, socialist health care persists only in Cuba and North Korea, while China and Vietnam have replaced the former socialist system with health insurance programs. In this section, we will review the alteration of the socialist form of health care in Russia and China.

Russia

Following the collapse of the old Soviet Union in 1991, the new Russian Federation passed legislation establishing a system of health insurance, consisting of compulsory and voluntary plans (Twigg 2000, 2002). The compulsory social health insurance plan is financed by central government subsidies for pensioners and the unemployed, along with contributions (3.1 percent of payrolls) from employers to cover workers. Health insurance is mandatory for all employees, provides the same basic benefits without choice, and is administered by 89 regional government health insurance funds that make payments to participating private insurance companies. Individuals or employers have a choice of insurance companies, and competition between these companies is expected to control costs and ensure quality services. There is also a voluntary plan of private insurance that anyone can purchase out of his or her own pocket that provides supplemental benefits. The intent is to move away from the former Soviet method of paying for health care directly out of the central government's budget and to replace it with a universal system of health insurance, providing basic benefits for all citizens in the form of payments to providers. One of the most important changes was to shift funding from the federal to the local level, so the financing of health care (about 60 percent) comes mainly from local budgets (which are based on both federal and local allocations) and the remainder from health insurance. This development marks a major change in financing health care delivery for the Russian people.

Prior to the collapse of communism, the health care delivery systems in the former Soviet Union and Eastern Europe were philosophically guided by Marxist–Leninist ideas for reshaping capitalism into socialism. The ultimate goal was the establishment of a classless society, featuring an end to class exploitation, private property, worker alienation, and economic scarcity. However, Marxist–Leninist ideology pertaining to health was never developed in depth. The Soviet state established in the aftermath of the 1917 revolution nevertheless faced serious health problems, including large-scale epidemics and famine. More out of practical than theoretical necessity, the Soviet government mandated that health care would be (1) the responsibility of the state; (2) provided without direct cost to the user; (3) controlled by a central authority; and (4) allocated priority for care to workers; with (5) an emphasis on preventive care (Cassileth, Vlassov, and Chapman 1995). Because of the critical need for doctors and a shortage of manpower resulting from industrial and military demands, large numbers of women, especially nurses with working-class backgrounds, were sent to medical schools where they were given cram courses and certified as physicians. William Knaus (1981:83) explains:

> Many had no ambitions beyond a weekly paycheck. The Soviet government responded in kind with a low wage scale and a social status for medicine that treated the new physician with no more respect given a factory worker. Professionalism was not rewarded nor even encouraged. Medicine became a job and women were the ones chosen to do it.

Russia has more doctors per capita than most countries (about 4.3 physicians for every 1,000 people in 2010), and some three-fourths are women. However, men hold the majority of academic positions in medicine and medical posts in the Ministry of Health. In 1987, four years before the collapse of the Soviet regime, the average salary for health care providers was about 30 percent less than the national average for all salaries. Doctors were paid about the same as high school teachers. Prominent physicians, however, had special privileges with respect to housing, vacations, schools for their children, access to restricted stores, and other benefits. The general public did not have a choice of physicians, as assignment to a medical practitioner was made on the basis of residence.

In order to receive more personal attention from their doctors and better care, patients typically provided gifts or bribes, which evolved into a second economy within the overall health care system. Mark Field (1993:167) referred to the bribery system as the "commercialization of Soviet medicine" and noted that it was paradoxical that payments by patients were reintroduced in a system designed to remove financial incentives from the patient–physician relationship. Russian doctors now have a payment structure based on income from insurance and patients for services rendered, but bribes still exist in some places because of low salaries. In 2013, the average salary for a physician in Moscow was $1,826 (or 66,000 rubles) a month, while doctors elsewhere in Russia were paid between $1,300 and $650 monthly.

The former Soviet health care system is now part of history, as the Russian Federation's new insurance-based structure has come into existence. Nevertheless, serious problems remain, including low financing of health care services and declining life expectancy. In the Russian Federation in the mid-1990s, less than 2 percent of the GDP was spent on health (Field 1995), and the figure was only 6.2 percent of the GDP in 2011. This is a lower percentage in comparison to other industrialized countries and less than one would expect, given the magnitude of health problems in the country.

From the end of World War II until the mid-1960s, health progress in the former Soviet Union was rapid and consistent. In Russia (the former Russian Soviet

Federated Socialist Republic in the old Soviet Union) life expectancy for males increased from 40.4 years in 1938 to 64.0 years in 1965; for females, life expectancy increased from 46.7 years to 72.1 over the same period. However, in the mid-1960s, ironically just as the former Soviet Union reached its highest point of economic development in relation to the West, life expectancy began a downward trend, largely brought on by rising mortality from heart disease among middle-age working-class males. With the collapse of the Soviet Union in 1991 and decline of Russia's standard of living in the 1990s, the decrease in life expectancy for both men and women accelerated. The longevity of women appeared to be most affected by stress and men by unhealthy lifestyles (Cockerham 2012).

Male life expectancy in Russia fell from 64.0 in 1965 to 61.4 in 1980, but improved to 64.9 (the highest ever) in 1987. Russian demographers credit this brief rise in male longevity to Premier Gorbachev's anti-alcohol campaign in the mid-1980s, which significantly curtailed both the production and consumption of vodka, along with making it more costly to purchase. Vladimir Shkolnikov and Alexander Nemtsov (1994) calculated the difference between observed and expected deaths by sex and age and found that longevity increased 3.2 years for males and 1.3 years for females during the campaign's duration, with the greatest advances occurring in 1986. Shkolnikov and Nemtsov (1994:1) concluded that "the rapid mortality decrease in the years 1984 to 1987 can be assumed to reflect a pure effect of reduced alcohol abuse on mortality, because there were no other significant changes in conditions of public health in that short period." But the campaign was discontinued in late 1987 because of its widespread unpopularity, and both alcohol consumption and male mortality correspondingly increased.

Following the 1991 collapse of the former Soviet Union, life expectancy for Russian males had dropped to 57.6 years by 1994, some 6.3 years less than the 1965 average. For females, there was a relatively slow but consistent upward trend between 1965 and 1989 from 72.1 years to 74.5 years. In 1991, in the new Russian Federation, females lived 74.3 years on average, but by 1994 life expectancy for women had fallen to 71.2 years. Consequently, both Russian men and women had a lower life expectancy in 1994 than their counterparts in 1965. Between 1995 and 1998, however, there was a slight increase in life expectancy for both Russian men and women because of a reduction in alcohol-related deaths (Shkolnikov, McKee, and Leon 2001). The most vulnerable people had died, and their premature deaths had less effect on life expectancy as a result. This was not a genuine improvement in longevity, as life expectancy figures resumed their downward movement from 61.8 years for males in 1998 to 58.9 years in 2005, only to finally recover to 64.6 years in 2012. Nevertheless, males averaged only 0.6 more years of life expectancy in 2012 compared to 1965—a period of 47 years. Longevity for females rose only 3.5 years during the same period. The gender gap in life expectancy in 2012 continued to be among the largest in the world, although shrinking somewhat, as the average Russian woman lived 11.6 years longer than the male. With rising death rates and falling birthrates, it is not surprising that Russia's population has declined from 147 million persons in 1989 to 143.4 million in 2013.

The decline of life expectancy in Russia and elsewhere in the old Soviet bloc countries was one of the most significant developments in world health in the late twentieth century. It has improved, but continues today in Russia, Belarus, and

Ukraine. This situation is without precedent in modern history. Nowhere else has health worsened so seriously and for so long in peacetime among industrialized nations. Ironically, the former socialist countries espoused an ideology of social equality that theoretically should have promoted health for all. However, the reverse occurred, and life expectancy turned downward in the region in the mid-1960s without completely recovering in some parts of the former Soviet Union. This is a surprising development, as such a prolonged decline in public health was completely unexpected.

The rise in mortality was greatest in Russia and came very late to East Germany, but virtually all former Soviet bloc countries were affected to varying degrees. The deaths largely stemmed from higher rates of heart disease and to a lesser extent from alcohol abuse and alcohol-related accidents. An unhealthy lifestyle appears to be the primary cause of the increase in heart disease in men and other health problems leading to the downturn in life expectancy (Cockerham 1997, 1999, 2000, 2006, 2007, 2012; Cockerham, Snead, and DeWaal 2002; Grigoriev et al. 2014; Manning and Tikhonoiva 2009; Medvedev 2000; Nazarova 2009; Pietilä and Rytkönen 2008; Rose 2009; Van Gundy, Shieman, Kelley, and Rebellion 2005). This lifestyle was characterized by extremely heavy alcohol and cigarette consumption, high-fat diets, and little or no leisure-time exercise, and was noted to be particularly common among middle-aged working-class males who were the principal victims of the rise in premature deaths. Thus, gender (male), age (middle age), and class (working class) were the key sociological variables in this health crisis. Medical treatment could not compensate for the damage to the circulatory system caused by unhealthy lifestyle practices, and the pathological effects they engendered overshadowed the contributions of infectious diseases, environmental pollution, and medically avoidable deaths to the increase in mortality. A health policy that failed to cope with the rise in heart disease and stress was also an important causal factor. The Soviet system lacked the flexibility, both administratively and structurally, to adjust to chronic health problems that could not be handled by the mass measures successful in controlling infectious ailments (Field 2000). Ultimately, the unhealthy lifestyle of a particular segment of the population appears to be the major social determinant of the downturn in life expectancy. In addition to the pervasiveness of unhealthy lifestyles, the poor performance of the health care system and government neglect of the population's social and material needs were also important (Grigoriev et al. 2014).

For example, the amount of taxed alcohol consumed in Russia annually is about 7 liters of pure alcohol per capita, but the real figure appears to be at least 13 to 15 liters when the consumption of unregistered imports and home-distilled beverages are taken into account (Nemtsov 2002). This is the highest per capita consumption of alcohol in the world. When it is noted that adult males consume 90 percent of the alcohol, yet comprise 25 percent of the population, it is apparent that the drinking practices of males far exceed per capita consumption and reflect a tremendous concentration of drinking. Not only is per capita consumption extraordinarily high, but also the type of alcohol typically consumed (vodka) and the drinking style (oriented toward drunkenness and binge drinking) are considerably more harmful than the moderate drinking of wine.

Cigarette consumption is also higher in Russia than in the West, and male deaths from lung cancer are extremely high by international standards (Oglobin and Brock 2003). About 53 percent of all Russian men and 20 percent of women smoke. However, in 2013, the Russian government banned smoking in public places as a health measure and beer was designated an alcoholic beverage, instead of a food, and was prohibited from being sold at street-corner kiosks. As for nutrition, the Russian diet has changed considerably since the 1960s, moving away from the consumption of cereals and potatoes toward much greater consumption of sugar and red meat. By 1990, over 36 percent of Russian food provided energy from fat, making it one of the fattiest diets in the world (Popkin et al. 1997). Further-more, men consume about 50 percent more fat than women (Shapiro 1995). There are few studies on healthy exercise, but existing data show exercise to be minimal (Palosuo 2000). As Russian medical sociologist Elena Dmitrieva (2005) concludes, Russia lacks a self-protective health culture. Trying to reduce smoking and alcohol consumption is a start.

China

The People's Republic of China remains a socialist country politically, but its eco-nomic transition from socialism to a market-driven economy has been accompa-nied by dramatic changes in its health care delivery system. China no longer has a socialist system of health care in which the state controls, organizes, finances, and allocates health care directly to all citizens free of charge. The Chinese health care system is now financed largely by fees paid by patients, employers, and health insur-ance companies (Chen 2005).

Prior to the 1949 revolution that brought the communists to power, there were few Western-trained physicians in China, and these doctors generally lived in major cities, where they commanded high fees for their work. Except for a few missionary doctors in the countryside, the bulk of the Chinese population received medical care from folk practitioners. There was a heavy death toll from disease, poor sanitation, and widespread ignorance about health matters. In 1949, the average life expec-tancy of a Chinese person was only 35 years.

Improvement in health became one of the major goals of the Communist Chinese government after it came to power following the civil war with nation-alist forces. One of the first public health measures was the "Patriotic Health Movement," in which millions of Chinese killed flies, removed trash, and worked to improve sanitation. Two other measures were also important. First, traditional Chinese medicine was revived, featuring the use of herbal medicines and techniques such as acupuncture, in which pain is controlled by the insertion of needles into certain designated points in the body. Even though its therapeutic value is not fully understood, traditional Chinese medicine is still used today throughout China, with considerable effectiveness for many health problems. China is the only country that consistently treats traditional and scientific medicine equally, making both of them legally available and requiring Western-style physicians to learn traditional methods.

Second, the so-called barefoot doctors movement was initiated, in which 1.8 million paramedical personnel were eventually trained in rudimentary medicine and sent to rural areas to provide basic medical treatment and assist in efforts at preventive medicine and public health. Through this movement, the majority of the population was able to have at least some routine access to basic health care.

China's attempts at improving its health care system suffered a serious setback during the Cultural Revolution of 1966 to 1970. The Cultural Revolution was intended by China's leaders to be a mass movement of the people that would expose corruption and rid the government of unnecessary bureaucracy. Many influential people were subjected to severe public criticism and even persecuted by revolutionary groups such as the Red Guards, whose membership included thousands of young students. Schools and universities were closed as young people abandoned their studies to participate in revolutionary activities. Factions developed within the movement itself, and this period of Chinese history is marked with chaos as power struggles were waged within the hierarchy of the government and the Communist party. There was a widespread disruption of work and education. For nearly four years, there was virtually no medical research or training of medical students. Thousands of doctors were forced to leave their positions and were sent into the countryside to work with peasants in agricultural communes. When medical education was resumed in 1970, the time for training was cut from eight years after high school to three years, with emphasis on practical and applied medicine. Almost anyone could gain admission to medical school, and few or no examinations were given during training. The quality of Chinese doctors declined accordingly, and the old system was returned, but many valuable years were lost in regard to both medical education and research.

Today, an extensive network of health care facilities exists in China. Neighborhood clinics are available in cities, and people with serious illnesses or injuries are referred to local and regional hospitals. Many factories have their own clinics and hospitals. Medical care for factory workers is paid by insurance that state-owned and some collectively owned factories have established with money obtained from the sale of goods. Employees for privately owned firms and the government also have health insurance. However, in rural areas, China's transition from a communal (collective farm) agricultural system in the 1980s to a household-centered approach (on state-owned land) led to the collapse of the collective farm health care system (Chen 2005). Without collective farming income, farm health clinics were dissolved, and many barefoot doctors left health care altogether or went into private practice. The financial burden in rural areas was shifted to individual households who had to pay for health care out of their pockets. Those who could not afford to pay went without care—as the Chinese government struggled to find an equitable and efficient way to deliver health services to rural areas. Finally, in 2009, a health reform plan was introduced to provide universal insurance coverage with comprehensive benefits in the cities and somewhat later in the countryside, with financing by contributions from employees, employers, and local governments. About 90 percent of the Chinese population now have health insurance (Lin 2012).

At present, the central government provides less than 1 percent of all health expenditures. The responsibility for health services was delegated to provincial and county governments. But the amount of money available covers only minimum wages for health care workers and capital investments for the construction of new facilities. The remaining expenses are to be covered by patient fees. Basic levels of health care tend to be provided below cost, but profits can be made from the sale of drugs and use of technology. Hospitals and health centers have to generate their own incomes from the services they provide to patients, but they control the allocation of profits. The result is the end of China's system of universal access to free health care and its replacement by a fee-for-service model. Although incomes have risen throughout China in recent decades, the urban and especially the rural poor are the most disadvantaged in obtaining health care. Social change has also influenced health in other ways.

Feinian Chen, Yang Yang, and Guangya Liu (2010) examined the effects of China's rapid modernization on socioeconomic disparities in health and found a pattern opposite to that of the United States. Chen and her colleagues determined that while disadvantaged circumstances over the life course of several Chinese age cohorts culminated in greater inequalities in health at older ages as in the United States, the pattern was strikingly different with respect to education and income within recent cohorts. Well-educated and higher-income Chinese tended to have *worse* health in these cohorts than less-educated and low-income persons. The difference is attributed to unhealthy lifestyle choices. Whereas higher socioeconomic (SES) groups in the United States have healthier lifestyles with respect to diet, smoking, alcohol use, and exercise, Chen et al. (2010:144) and others (Schafer and Kwon 2012) observed that in developing countries experiencing rapid economic development such as China, higher SES groups are more likely to have diets with high fat and sugar content and to be more sedentary, causing them to be more obese, and also to smoke and drink more. "With their rising purchasing power," states Chen and her associates (2010:144), "the socioeconomically advantaged adopt these unhealthy behaviors because they view these choices as privileges."

Consequently, in China, as in Russia, the lifestyles of certain segments of the class structure promote unhealthy outcomes. In the case of China, however, it is the more affluent, rather than the working class that are endangering their health through unhealthy lifestyle practices. Most recently, for example, China was been found to have the world's most rapid expansion of Type 2 diabetes as weight gain leads to this form of diabetes in Asians with much lower body-mass indexes than in whites and blacks (Xu et al. 2013). Approximately 114 million Chinese have Type 2 diabetes and another 493 million are estimated to be in a prediabetic stage. Another major problem that is emerging is the adverse effects of air pollution on health and longevity in northern China associated with rapid industrialization and urbanization, primarily the sustained use of coal to generate heat for homes and energy for factories. Automobile emissions are also a factor. Beijing, China's capital, has some of the worst air pollution in the world.

In 2011, the average life expectancy in China for males was 71.8 years and for females 75.2 years, while the infant mortality rate was 12.1 infant deaths per 1,000 live births in 2011. The infant mortality rate represents a significant improvement over 1991 when there were 50.2 infant deaths per 1,000 live births. Acute infectious diseases have generally been under control or eliminated, but a particular health problem within China that has threatened to become a global pandemic is the appearance of various forms of influenza-like diseases in recent years. First was SARS (severe acute respiratory syndrome) that initially appeared in Quangdong province in 2002, spreading to Beijing and Hong Kong in China, Hanoi in Vietnam, and Toronto in Canada in 2003. SARS infected 8,422 people and 918 died in a span of ten months. The disease was thought to have originated in markets where wild animals were slaughtered as delicacies for human food consumption (Cockerham and Cockerham 2010). Various strains of avian or bird influenza have subsequently appeared first in China, with the most recent strain, H7N9, emerging in 2013 and thought to have jumped from chickens to humans in an unusual chain of transmission. These newly emerging diseases have resulted in Chinese government health surveillance reforms to contain future outbreaks.

Heart disease and cancer are the major afflictions in most parts of the country. An increasingly important health problem now and in the future is lung cancer. China has an estimated 301 million smokers who account for one-third of the world's tobacco consumption. Some 52.9 percent of China's adult male population smokes, and the proportion of adult female smokers is about 2.4 percent (Li, Hsia, and Yang 2011). Lung cancer rates are increasing 4.5 percent a year, and smoking-related deaths are expected to reach around three million annually by 2025 or about 30 percent of the world's deaths from cigarettes. Already some 1.2 million Chinese die annually from smoking-related causes.

The government has initiated a nationwide campaign against smoking, but this effort is counter to the interests of the vast state-owned tobacco monopoly, which is the world's largest producer of cigarettes. Tax revenues from tobacco sales are the government's single largest source of income and many Chinese are employed in the tobacco industry. Consequently, the Chinese government is faced with an important dilemma: If smoking declines, a primary source of income will be reduced. Nevertheless, in 2014, China banned smoking in kindergartens, elementary and middle schools, and vocational schools. Universities were ordered to establish smoking areas and cigarettes could no longer be advertised or sold on campuses. An antismoking publicity campaign was also launched promoting a government measure to ban smoking in public places by 2015.

Conclusion

This review of the organization and social policy of health care in selected countries suggests that no nation has an ideal system of dealing with health problems. All nations are faced with rising demands for quality health care in the face of limited resources, and the high cost of care has presented special problems in achieving desired outcomes. Exact comparisons between nations in terms of the effectiveness of their respective health care delivery systems are difficult because of varying political structures, degree of technological advancement, social commitment to national health care, diet, and cultures, which have an impact on the overall health profile of a particular country.

Sweden and Japan, for example, appear to have especially effective approaches to the provision of health care when levels of life expectancy and infant mortality are considered. Yet, these countries have smaller and more homogeneous populations than large countries like the United States and have fewer social class differences. It is much easier for the Swedes to focus on health care and mobilize their financial resources to cope with it. Japan has been particularly successful with its health care system, which is both low cost and readily accessible to the general public. The Japanese have the highest life expectancy for women in the world and one of the highest for men. Economic conditions in Japan and Japanese lifestyles may be the primary factors in this development, but health care delivery has undoubtedly made a major contribution. Yet, the Japanese situation is one that other capitalist countries may not necessarily want to duplicate. This is because large business corporations have the expense of providing health benefits to their employees cost-free, people under 70 years of age in the national plan are responsible for up to 30 percent of the cost of their care monthly, and the use of prescription drugs is the highest in the world.

It is clear from the discussion in this chapter that the governments worldwide are under increasingly greater pressure to contain health care costs and yet maintain high-quality coverage for the entire population. One approach in Western Europe, influenced by the "internal market" measure introduced by Britain, has been to allow limited competition between providers within government-run health care systems to contract their services to purchasers, such as a foundation trust. These trusts, in turn, select the best and less costly providers and allocate their care to the people in their geographic areas. Efforts at reform are highly likely to continue in the twenty-first century as the numbers of elderly increase and place greater demands on health care systems, with fewer workers in the economy paying taxes to support those systems.

For the present, several general trends are appearing in developed societies, which are likely to have an effect on health care policy in the future. These trends are the following: (1) Considerable attention is being paid to the cost of health care, and controls over such costs are an important aspect of health policy. (2) Preventive medical services are receiving increasing emphasis in developed countries, as more attempts are being made to keep well people healthy. (3) Efforts are being made to design a more effective administration of large health care systems. (4) There is more demand and increased responsiveness on the parts of governments and policymakers to provide a health care system that meets national needs. While different countries are taking different approaches to solve health problems, all countries appear to be moving toward a system that will reduce inequities and control costs.

Critical Thinking Questions

1. How have health expenditures in the United States affected life expectancy and infant mortality?
2. Explain the basic features of socialized medicine in Canada, Britain, and Sweden.
3. Explain the basic features of decentralized medicine in Japan, Germany, and Mexico.
4. How does decentralized medicine differ from socialized medicine or are they both the same?
5. Describe the basic form of socialist medicine and explain the ways in which it was altered in Russia and China.
6. What is the difference between socialized and socialist medicine?

Suggested Readings

Amzat, Jimoh, and Oliver Razum (2014) *Medical sociology in Africa*. Dordrecht: Springer.
An outstanding new textbook on medical sociology written from an African perspective.
Bradby, Hannah (2012) *Medicine, health, and society*. London: Sage.
A recent British textbook on medical sociology presenting a theoretically informed introduction to the field.

Germov, John (ed.) (2009) *Second opinion: An introduction to health sociology*, 4th ed. Melbourne: Oxford University Press.

An Australian medical sociology textbook. Contains a wide range of well-designed chapters by different contributors on health and society in Australia.

Rose, Richard (2009) *Understanding post-communist transformation*. London: Routledge.

An informative account of the transition out of communism in the former Soviet-bloc countries, including the effects on health.

Segall, Alexander, and Christopher J. Fries (2011) *Pursuing health and wellness*. New York: Oxford University Press.

A theoretically grounded Canadian textbook on medical sociology with a focus on the social determinants of health.

References

Alter, David A., Theresa Stukel, Alice Chong, and David Henry (2011) "Lesson from Canada's universal care: Socially disadvantaged patients use more health services, still have poorer health." *Health Affairs* 30: 274–83.

Amzat, Jimoh, and Oliver Razum (2014) *Medical sociology in Africa*. Dordrecht: Springer.

Anesaki, Masahira, and Tsunetsugu Munakata (2005) "Health, illness, and health policy in Japan," pp. 441–55 in *The Blackwell companion to medical sociology*, W. Cockerham (ed.). Oxford, UK: Blackwell.

Bartley, Mel (2004) *Health inequality*. Cambridge, UK: Polity.

———— (2012) "Explaining health inequality: Evidence from the UK." *Social Science and Medicine* 74: 658–60.

Bradby, Hannah (2012) *Medicine, health and society*. London: Sage.

Burström, Bo (2012) "Sweden—Socioeconomic factors and health." *Social Science and Medicine* 74: 654–55.

Bury, Michael (2010) "The British health care system," pp. 412–33 in *The new Blackwell companion to medical sociology*, W. Cockerham (ed.). Oxford, UK: Wiley-Blackwell.

Cassileth, Barrie R., Vasily V. Vlassov, and Christopher C. Chapman (1995) "Health care, medical practice, and medical ethics in Russia today." *Journal of American Medical Association* 273: 1569–622.

Castro, Roberto (2005) "Medical sociology in Mexico," pp. 214–32 in *The Blackwell companion to medical sociology*, W. Cockerham (ed.). Oxford, UK: Blackwell.

Chen, Feinian, Yang Yang, and Guangya Liu (2010) "Social change and socioeconomic disparities in health over the life course in China: A cohort analysis." *American Sociological Review* 75: 126–50.

Chen, Meei-shia (2005) "The great reversal: Transformation of health care in the People's Republic of China," pp. 456–82 in *The Blackwell companion to medical sociology*, W. Cockerham (ed.). Oxford, UK: Blackwell.

Cockerham, Geoffrey B., and William C. Cockerham (2010) *Health and globalization*. Cambridge, UK: Polity.

Cockerham, William C. (1997) "The social determinants of the decline of life expectancy in Russia and Eastern Europe: A lifestyle explanation." *Journal of Health and Social Behavior* 38: 117–30.

———— (1999) *Health and social change in Russia and Eastern Europe*. London: Routledge.

———— (2000) "Health lifestyles in Russia." *Social Science and Medicine* 51: 1313–24.

———— (2000) "The sociology of health behavior and health lifestyles," pp. 159–72 in *Handbook of medical sociology*, 5th ed., C. Bird, P. Conrad, and A. Fremont (eds.). Upper Saddle River, NJ: Prentice Hall.

—— (2006) "Class matters: Health lifestyles in Post-Soviet Russia." *Harvard International Review* (Spring): 42–45.

—— (2007) "Health lifestyles and the absence of the Russian middle class." *Sociology of Health & Illness* 29: 457–73.

—— (2012) "The intersection of life expectancy and gender in a transitional state: The case of Russia." *Sociology of Health & Illness* 34: 943–57.

—— (2013) *Social causes of health and disease* (2nd ed.). Cambridge, UK: Polity.

Cockerham, William C., Hiroyuki Hattori, and Yukio Yamori (2000) "The social gradient in life expectancy: The contrary case of Okinawa in Japan." *Social Science and Medicine* 51: 115–22.

Cockerham, William C., M. Christine Snead, and Derek F. DeWaal (2002) "Health lifestyles in Russia and the socialist heritage." *Journal of Health and Social Behavior* 43: 42–55.

Dickinson, Harley D., and B. Singh Bolaria (2005) "The evolution of health care in Canada: Toward community or corporate control?" pp. 199–213 in *The Blackwell companion to medical sociology*, W. Cockerham (ed.). Oxford, UK: Blackwell.

Dmitrieva, Elena (2005) "The Russian health care experiment: Transition of the health care system and rethinking the sociology of medicine," pp. 320–33 in *The Blackwell companion to medical sociology*, W. Cockerham (ed.). Oxford, UK: Blackwell.

Evans, Robert G. (1986) "Finding the levers, finding the courage: Lessons from cost containment in North America." *Journal of Health Politics, Policy and Law* 11: 585–616.

Field, Mark G. (ed.). (1989) *Success and crisis in national health systems*. London: Routledge.

—— (1993) "The physician in the Commonwealth of Independent States: The difficult passage from bureaucrat to professional," pp. 162–83 in *The changing medical profession*, F. Hafferty and J. McKinley (eds.). New York: Oxford University Press.

—— (1995) "The health crisis in the former Soviet Union: A report from the 'post-war' zone." *Social Science and Medicine* 41: 1469–78.

—— (2000) "The health and demographic crisis in post-Soviet Russia: A two-phase development," pp. 11–42 in *Russia's torn safety nets: Health and social welfare during the transition*, M. Field and J. Twigg (eds.). New York: St. Martin's Press.

Grigoriev, Pavel, France Meslé, Vladimir M. Shkolnikov, Evgeny Andreev, Agnieszka Fihel, Marketa Pechholdova, and Jacques Vallin (2014) "The recent mortality decline in Russia: Beginning of the cardiovascular revolution?" *Population and Development Review* 40: 107–29.

Hemström, Örjan (2005) "Society, health, and health care in Sweden," pp. 298–318 in *The Blackwell companion to medical sociology*, W. Cockerham (ed.). Oxford, UK: Blackwell.

Hughes, David, and Peter Vincent-Jones (2008) "Schisms in the church: NHS systems and institutional divergence in England and Wales." *Journal of Health and Social Behavior* 49: 400–16.

Ikegami, Naoki, Byung-Kwang Yoo, Hideki Hashimoto, Masatoshi Matsumoto, Hiroya Ogata, Akira Babazono, Ryo Watanabe, Kenji Shibuya, Bong-Min Yang, Michael R. Reich, Yasuki Kobayashi (2011) "Japanese universal health coverage: Evolution, achievements, and challenges." *Lancet* 378: 1106–15.

Jarvis, Martin J., and Jane Wardle (1999) "Social patterning of individual health behaviours: The case of cigarette smoking," pp. 240–55 in *The social determinants of health*, M. Marmot and R. Wilkinson (eds.). Oxford, UK: Oxford University Press.

Kikuzawa, Sako, Sigrun Olafsdottir, and Bernice Pescosolido (2008) "Similar pressures, different contents: Public attitudes toward government intervention for health care in 21 countries." *Journal of Health and Social Behavior* 49: 385–99.

Kletke, Phillip R., David W. Emmons, and Kurt D. Gillis (1996) "Current trends in physicians' practice arrangements." *Journal of American Medical Association* 276: 555–60.

Knaul, Felicia Marie, Edurado González-Pier, Octavio Gómez-Dantés, David García-Junco, Héctor Arreola-Ornelas, Mariana Barraza-Lloréns, Rosa Sandoval, Francisco Caballero, Mauricio Hernández-Avila, Mercedes Juan, David Kershenobich, Gustavo Nigenda, Enrique Ruelas, Jaime Sepúlveda, Roberto Tapia, Guillermo Soberón, Salomón Chertorivski, Julio Frenk (2012) "The quest for universal health coverage: Achieving social protection for all in Mexico." *Lancet* 380: 1259–79.

Knaus, William A. (1981) *Inside Russian medicine.* Boston: Beacon Press.

Knesebeck, Olaf Von Dem, and Johannes Siegrist (2005) "Medical sociology in Germany," pp. 287–97 in *The Blackwell companion to medical sociology*, W. Cockerham (ed.). Oxford, UK: Blackwell.

Kosteniuk, Julie G., and Harley D. Dickinson (2003) "Tracing the social gradient in the health of Canadians: Primary and secondary determinants." *Social Science and Medicine* 57: 263–76.

Lahelma, Eero, Sara Arber, Katarina Kivela, and Eva Roos (2002) "Multiple roles and health among British and Finnish women: The influence of socioeconomic circumstances." *Social Science and Medicine* 54: 727–40.

Li, Quang, Jason Hsia, and Gonghaun Yang (2011) "Prevalence of smoking in China in 2010." *New England Journal of Medicine* 364: 2469–70.

Light, Donald W., and Alexander Schuller (eds.). (1986) *Political values and health care: The German experience.* Cambridge, MA: MIT Press.

Lin, Vivian (2012) "Transformation in the healthcare system in China." *Current Sociology* 60: 427–40.

Manning, Nick, and Nataliya Tikhonova (eds.). (2009) *Health and health care in the new Russia.* Farnham, UK: Ashgate.

Marmot, Michael (2004) *The status syndrome.* New York: Times Books.

McNeil, Donald G., Jr. (2010) "Dirt-poor nation, with a health plan." *New York Times* (June 15): D1, D6.

Medvedev, Roy (2000) *Post-soviet Russia*, G. Shriver (trans. and ed.). New York: Columbia University Press.

National Center for Health Statistics (2013) *Health United States, 2012.* Washington, DC: U.S. Government Printing Office.

———— (2014) *Health United States, 2013.* Washington, DC: US Government Printing Office.

Nazarova, Inna (2009) "Health and employment," pp. 147–70 in *Health and health care in the new Russia*, N. Manning and N. Tikhonova (eds.). Farnham, UK: Ashgate.

Nemtsov, A. V. (2002) "Alcohol-related human losses in Russia in the 1980s and 1990s." *Addiction* 97: 1413–25.

Nigenda, Gustavo, Lejeune Lockett, Cristina Manca, and Gerardo Mora (2001) "Non-biomedical health care practices in the state of Morelos, Mexico: Analysis of an emergent phenomenon." *Sociology of Health & Illness* 23: 3–23.

Nishi, Nobuo, Kae Makino, Hidebi Fukuda, and Kozo Tatarra (2004) "Effects of socioeconomic indicators on coronary risk factors, self-rated health, and psychological well-being among urban Japanese civil servants." *Social Science and Medicine* 58: 1159–70.

Nolte, Ellen, Rembrandt Scholz, Vladimir Shkolnikov, and Martin Mckee (2002) "The contribution of medical care to changing life expectancy in Germany and Poland." *Social Science and Medicine* 55: 1905–21.

Oglobin, Constatin, and Gregory Brock (2003) "Smoking in Russia: The 'Marlboro man' rides without 'Virginia Slims' for now." *Comparative Economic Studies* 45: 87–103.

Olafsdottir, Sigrun, and Jason Beckfield (2011) "Health and the social rights of citizenship; Integrating welfare-state theory and medical sociology," pp. 101–13 in *Handbook of health, illness, and healing*, B. Pescosolido, J. Martin, J. McLeod, and A. Rogers (eds.). Dordrecht: Springer.

Palosuo, Hannle (2000) "Health-related lifestyles and alienation in Moscow and Helsinki." *Social Science and Medicine* 51: 1325–41.

Pietilä, Ilkka, and Marja Rytkönen (2008) "Health is not a man's domain: Lay accounts of gender difference in life expectancy in Russia." *Sociology of Health & Illness* 30: 1070–85.

Popkin, Barry, Namvar Zohoori, Lenore Kohlmeier, Alexander Baturin, Arseni Martinchik, and Alexander Deev (1997) "Nutritional risk factors in the former Soviet Union," pp. 314–34 in *Premature death in the new independent states*, J. Bobadilla, C. Costello, and F. Mitchell (eds.). Washington, DC: National Academy Press.

Powell, Margaret, and Masahira Anesaki (1990) *Health care in Japan.* London: Routledge.

Quadagno, Jill (2010) "Institutions, interest groups, and ideology: An agenda for the sociology of health reform." *Journal of Health and Social Behavior* 51: 125–36.

Reid, Ivan (1998) *Social class differences in Britain.* Cambridge, UK: Polity.

Rose, Richard (2009) *Understanding post-communist transformation.* London: Routledge.

Rosenthal, Elizabeth (2013) "For medical tourists, simple math." *New York Times* (August 4): 1, 18.

Schafer, Markus H., and Soyoung Kwon (2012) "Cohorts and emerging health disparities: Biomorphic trajectories in China, 1989 to 2006." *Journal of Health and Social Behavior* 53: 515–32.

Segall, Alexander, and Christopher J. Fries (2011) *Pursing health and wellness: Healthy societies, healthy people.* Toronto: Oxford University Press.

Shapiro, Judith (1995) "The Russian mortality crisis and its causes," pp. 149–78 in *Russian economic reform at risk*, A. Aslund (ed.). London: Pinter.

Shaw, Mary, Danny Dorling, and George Davey Smith (1999) "Poverty, social exclusion, and minorities," pp. 211–39 in *The social determinants of health*, M. Marmot and R. Wilkinson (eds.). Oxford, UK: Oxford University Press.

Shkolnikov, Vladimir, and Alexander Nemtsov (1994) "The anti-alcohol campaign and variations in Russian mortality." Paper presented to the workshop on mortality and adult health priorities in the New Independent States, Washington, DC (November).

Shkolnikov, Vladimir, Martin Mckee, and David A. Leon (2001) "Changes in life expectancy in Russia in the mid-1990s." *Lancet* 357: 917–27.

Stevens, Fred (2010) "The convergence and divergence of modern health care systems," pp. 434–54 in *The new Blackwell companion to medical sociology*, W. Cockerham (ed.). Oxford, UK: Blackwell.

Twigg, Judith L. (2000) "Unfilled hopes: The struggle to reform *Russian health care* and its financing," pp. 43–64 in *Russia's torn safety nets: Health and welfare during the transition*, M. Field and J. Twigg (eds.). New York: St. Martin's Press.

——— (2002) "Health care reform in Russia: A survey of head doctors and insurance administrators." *Social Science and Medicine* 55: 2253–65.

Van Gundy, Karen, Scott Shieman, Margaret S. Kelley, and Cesar J. Rebellion (2005) "Gender role orientation and alcohol use among Moscow and Toronto adults." *Social Science and Medicine* 61: 2317–30.

Vogt, Peter (2014) "Longer life thanks to reunification." (September 9) Rostock, Germany: Max Planck Institute for Demographic Research.

Xu, Y., L. Wang, J. He, M. Li, T. Wang, L. Wang, Y. Jiang, M. Dai, J. Lu, M. Xu, Y. Li, N. Hu, J. Li, S. Mi, C. S. Chen, G. Li, Y. Mu, J. Zhao, L. Kong, J. Chen, S. Lai, W. Wang, W. Zhao, G. Ning, and 2010 China Noncommunicable Disease Surveillance Group (2013) "Prevalence and control of diabetes in Chinese adults." *Journal of American Medical Association* 310: 948–57.

CREDITS

Photo Credits

Chapter 1 Joseph Sohm/Visions of America/Corbis, p. 3; RGB Ventures/SuperStock/Alamy, p. 20; CQ-Roll Call, Inc./Getty Images, p. 22.

Chapter 2 Lou Linwei/Alamy, p. 29; forestpath/Shutterstock, p. 38; Fotoluminate LLC/Fotolia, p. 40.

Chapter 3 wavebreakmedia/Shutterstock, p. 54; Kayte Deioma/PhotoEdit, p. 56; Orange Line Media/Shutterstock.com, p. 57.

Chapter 4 Christopher Futcher/Getty Images, p. 78; iStock © UygarGeographic, p. 88; Robin Nelson/PhotoEdit, p. 100.

Chapter 5 Joe Patronite/The Image Bank/Getty Images, p. 113; Michael Ainsworth/KRT/Newscom, p. 129; Peter Turnley for Harper's/Corbis, p. 131; gradt/Fotolia, p. 133.

Chapter 6 Halfpoint/Fotolia, p. 142; Ariel Skelley/Alamy, p. 151; Three Lions/Getty Images, p. 155.

Chapter 7 Michael Siluk/The Image Works, p. 160; Mark Richard/PhotoEdit, p. 172; Image Point Fr/Shutterstock, p. 178.

Chapter 8 Dayna More/Shutterstock, p. 182; Comstock/Stockbyte/Getty Images, p. 187.

Chapter 9 Science Photo Library/Alamy, p. 212; Tom Wang/Fotolia, p. 217.

Chapter 10 Digital Vision/Getty Images, p. 240; Susan Van Etten/PhotoEdit, p. 247; Jonathan Nourok/PhotoEdit, p. 254.

Chapter 11 Zero Creatives/Alamy, p. 270; iStock © Geber86, p. 274; Keith/Newscom, p. 285.

Chapter 12 Ingram Publishing/Newscom, p. 291; Monkey Business/Fotolia, p. 301; RJ Sangosti/The Denver Post via Getty Images, p. 305.

Chapter 13 Lightwavemedia/Fotolia, p. 310; iStock © Dean Mitchell, p. 312; Cordelia Molloy/Science Source, p. 319.

Chapter 14 upixa/Shutterstock.com, p. 333; MPI/Stringer/Archive Photos/Getty Images, p. 338; Mark Richard/PhotoEdit, p. 345.

Chapter 15 Tony Savino/Corbis, p. 356; AP Photo/Charles Dharapak, p. 368.

Chapter 16 KIN CHEUNG/Reuters/Corbis, p. 383; TWPhoto/Corbis, p. 400; Dorothy Alexander/Alamy, p. 406.

Text Credits

Chapter 1 p. 4, Cockerham, William C. (2013a:1) *Social causes of health and disease*, 2nd ed. Cambridge, UK: Polity; p. 5, Light, Donald W., and Alexander Schuller (eds) (1986:9) *Political values and health care: The German experience. Cambridge*, MA: MIT Press; p. 7, Johnson, Malcolm (1975:229) "Medical sociology and sociological theory." *Social Science and Medicine* 9: 227–32; p. 8, Freidson, Eliot (1970b:62) *Professional dominance.* Chicago: Aldine; p. 9, Pescosolido, Bernice A., and Jennie J. Kronenfeld (1995:24) "Health, illness, and healing in an uncertain era: Challenges from and for medical sociology." *Journal of Health and Social Behavior* 36(Extra issue): 5–35; p. 12, Engels, Friedrich (1977:131) "The need for a new medical model: A challenge for biomedicine." *Science* 196: 129–35; p. 12, Foucault, Michel (1973) *The birth of the clinic.* London: Tavistock; p. 13, Mckeown, Thomas (1979:53)

The role of medicine. Oxford, UK: Blackwell; p. 14, Porter, Roy (1997:428) *The greatest benefit to mankind: A medical history of humanity.* New York: W. W. Norton; p. 14, Porter, Roy (1997:585) *The greatest benefit to mankind: A medical history of humanity.* New York: W. W. Norton; p. 15, Porter, Roy (1997:634) *The greatest benefit to mankind: A medical history of humanity.* New York: W. W. Norton; p. 16, Armelagos, George J., Peter J. Brown, and Bethany Turner (2005:755) "Evolutionary, historical and political economic perspectives on health and disease." *Social Science and Medicine* 61: 755–65; p. 17, Preston, Richard (1994:361) *The hot zone.* New York: Anchor Books; p. 19, Preston, Richard (1999:108) "West Nile mystery." *New Yorker* (October 18 & 25): 90–108; p. 21, Garrett, Laurie (1994:610) *The coming plague.* New York: Farrar, Straus & Giroux.

Chapter 3   p. 55, Reid, Ivan (1998:238) *Social class differences in Britain.* Cambridge, UK: Polity; p. 58, Swartz, David (1997:45) *Culture and power: The sociology of Pierre Bourdieu.* Chicago: University of Chicago Press; p. 59, Mirowsky, John, and Catherine E. Ross (2003:49) *Education, social status, and health.* New York: Aldine de Gruyter; p. 59, Herd, Pamela A., Brian Goesling, and James S. House (2007:236) "Socioeconomic position and health: The differential effects of education versus income on the onset versus progression of health problems." *Journal of Health and Social Behavior* 48: 223–38; p. 60, Carpiano, Richard M., Bruce G. Link, and Jo C. Phelan (2008:232) "Social inequality and health: Future directions for the fundamental cause explanation," pp. 232–63 in *Social class: How does it work?* A. Lareau and D. Conley (eds). New York: Russell Sage; p. 63, Wilkinson, Richard G. (1996:3) *Unhealthy societies.* London: Routledge; p. 64, Dolan, Alan (2007:726) "'Good luck to them if they get it': Exploring working class men's understandings and experiences of income inequality and material standards." *Sociology of Health and Illness* 29: 711–29; p. 66, Smith, James P. (1999:165) "Healthy bodies and thick wallets: The dual relation between health and economic status." *Journal of Economic Perspectives* 13:146–66; p. 68, Pearlin, Leonard I., Scott Schieman, Elena M. Fazio, and Stephen C. Meersman (2005:208) "Stress, health, and the life course: Some conceptual perspectives." *Journal of Health and Social Behavior* 46: 205–19; p. 69, Link, Bruce G., and Jo Phelan (1995:87) "Social conditions as fundamental causes of diseases." *Journal of Health and Social Behavior* 36(Extra issue): 80–94; p. 70, Link, Bruce G., and Jo Phelan (2000:37) "Evaluating the fundamental cause explanation for social disparities in health," pp. 33–47 in *Handbook of Medical Sociology*, 5th ed., C. Bird, P. Conrad, and A. Fremont (eds). Upper Saddle River, NJ: Prentice Hall; p. 71, Lutfey, Karen, and Jeremy Freese (2005:1355) "Toward some fundamentals of fundamental causality: Socio-economic status and health in the routine clinic visit for diabetes." *American Journal of Sociology* 110: 1326–72.

Chapter 4   p. 82, Annandale, Ellen C. (2010:103) "Health status and gender," pp. 97–112 in *The new Blackwell companion to medical sociology*, W. Cockerham (ed.). Oxford, UK: Oxford University Press; p. 83, Ross, Catherine E., John Mirowsky, and Patricia Ulbrich (1983:681) "Distress and the traditional female role: A comparison of Mexicans and Anglos." *American Journal of Sociology* 89:560–682; p. 85, Redelmeier, Donald A., and Jeffrey c. Kwong (2004:2541) "Death rates of medical school class presidents." *Social Science and Medicine* 8: 2537–43; p. 85, Auerbach, Judith and Anne Figert (1995:122) "Women's health research: Public policy and sociology." *Journal of Health and Social Behavior* 36(Extra issue): 115–31; p. 86, Verbrugge, Lois M. (1976:401) "Females and illness: Recent trends in sex differences in the United States." *Journal of Health and Social Behavior* 17: 387–403; p. 90, Rosenfield, Sarah (1989:77) "The effects of women's employment: Personal control and sex differences in mental health." *Journal of Health and Social Behavior* 30: 77–91; p. 100, Conley, Dalton, Kate W. Strully, and Neil G. Bennett (2003:34) *The starting gate: Birth weight and life chances.* Berkeley: University of California Press; p. 101, Robert, Stephanie A., and

James S. House (2000:84) "Socioeconomic inequalities in health: An enduring sociological problem," pp. 79–97 in *Handbook of Medical Sociology*, 5th ed., C. Bird, P. Conrad, and A. Fremont (eds). Upper Saddle River, NJ: Prentice Hall.

Chapter 5   Living at an epicenter of diabetes, defiance 116, Based on Thoits, Peggy A. (2010) "Stress and health: Major findings and policy implications." *Journal of Health and Social Behavior* 51: S41–53; p. 117, Cooley, Charles H. (1964) *Human nature and the social order*. New York: Schocken; p. 117, Volkart, E. H. (ed.) (1951) *Social behavior and personality*. New York: Social Science Research Council; p. 117, David Mechanic (1978:293) *Medical sociology*, 2nd ed. New York: The Free Press; p. 119, Durkheim, Emile (1950:13) *The rules of sociological method*. New York: The Free Press; p. 120, Durkheim, Emile (1951:256) *Suicide*. New York: The Free Press; p. 127, David Mechanic (1962:8) *Students under stress: A study of the social psychology of adaptation*. New York: The Free Press; p. 128, Turner, Bryan S. (2004:13) *The new medical sociology*. New York: W. W. Norton; p. 130, Tierney, Kathleen J., and Barbara Baisden (1979:36) *Crisis intervention programs for disaster victims: A source book and manual for smaller communities*. Rockville, MD: National Institute of Mental Health.

Chapter 6   p. 146, World Health Organization (1986:117) "Lifestyles and health." *Social Science and Medicine* 22: 117–24; p. 148, Crawford, Robert (1984:76) "A cultural account of health: Control, release, and the social body," pp. 60–103 in *Issues in the political economy of health care*, J. McKinley (ed.). New York: Tavistock; p. 148, Dahrendorf, Ralf (1979:73) *Life chances*. Chicago: University of Chicago Press. p. 149, Wickrama, K. A. S., Rand D. Conger, Lora Ebert Wallace, and Glen H. Elder, Jr (1999:260) "The inter-generational transmission of health-risk behaviors:Adolescent lifestyles and gender moderating effects." *Journal of Health and Social Behavior* 40: 258–72; p. 149, Kleinfield, N. R. (2006:A20) "Living at an epicenter of diabetes, defiance, and despair." *New York Times* (January 10): A1, A20; p. 150, Pampel, Fred C. (2009:526) "The persistence of educational differences in smoking." *Social Problems* 56: 526–42.

Chapter 7   p. 163, Mechanic, David (1995:1208) "Sociological dimensions of illness behavior." *Social Science and Medicine* 41: 1207–16; p. 167, Christakos, Nicholas A., and James H. Fowler (2008:2256–57) "The collective dynamics of smoking in a large social network." *New England Journal of Medicine* 358: 2249–58; p. 168, Pescosolido, Bernice A. (1992:1113) "Beyond rational choice: The social dynamics of how people seek help." *American Journal of Sociology* 97: 1096–138; p. 170, Seccombe, Karen, and Cheryl Amey (1995:179) "Playing by the rules and losing: Health insurance and the working poor." *Journal of Health and Social Behavior* 36: 168–81; p. 169, National Center for Health Statistics, 2011. p. 173, Dutton, Diana B. (1978:359) "Explaining the low use of health services by the poor: Costs, attitudes, or delivery systems?" *American Sociological Review* 43: 348–68; p. 174, Dutton, Diana B. (1978:361–62) "Explaining the low use of health services by the poor: Costs, attitudes, or delivery systems?" *American Sociological Review* 43: 348–68; p. 176, Conrad, Peter (2007:138) *The medicalization of society: On the transformation of human conditions into treatable disorders*. Baltimore: Johns Hopkins University Press; p. 177, Savage, Mathieu, Alex Dumas, and Stephen A. Stuart (2013:1222) "Fatalism and short-termism as cultural barriers to cardiac rehabilitation among underprivileged men." *Sociology of Health & Illness* 35: 1211–26; p. 180, Radley, Alan (1994:62) *Making sense of illness: The social psychology of health and disease*. London: Sage.

Chapter 8   p. 196, Freidson, Eliot (1970a:228) *Profession of medicine*. New York: Dodd, Mead; p. 197, Rier, David A. (2000:75) "The missing voice of the critically ill: A medical sociologist's first-person account." *Sociology of Health and Illness* 22: 68–93; p. 197, Rier, David A. (2000:71) "The missing voice of the critically ill: A medical sociologist's first-person account." *Sociology of Health and Illness* 22: 68–93; p. 197, Turner, Bryan S. (1996:214) *The body and society*, 2nd ed. Oxford, UK: Blackwell; p. 198, Joseph Davis, (2010:211) "Medicalization, Social Control, and the Relief of Suffering" in *The New Blackwell Companion to Medical Sociology*, William C. Cockerham (ed.) John Wiley & Sons; p. 198, Szasz, Thomas S. (1974:44–45) *The myth of mental illness*, rev. ed. New York: Harper & Row; p. 198, Twaddle, Andrew (1973:756) "Illness and deviance." *Social Science and Medicine* 7: 751–62; p. 199, Clarke, Adele E., Janet K. Shim, Laura Mamo, Jennifer Ruth Fosket, and Jennifer R. Fishman (2003:161) "Biomedicalization: Technoscientific transformation of health, illness, and U.S. biomedicine." *American Sociological Review* 68: 161–94; p. 199, Conrad, Peter (2005:10) "The shifting engines of medicalization." *Journal of Health and Social Behavior* 46: 3–14; p. 202, Campbell, John D. (1978:46) "The child in the sick role: Contributions of age, sex, parental status, and parental values." *Journal of Health and Social Behavior* 19: 35–51; p. 208, Becker, Howard S. (1973:179) *Outsiders: Studies in the sociology of deviance*, 2nd ed. New York: The Free Press; p. 209, Sontag, Susan (1978:3) *Illness as metaphor*. New York: Farrar, Straus, & Giroux; p. 209, Freund, Peter E. S., and Meredith B. Mcguire (1999:132) *Health, illness, and the social body*, 3rd ed. Englewood Cliffs, NJ: Prentice Hall; p. 210, Schieman, Scott, and Heather A. Turner (1998:171) "Age, disability, and the sense of mastery." *Journal of Health and Social Behavior* 39: 169–86; p. 211, Bury, Michael (2000:177) "On chronic illness and disability," pp. 173–83 in *Handbook of Medical Sociology*, 5th ed., C. Bird, P. Conrad, and A. Fremont (eds). Upper Saddle River, NJ: Prentice Hall; p. 211, Goffman, Erving (1963:3) *Stigma: Notes on the management of a spoiled identity*. Englewood Cliffs, NJ: Prentice-Hall.

Chapter 9 p. 219, Freidson, Eliot (1970a:258) *Profession of medicine*. New York: Dodd, Mead; p. 222, Katz, Pearl (1999:120) *The scalpel's edge: The culture of surgeons*. Boston: Allyn and Bacon; p. 222, Katz, Pearl (1999:120) *The scalpel's edge: The culture of surgeons*. Boston: Allyn and Bacon; p. 222, Warren, Mary Guptill, Rose Weitz, and Stephen Kulis (1998:364) "Physician satisfaction in a changing health care environment: The impact of challenges to professional autonomy, authority, and dominance." Journal of *Health and Social Behavior* 39: 356–67; p. 223, Cassell, Eric J., *Talking with Patients*, Volume 2: Volume 2 - Clinical Technique, 414 word excerpt, © 1985 Massachusetts Institute of Technology, by permission of The MIT Press; p. 224, Fitton, Freda, and H. W. K. Acheson (1979:75) *The doctor/patient relationship: A study in general practice*. London: Department of Health and Social Security; p. 225, Weitz, Rose (1999:214) "Watching Brian die: The rhetoric and reality of informed consent." *Health* 3: 209–27; p. 227, Davies, Karen (2003:734) "The body and doing gender: The relations between doctors and nurses in hospital work." *Sociology of Health and Illness* 25: 720–42; p. 228, Hammond, Judith (1980:39) "Biography building to insure the future: Women's negotiation of gender relevancy in medical school." *Symbolic Interaction* 3: 35–49; pp. 228–229, Hinze, Susan W. (1999:236) "Gender and the body of medicine or at least some body parts: (Re)constructing the prestige hierarchy of medical specialties." *Sociological Quarterly* 40: 217–40; p. 230, Riska, Elianne (2010:348) "Health professions and occupations," pp. 337–54 in *The new Blackwell companion to medical sociology*, W. Cockerham (ed.). Oxford, UK: Blackwell; p. 230, Williams, Alex (2008:8) "The falling-down professions." *New York Times* Sunday Styles (January 6): 2, 8; p. 236, Barker, Kristin K. (2008:21) "Electronic support groups, patient-consumers, and medicalization: The case of contested illness." Journal of *Health and Social Behavior* 49: 20–38; p. 240, Conrad, Peter, and Jonathan Gabe (1999:514) "Introduction: Sociological perspectives on the new genetics: An overview." *Sociology of Health and Illness* 21: 505–16.

Chapter 10 p. 250, Goode, William J. (1960:903) "Encroachment, charlatanism, and the emerging profession: Psychology, sociology, and medicine." *American Sociological Review* 25: 902–14; p. 251, Brown, E. Richard (1979:62–63) *Rockefeller medicine men: Medicine and capitalism in America*. Berkeley: University of California Press. 62–63; p. 252, Brown, E. Richard (1979:73) *Rockefeller medicine men: Medicine and capitalism in America*. Berkeley: University of California Press. 73; p. 252, Brown, E. Richard (1979:73) *Rockefeller medicine men: Medicine and capitalism in America*. Berkeley: University of California Press. 73; p. 252, Stevens, Rosemary (1971:135) *American medicine and the public interest*. New Haven, CT: Yale University Press; p. 254, Light, Donald W. (2004:6) "Introduction: Ironies of success—A new history of the American health care 'system.' "Journal of *Health and Social Behavior* 45 (Extra issue): 1–24. 6; p. 254, Hafferty, Frederic W., and Donald W. Light (1995:138) "Professional dynamics and the changing nature of medical work." Journal of *Health and Social Behavior* 36 (Extra issue): 132–53; p. 255, Hafferty, Frederic W., and Donald W. Light (1995:138) "Professional dynamics and the changing nature of medical work." Journal of *Health and Social Behavior* 36 (Extra issue): 132–53; p. 256, Stevens, Rosemary (1971:67) *American medicine and the public interest*. New Haven, CT: Yale University Press; p. 257, Light, Donald W. (2004:8) "Introduction: Ironies of success—A new history of the American health care 'system.' "Journal of *Health and Social Behavior* 45 (Extra issue): 1–24. 6; p. 258, Becker, Howard S., Blanche Greer, Everett C. Hughes, and Anselm Strauss (1961:72) *Boys in white: Student culture in medical school*. Chicago: University of Chicago Press. p. 260, Timmermans, Stefan, and Neetu Chawla (2009:152) "Evidence-based medicine and medical education," pp. 139–55 in *Handbook of the Sociology of Medical Education*, C. Brosnan and B. Turner (eds). London: Routledge; p. 260, Haas, Jack, and William Shaffir (1977:71) "The professionalization of medical students: Developing competence and a cloak of competence." *Symbolic Interaction* 1: 71–88; p. 261, Jagsi, Reshma, and Rebecca Surender (2004:2184) "Regulation of junior doctors' work hours: An analysis of British and American doctors' experiences and attitudes." *Social Science and Medicine* 58: 281–91; p. 261, Light, Donald W. (1979:320) "Uncertainty and control in professional training." Journal of *Health and Social Behavior* 20: 310–22; p. 262, Rothman, Ellen Lerner (1999:155) *White coat: Becoming a doctor at Harvard Medical School*. New York: HarperCollins. p. 262, Rothman, Ellen Lerner (1999:167) *White coat: Becoming a doctor at Harvard Medical School*. New York: HarperCollins. p. 264, Hall, Oswald (1948:330) "The stages of a medical career." *American Journal of Sociology* 53: 327–36; p. 265, Freidson, Eliot (1960:378) "Client control and medical practice." *American Journal of Sociology* 65: 374–82; p. 266, Duff, Raymond S., and August B. Hollingshead (1968:46) *Sickness and society*. New York: Harper & Row; p. 266, Hafferty, Frederic W., and Donald W. Light (1995:141) "Professional dynamics and the changing nature of medical work." Journal of *Health and Social Behavior* 36 (Extra issue): 132–53.

Chapter 11 p. 271, Pescosolido, Bernice A., Steven A. Tuch, and Jack K. Martin (2001:13) "The profession of medicine and the public: Examining Americans' changing confidence in physician authority from the beginning of the 'health care crisis' to the era of health care reform." Journal of *Health and Social Behavior* 42: 1–16; p. 273, Freidson, Eliot (1960:379) "Client control and medical practice." *American Journal of Sociology* 65: 374–82; p. 273, Millman, Marcia (1977b) *The unkindest cut*. New York: Morrow; p. 276, Freidson, Eliot (1975:251) *Doctoring together*. New York: Elsevier North-Holland; p. 277, Light, Donald W. (2000:204) "The medical profession and organizational change: From professional dominance to contervailing power," pp. 201–16 in *Handbook of Medical Sociology*, 5th ed., C. Bird, P. Conrad, and A. Fremont (eds). Upper Saddle River, NJ: Prentice Hall; p. 278, Mckinlay, John B (1999:1) *"The end of the Golden age of doctoring."* New England Research Institutes Newsletter (Summer): 1, 3; p. 279, Waitzkin, Howard (2000:272) "Changing patient–physician relationships in the changing health-policy environment," pp. 271–83 in

Handbook of Medical Sociology, 5th ed., C. Bird, P. Conrad, and A. Fremont (eds). Upper Saddle River, NJ: Prentice Hall; p. 281, Starr, Paul (1982:436) *The social transformation of American medicine*. New York: Basic Books; p. 282, Starr, Paul (1982:446) *The social transformation of American medicine*. New York: Basic Books; p. 282, Starr, Paul (1982:445) *The social transformation of American medicine*. New York: Basic Books; p. 283, Ritzer, George, and David Walczak (1988:6) "Rationalization and the deprofessionalization of physicians." *Social Forces* 67: 1–22; p. 284, Light, Donald W (1989:470) "Social control and the American health care system," pp. 456–74 in *Handbook of Medical Sociology*, 4th ed., H. Freeman and S. Levine (eds). Englewood Cliffs, NJ: Prentice Hall; p. 284, Hafferty, Frederic W., and Donald W. Light (1995:138) "Professional dynamics and the changing nature of medical work." Journal of *Health and Social Behavior* 36 (Extra issue): 132–53; p. 284, Rosenberg, Charles E. (2007:1) *Our present compliant: American medicine*, then and now. Baltimore: Johns Hopkins University Press; p. 286, Kletke, Phillip R., David W. Emmons, and Kurt D. Gillis (1996:560) "Current trends in physicians' practice arrangements." *JAMA* 276: 555–60.

Chapter 12   p. 295, Strauss, Anselm (1966) "Structure and ideology of the nursing profession," pp. 60–104 in *The Nursing Profession*, F. Davis (ed.). New York: John Wiley; p. 298, Davis, Fred (1972:46) *Illness, Interaction, and the Self*. Belmont, CA: Wadsworth; p. 298, Davis, Fred (1972:46) *Illness, Interaction, and the Self*. Belmont, CA: Wadsworth; p. 298, Porter, Sam (1992:523) "Women in a women's job: The gendered experience of nurses." *Sociology of Health & Illness* 14: 510–27; p. 299, Brannon, Robert L. (1994b:170) "Professionalization and work intensification." *Work and Occupations* 21: 157–78; p. 299, Rank, Steven G., and Cardell K. Jacobson (1977:191) "Hospital nurses' compliance with medication overdose orders: A failure to replicate." Journal of *Health and Social Behavior* 18: 188–93; p. 302, Aiken, Linda H., and Douglas M. Sloane (1997:218) "Effects of specialization and client differentiation on the status of nurses: The case of AIDS." Journal of *Health and Social Behavior* 38: 203–22; p. 303, Schulman, Sam (1972:236) "Mother surrogate—After a decade," pp. 233–39 in *Patients, Physicians and Illness*, E. Jaco (ed.). New York: The Free Press.

Chapter 13   p. 316, Allen, Gillian, and Roy Wallis (1976:134–35) "Pentecostalists as a medical minority," pp. 110–37 in *Marginal Medicine*, R. Wallis and P. Morley (eds). New York: The Free Press; p. 316, Glik, Deborah C. (1990:161) "The redefinition of the situation: The social construction of spiritual healing experiences." *Sociology of Health & Illness* 12: 151–68; p. 316, Glik, Deborah C. (1990:157) "The redefinition of the situation: The social construction of spiritual healing experiences." *Sociology of Health & Illness* 12: 151–68; p. 318, Idler, Ellen L. (2010:138–39) "Health and religion," pp. 133–58 in The new Blackwell companion to medical sociology, W. Cockerham (ed.). Oxford, UK: Wiley-Blackwell. p. 318, Abrums, Mary (2000:104) "Jesus will fix it after a while: Meanings and health." *Social Science and Medicine* 50: 89–105; p. 321, Snow, Loudell F. (1978:79) "Sorcerers, saints and charlatans: Black folk healers in urban America." *Culture, Medicine, and Psychiatry* 2: 69–106; p. 322, Roebuck, Julian, and Robert Quan (1976:157) "Health-care practices in the American Deep South," pp. 141–61 in *Marginal Medicine*, R. Wallis and P. Morely (eds). New York: The Free Press; p. 322, Snow, Loudell F. (1993:73) *Walkin' over medicine*. Boulder, CO: Westview Press; p. 325, Levy, Jerrold E. (1983:132) "Traditional Navajo health beliefs and practices," pp. 118–78 in *Disease change and the role of medicine: The Navajo experience*, J. Kunitz (ed.). Berkeley: University of California Press.

Chapter 14   p. 344, Georgopoulos, Basil F., and Floyd C. Mann (1972:308) "The hospital as an organization," pp. 304–11 in *Patients, physicians and illness*, 2nd ed., E. Jaco (ed.). New York: Macmillan; p. 344, Strauss, Anselm, Leonard Schatzman, Danuta Ehrlich, Rue Bucher, and Melvin Sabshin (1963:154) "The hospital and its negotiated order," pp. 147–69 in

The hospital in modern society, E. Freidson (ed.). New York: The Free Press; p. 346, Mckevitt, Christopher, and Myfanwy Morgan (1997:649) "Anomalous patients: The experiences of doctors with an illness." *Sociology of Health & Illness* 19: 644–67; p. 347, Mckevitt, Christopher, and Myfanwy Morgan (1997:650) "Anomalous patients: The experiences of doctors with an illness." *Sociology of Health & Illness* 19: 644–67; p. 347, Carey, Benedict (2005:A12) "In the hospital, a degrading shift from person to patient." *New York Times* (August 16): A1, A12; p. 353, Stevens, Rosemary (1989:324) *In sickness and in wealth: American hospitals in the twentieth century*. New York: Basic Books.

Chapter 15 p. 361, Stevens, Rosemary (1971:438–39) *American medicine and the public interest. New Haven*, CT: Yale University Press; p. 365, Mechanic, David (2006:22) *The truth about health care: Why reform is not working in America*. New Brunswick, NJ: Rutgers University Press; p. 365, Light, Donald W (2004:19) "Introduction: Ironies of success—A new history of the American health care 'system.'" Journal of *Health and Social Behavior* 45 (Extra issue): 1–24. 19; p. 376, Gold, Marsha R. (1999:14) "The changing US health care system: Challenges for responsible public policy." *Milbank Quarterly* 77: 3–37; p. 376, Warren, Mary Guptill, Rose Weitz, and Stephen Kulis (1998:364) "Physician satisfaction in a changing health care environment: The impact of challenges to professional autonomy, author-ity, and dominance." Journal of *Health and Social Behavior* 39: 356–67; p. 377, Mechanic, David (2004:83) "The rise and fall of managed care." Journal of *Health and Social Behavior* 45 (Extra issue): 76–86; p. 377, Turner, Bryan S. (1988:52) *Status*. Milton Keynes, UK: Open University Press; p. 378, Starr, Paul (1994:xxxvi–xxxvii) *The Logic of Health Care Reform*, rev. and enl. ed. New York: Penguin Books; p. 379, Myles, John F. (1984:30) *Old Age in the Welfare State*. Boston: Little, Brown.

Chapter 16 p. 392, Evans, Robert G. (1986:597) "Finding the levers, finding the courage: Lessons from cost containment in North America." Journal of *Health Politics, Policy and Law* 11: 585–616; p. 401, Powell, Margaret, and Masahira Anesaki (1990:174) *Health care in Japan*. London: Routledge; p. 408, Knaus, William A. (1981:83) *Inside Russian Medicine*. Boston: Beacon Press; p. 409, Shkolnikov, Vladimir, and Alexander Nemtsov (1994:1) "The anti-alcohol campaign and variations in Russian mortality." *Paper Presented to the Workshop on Mortality and Adult Health Priorities in the New Independent States*, Washington, DC (November); p. 413, Chen, Feinian, Yang Yang, and Guangya Liu (2010:144) "Social change and socioeconomic disparities in health over the life course in China: A cohort anaylsis." *American Sociological Review* 75: 126–50.

NAME INDEX

427

SUBJECT INDEX